X

Developing the Curriculum

SEVENTH EDITION

Developing the Curriculum

Peter F. Oliva

PEARSON

Boston   New York   San Francisco
Mexico City   Montreal   Toronto   London   Madrid   Munich   Paris
Hong Kong   Singapore   Tokyo   Cape Town   Sydney

Series Editor: *Kelly Villella Canton*
Series Editorial Assistant: *Christine Pratt Swayne*
Marketing Manager: *Krista Clark*
Production Editor: *Mary Beth Finch*
Editorial Production Service: *Omegatype Typography, Inc.*
Composition Buyer: *Linda Cox*
Manufacturing Buyer: *Linda Morris*
Electronic Composition: *Omegatype Typography, Inc.*
Interior Design: *Omegatype Typography, Inc.*
Cover Administrator: *Linda Knowles*

For related titles and support materials, visit our online catalog at www.ablongman.com.

Between the time website information is gathered and then published, it is not unusual for some sites to have closed. Also, the transcription of URLs can result in typographical errors. The publisher would appreciate notification where these errors occur so that they may be corrected in subsequent editions.

Library of Congress Cataloging-in-Publication Data

Oliva, Peter F.
   Developing the curriculum / Peter F. Oliva. — 7th ed.
      p. cm.
   Includes bibliographical references and index.
   ISBN-13: 978-0-205-59350-7 (hardcover)
   ISBN-10: 0-205-59350-X (hardcover)
  1. Curriculum planning—United States. 2. School supervision—United States. I. Title.

  LB2806.15.O45 2009
  375'.001—dc22
                                                2007036161

Printed in the United States of America

10 9 8 7 6 5 4 3 2   RRD-VA   12 11 10 09

For my wife, Ruth;
our children, Eve and Marc;
and our grandchildren,
Gregory, Cory, Anthony, and Amanda

About the Author

Peter F. Oliva, formerly professor and chairperson at Southern Illinois University, Florida International University, and Georgia Southern University, is author of numerous articles in education journals and several textbooks, and co-author of *Supervision for Today's Schools* (8th ed.). He has served as a high school teacher and guidance counselor, and as a professor of education at the University of Florida, University of Mississippi, University of Hawaii, and Indiana State University. He has taught summer sessions at Portland State College, Miami University of Ohio, and Western Michigan University. He has also served as a part-time instructor supervising interns at the University of Central Florida.

Contents

6 Philosophy and Aims of Education   145

7 Needs Assessment   183

Instructional Goals and Objectives   307

Selecting and Implementing Strategies of Instruction   334

Evaluating Instruction   370

Evaluating the Curriculum   408

Part IV   CURRICULUM DEVELOPMENT: Products and Issues

Curriculum Products   458

Issues in Curriculum Development   471

Preface

Now in its seventh edition, *Developing the Curriculum* remains a comprehensive analysis of the *process* of curriculum development, a distinguishing feature of this text. The book's major purpose is to give students a comprehensive view of the field of curriculum development by illuminating how various curriculum workers collaborate when developing the curriculum. Although the same overall structure remains in place, a number of changes have been made in this seventh edition to make the book more current and more useful in the university classroom:

- Thorough updating to reflect changes that have taken place since the previous edition was published, including Table 2.1, "Forces Affecting Curriculum and Instruction," in Chapter 2; mention of smaller learning communities, change in the status of some middle schools, and instruction through cyberspace in Chapter 9; recent National Assessment of Educational Progress and international assessments in Chapter 12; updating of material on standards and assessment and further discussion of smaller learning communities in Chapter 15; and recent references citing views and data from curriculum specialists, education writers, private organizations, and governmental agencies (for example, on interpretations of curriculum in Chapter 1, on census data in Chapter 4, on measurement in Chapter 12, on curriculum evaluation in Chapter 13, and on curriculum issues in Chapter 15).
- Comprehensive reorganization of Chapter 15, "Issues in Curriculum Development," reducing the number of issues from fourteen to twelve. Service-learning has been considered less of an issue at present and dropped. Cultural literacy/core knowledge has been shifted to a new category, Academic Area Initiatives, where the reader will also find discussion of diversification of programs. Alternative School Arrangements includes updated material on vouchers, charter schools, and home-schooling.
- Greater attention to technology in education, especially in Chapters 9 and 11. Many references to technological developments throughout the text. Numerous helpful websites at end of chapter narratives and in chapter endnotes.
- Expanded discussion of the impact of No Child Left Behind Act (NCLB), including frequent references to NCLB in Chapters 6, 9, 12, and 15.

- Extensive updating of the Appendix of Resources for Further Research, including Curriculum Journals, change in ERIC, change in the U.S. Department of Education's Institute of Education Sciences, Internet Resources in Education, Regional Educational Laboratory Program, and Research and Development Centers.

Like preceding editions, this book is intended for students in courses such as Curriculum Development, Curriculum Planning, and Curriculum Improvement. Preservice and inservice curriculum coordinators, principals, assistant principals for curriculum, department chairpersons, instructional team leaders, and grade coordinators will benefit from this practical guide to curriculum development. The book contains a great deal of information and suggestions useful to these professionals. In addition, numerous examples of practices from actual schools and school systems appear throughout the book.

The text follows a particular sequence: It begins with an examination of the theoretical dimensions of curriculum development, looks at roles of various personnel who have primary responsibility for developing the curriculum, and describes a number of models of curriculum development, including the author's model. Subsequent chapters outline a step-by-step process for engaging in curriculum development. The process of curriculum development is examined from stating philosophical beliefs and broad aims of education to specifying curriculum and instructional goals and objectives, implementing curriculum and instruction, and evaluating instruction and the curriculum.

Each chapter begins with a number of cognitive objectives to be achieved by the student on completion of study of the chapter. Several questions for discussion are found at the end of each chapter. Exercises that follow discussion questions are designed to serve two purposes: (1) to reinforce the objectives of each chapter and (2) to extend the treatment of topics beyond the material presented in the chapter. To further enhance the usefulness of the text, chapters conclude with additional references, including websites, videos, kits, and a bibliography of pertinent books and journal articles for further research and study. A short appendix at the end of the book provides important sources of curriculum and other educational data.

One clarifying note about the structure of the book: You will encounter the rubrics of Curriculum Past, Curriculum Present, and Curriculum Future in Chapter 9. The book returns to Curriculum Present and, to a lesser extent, Curriculum Future in Chapter 15. In Curriculum Present, Chapter 9, I include a number of recent developments that are more established and less controversial. However, in Chapter 15 I present a number of recent developments and issues that engender considerable disagreement among people. Here I call attention to the issues, synthesize principal positions pro and con, and direct attention to sources of additional information.

It was my aim to provide a useful, well-researched, and readable book on the complex field of curriculum development. This textbook, with its questions for discussion, exercises, recommended materials, websites, videos, and bibliographies, offers a helpful teaching aid for instructors and a reliable sourcebook for students in courses in curriculum development.

Acknowledgments

Many people have contributed to the writing and publishing of this and earlier editions of this textbook. Through their insights into curriculum and instruction, and into education in general, teachers, administrators, students, and colleagues with whom I have worked have helped to shape my thinking. I am deeply indebted to the reviewers, who so generously gave of their time to review the manuscripts of all editions. Specifically, I'd like to thank and acknowledge the most recent group of reviewers: Mary Lynn Collins, Nova Southeastern University; Lesia Lennex, Morehead State University; and Allen R. Warner, University of Houston. I especially wish to thank my editor, Kelly Villella Canton, and my assistant editor, Angela Pickard, at Allyn and Bacon for their continuing encouragement and support.

As always, I welcome comments from users of the book.

Peter F. Oliva
124 Carriage Hill Drive
Casselberry, FL 32707

Curriculum and Instruction Defined

AFTER STUDYING THIS CHAPTER YOU SHOULD BE ABLE TO:

1. Define curriculum.
2. Define instruction.
3. Explain in what ways curriculum can be considered a discipline.
4. Create or select a model of the relationship between curriculum and instruction and describe your creation or selection.

CONCEPTIONS OF CURRICULUM

Gaius Julius Caesar and his cohorts of the first century B.C. had no idea that the oval track on which the Roman chariots raced would bequeath a word used almost daily by educators twenty-one centuries later. The track—the *curriculum*—has become one of the key concerns of today's schools, and its meaning has expanded from a tangible racecourse to an abstract concept.

In the world of professional education, the word *curriculum* has taken on an elusive, almost esoteric connotation. This poetic, neuter word does possess an aura of mystery. By contrast, other dimensions of the world of professional education like administra*tion*, instruc*tion*, and supervi*sion* are strong, action-oriented words. Administration is the *act* of administering; instruction is the *act* of instructing; and supervision is the *act* of supervising. But in what way is *curriculum* an act? While administrators administer, instructors instruct, and supervisors supervise, no school person *curricules*, and though we can find the use of the term *curricularist*,[1] it is only a rare *curricularist* who *curricularizes*.

The quest for a definition of curriculum has taxed many an educator. As long ago as 1976, Dwayne Huebner ascribed ambiguity and a lack of precision to the term *curriculum*.[2] In the 1980s Elizabeth Vallance observed, "The curriculum field is by no means clear; as a discipline of study and as a field of practice, *curriculum* lacks clean boundaries. . . ."[3] At the turn of the century Arthur W. Foshay attributed a lack of specificity to the curriculum.[4] Indeed, curriculum seems at times analogous to the blind men's elephant. It is the pachyderm's trunk to some; its thick legs to others; its pterodactyllike flopping ears to some people; its massive, rough sides to other persons; and its ropelike tail to still others.

Though it may be vehemently denied, no one has ever seen a curriculum, not a real, total, tangible, visible entity called a curriculum. The interested observer may have seen a written plan that may have been called a curriculum. Somehow the observer knows, probably by word of mouth, that in every school in which teachers are instructing students a curriculum exists. A written plan provides the observer with an additional clue to the existence of a certain something called a curriculum. But if by some bit of magic the observer could lift the roof of a school in session and examine the cross section thereof, the curriculum would not be apparent. What the observer would immediately perceive would be many instances of teacher–pupil interaction we call *instruction*.

The search for evidence of the mysterious creation called curriculum is not unlike efforts to track down Bigfoot, the Bear Lake Monster, the Florida Everglades Skunk Ape, Lake Champlain's Champ, the Yeti, the Almasty, South Bay Bessie, Scotland's Loch Ness Monster, or Sweden's Great Lake Monster. Bigfoot, the Yeti, and the Almasty, have left their tracks in the mud and the snow; Champ, Bessie, and Nessie have rippled the waters of their lakes; but no one has yet succeeded in producing incontrovertible photographs of these reputed creatures.

Nor has anyone ever photographed a curriculum. Shutterbugs have instead photographed pupils, teachers, and other school personnel. Perhaps if someone videotaped every instance of behavior in every classroom, corridor, office, and auxiliary room of a school every day and then investigated this record as thoroughly as military leaders analyze air reconnaissance photos, a curriculum could be discerned.

Certification and Curriculum

State certification laws compound the problem of defining curriculum because few, if any, professionals can become certified in *curriculum*. Whereas all professionals in training must take courses of one type or another called *curriculum*, there is not a certifiable field labeled *curriculum*. Professionals are certified in administration, guidance, supervision, school psychology, elementary education, and many teaching fields. But in *curriculum* per se? Not as a rule, although courses in the field of curriculum are mandated for certification in certain fields of specialization, such as administration and supervision.

Nevertheless, numbers of curriculum workers, consultants, coordinators, and even professors of curriculum can be identified. These specialists, many of whom may hold state certification in one or more fields, cannot customarily hang on the wall a certificate that shows that endorsement has been granted in a field called *curriculum*.

While a certifiable field of specialization called curriculum may be lacking, the word itself is treated as if it had tangible substance, for it can undergo a substantial variety of processes. Curriculum—or its plural, curricula or curriculums (depending on the user's penchant or abhorrence for the Latin)—is built, planned, designed, and constructed. It is improved, revised, and evaluated. Like photographic film and muscles, the curriculum is developed. It is also organized, structured, and restructured, and, like a wayward child, reformed. With considerable ingenuity the curriculum planner—another specialist—can mold, shape, and tailor the curriculum.

Interpretations of Curriculum

The amorphous nature of the word *curriculum* has given rise over the years to many interpretations. Madeleine R. Grumet labeled curriculum as a "field of utter confusion."[5] Depending on their philosophical beliefs, persons have conveyed these interpretations, among others:

- Curriculum is that which is taught in school.
- Curriculum is a set of subjects.
- Curriculum is content.
- Curriculum is a program of studies.
- Curriculum is a set of materials.
- Curriculum is a sequence of courses.
- Curriculum is a set of performance objectives.
- Curriculum is a course of study.
- Curriculum is everything that goes on within the school, including extra-class activities, guidance, and interpersonal relationships.
- Curriculum is that which is taught both inside and outside of school directed by the school.
- Curriculum is everything that is planned by school personnel.
- Curriculum is a series of experiences undergone by learners in school.
- Curriculum is that which an individual learner experiences as a result of schooling.

In the foregoing definitions you can see that curriculum can be conceived in a narrow way (as subjects taught) or in a broad way (as all the experiences of learners, both in school and out, directed by the school). The implications for the school to be drawn from the differing conceptions of curriculum can vary considerably. The school that accepts the definition of curriculum as a set of subjects faces a much simpler task than the school that takes upon itself responsibilities for experiences of the learner both inside and outside of school.

A variety of nuances are perceived when the professional educators define curriculum. The first definition, for example, given in Carter V. Good's *Dictionary of Education* describes curriculum as "a systematic group of courses or sequences of subjects required for graduation or certification in a field of study, for example, social studies curriculum, physical education curriculum. . . ."[6]* Let's see how a few writers on the subject define curriculum. One of the earliest writers on curriculum, Franklin Bobbitt, perceived curriculum as

> . . . that *series of things which children and youth must do and experience* by way of developing abilities to do the things well that make up the affairs of adult life; and to be in all respects what adults should be.[7]

Hollis L. Caswell and Doak S. Campbell viewed curriculum not as a group of courses but as "all the experiences children have under the guidance of teachers."[8] J. Galen Saylor, William M. Alexander, and Arthur J. Lewis offered this definition: "We define curriculum as a plan for providing sets of learning opportunities for persons to be educated."[9]

The Saylor, Alexander, and Lewis definition parallels the one given by Foshay as "a plan for action by students and teachers,"[10] and by Hilda Taba in a discussion of criteria for providing sets of learning opportunities for curriculum development: "A curriculum is a plan for learning."[11] She defined curriculum by listing its elements:

> All curricula, no matter what their particular design, are composed of certain elements. A curriculum usually contains a statement of aims and of specific objectives; it indicates some selection and organization of content; it either implies or manifests certain patterns of learning and teaching, whether because the objectives demand them or because the content organization requires them. Finally, it includes a program of evaluation of the outcomes.[12]

Ronald C. Doll defined the curriculum of a school as:

> . . . the formal and informal content and process by which learners gain knowledge and understanding, develop skills, and alter attitudes, appreciations, and values under the auspices of that school.[13]

Daniel Tanner and Laurel N. Tanner proposed the following definition:

> The authors regard curriculum as *that reconstruction of knowledge and experience that enables the learner to grow in exercising intelligent control of subsequent knowledge and experience.*[14]

Albert I. Oliver equated curriculum with the educational program and divided it into four basic elements: "(1) the program of studies, (2) the program of experiences, (3) the program of services, and (4) the hidden curriculum."[15]

The programs of studies, experiences, and services are readily apparent. To these elements Oliver has added the concept of a hidden curriculum, which encompasses values promoted by the school, differing emphases given by different teachers within the same

*From *Dictionary of Education*, Carter V. Good, ed. Copyright © 1973 by McGraw-Hill. Reproduced with permission of The McGraw-Hill Companies, Inc.

subject areas, the degree of enthusiasm of teachers, and the physical and social climate of the school.

A different approach to defining curriculum was taken by Robert M. Gagné, who wove together subject matter (content), the statement of ends (terminal objectives), sequencing of content, and preassessment of entry skills required of students when they begin the study of the content.[16] Mauritz Johnson, Jr. agreed basically with Gagné when he defined curriculum as a "structured series of intended learning outcomes."[17] Johnson perceived curriculum as "the output of a 'curriculum development system' and as an input into an 'instructional system.'"[18]

Geneva Gay, writing on desegregating the curriculum, offered a broad interpretation of curriculum:

> If we are to achieve equally, we must broaden our conception to include the entire culture of the school—not just subject matter content.[19]

Evelyn J. Sowell offered the definition: "what is taught to students, both intended and unintended information, skills, and attitudes"[20] whereas Herbert K. Kliebard observed that "what we call *the* American curriculum is actually an assemblage of competing doctrines and practices."[21]

Jon Wiles and Joseph Bondi also saw "the curriculum as a desired goal or set of values that can be activated through a development process culminating in experiences for students."[22]

Expressing the view that the word "'curriculum' has come to mean only a course of study," D. Jean Clandinin and F. Michael Connelly held curriculum to be no less than "a course of life" led by teachers as curriculum makers.[23]

Departing from a definition of curriculum as "school materials," William F. Pinar, William M. Reynolds, Patrick Slattery, and Peter M. Taubman described curriculum as "symbolic representation."[24] Said these authors:

> Curriculum understood as symbolic representation refers to those institutional and discursive practices, structures, images, and experiences that can be identified and analyzed in various ways, i.e., politically, racially, autobiographically, phenomenologically, theologically, internationally, and in terms of gender and deconstruction.[25]

More recently, concerning the various interpretations of curriculum, Peter S. Hlebowitsh commented, "When we begin to think about the curriculum as a strictly professional and school-based term, a number of different interpretive slants on what comprises the curriculum comes into play."[26]

Definitions by Purposes, Contexts, and Strategies

Differences in substance of definitions of curriculum, while they exist, are not as great or as common as differences in what the curriculum theorists include in their conceptions of the term. Some theorists elaborate more than others. Some combine elements of both curriculum and instruction, a conceptual problem that will be examined later in this chapter. Others find a definition of curriculum in (1) purposes or goals of the curriculum, (2) contexts within which the curriculum is found, or (3) strategies used throughout the curriculum.

Purposes.   The search for a definition of curriculum is clouded when the theoretician responds to the term not in the context of what curriculum is but what it *does* or *should do*—that is, its purpose. On the purposes of the curriculum we can find many varying statements.

When curriculum is conceptualized as "the development of reflective thinking on the part of the learner" or "the transmission of the cultural heritage," purpose is confused with entity. This concept could be stated more correctly: "The purpose of the curriculum is transmission of the cultural heritage," or "The purpose of the curriculum is the development of reflective thinking on the part of the learner." A statement of what the curriculum is meant to achieve does little to help us sharpen a definition of what curriculum is.

Contexts.   Definitions of curriculum sometimes state the settings within which it takes shape. When theoreticians speak of an essentialist curriculum, a child-centered curriculum, or a reconstructionist curriculum, they are invoking two characteristics of the curriculum at the same time—purpose and context. For example, an essentialistic curriculum is designed to transmit the cultural heritage, to school young people in the organized disciplines, and to prepare boys and girls for the future. This curriculum arises from a special philosophical context, that of the essentialistic school of philosophy.

A child-centered curriculum clearly reveals its orientation—the learner, who is the primary focus of the progressive school of philosophy. The development of the individual learner in all aspects of growth may be inferred but the plans for that development vary considerably from school to school. The curriculum of a school following reconstructionist philosophical beliefs aims to educate youth in such a way that they will be capable of solving some of society's pressing problems and, therefore, change society for the better. Setting forth a "feminist argument," Madeleine R. Grumet argued that *"what is the most fundamental to our lives as men and women sharing a moment on this planet is the process and experience of reproducing ourselves."*[27] Holding the view that "schools are ritual centers cut off from the real living places where we love and labor,"[28] she defined curriculum as a "project of transcendence, our attempt while immersed in biology and ideology to transcend biology and ideology."[29] Again we see a particular orientation or context within which the curriculum is lodged.

Strategies.   While purpose and context are sometimes offered as definitions of curriculum, an additional complexity arises when the theoretician equates curriculum with instructional strategy. Some theoreticians isolate certain instructional variables, such as processes, strategies, and techniques, and then proceed to equate them with curriculum. The curriculum as a problem-solving process illustrates an attempt to define curriculum in terms of an instructional process—problem-solving techniques, the scientific method, or reflective thinking. The curriculum as group living, for example, is an effort at definition built around certain instructional techniques that must be used to provide opportunities for group living. The curriculum as individualized learning and the curriculum as programmed instruction are, in reality, specifications of systems by which learners encounter curricular content through the process of instruction. Neither purpose, context, nor strategy provides a clear basis for defining curriculum.

In a class by itself is the definition of curriculum as ends or terminal objectives. W. James Popham and Eva L. Baker classified curriculum as ends and instruction as means when they said, "Curriculum is all the planned learning outcomes for which the school is responsible."[30] In designing the curriculum, planners would cast these outcomes or objectives in operational or behavioral terms.

The operational or behavioral objectives are, in effect, instructional objectives. According to the proponents of behavioral objectives, a compilation of all the behavioral objectives of all the programs and activities of the school would constitute the curriculum. The curriculum would then be the sum total of all instructional objectives. You will encounter in this text an approach that distinguishes curriculum goals and objectives from instructional goals and objectives. You will see later that curriculum objectives are derived from curriculum goals and aims of education, and instructional objectives are derived from instructional goals and from curriculum goals and objectives. Both curriculum objectives and instructional objectives can be stated in behavioral terms.

Some advocates of behavioral objectives seem comfortable with the notion that once the terminal objectives (the ends) are clearly specified, the curriculum has been defined. From that point on instruction takes over. This view of curriculum as specification of objectives is quite different, for example, from the concept of the curriculum as a plan, a program, or a sequence of courses.

In this text curriculum is perceived as a plan or program for all the experiences that the learner encounters under the direction of the school. In practice, the curriculum consists of a number of plans, in written form and of varying scope, that delineate the desired learning experiences. The curriculum, therefore, may be a unit, a course, a sequence of courses, the school's entire program of studies—and may be encountered inside or outside of class or school when directed by the personnel of the school.

RELATIONSHIPS BETWEEN CURRICULUM AND INSTRUCTION

The search to clarify the meaning of curriculum reveals uncertainty about the distinctions between curriculum and instruction and their relationships to each other. We may simplistically view curriculum as that which is taught and instruction as the means used to teach that which is taught. Even more simply, curriculum can be conceived as the "what" and instruction as the "how." We may think of the curriculum as a program, a plan, content, and learning experiences, whereas we may characterize instruction as methods, the teaching act, implementation, and presentation.

Distinguishing instruction from curriculum, Johnson defined instruction as "the interaction between a teaching agent and one or more individuals intending to learn."[31] James B. Macdonald viewed curricular activity as the production of plans for further action and instruction as the putting of plans into operation. Thus, according to Macdonald, curriculum planning precedes instruction, a premise with which I am in agreement.[32]

In the course of planning for either the curriculum or instruction, decisions are made. Decisions about the curriculum relate to plans or programs and thus are *programmatic*, while those about instruction (and thereby implementation) are *methodological*. Both curriculum and instruction are subsystems of a larger system called schooling or education.

Models of the Curriculum–Instruction Relationship

Definitions of the two terms are valuable but can obscure the interdependence of these two systems. They may be recognized as two entities, but like cojoined twins, one may not function without the other. That the relationship between the "what" and the "how" of education is not easily determined can be seen in several different models of this relationship. For lack of better terminology, the following labels are coined for these models: (1) dualistic model, (2) interlocking model, (3) concentric models, and (4) cyclical model.

Dualistic Model. Figure 1.1 depicts the dualistic model. Curriculum sits on one side and instruction on the other and never the twain shall meet. Between the two entities lies a great gulf. What takes place in the classroom under the direction of the teacher seems to have little relationship to what the master plan says should go on in the classroom. The planners ignore the instructors and in turn are ignored by them. Discussions of curriculum are divorced from their practical application to the classroom. Under this model the curriculum and the instructional process may change without significantly affecting one another.

Interlocking Model. When curriculum and instruction are shown as systems entwined, an interlocking relationship exists. No particular significance is given to the position of instruction or curriculum in either of the versions of this model presented in Figure 1.2. The same relationship is implied no matter which element appears on the left or the

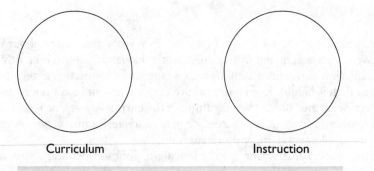

Curriculum   Instruction

FIGURE 1.1 The Dualistic Model

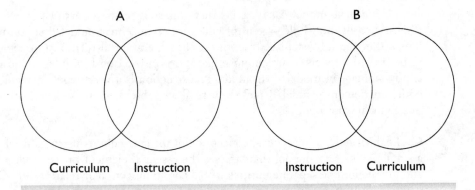

A

B

Curriculum   Instruction   Instruction   Curriculum

FIGURE 1.2   The Interlocking Model

right. These models clearly demonstrate an integrated relationship between these two entities. The separation of one from the other would do serious harm to both.

Curriculum planners would find it difficult to regard instruction as paramount to curriculum and to determine teaching methods before program objectives. Nevertheless, some faculties proceed as if instruction were primary by dispensing with advance planning of the curriculum and by letting it more or less develop as it unfolds in the classroom.

Concentric Models.   The preceding models of the relationship between curriculum and instruction reveal varying degrees of independence from complete detachment to interlocking relationships. Mutual dependence is the key feature of concentric models. Two conceptions of the curriculum–instruction relationship that show one as the subsystem of the other can be sketched (Figure 1.3). Variations A and B both convey the idea that one of the entities occupies a superordinate position while the other is subordinate.

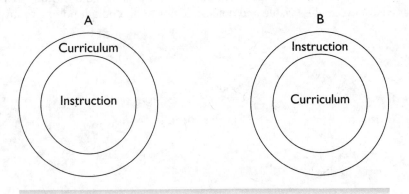

A

Curriculum

Instruction

B

Instruction

Curriculum

FIGURE 1.3   The Concentric Model

Concentric model A makes instruction a subsystem of curriculum, which is itself a subsystem of the whole system of education. Concentric model B subsumes curriculum within the subsystem instruction. A clear hierarchical relationship comes through in both these models. Curriculum ranks above instruction in model A and instruction is predominant in model B. In model A instruction is a very dependent portion of the entity curriculum. Model B makes curriculum subservient to and derivative from the more global instruction.

Cyclical Model.   The cyclical conception of the curriculum–instruction relationship is a simplified systems model that stresses the essential element of feedback. Curriculum and instruction are separate entities with a continuing circular relationship. Curriculum makes a continuous impact on instruction and, vice versa, instruction has impact on curriculum. This relationship can be schematically represented as in Figure 1.4. The cyclical model implies that instructional decisions are made after curricular decisions, which in turn are modified after instructional decisions are implemented and evaluated. This process is continuous, repetitious, and never-ending. The evaluation of instructional procedures affects the next round of curricular decision making, which again affects instructional implementation. While curriculum and instruction are diagrammed as separate entities, with this model they are not to be conceived as separate entities but as part of a sphere—a circle that revolves, causing continuous adaptations and improvements of both entities.

Each curriculum–instruction model has its champions who espouse it in part or in whole, in theory or in practice. Yet how can we account for these numerous conceptions, and how do we know which is the "right" one to hold?

Common Beliefs.   As newer developments occur in education, as research adds new insights on teaching and learning, as new ideas are developed, and as times change, beliefs about curriculum and instruction also undergo transformation. The "rightness" or "wrongness" of concepts like curriculum and instruction cannot be established by an individual educator or even by a group of educators. One index of "correctness" might be the prevailing opinion of most educators at a particular stage in history—a rather pragmatic but nevertheless viable and defensible position. Though no one to my knowledge

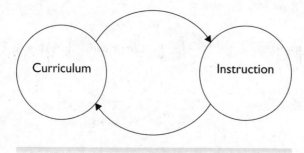

FIGURE 1.4   The Cyclical Model

has made a count of prevailing postulates regarding curriculum and instruction, most theoreticians today appear to agree with the following comments:

- Curriculum and instruction are related but different.
- Curriculum and instruction are interlocking and interdependent.
- Curriculum and instruction may be studied and analyzed as separate entities but cannot function in mutual isolation.

In my judgment, serious problems are posed by the dualistic conceptual model of the relationship between curriculum and instruction with its separation of the two entities and by concentric models that make one a subsystem of the other.

Some curriculum workers feel comfortable with an interlocking model because it shows a close relationship between the two entities. Of all the curriculum–instruction models that have crossed my path, however, I feel that the cyclical has much to recommend it for its simplicity and for its stress on the need for the continuous influence of each entity on the other.

CURRICULUM AS A DISCIPLINE

In spite of its elusive character, curriculum is viewed by many, including me, as a discipline—a subject of study—and even, on the graduate level of higher education, as a major field of study. Curriculum is then both a field within which people work and a subject to be taught. Graduate and, to some extent, undergraduate students take courses in curriculum development, curriculum theory, curriculum evaluation, secondary school curriculum, elementary school curriculum, middle school curriculum, community college curriculum, and, on fewer occasions, university curriculum.

Can there be a discipline called curriculum? Are the many college courses in curriculum mere frosting, as some of the critics of teacher education maintain, or is there cake beneath the surface? Is there a curriculum field or occupation to which persons can devote their lives?

The Characteristics of a Discipline

To arrive at a decision as to whether an area of study is a discipline, the question might be raised, "What are the characteristics of a discipline?" If the characteristics of a discipline can be spelled out, we can determine whether curriculum, for example, is a discipline or not.

Principles. *Any discipline worthy of study has an organized set of theoretical constructs or principles that governs it.* Certainly, the field of curriculum has developed a significant set of principles, tried and untried, proved and unproved, many of which are appropriately the subjects of discussion in this text. Balance in the curriculum, discussed in Chapter 13, is a construct or concept. Curriculum itself is a construct or concept, a verbalization of an extremely complex idea or set of ideas. Using the constructs of balance and curriculum, we can derive a principle or rule that, stated in simple terms, says, "A curriculum that provides maximum opportunities for learners incorporates the concept of balance." Sequencing of courses, behavioral objectives, integrated studies, multiculturalism, and a whole-language approach to the teaching of language arts are examples of constructs incorporated into one or more curriculum principles.

A major characteristic of any theoretical principle is its capacity for being generalized and applied in more than one situation. Were curriculum theories but one-shot solutions to specific problems, it would be difficult to defend the concept of curriculum as a discipline. But the principles of curriculum theory are often successful efforts to establish rules that can be repeated in similar situations and under similar conditions. Many people will agree, for example, that the concept of balance should be incorporated into every curriculum. We encounter more controversy, however, over a principle that might be stated as, "The first step in curriculum planning is the specification of behavioral objectives." Though some maintain this principle has become universal practice and therefore, might be labeled "truth," it has been tried and accepted by many educators, rejected by some, and tried and abandoned by others.

Knowledge and Skills.   *Any discipline encompasses a body of knowledge and skills pertinent to that discipline.* The field of curriculum has adapted and borrowed subject matter from a number of pure and derived disciplines. Figure 1.5 schematically shows areas from which the field of curriculum has borrowed constructs, principles, knowledge, and skills. Selection of content for study by students, for example, cannot be done without referring to the disciplines of sociology, psychology, and subject areas. Organization of the curriculum depends on knowledge from organizational theory and management, which are aspects of administration. The fields of supervision, systems theory, technology, and communications theory are called on in the process of curriculum development. Knowledge from many fields is selected and adapted by the curriculum field.

The "child-centered curriculum" as a concept draws heavily on what is known about learning, growth, and development (psychology and biology), on philosophy (particularly from one school of philosophy, progressivism), and on sociology. The "essentialist curriculum" borrows from the subject areas of philosophy, psychology, and sociology, and the academic disciplines.

You might ask whether the field of curriculum contributes any knowledge of its own to that borrowed from other disciplines. Certainly, a good deal of thinking and research is going on in the name of curriculum. New curricular ideas are being generated continuously. These ideas, whether they be cooperative learning, computer literacy, or character education (to mention but three fairly recent concepts), borrow heavily from other disciplines.

The skills used by curriculum specialists are also borrowed from other fields. Let's take an example from the field of social psychology. Generally accepted is the notion that a curriculum changes only when the people affected have changed. This principle, drawn from the field of social psychology, and applied in the field of curriculum development, was perhaps most dramatically demonstrated by the Western Electric researches conducted by industry in the 1930s.[33] Here researchers discovered that factory workers assembling telephone relays were more productive when they

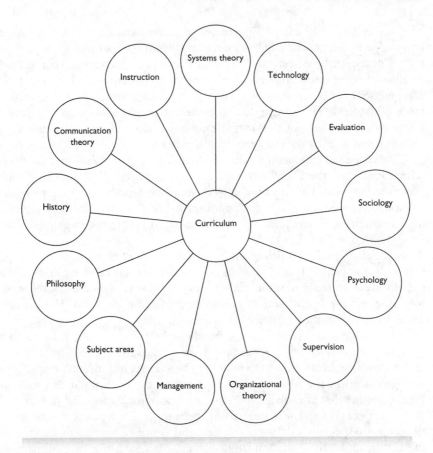

FIGURE 1.5 Sources of the Curriculum Field

were consulted and made to feel of value to the organization. Making the workers feel important resulted in greater productivity than manipulating the physical environment, for example, lighting in the factory. The feeling of being part of the research studies also created its own aura, the so-called Hawthorne effect, named for the Western Electric's Hawthorne plant in Chicago. Since the feeling of involvement can in itself contribute to high productivity, this effect is one that researchers learn to discount, for it can obscure the hypothesized or real causes for change. However, the educational practitioner who is aware of the Hawthorne effect may take advantage of it to promote learning.

Criticisms have been made of the Western Electric researches.[34] In spite of the criticisms, however, the findings still appear generally sound. An instructional leader—let's call him or her a supervisor—is the person who acts as a catalyst or agent for bringing about change in people. How does the supervisor do this? He or she makes use of knowledge and skills from a number of fields: communication theory, psychology of groups, and other areas. How does the supervisor help teachers to carry out the change once they have subscribed to it? He or she applies principles and skills from management, from knowledge of the structure of disciplines, and from other areas.

Consequently, we can conclude that the field of curriculum requires the use of an amalgamation of knowledge and skills from many disciplines. That curriculum theory and practice are derived from other disciplines does not in any way diminish the importance of the field. The observation of its derived nature simply characterizes its essence. Curriculum's synthesis of elements from many fields in some ways makes it both a demanding and an exciting arena in which to work.

In a cyclical fashion the derived discipline of *curriculum* in turn makes its own potent impact on the disciplines from which it is derived. Through curricular research, experimentation and application, subject areas are modified; learning theories are corroborated, revised, or rejected; administrative and supervisory techniques are implemented or changed; and philosophical positions are subjected to examination.

Theoreticians and Practitioners. *A discipline has its theoreticians and its practitioners.* Certainly, the field of curriculum has an array of workers laboring in its name. Mention has already been made of some of the titles they go by: planners, consultants, coordinators, directors, and professors of curriculum, to name but a few. We can include them under the generic title of curriculum specialist.

Curriculum specialists make a number of distinctive contributions to their field. Specialists know what types of curricula have worked in the past, under what conditions, and with what success. Since the name of the game is improvement, specialists must be well grounded in the historical development of the curriculum and must possess the capacity to use that knowledge to help the schools avoid historical pitfalls.

Curriculum specialists generate or help to generate new curriculum concepts. In this capacity specialists draw on the past and conceive new arrangements, adaptations of existing approaches, or completely new approaches. Alternative forms of schools, for example, are newer arrangements and approaches for the same general goal—education of the young.

While curriculum specialists are indulging in the "big think," hoping to bring to light new theories—a worthy goal not to be dismissed lightly—other, and perhaps more, curriculum specialists are experts in application of theory and research. They know techniques of curriculum planning that are most likely to result in higher achievement on the part of learners. They are familiar with variations in the organizational patterns. They must be not only knowledgeable but also creative and able to spark innovations that give promise of bringing about higher achievement in learners.

The concept of "core" curriculum dating from the 1930s and the 1940s, for example, that integrated two or more subjects, was a promising, creative innovation. In one of its shapes the core curriculum, which we will discuss in Chapter 9, fused English and social studies into a block of time—ordinarily two to three periods—at the junior high school level, using content based on adolescent needs and interests. But was this innovative concept truly original, unique to the field of curriculum, or was it adapted and drawn from a variety of disciplines? Examination of the subconcepts of the core curriculum shows that it owed a great deal to other disciplines. The adolescent-needs base followed in some core programs came from student-centered, progressive learning theories, as did the problem-solving approach used in instruction. One reason for the inauguration of this type of core curriculum in schools in the 1930s and 1940s could be attributed to dissatisfaction with the subject matter, as evidenced by, among other factors, the low holding power of schools of the times.

CURRICULUM SPECIALISTS

Curriculum specialists often make a unique contribution by creatively transforming theory and knowledge into practice. Through their efforts a new, at first experimental, approach gradually becomes a widespread practice. As students of the discipline of curriculum, they also examine and reexamine theory and knowledge from their field and related fields. Awareness of past successes and failures elsewhere helps those who work in the field of curriculum to chart directions for their own curricula.

Curriculum specialists are in the best position to stimulate research on curricular problems. Specialists carry out and encourage study of curricular problems, comparisons of plans and programs, results of new patterns of curriculum organization, and history of curriculum experiments, to indicate but a few areas of research. Specialists encourage the use of results of research to continue efforts to improve the curriculum.

While classroom teachers daily concern themselves with problems of curriculum and instruction, the curriculum specialist is charged with the task of providing leadership to the teachers. Since there are so many different types of specialists in so many different locations, you will find it difficult to generalize on their roles. Some curriculum workers are generalists whose roles may be limited to leadership in curricular or programmatic planning or whose roles may also encompass instructional planning and decision making.

Some curriculum workers confine their spheres of action to certain levels or subjects, such as elementary, middle, or secondary school curriculum; community college curriculum, special education, science education, early childhood education; and others. What can be observed is that the roles the curriculum leader plays are shaped by the job, by the supervising administrator, and by the specialist himself or herself. At varying times the curriculum specialist must be

- a philosopher
- a psychologist
- a sociologist
- a human relations expert
- a technology expert
- a theoretician
- a historian
- a scholar in one or more disciplines
- an evaluator
- a researcher
- an instructor
- a systems analyst

Supervisors

An additional clarification should be made at this point—that is, the relationship between the roles of persons designated as curriculum specialists and those persons who are called supervisors. Some consider the titles synonymous.

In this text a *supervisor* is perceived as a specialist who works in three domains: instructional development; curriculum development; and staff, primarily teacher, development.[35] When the supervisor works in the first two domains, he or she is an instructional/curriculum specialist or often referred to as an "instructional supervisor." Thus, the curriculum worker or specialist is a particular type of supervisor, one with more limited responsibilities than a general supervisor. Both the curriculum specialist and the supervisor fulfill similar roles when they work with teachers in curriculum development and instructional development, but the curriculum specialist is not primarily concerned with such activities as organizing inservice programs and evaluating teachers, which are more properly responsibilities of the general supervisors.

Role Variations

As with so many jobs in the field of education, difficulty arises in attempting to draw firm lines that apply under all conditions and in all situations. To understand more fully the roles and functions of educational personnel, we must examine local practice. Teachers, curriculum specialists, and supervisors all engage in activities to improve both curriculum and instruction. At times their roles are different and at other times their roles are similar. These personnel, all specialists in their own right, frequently trade places to accomplish the task of improvement. Sometimes they are one and the same person—the teacher who is his or her own curriculum specialist and supervisor. Whatever the structure of leadership for the improvement of curriculum and instruction, all teachers and all specialists must ultimately participate in this challenging task. Since curriculum and instruction are the mind and heart of schooling, all personnel, all students, and the community as well participate in the improvement of what is offered by the school and how it is implemented.

Chapters 3 and 4 will describe roles of personnel involved in curriculum development, including teachers, students, department heads, lead teachers, team leaders, grade coordinators, administrators, curriculum specialists, supervisors, and laypersons.

Summary

Curriculum and instruction are viewed as separate but dependent concepts. Curriculum is defined in a variety of ways by theoreticians. This text follows the concept of curriculum as a plan or program for the learning experiences that the learner encounters under the direction of the school.

Instruction is perceived in these pages as the means for making the curriculum operational, that is, the techniques that teachers use to make the curriculum available to the learners. In short, curriculum is program and instruction is method.

A number of models showing the relationship between curriculum and instruction have been discussed. While all models have their strengths and weaknesses, the cyclical model seems to have particular merit for its emphasis on the reciprocity between curriculum and instruction.

Planning should begin with the programmatic—that is, with curriculum decisions, rather than with instructional decisions. Appropriate planning begins with the broad aims of education and proceeds through a continuum that leads to the most detailed objectives of instruction.

Curriculum is perceived as a discipline, albeit a derived one that borrows concepts and principles from many disciplines.

Many practitioners work in the field of curriculum, including specialists who make a career of curriculum planning, development, and research. Teachers, curriculum specialists, and instructional supervisors share leadership responsibilities in efforts to develop the curriculum.

As a discipline, curriculum possesses (1) an organized set of principles, (2) a body of knowledge and skills for which training is needed, and (3) its theoreticians and practitioners.

Questions for Discussion

1. Does it make any difference which definition of curriculum you adopt? Why? Give examples of the effects of following different definitions of curriculum.

2. Should curriculum be an area certified (credentialed) by the state? Why?

3. What is the purpose of distinguishing curriculum from instruction?

4. In what fields must a curriculum specialist have expertise?

5. Does planning start with the curriculum or with instruction? Why?

Exercises

1. Locate and report three definitions of curriculum that differ from those quoted in this chapter.

2. Describe the characteristics of a discipline.

3. Describe whether curriculum is a discipline, a pseudodiscipline, or not a discipline, and state your reasons for your decision.

4. Make a brief presentation on the distinctions between a curriculum specialist and a supervisor, using selected quotations from the professional literature or from persons in positions with those titles.

5. Show the differences, if any, between the terms *curriculum worker, curriculum specialist, curriculum planner, curriculum coordinator, curriculum consultant*, and *instructional supervisor.*

6. Locate in the literature and describe one or more models of the relationship between curriculum and instruction that are different from those that appear in this chapter.

7. Describe your own model of the relationship between curriculum and instruction.

8. Report on the purposes and activities of the Association for Supervision and Curriculum Development, the Council of Professors of Instructional Supervision, and Professors of Curriculum.

9. Take each of the disciplines from which the field of curriculum borrows and describe at least one contribution (principle, construct, concept, or skill) borrowed from that discipline.

10. Decide whether there are any sources of the curriculum field not shown in Figure 1.5.

11. State what you believe is meant by the following terms: *curriculum planning, curriculum development, curriculum improvement, curriculum revision, curriculum reform,* and *curriculum evaluation.*

12. Report on the Western Electric researches mentioned in this chapter and explain their significance for curriculum development. Include in your answer your description of the Hawthorne effect. Evaluate some of the criticisms of the Western Electric researches.

13. Consult one or more of the following references (see bibliography) on the meaning of "hidden curriculum": James A. Beane et al.; Henry Giroux and David Purpel; Kenneth T. Henson; John D. McNeil; Albert I. Oliver; Allan C. Ornstein; and Francis P. Hunkins.

14. Explain what George S. Morrison means by formal curriculum, informal curriculum, hidden curriculum, and integrated curriculum (see bibliography).

15. Define types of curricula described by Allan A. Glatthorn and by John I. Goodlad (see bibliography).

Websites

Association for Supervision and Curriculum Development: http://www.ascd.org

Endnotes

1. See, for example, Peter S. Hlebowitsh, *Designing the School Curriculum* (Boston: Allyn and Bacon, 2005), p. 2 and Daniel Tanner and Laurel Tanner, *Curriculum Development: Theory into Practice*, 4th ed. (Upper Saddle River, N.J.: Merrill/Prentice Hall, 2007), p. 135.

2. Dwayne Huebner, "The Moribund Curriculum Field: Its Wake and Our Work," *Curriculum Inquiry* 6, no. 2 (1976): 156.

3. Elizabeth Vallance, "Curriculum as a Field of Practice," in Fenwick W. English, ed., *Fundamental Curriculum Decisions*, 1983 Yearbook (Alexandria, Va.: Association for Supervision and Curriculum Development, 1983), p. 159.

4. Arthur W. Foshay, *The Curriculum: Purpose, Substance, Practice* (New York: Teachers College Press, 2000), p. xv.

5. Madeleine R. Grumet, *Bitter Milk: Women and Teaching* (Amherst, Mass.: The University of Massachusetts Press, 1988), p. 4.

6. Carter V. Good, ed., *Dictionary of Education*, 3rd ed. (New York: McGraw-Hill, 1973), p. 157.

7. Franklin Bobbitt, *The Curriculum* (Boston: Houghton Mifflin, 1918), p. 42.

8. Hollis L. Caswell and Doak S. Campbell, *Curriculum Development* (New York: American Book Company, 1935), p. 66.

9. J. Galen Saylor, William M. Alexander, and Arthur J. Lewis, *Curriculum Planning for Better Teaching and Learning*, 4th ed. (New York: Holt, Rinehart and Winston, 1981), p. 8.

10. Ibid.

11. Hilda Taba, *Curriculum Development: Theory and Practice* (New York: Harcourt Brace Jovanovich, 1962), p. 11.

12. Ibid., p. 10.

13. Ronald C. Doll, *Curriculum Improvement: Decision Making and Process*, 9th ed. (Boston: Allyn and Bacon, 1996), p. 15.

14. Daniel Tanner and Laurel Tanner, *Curriculum Development: Theory into Practice*, 4th ed. (Upper Saddle River, N.J.: Merrill/Prentice Hall 2007), p. 99.

15. Albert I. Oliver, *Curriculum Improvement: A Guide to Problems, Principles, and Process*, 2nd ed. (New York: Harper & Row, 1977), p. 8.

16. See Robert M. Gagné, "Curriculum Research and the Promotion of Learning," *AERA Monograph Series on*

Evaluation: Perspectives of Curriculum Evaluation, no. 1 (Chicago: Rand McNally, 1967), p. 21.

17. Mauritz Johnson, Jr., "Definitions and Models in Curriculum Theory," *Educational Theory* 17, no. 2 (April 1967), p. 130.

18. Ibid., p. 133.

19. Geneva Gay, "Achieving Educational Equality Through Curriculum Desegregation," *Phi Delta Kappan* 72, no. 1 (September 1990): 61–62.

20. Evelyn J. Sowell, *Curriculum: An Integrative Introduction* (Englewood Cliffs, N.J.: Merrill, 1996), p. 367.

21. Herbert M. Kliebard, "The Effort to Reconstruct the Modern American Curriculum," in *The Curriculum: Problems, Politics, and Possibilities*, 2nd ed., in Landon E. Beyer and Michael W. Apple, eds. (Albany, N.Y.: State University of New York Press, 1998), p. 21.

22. Jon Wiles and Joseph Bondi, *Curriculum Development: A Guide to Practice*, 7th ed. (Upper Saddle River, N.J.: Merrill/Prentice Hall, 2007), p. 5.

23. D. Jean Clandinin and F. Michael Connelly, *Teacher as Curriculum Maker*, in Phillip W. Jackson, ed., *Handbook of Research on Curriculum: A Project of the American Educational Research Association* (New York: Macmillan, 1992), p. 393.

24. William F. Pinar, William M. Reynolds, Patrick Slattery, and Peter M. Taubman, *Understanding Curriculum: An Introduction to the Study of Historical and Contemporary Curriculum Discourses* (New York: Peter Lang, 1996), p. 16.

25. Ibid.

26. Peter S. Hlebowitsh, *Designing the Curriculum* (Boston: Allyn and Bacon, 2005), p. 1.

27. Grumet, *Bitter Milk: Women and Teaching*, pp. 3–4.

28. Ibid., p. 21.

29. Ibid., p. 20.

30. W. James Popham and Eva L. Baker, *Systematic Instruction* (Englewood Cliffs, N.J.: Prentice-Hall, 1970), p. 48.

31. Johnson, "Definitions," p. 138. See also Saylor, Alexander, and Lewis, *Curriculum Planning*, pp. 9–10, for a definition of instruction.

32. James B. Macdonald and Robert R. Leeper, eds., *Theories of Instruction* (Alexandria, Va.: Association for Supervision and Curriculum Development, 1965), pp. 5–6.

33. See F. J. Roethlisberger and William J. Dickson, *Management and the Worker* (Cambridge, Mass.: Harvard University Press, 1939) for discussion of the Western Electric researches.

34. See, for example, Berkeley Rice, "The Hawthorne Defect: Persistence of a Flawed Theory," *Psychology Today* 16, no. 2 (February 1982): 70–74.

35. See also George E. Pawlas and Peter F. Oliva, *Supervision for Today's Schools*, 8th ed. (Hoboken, N.J.: Wiley, 2008).

Bibliography

Armstrong, David G. *Developing and Documenting the Curriculum*. Boston: Allyn and Bacon, 1989.

Beane, James A., Toepfer, Conrad F., Jr., and Alessi, Samuel J., Jr. *Curriculum Planning and Development*. Boston: Allyn and Bacon, 1986.

Beauchamp, George A. *Curricular Theory*, 4th ed. Itasca, Ill.: F. E. Peacock, 1981.

Beyer, Landon E. and Apple, Michael W., eds. *The Curriculum: Problems, Politics, and Possibilities*, 2nd ed. Albany, N.Y.: State University of New York Press, 1998.

Bobbitt, Franklin. *The Curriculum*. Boston: Houghton Mifflin, 1918.

Caswell, Hollis L., and Campbell, Doak S. *Curriculum Development*. New York: American Book Company, 1935.

Clandinin, D. Jean and Connelly, F. Michael. "Teacher as Curriculum Maker." In Philip W. Jackson, ed., *Handbook of Research on Curriculum: A Project of the American Educational Research Association*. New York: Macmillan, 1992, pp. 363–401.

Doll, Ronald C. *Curriculum Improvement: Decision Making and Process*, 9th ed. Boston: Allyn and Bacon, 1996.

Eisner, Elliot W. *The Educational Imagination: On the Design and Evaluation of School Programs*, 2nd ed. New York: Macmillan, 1985.

Foshay, Arthur W. *The Curriculum: Purpose, Substance, Practice*. New York: Teachers College Press, 2000.

Gagné, Robert M. "Curriculum Research and the Promotion Learning." *AERA Monograph Series on Evaluation: Perspectives of Curriculum Evaluation*, no. 1. Chicago: Rand McNally, 1967.

Gay, Geneva. "Achieving Educational Equality Through Curriculum Desegregation." *Phi Delta Kappan* 72, no. 1 (September 1990): 61–62.

Giroux, Henry A., Penna, Anthony N., and Pinar, William F., eds. *Curriculum and Instruction: Alternatives in Education*. Berkeley, Calif.: McCutchan, 1981.

———— and Purpel, David, eds. *The Hidden Curriculum and Moral Education.* Berkeley, Calif.: McCutchan, 1983.

Glatthorn, Allan A. *Curriculum Leadership.* Glenview, Ill.: Scott, Foresman, 1987.

Goodlad, John I. and associates. *Curriculum Inquiry: The Study of Curriculum Practice.* New York: McGraw-Hill, 1979.

Grumet, Madeleine R. *Bitter Milk: Women and Teaching.* Amherst, Mass.: The University of Massachusetts Press, 1988.

Henson, Kenneth T. *Curriculum Planning: Integrating Multiculturalism, Constructivism, and Education Reform,* 3rd ed. Long Grove, Ill.: Waveland Press, 2006.

Hlebowitsh, Peter S. *Designing the School Curriculum.* Boston: Allyn and Bacon, 2005.

Huebner, Dwayne. "The Moribund Curriculum Field: Its Wake and Our Work." *Curriculum Inquiry* 6, no. 2 (1976): 156.

Jackson, Philip W., ed. *Handbook of Research on Curriculum: A Project of the American Educational Research Association.* New York: Macmillan, 1992.

Johnson, Mauritz, Jr. "Definitions and Models in Curriculum Theory." *Educational Theory* 17, no. 2 (April 1967): 127–140.

Kliebard, Herbert M. "The Effort to Reconstruct the Modern American Curriculum." In Landon E. Beyer and Michael W. Apple, eds., *The Curriculum: Problems, Politics, and Possibilities,* 2nd ed. Albany, N.Y.: State University of New York Press, 1998.

Macdonald, James B. and Leeper, Robert R., eds. *Theories of Instruction.* Alexandria, Va.: Association for Supervision and Curriculum Development, 1965.

Marshall, J. Dan, Sears, James T., and Schubert, William H. *Turning Points in Curriculum: A Contemporary American Memoir.* Upper Saddle River, N.J.: Merrill, 2000.

McNeil, John D. *Curriculum: A Comprehensive Introduction,* 5th ed. New York: HarperCollins, 1996.

Morrison, George S. *Contemporary Curriculum K–8.* Boston: Allyn and Bacon, 1993.

Oliver, Albert I. *Curriculum Development: A Guide to Problems, Principles, and Process,* 2nd ed. New York: Harper & Row, 1977.

Ornstein, Allan C. and Behar, Linda S., eds. *Contemporary Issues in Curriculum.* Boston: Allyn and Bacon, 1995.

———— and Hunkins, Francis P. *Curriculum Foundations, Principles, and Issues,* 2nd ed. Boston: Allyn and Bacon, 1993.

Pawlas, George E. and Oliva, Peter F. *Supervision for Today's Schools,* 8th ed. Hoboken, N.J.: Wiley, 2008.

Pinar, William F., Reynolds, William M., Slattery, Patrick, and Taubman, Peter M. *Understanding Curriculum: An Introduction to the Study of Historical and Contemporary Discourses.* New York: Peter Lang, 1996.

Popham, W. James and Baker, Eva L. *Systematic Instruction.* Englewood Cliffs, N.J.: Prentice-Hall, 1970.

Posner, George J. *Analyzing the Curriculum.* New York: McGraw-Hill, 1992.

Rice, Berkeley. "The Hawthorne Defect: Persistence of a Flawed Theory." *Psychology Today,* 16, no. 2 (February 1982): 70–74.

Roethlisberger, F. J. and Dickson, William J. *Management and the Worker.* Cambridge, Mass.: Harvard University Press, 1939.

Saylor, J. Galen, Alexander, William M., and Lewis, Arthur J. *Curriculum Planning for Better Teaching and Learning,* 4th ed. New York: Holt, Rinehart and Winston, 1981.

Schubert, William H. *Curriculum: Perspective, Paradigm, and Possibility.* New York: Macmillan, 1986.

————, Schubert, Ann Lynn Lopez, Thomas, Thomas P., and Carroll, Wayne M. *Curriculum Books: The First Hundred Years,* 2nd ed. New York: Peter Lang, 2002.

Schwab, Joseph J. *The Practical: A Language for Curriculum.* Washington, D.C.: National Education Association, Center for the Study of Instruction, 1970.

Slattery, Patrick. *Curriculum Development in the Postmodern Era.* New York: Garland Publishing, 1995.

Smith, B. Othanel, Stanley, William O., and Shores, J. Harlan. *Fundamentals of Curriculum Development,* rev. ed. New York: Harcourt Brace Jovanovich, 1957.

Sowell, Evelyn J. *Curriculum: An Integrative Introduction.* Englewood Cliffs, N.J.: Merrill, 1996.

Taba, Hilda. *Curriculum Development: Theory and Practice.* New York: Harcourt Brace Jovanovich, 1962.

Tanner, Daniel and Tanner, Laurel. *Curriculum Development: Theory into Practice,* 4th ed. Upper Saddle River, N.J.: Merrill/Prentice Hall, 2007.

Tyler, Ralph W. *Basic Principles of Curriculum and Instruction.* Chicago: University of Chicago Press, 1949.

Vallance, Elizabeth. "Curriculum as a Field of Practice." In Fenwick W. English, ed., *Fundamental Curriculum Decisions,* 1983 Yearbook, 154–164. Alexandria, Va.: Association for Supervision and Curriculum Development, 1983.

Walker, Decker. *Fundamentals of Curriculum: Passion and Professionalism,* 2nd ed. Mahwah, N.J.: Lawrence Erlbaum Associates, 2003.

Wiles, Jon and Bondi, Joseph. *Curriculum Development: A Guide to Practice,* 6th ed. Upper Saddle River, N.J.: Merrill/Prentice Hall, 2007.

2 Principles of Curriculum Development

AFTER STUDYING THIS CHAPTER YOU SHOULD BE ABLE TO:

1. Describe the ten axioms for curriculum development discussed in this chapter.
2. Illustrate in what way the curriculum is influenced by changes in society.
3. Describe limitations affecting curriculum changes in a school system and within which curriculum workers must function.

CLARIFICATION OF TERMS

Education is one of the institutions the human race has created to serve certain needs, and, like all human institutions, it responds or should respond to changes in the environment. The institution of education is activated by a curriculum that itself changes in response to forces affecting it. The curriculum of the cave dweller, albeit informal and unstructured, was quite different from increasingly formal types of schooling that the human race invented over subsequent periods of history. Techniques for coping with the woolly mammoth may well have been of paramount concern to prehistoric man.[1] But the woolly mammoth has disappeared, and men and women today must learn to cope with other sources of anxiety like poverty, crime, drug addiction, job insecurities, homelessness, environmental problems, health problems, natural distasters, decreasing natural resources, intercultural and international conflicts, and the military and industrial hazards of nuclear power. At the same time humankind must learn to apply the technological tools that are proliferating in both number and complexity at an astronomical rate—a cause of anxiety in itself—to solve these and other problems.

Although no educator—teacher, curriculum coordinator, administrator, or professor—would dream of arguing that techniques for coping with the woolly mammoth should be part of the curriculum of schools at the dawn of the twenty-first century A.D., in the third century of the American republic, the woolly mammoth syndrome still persists. Schools "woolly mammoth" children when they offer a curriculum that does the following:

- Allows learners to leave school without an adequate mastery of the basic skills.
- Ill equips learners to find and hold employment when they finish school.
- Fails to promote attitudes of respect for others, cooperation with others, responsibility for one's actions, tolerance for others, and preservation of the environment.
- Holds learners to low expectations.
- Uses materials that show all children as members of healthy, happy, prosperous, white, Anglo-Saxon, Protestant families joyously living in the suburbs.
- Leaves out the practical knowledge and skills necessary for survival and success in a complex, technological society, such as computer science, knowledge about insurance and taxes, writing a résumé and letter of application for a job, interviewing for a position, intelligent consumerism, and listening and discussion skills.
- Omits exposure to the fine arts, including the development of aesthetic appreciation.
- Distorts truths of the past ("Honest Abe had no faults"), the present ("Every person who is willing to work can find an adequate job"), and the future ("There is no need for residents of fast-growing sections of the country to worry about running out of potable water").
- Appeals to short-term interests of students and ignores long-range needs; or, vice versa, appeals to long-range needs and ignores short-term interests.
- Ignores the health needs of children and youth.

If the curriculum is perceived as a plan for the learning experiences that young people encounter under the direction of the school, its purpose is to provide a vehicle for ordering and directing those experiences. This process of providing the vehicle and keeping it running smoothly is known as *curriculum development*.

It may be helpful at this point to review the slight distinctions among the following terms: *curriculum development, curriculum planning, curriculum improvement*, and *curriculum evaluation. Curriculum development* is the more comprehensive term; it includes planning, implementation, and evaluation. Since curriculum development implies change and betterment, *curriculum improvement* is often used synonymously with curriculum development, though in some cases improvement is viewed as the result of development.

Curriculum planning is the preliminary phase of curriculum development when the curriculum workers make decisions and take actions to establish the plan that teachers and students will carry out. Planning is the thinking or design phase.

Curriculum implementation is translation of plans into action. During the stage of curriculum planning certain patterns of curriculum organization or reorganization are chosen. These patterns are put into operation at the implementation stage. Ways of delivering the learning experiences, for example, using teaching teams, are taken out of the planning context and made operational. Since curriculum implementation translates plans into action in the classroom, thereby transforming the realm of curriculum into the realm of instruction, the role of the teacher changes from curriculum worker to instructor.

Those intermediate and final phases of development in which results are assessed and successes of both the learners and the programs are determined are *curriculum evaluation*. On occasion, *curriculum revision* is used to refer to the process for making changes in an existing curriculum or to the changes themselves and is substituted for *curriculum development* or *improvement*. We shall return to the distinctions among curriculum planning, implementation, and evaluation when models of curriculum development are diagrammed and discussed in Chapter 5.

Through the process of curriculum development we can discover new ways for providing more effective pupil learning experiences. The curriculum developer continuously strives to find newer, better, and more efficient means to accomplish the task of educating the young.

TYPES OF CURRICULUM DEVELOPERS

Some curriculum developers excel in the conceptualizing phase (planning), others in carrying out the curricular plan (implementation), and still others in assessing curriculum results (evaluation). Over the centuries the human race has had no shortage of curriculum developers. In a positive vein Moses, Jesus, Buddha, Confucius, and Mohammed could all be called curriculum consultants. They had their respective conceptions of the goals of the human race and recommended behavior that must be learned and practiced to achieve those goals. On the negative side, at a later period in history, Hitler, Stalin, Mussolini, and Mao Zedong had definite notions and programs to train the young in what to believe and how to behave in a totalitarian society. On the current scene, the curriculum of the madrassas of Moslem countries diverges widely from that of Western nations.

The ranks of the politicians in a democracy have produced curriculum consultants, some more astute than others. To the weary professional curriculum worker, it sometimes seems that every federal, state, and local legislator is a self-appointed, self-trained curriculum consultant who has his or her own pet program to promulgate. The statutes of the state legislatures, as we shall see in Chapter 3, provide numerous examples of legislative curriculum making.

Singling out all the politicians who have turned themselves into curriculum consultants through the years would be impossible. But the kite-flier who experimented with electricity, invented a stove, created a new educational institution called the Academy, and in between found time to participate in a revolution—Benjamin Franklin—made some farsighted curriculum proposals for his academy. Franklin's statement of recommendations almost seems to have been drawn out of a report on a high school's program of studies by a present-day visiting committee of a regional accrediting association. Franklin proposed for his academy (later to become the University of Pennsylvania) a curriculum much more suited to its time than its predecessor, the Latin Grammar School.[2]

Curriculum advisers have been found not only among politicians but also among academicians, journalists, the clergy, and the public at large. Professional educators have received a great deal of both solicited and unsolicited help in shaping school curricula. An unending procession of advisers from both within and outside the profession of education over many decades has not been at a loss to advocate curriculum proposals. No matter how significant or minor, no matter how mundane or bizarre, all proposals have shared one common element: advocacy of change.

What has led so many people to be dissatisfied with so much of what education is all about? Why is the status quo rarely a satisfactory place to be? And why does it turn out, as will be illustrated, that yesterday's status quo is sometimes tomorrow's innovation? For answers to these questions some general principles of curriculum development should be considered by teachers and specialists who participate in efforts to improve the curriculum.

SOURCES OF CURRICULUM PRINCIPLES

Principles serve as guidelines to direct the activity of persons working in a particular area. Curriculum principles are derived from many sources: (1) empirical data, (2) experimental data, (3) the folklore of curriculum, composed of unsubstantiated beliefs and attitudes, and (4) common sense. In an age of science and technology, the attitude often prevails that all principles must be scientifically derived from the results of research. Yet even folklore and common sense can have their use. The scientist has discovered, for example, that some truths underlie ancient folk remedies for human maladies and that old wives' tales are not always the ravings of demented witches. While a garland of garlic hung around the neck may or may not fend off vampires and asafetida on the end of a fishline may or may not lure fish onto the hook, the aloe plant does, after all, yield a soothing ointment for burns, and the peppermint herb has relieved many a stomachache.

Common sense, which is often distrusted, combines folklore, generalizations based on observation, and learning discovered through experimentation with intuition and reasoned guesses. It can function not only as a source of curriculum principles but as a methodology as well. For example, Joseph J. Schwab proposed a commonsense process he called "deliberation" to deal with curriculum problems. Minimizing the search for theoretical constructs and principles, his method depends more on practical solutions to specific problems.[3] Schwab pointed out the pitfalls of relying on theory alone. He rejected "the pursuit of global principles and comprehensive patterns, the search for stable sequences and invariant elements, the construction of taxonomies of supposedly fixed or recurrent kinds" and recommended "three other modes of operation . . . the practical, the quasi-practical, and the eclectic."[4]

Of particular interest is Schwab's contrast of the theoretical and practical modes. Schwab explained:

> The end or outcome of the theoretical is knowledge, general or universal statements which are supposed to be true, warranted, confidence-inspiring. Their truth, warrant, or untrustworthiness is held, moreover, to be durable and extensive. . . . The end or outcome of the practical, on the other hand, is a *decision*, a selection and guide to possible action.

Decisions are never true or trustworthy. Instead a decision (before it is put into effect) can be judged only comparatively, as probably better or worse than alternatives. . . . A decision, moreover, has no great durability or extensive application. It applies unequivocally only to the case for which it is sought.[5]

When curriculum planning is based on deliberation, judgment and common sense are applied to decision making. Some professional educators have faulted the application of common sense or judgment as a methodology, so imbued are they with a scientific approach to problem solving. In 1918 Franklin Bobbitt took note of scientific methodology in curriculum making, citing the application of measurement and evaluation techniques, diagnosis of problems, and prescription of remedies.[6] At a later date Arthur W. Combs was moved to warn against too great a reliance on science for the solution of all educational problems.[7] Whereas science may help us find solutions to some problems, not all answers to educational problems of the day can be found in this way. Certainly, hard data are preferred over beliefs and judgments. But there are times in the absence of hard data when curriculum workers must rely on their intuition and make judgments on the basis of the best available evidence.

Unless a principle is established that is irrefutable by reason of objective data, some degree of judgment must be brought into play. Whenever judgment comes into the picture, the potential for controversy arises. Consequently, some of the principles for curriculum development provoke controversy, while others are generally accepted as reasonable guidelines. Controversy occurs as often as a result of differing values and philosophical orientations of curriculum workers as it does from lack of hard data for making decisions.

TYPES OF PRINCIPLES

Curriculum principles may be viewed as whole truths, partial truths, or hypotheses. While all function as operating principles, they are distinguished by their known effectiveness or by degree of risk. It is important to understand these differences before examining the major guiding principles for curriculum development.

Whole Truths

Whole truths are either obvious facts or concepts proved through experimentation, and they are usually accepted without challenge. For example, few will dispute that students will be able, as a rule, to master an advanced body of content only after they have developed the prerequisite skills. From this principle come the practices of preassessment of entry skills and sequencing of content.

Partial Truths

Partial truths are based on limited data and can apply to some, many, or most situations, but they are not always universal. Some educators assert, for example, that student achievement is higher when students are grouped homogeneously for instruction. Some learners may achieve better results when placed in groups of like ability, but others may not. The practice of homogeneous or ability grouping may be successful with some groups but not with others. It may permit schools to achieve certain goals of education, such as mastery of content, but prevent them from achieving other goals, such as enabling students to learn to live and work with persons of differing levels of ability. Partial truths are not "half-truths," containing falsehoods, but they do not always tell the whole story.

Hypotheses

Finally, some principles are neither whole nor partial truths but are *hypotheses* or tentative working assumptions. Curriculum workers base these ideas on their best judgments, folklore, and common sense. As one example, teachers and administrators have talked for many years about optimum size for classes and for schools. Educators have advocated class sizes of as few as twenty-five students in high school classes and fewer in elementary classes. They have been less certain as to how many pupils should be housed in a single school. Figures used as recommendations for class and school size are but estimates based on best judgments. School planners have reasoned that for purposes of economy and efficiency, class and school sizes can be too small. They also know from intuition or experience that class and school sizes can grow so large as to create situations that reduce educational productivity. However, the research delivers no magic number that will guarantee success in every course, classroom, and school.

While practice based on whole truth is a desideratum, the use of partial truths and the application of hypotheses contribute to the development of the field. Growth would be stymied if the field waited until all truths were discovered before any changes were made. Judgments, folklore, and common sense make the curriculum arena a far more stimulating place to work than if everything were already predetermined. If all theories, beliefs, and hypotheses could be either proved or disproved—a most improbable event—we would have reached that condition of perfection that would make life among the curriculum developers exceedingly dull.

TEN AXIOMS

Instead of talking in terms of whole truths and partial truths, since so many of the principles to which practitioners subscribe have not been fully tested, we might be more accurate if we speak of *axioms* or *theorems*. As students of mathematics know well, both axioms and theorems serve the field well. They offer guidelines that establish a frame of reference for workers seeking ways of operating and resolving problems. Several generally accepted axioms that apply to the curriculum field may serve to guide efforts that curriculum workers make for the purpose of improving the curriculum.

Inevitability of Change

Axiom 1.   *Change is both inevitable and necessary, for it is through change that life forms grow and develop.* Human institutions, like human beings themselves, grow and develop in proportion to their ability to respond to change and to adapt to changing conditions. Society and its institutions continuously encounter problems to which they must respond or perish. Forrest W. Parkay, Eric J. Anctil, and the late Glen T. Hass called attention to the following major contemporary problems facing society, all of which remain continuing issues:

- changing values and cultural diversity
- changing values and morality
- family
- Microelectronics Revolution
- changing world of work
- equal rights
- crime and violence
- lack of purpose and meaning
- global interdependence[8]

The public school, one of our society's fundamental institutions, faces a plethora of contemporary problems, some of which threaten its very existence. We need cite only the intense competition from both secular and sectarian private schools; proposals for tax credits and vouchers which may be used at any school, public, private, or parochial; the advent of charter schools; and the increase in the number of home schools to illustrate the scope of problems currently confronting the public school. Change in the form of responses to contemporary problems must be foremost in the minds of curriculum developers.

Curriculum as a Product of Its Time

Axiom 2. The second axiom is a corollary of the first. Quite simply, a *school curriculum not only reflects but also is a product of its time.* Though it may seem to some that the curriculum is a tortoise moving infernally s-l-o-w-l-y, it has really undergone more transformations than the number of disguises assumed by a skilled master change artist.

Prior to the advent of television, computer networks, and other sophisticated media, curriculum change came relatively slowly; in fact, it sometimes took decades, but today news and ideas flash across the country, indeed across the world, instantaneously. It did not take decades for thousands of schools throughout the country to put into practice (and in some cases later abandon) team teaching, instructional television, open-space education, values clarification, behavioral objectives, computer literacy, cooperative learning, and whole language, to mention only a few curricular innovations.

Clearly, the curriculum responds to and is changed by social forces, philosophical positions, psychological principles, accumulating knowledge, and educational leadership at its moment in history. Changes in society clearly influence curriculum development as, for example, the increased pluralism of our nation, the rapid growth of technology, and the need for health education. You will note the pervasive effects of social forces when we discuss programs and issues in Chapters 9 and 15.

The impact of the rapid accumulation of knowledge may be one of the more dramatic illustrations of forces affecting the curriculum. Certainly some adaptations in the school's program ought to be made as a result of discoveries of lifesaving vaccines and medications; inventions such as the computer, the laser, the multipurpose cell phone; the digital camera; high-definition television; interactive video; scientific accomplishments like the moon landings; the Mars flights; the Galileo probes; the Cassini and Genesis missions; shuttles to and from the space station; and other land, sea, and space explorations.

The presence of persuasive educational groups and individuals has been responsible for the adoption of curricular innovations at given moments in history and in numerous cases has caused permanent and continuing curriculum change. The effects of the *Cardinal Principles of Secondary Education* by the Commission on the Reorganization of Secondary Education, *Education for All American Youth* by the Educational Policies Commission, and *A Nation at Risk* by the National Commission on Excellence in Education are illustrations of the impact persuasive groups have on the curriculum.

We may even point to individuals over the course of history, speaking either for themselves or for groups that they represented, who can be credited (or blamed, depending on one's perspective) for changes that have come about in the curriculum. Who can calculate the impact on education, for example, of Benjamin Franklin in the eighteenth century or Horace Mann in the nineteenth? What would the progressive education movement of the early twentieth century have been without John Dewey, William H. Kilpatrick, and Boyd Bode? How many secondary schools in the late 1950s and early 1960s "Conantized" their programs on the recommendations of James B. Conant, the former president of Harvard University? What impact has Maria Montessori had on elementary school programs? What responses of the curriculum in the latter half of the twentieth century can be traced to the teachings of Jean Piaget and of B. F. Skinner? What changes will come about as a result of recommendations made by Mortimer J. Adler, Ernest L. Boyer, John I. Goodlad, and Theodore R. Sizer? (In Chapter 9 we will examine some of these recommendations.)

We could fashion for ourselves a little chart—see Table 2.1—to illustrate the effects of several forces during periods of history on both the curriculum and instruction. In barest skeletal form we might break American educational history into three periods: 1650–1750, 1750–1850, and 1850 to the present. We might then chart some of the curricular and instructional responses to philosophical, psychological, and sociological forces of their time as the table shows. These forces and responses often overlap from one period to the next.

We could embellish the chart by refining the periods of history and adding other elements, but this skeletal description serves to illustrate that a curriculum is the product of its time or, as James B. Macdonald noted, "any reforms in institutional setting . . . are intricately related to multiple social processes and set in the context of a general cultural ethos."[9]

Consequently, the curriculum planner of today must identify and be concerned with forces that impinge on the schools and must carefully decide how the curriculum should change in response to these often conflicting forces.

TABLE 2.1 Forces Affecting Curriculum and Instruction

Period	Forces	Curricular Responses	Instructional Responses
1650–1750	*Philosophy* Essentialism *Psychology* Faculty psychology—mind as a muscle *Sociology* Theocracy—Calvinist Male chauvinism Agrarian society Rich–poor dichotomy	Latin Grammar School: School for boys The Bible The three R's Classical curriculum	Strict discipline Rote learning Use of sectarian materials Mental discipline

1750–1850	*Philosophy*
	Essentialism
	Utilitarianism
	
	Psychology
	Faculty psychology
	
	Sociology
	Industrial Revolution
	Westward movement
	Rise of middle class
	Increased urbanization
		Academy
		Education for girls
		Instruction in:
		    English
		    Natural history
		    Modern languages plus
		        three R's and classical
		        curriculum
		Tax-supported schools
		Kindergartens
			Mental discipline
			Recitation
			Strict discipline
			Some practical applications

1850 to present	*Philosophy*
	Essentialism
	Progressivism
	
	Psychology
	Behavioristic
	Experimental
	Gestalt
	Perceptual
	
	Sociology
	Settling the West
	Mechanized society
	Urbanization
	Immigration
	Armed conflicts
	Civil rights
	Big business
	Big labor
	Equal rights
	Changes in family
	Environmental problems
	Diminishing resources
	Rapid growth of
	    technology
		1850–1925:
		High schools
		1925–1950:
		Child-centered curriculum
		Experimentalism
		Centralization and
		    consolidation of schools
		Life adjustment
		1950 to present:
		Career education
		Open-space education
		Basic skills
		Alternative schooling
		Magnet schools
		Charter schools
		Home schools
		Middle schools
		Standards
		Computer education
		Values/character education
		Environmental education
		Multicultural education
		Global education
			Practical applications
			Problem-solving methods
			Attention to whole child
			
			Individualization and
			    groupings for instruction
			Mediated instruction
			Education for self-
			    discipline
			Achievement testing
			Effective teaching models
			Cooperative learning
			Whole language
			Use of community
			    resources
			Computer-assisted
			    instruction
			Integrated studies

(continued)

TABLE 2.1   Continued

Period	Forces	Curricular Responses	Instructional Responses
1850 to present (continued)	Space exploration Public demand for schools' accountability Unemployment Drug and alcohol abuse Crime Homeless persons Racial tensions/ethnic conflicts Movements for human rights Persons with disabilities Aging population Sexual behavior Religious differences Growth of democratic movements worldwide Economic crises Global warming End of cold war AIDS Continuing health needs Globalization International tensions, conflicts, and crises Terrorism	Health education/clinics Sexuality education Adult education Literacy education Bilingual education Consumer education Cultural literacy (core knowledge) Community service Smaller schools/schools-within-schools Technological education	State assessment/exit exams Online instruction

Concurrent Changes

Axiom 3.   *Curriculum changes made at an earlier period of time can exist concurrently with newer curriculum changes at a later period of time.* The classical curriculum of the Latin Grammar School was continued, in spite of the reluctance of Benjamin Franklin, in the Academy. Indeed, even the first high school, established in Boston in 1821, was known as the English Classical School. It was not until three years later that the English Classical School became the English High School.

Curriculum revision rarely starts and ends abruptly. Changes coexist and overlap for long periods of time. Ordinarily, curricular developments are phased in gradually and phased out the same way. Because competing forces and responses occur at different periods of time and continue to exist, curriculum development becomes a frustrating, yet challenging task.

Differing philosophical positions on the nature of humankind, the destiny of the human race, good and evil, and the purposes of education have existed at every period of history. The powerful schools of essentialism and progressive thought continually strive to capture the allegiance of the profession and the public. The college preparatory curriculum, for example, vies with the vocational curriculum for primacy. Instructional strategies that are targeted at the development of the intellect compete with strategies for treating the child in body, mind, and spirit. Even the discredited tenets of faculty psychology ("mind as a muscle," mental discipline) linger in school practices.

The competing responses to changing conditions have almost mandated an eclecticism, especially in the public schools. Curriculum developers select the best responses from previous times or modify them for future times. Except at the most trivial level, either/or choices are almost impossible to make in complex social areas like education. Yet some people continue to look for and argue for either/or solutions. To some, instruction will suffer if all teachers do not write behavioral objectives. To others, the growth of preadolescents will surely be stunted unless they are educated in a middle school. Some elementary school administrators seek to provide a quality education with teaching teams. Others hold firmly to the traditional self-contained classroom. Public sentiment in the early 2000s identifies state and national assessments as the cure for the ills of public schooling.

Some themes are repeated through history. Critics have, for example, lambasted the schools periodically for what they conceive as failure to stress fundamental subject matter.[10] The history of curriculum development is filled with illustrations not only of recurrent philosophical themes, like the subject matter cacophony, but also with recurrent and cyclical curricular responses. Many of our schools have changed from an essentialistic to a progressive curriculum and back again.

Schools have moved from self-contained to open space to self-contained; elementary schools have shifted from self-contained to nongraded to self-contained; schools have taught the "old math," then the "new math," and afterwards reverted to the former; they have followed the phonics method of teaching reading, changed to "look/say" methods, then gone back to phonics; they have stressed modern languages, then abandoned them, then reincorporated them in the curriculum. On the other hand, some schools, particularly the essentialistic, have remained unchanged while social transformations have swirled around them.

The schools of the early days in America stressed basic skills taught in a strict disciplinary climate. The early twentieth century schools went beyond basic skills—some would say away from basic skills—to concern for pupils' diverse needs and interests in a more permissive environment. Schools of the present emphasize the basic skills, especially reading and mathematics; subject matter; academic achievement; pupil assessment; and codes of conduct as well as personal development in a culturally diverse society.

As curricular themes are often recapitulated, some teachers and curriculum developers are disposed to maintain the status quo, concluding that their current mode of operation, while it may be out of favor at the present moment, will be in style again sometime in the future. "Why change and then have to change back?" they ask.

When the status quo no longer serves the needs of the learners or of society, the maintenance of the status quo is inexcusable, for it prohibits responses appropriate to the times. Even if prior responses return at a later date, they should result from a reexamination of the forces of that particular time. Thus, the reemergence of prior responses will be new responses, not *old* in the sense of being unchanging and unchangeable.

Change in People

Axiom 4.   *Curriculum change results from changes in people.* Thus, curriculum developers should begin with an attempt to change the people who must ultimately effect curriculum change. This effort implies involving people in the process of curriculum development to gain their commitment to change. Sad experience over a long period of time has demonstrated that changes handed down from on high to subordinates do not work well as a rule. Not until the subordinates have internalized the changes and accepted them as their own can the changes be effective and long lasting. Many school personnel lack commitment because they are denied this involvement in change and their contributions to change have been deprecated.

The importance of effecting change in people has been stressed by curriculum experts for many years. Alice Miel, for example, wrote:

> To change the curriculum of the school is to change the factors interacting to shape the curriculum. In each instance this means bringing about changes in people—in their desires, beliefs, and attitudes, in their knowledge and skill. Even changes in the physical environment, to the extent that they can be made at all, are dependent upon changes in the persons who have some control over that environment. In short, the nature of curriculum change should be seen for what it really is—a type of social change, change in people, not mere change on paper.[11]

A lack of enthusiastic support from those affected by change spills over to the students, who often adopt negative attitudes as a result.

Some curriculum planners interpret this axiom to mean that one hundred percent commitment of all affected parties must be achieved before a curriculum change can be implemented. Would that it were possible to obtain one hundred percent consensus on any issue in education! Somewhere between a simple majority and universal agreement would appear to be a reasonable expectation. Involvement of persons affected in the process itself will succeed in garnering some support even from those who may disagree with the final curricular product.

The curriculum planner should ensure that all persons have an opportunity to contribute to a proposed change before it is too far along and irreversible. No persons should be involved in the charade practiced in some school systems whereby teachers and others are brought into the planning process for window dressing when it is a foregone conclusion that the curriculum change will be implemented whether the participants accept it or not. The "curriculum planner knows best" attitude has no place in curriculum design and implementation.

Today we commonly witness the practice of empowering teachers and laypersons, that is, enabling them to exercise a degree of control over what happens in their schools.

For further discussion of empowerment, see Chapter 4, which expands on the process for instituting and effecting curriculum change.

Cooperative Endeavor

Axiom 5. *Curriculum change is effected as a result of cooperative endeavor on the part of groups.*

Although an individual teacher working in isolation might conceivably, and some-times does, effect changes in the curriculum by himself or herself, large and fundamental changes are brought about as a result of group decision. Numerous authorities over the years have underscored the group nature of curriculum development.[12]

Several groups or constituencies are involved in curriculum development in differ-ing roles and with differing intensities. Students and laypersons often, though perhaps not as frequently as might be desired, join forces with educational personnel in the com-plex job of planning a curriculum.

Teachers and curriculum specialists constitute the professional core of planners. These professionally trained persons carry the weight of curriculum development. They work together under the direction of the school administrator whose task it is to oversee their activities and to facilitate their efforts at all stages of development. The administra-tor may take the bows for the school's successful activities but by the same token will also receive barbs for efforts gone awry.

Students enter the process of curriculum development as direct recipients of both benefits and harm that result from curriculum change, and parents are brought in as the persons most vitally concerned with the welfare of their young. More often than in days gone by, administrators, either willingly on their own or by directives from higher au-thority, invite students and parents to participate in the process of curriculum planning. Some school systems go beyond parents of children in their schools and seek represen-tation from the total community, parents and nonparents alike. People from the com-munity are asked more frequently now what they feel the schools should offer and what they believe the schools are omitting from their programs.

Generally, any significant change in the curriculum should involve all the afore-mentioned constituencies, as well as the school's noncertificated personnel. The more people affected by the change, the greater its complexity and costs, the greater the num-ber of persons and groups that should be involved. The roles of various individuals and groups in curriculum development are examined in Chapter 4.

Although some limited gains certainly take place through independent curriculum development within the walls of a classroom, significant curriculum improvement comes about through group activity. Results of group deliberation are not only more extensive than individual efforts, but the process by which the group works together allows group members to share their ideas and to reach group consensus. In this respect group mem-bers help each other to change and to achieve commitment to change. Carl D. Glickman averred: "Any comprehensive changes made without the understanding and support of at least a core majority of educators and parents will fail, not necessarily because of the changes themselves but because of the way they came about."[13] Drawing on a report from Public Agenda by Jean Johnson and John Immerwahr,[14] Glickman affirmed that the public wants to maintain the status quo and stressed the importance of involving parents and citizens in curriculum planning when he said:

> The hard facts are that most parents and citizens do not believe in or want much alternation in their schools' educational structures. They want grade levels, letter grades, ability grouping, single classrooms, and textbooks. They want today's school to look like the schools they attended. They want teachers to emphasize the basic skills and direct instruction. They are skeptical about new ways of assessing student learning, group or cooperative learning, critical thinking, and student problem solving. . . . Regardless of how insupportable is the case for keeping schools as they are, without a way for educators, parents, and citizens to understand, discuss, and participate in new possibilities, change efforts for the long term will be for naught.[15]

In analyzing the failures of curriculum reform efforts Larry Cuban made clear that "defining the official school curriculum (as opposed to the 'taught,' 'learned,' and 'tested' curricula) is one of the few endeavors left that allows groups in a democratic society, continually pulled this way and that by highly prized but competing values to debate what they want for the next generation."[16]

Decision-Making Process

Axiom 6. *Curriculum development is basically a decision-making process.* Curriculum planners, working together, must make a variety of decisions, including the following:

1. *Choices among disciplines.* The absence of philosophy, anthropology, Eastern languages, driver education, and sometimes even art, music, and physical education from the curriculum of schools indicates that choices have been made about the subjects to which students will be exposed.
2. *Choices among competing viewpoints.* Planners must decide, for example, whether they agree that bilingual education best serves the needs of segments of society. If they decide in the positive, they must further decide what type of bilingual education is appropriate for their schools. Planners must make decisions about programs such as interscholastic athletics for girls; whether pupils with learning disabilities should be assigned to special classes; whether to group pupils by ability, achievement, age, or heterogeneously; and whether programs of sexuality education should be offered.
3. *Choices of emphases.* Shall a school system, for example, give extra help to poor readers? Shall school systems provide programs for the gifted? Shall extra efforts be made for disadvantaged students? Should school funds be diverted from one group of students to aid another group?
4. *Choices of methods.* What is the best way, for example, to teach reading? phonics? look/say? "systems" reading? whole language? What is the best way to teach writing? Shall methods emphasize skills or creativity and self-esteem? What are the

more effective materials to use? How do we eliminate ethnic and cultural bias from the curriculum?

5. *Choices in organization.* Is a nongraded school, for example, the better approach to an organizational arrangement that will provide maximum opportunities for learners? Should alternative forms of schooling within and outside the system be provided? Shall elementary programs be delivered in an open-space or pod setting, with totally self-contained classrooms, or with the use of resource persons to assist a teacher in a self-contained classroom? Should schools operate year-round and if so, shall they be single track or multitrack? What can we do to reduce class sizes?

Two necessary characteristics of a curriculum planner are the ability to effect decisions after sufficient study of a problem and the willingness to make decisions.[17] The indecisive person had best not gravitate to a career as a curriculum planner. Those persons for whom every *i* must be dotted and every *t* crossed before a move can be made are far too cautious for curriculum planning. Every decision involves calculated risk, for no one—in spite of what some experts may claim—has all the answers to all the problems or a single panacea for every problem. Some decisions will end in dismal failure. But unless the test is made, it can never be known what will succeed and what will not. The most that can be expected of a fallible human being is that decisions will be made on the basis of available evidence that suggests success for the learners and that promises no harm for them as a result of a decision taken. In the history of curriculum development we can find evidence of many roads that were not taken. Those roads might have turned out to be expressways to learning, though of course, the pessimistic champion of the status quo would assure us that the roads not taken would have been overgrown ruts that ended at the brink of a precipice or circular paths that would lead us right back to where we were.

The curriculum planner needs to be aware as John D. McNeil pointed out, that "curriculum decision making is a political process."[18] Although the task of making curricular choices may be difficult in complex, advanced societies, the opportunity to make choices from among many alternatives is a luxury not found in every country.

Continuous Process

Axiom 7. *Curriculum development is a never-ending process.* Curriculum planners constantly strive for the ideal, yet the ideal eludes them. Perfection in the curriculum will never be achieved. The curriculum can always be improved, and many times better solutions can be found to accomplish specific objectives. As the needs of learners change, as society changes, as technology unfolds, and as new knowledge appears, the curriculum must change. Curriculum evaluation should affect subsequent planning and implementation. Curriculum goals and objectives and plans for curricular organization should be modified as feedback reveals the need for modification.

Curriculum development is not finished when a single curricular problem has been temporarily solved nor when a newer, revised program has been instituted. Continual monitoring is necessary to assure that the program is on track and the problem does not recur. Further, adequate records should be kept by curriculum committees so that curriculum workers in future years will know what has been attempted and with what results.

Comprehensive Process

Axiom 8.   *Curriculum development is a comprehensive process.* Historically, curriculum revision has been a hit-or-miss procedure: patching, cutting, adding, plugging in, shortening, lengthening, and troubleshooting. In agreeing with the necessity for comprehensive planning, Hilda Taba explained:

> Some commentators have pointed out that the whole history of curriculum revision has been piecemeal—a mere shifting of pieces from one place to another, taking out one piece and replacing it with another without a reappraisal of the whole pattern. The curriculum has become "the amorphous product of generations of tinkering"—a patchwork. This piecemeal approach is continuing today, when additions and revisions in certain areas are made without reconsidering the entire pattern, and when attention in one part of the school system is recommended without corresponding changes in the next.[19]

Curriculum planning has often been too fragmentary rather than comprehensive or holistic. Too many curriculum planners have focused on the trees and not seen the forest. The popular expression that the whole is greater than the sum of its parts applies well to curriculum development. Although parts of the curriculum may be studied separately, planners must frequently and periodically view the macrocurriculum, that is, the curriculum as a whole, as distinguished from the sum of its parts.

Curriculum development spills not only into the forest but also beyond. A comprehensive view encompasses an awareness of the impact of curriculum development not only on the students, teachers, and parents directly concerned with a programmatic change but also on the innocent bystanders, those not directly involved in the curriculum planning but affected in some way by the results of planning. Sexuality education, for example, may affect not only teachers, students, and parents of students for whom the program is intended but also teachers, students, and parents of those who are not scheduled for the instruction. Some from the groups involved may not wish to be included. Some from the groups not in the program may wish to receive the instruction. Some from both groups may reject the subject as inappropriate for the school.

The comprehensive approach to curriculum planning requires a generous investment of physical and human resources. Curriculum workers must engage in, without meaning to be redundant, planning for curriculum planning or what some people might refer to as "preplanning." Some predetermination must be made prior to initiating curriculum development as to whether the tangible resources, the personnel, and sufficient time will be available to allow a reasonable expectation of success. Not only must personnel be identified, but their sense of motivation, energy level, and other commitments must also be taken into consideration by the curriculum leaders. Perhaps one of the reasons that curriculum development has historically been fragmentary and piecemeal is the demand the comprehensive approach places on the school's resources.

Systematic Development

Axiom 9. *Systematic curriculum development is more effective than trial and error.* Curriculum development should ideally be made comprehensive by looking at the whole canvas and should be made systematic by following an established set of procedures. That set of procedures should be agreed upon and known by all those who participate in the development of the curriculum. Curriculum planners are more likely to be productive and successful if they follow an agreed-upon model for curriculum development that outlines or charts the sequence of steps to be followed. In Chapter 5 we will examine several models for curriculum development.

If the curriculum worker subscribes to the foregoing axioms and consents to modeling his or her behavior on the basis of these axioms, will success be guaranteed? The answer is an obvious no, for there are many limitations on curriculum workers, some of which are beyond their control. Among the restrictions on the curriculum planner are the style and personal philosophy of the administrator, the resources of the school system, the degree of complacency in the school system and community, the presence or absence of competent supervisory leadership, the fund of knowledge and skills possessed by the participants in curriculum development, and the availability of professional materials and resource persons.

One of the great limitations—sometimes overlooked because it is so obvious and encompassing—is the existing curriculum. Many treatises have been written by curriculum experts on the characteristics of different types of curriculum. The earmarks of an activity curriculum, a subject matter curriculum, a broad-fields curriculum, and variations of core curriculum are described in the literature in detail.[20] From a purely cognitive base such discussions are useful. But the inference is sometimes drawn that the choice of a type of curriculum is an open one—that if the planners know and believe in the characteristics of an activity curriculum, for example, they will have the option of organizing and implementing that type of curriculum. It is as if a curriculum planner could start from scratch and design a totally new curriculum, which is rarely the case, and which leads us to the tenth axiom.

Starting from the Existing Curriculum

Axiom 10. *The curriculum planner starts from where the curriculum is, just as the teacher starts from where the students are.* Curriculum change does not take place overnight. Few quantum leaps can be found in the field of curriculum, and this condition may be a positive value rather than a negative one, for slow but steady progress toward change allows time for testing and reflection.

Since most curriculum planners begin with already existing curricula, we would be more accurate if, instead of talking about curriculum organization, we talked about curriculum reorganization. The investment of thought, time, money, and work by previous planners cannot be thrown out even if such a drastic remedy appeared valid to a new set of planners. The curriculum worker might well follow the advice in the *Book of Common Prayer,* where the believer is told to "hold fast to that which is good."

Summary

The system that we call education responds to changes as conditions in its suprasystem (society) change. Curriculum change is a normal, expected consequence of changes in the environment.

It is the responsibility of curriculum workers to seek ways of making continuous improvement in the curriculum. The task of the curriculum worker is facilitated if the worker follows some generally accepted principles for curriculum development. Ten general principles or axioms are presented in this chapter. The principles stem not only from disciplines outside of professional education but also from the folklore of curriculum, observation, experimental data, and common sense.

Axioms suggested as guidelines to curriculum developers are:

- Curriculum change is inevitable and desirable.
- The curriculum is a product of its time.
- Curriculum changes of earlier periods often coexist and overlap curriculum changes of later periods.
- Curriculum change results only as people are changed.
- Curriculum development is a cooperative group activity.
- Curriculum development is basically a process of making choices from among alternatives.
- Curriculum development never ends.
- Curriculum development is more effective if it is a comprehensive, not piecemeal, process.
- Curriculum development is more effective when it follows a systematic process.
- Curriculum development starts from where the curriculum is.

Both teachers and curriculum specialists fill roles as curriculum workers in cooperation with other school personnel. Teachers, curriculum specialists, supervisors, administrators, students, parents, and other community representatives can all play significant roles in effecting curriculum change.

Curriculum developers start from the given and work within specific parameters. Ordinarily, change is relatively slow, limited, and gradual.

Questions for Discussion

1. In what ways is today's public school curriculum suitable for the times?

2. In what ways is today's public school curriculum not suitable for the times?

3. What are some curriculum principles derived from common sense?

4. Are there any curriculum developments that have been based on whole truths? If so, give examples.

5. Are there any curriculum developments that have been based on false premises? If so, give examples.

Exercises

1. Develop your own chart of the effects of forces on curriculum and instruction by periods of history of the United States. Your chart should expand on the periods of history and present additional details.

2. Formulate and support one or two additional axioms pertaining to curriculum development. These may be original ones that you will be able to defend, or they may be axioms drawn from the professional literature.

3. Look up and write a paper on the contributions of one of the following persons to the development of curriculum thought or practice: Franklin Bobbitt, Boyd Bode, John Dewey, Robert Hutchins, William H. Kilpatrick, Jean Piaget, B. F. Skinner, and Ralph Tyler.

4. Look up and write a paper on one of the following groups and describe its impact on curriculum development in the United States: the Committee of Ten, the Commission on the Reorganization of Secondary Education, the Educational Policies Commission, the National Science Foundation, and the National Commission on Excellence in Education.

5. Choose three social developments, events, pressures, or forces in the United States within the last fifteen years that have caused changes in the school's curriculum, and briefly explain those changes.

6. Look up one or more books or articles by an author who has been critical of public education (such as Arthur Bestor, Rudolph Flesch, Paul Goodman, John Holt, John Keats, James D. Koerner, Jonathan Kozol, Max Rafferty, Hyman Rickover, and Mortimer Smith in the 1950s; George B. Leonard in the 1960s; Paul Cooperman, Ivan Illich, and Charles E. Silberman in the 1970s; Richard Mitchell, E. D. Hirsch, Jr., Diane Ravitch, and Chester E. Finn, Jr. in the 1980s; William J. Bennett, Lynne V. Cheney, Lewis J. Perelman, Harold W. Stevenson and James W. Stigler, Thomas Toch, and Ernest R. House in the 1990s; and Diane Ravitch and Jon Wiles and John Lundt in the 2000s) and summarize their criticisms in a written or oral report. Tell where you believe they were right and where you believe they were wrong.

7. Read *The Practical: A Language for Curriculum* by Joseph J. Schwab and explain to the class what Schwab meant by three modes of operation for curriculum development: the practical, the quasi-practical, and the eclectic. Tell what Schwab meant when he said, "The field of curriculum is moribund." State whether you agree with Schwab. (See bibliography.)

8. Consult some references on the history of American education and prepare comparative descriptions of the curriculum of (1) the Latin Grammar School, (2) the Academy, and (3) the English High School.

9. Explain what Larry Cuban meant by the four curricula: official, taught, learned, and tested. (See bibliography.)

Endnotes

1. For delightful reading, the little classic by Harold Benjamin (J. Abner Peddiwell) entitled *The Saber-Tooth Curriculum* (New York: McGraw-Hill, 1939) is recommended.

2. For discussion of the Academy, see Peter S. Hlebowitsh, *Foundations of American Education: Purpose and Promise*, 2nd ed. (Belmont, Calif.: Wadsworth, 2001), pp. 208–210.

3. Joseph J. Schwab, *The Practical: A Language for Curriculum* (Washington, D.C.: National Education Association, Center for the Study of Instruction, 1970).

4. Ibid., p. 2.

5. Ibid., pp. 2–3.

6. See Franklin Bobbitt, *The Curriculum* (Boston: Houghton Mifflin, 1918), pp. 41–42.

7. See Arthur W. Combs, *The Professional Education of Teachers* (Boston: Allyn and Bacon, 1965), p. 74.

8. Forrest W. Parkay, Eric J. Anctil, and Glen Hass, *Curriculum Planning: A New Approach*, 5th ed. (Boston: Allyn and Bacon, 2006), pp. 52–57.

9. James B. Macdonald, "Curriculum Development in Relation to Social and Intellectual Systems," in Robert M. McClure, ed., *The Curriculum: Retrospect and Prospect*, 70th Yearbook, Part I, National Society for the Study of Education (Chicago: University of Chicago Press, 1971), pp. 98–99.

10. See, for example, Arthur Bestor, *Educational Wastelands: The Retreat from Learning in Our Public Schools* (Urbana, Ill.: University of Illinois Press, 1953); Hyman Rickover, *Swiss Schools and Ours: Why Theirs Are Better* (Boston: Little, Brown, 1962); Richard Mitchell, *The Graves of Academe* (Boston: Little, Brown, 1981); and William J. Bennett, *The De-Valuing of America: The Fight for Our Children and Our Culture* (New York: Summit Books, 1992).

11. Alice Miel, *Changing the Curriculum: A Social Process* (New York: D. Appleton Century, 1946), p. 10.

12. See, for example, Albert I. Oliver and Joseph J. Schwab. (See bibliography.)

13. Carl D. Glickman, *Revolutionizing America's Schools* (San Francisco: Jossey-Bass, 1998), p. 38.

14. Jean Johnson and John Immerwahr, *First Things First: What Americans Expect from the Public Schools: A Report from Public Agenda* (New York: Public Agenda, 1994).

15. Glickman, *Revolutionizing*, p. 39.

16. Larry Cuban, "The Lure of Curricular Reform and Its Pitiful History," *Phi Delta Kappan* 75, no. 2 (October 1993): 183.

17. For description of a decision-making process, see Chapter 13 of this text regarding material from Phi Delta Kappa Committee on Evaluation, Daniel L. Stufflebeam, committee chairman, *Educational Evaluation and Decision Making* (Itasca, Ill.: F. E. Peacock, 1971).

18. John D. McNeil, *Curriculum: A Comprehensive Introduction*, 5th ed. (New York: HarperCollins, 1996), p. 290.

19. Hilda Taba, *Curriculum Development: Theory and Practice* (New York: Harcourt Brace Jovanovich, 1962), p. 8.

20. See B. O. Smith, William O. Stanley, and J. Harlan Shores, *Fundamentals of Curriculum Development*, rev. ed. (New York: Harcourt Brace Jovanovich, 1957). See also Chapter 9 of this text.

Bibliography

Adler, Mortimer J. *The Paideia Proposal: An Educational Manifesto.* New York: Macmillan, 1982.

Anderson, Vernon E. *Principles and Procedures of Curriculum Improvement*, 2nd ed. New York: Ronald Press, 1965.

Beane, James A., Toepfer, Conrad F., Jr., and Alessi, Samuel J., Jr. *Curriculum Planning and Development.* Boston: Allyn and Bacon, 1986.

Benjamin, Harold R. W. (Peddiwell, J. Abner). *The Saber-Tooth Curriculum.* New York: McGraw-Hill, 1939.

Bennett, William J. *The De-Valuing of America: The Fight for Our Children and Our Culture.* New York: Summit Books, 1992.

Bestor, Arthur. *Educational Wastelands: The Retreat from Learning in Our Public Schools.* Urbana, Ill.: University of Illinois Press, 1953.

Bobbitt, Franklin. *The Curriculum.* Boston: Houghton Mifflin, 1918. Also, New York: Arno Press and the New York Times, 1975.

Boyer, Ernest L. *High School: A Report on Secondary Education in America.* New York: Harper & Row, 1983.

Charters, W. W. *Curriculum Construction.* New York: Macmillan, 1923. Also, New York: Arno Press and the New York Times, 1971.

Commission on the Reorganization of Secondary Education. *Cardinal Principles of Secondary Education.*

Washington, D.C.: U.S. Office of Education, Bulletin 35, 1918.

Cuban, Larry. "The Lure of Curriculum Reform and Its Pitiful History." *Phi Delta Kappan* 75, no. 2 (October 1993): 182–185.

Davis, O. L., Jr. *Perspectives on Curriculum Development 1776–1976.* 1976 Yearbook. Alexandria, Va.: Association for Supervision and Curriculum Development, 1976.

Doll, Ronald C. *Curriculum Improvement: Decision Making and Process,* 9th ed. Boston: Allyn and Bacon, 1996.

Draper, Edgar Marion. *Principles and Techniques of Curriculum Making.* New York: D. Appleton-Century, 1936.

Educational Policies Commission. *Education for All American Youth.* Washington, D.C.: National Education Association, 1944.

Firth, Gerald R. and Kimpston, Richard D. *The Curricular Continuum in Perspective.* Itasca, Ill.: F. E. Peacock, 1973.

Frymier, Jack R. and Hawn, Horace C. *Curriculum Improvement for Better Schools.* Worthington, Ohio: Charles A. Jones, 1970.

Glickman, Carl D. *Revolutionizing America's Schools.* San Francisco: Jossey-Bass, 1998.

Goodlad, John I. *A Place Called School: Prospects for the Future.* New York: McGraw-Hill, 1984.

Gwynn, J. Minor and Chase, John B., Jr. *Curriculum Principles and Social Trends,* 4th ed. New York: Macmillan, 1969.

Hass, Glen. *Curriculum Planning: A New Approach,* 5th ed. Boston: Allyn and Bacon, 1987.

Henson, Kenneth T. *Curriculum Planning: Integrating Multiculturalism, Constructivism, and Education Reform,* 3rd ed. Long Grove, Ill.: Waveland Press, 2006.

Herrick, Virgil E. and Tyler, Ralph W. *Toward Improved Curriculum Theory.* Supplementary Educational Monograph, no. 71, March, 1950. Chicago: University of Chicago Press, 1950.

Hlebowitsh, Peter S. *Foundations of American Education: Purpose and Promise,* 2nd. ed. Belmont, Calif.: Wadsworth, 2001.

Johnson, Jean and Immerwahr, John. *First Things First: What Americans Expect from the Public Schools: A Report from Public Agenda.* New York: Public Agenda, 1994.

Leonard, Gorge B. *Education and Ecstasy with the Great School Reform Hoax.* Berkeley, Calif.: North Atlantic Books, 1987.

Macdonald, James B., Anderson, Dan W., and May, Frank B. *Strategies of Curriculum Development: Selected Writings of the Late Virgil E. Herrick.* Columbus, Ohio: Merrill, 1965.

McClure, Robert M., ed. *The Curriculum: Retrospect and Prospect.* 70th Yearbook. Chicago: National Society for the Study of Education, University of Chicago Press, 1971.

McNeil, John D. *Curriculum: A Comprehensive Introduction,* 5th ed. New York: HarperCollins, 1996.

Miel, Alice. *Changing the Curriculum: A Social Process.* New York: D. Appleton-Century, 1946.

Mitchell, Richard. *The Graves of Academe.* Boston: Little, Brown, 1981.

The National Commission on Excellence in Education, David P. Gardner, chairman. *A Nation at Risk: The Imperative for Educational Reform.* Washington, D.C.: U.S. Government Printing Office, 1983.

Oliver, Albert I. *Curriculum Improvement: A Guide to Problems, Principles, and Process,* 2nd ed. New York: Harper & Row, 1977.

Parkay, Forrest W., Anctil, Eric J., and Hass, Glen T. *Curriculum Planning: A Contemporary Approach,* 8th ed. Boston: Allyn and Bacon, 2006.

Perelman, Lewis J. *School's Out: Hyperlearning, the New Technology, and the End of Education.* New York: William Morrow, 1992.

Phi Delta Kappa Commission on Evaluation, Daniel L. Stufflebeam, committee chairman. *Educational Evaluation and Decision Making.* Itasca, Ill.: F. E. Peacock, 1971.

Posner, George and Rudnitzky, Alan N. *Curriculum Design: A Guide to Curriculum Development for Teachers,* 7th ed. Boston: Allyn and Bacon, 2006.

Rubin, Louis, ed. *Curriculum Handbook: The Disciplines, Current Movements, and Instructional Methodology.* Boston: Allyn and Bacon, 1977.

———. *Curriculum Handbook: Administration and Theory.* Boston: Allyn and Bacon, 1977.

Rickover, Hyman. *Swiss Schools and Ours: Why Theirs Are Better.* Boston: Little, Brown, 1962.

Saylor, J. Galen, Alexander, William M., and Lewis, Arthur J. *Curriculum Planning for Better Teaching and Learning,* 4th ed. New York: Holt, Rinehart and Winston, 1981.

Schwab, Joseph J. *The Practical: A Language for Curriculum.* Washington, D.C.: National Education Association, Center for the Study of Instruction, 1970.

Sizer, Theodore R. *Horace's Compromise: The Dilemma of the American High School.* Boston: Houghton Mifflin, 1984.

Smith, B. O., Stanley, William O., and Shores, J. Harlan. *Fundamentals of Curriculum Development,* rev. ed. New York: Harcourt Brace Jovanovich, 1957.

Taba, Hilda. *Curriculum Development: Theory and Practice.* New York: Harcourt Brace Jovanovich, 1962.

Tanner, Daniel and Tanner, Laurel N. *Curriculum Improvement: Theory into Practice*, 4th ed. Upper Saddle River, N.J.: Merrill/Prentice Hall, 2007.

Turney, David. "Sisyphus Revisited." *Perspectives on Curriculum Development 1776–1976.* 1976 Yearbook. Alexandria, Va.: Association for Supervision and Curriculum Development, 1976.

Unruh, Glenys H. *Responsive Curriculum Development: Theory and Action.* Berkeley, Calif.: McCutchan, 1975.

Verduin, John R., Jr. *Cooperative Curriculum Improvement.* Englewood Cliffs, N.J.: Prentice-Hall, 1967.

Walker, Decker F. *Fundamentals of Curriculum: Passion and Professionalism*, 2nd. ed. Mahwah, N.J.: Lawrence Erlbaum Associates, 2003.

——— and Soltis, Jonas F. *Curriculum and Aims*, 4th ed. New York: Teachers College Press, 2004.

Wiles, Jon and Bondi, Joseph C. *Curriculum Development: A Guide to Practice*, 7th ed. Upper Saddle River, N.J.: Merrill/Prentice Hall, 2007.

Zais, Robert S. *Curriculum: Principles and Foundations.* New York: Harper & Row, 1976.

3 Curriculum Planning: A Multilevel, Multisector Process

AFTER STUDYING THIS CHAPTER YOU SHOULD BE ABLE TO:

1. Describe types of curriculum planning that are conducted at five levels and in three sectors.
2. Describe an organizational pattern for curriculum development at the individual school level.
3. Describe an organizational pattern for curriculum development at the school district level.

ILLUSTRATIONS OF CURRICULUM DECISIONS

Daily, curriculum decisions like the following are being made in some school district somewhere in the United States:

- An elementary school uses computer-assisted instruction in teaching the basic skills.
- Computer laboratories have been established in both the middle and senior high schools of the same school district.
- A middle school has decided to incorporate more material on the achievements of various ethnic groups into its social studies program.

43

- An entire school district has decided to put a program of sexuality education into the curriculum at all levels.
- A senior high school faculty is concentrating on the development of students' thinking skills.
- A school system has revised a plan for bilingual education.
- An elementary school has decided to replace its reading series with that of another publisher.
- A school district prepares pupils to take a state-mandated test.
- A school district has put into operation a program of character education.
- A school system has approved a plan for meeting the needs of the academically talented and gifted.
- The secondary schools of a district have put into operation a plan for increasing opportunities for girls to participate in team sports and for placing these sports on a par with boys' athletic activities.
- An urban school district is establishing a magnet secondary school that will emphasize science, mathematics, and technology.

Variations among Schools

Countless curricular decisions like those in the preceding examples are made constantly. Some decisions are relatively simple—adding a course here, deleting a course there, or making some minor changes of content. Other decisions are sweeping and far-reaching—for example, the institution or abandonment of open-education plans or the conversion of a 6–3–3 plan for school organization (six years of elementary school, three of junior high, and three of senior high) to a 4–4–4 plan (four years each of elementary, middle, and high school). These changes are both administrative and curricular decisions.

Some of the more dynamic school systems maintain a lively pace of curriculum decision making and are continuously effecting changes in the curriculum as a result of these decisions. Often more than one type of change occurs simultaneously in some districts and schools.

Some systems follow a reasoned, measured process for arriving at planning decisions and carrying out those decisions; others enter into an almost frenzied, superheated process in which dozens of curricular ideas are dancing around without decisions or resolution; other school districts demonstrate lethargy and apathy toward curricular decision making and are, for all intents and purposes, stagnant.

The foregoing illustrations of curriculum decisions are typical examples occurring within individual school districts. These illustrations of curriculum decisions could apply to multiple school districts scattered throughout the United States.

How can we account for the simultaneous development of curriculum plans in different parts of the country? Shall we attribute it to legal pressures from federal or state sources? Among the foregoing illustrations only three—bilingual education programs, increased opportunities for girls to participate in team sports, and preparation for a state test—may be said to have evolved as a result of legal processes. In 1974 the United States Supreme Court opened the doors to bilingual education programs with its decision in the *Lau v. Nichols* case.[1] As a consequence of this decision the San Francisco school system was required to provide special instruction to children of Chinese ancestry who were having difficulty with the English language. Furthermore, federal funds have been appropriated to assist school systems to develop and implement bilingual education programs. The participation of girls in team sports has been advanced through enactment by the U.S. Congress of Title IX of the Educational Amendments of 1972, which bars discrimination on the basis of gender. With added pressure from the No Child Left Behind Act of 2001, states, setting academic standards, have been instituting tests at the elementary through high school levels. Certainly, federal and state legislation and court decisions have brought about curricular change, as we will explore more fully later. But we must also look elsewhere for other causes or partial causes of simultaneous development of curricular plans.

Simultaneous Developments

Though it is unlikely, similar curriculum developments in different school systems may unfold at the same time by pure chance. This situation resembles that of two astronomers, unknown to each other and separated by oceans, who suddenly discover a new planet, or two scientific researchers who find within days of each other a cure for a disease plaguing humankind.

It is more likely that our country's efficient systems of transportation and communication can be pointed to as principal reasons for concurrent curriculum development. These pervasive technological systems make possible the rapid transmission of the beneficial pollen (or not so beneficial virus, depending on one's point of view) of curricular ideas.

These gigantic systems have an impact on all the constituencies of a school district—the administrators, teachers, students, parents, and other members of the community. Transportation makes it possible for people from all parts of the country to get together in formal and informal settings and discuss contemporary problems of the schools. It would be interesting, for example, to measure the effects of national professional conferences on the spread of curricular innovation. Although the pessimist would assert that a great deal of drivel flows at many professional conferences, enough seeds of wisdom are shared and taken back home where they are planted, nurtured, and brought to fruition. Could not several of the preceding illustrations have come about through the exchange of ideas on a person-to-person basis at a state, regional, or national meeting?

With possibly an even greater impact, communication systems permit the dissemination of reports of educational and social problems in various parts of the country and descriptions of how communities have sought to cope with these problems. The ubiquitous computer and a dazzling and seemingly never-ending array of technological devices keep us apprised of developments around the world. The commercial press and television consistently make the public aware of social problems that call for some curricular responses, such as military conflicts, AIDS, drug abuse, crime, unemployment, ethnic tensions, environmental hazards, and the lack of basic skills on the part of young people. The media have been instrumental in revealing widespread dissatisfaction with the public schools to the point where lay constituencies are demanding that curriculum changes be made or parents be issued vouchers so their children may attend nonpublic schools of their choice.

While the commercial media are pointing out social problems and, on occasion, educational responses to these problems, the professional media are engaged in healthy dialogue. The United States is blanketed with professional journals filled with educators' philosophical positions; proposals for change; and reports of projects, research, and experimentation. National and state professional organizations, the United States Department of Education, and state departments of education frequently release monographs, guides, and research reports of promising curricular projects. Both popular and professional books on education make their contributions to the quest for curricular solutions to many social and educational problems. Who is to assess, for example, the impact made on the schools by educators such as Earl Kelley, who stressed the importance of an individual's self-concept;[2] Ralph Tyler, who suggested a systematic way of arriving at instructional objectives;[3] Benjamin Bloom and his associates, who offered a way of classifying educational objectives and advocated mastery learning;[4] James B. Conant, who made recommendations that were widely adopted by secondary schools;[5] Jerome S. Bruner, who wrote on the structure of disciplines;[6] Theodore Sizer, who founded the Coalition of Essential Schools;[7] and John I. Goodlad, who directed an extensive study of schools and made recommendations for improvement?[8]

Through modern means of communication and transportation, curriculum innovations—good, bad, and indifferent—are transmitted rapidly to a world thirsty for new and better ways of meeting its educational obligations to children and youth. It is extremely difficult in an enterprise as large as education to pinpoint the source of a particular curriculum change, and it is not usually necessary to do so. What is important to the student and practitioner in curriculum planning is to understand that processes for effecting change are in operation. These processes extend beyond the classroom, the school, even the school district.

LEVELS OF PLANNING

Curriculum planning occurs on many levels, and curriculum workers—teachers, supervisors, administrators, or others—may be engaged in curriculum efforts on several levels at the same time. The levels of planning on which teachers function can be conceptualized as shown in Figure 3.1.[9] All teachers are involved in curriculum planning at the classroom level, most teachers participate in curriculum planning at the school level, some take part at the district level, and fewer and fewer engage in planning at the state, regional, national, and international levels. A few teachers, however, do participate in curriculum planning at all levels.

Importance of Classroom Level

The model in Figure 3.1, with its ascending stairs and even with its use of the term "levels," may lead to some erroneous conclusions. You might decide, since the steps clearly sketch a hierarchy, that planning at the classroom level is least important and planning at

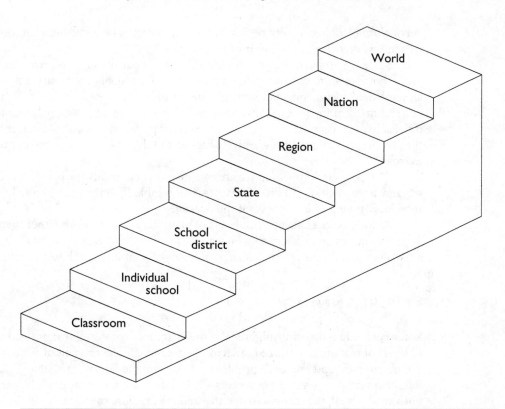

FIGURE 3.1 Levels of Planning

each successive level is increasingly more important. Nothing could be further from the truth. If we are concerned about levels of importance, and indeed we are, we should concede that classroom planning is far more important than any of the successive steps. At the classroom level, the results of curriculum planning make their impact on the learners.

In some ways it would appear pertinent if we turned the model around and placed classroom planning at the top and international planning at the bottom. Unfortunately, reversing the step model would introduce another possible misinterpretation. Since the classroom is the focal point for curriculum planning and the main locale for curriculum development efforts, this stage is shown as the first step. Designating the international level as the initial step would be extremely inaccurate since very few teachers or curriculum specialists work at that level and then usually only after they have demonstrated competence in the other levels.

The step model may convey to some readers that curriculum workers move through each stage or level in a fixed sequence. Although most teachers are involved in curriculum planning at both the classroom and school levels, some will proceed no further than those two levels. Some teachers and curriculum specialists work in sequence from one level to the next or simultaneously at all levels, whereas others may skip whole levels. Although curriculum planning usually begins in the classroom, it may start at whatever level curriculum workers feel a need to initiate change.

Since the steps in the preceding model are of equal width and rise, the model can give the impression that curriculum planners have an equal opportunity to participate at all levels and spend equal amounts of time in planning at each level. Opportunities for curriculum planning become fewer at each successive step up the staircase. Consequently, if the step model is retained to show the levels of planning, it would be better to visualize the rise between steps as progressively higher and the width of each step as progressively narrower.

The persons with whom we are most concerned in this textbook—the curriculum workers at the school and district levels—will be able to devote only limited time to curriculum planning at levels beyond the district.

As long as we conceptualize levels of planning as loci of work rather than of importance and understand that curriculum specialists do not necessarily work at all levels or in a fixed sequence of levels, the concept of levels of planning is valid and useful.

SECTORS OF PLANNING

Some curriculum theorists might feel somewhat more comfortable if, instead of speaking of levels of planning, we talked of sectors of planning. The concept of sectors eliminates the hierarchical and sequence problems of the step model and says simply that curriculum planning goes on in eight sectors—the classroom, the team/grade/department, the individual school, the school district, the state, the region, the nation, and the world. The sector model, illustrated in Figure 3.2, shows teachers and curriculum workers spending the largest part of their time in the individual school and school district and decreasing amounts of their time in sectors beyond the district boundaries. The broken lines signify that an individual teacher or curriculum planner may work at separate times or simultaneously in more than one sector. On the other hand, the teacher or curriculum planner may confine himself or herself to the classroom sector.

Models of levels or of sectors of planning address the questions of where decisions are made and what organizational processes are used for developing plans. These models do not, of course, answer the questions of why decisions are made, a topic explored in later chapters.

In discussing levels or sectors of planning, we should distinguish between levels or sectors in which individual planners work and those where decisions are actually made. These are not necessarily the same. Let's take, for example, the case of a fifth-grade teacher. This teacher may possess sufficient leadership skills, motivation, and knowledge to become involved in curriculum planning either at successive times or simultaneously in the classroom, team/grade/department, school, and district levels. This individual may be involved at each level in making curriculum decisions that affect him or her as well as others in the school system.

On the other hand, this fifth-grade teacher may be engaged in curriculum planning at only the classroom level and may not be actively involved in the process above that

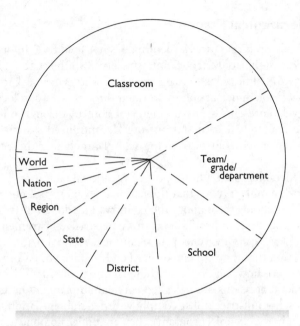

FIGURE 3.2   Sectors of Planning

level. Nevertheless, decisions about classroom curriculum that the individual teacher wishes to make must often be referred to a higher level of decision making, especially if these decisions will affect other teachers. For example, the individual teacher cannot unilaterally replace an adopted textbook that is part of an articulated series used at several grade levels. Decision making, then, will and must take place at higher levels whether or not the individual teacher actively participates in them.

A Hierarchical Structure

Since many curriculum decisions must be, in effect, ratified at successive levels, we do have a hierarchical structure in operation throughout the United States. Each successive level of the hierarchy, up to and including the state level, possesses the power to approve or reject curriculum proposals of the level below it.

In practice, responsibility for curriculum planning is spread across the levels of classroom, school, district, and state. Whereas teachers and curriculum specialists may participate in curriculum projects at the state level, their curriculum efforts at that level are purely advisory. Only the state board of education, the state department of education, or the state legislature can mandate incorporating the projects' results in the schools' programs. School systems must follow specific state regulations and statutes after which, allowing for state curriculum mandates, they may then demonstrate initiative in curriculum planning.

Limitations of Hierarchical Structure

Beyond the state level, hierarchical power structure does not hold true. In our decentralized system of education, authority for education is reserved to the states. The regional, national (with appropriate qualifications), and international sectors may seek to bring about curriculum change only through persuasion by working through state and local levels.

The national level represents a unique blend of control through both authority and persuasion. Some maintain that in spite of our decentralized system, the federal government exercises too much control over the schools, including the curriculum of those schools.

The history of federal legislation in support of vocational education and education of the handicapped, for example, reveals that the national level exerts a potent influence on the curriculum of the schools throughout the country. The dollar, distributed by the federal government is, of course, in itself a powerfully persuasive instrument. However, officials at the national level can intervene in state and local school matters only subsequent to federal legislation that they are empowered and required to enforce.

It is a moot question, however, whether the enactment of federal legislation and the enforcement of federal decisions can be called curriculum planning in its true sense. For example, whereas school districts must comply with federal legislation that bans all forms of discrimination in the schools' programs, they are under no obligation to submit grant proposals for optional types of aid.

Consequently, we might design a model that shows the levels of curriculum planning through the state level and the sectors beyond the state level. Such a model is shown in Figure 3.3.

CURRICULUM EFFORTS AT THE VARIOUS LEVELS

When the graduates of teacher education programs, with degrees and state certificates fresh in hand, sign contracts for their first teaching positions, they generally have only the vaguest of notions of the extent to which they will be involved in curriculum planning and development. Teacher education institutions do not ordinarily require courses in curriculum development at the undergraduate level. A typical preservice training program, ignoring the problem of differing delivery systems, consists of general education (liberal studies); foundations of education (social, psychological, philosophical, and historical) or introduction to education; methods of teaching (both general and specific); and student teaching in addition to a field of specialization (elementary or middle school education or secondary school academic discipline). Some teacher candidates are exposed to an undergraduate course in curriculum, which provides them with an overview of the sources of the curriculum; presents a survey of programs in elementary, middle, and secondary education; and raises some curriculum issues. Despite their limited undergraduate training in curriculum development, teachers engage in instructional and curricular decision making from day one. Novice teachers are, as a rule, reasonably well trained to make the instructional or methodological decisions but are less well equipped to make the curricular or programmatic decisions, even though they may be well grounded in subject matter.

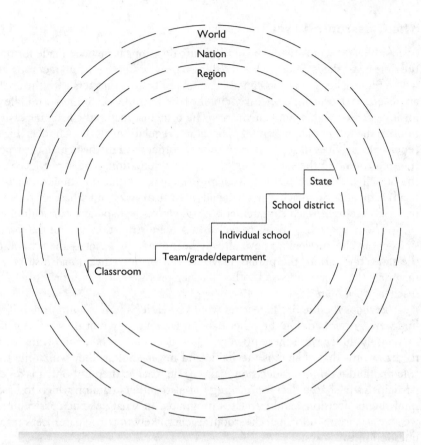

FIGURE 3.3   Levels and Sectors of Planning. For purposes of simplicity this figure does not show two levels—the area level that is a subdivision of the district and the intermediate unit that is a level between the district and the state. The area level is found in large urban school systems and the intermediate level, primarily a service unit, in some states.

Teachers and curriculum specialists work within and across many levels and sectors. Each level performs distinct curricular efforts and has its own organizational processes for making curriculum decisions. Let's examine these levels more fully and point to the internal structures professionals have created to improve the curriculum. By contrast, in Chapters 4 and 7 you will see how external structures—those outside the teaching profession itself—impinge on internal structures.

For curriculum decision making to take place, appropriate organizational structures are essential. In the following pages of this chapter we will examine such structures in some detail. In Chapter 4 you will find a fuller treatment of the roles of various individuals and groups in the curriculum development process.

The Classroom Level

At first blush it seems that all programmatic decisions have been made for the teacher at the time he or she is employed. A full-blown program is already in operation at the school where the teacher is to be assigned. The school board contracts with the applicant to fill an advertised position, be it early childhood education, sixth grade, middle school English, or senior high school chemistry. The principal makes the teaching assignment and informs the teacher about school policies and regulations. If the school is large enough to require the services of supervisory personnel other than the principal, the teacher may be referred to one of the supervisors for further orientation. The supervisor designated by the principal (for example, the assistant principal, a grade coordinator, or a department head) acquaints the teacher with the adopted textbooks and whatever other curriculum materials are used, such as statements of objectives, syllabi, and curriculum guides.

The new teacher begins to feel with some justification as if all the important decisions about the curriculum have already been made by others—the school, the district, the state, the nation, the public. Have we not in our educational history encountered materials that were supposed to be "teacher-proof"? No need for a teacher at all with teacher-proof materials!

Perhaps the life of the teacher would be easier and less complicated if the curriculum were prescribed. On the other hand, it is safe to say that the teacher's life would be immensely duller were there no curriculum decisions to be made. If teachers subscribe to the axioms that change is inevitable and never-ending, they will come to view their role first and foremost as decision maker. The teacher then not only makes decisions or participates in shared decision making but also gathers data on which to base decisions, implements decisions, and evaluates programs. In what specific curriculum endeavors, we may ask, is the individual classroom teacher likely to participate? Let's respond to that question in two ways.

Two Cases.   First, let us take the hypothetical cases of two high-powered, experienced, highly motivated teachers—a fourth-grade teacher and a tenth-grade teacher of social studies. We will further posit that (l) the fourth-grade teacher is a male and the tenth-grade teacher, a female, (2) both are employed in the same school district, and (3) both participate in curriculum planning at all levels and sectors. Our fourth-grade teacher, whom we will refer to as Teacher F, is the grade coordinator in a school that houses three sections of the fourth grade. Our tenth-grade teacher, Teacher N, is a member of a social studies department numbering eight faculty members. We will examine their curriculum development activities at one point in time—the cold and windy month of March.

During this period Teacher F was selecting supplementary materials for his pupils' science lessons (classroom level). He was reviewing with the other teachers the next day's mathematics lesson for slower students in the classes and examining a new fourth-grade reading program (grade level). He was also participating in making recommendations for implementing a new human growth and development program in the school (school level), serving on a committee studying ways to implement federal legislation regarding the handicapped (district level), serving on a statewide committee to define minimal competencies in language arts (state level), taking part in a panel discussion at a regional conference on effective teaching (regional level), finishing a proposal for federal funding of a project for children-at-risk (national sector and local level), and planning activities for a program on contributions of immigrants to American culture (international sector and local level).

While Teacher F has been making his contributions toward keeping the curriculum of his school system lively, Teacher N has been no less occupied. She has just finished resequencing the content of a course in geography that she regularly teaches (classroom level); is working with all the tenth-grade social studies teachers on a new course in consumer economics (department level); will attend later in the week as her department representative a meeting of the school's curriculum council to discuss ways for the school to use community resources more effectively (school level); has been serving on the same district committee as Teacher F, which is charged with the task of making recommendations for an improved curriculum for the physically challenged (district level); has been invited to participate on a committee to consider changes in the state's minimal requirements for high school graduation (state level); served a week ago on a visiting committee for a distant high school that is seeking accreditation (regional sector); has been notified by the National Endowment for the Humanities that a proposal she submitted will be funded (national sector and local level); and has been invited by the World Council for Gifted and Talented Children to present a paper at a conference in Europe (international sector). While relatively few teachers have the opportunity, ability, or perhaps the inclination to participate in curriculum efforts at all levels and in all sectors suggested by these two hypothetical cases, none of these curricular activities is beyond the realm of possibility. Teachers have engaged in activities like these at some time or other.

A second way to respond to the question "In what specific endeavors is the individual classroom teacher likely to participate?" is to survey typical curriculum efforts that take place at each level and in each sector. An examination of some of the curriculum responsibilities at the classroom level reveals that the individual teacher has a rather large task cut out for him or her. A number of tasks in curriculum development at the classroom level may be identified.

Tasks of Teachers. Teachers carry out activities in curriculum design when they write curricular goals and objectives, select subject matter (content), choose materials, identify resources in the school and community, sequence or resequence the subject matter, decide on the scope of the topics or course, revise the content, decide on types of instructional plans to use, construct the plans, try out new programs, create developmental and remedial programs in reading or other subject matter, seek ways to provide for all kinds of individual differences in the classroom, incorporate content mandated by levels above the classroom, and develop their own curricular materials.

Curriculum implementation is equated by some curriculum experts with instruction. Some hold the view that curriculum implementation does not start until the teacher interacts with the students. I would include in this concept the final stages of curriculum planning or design when the nitty-gritty decisions are made about how programs will be put into operation and how instruction will be designed and presented. Within this context teachers are occupied at the classroom level when they select appropriate emphases within the subjects, decide which students will pursue what subject matter, allot times for the various topics and units to be taught, determine if the facilities are appropriate and how they will be modified (if necessary), decide how materials and resources may best be made available to the learners, assign duties to volunteer aides, write instructional goals and objectives, and select and carry out strategies for classroom presentation and interaction.

Teachers have the responsibility of evaluating both the curriculum and instruction. In some ways it is difficult to separate the two dimensions of evaluation and to tell where instructional evaluation ceases and curriculum evaluation begins. In a very real sense evaluating instruction is evaluating curriculum implementation. We may clarify the distinctions between the two dimensions of evaluation in the following way: *Curriculum evaluation* is the assessment of programs, processes, and curricular products (material, not human). *Instructional evaluation* is (1) the assessment of student achievement before, during, and at the end of instruction and (2) the assessment of the effectiveness of the instructor. Thus, teachers work at the task of curriculum evaluation when they seek to find out if the programs are meeting the curriculum objectives; try to learn if the programs are valid, relevant, feasible, of interest to the learners, and in keeping with the learners' needs; review the choices of delivery systems, materials, and resources; and examine the finished curriculum products, such as guides, unit plans, and lesson plans, that they have created. Teachers conduct instructional evaluation when they assess the learners' entry skills before the start of instruction; give progress tests; write, administer, score, and interpret final achievement tests; and permit students to evaluate their performance as instructors.

These examples of activities transpiring at the classroom level demonstrate that curriculum planning and development are complex and demanding responsibilities of the teacher. As we discuss curriculum planning at the various levels in the following pages of this chapter, it may seem that individual teachers have little autonomy. Surely, many hold that view, and to some extent there is truth in that belief. The impingement of federal, state, and local school system mandates affecting the teachers' prerogatives in the areas of curriculum and instruction is a serious concern. In spite of the infringement on the teachers' professional responsibilities, many curricular and instructional decisions remain to be made, especially in selecting delivery systems, adapting techniques to students' learning styles, diagnosing student problems, and prescribing remediation.

Teachers may take comfort from the fact that they have at least as a group, if not individually, considerable opportunity to shape curricular decisions at the classroom, local school, and district levels and some opportunity at the state level.

The Team, Grade, and Department Level

One of the axioms in Chapter 2 stated that curriculum development is essentially a group undertaking. Once the teacher leaves the sanctuary of the self-contained elementary, middle, or secondary school classroom and joins other teachers, curriculum development takes a new turn. It calls for a cooperative effort on the part of each teacher, places a limit on solitary curriculum planning, and calls for a more formal organizational structure. It is at the team, grade, or department level that curriculum leadership begins to emerge, with leaders coming to be distinguished from followers.

For decades the graded school system with its orderly hierarchical structure and self-contained classrooms has been and continues to be the prevailing model of school organization. In the late 1970s, however, the self-contained classroom with its one teacher and one group of students was jostled by the appearance of open-space or open-area schools. Scores of elementary, middle, and junior high schools were built as or converted into open-space facilities. In these schools, in place of walled, self-contained classrooms came large open spaces in which the learning activities of a large group of youngsters were directed by a team of teachers assisted in some cases by paraprofessionals. A semblance of territoriality was created by assigning each of the members of the teaching team to a particular group of youngsters whose home base was a sector of the large open area. In theory and in practice, groups and subgroups were formed and reformed continuously depending on their learning needs, goals, and interests and on the teachers' individual competencies. Although open-space schools can still be found, the movement has reversed itself, and in many cases open classrooms have been converted or reconverted into self-contained classrooms. Sentiment among teachers, parents, and students has continued to favor the self-contained classroom.

Specific curriculum innovations are discussed in this text primarily to delineate the process of curriculum development and to help the curriculum worker to effect and evaluate curriculum change. Organizational patterns appear in this chapter to illustrate teachers' participation in curriculum planning at various levels beyond the classroom. Teachers in schools organized into self-contained units participate at the grade or department level. Teachers in open-space elementary schools share curriculum planning responsibilities at both the team and grade levels. Teachers in middle schools customarily take part in curriculum development at the team (usually interdisciplinary), grade, and department levels. Secondary school teachers join with their colleagues in curriculum planning primarily at the department level, also on the grade level, and, in the case of team teaching efforts, at the team level.[10]

With the children for whom they are specifically responsible in mind, the teachers in a team, given grade, or particular department are called on to make curricular decisions such as the following:

- determining content to be presented
- sequencing subject matter
- adapting instruction for exceptionalities
- establishing or revising team, grade, or departmental objectives
- selecting materials and resources suitable to the children under their supervision
- creating groupings and subgroupings of learners
- establishing a means of coordinating progress of students in the various sections and classrooms
- writing tests to be taken by students of the team, grade, or department

- writing curriculum materials for use by all teachers
- agreeing on team-wide, grade-wide, and department-wide programs that all students and teachers will attend
- agreeing on ways students can learn to demonstrate socially responsible behavior and self-discipline
- agreeing on or reviewing minimal standards that pupils must demonstrate in the basic skills
- cooperating in the establishment and use of laboratories and learning centers
- agreeing on implementation of the school's marking practices
- agreeing on the institution of new programs and abandonment of old programs within their jurisdiction
- planning tutorial programs for students who do not do well on state exams
- evaluating their programs, students, and instructors

These are but a sampling of the many kinds of cooperative decisions that members who constitute the team, grade, or department must make. Team leaders or lead teachers, grade coordinators, or chairpersons are generally free to make many, though not all, decisions that affect only their own classes. When a decision is likely to have an impact on teachers other than the individual classroom teacher, it becomes a matter for joint deliberation by the parties to be affected or, at higher levels, by their representatives.

To enable the decision-making process to become more efficient, curriculum leaders either emerge or need to be designated. Team leaders or lead teachers, grade coordinators, or chairpersons are appointed by the principal or elected by the teachers themselves. Those administrators who are inclined to a bureaucratic approach to administration prefer the former system, and those who are disposed to a collegial approach permit the latter system. In either case, if the most experienced and skilled teachers are chosen for leadership positions, they may establish themselves as curriculum specialists, key members of a cooperating group of curriculum workers.

Patterns of organizational interaction among teachers, teams, grades, and departments with the principal vary from school to school and from school district to school district.

In the less common small school with only one class of each grade with one teacher in a self-contained unit, the individual teacher is both the leader and follower and has sole responsibility for making curriculum decisions (with the administrator's cooperation and approval) for the classroom and grade levels, in this case identical. The teacher and principal, who is viewed by many as the school's instructional leader, relate to each other directly. Although the presence of a single section of a particular grade prevents cooperative curriculum planning within grade levels, cooperation is possible, if the principal encourages it, at the school level and across grade levels.

In some schools housing multiple sections of each grade the principal follows the model of the less common small school, trying to relate to each teacher on an individual basis and not encouraging cooperative planning by the faculty within and across grade levels. Interchange among those affected by curriculum change is essential to intelligent and effective curriculum planning.

Curriculum matters that can be settled and contained within a team, grade, or department are handled at that level. However, curriculum planning sends out waves that affect, sometimes even engulf, persons beyond the planners and the client group for whom the plans were made. Hence, we must look to the next level—the school level—for curriculum decision making that transcends the team, grade, or department.

The School Level

Although many curriculum decisions may be made at the classroom or team/grade/department level, other decisions can be reached only at a schoolwide level. The institution must provide some mechanism whereby the curriculum is articulated and integrated. The administrator must ensure a process whereby the implications of curriculum decisions made anywhere within the institution will be understood and, hopefully, agreed to by the faculty as a whole.

Of all the levels and sectors of curriculum planning, the individual school has emerged as the most critical. Current administrative philosophy promotes an approach to school administration known generally as "school-based (or site-based) management" in which authority is decentralized and the school principal is granted considerable autonomy over not only curriculum planning but also the budget, hiring and firing of school personnel, inservice education of staff, and supervision and evaluation of staff.[11] Several writers have identified the individual school as the primary locus for curriculum change. Alice Miel long ago observed, "If really widespread participation is desirable, there appears to be no better way than to make the individual school the unit of participation, the primary action agency in curriculum development."[12] Almost forty years later Goodlad endorsed the concept of the school as the unit for improvement.[13]

The decade of the 1980s, with its quest for reform of the schools, saw many states shift more and more decision making to the state level as they grappled for ways to improve their schools. Local schools felt the pressure of state curricular mandates that in some cases went beyond the specification of subjects and units to the specification of instructional objectives to be accomplished at every level in every course.

Emphasis in the 1990s shifted away from heavy centralized state and district administration toward more responsibility for operation of the schools on the local school level. Tight state budgets as well as educational reasons such as espousal of principles of school-based management accelerated the move toward decentralization from state to local level. Today pressures, especially from the federal level's No Child Left Behind Act of 2001, have forced states into renewing closer direction of their school systems.

The preceding chapter demonstrated that curriculum specialists conceive of curriculum development as a cooperative group undertaking. Given the many dimensions of the school administrator's job, intensified by the concept of school-based management, a participatory approach to administration is sound not only philosophically but also practically. Shared decision making, whether in respect to curriculum planning or to other aspects of the administrator's job, makes for a more efficient and effective school.

Foreign observers are often amazed, if not shocked, by the uniqueness of each American school. Two elementary schools in the same community, for example, may be completely different in ambience, student body, staffing, scheduling, resources, and to some extent, curricula. Achievement levels, motivation of the students, enthusiasm of the faculty, leadership skills of the principal, neighborhood, support from the parents, and curricular emphases make for differences from school to school. Consequently, Americans are not surprised when they find that organizational arrangements differ school by school within the nation, within the state, indeed, within the same locality. Educational diversity is both a blessing and a dilemma for curriculum planners. It is a strength of our system of education in that it permits schools to respond to needs evidenced in the individual school and locality. It presents a problem for curriculum workers who seek to create state and even national curricula that specify commonalities, minimal competencies, and proficiency levels.

Constituencies of the School.   To varying degrees, the democratic process is accepted more and more in school systems across the country. Nowhere is its presence more clearly felt than in the participatory procedures that seek to involve the major constituencies of the school in curriculum development. Usually identified as the principal constituencies are the administrators and their staffs, teachers, students, and citizens of the community. On occasion, nonprofessional employees of the school system are acknowledged in this way and become involved in the planning process—but rarely as major participants.

Some time ago Jack R. Frymier and Horace C. Hawn stated a principle that summarizes the belief in the necessity for involving persons in curriculum planning on a broad scale:

> *People Who Are Affected Must Be Involved.* Involvement is a principle fundamental to democracy and to learning theory. The very essence of democracy is predicated upon the assumption that those who are affected by any change should have some say in determining just what that change shall be. This is guaranteed in our political-social system through citizen participation and through our efforts to persuade representatives once they have been chosen. Devising ways of involving people in decision making is a difficult and time-consuming chore, but *unless decisions are made democratically they will be less than the best.* . . . Significant and lasting change can only come about by such involvement. All who are affected by curriculum development and change must have a genuine opportunity to participate in the process.[14]

Robert S. Zais raised a question, however, about the validity of the participatory model of curriculum decision making. Speaking of the democratic "grass-roots model,"[15] Zais said:

> The grass-roots model of curriculum engineering[16] . . . is initiated by teachers in individual schools, employs democratic group methods of decision making, proceeds on a "broken front," and is geared to the specific curriculum problems of particular schools or even classrooms.
>
> The intensely democratic orientation of the grass-roots model is responsible for generating what have probably become the curriculum establishment's two least-questioned axioms: First, that a curriculum can be successfully implemented only if the teach-

ers have been intimately involved in the construction and development processes, and second, that not only professional personnel, but students, parents, and other lay members of the community must be included in the curriculum planning process. To deny the validity of either of these claims (neither of which has been satisfactorily demonstrated) is not necessarily to deny *any* role to teachers or lay participants; rather it is to suggest the need to define more precisely the *appropriate* role that administrators, teachers, curriculum specialists, and nonprofessionals should play in curriculum engineering.[17]

Decisions and Organizational Patterns. Curriculum committees or councils exist in many schools. The school's curriculum committee meets and makes recommendations on such matters as the following:

- adding new programs for the school, including interdisciplinary programs
- deleting existing programs
- revising existing programs
- increasing classroom use of computers throughout the school, including online instruction and research
- conducting schoolwide surveys of teacher, student, and parental opinion
- evaluating the school's curriculum
- planning ways to overcome curricular deficiencies
- planning for school accreditation
- choosing articulated series of textbooks
- using library and learning centers
- planning for exceptional children
- verifying the school's compliance with state mandates and federal legislation
- sanctioning schoolwide events like career days and science fairs
- supervising assessment of student achievement
- reviewing recommendations of accrediting committees and planning for removal of deficiencies
- reducing absenteeism
- increasing the holding power of the school

Although curriculum specialists may not agree to what degree they should encourage or permit the involvement of various constituencies, how each group will be constituted, and which group has the primary role, the literature on curriculum development almost unanimously endorses the concept of the democratic, participatory approach. Although it is possible that the collective judgment of specialists in the field could be in error, their judgments—based on experience, training, observation, and research—provide a foundation for accepting the validity of the democratic approach to curriculum development.

Several organizational arrangements exist on the school level for considering curriculum matters. Patterns differ regarding the degree to which the administrator shares decision making with teachers.

We should not forget that in any organizational model in which decision making is shared, groups other than the duly appointed administrators serve only in advisory capacities. Both professionally and legally the administrator does not and cannot surrender "line" authority for making ultimate decisions and supervising the staff. Patterns of organizing for curriculum development at the local school level maintain the customary line-and-staff relationship that exists at the team/grade/department level and at the school district level.

In some school districts citizens of the community and students join forces with the faculty and administrators to produce collaborative patterns. Some principals keep the three constituencies separate. Others integrate all three constituencies into one expanded curriculum committee and incorporate the total faculty within the model.

Integrated, collaborative models appear the most democratic, but it would be wrong to conclude that it is, therefore, the most efficient. As anyone who has grappled with the concept of "parity" as dictated by some federal programs—public school teachers, university specialists, and laypeople working together as equal partners from proposal stage to final evaluation—has discovered, "parity" is not necessarily the most efficient way to do business. In reference to the expanded curriculum committee the professionals—the teachers and administrators—must often talk a language filled with concepts that must be explained to lay citizens and students and must make distinctions between desired outcomes and processes. Technical decisions that must be made are often beyond the competence of lay citizens and students. Only if an expanded curriculum committee is composed of persons who are well informed about the processes of education and are highly motivated can this pattern meet with any degree of success.

Students and laypeople often participate with teachers and administrators on school-level committees. In the next chapter, we will examine the roles of these constituent groups in curriculum development. We might ask at this point: What are typical curriculum tasks of the schoolwide curriculum committee? The school curriculum committee or council must articulate its work with curriculum development efforts at the classroom and team/grade/department levels and, in effect, coordinate the work of lower levels. It receives proposals for curricular change from the lower levels, especially proposals that affect more than one team, grade, or department or that are interdisciplinary in nature.

The school curriculum council considers proposals that require human and material resources, budgetary expenditures, and changes in staffing. The council conducts or supervises assessment of the educational needs of pupils. It coordinates the development of a statement of school philosophy. It specifies and regularly reviews curriculum goals and objectives for the school.

The curriculum council plans the evaluation of the curriculum. It studies results of student assessment and proposes changes based on the data gathered. The council studies the educational needs of the community and implements programs to meet legitimate needs. The council seeks solutions to short-range curricular problems while also establishing and refining long-range plans.

The council is both proactive and reactive in its manner of operating. Whereas it may react to proposals presented by both the principal and the faculty, it also generates its own proposals and possible solutions to curricular problems.

At the time of a pending school evaluation by a regional accreditation team, the curriculum council may act as a steering committee and assign specific tasks to various committees. The council coordinates an intensive self-study prior to the visit of the accrediting team.

The council must ensure articulation between and among the various teams, grades, and departments of the school, making certain that teachers are following agreed-upon sequences and meeting minimal prescribed objectives. Requests from higher levels and various sectors for the school's cooperation on curriculum projects are routed to the curriculum council.

The local school curriculum council occupies a strategic position and fulfills a key role in the process of curriculum development. Of all groups at all levels and sectors of planning, the schoolwide curriculum council is in the position to make significant contributions to curriculum improvement.

Limitation to Decentralization.   A decentralized site-based approach to management, per se, is no greater guarantee of successful curriculum making than is a centralized approach orchestrated by the district or state level. Michael G. Fullan called attention to the need for coordinating top-down and bottom-up strategies.[18] Site-based management and shared decision making should not be perceived as the delegation of all authority and responsibility to the individual school. A bottom-up approach without cooperation of higher levels may be no more successful in effecting lasting curriculum improvement than a top-down approach without cooperation of lower levels. Commented Fullan, "In sum, decentralized initiatives, as far as the evidence is concerned, are not faring much better than centralized reforms."[19] Efforts toward empowerment at the local level have sought to balance the heavier control formerly exerted by district and state levels. However, the local school cannot work in isolation. Collaboration among levels and sectors remains essential.

The School District Level

None of the previously discussed levels—classroom, team/grade/department, or individual school—can work as isolated units. They function within the context of the school district under the direction of the duly constituted school board and its administrative officer, the superintendent. Their efforts must be coordinated among themselves and with the central district office. Goals and objectives of the subordinate units must mesh with those of the district level. Consequently, the superintendent must provide a mechanism whereby district-level curriculum planning may be conducted.

Curriculum planning on a districtwide level is often conducted through the district curriculum council composed of teachers, administrators, supervisors, laypersons, and, in some cases, students. The size of the district curriculum council and the extent of its representation depend on the size of the school district. Representatives may be either elected by members of their respective groups or appointed by district-level administrators, frequently on the recommendation of school principals.

Decisions and Organizational Patterns.   Districtwide committees meet to consider problems such as these:

- adding new programs for the district
- abandoning districtwide programs
- reviewing student achievement in the various schools and recommending ways to improve programs of any deficient schools
- writing or reviewing proposals for state and federal grants
- gathering data on student achievement for presentation to parent groups and lay advisory councils
- supervising district compliance with state mandates and federal legislation
- recommending distribution of technological equipment among schools of the district
- evaluating programs on a districtwide basis
- articulating programs between levels
- instituting smaller schools and single-sex schools and classes

Patterns of organization at the school district level increase in complexity as the size of the school district increases. Some districts use a curriculum council composed of professionals only—administrators and supervisors named by the superintendent and teachers selected by their principals or elected by their faculties to represent them on the council. Subcommittees of professionals from anywhere in the school system are appointed by the curriculum council to conduct specific phases of curriculum development. The community advisory council serves in an advisory capacity to the superintendent and may or may not consider curriculum matters. Subordinate school units are responsible to the superintendent through the principals.

Some school districts extend membership on the curriculum council to students and laypersons. Large urban school districts often break the organizational pattern into subordinate areas headed by area superintendents.

Sequence for Decision Making.   We might visualize the sequence for decision making by the curriculum groups at the various levels within a school system in the form of waves starting in the individual teacher's classroom and terminating with the district curriculum council, as pictured in Figure 3.4.

Teachers new to a school system should be informed by curriculum supervisors and/or mentors of the district's structures for curriculum development. Teachers should be aware not only of the process of curriculum development in the district but also of the opportunities for curricular leadership.

Each level receives information, ideas, and proposals from the lower levels and, in turn, sends information, ideas, and proposals to them. Each level acts within the limitations of its own "territory." Councils at any level may initiate action as well as react to suggestions made to them. Councils must be responsive to both subordinate and higher levels. If a council wishes to initiate a plan that affects lower levels, it must involve persons from those levels beginning at the earliest planning stages. If a council wishes

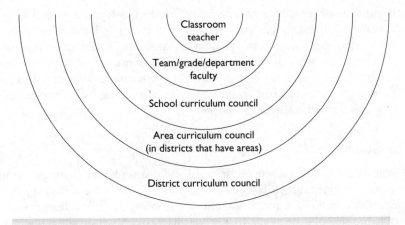

FIGURE 3.4 Sequence of Decision Making

to initiate or endorse a plan that goes beyond its "territory" or that might be likely to create repercussions anywhere in the system, it must seek approval at higher levels.

Before we discuss curriculum development at the next level—the state—we should consider the following observations about varying organizational patterns or models for curriculum development:

- Although an administrator—the principal or superintendent—is ordinarily depicted in schematics at the top, organizational patterns should not be considered simply administrative models in which orders are given by the administrator to his or her subordinates. From administrator to curriculum committees, exchange should be a two-way rather than a one-way process. The administrator holds the power for final decision making and must take the consequences if decisions prove to be unwise. The administrator's presence at the top of a pattern does not in itself make the pattern undemocratic.

  The key difference between a democratic and an undemocratic process is the involvement of people. No worthy administrator can turn over the decision-making process completely to others, yet every administrator can seek to obtain the widest possible participation of people in that process.

- Organizational patterns are but models that reflect the work of curriculum development to be carried out by the professionals in the school system and by others whose aid they solicit. Many patterns exist. Zais, for example, analyzed a number of existing and proposed models for curriculum development.[20]

- Realistically, we must admit that a significant amount of curriculum change is brought about *outside* of the established structure. Individual teachers and small committees often effect changes that are well received and disseminated through the school system and sometimes beyond. B. Frank Brown observed many years ago that a few teachers, by their example, may be instrumental in bringing about curriculum revision, a process he referred to as "spinning out."[21] The public and teachers' organizations are often ahead of the designated curriculum leaders.

- Patterns mentioned in this chapter are models of structure—the organizational arrangements whereby the professionals and those who assist them may apply their knowledge and skills to curriculum improvement. We should distinguish these organizational patterns from models for the process of curriculum development, which we will consider in Chapter 5.

The State Level

To many curriculum workers on the local and district levels, participation in curriculum development beyond their boundaries seems like a remote undertaking. Administrators, teachers, and others are aware, sometimes painfully, that curriculum revision does go on outside the school district and that it does have an impact on the schools of the district. Although state involvement in curricular and instructional development has varied over the years, relatively few school personnel in proportion to the number of employees are actively involved in curriculum making outside the district and then rarely on a sustaining basis.

As we move further and further away from the district level, the percentage of school personnel actively and continuously participating in curriculum development shrinks in size. Were the state not in a superordinate position over the local school districts and were the state not directly responsible for the educational system within its borders, we should classify the state as a sector rather than a level. Clearly, however, under the Tenth Amendment to the U.S. Constitution and under the state constitutions, the state holds primary power over education.

Channels within Education. The state operates in the arena of curriculum development through a number of channels within the education profession. The state department of education and school people from the various districts of the state who are called on to assist the state department of education constitute the professional channel for curriculum development under the aegis of the state.

State Departments of Education. The state department of education, often a large bureaucracy that is sometimes criticized for its size and power, exercises direct responsibility over the curriculum of the schools of the state. Led by a chief state school officer (superintendent or commissioner of education), the state department of education—an agency of the executive branch of the state government—consists of a number of assistant superintendents, heads of branches, curriculum specialists, and other staff members. The state department of education provides general leadership to the schools; it interprets, enforces, and monitors legislated regulations as well as its own regulations that attain the force of law.

The state department of education wields great power over the districts of the state. In curriculum matters it accredits and monitors school programs, disburses state and federal-through-state moneys for specific programs, enforces standards for high school graduation, and sets specifications for amounts of time to be devoted to specific content areas. The state department of education develops statewide standards of philosophy, goals, and objectives. Additionally, the state department of education makes available consultant help to the individual schools and districts and conducts evaluation of school programs.

At times, decisions are made on the state level without advance consultation with the local school personnel of the state. At other times, however, the state department of education seeks advice and assistance from individuals and from ad hoc committees that they create for the purpose of studying specific problems and recommending solutions. Administrators and teachers are often asked to participate in organizing, conducting, or attending conferences and workshops held throughout the state on specific topics—for example, drug abuse, programs for the physically challenged, eliminating gender discrimination, writing curriculum guides, conducting research studies, identifying teacher competencies, specifying minimal competencies that students are expected to achieve at each grade level, and selecting textbooks for state adoption.

The state department of education takes a leadership role in disseminating information regarding curriculum innovations and practices among the schools of the state. It issues both regular and periodic bulletins, monographs, and newsletters, frequently containing articles written by persons from local school districts, to keep school personnel throughout the state up-to-date on recent developments in curriculum, instruction, and other matters.

The state's presence in all school matters is a commanding one especially in an era of emphasis on standards and testing.

State Professional Organizations.   In a less formal way curriculum workers find opportunities for curriculum planning and consideration of curriculum problems through activities of the state professional organizations. Conference programs of such organizations as the state chapters of the National Council of Teachers of English, the National Council for the Social Studies, and the Association for Supervision and Curriculum Development customarily focus on curriculum concerns. Although conference participants may engage in curriculum planning in only the most rudimentary and often passive way, the sharing of curriculum ideas often lays the groundwork for subsequent curriculum reform. This type of curriculum activity cannot, of course, be equated with more structured efforts under the state department of education. Nor can we truly label the examination of curriculum problems by state professional organizations as a level of planning since no element of authority exists in this type of voluntary activity. More appropriately, the state professional organizations constitute a sector that seeks to effect curriculum change through research, example, and persuasion. Nevertheless, we would be remiss if we did not credit state professional organizations for the influence they often exert in bringing about changes in the curriculum of the local school systems of the state.

Channels outside of Education.   Other departments of the executive branch, the state legislature, and the state judicial branch form channels outside the profession of education that have an impact on the curriculum of all the schools of the state. Within the executive branch the governor and the state board of education wield tremendous power over the state educational system. The governor presents a budget to the legislature in which he or she recommends supporting or curtailing programs. The state board sets policies that bind all the schools of the state.

Legislative Decisions.   State legislatures throughout the country consistently demonstrate a penchant for curriculum making. Mandates from the state legislatures in some cases with leadership from the executive branch have been the prime movers for educational reform in the 1980s and early 1990s. Since the 1990s states have been reviewing their educational system, making modifications, for example, in requirements for high school graduation and assessments of educational achievement.

The legislature of the state of Florida provides an example of legislative curriculum making. Among the many curriculum prescriptions are the following extractions from Florida statutes.

Florida Statute 233.061, addressing a wide variety of designated needs, required instruction on the following:

> Declaration of Independence
> Arguments in support of a republican form of government
> U.S. Constitution and its relation to government structure
> Flag education, including proper display and salute
> The elements of civil government
> History of the Holocaust
> History of African Americans
> The elementary principles of agriculture
> The true effects of all alcoholic and intoxicating liquors, beverages, and narcotics
> Kindness to animals
> The history of the state
> The conservation of natural resources
> Comprehensive health education
> The study of Hispanic contributions to the United States
> The study of women's contributions to the United States

Florida Statute 233.0612, authorized school districts to provide the following instruction:

> Character development and law education
> The objective study of the Bible and religion
> Traffic education
> Free enterprise and consumer education
> Programs to encourage patriotism and greater respect for country
> Drug abuse resistance education
> Comprehensive health education
> Care of nursing home patients
> Acquired immune deficiency syndrome

Voting instruction, including the use of county voting machines
Before-school and after-school programs

In mandating character-development education in the spring of 1999 the Florida legislature became very specific, stipulating for the elementary schools a secular character-development program similar to those of Character Counts![22]

Florida Statute 229.57, made sweeping provision, later modified, for state assessment of student progress when it directed the state commissioner of education to:

> Develop and administer in the public schools a uniform, statewide program of assessment to determine, periodically, educational status and progress and the degree of achievement of approved minimum performance standards. The uniform statewide program shall consist of testing in grades 3, 5, 8, and 11. . . .

Although some legislation is a result of grassroots movement within the state and some statutes evolve from recommendations made by the state superintendent of public instruction and the state department of education, many acts of the state legislature stem from the personal beliefs and desires of the legislators themselves. Even the state judicial branch finds itself entangled in curriculum decision making from time to time. Two famous cases may serve to illustrate involvement of the state courts in curriculum making.

The Supreme Court of Michigan ruled in 1874 in a case brought against the school district of Kalamazoo by a taxpayer of that community that the school board of Kalamazoo could, indeed, spend public funds to provide a secondary school education for youth of their district.[23]

In 1927 the Supreme Court of Tennessee replied to the appeal of defense attorneys of John Thomas Scopes of the world-famous "monkey trial" by upholding the constitutionality of the Tennessee law that forbade teaching in the public schools any theory that denied human creation by a Divine Being.[24] Periodically, state legislatures have attempted to mandate the teaching of "scientific creationism" or, more currently, "intelligent design" in the public schools as a counterbalance to the theory of evolution. The scientific creationism/evolution issue, to which we will return in Chapter 15, continues to surface in some state executive and legislative bodies.

SECTORS BEYOND THE STATE

When curriculum planners leave the state level and move onto the broader scene, they work in quite a different context. Participation in planning in the regional, national, and international sectors is ordinarily a voluntary activity. Except in the case of federal legislation, information sharing and persuasion rather than statutory power are the tools of the regional, national, and international sectors. No assurance of any kind exists that curriculum decisions reached in these sectors will or can be put into operation in the schools.

Although fewer opportunities exist for curriculum workers to engage in planning in the regional, national, and international sectors, the opportunities that do arise can be exciting for the participants.

The Regional Sector

Participation in planning in the regional, national, and international sectors is not comparable to that in the previously described levels. On occasion, curriculum specialists of a particular region of the United States, from around the nation, or even from a number of foreign countries may assemble and develop curriculum materials that they will then disseminate or try out in their own schools. Notable illustrations of this type of cooperative endeavor were the efforts of the scholars from various parts of the country who in the late 1950s developed the so-called new math and new science programs.

As a general rule, curriculum activities in the regional, national, and international sectors are more likely to consist of sharing problems, exchanging practices, reporting research, and gathering information. Conferences of the professional organizations—for example, the South Atlantic Modern Language Association—are the most common vehicle whereby school personnel participate in regional curriculum study. With considerable frequency teachers, administrators, and curriculum specialists are invited to take part in the activities of the regional associations (New England, Middle States, North Central, Northwest, Southern, and Western) that accredit schools and colleges. This participation consists of three types. First, participants are elected or invited to serve on various committees and commissions of the associations—for example, the Commission on Elementary Schools, the Commission on Secondary Schools, and the regional associations' state committees. Second, committees of professionals review, revise, and write for each subject area the criteria that schools follow in evaluating their programs. The third and most extensive of the three types of participation is service on accreditation visiting committees that go into schools in the region to ascertain strengths and weaknesses of the schools' programs and to make recommendations for improvements and accreditation of the schools.

Much of the participation in which school personnel take part in the regional sector falls into the category of curriculum evaluation in contrast to planning or implementation of the curriculum.

The National Sector

The U.S. Congress. Although education in the United States is a function reserved to the states by the Tenth Amendment to the Constitution, we cannot minimize the profound effect of congressional legislation on the administration and curriculum of our schools. The Congress has engaged in curriculum development with passage of laws related to reading, bilingual education, vocational education, exceptionalities, and gender, to name but a few areas of congressional interest.

The Congress occasionally takes focus on topics that it wishes included in the curriculum, for example, by slipping a notice in an omnibus appropriation bill in 2004 requiring all schools to conduct a program every year on Constitution Day, September 17 (or during the preceding or following week if September 17 falls on a weekend or holiday), to teach about the U.S. Constitution.

U.S. Department of Education. The national scene is peppered with a variety of public, private, and professional curriculum activities, and school personnel from the state level and below play key roles in some of these activities. In the public governmental sector, the Department of Education exercises a strong influence. Called the United States Office of Education until education was separated from the U.S. Department of Health, Education, and Welfare in 1980 during President Jimmy Carter's administration, the Department of Education with its large bureaucracy gathers data, disseminates information, provides consultative assistance, sponsors and conducts research, funds projects, and disburses money appropriated by Congress. Local school people find the opportunity to participate in national curriculum efforts by writing and submitting proposals for grants to conduct curricular research or to put particular programs into operation in their school systems.

Federal Funding. To choose recipients of funds for proposals awarded competitively, the Department of Education calls in readers who are specialists in the particular fields in which grants are being given. These readers evaluate and make recommendations on proposals to be awarded by the specific office within the Department of Education. Persons from all over the United States journey to Washington (or sometimes to other sites) to read proposals. In so doing, they grow professionally and bring back new ideas for curriculum development in their own institutions.

Federal funding permits numerous committees to carry out curriculum projects that the U.S. Congress deems significant. Title I of the Elementary and Secondary Education Act of 1965 (which later became Chapter 1 of the Education Consolidation and Improvement Act of 1981), for example, provided for programs to aid the culturally disadvantaged. The No Child Left Behind Act of 2001 (NCLB), an extension of the Elementary and Secondary Education Act, included among its titles an initiative known as *Reading First*, which provided grants to the states to improve reading standards. To promote the Reading First Program during the winter of 2002, the U.S. Department of Education conducted three Reading First Leadership Academies for state policymakers and educational leaders. Possible loss of federal funding under NCLB has motivated, some would say "pressured," school systems throughout the country to strive to raise all students to "proficiency level" as determined by state tests, to secure "highly qualified" teachers, and to offer alternative arrangements for children who are not making "adequate yearly progress."

Grants from the federal government over the years have enabled national study groups to prepare curriculum materials, some of which (as in foreign languages, mathematics, and science) have been used extensively.

Federal aid has stimulated and resulted in the involvement of curriculum workers both directly as participants and indirectly as consumers of products and services of the Educational Resources Information Center (ERIC), the Regional Educational

Laboratories, Research and Development Centers, and the National Centers within the U.S. Department of Education's Institute of Education Sciences.[25]

Local schools in various regions of the country have participated in curriculum evaluation on a national scale through the National Assessment of Educational Progress, which is funded by the Institute of Education Sciences. Under the direction of the National Assessment of Educational Progress (NAEP), objectives have been specified, criterion-referenced measurement instruments have been created, and assessments have been conducted in a number of subject areas.[26] From these data curriculum developers in the local school systems can draw inferences about appropriate objectives of the areas tested, achievements of pupils in their region as compared to other regions, and their own state and local assessment programs.

Historically, the U.S. Department of Education has exercised a degree of leadership in curriculum development for the schools of the nation. Downsizing of government for budgetary and political reasons set in with such force at the federal level during the 1990s that in the spring of 1995 the survival of the U.S. Department of Education was in doubt. Supervising the provisions of NCLB, however, plays a strong role in current attempts to reform American education.

In this discussion of curriculum efforts on a national scale, I have mentioned the executive branch of the U.S. government (the Department of Education) and the legislative branch (the Congress). We should not neglect to note that on occasion the judicial branch of the federal government assumes the role of curriculum maker. For example, the U.S. Supreme Court has ruled that public schools may not conduct sectarian practices,[27] that released time for religious instruction under certain conditions is permissible,[28] that the theory of evolution may be taught,[29] that special instruction in English must be given to non-English-speaking pupils,[30] that prayer in the public schools is a violation of the First Amendment of the U.S. Constitution,[31] and that Cleveland's school voucher program does not infringe on the principle of separation of church and state.[32] The U.S. Supreme Court justices do not seek the role of curriculum specialists but by virtue of the cases that come before them sometimes find themselves in that role.

Professional Education Associations.   The professional education associations afford opportunities for educators to engage in curriculum deliberations. The National Education Association (NEA) has repeatedly called together influential groups to evaluate purposes and programs of the schools. The NEA's Committee of Ten, for example, issued a report in 1893 that recommended the same courses (foreign languages, history, mathematics, and science) and the same allotment of time for each course for both college-bound and non-college-bound students.[33] Decker F. Walker and Jonas F. Soltis commented on the influence of the Committee of Ten's report:

> Even today, the college preparatory high school curriculum in most schools strongly resembles the recommendations made by this Committee a hundred years ago.[34]

One of the more significant attempts at curriculum decision making at the national level was the National Education Association's appointment of the Commission on the

Reorganization of Secondary Education, which produced in 1918 one of the most influential and foresighted documents in the history of American education. The document, *Cardinal Principles of Secondary Education*, made nineteen generalizations or principles, some of which applied at all levels of education. In speaking of the role of secondary education in achieving the main objectives of education the Commission listed (in Principle IV) seven objectives that have become widely known and discussed as the *Seven Cardinal Principles*.[35]

These seven objectives were:

1. health
2. command of fundamental processes [currently known as the basic skills]
3. worthy home membership
4. vocation
5. citizenship
6. worthy use of leisure
7. ethical character

The Commission's report, possessing no authority other than its persuasiveness, was broadly received and accepted as a valid statement of goals for secondary education of its time. Many high schools have attempted to implement the Commission's Cardinal Principles. Although some criticism of the Seven Cardinal Principles exists, many educators feel that this statement of the purposes of secondary education is as relevant today as it was when first issued so many years ago.[36]

Between 1938 and 1961 the prestigious Educational Policies Commission of the National Education Association formulated statements of the purposes of education. Three of these statements have had an enduring effect on American education.

In 1938 the Educational Policies Commission defined the purposes of education as fourfold: self-realization, human relationship, economic efficiency, and civic responsibility.[37] Six years later, in the midst of World War II, the Educational Policies Commission released its report *Education for All American Youth*, which set forth ten imperative needs of American youth.[38]

Refining the earlier Seven Cardinal Principles, the Educational Policies Commission in 1944 stated the purposes of secondary education as follows:

1. All youth need to develop salable skills.
2. All youth need to develop and maintain good health, physical fitness, and mental health.
3. All youth need to understand the rights and duties of the citizen of a democratic society.
4. All youth need to understand the significance of the family.
5. All youth need to know how to purchase and use goods and services intelligently.
6. All youth need to understand the methods of science.
7. All youth need opportunities to develop their capacities to appreciate beauty in literature, art, and music.

8. All youth need to be able to use their leisure time well.

9. All youth need to develop respect for other people, to grow in their insight into ethical values and principles, to be able to live and work cooperatively with others, and to grow in the moral and spiritual values of life.

10. All youth need to grow in their ability to think rationally, to express their thoughts clearly, and to read and listen with understanding.[39]

Once again, this time in 1961, the Educational Policies Commission turned its attention to the purposes of education and decided that the central purpose of American education was to develop the ability to think.[40]

On the current scene, the Association for Supervision and Curriculum Development (ASCD), a professional association with a special interest in curriculum improvement, engages its members and others in numerous curriculum studies. It disseminates the results of studies through its journals, yearbooks, and monographs. Of special help to persons interested in the curriculum field are the ASCD's National Curriculum Study Institutes in which participants under the leadership of recognized experts focus on particular curriculum problems. Its online newsletter *Smart Brief*, five days a week, provides links to articles in the press on significant up-to-the-minute educational events and issues.

Development of curricula in certain specialized fields has been made possible by the National Science Foundation in cooperation with professional associations. The National Science Foundation, the American Mathematical Society, the National Council of Teachers of Mathematics, and the Mathematical Association of America joined forces in the 1950s to produce the School Mathematics Study Group (SMSG) program for grades four through twelve. Involved in the production of this program were mathematicians, mathematics educators, and high school teachers. At about the same time and through a similar collaborative effort, the American Institute of Biological Sciences, with financial backing by the National Science Foundation, brought forth the Biological Sciences Curriculum Study (BSCS) programs (in three versions) for high school biology.

Professional education organizations have made and continue to make significant contributions to the curriculum field.

Private Foundations and Business Corporations.   Over the years a goodly number of private foundations and organizations sponsored by business and industrial corporations have demonstrated a keen interest in supporting projects designed to improve education in the United States. The Ford Foundation has given generous backing to experimentations with novel staff patterns in the schools and the use of educational television. The Kellogg Foundation has zeroed in on studies of educational administration. As examples of foundations' interest in the curriculum of the schools we might mention the Carnegie Corporation's support in the field of mathematics and the Alfred P. Sloan Foundation's aid in the field of science. In the early 1950s the Carnegie Corporation financially aided professors in arts and sciences, education, and engineering at the University of Illinois to develop a school mathematics program for grades nine through twelve, which became known as the University of Illinois Committee on School Mathematics (UICSM) math. Shortly thereafter, in the late 1950s, the Carnegie Corporation funded another mathematics project: the development of a program for grades seven and eight by teachers of mathematics, mathematicians, and mathematics educators at the University of Maryland.

The Alfred P. Sloan Foundation entered into curriculum development in the late 1950s by supporting, along with the National Science Foundation and the Ford Foundation's Fund for the Advancement of Education, the production of a new program for high school physics known as Physical Science Study Committee (PSSC) physics.

Several observations can be made about these illustrations of national curriculum development in mathematics and science. First, these programs were created through the collaboration of scholars and practitioners, professors and teachers, combinations that have been tried with rather low frequency, unfortunately. Second, all these undertakings took considerable effort and cost a significant amount of money. Without the largesse of the federal government, public and private foundations, and professional organizations, these materials would most probably never have seen the light of day. Third, as you may have already noted, all these aforementioned developments occurred in the decade of the 1950s and continued into the early 1960s. The 1950s were a time when there was a great deal of ferment in education, and money flowed into educational pursuits as if from the proverbial horn of plenty. As a response to the technology of the former Soviet Union and in the name of national defense, the availability of funds for educational projects and research made the 1950s a heady time for educators. No such concerned collaborative activity on such a broad scale has occurred since, and we may well ponder whether it is ever likely to happen again. Finally and most significantly, in spite of the curriculum fervor of the 1950s (Could it be *because* of the fervor of the 1950s?), some of the new math and new science programs have gone into eclipse, causing us to muse with François Villon, "Where are the snows of yesteryear?"

In the 1980s the Carnegie Corporation with the Atlantic Richfield Foundation funded the study of American high schools directed by Ernest L. Boyer, president of the Carnegie Foundation for the Advancement of Teaching.[41] Six philanthropic foundations—the Charles E. Culpepper Foundation, the Carnegie Corporation, the Commonwealth Fund, the Esther A. and Joseph Klingenstein Fund, the Gates Foundation, and the Edward John Noble Foundation—supported Theodore R. Sizer's study of the American high school. Cosponsors of Sizer's study were the National Association of Secondary School Principals and the National Association of Independent Schools.[42]

Funds for John Goodlad's study of schooling in America were provided by eleven foundations, including the Danforth Foundation, the Ford Foundation, the International Paper Company Foundation, the JDR[3rd] Fund, the Martha Holden Jennings Foundation, the Charles F. Kettering Foundation, the Lilly Endowment, the Charles Stewart Mott Foundation, the Needmore Fund, the Rockefeller Foundation, and the Spencer Foundation; funding was also provided by Pedamorphosis, Inc., the National Institute of Education, and the U.S. Office of Education.[43]

The Danforth Foundation, which long concerned itself with professional growth and development of secondary school administrators, has over the years also taken an interest in promoting international education in the schools. The John D. and Catherine T. MacArthur Foundation aided the Paideia Group, which issued the *Paideia Proposal*, calling for the same course of study for all students in the twelve years of basic schooling, the only exception being the choice of a second language.[44]

In recent years Microsoft Corporation has made available without charge to K–12 schools software to enable them to become familiar with the Internet. Microsoft joined forces with MCI to offer schools the opportunity to establish an informative Web page or register Web pages with Global SchoolNet Foundation's *Global Schoolhouse*. Presently, the Bill and Melinda Gates Foundation lends support in the fields of education, as, for example, with its Gates Millennium Scholars Program and efforts to promote smaller schools, and global health, as, for example, combatting AIDS.

The Oklahoma Foundation for Excellence has directed efforts to prevent students from dropping out of school and made awards recognizing excellence among students and teachers in the public schools of Oklahoma while the Steppingstone Foundation has sought to help scholars in Boston and Philadelphia schools. The DeWitt-Wallace Reader's Digest Fund has extended grants to nonprofit charitable organizations that seek to improve opportunities and services for youth in the areas of education and career development.

You can readily see that private foundations and business corporations play a significant role in promoting change in the school's curriculum.

Other Influential Voices.   In 1990 President George H. W. Bush and the National Governors Association set forth six national educational goals that resulted in the America 2000 legislation. Expanding on the Bush reform efforts, the U.S. Congress in 1994 enacted President Bill Clinton's educational reform package known as Goals 2000 Educate America Act, which added two goals beyond the earlier six and authorized funding to promote achievement of those goals. Further educational reform is the goal of the No Child Left Behind Act passed by the U.S. Congress in 2001 and signed into law by President George W. Bush in January 2002. We will return to these goals and their significance in Chapter 6.

Tests and Texts.   Before we leave the national sector, we should mention an aspect of curriculum development that has evoked considerable discussion. Standardized tests of achievement and textbooks used in the schools have played a great part in molding the contemporary curriculum. Combined with the movement toward specification of competencies for high school graduation, achievement tests profoundly affect what is being taught and how it is being taught. Under these conditions, curriculum decisions have been, in effect, put into the hands of the test makers and textbook writers. Some curriculum experts see the reliance on tests and textbooks marketed throughout the country as constituting a "national curriculum." As long ago as 1985, Elliot W. Eisner expressed concern about the influence of the testing movement:

> One may wax eloquent about the life of the mind and the grand purposes of education, but must face up to the fact that school programs are shaped by other factors as well. Communities led to believe that the quality of education is represented by the reading and math

scores students receive come to demand that those areas of the curriculum be given the highest priority. When this happens, teachers begin to define their own priorities in terms of test performance. Indeed, I do not believe it is an exaggeration to say that test scores function as one of the most powerful controls on the character of educational practice.[45]

State testing required under the terms of NCLB today reinforces Eisner's observation. Other educators identify federal aid for specific categories as creating types of national curricula. Considerable activity in planning, implementing, and evaluating curriculum transpires in the national sector. Although curriculum activities on the national scene are many and diverse, opportunities for personal involvement are rather limited for the rank-and-file teacher and curriculum specialist. Their roles are more often as recipients of curriculum plans developed by others, implementors of plans, and sometimes evaluators.

The Public.   We would be remiss if we did not include the public in our survey of groups that influence curriculum development. We have but to examine some of the controversial issues discussed in Chapter 15 as evidence of public participation in efforts to change the curriculum.

Most often the public's efforts are diffuse with subgroups advocating change of one type whereas other subgroups take opposite positions. The public's views, however, succeed in effecting change when issues are put before them, albeit from legislator-curriculum planners, in the form of proposals to be voted on by the voting public. The electorate of California, for example, in the spring of 1998 voted to remove bilingual education from the public schools. Citizens of Florida in 2002 approved a highly controversial amendment to the state constitution limiting class size in all grades.

The International Sector

International Professional Associations.   Involvement of American curriculum workers on the international scene is made possible through membership in international professional associations, primarily those based in the United States. The International Reading Association, for example, attracts reading specialists from around the world but primarily from the United States and Canada. The World Council for Gifted and Talented Children holds conferences in various parts of the world. Two of the more pertinent international organizations for individuals interested in curricular activities on a cross-national scale are the World Council for Curriculum and Instruction and the International Association for the Advancement of Curriculum Studies. The American Association for the Advancement of Curriculum Studies is a member of the latter. Sponsoring periodic conferences in various parts of the world, these international organizations offer opportunities for individuals interested in curriculum studies to exchange ideas and develop an understanding of one another's educational systems and problems.

If teachers and administrators are willing to spend a period of time abroad, they can become intimately involved in curriculum development overseas by accepting employment in the U.S. Department of Defense Schools (which, given current retrenchments in the defense establishment, are shrinking in numbers) or in the private American Community/International Schools whose curricula are mainly those offered stateside.

Or they may become active in developing curricula of foreign national schools through employment with the Peace Corps or the Agency for International Development.

The United Nations Educational, Scientific, and Cultural Organization (UNESCO), with headquarters in Paris, affords opportunities for curriculum study, research, teaching, and technical assistance from members of the United Nations. The Institute of International Education in New York City directs an international exchange of students and teachers supported in part by Fulbright funds. The Council for International Exchange of Scholars in Washington, D.C., administers Fulbright grants that enable faculty from institutions of higher education to conduct research and teach in foreign countries.

Opportunities for firsthand participation in actual curriculum construction on a cross-national basis are rare, and this dearth of opportunity is, perhaps, to be expected. The curricular needs and goals of education in various countries are so divergent as to make impractical the building of a particular curriculum that will fit the requirements of the educational system of every country.

International Studies of Student Achievement.   Significant efforts primarily in the realm of assessment of student achievement should be noted. Studies comparing achievement of students in a number of countries and in a variety of disciplines have been conducted by the International Association for Evaluation of Educational Achievement (IEA) and the International Assessment of Educational Progress (IAEP). You will find discussion of international comparative studies in Chapter 12 of this text.

Comparative Textbook Studies.   One of the more interesting international curriculum studies of modern times was the United States and the then USSR Textbook-Study Project sponsored by the National Council for the Social Studies, the Council of Chief State School Officers, the Association of American Publishers, the Association for the Advancement of Slavic Studies, and the former Soviet Union's Ministry of Education.[46] Begun in 1977 as a phase of cultural exchange agreements between the two countries, the project ceased functioning after the Soviet march into Afghanistan in 1979. The project resumed operation in 1985, drafted a report in 1987, and presented a subsequent report on the conclusion of a seminar in Moscow in 1989.

Educators from both countries examined history and geography textbooks used in the secondary schools of each country to ascertain what one nation's students were taught about the other nation. These educators searched for errors of fact and distortions in the textbooks. Project efforts pointed to the need for textbooks published in each country to present a more accurate picture of the other country. The need for comparative studies of this nature is revealed and reinforced by China's protest in 2005 over Japan's junior high school textbooks that minimize Japan's destructive role in China during World War II. This exciting approach to international curriculum study could well furnish a model that the United States could and, I believe, should replicate with other countries.

Global Awareness.   The frenzied pace of economic and technological globalization increases the need for a curriculum and international exchange of students and teachers to foster global awareness and understanding.

Various commissions and organizations such as the President's Commission on Foreign Languages and International Studies (1970s)[47] and the National Commission on Excellence in Education (1980s)[48] have promoted the teaching of foreign languages as one dimension of global education. Problems on an international scale from global warming to military conflicts have caused Americans to recognize the necessity for learning about the culture of other peoples, sharing ideas, and working cooperatively.

A rationale for global education was the focus of the 1991 Yearbook of the Association for Supervision and Curriculum Development. The Yearbook includes descriptions of ways to introduce global studies into the curriculum.[49]

Although opportunities for actual curriculum development on the international scene are limited, many opportunities exist for school personnel to study and compare curricula of the world's nations. Professional organizations like Phi Delta Kappa, the National Education Association, the Association for Supervision and Curriculum Development, and the Comparative and International Education Society conduct frequent study tours for those interested in examining firsthand the curricula of other countries and meeting their educational leaders. Many teachers have taken advantage of opportunities to serve as leaders of educational study tours abroad. Furthermore, development of both awareness and understanding of other cultures (both within and outside of our borders) remains a high priority of our elementary and secondary curricula. Through exchange of personnel, countries come to realize that they have much to learn from each other not only in education but in other dimensions of living as well.

Summary

Curriculum planning is viewed as occurring on five levels: classroom, team/grade/department, individual school, school district, and state. Each level in ascending order exercises authority over levels below it.

In addition, planning takes place in regional, national, and world sectors. Sectors are distinguished from levels because powers of the sectors over the five levels are nonexistent or limited.

Teachers and curriculum specialists will find their most frequent opportunities to participate actively in curriculum development at the first four levels. Some curriculum workers are called on by the state to serve on curriculum projects. A limited number of school-based persons take part in a variety of curriculum efforts sponsored by regional, national, and international organizations and agencies.

This chapter discusses a variety of organizational patterns for carrying out curriculum activities in the individual school and school district. A teacher or curriculum specialist may be requested to serve on a number of curriculum committees and councils within a school system.

Forces outside the schools also influence curriculum decision making. Curriculum development is perceived as a multilevel, multisector process and as a collaborative effort.

Questions for Discussion

1. To what degree should teachers be involved in curriculum planning at the individual school level? at the district level?

2. What are the strengths and limitations of the concept of levels of planning?

3. What are the strengths and limitations of the concept of sectors of planning?

4. What do you believe is the best way for organizing a curriculum council on the individual school level?

5. What do you believe is the best way for organizing a curriculum council on the school district level?

Exercises

1. Chart the organizational pattern for curriculum development in your school and district.

2. Write a short paper describing the extent to which the organizational patterns operating in your school system can be called participatory.

3. Tell how curriculum committees and councils, if any, are selected and constituted in your school district.

4. Describe any curricular changes within the last three years brought about by an individual teacher in his or her classroom.

5. Describe activities of a team, grade, or department of a school faculty in the last three years in the area of curriculum development.

6. Describe the roles and powers of (a) the state superintendent of public instruction, (b) the state board of education, and (c) the state department of education in curricular and instructional matters within your state.

7. Study an organizational chart of your state department of education and identify those offices that are charged with providing curricular and instructional leadership in the state. Describe some of the services of these offices.

8. Report on several programs that have come about or been affected as a result of state legislation.

9. Describe any curriculum developments that have come about as a result of regional activities.

10. Report on the purposes and activities of the accrediting associations of your region.

11. Report on several programs that have come about or been affected as a result of federal legislation.

12. Describe any support that may have come to schools of your community and/or state from private foundations or business/industrial corporations.

13. Report on any national curriculum studies that you would call significant.

14. Report on at least two state and two federal court decisions that have had an impact on the curriculum of your school system.

15. Describe any curriculum development in your school that might be attributed to international influences.

16. Report on the purposes and recent activities of at least two state, two national, and two international professional organizations concerned with curriculum development.

17. Write a description of the processes by which textbooks are selected in your state or district.

18. If you work in a private school and if your school is accredited by an association or associations other than the regional association, describe the purpose and activities of that association or associations.

19. In Chapter 11 of his book, John D. McNeil (see bibliography) discusses the politics of curriculum making. Report several ways in which curriculum making is a political process.

20. Describe what Michael W. Apple meant by "Curriculum . . . is the social product of contending forces." (See bibliography.) See also Chapter 4, "Understanding Curriculum as Political Text," in William F. Pinar et al. (see bibliography).

21. Describe any program of global studies in any school with which you are familiar or that you can find in the literature.

Organizations

Association for Supervision and Curriculum Development, 1703 N. Beauregard St., Alexandria, Va. 22311-1714. Journals: *Educational Leadership* and *Journal of Curriculum and Supervision*. Website: http://www.ascd.org.

National Education Association, 1201 16th St., N.W., Washington, D.C. 20036. Journal: *NEA Today*. Website: http://www.nea.org.

Phi Delta Kappa, Box 789, Bloomington, Ind. 47402. Journal: *Phi Delta Kappan*. Website: http://www.pdkint.org.

Websites

American Association for the Advancement of Curriculum Studies: http://aaacs.info

American Association of School Administrators: http://aasa.org

Association for Supervision and Curriculum Development *Smart Brief*: http://wwwsmartbrief.com/ascd

Coalition of Essential Schools: http://essentialschools.org

Comparative and International Education Society: http://www.cies.ws

Council for International Exchange of Scholars: http://www.cies.org

Bill and Melinda Gates Foundation: http://www.gatesfoundation.org

Global School Net Foundation: http://www.globalschoolnet.org

Institute of International Education: http://www.iie.org

International Association for the Advancement of Curriculum Studies: http://www.iaacs.org

International Association for the Evaluation of Educational Achievement: http://www.iea.nl

National Assessment of Educational Progress: http://nces.ed.gov/nationsreportcard

National Association of Elementary School Principals: http://www.naesp.org

National Association of Independent Schools: http://www.nais.org

National Association of Secondary School Principals: http://www.nassp.org

National Middle School Association: http://www.nmsa.org

United Nations Educational, Scientific, and Cultural Organization: http://www.unesco.org

U.S. Department of Education: http://www.ed.gov

World Council for Curriculum and Instruction: http://www.wcci-international.org

World Council for Gifted and Talented Children: http://www.worldgifted.ca

Endnotes

1. *Lau v. Nichols*, 414 U.S. 563 (1974).
2. Earl C. Kelley, *Education for What Is Real* (New York: Harper & Row, 1947).
3. Ralph W. Tyler, *Basic Principles of Curriculum and Instruction* (Chicago: University of Chicago Press, 1949).
4. Benjamin S. Bloom, ed., *Taxonomy of Educational Objectives: The Classification of Educational Goals: Hand-book I: Cognitive Domain* (White Plains, N.Y.: Longman, 1956). Benjamin S. Bloom, J. Thomas Hastings, and George F. Madaus, *Handbook on Formative and Summative Evaluation of Student Learning* (New York: McGraw-Hill, 1971).
5. James B. Conant, *The American High School Today* (New York: McGraw-Hill, 1959).

6. Jerome S. Bruner, *The Process of Education* (Cambridge, Mass.: Harvard University Press, 1960).

7. Theodore R. Sizer, *Horace's Compromise: The Dilemma of the American High School* (Boston: Houghton Mifflin, 1984).

8. John I. Goodlad, *A Place Called School: Prospects for the Future* (New York: McGraw-Hill, 1984).

9. Adapted from Peter F. Oliva, *The Secondary School Today*, 2nd ed. (New York: Harper & Row, 1972), p. 280.

10. See Chapter 9 of this text for a discussion of the graded school, open-space schools, team teaching, and other organizational arrangements.

11. See Priscilla Wohlstetter, "Getting School-Based Management Right: What Works and What Doesn't," *Phi Delta Kappan* 77, no. 1 (September 1995): 22–26.

12. Alice Miel, *Changing the Curriculum: A Social Process* (New York: D. Appleton Century, 1946), p. 69.

13. Goodlad, *A Place Called School*, pp. 31 and 318–319.

14. Jack R. Frymier and Horace C. Hawn, *Curriculum Improvement for Better Schools* (Worthington, Ohio: Charles A. Jones, 1970), pp. 28–29.

15. Zais attributes the classification "grass-roots model" to B. Othanel Smith, William O. Stanley, and J. Harlan Shores, *Fundamentals of Curriculum Development* (New York: Harcourt Brace Jovanovich, 1957). See Robert S. Zais, *Curriculum: Principles and Foundations* (New York: Harper & Row, 1976), p. 448.

16. Zais refers to the definition of "curriculum engineering" by George A. Beauchamp, *Curriculum Theory*, 2nd ed. (Wilmette, Ill.: Kagg Press, 1968), and uses the term to encompass "curriculum construction," "curriculum development," and "curriculum implementation." Zais, *Curriculum*, p. 18. See also the third edition of Beauchamp's *Curriculum Theory* (1975), Chapter 7.

17. Zais, *Curriculum*, pp. 448–449.

18. Michael G. Fullan, "Coordinating Top-Down and Bottom-Up Strategies for Educational Reform," in Richard F. Elmore and Susan H. Fuhrman, eds., *The Governance of Curriculum*, 1994 Yearbook (Alexandria, Va.: Association for Supervision and Curriculum Development, 1994), pp. 186–202.

19. Ibid., p. 189.

20. Zais, *Curriculum*, Chapter 19.

21. B. Frank Brown, *The Nongraded High School* (Englewood Cliffs, N.J.: Prentice-Hall, 1963), pp. 209–210.

22. See Chapter 6 for reference to Character Counts! Coalition.

23. *Stuart v. School District No. 1, Village of Kalamazoo*, 30 Mich. 69 (1874).

24. See Lyon Sprague de Camp, *The Great Monkey Trial* (Garden City, N.Y.: Doubleday, 1968).

25. For recent lists of centers and laboratories see the Appendix.

26. See Chapter 12 of this text for additional details about the National Assessment of Educational Progress.

27. *Illinois ex rel McCollum v. Board of Education*, 333 US 203, 68 S Ct. 461 (1948).

28. *Zorach v. Clauson*, 343 US 306, 72 S. Ct. 679 (1952).

29. *Epperson v. Arkansas*, 393 US 97, 89 S. Ct. 266 (1968).

30. *Lau v. Nichols*, 414 US 663 (1974).

31. *School District of Abington Township, Pa. v. Schempp & Murray v. Curlett*, 374 US 203, 83 S. Ct. 1560 (1963).

32. *Zolman et al. v. Simmons-Harris et al.* 536 US 639 (2002).

33. National Education Association, *Report of the Committee of Ten on Secondary School Studies* (Washington, D.C.: National Education Association, 1893).

34. Decker F. Walker and Jonas F. Soltis, *Curriculum and Aims*, 4th ed. (New York: Teachers College Press, 2004), p. 28.

35. Commission on the Reorganization of Secondary Education, *Cardinal Principles of Secondary Education* (Washington, D.C.: United States Office of Education, Bulletin no. 35, 1918), pp. 5–10.

36. For criticism of the Seven Cardinal Principles, see Chapter 9 of this text.

37. Educational Policies Commission, *The Purposes of Education in American Democracy* (Washington, D.C.: National Education Association, 1938).

38. Educational Policies Commission, *Education for All American Youth* (Washington, D.C.: National Education Association, 1944).

39. Educational Policies Commission, *American Youth*, pp. 225–226.

40. Educational Policies Commission, *The Central Purpose of American Education* (Washington, D.C.: National Education Association, 1961).

41. Ernest L. Boyer, *High School: A Report on Secondary Education in America* (New York: Harper & Row, 1983).

42. Theodore R. Sizer, *Horace's Compromise: The Dilemma of the American High School* (Boston: Houghton Mifflin, 1984).

43. Goodlad, *A Place Called School*.

44. Mortimer J. Adler, *The Paideia Proposal: An Educational Manifesto* (New York: Macmillan, 1982).

45. Elliot W. Eisner, *The Educational Imagination: On the Design and Evaluation of School Programs*, 2nd ed. (New York: Macmillan, 1985), p. 4.

46. Robert Rothman, "Americans, Soviets Critique Texts." *Education Week* 7, no. 12 (November 25, 1987): 5; and Oliva's correspondence from the National Council for the Social Studies, dated December 4, 1990.

47. See Malcolm G. Scully, "Require Foreign-Language Studies, Presidential Panel Urges Colleges," *The Chronicle of Higher Education* 19, no. 11 (November 13, 1979): 1 ff.

48. National Commission on Excellence in Education, *A Nation at Risk: The Imperative for Educational Reform* (Washington, D.C.: U.S. Government Printing Office, 1983), p. 26.

49. Kenneth A. Tye, ed., *Global Education: From Thought to Action.* 1991 Yearbook (Alexandria, Va.: Association for Supervision and Curriculum Development, 1990). See also "The World in the Classroom," *Educational Leadership* 60, no. 2 (October 2002): 6–69 and Sharon Lynn Kagan and Vivien Stewart, eds., "Education in a Global Era," *Phi Delta Kappan* 87, no. 3 (November 2005): 184–245.

Bibliography

Adler, Mortimer J. *The Paideia Proposal: An Educational Manifesto.* New York: Macmillan, 1982.

Apple, Michael W. "Social Crisis and Curriculum Accords." *Educational Theory* 38, no. 2 (Spring 1988): 191–201.

Association for Supervision and Curriculum Development. "Making Connections Through Global Education." *Curriculum Update* (summer 1998): 8.

Ayers, William. "*Perestroika* in Chicago's Schools" *Educational Leadership* 48, no. 8 (May 1991): 69–71.

Beauchamp, George A. *Curriculum Theory,* 4th ed. Itasca, Ill.: F. E. Peacock, 1981.

Bloom, Benjamin S., ed. *Taxonomy of Educational Objectives: The Classification of Educational Goals: Handbook I: Cognitive Domain.* White Plains, N.Y.: Longman, 1956.

———, Hastings, J. Thomas, and Madaus, George F. *Handbook on Formative and Summative Evaluation of Student Learning.* New York: McGraw-Hill, 1971.

Boyer, Ernest L. *High School: A Report on Secondary Education in America.* New York: Harper & Row, 1983.

Brown, B. Frank. *The Nongraded High School.* Englewood Cliffs, N.J.: Prentice Hall, 1963.

Bruner, Jerome S. *The Process of Education.* Cambridge, Mass.: Harvard University Press, 1960.

Carroll, Joseph M. "The Copernican Plan: Restructuring the American High School." *Phi Delta Kappan* 71, no. 5 (January 1990): 358–365.

Commission on the Reorganization of Secondary Education. *Cardinal Principles of Secondary Education.* Washington, D.C.: United States Office of Education, Bulletin no. 35, 1918.

Conant, James B. *The American High School Today.* New York: McGraw-Hill, 1959.

David, Jane L. "Synthesis on Research on School-Based Management." *Educational Leadership* 46, no. 8 (May 1989): 45–53.

Doll, Ronald C. *Curriculum Improvement: Decision Making and Process,* 9th ed. Boston: Allyn and Bacon, 1996.

Educational Policies Commission. *The Central Purpose of American Education.* Washington, D.C.: National Education Association, 1961.

———. *Education for All American Youth.* Washington, D.C.: National Education Association, 1944.

———. *The Purposes of Education in American Democracy.* Washington, D.C.: National Education Association, 1938.

Eisner, Elliot W. *Confronting Curriculum Reform.* Boston: Little, Brown, 1971.

———. *The Educational Imagination: On the Design and Evaluation of School Programs,* 2nd ed. New York: Macmillan, 1985.

Elmore, Richard F. and Fuhrman, Susan H., eds. *The Governance of Curriculum,* 1994 Yearbook. Alexandria, Va.: Association for Supervision and Curriculum Development, 1994.

Firth, Gerald R. and Kimpston, Richard D. *The Curricular Continuum in Perspective.* Itasca, Ill.: F. E. Peacock, 1973.

Frymier, Jack R. and Hawn, Horace C. *Curriculum Improvement for Better Schools.* Worthington, Ohio: Charles A. Jones, 1970.

Fuhrman, Susan H. "Legislation and Education Policy." In Richard F. Elmore and Susan H. Fuhrman, eds., *The Governance of Curriculum,* 1994 Yearbook. Alexandria, Va.: Association for Supervision and Curriculum Development, 1994.

Fullan, Michael G. "Coordinating Top-Down and Bottom-Up Strategies for Educational Reform." In Richard F. Elmore and Susan H. Fuhrman, eds., *The Governance of Curriculum,* 1994 Yearbook. Alexandria, Va.: Association for Supervision and Curriculum Development, 1994.

Gomez, Joseph J. "The Path to School-Based Management Isn't Smooth, but We're Scaling the Obstacles One by One." *American School Board Journal* 176, no. 10 (October 1989): 20–22.

Goodlad, John I. *A Place Called School: Prospects for the Future.* New York: McGraw-Hill, 1984.

Kelley, Earl C. *Education for What Is Real.* New York: Harper & Row, 1947.

Kimbrough, Ralph B. and Nunnery, Michael Y. *Educational Administration: An Introduction*, 3rd ed. New York: Macmillan, 1988.

McNeil, John D. *Contemporary Curriculum in Thought and Action*, 6th ed. Hoboken, N.J.: Wiley, 2006.

Mendez, Roy. "The Curriculum Council: One Way to Develop the Instructional Leadership Role." *NASSP Bulletin* 67, no. 464 (September 1983): 18–21.

Miel, Alice. *Changing the Curriculum: A Social Process.* New York: D. Appleton Century, 1946.

National Commission on Excellence in Education. *A Nation at Risk: The Imperative for Educational Reform.* Washington, D.C.: U.S. Government Printing Office, 1983.

National Education Association. *Report of the Committee of Ten on Secondary School Studies.* Washington, D.C.: National Education Association, 1893.

Oliva, Peter F. *Developing the Curriculum*, 5th ed. (New York: Longman, 2001), pp. 59–73.

———. *The Secondary School Today*, 2nd ed. New York: Harper & Row, 1972.

Oliver, Albert I. *Curriculum Improvement: A Guide to Problems, Principles, and Process*, 2nd ed. New York: Harper & Row, 1977.

Pinar, William F., Reynolds, William M., Slattery Patrick, and Taubman, Peter M. *Understanding Curriculum: An Introduction to the Study of Historical and Contemporary Curriculum Discourses.* New York: Peter Lang, 1996.

Prasch, John. *How to Organize for School-Based Management.* Alexandria, Va.: Association for Supervision and Curriculum Development, 1990.

"Restructuring Schools to Match a Changing Society." *Educational Leadership* 45, no. 5 (February 1988): 3–79.

"Restructuring Schools: What's Really Happening." *Educational Leadership* 48, no. 8 (May 1991): 3–76.

Rothman, Robert. "Americans, Soviets Critique Texts," *Education Week* 7, no. 12 (November 25, 1987): 5.

Rubin, Louis, ed. *Curriculum Handbook: The Disciplines, Current Movements, and Instructional Methodology.* Boston: Allyn and Bacon, 1977.

Scully, Malcolm G. "Require Foreign-Language Studies, Presidential Panel Urges Colleges," *The Chronicle of Higher Education* 19, no. 11 (November 13, 1979): 1ff.

Shanker, Albert. "The End of the Traditional Model of Schooling—And a Proposal for Using Incentives to Restructure Our Public Schools." *Phi Delta Kappan* 71, no. 5 (January 1990): 344–357.

Silberman, Charles E. *Crisis in the Classroom: The Remaking of American Education.* New York: Random House, 1970.

Sizer, Theodore F. *Horace's Compromise: The Dilemma of the American High School.* Boston: Houghton Mifflin, 1984.

Smith, B. Othanel, Stanley, William O., and Shores, Harlan J. *Fundamentals of Curriculum Development.* New York: Harcourt Brace Jovanovich, 1957.

Sprague de Camp, Lyon. *The Great Monkey Trial.* Garden City, N.Y.: Doubleday, 1968.

Tanner, Daniel and Tanner, Laurel. *Curriculum Development: Theory into Practice*, 4th ed. Upper Saddle River, N.J.: Merrill/Prentice Hall, 2007.

Tye, Kenneth A., ed. *Global Education from Thought to Action.* 1991 Yearbook. Alexandria, Va: Association for Supervision and Curriculum Development, 1990.

Tyler, Ralph W. *Basic Principles of Curriculum and Instruction.* Chicago: University of Chicago Press, 1949.

Walker, Decker F. *Fundamentals of Curriculum: Passion and Professionalism*, 2nd ed., Mahwah, N.J.: Lawrence Erlbaum Associates, 2003.

——— and Soltis, Jonas F. *Curriculum and Aims*, 4th ed. New York: Teachers College Press, 2004.

Wiles, Jon and Bondi, Joseph C. *Curriculum Development: A Guide to Practice*, 7th ed. Upper Saddle River, N.J.: Merrill/Prentice Hall, 2007.

Wohlstetter, Priscilla. "Getting School-Based Management Right: What Works and What Doesn't," *Phi Delta Kappan* 77, no. 1 (September 1995): 22–26.

"The World in the Classroom," *Educational Leadership* 60, no. 2 (October 2002): 60–69.

Zais, Robert S. *Curriculum: Principles and Foundations.* New York: Harper & Row, 1976.

Curriculum Planning: The Human Dimension

THE SCHOOL AS A UNIQUE BLEND

Let us for a few moments step into the shoes of the superintendent of a hypothetical school district. It is mid-May. The school year is almost over and summer school plans are ready to be implemented. The superintendent has just concluded a meeting with his principals on the budget and staffing needs for next year. In thirty minutes he will meet with an assistant superintendent and one of the principals of the district, who intend to bring charges of insubordination against one of the teachers in the principal's school. For a half hour the superintendent muses on what improvements in curriculum and instruction have been accomplished in the school district this year. Since his energies have been channeled into public relations, budgeting, personnel problems, transportation, new buildings, and other administrative matters, he has delegated responsibility for curriculum and instruction. He holds in his hands the assistant superintendent's report updating developments in the district this year.

The superintendent is struck by the large amount of time and effort that the school district is expending toward improving curriculum and instruction. He is impressed by the sizable number of people involved in this activity. He notes that most teams of teachers meet practically daily; most grade faculties or departments meet as groups regularly, some of them on a weekly basis; every school has its own curriculum council, which meets at least once a month; a number of curriculum committees meet at various times on districtwide problems of curriculum and instruction. The superintendent certainly cannot fault the quantity of effort expended by the professionals in curriculum development.

As to quality, he is less certain. He reviews some of the accomplishments to date and is struck by the unevenness of developments from school to school. The accomplishments at some schools far outshine those of others. Several innovative programs are in experimental stages in some schools. Other schools have defined their philosophies, goals, and objectives. Some have conducted thorough reexaminations of their curricula, whereas others have been content with the status quo. Several groups of teachers have revised their particular curricula. Other groups have developed some new curriculum guides. Some schools have responded to previously unmet curricular needs of their students, and others have failed to come up with solutions to some of their more pressing curricular problems. The superintendent is surprised (though he realizes that he should not be) that a few schools obviously surpass the others in both quantity and quality of curriculum efforts. A few schools have tackled curriculum development with a vigor that has effected significant change. He finds repeated references in the report to positive changes made by a few schools. He concludes that some schools are imbued with the spirit of change and are willing to move forward and out, while others find the established ways of operating more comfortable. The superintendent wonders why such great variations in curriculum development exist from school to school. Whom should he credit in those schools that seem to be engaged in productive curriculum efforts? The principals? The teachers? The curriculum leaders, whoever they are? The students? The parents? The signs of the zodiac? Just plain luck? Or a combination of all these factors?

The superintendent is aware that schools differ considerably from one another. Their physical facilities, resources, and locales all differ. Yet these more or less tangible factors do not explain the great differences in strides made by schools in curriculum and instruction. Yes, we may say that schools differ in many ways, but schools are only brick, concrete, mortar, steel, wood, glass, and a host of other building materials. It is not the schools that differ as much as the people who either support them or operate within them. The superintendent must credit not the schools in the abstract but the people who make them function. In his short period of reflection, the superintendent reinforces a long-held, verified belief—that curriculum development is a "people" process, a human endeavor. Curriculum development is a process in which the human players accept and carry out mutually reinforcing roles. Given a predisposition to change and a subtle blending of skills and knowledge, a faculty can achieve significant successes in curriculum improvement even in a substandard physical environment. The "people" factor far outweighs the physical setting.

Differences among Faculty

Let's leave the meditating superintendent and focus our attention on another place, another time. It is early in the school year. The principal of a medium-size secondary school is presiding over the initial organizational meeting of the school's curriculum council. Representatives of the nine departments of the school are about to elect their chairperson. With freshness, high spirits, and a modicum of levity, the curriculum council is getting under way. The principal wonders what progress the school will make this year in curriculum improvement. She realizes as she looks around the room that success in improving the curriculum depends largely on human differences among individual curriculum workers and between curriculum groups.

Each school is characterized by its own unique blend of persons, each with different skills, knowledge, experience, and personality. The principal mentally lists some of the ways individuals within the curriculum council, which represents the faculty, differ. Certainly, the philosophical beliefs of the various council members diverge greatly. It will take considerable effort to reach some kind of consensus on the goals of this school, let alone the general goals of education. The council members differ in their knowledge about and ability to apply learning theory. Some are outstanding instructors, others only passable. Variations exist in the members' knowledge of curriculum history and theory and in experience in curriculum development.

Some younger members, new to teaching and the particular school, are less knowledgeable about children in general and in this setting than older teachers who have taught several years, many of them in this school. As soon as the council settles down to work it becomes apparent that there are great differences in individuals' skills in interacting with others; in the leadership skills of the various council members; in the followership skills; in organizational, writing, and oral skills.

Some of the council members will show themselves as being more perceptive of parental roles and the needs of the community. Personal traits like friendliness, reliability, motivation, sense of humor, enthusiasm, and frustration level are significant differences among individuals that contribute to the success or failure of group efforts like curriculum development. Outside commitments, family obligations, and allocations of time differ from person to person and can affect the process of curriculum planning.

The human variables in the process are many and complex. Success or failure will depend to a great extent on how the council members relate to one another, on how each member relates to other teachers on the faculty, and how they, in turn, relate to one another. The way the council and faculty interact with parents, others in the community, and the students can make or break curriculum efforts.

Dependent Variables

The differences among individuals and groups participating in curriculum development are dependent rather than independent variables. The presence or absence of a particular skill or trait and the degree to which an individual possesses it have an impact on all other individuals who take part in the process. Not only are the leaders' leadership skills and the followers' followership skills significant in themselves, but the manner in which they come together is even more important. Competence in leadership must ideally be met with competence in followership. Whether in military service, industry, or education, a superb leader is going nowhere without committed followers. In the same manner superb followers are going nowhere without competent leadership.

In accounting for success or failure in a cooperative enterprise, we should also look to differences among groups as well as among individuals. It is trite but pertinent to say that the whole is greater than the sum of its parts. A group is not simply the addition of each individual member to make a sum but something more than the sum, something special created by an inexplicable meshing of the human elements. Working together, members of a group must become unified as they move toward common goals in a spirit of mutual respect. Thus, a curriculum council *as a group* can demonstrate competence in leadership. Success in curriculum development is more likely to be achieved when the leadership skills of the council interface with those of the faculty, resulting in a total team approach to the solution of curriculum problems. When we compare schools' achievements in curriculum improvement, we quickly discover great variations in the leadership skills of (1) the person or persons directing the curriculum study, (2) the curriculum committees or councils, (3) the total faculty, and (4) the preceding three entities working together. The contributions to curriculum improvement that may be made by students, parents, and others from the community enhance the work of the professionals.

THE CAST OF PLAYERS

We would not be far off the mark if we perceived the process of curriculum development as a continuing theatrical production in which actors play specific roles. Some of these roles are determined by society and the force of law; others are set by players themselves. Some roles are mandated, whereas others spring out of the players' personalities.

When discussing roles of various groups, J. Galen Saylor and William M. Alexander applied the analogy of drama to the process of curriculum planning:

> In addition to leading roles of students and teachers in the curriculum planning drama, important supporting actors include the members of lay advisory groups, curriculum councils and committees, teacher teams, and curriculum development units. . . . all of these roles are affected by their interaction with various groups and agencies outside the curriculum theatre.[1]

Although the metaphor of curriculum planning as drama can be overworked, we must admit that a good deal of role-playing does occur, much of it unconsciously, in the group process itself. For the moment, let's talk about the conscious roles the curriculum participants are called on to play. For purposes of analysis we will focus our attention on roles of constituent groups (administrators, students, laypeople, curriculum workers: teachers, curriculum consultants, and supervisors). To achieve clarity we will focus on the individual school level. When we discuss below roles of administrators, teachers, and students in curriculum development, we should keep in mind the interactions among these constituencies not only in curriculum development but also in the total life of the school. We should be developing as Roland S. Barth termed it, a "community of learners," striving for high standards in an atmosphere of low anxiety.[2]

Addressing the concept of schools as communities, indeed, the concept of "community as curriculum,"[3] Thomas J. Sergiovanni and Robert J. Starratt drew the inferences from "conditions of late or post-modernity" that "there needs to be a curriculum *of* community, a curriculum that intentionally and explicitly attends to the building up of knowledge, skills, and dispositions which constitute the work of becoming and sustaining a community."[4]

Role of the Administrator

As long ago as the mid-1950s the Southern States Cooperative Program in Education, sponsored by the W. K. Kellogg Foundation, listed "instructional and curriculum development" as the number one critical task for administrators.[5] With research on effective teaching and effective schools that pointed to the crucial importance of effective leadership, the decade of the 1980s brought a plethora of articles and speeches stressing the role of the principal as *instructional leader*—the term in this context shorthand for both curriculum and instruction. We are concerned at the moment about the administrator's role in curriculum development.

Whether the chief administrator of the school, the principal, serves actively as leader in the process of curriculum development or passively by delegating leadership responsibilities to subordinates, efforts are doomed to failure without his or her support. Although some school administrators claim, in keeping with some current conceptions of the administrator's role, that they are instructional leaders, others admit that they are primarily managers.

Although the role of the principal as instructional leader is recognized by many, perhaps most, administrators as an important task, instructional and curriculum development do not head the list of priorities of many school principals. Thelbert L. Drake and William H. Roe observed that the principal is torn between his or her desired role as instructional leader and his or her actual role as administrator and manager.[6]

The reasons for the low priority assigned by many principals to what used to be their main raison d'être are found both within the personality of the principal and in the pressure from outside forces. Some of the factors that lead principals away from spending time on instructional leadership are the priority that the higher officers place on efficiency of operation, limitations placed on principals' fields of operation by teachers' organizations, and preservice programs for administrators that emphasize business and personnel management, minimizing curriculum and instructional development.

Glenys G. Unruh observed that training programs for administrators may be at least partially at fault for the lower priority placed on curriculum and instruction by some principals.[7] With continuing emphasis on the individual school as the locus of change, on public demand for improvement in students' achievement, on state and federal mandates, and on the assessment of teacher performance, there are signs that the principals' priorities have shifted somewhat. Professional associations for administrators recognize the importance of instructional leadership. Preservice and inservice education programs for school administrators are incorporating training in the technical, supervisory, and human relations skills needed by the instructional leader. Thus, more and more principals will be able to play a direct, central role in curriculum development. Hopefully, instructional leadership will eventually top the list of tasks actually performed by all principals.

Whether the principal plays a direct or indirect role, his or her presence is always keenly felt by all the players. The participants are aware that the principal by both tradition and law is charged with responsibility for conducting all the affairs of the school and for decision making in that school. In that sense, all curriculum groups and subgroups of the school are advisory to the principal.

"Theory X" and "Theory Y." Through management style the principal exerts a force on all operations within the school. The success of the curriculum developers may depend to some extent on whether the principal is a "Theory X" or "Theory Y" person. Douglas McGregor has classified into the categories Theory X and Theory Y two sets of assumptions that he believes managers have about people.[8] These theories are widely quoted in the literature on management. According to McGregor, managers following Theory X believe the following:

- The average person dislikes work and tries to avoid it.
- Most people must be forced to work and threatened with punishment to get them to work.
- The average person lacks ambition and avoids responsibility.
- The average person must be directed.
- The need for security is the chief motivation of the average person.

Authority, control, task maintenance, and product orientation dominate the thinking of the Theory X administrator. On the other hand, the administrator who subscribes to Theory Y holds these beliefs:

- The average person welcomes work.
- The average person seeks responsibility.
- Most people will demonstrate self-reliance when they share a commitment to the realization of common objectives.
- The average person will be committed to an organization's objectives if he or she is rewarded for that commitment.
- Creativity in problem solving is a trait found rather widely among people.

Whereas the typical administrator will be more inclined toward one theory, he or she will manifest behavior that will at times lean toward the other. There are occasions, for example, when the Theory Y administrator must exercise authority and follow Theory X principles. Nevertheless, the position among many specialists in curriculum development, supervision, and administration counsels a Theory Y approach. Thomas J. Sergiovanni and Fred D. Carver counseled: "In our view, the unique role of the school as a humanizing and self-actualizing institution requires that school executives adopt the assumptions and behavior manifestations of Theory Y."[9]

The human relations–oriented principal nurtures the curriculum development process by establishing a climate in which the planners feel valued and in which they satisfy, to use Abraham Maslow's term, "the need for self-actualization."[10] The principal must encourage and facilitate the process. Since the principal holds the power for final decision making within the school, he or she must give serious consideration to recommendations made by the school's curriculum study groups. Further, the principal must always demonstrate sincere interest in the curriculum development process. Personal traits such as a negative attitude or indifference by the school's chief administrator will effectively block progress in improving the school's curriculum. The principal's personality may, indeed, be a more powerful determinant of progress than his or her training, knowledge, or conscious intentions.

Theory Y principals might well find compatible with their views of administration some of the principles of Theory Z organizations.[11] Based on practices traditionally followed by Japanese business and industry, Theory Z organizations emphasize collective decision making and responsibility over individual decision making and responsibility. Theory Z organizations welcome the establishment of "quality control circles," or simply, "quality circles," small groups of employees whose task it is to study and propose ways of solving problems and improving the effectiveness of the organization.[12]

Regardless of their style or approach—and here we may generalize to all levels of the school system—administrators and their assistants must assume responsibility for providing leadership in many areas. They must establish the organizational framework so that curriculum development may proceed, secure facilities and needed resources, coordinate efforts of the various groups, offer consultative help, keep the groups on task, resolve conflicts, communicate school needs to all groups, maintain a harmonious working climate, assure collection of needed data, provide for communication among groups, advise groups on the latest developments in education, and make final decisions for their particular level.

Role of Students

Before turning our attention to the main participants in the curriculum development process (the curriculum leaders and their fellow workers), let's briefly consider the roles of two supporting groups—the students and the adult citizens from the community. With increasing frequency, students, depending upon their maturity, are participating both directly and indirectly in the task of improving the curriculum. In some cases, notably at the high school level (and above), students are accorded membership on curriculum councils. More commonly, student input is sought in a more indirect fashion. There are still many administrators and teachers who take a dim view of sharing decision making with the student clientele. On the other hand, it is becoming increasingly more common for administrators and teachers to solicit student reactions to the curriculum. Surveys are conducted to obtain student perceptions of their programs; individual students and groups are interviewed. Suggestions for improvement in the curriculum and for ways of meeting students' perceived needs are actively sought.

The recipient of the program—the student—is often in the best position to provide feedback about the product—the curriculum. Advice from the student constituency of the school may well provide clues for intelligent curriculum decision making.

Some schools seek information and advice from the chosen student leaders—the student government—whereas others look toward a wider sampling of opinion about programs. Even in those schools in which student input is not actively sought and in which channels have not been established for gathering data from students, the learners speak loudly by their achievements in class. When standardized and state assessment test scores are consistently below grade level, the faculty can conclude that some adjustments are necessary in respect to either the curriculum or instruction. When diagnostic tests reveal deficiencies on the part of learners, something is being conveyed about the school's program.

In Chapter 7 we will consider the student as a source of the curriculum. Here we are primarily concerned with the student's role as a participant in curriculum development.

Student Involvement.   Student involvement in curriculum improvement has grown in recent years along with the concomitant movement toward students' rights. Ronald Doll spoke of the connection between student participation in curriculum development and the students' rights movement as follows:

> The revolutionary movement in colleges in the 1960s had almost immediate effect on many high schools and indeed on some elementary schools. Student rights came to include the right to participate with adults in planning the uses to which pupils' time in schools was to be put. . . . To some teachers and principals, pupils' newly acquired status represented a refreshing view of human potential and a deserved position in the educational hierarchy; to others it seemed an especially time-consuming and plaguing form of contemporary insanity.[13]

Students can help out greatly by indicating to the professional curriculum planners how they perceive a new proposal or program. They can provide input from the standpoint of the recipients of the program, the persons for whom the program was designed. The more alert students can point out pitfalls that the professional planners might be able to avoid. The students can communicate reactions of their peers and they can further relate the nature and purpose of curriculum changes to their parents and other citizens of the community. Students can excel in describing how they perceive a development and how they feel about it.

The degree to which students may participate and the quality of that participation depend on a number of variables such as intelligence, motivation, and knowledge. The most significant variable is the students' maturity. For that reason students in senior high schools and in higher education find more opportunities to take part in curriculum development than students in elementary, middle, and junior high schools.

A particularly valuable contribution to curriculum improvement that students can make is to evaluate the teachers' instruction. Although some teachers resist student evaluations of their performance, evaluations done anonymously by the learners can provide valuable clues for modifying a curriculum and improving methods of instruction.

Although students do enter actively into the process of curriculum development in some school systems, their involvement by and large still tends to be sporadic and ancillary. Sporadic, too, are opportunities for students to make input by serving on local district and state school boards. We find inconsistencies throughout the country in the practice of student service on school boards.

Some states prohibit outright student membership and voting rights on district or state school boards. Some allow membership on district or state school boards without the right to vote. Others allow membership and voting on district but not state school boards. California, however, permits students to serve and vote on both district and state school boards.

Membership and voting rights on district and state school boards enable students to make known their views on curricular, instructional, and other needs of their school systems.[14]

Role of Residents of the Community

The roles of parents and other members of the community in the affairs of the school have changed considerably over the years. Historically, the community *was* the school. Parents tutored their young at home for lack of or in preference to a formal school; the well-to-do imported tutors from Europe to live in their homes and to instruct their children. The church provided instruction in its religious precepts, and young men learned trades as apprentices on the job. Women in colonial America would bring youngsters into their homes and for a small payment from each of their families, teach them the three R's.[15]

As formal schools evolved, the community turned the task of educating the young (for many years only the young white males) over to the school. A gap opened between the community and the school. Both the community and the institution it established developed the attitude that the community should get on with its business and leave teaching to those who know how to do it best—the school personnel. An invisible wall was erected between community and school, resembling the one between church and state.

Some parents with their state's consent have turned in recent years to instructing their children at home. Today, the homeschool movement, discussed in Chapter 15, is significant enough to be of concern to the public schools.

Erosion of the Wall between School and Community. Although some school administrators prefer to cling to an outmoded concept of community/school relationships, the wall separating school from community has crumbled. The process of erosion began slowly and has accelerated in recent years. The involvement of parents and other community members can be readily observed in school affairs today. The literature on professional education is filled with discussions of the necessity for involving the community in the educational process.

For the greater part of the twentieth century, community involvement was interpreted as passive support to the schools. The school would send bulletins and notices home to inform parents about issues and activities. The Parent-Teacher Association (PTA) would meet and discuss educational issues, hear about the school's achievements, and plan a rummage sale to raise funds for some school improvement. With much fanfare the school would conduct a "Back-to-School Night," which brought in parents in record numbers. Booster clubs would raise money for athletics and the band. During this period the community rarely participated in decision making even of an advisory nature. The old sentiment prevailed that school matters were best left to the school people. The community's role was to support and strengthen decisions made by the school.

Erosion of the wall between school and community was hastened when administrators and teachers began to realize that the community might supply the schools with certain types of information that could aid in decision making. Consequently, still resorting to a somewhat passive role for the community, the school sent home questionnaires for parents to fill out and return. While the school and community were taking careful, modest steps toward bridging the gulf between them, American society through the twentieth century was bubbling. First, the sociologists and then the educators began to subject the American community to intense scrutiny, identifying networks of influential persons who are referred to in the literature as "the power structure."[16] Educators started to give attention to the politics of education as they realized that the school was as much a part of the total political structure as other social institutions. The astute school administrator became intensely conscious of public relations and sought to involve community members in support of the school. Some might say that the educators' attention to community concerns was more effect than cause as discontent, anxiety, and pressure on educators from outside the schools had been growing and increasing in intensity for several decades.

Social Problems.   Wars, terrorism, revolutions, the greying of the population, high unemployment rates, the collapse of business icons, the prevalence of illicit drugs, increased international tensions, and the ascendance of the United States as the world's only superpower all created problems for the schools—problems that could no longer be solved by the schools themselves. With America's social and economic problems came a disenchantment with the programs of the schools and the low achievement of the pupils. From this dissatisfaction arose the concept of accountability of school personnel for the success or failure of their products—the students.

Today, community involvement in school activities—beyond the duly constituted boards of education—is widespread, encouraged, and generally valued. Members of the community aid in curriculum development in a variety of ways. Parents and other citizens serve on numerous advisory committees. Schools frequently call on parents and others to serve as resource persons and volunteer aides. Across the country, especially in urban areas, local businesses have entered into partnerships with the schools, supplementing and enriching the schools' curricula by providing expertise, materials, and funds.

The school principal always faces a dilemma in deciding how laypeople should be involved and who these people should be. Some principals seek the participation of parents of children in their own schools. Some try to involve a broader spectrum of the community, including parents and nonparents and representatives from all socioeconomic levels of the area served by the schools. Some limit participation by plan or by default to parents who happen to be available to attend meetings during the day. The chief participants under this condition tend to be middle-class homemakers. Some principals seek out the community decision makers from among the citizens who make up the power structure.

State and National Initiatives.   State and national efforts have supplemented local initiatives to involve the community in school affairs. States have empowered schools and school districts to create advisory councils. The Florida legislature, for example, in 1976 not only established school advisory councils but also charged the principal of every public school in the state with the responsibility of publishing by November 1 of each year an annual report of school progress that must be distributed to the parent or guardian of each student in the school.[17]

Amending the 1976 legislation on school advisory councils, the Florida legislature in 1993 required school boards to establish school (or district in the case of student populations of less than 10,000) advisory councils whose task it is to assist in preparation and evaluation of mandated school improvement plans and to help the principal on request in preparing the school's annual budget. The statute set forth the composition of the councils to reflect the socioeconomic demographics of the community.

Each advisory council shall be composed of the principal and an appropriately balanced number of teachers, education support employees, students, parents, and other business and community citizens who are representative of the ethnic, racial, and economic community served by the school.[18]

Local, state, and federal initiatives have promoted the involvement of members of the community in affairs of the school. The universal use of program advisory groups in connection with federally funded vocational education programs, for example, has exerted a significant influence on the curriculum of local school systems.

Looking to the future, Roald F. Campbell, Luvern L. Cunningham, Raphael O. Nystrand, and Michael D. Usdan identified community groups with which administrators must be concerned and made the following prediction:

Interest groups representing blacks, American Indians, and other ethnic groups will continue to focus on the schools as a major mechanism for equalizing educational, social, and economic opportunities for their constituencies.

Taxpayer groups, concerned about periodic inflation, recession, and energy shortages in an uncertain economy, will continue to scrutinize school expenditures.[19]

Hispanics, comprising the fastest-growing minority group as shown by data of the U.S. Bureau of the Census, are projected to constitute 24 percent of the U.S. population by July 1, 2050.[20] Census data released in May 2006 reported almost one in every three U.S. residents was part of a group other than single-race non-Hispanic white.[21] Assuming current trends, the Bureau of the Census projects minority groups as constituting about one-half of the projected 419 million U.S. population by 2050.[22]

The wise administrator realizes that strong community support can make his or her job much simpler and for that reason devotes considerable time to building that support. Some schools have been turned into community schools in which the resources of the school are shared with the community and vice versa.

Models for community participation in school affairs differ widely from state to state. In some communities residents play a purely advisory role; in others they share directly in the decision-making process. In some localities members of the community serve on standing committees that meet regularly; in other locations they serve on ad hoc groups that undertake a specific task and are then disbanded. In some school districts parents and others are invited to address themselves to any and all problems of the schools, whereas in other communities their areas of responsibility are clearly defined.

Members of the community can serve the schools in a variety of ways. They may be consulted in the curriculum designing stage. They may participate as resource persons, volunteer tutors, and school aides. The resources of individuals, businesses, institutions, and other agencies are tapped to enhance the learning experiences of the students.

With guidance from the school, parents can assist their children in their studies at home. By posting school news and homework assignments on the Web, schools strengthen ties with the community.

Parents and others share in curriculum development by responding to surveys sent out by the school. They are able to describe the effect of new programs on their children and can be very specific in telling teachers about problems their children are experiencing.

They may invite children to their places of work and thereby contribute to the children's knowledge of the world around them. They may supervise student work experiences in the community.

Parents and others can inform the professional planners about potential conflicts that are likely to arise in the community over teaching of controversial issues. They can help the school authorities review instructional materials and books for bias and distortion. Parents and other residents are often able to suggest programs that would help meet certain educational needs in the community. By actively seeking citizen participation, the principal is able to develop a reservoir of goodwill toward the school that will stand him or her in good stead when problems inevitably develop. The principal is more readily able to gain support for new programs and to defuse potential controversies if parents and others perceive the school as their institution and as a place where their voices may be heard and their opinions valued. Community participation in curriculum development is a natural consequence of the American public's political power.[23]

Role of the Curriculum Workers

Primary responsibility for curriculum development is assigned to teachers and their elected or appointed leaders, both of whom we will refer to as "curriculum workers." This group of persons working together carries the heaviest burden in seeking to improve the curriculum. In Chapter 3 we saw that curriculum groups function at several levels and in several sectors. To make the following discussion clearer, however, let's conceptualize the curriculum council of a particular school. Let's choose an elementary school with grades kindergarten through six that is fortunate enough to have a full-time curriculum coordinator on its staff. By agreement of the total faculty, the grade coordinators (seven of them) join with the curriculum coordinator (appointed by the principal) to form the school's curriculum council. In our hypothetical school, by tacit understanding between the principal and the faculty, the coordinator serves as chairperson or leader of the council.

Let's imagine that we are neutral observers watching this council at its first session of the year. We watch the group get organized; we listen to its discussion; we study the faces of the council members; we observe the interplay between the coordinator and the council members and among the council members themselves. We cannot help speculating about whether this curriculum group will have a productive year. The question crosses our mind, "What conditions make for a productive year in curriculum development?" We wonder, "Could we predict whether a curriculum council is likely to be productive?"

After a great deal of thought, we might conclude that success in terms of productivity is more likely to come about if the group:

- sets its goals at the beginning of its work
- is made up of compatible personalities
- has members who bring to the task expertise, knowledge, and technical competence
- is composed of persons who are motivated and willing to expend time and energy

- accepts its appropriate leadership and followership roles
- has persons who can communicate with each other
- has developed skills in decision making
- has members who keep their own personal agendas in appropriate relationship to the group's goals

What are the roles, we may ask, of those persons whom we call curriculum workers? How do teachers function in curriculum development? What role does the curriculum leader play?

Role of the Teachers.   Throughout this text teachers are repeatedly seen as the primary group in curriculum development. Numerous examples are given of teacher involvement in curriculum development. Teachers constitute either the majority or the totality of the membership of curriculum committees and councils. Teachers participate at all stages in curriculum development. They initiate proposals and carry them out in their classrooms. They review proposals, gather data, conduct research, make contact with parents and other laypeople, write and create curriculum materials, evaluate resources, try out new ideas, obtain feedback from learners, and evaluate programs. Teachers serve on committees mainly at the classroom, team/grade/department, school, and district levels or sectors and on occasion may serve at other levels or sectors.

New teachers typically view themselves primarily as instructors and are often scarcely aware of the responsibilities that are likely to be expected of them in the curriculum area. Beginning teachers' lack of awareness of their professional obligations in curriculum development is not surprising given that preservice teacher education programs, as a rule and understandably, emphasize the mastery of instructional skills over curriculum development competencies.

At the very least, preservice teachers should be oriented to the obligations and opportunities they will encounter in curriculum development. Becoming aware that they will serve on various councils and committees, that curriculum development takes place at many levels and in many sectors, and that instruction and curriculum are different domains, both worthy of involvement, should be part of their training. Thus, the teachers, in cooperation with the administrators and other professionals, can bring appropriate knowledge and skills to bear in efforts to improve the curriculum. *Only* the teachers, by their presence at the classroom level, can ensure that curricular plans are carried out.

Assumption of a primary role by teachers not only in curriculum development but also in the general affairs of the school is the goal of efforts at "empowerment," which permits teachers as professionals to take part in the decision-making process.[24] The empowerment movement, which gained momentum in the 1980s and 1990s, seeks to raise the status of teachers and thereby improve the school's program and effectiveness.

Empowerment of teachers is a fundamental and essential aspect of the more recent conception of school administration referred to as "site-based management." Following the practices of site-based management, administrators literally share their power with teachers.[25]

Although critics of empowerment argue that teacher involvement in decision making is an unnecessary demand on teachers' time, an inappropriate role, or an infringement on administrative authority, industrial research of the 1930s and the success of Japanese quality circles in recent years have revealed that meaningful involvement in decision making enhances worker morale and consequently increases production.[26] Translated into school terms, this principle indicates that when teachers find themselves to be valued professionals whose opinions carry some weight, they will be more satisfied with their profession. This improvement in teacher morale, in turn, will increase school productivity—that is, student achievement. George H. Wood connected the empowerment of teachers to the empowerment of students when he said, "Only by linking democracy to empowerment, that is, working for the democratic empowerment of *students* will teachers find a genuine sense of empowerment themselves."[27]

Role of the Curriculum Leader.   As we consider the complexities in carrying out curriculum development we become keenly aware of the curriculum leader's responsibility for the success or failure of the work of a curriculum committee or council. The curriculum leader most often is a member of the faculty but can be an outsider. It is perhaps inaccurate here to refer to a curriculum leader as *the* curriculum leader. A person may serve as a leader for a period of time and then give way to another leader for any number of sound reasons. Some teachers may serve as leaders at one level, such as the grade, whereas others may serve as leaders at another level, such as the school. In a democratic organization individuals serve as either leaders or followers as the situation demands.

The curriculum leader (coordinator) may also come from outside the teacher group, as in the case of central office supervisors, curriculum consultants, directors of instruction, and assistant principals for curriculum. Perhaps even in these cases it would be useful to think of the teachers and leaders from outside the faculty as constituting the "extended family," for they are all colleagues, albeit with different functions and duties. The leadership position is filled either by appointment by an administrator or supervisor, election by the group's members, or self-selection from the group.

The principles discussed in the following pages apply to all curriculum leaders regardless of whether they come from inside or outside the teacher group. We may begin to look at the role of the curriculum leader by asking ourselves what special knowledge and skills the leader must bring to the task. The curriculum coordinator must:

- possess a good general education
- have a good knowledge of both general and specific curricula
- be knowledgeable about resources for curriculum development
- be skilled in research and knowledgeable about locating pertinent research studies
- be knowledgeable about the needs of learners, the community, and the society
- be a bit of philosopher, sociologist, and psychologist
- know and appreciate the individual characteristics of participating colleagues

Most significantly, the curriculum coordinator must be a specialist in the group process, possessing a unique set of skills. Many treatises on the functioning of groups reveal that managing groups effectively is not a trivial task. It is an enormously complicated effort that brings into play all the subtleties of environment and personality. Curriculum development is an exercise in group process, a human endeavor that can lead to both joy and frustration.

Success in curriculum improvement depends, of course, on the concerted effort of both group members and leaders. We will focus our attention, however, on the curriculum leader; no matter how well intentioned, motivated, and skilled the followers of the group are, group effort cannot succeed without competent leadership.

THE CURRICULUM LEADER AND GROUP PROCESS

Neither technical expertise nor knowledge about curriculum theory can substitute for a curriculum leader's knowledge of and aptitude for group process. What, then, we might ask, are some of the basic principles from the research on group process that would help those who take a leadership role in curriculum development? What skills and knowledge about group process are essential to the job? Four sets or clusters of group process skills appear to be of particular significance:

1. *The change process.* The leader must be knowledgeable about the process of effecting change and be able to translate that knowledge into practice with the group. He or she must demonstrate effective decision-making skills and be able to lead group members in demonstrating them.
2. *Interpersonal relations.* The leader must be knowledgeable about group dynamics. He or she must exhibit a high degree of human relations skills, be able to develop interpersonal skills among members of the group, and be able to establish a harmonious working climate.
3. *Leadership skills.* The leader must demonstrate leadership skills, including organizational skills and the ability to manage the process. He or she must help members of the group to develop leadership skills so that they may assume leadership roles when necessary.
4. *Communication skills.* The leader must communicate effectively and be able to lead members of the group in communicating effectively. He or she must be a proficient discussion leader.

The Change Process

Axiom 1 in Chapter 2 presented the proposition that change is both inevitable and desirable. Human institutions, like human beings, must change if they are to continue growing and developing. Institutions, however, tend to preserve the status quo.

Gail McCutcheon cited the ease and comparative safety of the status quo, the requirements of time and effort, the lack of rewards, established school policies, and routines as impediments to change.[28] Nevertheless, neither the status quo nor regression to outmoded practices is a defensible position for living institutions like the schools. They must constantly seek to better themselves.

Curriculum development is the planned effort of a duly organized group (or groups) that seeks to make intelligent decisions in order to effect change in the curriculum. Planned change, far different from trial and error or natural evolution, implies a systematic process to be followed by all participants. Let's begin our examination of the change process by looking at the variables that exist within organizations and that have an impact upon that process.

Four Variables.   Harold J. Leavitt and Homa Bahrami identified four organizational variables: "structure," "information and control methods (i.e., the technology of managing)," "people," and "task."[29]

.Every organization establishes its own *structure*. In Chapter 3 we considered some of the organizational patterns that schools have adopted to carry out curriculum development. As already noted, structures differ considerably among school systems and among individual schools. A school's organizational structure is shaped not only by the tasks to be accomplished but also by the idiosyncrasies of administrators, supervisors, and teachers. No single organizational structure will satisfy the personal and professional needs of participants in every school system. Determination of the appropriate organizational structure is one of the prior decisions that curriculum developers must make.

The element of *technology of managing* encompasses both the technological equipment at the school's disposal and the procedures followed to accomplish the school's task.

The human variable—*the people*—sets the operation in motion and carries on the task. The differences in people make each school's efforts at curriculum development a unique undertaking. The persons essential to the curriculum development process have been discussed earlier in this text. Experts in the social science of human behavior refer to the main characters in the change process as the *change agent* and the *client system*. In their language a change agent is a person trained in the behavioral sciences who helps an organization change. The client system consists of those persons in the organization with whom the change agent works and who may, themselves, undergo change. This point reinforces Axiom 4 in Chapter 2, which postulates that curriculum change results from changes in people.

Although behavioral scientists argue about whether the change agent must come from within or outside the system, in practical terms schools will ordinarily use their own personnel for developing the curriculum.

Robert J. Alfonso, Gerald R. Firth, and Richard F. Neville identified change theory as one of four theoretical fields assumed to have implications for the behavior of instructional supervisors. They took the position that a school system should designate the supervisor responsible for promoting change and that the supervisor be conversant with change theory and willing to devote "a significant amount of time, effort, and creative thought to the change process."[30] If an outside change agent is brought in, they warned:

> Simply "importing" a change agent will not assist the supervisor markedly unless teachers perceive such a person as connected to the system or to the supervisor in some acceptable way.[31]

What are the typical functions of a change agent? Warren G. Bennis listed normative goals of change agents including such tasks as improving interpersonal relationships among managing personnel, helping in resolving conflicts, and reducing tensions among workers.[32]

The *task* of the school is set out in numerous pronouncements of mission, aims, goals, and objectives, for example, the cardinal principles, the ability to think, the transmittal of the cultural heritage, and so on. More accurately, we should speak of the *tasks* of the school rather than *task*. The school performs many tasks in a number of curriculum development areas and provides a vital service—the education of the young. Although the school is not engaged in the tasks of manufacturing and selling products for profit, it does turn out products—a quite different kind of product—the learners themselves, human beings whose behavior is modified as a result of exposure to the school curriculum. Leadership calls for the judicious integration of these four variables.

Kurt Lewin viewed organizations as being in a state of balance or equilibrium when forces of change (driving forces) and forces of resistance (restraining forces) are equal in strength.[33] Changes occur when the organization is forced into a state of disequilibrium. This state of imbalance may be accomplished by augmenting the driving forces or by reducing the restraining forces—either action breaks the force field that maintains the organization in equilibrium.

Following his concept of the force field, Lewin proposed a simple strategy consisting of three steps. Or was it so simple? Lewin suggested that existing targets of change be unfrozen, then changes or innovations made, and finally the new structures refrozen until the start of a new cycle.

How shall we go about unfreezing old programs and practices—in effect, changing old habits? How would we move, for example, from the junior high school to the middle school; from independent to cooperative learning; from discrete linguistic concepts to whole language; from exclusive stress on cognitive learning to provision for cognitive, affective, and psychomotor learning; from emphasis on convergent thinking to more on divergent thinking; or from rote learning to critical thinking? How do we thaw out old patterns?

When we identify the barriers or impediments to change and eliminate those barriers, we can set the organization into disequilibrium. Table 4.1 lists several commonly encountered barriers and suggest tactics for overcoming them. Uppermost in the minds of curriculum planners must be the purpose of change: improvement in the organization, not change for change's sake nor for creating an image of newness per se but for bettering the products of the school.

Decision Making.   Axiom 6 of Chapter 2 takes the position that curriculum development is basically a decision-making process. A lack of skills in decision making on the part of a curriculum leader and group can be a formidable barrier to change. Are there any principles of decision making that could be helpful to curriculum study groups? Let's turn to Daniel L. Stufflebeam and the Phi Delta Kappa National Study Committee on Evaluation, which Stufflebeam chaired, for guidance on the process of decision making.[34]

Stufflebeam and his committee ventured that the process of decision making consists of four stages—awareness, design, choice, and action—during which four kinds of decisions must be made—planning, structuring, implementing, and recycling.

Planning decisions are made "to determine objectives." They "specify *major changes that are needed in a program.*" Structuring decisions are made "to design procedures."

TABLE 4.1 Common Barriers to Change

Barriers	Tactics
Fear of change on the part of those likely to be affected	The group should proceed slowly. Leader gives repeated reassurance to those affected by change. Involvement of those affected in decision making. The changed status must be made more attractive than the old pattern.
Lack of clear goals	The group must set clear goals before proceeding further.
Lack of competent leadership	Superiors must appoint or peers must elect persons as leaders who are most qualified. Leaders who prove to be incompetent should be removed.
Lack of ability of group members to function as a group	Training in group process should be conducted.
Lack of research on problems before the group	The leader should have the ability to conduct research, to locate pertinent research data, and to interpret research studies to the group.
A history of unsuccessful curriculum efforts	The group must be made to feel that progress is being made continuously.
Lack of evaluation of previous curriculum efforts	Efforts should be made to evaluate previous efforts, and an evaluation plan for current efforts must be designed.
Negative attitudes from the community	School personnel must call parents and citizens in for discussion, involve them in the process, and try to change their attitudes.
Lack of resources	Adequate resources both to carry out curriculum planning and to implement plans decided on must be available. Personnel needed must be available.
External pressures such as state and federal legislation, regional accreditation, and regulations of the state department of education	Efforts must be made to work within the framework of laws and regulations or to try to get the laws and regulations changed. Responses to laws and regulations, which are broad and general, may vary from school to school.
Lack of experience or knowledge about a particular curricular problem	The group may call in consultants for assistance, or the school may provide training for its personnel.

They "specify the *means to achieve the ends* established as a result of planning decisions." Implementing decisions are made "to utilize, control, and refine procedures." Decisions on implementation are "those involved in *carrying through the action plan*." Recycling decisions are made "to judge and react to attainments." "These are decisions used in determining the relationship of attainments to objectives and whether to continue, terminate, evolve, or drastically modify the activity."[35]

From the time a perceptive staff member in a school first starts to feel uneasy about a program and senses that something is not right and change is needed, decisions must be made constantly. Since decision making never ends, skills in the process need to be developed.

Concluding "any kind of educational innovation, including curriculum change, is never a simple matter," Colin J. Marsh and George Willis pointed to differences in organizational climate, staff, student body, and community views as affecting the change process.[36]

Creative Individuals. Although the literature on change stresses the necessity of group involvement, change can be and often is brought about by creative individuals and small groups working independently. Many of our great inventors, for example, have been individualists.

What sometimes happens is that an individual experiments with a new idea; a few others who like the idea adopt it; success with the idea builds on success and the idea is widely translated into practice. Creative individual enterprise should be encouraged by administrators and faculty as long as the implications of the activity do not invade areas outside the individual's own sphere. When creative endeavor begins to force demands on others without their sanction or involvement, independence must give way to cooperation.

In summary, curriculum leaders guide cooperating workers in bringing about change. In so doing they must exhibit skill in directing the change process. Both leaders and followers must have skill in decision making if positive curricular changes are to be effected.

Interpersonal Relations

The principal's reminder, "faculty meeting today at 3:30 P.M.," is normally greeted with less than enthusiasm. The typical teacher responses are likely to be "Oh, no, not again!" "I hope it's short," and "Faculty meetings are such a waste of time." At best these group meetings are received with a quiet resignation. Why does a group effort like a faculty meeting, which should be such a potent instrument for group deliberation, provoke such widespread dissatisfaction?

Let's try to answer that question by picturing a typical faculty meeting of a secondary school. Some fifty faculty members shuffle into a classroom and take their seats while the principal stands at the desk at the front of the room.

We observe the faculty meeting in session and take some notes:

- The classroom is crowded and the pupils' desks are uncomfortable for some of the faculty, particularly the heavier teachers.
- The straight rows are not conducive to group discussion.
- No refreshments were provided to help set a pleasant tone for the meeting.
- It is difficult to understand the purpose of the meeting. Is it information-giving on the part of the principal? A sermon from the principal on responsibilities? An effort to gain faculty approval of policies? An attempt to get faculty opinion on an issue?
- One teacher in the back was reading the daily newspaper.

- One teacher by the window was grading papers.
- Two teachers were talking about an incident that took place in one of the teachers' classrooms that day.
- One teacher, tired, sat with her eyes closed during the meeting.
- The football coaches were absent.
- A couple of teachers spoke repeatedly, whereas the majority remained silent.
- Several teachers watched the clock on the wall.
- The principal became visibly annoyed with the comment of one teacher.
- A restlessness among the teachers was apparent after the first thirty minutes.
- The group rushed out of the room as soon as the meeting ended.

None of the behaviors at this hypothetical meeting was unusual. The behaviors were quite predictable and to a great extent preventable. The general faculty meeting is but one of many group configurations in which teachers and administrators will participate. If the administrator fosters a collegial approach to administration, teachers will find themselves working on a number of committees for a variety of purposes, including curriculum development.

Most new teachers do not fully realize the extent to which teaching is a group-oriented career. Training in group process, for example, is conspicuous by its absence in preservice programs. The mind-set that novice teachers have developed about teaching pictures the teacher as an *individual* planner, presenter, and evaluator. When they begin teaching, they are unaware of the degree to which teaching involves *group* activities in which responsibilities must be shared.

Whereas beginning teachers realize from student teaching that they work with groups of children, they are often not ready to work cooperatively with their professional colleagues. A preparation program for teachers should seek to develop an appreciation of the necessity of working in groups, an attitude of willingness to work cooperatively, an understanding of the working or dynamics of a group, and skills of group participation. If these cognitive and affective objectives are not achieved in preservice teacher education, their attainment should be sought in inservice education programs.

Let's try to improve our understanding of the composition and functioning of groups by examining some of the salient characteristics of group dynamics. We shall not belabor the question of defining *group* but will call two or more persons working together for a mutual purpose a group. The faculty as a body, curriculum councils, departments, advisory committees, and teams are illustrations of formal groups.

Informal groups are self-constituted, ad hoc, impromptu collections of individuals who gather together for some immediate purpose and later disband. Protest groups and cliques of teachers are illustrations of informal groups. Although we are primarily concerned with the functioning of formally constituted groups, we should not overlook the possible impact of informal groups. It is quite possible, for example, for the formal and informal groups within a school to be working at cross purposes. The wise curriculum leader seeks to identify informal groups that may have an impact on curriculum development efforts and to channel their energies into the deliberations of the formal structure.

Recall that in the illustration of the hypothetical secondary school faculty meeting, the sense of purpose was unclear. Both the general purpose and the specific goals of the group must be known. Groups are organized most frequently for the following purposes:

- To receive instructions or information. Faculty meetings are often used for this purpose.
- To help individuals develop personally or professionally. Sensitivity groups, study groups, and workshops in pedagogy are examples of groups with this purpose.
- To recommend solutions to problems. Making such recommendations is a major purpose of curriculum improvement groups.
- To produce something. Curriculum committees, for example, may be charged with the task of creating new programs or writing curriculum guides.
- To resolve conflicts. Curriculum development efforts sometimes result in disagreements among factions, necessitating new groups to resolve these differences.

To some extent all these purposes operate in curriculum development. However, the latter three are the primary purposes, which make curriculum committees action- or task-oriented rather than ego- or process-oriented groups. In all human groups we find individuals who are there to serve the social needs of the organizations—that is, the fulfillment of the group's task—and others who are there to satisfy their own ego needs.

One of the great difficulties for the curriculum leader is keeping a group "on task." Challenging this goal are the many individuals who are impelled to satisfy their own personal needs in a group setting, behavior referred to as "processing." Some processing is essential in any group, particularly early in the group's activity when individuals are getting to know each other and trying to analyze the task. The curriculum leader must ensure some, though not equal, balance between "task orientation" and "process orientation." He or she must see to it that a group moves on with its task while permitting individuals to achieve personal satisfaction as members of the group. Excessive stress on either approach can lead to frustration and withdrawal.

The curriculum leader who is, of course, a key—or *the* key—member of a curriculum planning group, must be aware of the presence of three types of behavior within a group. First, each group is composed of individuals who bring their own individual behaviors to the group. Some will maintain these behaviors, sometimes consciously and at other times subconsciously, regardless of the group setting. Thus, the teacher who is habitually punctual, conscientious, confident, or complaining is likely to bring those traits into the group setting. Some traits have a positive impact on the group, others, a negative one.

Individuals bring their motivations, often covert, into group efforts—their personal desires, feelings, or goals, commonly referred to as the "hidden agenda." Individuals may react negatively to a curriculum proposal, for example, not because they object to the proposal per se but because they dislike the person who made the proposal. Individuals may attack a proposal because they feel their ideas have not been adequately considered. Individuals may strive to ask a group member embarrassing questions because they perceive that person as a potential rival for a leadership position. The curriculum leader must constantly attempt to channel negative behaviors into constructive paths or to eliminate them where possible. He or she must often act as mediator to ensure that the individuals' hidden agendas do not sabotage the official agenda.

Second, individuals in groups often behave in ways that are quite different from their individual behaviors. We have only to turn to studies of mob psychology to demonstrate that individuals change their behavior in group situations. Have we never observed, for example, a group of otherwise sweet, innocent elementary school youngsters taunting a classmate? Have we never seen an otherwise cautious adolescent driver become reckless when driving a car filled with friends? The presence of companion human beings who read and evaluate an individual's behavior causes that individual to behave in a way in which he or she perceives the group members wish him or her to act.

We see great contrasts in behavior between the individual who relies on his or her own inner resources (the inner-directed personality) and the individual who takes cues from those around him or her (the outer-directed personality). Although few individuals are completely immune to outer-direction in our society, some individuals are more adept than others at weighing external influences before acting on them. Some individuals are aware when they are being manipulated by others, whereas others are highly subject to suggestion. Not only do personal behaviors sometimes change in a group setting, but also individuals assume, as we shall soon see, special roles that they do not and cannot perform in isolation.

Third, the group itself assumes a personality of its own. We already noted that the functioning of the group is more than the sum of the functioning of each of the individuals who make up the group. The individuals interact with and reinforce each other, creating a unique blend. In this respect some departments of a school are perceived as being more productive (pick your own word: creative, enthusiastic, reactionary, innovative, obstreperous) than others, just as schools are perceived as being different from one another.

The curriculum leader must try to develop pride in the group as a team organization by promoting group morale and by helping the group feel a sense of accomplishment. The group concept is fostered when

- interaction among group members is frequent, on a high professional level, friendly, and harmonious
- personal conflicts among group members are infrequent or nonexistent
- leadership is allowed to develop from within the group so that the group capitalizes on the strengths of its members
- constructive dissent is encouraged
- the group realizes that it is making progress toward meeting its goals, which points out again the necessity for clearly specifying the goals the group expects to attain
- the group feels some sense of reward for accomplishment

Perhaps the most satisfying reward for a group is to see its recommendations translated into practice. A word of appreciation from the administrator also goes a long way in securing the continuous motivation of teachers to participate in curriculum development.

Responding to Teacher Concerns.   Fundamental to successful change, be it curricular or other, is an understanding of concerns of individuals who form a group. The

Concerns-Based Adoption Model (CBAM) developed at the Research and Development Center for Teacher Education at the University of Texas illuminates the necessity for analyzing concerns among individuals in a group that intends to effect change. CBAM targets the personal concerns of individuals in the group.

Gene E. Hall and Susan Loucks described seven stages of concern during the change process from simple awareness of an innovation to be considered to refocusing on benefits of the innovation.[37] The perceptive curriculum leader is aware of these concerns and guides the members constituting the group through the seven stages to shifting concerns away from themselves to successful implementation of the innovation.

Roles Played by Group Members.   Many years ago Kenneth D. Benne and Paul Sheats developed a classification system for identifying functional roles of group members.[38] They organized their classification system into three categories: group task roles, group building and maintenance roles, and individual roles. Group members take on task roles when they seek to move the group toward attaining its goals and solving its problems. Group members play group building and maintenance roles when they are concerned with the functioning of the group. Group members indulge in individual roles to satisfy personal needs.

Since the Benne-Sheats classification system stands as one of the most creative and comprehensive expositions of roles played by group members, its categories and roles are reproduced here:

Group Task Roles
a. Initiator-contributor. Suggests ideas, ways of solving problems, or procedures.
b. Information seeker. Seeks facts.
c. Opinion seeker. Asks opinions about the values of the suggestions made by members of the group.
d. Information giver. Supplies facts as he or she sees them.
e. Opinion giver. Presents his or her own opinions about the subject matter under discussion.
f. Elaborator. States implications of suggestions and describes how suggestions might work out if adopted.
g. Coordinator. Tries to synthesize suggestions.
h. Orienter. Lets group know when it is off task.
i. Evaluator-critic. Evaluates suggestions made by group members as to criteria which he or she feels important.
j. Energizer. Spurs the group to activity.
k. Procedural technician. Performs the routine tasks that have to be done such as distributing materials.
l. Recorder. Keeps the group's record.

Group Building and Maintenance Roles
a. Encourager. Praises people for their suggestions.
b. Harmonizer. Settles disagreements among members.
c. Compromiser. Modifies his or her position in the interests of group progress.

    d. Gatekeeper. Tries to ensure that everybody has a chance to contribute to the discussion.

    e. Standard setter or ego ideal. Urges the group to live up to high standards.

    f. Group observer and commentator. Records and reports on the functioning of the group.

    g. Follower. Accepts suggestions of others.

Individual Roles

    a. Aggressor. Attacks others or their ideas.

    b. Blocker. Opposes suggestions and group decisions.

    c. Recognition-seeker. Seeks personal attention.

    d. Self-confessor. Expresses personal feelings not applicable to the group's efforts.

    e. Playboy. Refrains from getting involved in the group's work with sometimes disturbing behavior. [Since the term *playboy* may give a different connotation in today's climate, we might want to use a term like *frivolous* or *noncommitted individual*.]

    f. Dominator. Interrupts others and tries to assert own superiority.

    g. Help-seeker. Tries to elicit sympathy for himself or herself.

    h. Special interest pleader. Reinforces his or her position by claiming to speak for others not represented in the group.

A group will be more effective if the individual and negative roles are minimized or eliminated. Groups can be helped by the leader or by an outside consultant through exposing them to group dynamics theory and a classification system such as the Benne-Sheats model. Help of a more personal nature can be achieved through group interaction that permits feedback to its members. This feedback could be in the form of simple analysis of interaction skills possessed by the various members. Certainly, a group will be more productive if its members already possess a high degree of interaction skill. If, however, a group appears to lack skills in interaction or human relations, it may be advisable to depart from the group's task long enough to seek to develop some fundamental interpersonal skills.

A trained observer who records the performance of individuals participating in a group can provide valuable feedback. To record the performance of individuals in a group the observer can create a simple checksheet by listing the task, building/maintenance, and individual roles in a column on the left and the names of members across the top. The observer then records with a tally the frequency with which a participant plays a particular role.

After the observation period members would be furnished feedback about their performance. The observer must exercise great tact in how he or she presents the information. Some of the individual roles are particularly unflattering, and it will be difficult for some individuals to accept the fact that they behave in this way. Therefore, negative feedback should be supplied to individuals only on request and in confidence.

Task-Oriented Groups.   Curriculum development groups are or should be essentially task-oriented groups. They are given a specific job to do, carry it out, and then either accept another job or cease to function. Their productivity should be measured first in the quality of improvement that takes place in the curriculum and second in the personal and professional growth of the participants.

Curriculum development consists of a continuing series of interpersonal experiences. Both leaders and followers are obligated to make the process successful. With a modicum of training, professional persons should be able to bury their hidden agendas and to eliminate or suppress negative behaviors that disrupt the group's effort. Fortunately, some human beings have learned during their formative years to demonstrate human relations skills like warmth, empathy, valuing others' opinions and beliefs, intellectual honesty, patience, mutual assistance, and respect for others as persons. They have learned to accept responsibility and to refrain from blaming others for their own deficiencies. They have learned to put aside their own ego needs in deference to the needs of the group. They have learned to enjoy and take pride in group accomplishments. Others who demonstrate a low level of performance in these skills should be encouraged to participate in a human relations training program to improve their interpersonal skills.

Remember that curriculum development is ordinarily a voluntary undertaking. Curriculum workers might ask themselves what motivated them to agree to serve in a group devoted to curriculum improvement. They might uncover motives like the following:

- a desire to please the administrator
- a desire to work with certain colleagues
- a desire to be where the action is
- a desire to grow professionally
- a desire to make a professional contribution to the school system
- a desire to make use of one's skills and talents
- a desire for a new experience
- a desire to socialize
- a desire to use the group as a sounding board for personal beliefs and values

The reasons why individuals agree to participate in group activity are many and varied, sometimes verbalized but often not; sometimes valid in terms of the group's goals, sometimes not. Individuals who are motivated and possess the necessary personal and professional skills should be encouraged to take part in curriculum development.

Characteristics of Productive Groups.   From examining the wealth of literature on group dynamics and group process, how might we summarize the characteristics that make for group effectiveness or productivity? We have already noted in Chapter 1 that research conducted in the Hawthorne plant of the Western Electric Company in Chicago produced evidence that involvement of workers in planning and carrying out a project led to greater productivity. Research by Kurt Lewin, Ronald Lippitt, and Ralph K. White on groups of eleven-year-old children showed their productivity to be greater in a democratic group climate than in an authoritarian or laissez-faire one.[39] Rensis Likert saw a supportive environment, mutual confidence and trust among group members, and a sharing of common goals as contributing to group effectiveness.[40] Ned A. Flanders's studies of classroom verbal interaction led users of his instrument for observing this process to conclude that group leaders need to decrease their own verbal behavior and stimulate members of the group to interact more.[41] John Dewey[42] and Daniel L. Stufflebeam and associates[43] wrote of the importance of the skill of problem solving or decision making. Warren G. Bennis, Kenneth D. Benne, and Robert Chin advocated skill in planning for change.[44] Fred E. Fiedler concentrated on the effectiveness of the leader,[45] and Kimball Wiles gave attention to skill in communication as essential to group effectiveness.[46] These latter two sets of skills will be discussed in the next section, but first, based on the foregoing principles, we might conclude that a group is effective when

- leaders and members support each other
- trust is apparent among members
- goals are understood and mutually accepted
- adequate opportunity exists for members to express their own feelings and perceptions
- roles played by group members are essentially positive
- hidden agendas of members do not disrupt the group
- leadership is competent and appropriate to the group
- members possess the necessary expertise
- members have the necessary resources
- members share in all decision making
- communication is at a high level
- leadership is encouraged from within the group
- progress in accomplishing the task is noticeable and significant
- the group activity satisfies members' personal needs
- leaders seek to release potential of the members
- the group manages its time wisely

Leadership Skills

Let's attend the meeting of a school's curriculum committee as a guest of the curriculum coordinator who is serving as chairperson. It is early in the year. We take a seat in the back of the room and in the course of less than an hour we observe the following behaviors:

- Two teachers are discussing an action of the principal.
- Each person speaks as long as he or she wishes, sometimes going on at length.
- The coordinator engages in dialogue with one individual, ignoring the group.
- Several members ask whether this discussion is in keeping with the group's purposes.
- The coordinator pushes his ideas and is visibly annoyed when someone disagrees with him.
- Two teachers become involved in arguing with each other.
- The coordinator steers the group toward a proposal that he has offered.
- The meeting breaks up without closure and without identifying next steps.

We might conclude that this session of the curriculum committee was less than productive. Would we attribute this lack of productivity to deficiencies on the part of the group members? To lack of leadership on the part of the coordinator? To both? Certainly, group productivity arises from a harmonious blend of skills by group members and the group leader, yet a heavy burden for the productivity of the group rests with the leader. This person has been chosen to set the pace, to provide expertise, and to channel the skills of others. The skilled leader would have been able to avoid and resolve some of the unproductive situations that developed in this curriculum committee.

Traits of Leaders.   When asking ourselves and others what traits a leader should possess, we would probably garner the following responses:

- intelligent
- experienced
- assertive
- articulate
- innovative
- dynamic
- charismatic

Some would say, "You must be in the right place at the right time." Others, perhaps more cynical, would say a leader must be

- a politician
- a climber
- a friend of a person in power

Like Laurence J. Peter, Jr., some people would observe that persons rise to their level of incompetence.[47]

What the research has found, however, is that it is almost impossible to ascribe any single set of traits to all persons in positions of leadership. Generalizing that leaders tend to possess, among other traits, slightly above average intelligence as well as requisite personal and administrative skills, Ralph B. Kimbrough and Michael Y. Nunnery concluded that the possession of certain traits does not guarantee success as an administrator nor does their absence rule out success.[48]

Commenting on trait theory, the attempt to predict successful leaders through judging their personal, social, and physical characteristics, Robert H. Palestini noted the theory's popularity in the 1940s and 1950s.[49] Among the traits considered significant were "drive, desire to lead, honesty and integrity, self-confidence, cognitive ability, and knowledge of the business they are in."[50] Palestini opined, "The trait approach has more historical than practical interest to managers and administrators, even though recent research has once again tied leadership effectiveness to leader traits."[51]

Two Approaches.   Leaders tend to lean toward one of two basic approaches to administration: the bureaucratic or the collegial. The first approach has been labeled autocratic; the second, democratic. Edgar L. Morphet, Roe L. Johns, and Theodore L. Reller discussed the assumptions that underlie these two approaches. According to these authors, leaders who follow what they termed the "traditional, monocratic, bureaucratic approach" hold to a line-and-staff plan of organization that places responsibility and authority at the top, that encourages competition, and that allows individuals to be expendable.[52] On the other hand, according to Morphet, Johns, and Reller, leaders who follow what they called the "emerging, pluralistic, collegial approach" believe that power, authority, and decision making can be shared, that consensus leads to unity within the organization, and that individuals are not expendable.[53]

In contrasting these two approaches to administration Morphet, Johns, and Reller noted that the traditional approach operates in a closed climate, whereas the democratic approach functions in an open climate. The traditional approach relies on centralized authority with a fixed line-and-staff structure. Authority is spread out and shared under the pluralistic approach; the structure, while sometimes more complex than the traditional structure, is more flexible to allow for maximum participation of members of the organization. The flow of communication is much different under these two approaches. The autocratic or authoritarian approach is imbued with the philosophy of going through channels. Messages may originate from the top of the echelon, which is most common, or from the bottom. Messages from the top pass down through intermediate echelons but may not be stopped by these echelons. On the other hand, messages originating from the bottom proceed through intermediate echelons and may be stopped by any echelon. Subordinates are required to conduct business through channels and may not with impunity "go over the head" of their immediate supervisor. Under a pluralistic approach communications may flow in any direction—up, down, circularly, or horizontally. They may skip echelons and may be referred to persons outside the immediate chain of command. The pluralistic administrator is not "hung up" on channels and personal status. It is the traditional approach that begets the "organization man."

Morphet, Johns, and Reller cautioned, in comparing these two approaches, "It should not be inferred, however, that democratic administration is *ipso facto* good and that authoritarian administration is *ipso facto* bad. History provides numerous examples of successful and unsuccessful democratic administration and successful and unsuccessful authoritarian administration."[54] They noted, though, that some studies reveal monocratic organizations to be less innovative than pluralistic ones.

Some people would identify the traditional leader as an adherent to Theory X; they would classify the pluralistic leader as a follower of Theory Y. Leaders in organizations of the Theory Z type are largely Theory Y practitioners who structure their organizations to secure maximum involvement and commitment from the workers. The pluralistic assumption that the individual is not expendable, for example, has been interpreted in Japanese Theory Z organizations as a guarantee of lifetime employment in the organization in return for full commitment to that organization in the realization of its goals.[55] This guarantee has become less certain in the economic stress of the late 1990s and early 2000s.

Leadership style is a potent factor in the productivity of groups. A classic study of the impact of leadership is the previously mentioned research conducted by Lewin, Lippitt, and White, who studied the effects of three different styles of adult leadership on four groups of eleven-year-old children. They examined the effects of "authoritarian," "democratic," and "laissez-faire" leadership.

> Under the authoritarian leadership, the children were more dependent upon the leader, more discontent, made more demands for attention, were less friendly, produced less work-minded conversation than under the democratic leadership. There was no group initiative in the authoritarian group climate.
>
> The laissez-faire atmosphere produced more dependence on the leader, more discontent, less friendliness, fewer group-minded suggestions, less work-minded conversation than under the democratic climate. In the absence of the laissez-faire leader, work was unproductive. The laissez-faire group was extremely dependent upon the leader for information. The converse of these situations was true for the democratic group climate. In addition, relations among the individuals in the democratic leadership atmosphere were friendlier. Those under the democratic leadership sought more attention and approval from fellow club members. They depended upon each other for recognition as opposed to recognition by the leader under the authoritarian and laissez-faire systems. Further, in the absence of the leader the democratic group proceeded at their work in productive fashion.[56]

Thus, if a curriculum leader seeks commitment from a group, the authoritarian and laissez-faire approaches are not likely to be effective. The curriculum leader's power (what little there is) is conferred by the group, especially if the leadership is encouraged from *within* the group. The democratic approach is, indeed, the only viable approach open to the curriculum leader who is a staff and not a line person propped up by external authority.

Task- and Relationship-Oriented Leaders. Fred E. Fiedler studied the age-old question of whether successful leadership results from personal style or from the circumstances of the situation in which the leader finds himself or herself.[57] Fiedler spoke of the need for an appropriate match between the leader's style and the group situation in which he or she must exercise leadership. Developing what is called a "contingency model," Fiedler classified leaders as task-oriented or relationship-oriented. We might substitute human relations oriented for the latter term. In some respects this classification resembles the dichotomy between the autocratic and democratic leader. The task-oriented leader keeps the goals of the organization always in front of him or her and the group. The needs of the organization take precedence over the needs of individuals. The superordinate–subordinate relationship is always clear. The relationship-oriented leader is less task oriented and more concerned with building harmonious relationships among the members of the organization. He or she possesses a high degree of human relations skill and is less conscious of status.

Persons exhibiting either of these two styles may find themselves in organizations that are either structured or unstructured, or in mixed situations possessing elements of both structure and lack of structure. Successful leadership depends on the fortuitous combination of both style and circumstance. Fiedler found that task-oriented leaders perform better than relationship-oriented leaders at both ends of the continuum from structure to lack of structure. They perform well in structured situations where they possess authority and influence and in unstructured situations where they lack authority and influence. Relationship-oriented persons function best in mixed situations in which they possess moderate authority and influence.

Leadership, then, arises from the exigencies of a situation. Stephen J. Knezevich, for example, espoused a situational view of leadership when he said:

> A person is selected to perform the leadership role because of possessing a set of sensitivities, insights, or personal qualities the group may require for realization of group objectives and decisions. . . . The leader is selected and followed because of being capable to achieve what the followers need or want. A leader successful in one community with a unique set of educational needs may not experience similar success when moved to another with a markedly different set of educational problems, personnel, and value orientations. Changing the situation, or group's nature and purposes, results in a significant variation in leader characteristics desired that upsets all but the broadest interpretations of personal attributes.[58]

When a group member who has been in the role of follower assumes the role of leader that person is then expected to demonstrate democratic behaviors associated with his or her new status of leadership. If the original leader remains a part of the group, he or she then assumes the role of follower. Some status leaders find it difficult to surrender power and are compelled to be constantly on center stage. Such behavior will effectively prevent leadership from developing within the group and is likely to impede its progress. When the original leader resists being replaced, the leader's superior with executive, line power may have to correct the situation by urging changes in the original leader's behavior or by removing him or her from the scene.

The research on leadership thus suggests that the leader in curriculum development should

- seek to develop a democratic approach
- seek to develop a relationship-oriented style
- move between a task-oriented and relationship-oriented style as the situation demands (Jacob W. Getzels, James M. Lipham, and Roald F. Campbell called this flexible style "transactional"[59])
- keep the group on task and avoid excessive processing
- avoid a laissez-faire approach
- encourage the development of leadership from within the group
- maintain openness and avoid a defensive posture
- fulfill his or her role as a change agent by serving as

adviser	interpreter
expert	reinforcer
mediator	spokesperson
organizer	intermediary
explainer	summarizer
discussion leader	team builder

Even with the best leadership some groups experience great difficulties in moving toward accomplishment of their goals. Without effective leadership little can be expected of groups in terms of productivity.

W. Edwards Deming, whose ideas on management are credited with helping Japan's rise as an industrial power, blended industrial management principles into a concept known as Total Quality Management (TQM). Although Deming's ideas applied to industry, TQM when applied to education would incorporate principles of shared-management, the notion that quality should be determined in process rather than tested at the end of the process, learners should share responsibility in evaluating their own work, abandonment of performance ratings of individuals, and participation of group members in finding solutions to problems. You have encountered some of these principles earlier in this chapter when we discussed quality circles.[60] William Glasser, in a vein similar to Deming's, pointed out obstacles to quality schools in the presence of too much "boss-management," too much coercion, not enough cooperative learning, too much traditional testing, too little emphasis on enhancing the ability to use knowledge, and too little opportunity for learners to evaluate the quality of their work.[61] Neither American industry nor education has fully implemented all principles of quality management. However, we see some evidence in performance assessment, cooperative learning, and constructivist psychology, which encourages the learners to take responsibility for formulating their own knowledge under the guidance of the teacher.

Communication Skills

Curriculum development is primarily an exercise in verbal behavior—to some degree written but to a greater degree oral. Through the miraculous gift of language one human being is able to communicate his or her thoughts and feelings to another. Much of the world's business—particularly in a democratic society—is transacted through group discussions. Sometimes it seems as if most administrators, including school personnel, spend the majority of their hours participating in groups, for the standard response to callers is "Sorry, he's [she's] in a meeting."

Thoughts are communicated verbally in the form of oral activity, handwritten, printed or electronic documents; visually in the form of pictures, diagrams, charts, and the like; and nonverbally in the form of gestures and actions. Styles of oral communication differ from individual to individual and from group to group. Styles vary among ethnic, regional, and national groups. The choice of words, the loudness or softness of speech, and the rapidity of the spoken language differ from person to person and from group to group. We find differences in "accent" and in tone or intonation. The flexibility of language, both a strength and a problem, can be seen in a simple example. By using the same words but by varying the intonation or stress pattern, a speaker can convey different meanings as follows:

- *They* said that.
- They *said* that.
- They said *that*.
- They said *that*?

Individuals from some cultures are said to "talk with their hands," indicating frequent use of nonverbal behavior, whereas individuals from other cultures are taught not to be so expressive. Proficiency in communication skills by both the leader and the group members is essential to successful curriculum development. They must demonstrate proficiency in both oral and written communication. At the same time, they must be aware of their own nonverbal behavior and be skilled at reading other people's.

The leader must demonstrate proficiency in two ways: He or she must possess a high degree of communication skill and must also be able to help group members to increase their proficiency in communicating.

For purposes of our discussion, we will assume that the school or district curriculum committees, in which we are most interested, operate through the medium of the English language and that, although they represent a variety of ethnic groups and national origins, they possess at least average proficiency in English language usage. What we have to say about communication goes beyond the mere mechanics of grammar, syntax, spelling, vocabulary, and sentence structure. Deficiencies in the linguistic aspects of communication can be remedied perhaps more easily than some of the more complex psychological, social, and cultural aspects.

It is safe to conjecture that even in a group in which all members possess an excellent command of the language, communication leaves something to be desired. Have you ever sat, for example, in group meetings where

- two people talk at the same time?
- one member consistently finishes sentences for people?
- one member jumps into the discussion without recognition from the chair, elevates his or her voice, and continues to do so until he or she has forced others to be silent?
- one member, angered with the way the discussion is going, gets up and stomps out of the room?
- members snicker and make snide remarks whenever a particular member of the group speaks?
- one member drones on *ad infinitum*?
- one member cannot resist displaying his or her advanced knowledge of the subject under discussion?
- one member becomes sullen when another disagrees with his or her ideas?
- the leader has to explain a point three times before all group members seem to understand?

Do you recognize any of these people? Some of them are, of course, playing the roles discussed earlier. It is possible that many, even most, of the members thought they were communicating something to the group while they were speaking. It is highly probable that what they were communicating was much different from what they thought they were.

Two people vying for the floor may communicate that they both are individuals who demand attention. Or shall we say that they possess a trait, lauded by some, called "assertiveness"? The member who finishes others' sentences may communicate that it is necessary for him or her to think for others. The member who stomps out of the room might attempt to convey that he or she is a person who sticks to his or her principles. More likely, in rejecting the group, the person will be perceived as a "sore loser." We communicate not only through words but through our actions as well.

Common Misunderstandings. We should clear up some common misunderstandings about communication. First, skill in speaking is sometimes mistaken for communication. The ability to respond quickly and fully—to think on one's feet—is an attribute desired, some say required, of a leader. However, facility in speaking does not ensure that a message is getting across. One need only listen to some political leaders to make the distinction between the ability to articulate and the ability to communicate. People place great stress on oral skills, often to such an extent that they do not realize they are accepting form in the place of substance. A glib tongue may obfuscate a topic under discussion. A speaker should strive to be both articulate and communicative.

Second, group interaction is sometimes taken for communication. Comments like "We had a lively discussion" are meaningless unless we know whether the discussion led to understanding and decision making. Processing, the sharing of personal feelings and opinions, is sometimes equated with communication. Interaction for interaction's sake cannot be accepted as a legitimate activity for work in curriculum development.

Third, the assumption that communication is full, clear, and completely understood is often made without sufficient evidence. Alfonso, Firth, and Neville advised supervisors against making such an assumption: "Communication will always be inaccurate because sender and receiver can never share common perceptions. Supervisors often operate on the assumption that communication is perfect. Instead, they should function on the basis that communication is imperfect and must always be so."[62]

How many times have we heard the words of a speaker, understood them all, yet not comprehended what the speaker was saying? How many times have we heard a member of a group tell another, "I hear you," but mean, "Even though I hear you, I do not know what you are saying"?

What are some common problems people experience in trying to communicate and what can be done to solve them? Let's create three categories: (1) problems with oral communication or those that oral and written communication share, (2) problems with written communication, and (3) problems brought about by nonverbal behavior or the absence thereof.

Oral Communication. Difficulties in oral communication can arise in the following situations:

1. *Members of the group either unintentionally or deliberately fail to come to the point.* They talk around instead of to an issue. Sometimes they engage in avoidance behavior—that is, they resist coming to grips with the issue. The curriculum leader must help group members to address the issues and to come to the point. When some group members prattle on, others in the group become bored and frustrated. The burden of keeping the group's attention on the issues falls on the group leader.

2. *Members of the group use fuzzy, imprecise language.* They use words with many interpretations, like "relevance," without defining them. They use "psychobabble," like "Tell me where you're coming from" and "I'm into behavioral objectives." They employ without defining words of low frequency, like "nomothetic," "synergy," and "androgogy," that some members of the group may not understand. They lapse into pedagese, like "Each child must develop his or her personal curriculum," without venturing to explain how this may be done. They borrow Madison Avenue jargon, like "Let's run it up the flagpole," or they turn to sports analogies, like "What's the game plan?" The group leader must be alert to difficulties members may have in following a discussion. He or she must ask speakers to repeat and clarify statements and questions as necessary. The leader must keep in mind that some members hesitate to ask for clarifications themselves, feeling that in so doing they may expose their own ignorance.

3. *Members of the group select out of a discussion those things that they wish to hear.* It is a well-known fact that we hear and see selectively. We hear and see those people and things that we wish to hear and we see and reject those people and things that we do not want to see or hear. The leader must help group members to see all facets of a problem, calling attention to points they may have missed.

4. *Members fail to express themselves, particularly if they disagree with what has been said.* Some persons hold back their views from a sense of insecurity. They feel that their opinions are not worthwhile, or they fear embarrassment or ridicule. They may not wish to seem in disagreement with status persons who are in a position to reward or punish them. The group leader must assure members that dissent is possible and encouraged. The leader must foster a climate in which each person can express himself or herself without fear.

5. *Members fail to follow an orderly process of discussion.* Communication is impossible when group members are unwilling to discipline themselves and do not take turns in discussing, listening to each other, and respecting each other's views. The group leader must enforce order during the discussion process to ensure that everyone who wishes to be heard has an opportunity.

6. *Discussion is shut off and the group presses for a premature vote.* The group should be striving to reach consensus on issues. The goal is commitment of as many persons as possible. The group leader should keep the goal of consensus in front of the group. Close votes on issues should be reexamined, if possible. A vote may (or may not) secure compliance on the part of the people affected; it does not guarantee, however, commitment that is so necessary to curriculum improvement.

7. *Sessions break up without some sort of closure.* If next steps are not clear, members leave the group sessions confused. The leader has the responsibility for seeking closure on issues when possible, for summarizing the group's work, and for calling the group's attention to next steps.

8. *The communication flow is primarily from leader to members.* The leader should resist the temptation to dominate a discussion and to foist his or her views on the group. He or she should ensure that communication is initiated by members of the group to the leader and to each other as well as from the leader to group members.

9. *Acrimony, hostility, and disharmony exist within a group.* When these conditions occur, the leader must spend time developing a pleasant, harmonious group climate before positive communication can take place among members. Members must learn to work together in an atmosphere of trust and mutual respect. The leader should seek to promote a relaxed, threat-free atmosphere.

Written Communication.   In the course of a group's activity there will be occasions on which the leader and members of the group will wish and need to communicate in written form between group sessions. They will also need to communicate in writing with persons outside the work group. Difficulties arise with this form of communication when the following situations occur:

1. *The writer cannot sense the impact of his or her words in a written communication.* Extra care needs to be taken when structuring a written message. Writers of memos must weigh their choice of words and manner of phrasing their thoughts. Some messages are unintentionally blunt or curt and cause negative responses in the receivers. A message when put in writing may give a far different impression from what the writer intended. The writer should review any written communication in the light of the impact it would have on him or her if he or she were the recipient.

2. *Written communications are excessive in number.* Some persons indulge in memorandum writing with almost the same frequency as some individuals write letters to the editor of a newspaper. Some vent their own frustrations in memo after memo. Some people believe that every thought, word, and deed must be committed to writing in order to (a) preserve them for posterity, (b) maintain an ongoing record for current use, or (c) cover one's posterior, as is crudely suggested. Some recipients—or intended recipients—will not take any action unless they have information in written form. Some organizations have almost immobilized themselves with the ubiquitous memo to the point where there are many communiqués but little communication. The leader should encourage the use of memoranda and other written communications as needed and discourage their excessive use. Courtesy, clarity, and brevity should be earmarks of written communications.

3. *The use of English is poor.* Many memoranda, particularly from professional people, lose their impact because of poor English usage. Inaccurate spelling, improper grammar, and poor sentence structure can detract from the message contained in the memoranda and can subject the writers to unnecessary criticism.

Special precautions must be taken when the medium of e-mail is used to deliver messages. E-mail conventions (e.g., the avoidance of sending messages all in capital letters which can be interpreted as shouting) must be observed to prevent misunderstandings. Further, writers of e-mail must keep in mind that there is no clarifying, correcting, or softening of a message once they've hit the Send button.

The writing of intelligible memoranda that do not create negative responses on the part of recipients is an art that, at least in a cooperative activity like curriculum development, should serve only to supplement, not replace, oral communication.

Face-to-face communication is ordinarily—barring the need for complex or technical data—a far more effective means than writing for conveying ideas among members of small groups of peers such as a typical curriculum development group. Even in the case of complex or technical data presented in written form, follow-up discussion is usually necessary.

Nonverbal Behavior. Human beings communicate with each other without the use of words. A smile, a frown, a wave, a shrug, and a wink all say something. Nonverbal behavior is shaped both biologically and culturally. Most human beings start out life with basically the same physiological equipment—two eyes, arms, legs, and so on. But what they do with that equipment is shaped by the culture in which they grow and develop. Thus, it is possible for every human being to smile, but some individuals within a single culture are more prone to smiling than others, and members of a particular culture are more prone to smile than members of another culture. South American Indians, for example, are much more stoic and reserved than the more expressive Latinos of Spanish origin.

Nonverbal behavior is less studied and less understood than verbal behavior. We have great need in our teacher education programs for training in understanding the differences in nonverbal behavior between members of the U.S. culture and foreign cultures in the United States. In our pluralistic society many social and work groups are composed of persons from varying subcultures: white, black, Hispanic, Native American, and Asian, among others. Every individual brings to a group his or her culturally determined ways of behaving. While some cultures prize assertiveness, others stress deference. Signs of respect are accorded to age, status, and experience more often in some cultures than in others. Attitudes of both males and females toward children and of one gender toward the other vary among cultures. Some cultures value physical closeness among individuals and gregariousness. Other cultures strive to maintain distance among individuals both physically and socially. These attitudes are shown in both verbal and nonverbal behavior. Accepted styles of dress vary from culture to culture and even from subculture to subculture.

We need to learn to perceive what our colleagues are trying to communicate to us by the expression on their faces, by the look in their eyes, by the way they hold their mouths or heads, by the movement of their hands, and by the fidgeting of their legs. A group leader should be able to detect fatigue, boredom, hostility, and sensitivity on the part of members of the organization. He or she should be able to sense when one individual is stepping on another's toes and turn the discussion to constructive paths. He or she should strive to effect signs of pleasure, not pain, among members of the group. The leader must be especially cautious of nonverbal signals he or she gives and must make every effort to ensure that those signals are positive. Finally, for successful curriculum development both the leader and group members must exhibit a high degree of skill in all modes of communication.[63]

Summary

This chapter focused on the roles played by various persons and groups participating in curriculum development at the individual school level. Some principals perceive themselves as instructional leaders and take an active part in curriculum development, whereas others delegate that responsibility. A Theory X administrator emphasizes authority and control, whereas a Theory Y administrator follows a human relations approach. Theory Y leaders may adopt Theory Z principles.

Students in some schools, depending on their maturity, participate in curriculum improvement by serving on committees and by providing data about their own learning experiences.

Parents and other citizens participate in curriculum work by serving on advisory committees, responding to surveys, providing data about their children, and serving as resource persons in school and out.

The professional personnel—teachers and specialists—share the greatest responsibility for curriculum development. Both leaders and followers need to develop skills in group process. Among the competencies necessary for the curriculum leader are skills in producing change, in decision making, in interpersonal relationships, in leading groups, and in communicating.

Questions for Discussion

1. What evidence is there that today's principals either are or are not instructional leaders?

2. What are some community groups with which school administrators and supervisors should be concerned?

3. What are the characteristics of a school as a community of learners?

4. Should students be allowed to participate on district or state curriculum councils and boards and, if so, should they be allowed to vote?

5. How would you as a curriculum leader proceed to bring about change in the curriculum?

Exercises

1. Write a paper stating the pros and cons and showing your position on the role of the principal as instructional leader.

2. List qualities and qualifications needed by a curriculum leader.

3. Explain what is meant by Theory X, Theory Y, and Theory Z, and draw implications of these theories for curriculum development.

4. Report on ways students are involved in curriculum development in a school district with which you are familiar.

5. Report on ways parents and others from the community are involved in curriculum development in a school district with which you are familiar.

6. Explain the meaning of the term "power structure," and draw implications of the power structure for curriculum development.

7. Analyze the power structure of a community that you know well.

8. Write an essay on the curriculum leader as a change agent.

9. Write a brief report on ways to unfreeze curricular patterns.

10. Identify roles played by group members and how the curriculum leader copes with each. (You should make an effort to describe roles in addition to those mentioned in this chapter.)

11. Describe common barriers to educational change and suggest ways the curriculum leader may work to eliminate them.

12. List steps in the decision-making process.

13. Create an observation chart based on the Benne-Sheats classification system discussed in this chapter and use it in observing a discussion group in action. (You might want to try using this system at a school board meeting.)

14. Observe a discussion group in action and record evidence of task orientation and process orientation. Conjecture on hidden agendas present in the group.

15. Observe a discussion group in action and evaluate the effectiveness of the leader, using criteria discussed in this chapter.

16. Choose a particular culture and report on the meaning of gestures used within that culture.

17. Analyze the gestures you use, if any. If you do not use any gestures, account for this lack of use.

18. Explain the ten kinds of human activity that Edward T. Hall labeled Primary Message Systems (see bibliography).

19. Explain and demonstrate examples of body language as described by Julius Fast (see bibliography).

20. Prepare a written or oral report on the Concerns-Based Adoption Model (CBAM) developed by the University of Texas Research and Development Center for determining stages of teacher concerns about an innovation and levels of teacher use of innovations. See references to Gene E. Hall and Susan Loucks and to Hall, Loucks, Rutherford, and Newlove in the bibliography. See also a description of this model in John P. Miller and Wayne Seller (see bibliography).

Websites

Center on Education Policy: http://www.cep-dc.org

Concerns-Based Adoption Model:
   http://www.mentoring-association.org/members only/CBAM.html

http://www.nationalacademies.org/rise/backg.htm

Sound Out: http://www.soundout.org

Endnotes

1. J. Galen Saylor and William M. Alexander, *Planning Curriculum for Schools* (New York: Holt, Rinehart and Winston, 1974), p. 59.

2. Roland S. Barth, *Improving Schools from Within: Teachers, Parents, and Principals Can Make a Difference* (San Francisco: Jossey-Bass, 1990).

3. Thomas J. Sergiovanni and Robert J. Starratt, *Supervision: A Redefinition*, 8th ed. (Boston: McGraw-Hill, 2007), p. 56.

4. Ibid, pp. 56–57.

5. Southern States Cooperative Program in Educational Administration, *Better Teaching in School Administration* (Nashville, Tenn.: McQuiddy, 1955).

6. Thelbert L. Drake and William H. Roe, *The Principalship*, 6th ed. (Upper Saddle River, N.J.: Merrill/Prentice Hall, 2003), p. 22.

7. Glenys G. Unruh, "Curriculum Politics," in Fenwick W. English, ed. *Fundamental Curriculum Decisions*. 1983 Yearbook (Alexandria, Va.: Association for Supervision and Curriculum Development, 1983), p. 109.

8. Douglas M. McGregor, *The Human Side of Enterprise* (New York: McGraw-Hill, 1960).

9. Thomas J. Sergiovanni and Fred D. Carver, *The New School Executive: A Theory of Administration*, 2nd ed. (New York: Harper & Row, 1980), p. 49.

10. Abraham H. Maslow, *Motivation and Personality*, 2nd ed. (New York: Harper & Row, 1970), p. 46.

11. See William G. Ouchi, *Theory Z: How American Businesses Can Meet the Japanese Challenge* (Reading, Mass.: Addison-Wesley, 1981).

12. Ibid., pp. 261–268. For a view of the negative side of Japanese management, see Joel Kotkin and Yoriko Kishimoto, "Theory F," *Inc.* 8, no. 4 (April 1986): 53–60.

13. Ronald C. Doll, *Curriculum Improvement: Decision Making and Process*, 9th ed. (Boston: Allyn and Bacon, 1996), p. 423.

14. See data from *Sound Out*, a program of Common Action, a nonprofit corporation registered in the State of Washington, *Students on School Boards: The Law*, http://www.soundout.org/schoolboardlaw.html, accessed 9/1/06.

15. This practice is commonly referred to in the literature on the history of education as the "dame school" or "kitchen school."

16. See the following: Robert S. Lynd, *Middletown: A Study in American Culture* (New York: Harcourt Brace Jovanovich, 1929) and Robert S. Lynd and Helen M. Lynd, *Middletown in Transition: A Study in Cultural Conflicts* (New York: Harcourt Brace Jovanovich, 1937); Ralph B. Kimbrough, *Community Power Structure and Analysis* (Englewood Cliffs, N.J.: Prentice-Hall, 1964); Ralph B. Kimbrough and Michael Y. Nunnery, *Educational Administration: An Introduction*, 3rd ed. (New York: Macmillan, 1988), Chapter 13.

17. Florida Statute 229.575 (3).

18. Florida Statute 229.58 (1).

19. Roald F. Campbell, Luvern L. Cunningham, Raphael O. Nystrand, and Michael D. Usdan, *The Organization and Control of American Schools*, 6th ed. (Columbus, Ohio: Merrill, 1990), pp. 329–342.

20. "Hispanic Americans by the Numbers," http://www.infoplease.com/spot/hhmcensus1.html, accessed 9/1/06.

21. http://www.census.gov/Press-Release/www/releases/archives/population/006808.html, accessed 9/3/06.

22. http://www.census.gov/Press-Release/www/releases/archives/population/001720.html, accessed 9/3/06.

23. For discussion of limitations on the state's power to compel school attendance, you may wish to read *Teach Your Own: A Hopeful Path for Education* (New York: Delacorte Press/Seymour Lawrence, 1981) by John Holt, an advocate of home schooling. See also Chapter 15 of this text.

24. See Gene Maeroff, *The Empowerment of Teachers: Overcoming the Crisis of Confidence* (New York: Teachers College Press, 1988). See also G. Alfred Hess, Jr., ed., *Empowering Teachers and Parents: School Restructuring Through the Eyes of Anthropologists* (Westport, Conn.: Bergin & Garvey, 1992). See also Paula M. Short and John T. Greer, *Leadership in Empowered Schools: Themes from Innovative Efforts* (Upper Saddle River, N.J.: Merrill, 1997).

25. Richard A. Gorton, Judy A. Alston, and Petra E. Snowden, *School Leadership & Administration: Important Concepts, Case Studies, and Simulations*, 7th ed. (Boston: McGraw-Hill, 2007).

26. See F. J. Roethlisberger and William J. Dickson, *Management and the Worker* (Cambridge, Mass.: Harvard University Press, 1939); see also William G. Ouchi, endnote 11 of this chapter.

27. George H. Wood, "Teachers as Curriculum Workers," in James T. Sears and J. Dan Marshall, eds., *Teaching and Thinking About Curriculum: Critical Inquiries* (New York: Teachers College Press, 1990), p. 107.

28. Gail McCutcheon, "Curriculum Theory/Curriculum Practice: A Gap or the Grand Canyon?" in Alex Molnar, ed., *Current Thought on the Curriculum*. 1985 Yearbook (Alexandria, Va.: Association for Supervision and Curriculum Development, 1985), p. 46.

29. Harold J. Leavitt and Homa Bahrami, *Managerial Psychology: Managing Behavior in Organizations*, 5th ed. (Chicago: University of Chicago Press, 1988), pp. 246–256.

30. Robert J. Alfonso, Gerald R. Firth, and Richard F. Neville, *Instructional Supervision: A Behavior System*, 2nd ed. (Boston: Allyn and Bacon, 1981), p. 283.

31. Ibid., p. 284.

32. See Warren G. Bennis, "Theory and Method in Appying Behavioral Science in Panned Organizational Change," *Journal of Applied Behavioral Science* 1, no. 4 (1965): 347–348.

33. See Kurt Lewin, *Field Theory in Social Science* (New York: Harper Torchbooks, 1951). Also in Kurt Lewin, "Frontiers in Group Dynamics," *Human Relations* 1 (1947): 5–41.

34. Daniel L. Stufflebeam et al., *Educational Evaluation and Decision Making* (Itasca, Ill.: F. E. Peacock, 1971), especially Chapter 3.

35. Ibid., pp. 80–84.

36. Colin J. Marsh and George Willis, *Curriculum: Alternative Approaches, Ongoing Issues*, 3rd. ed. (Upper Saddle River, N.J.: Merrill/Prentice Hall, 2003), p. 175.

37. Gene E. Hall and Susan Loucks, "Teacher Concerns as a Basis for Facilitating and Personalizing Staff Development," *Teachers College Record* 80, no. 1 (September 1978): 36–53.

38. Kenneth D. Benne and Paul Sheats, "Functional Roles of Group Members," *Journal of Social Issues* 4, no. 2 (Spring 1948): 43–46.

39. Kurt Lewin, Ronald Lippitt, and Ralph K. White, "Patterns of Aggressive Behavior in Experimentally Created Social Climates," *Journal of Social Psychology* 10 (May 1939): 271–299.

40. Rensis Likert, *New Patterns of Management* (New York: McGraw-Hill, 1961).

41. Ned A. Flanders, *Analyzing Teacher Behavior* (Reading, Mass.: Addison-Wesley, 1970).

42. John Dewey, *How We Think*, rev. ed. (Lexington, Mass.: D. C. Heath, 1933).

43. Stufflebeam et al., *Educational Evaluation*.

44. Warren G. Bennis, Kenneth D. Benne, and Robert Chin, eds., *The Planning of Change*, 4th ed. (New York: Holt, Rinehart and Winston, 1985).

45. Fred E. Fiedler, *A Theory of Leadership Effectiveness* (New York: McGraw-Hill, 1967).

46. Kimball Wiles, *Supervision for Better Schools*, 3rd ed. (Englewood Cliffs, N.J.: Prentice-Hall, 1967). See also John T. Lovell and Kimball Wiles, *Supervision for Better Schools*, 5th ed., 1983.

47. See Laurence J. Peter, Jr., and Raymond Hull, *The Peter Principle: Why Things Always Go Wrong* (New York: William Morrow, 1969).

48. Kimbrough and Nunnery, *Educational Administration*, p. 357.

49. Robert H. Palestini, *Educational Administration: Leading with Mind and Heart*, 2nd ed. (Lanham, Md.: Rowman & Littlefield Education, 2005).

50. Ibid.

51. Ibid.

52. Edgar L. Morphet, Roe L. Johns, and Theodore L. Reller, *Educational Organization and Administration: Concepts, Practices, and Issues*, 4th ed. (Englewood Cliffs, N.J.: Prentice-Hall, 1982), pp. 77–79.

53. Ibid., pp. 80–82.

54. Ibid., p. 85.

55. See Ouchi, *Theory Z.*

56. Lewin, Lippitt, and White, "Patterns of Aggressive Behavior." Quoted from Peter F. Oliva, "High School Discipline in American Society," *NASSP Bulletin* 40, no. 26 (January 1956): 7–8.

57. See Fiedler, *Theory of Leadership*. Also, "Style or Circumstance: The Leadership Enigma," *Psychology Today* 2, no. 10 (March 1969): 38–43.

58. Stephen J. Knezevich, *Administration of Public Education*, 4th ed. (New York: Harper & Row, 1984), p. 66.

59. Jacob W. Getzels, James M. Lipham, and Roald F. Campbell, *Educational Administration as a Social Process* (New York: Harper & Row, 1968).

60. See W. Edwards Deming, *Out of the Crisis: Productivity and Competitive Position* (Cambridge, Mass.: Massachusetts Institute of Technology Press, 1986). See also Kenneth T. Delavigne and J. Daniel Robertson, *Deming's Profound Changes: When Will the Sleeping Giant Awaken?* (Englewood Cliffs, N.J.: Prentice-Hall, 1994).

61. William Glasser, *The Quality School: Managing Students Without Coercion*, 2nd, expanded ed. (New York: HarperPerennial, 1992). See also William Glasser, "The Quality School," *Phi Delta Kappan* 71, no. 6 (February 1990): 424–435.

62. Alfonso, Firth, and Neville, *Instructional Supervision*, p. 175.

63. For interesting analyses of some aspects of nonverbal behavior see Edward T. Hall, *The Silent Language* (Garden City, N.Y.: Doubleday, 1959); Julius Fast, *Body Language* (New York: M. Evans, 1970); and Desmond Morris, Peter Collett, Peter Marsh, and Marie O'Shaughnessy, *Gestures: Their Origin and Distribution* (New York: Stein and Day, 1979).

Bibliography

Alfonso, Robert J., Firth, Gerald R., and Neville, Richard F. *Instructional Supervision: A Behavior System*, 2nd ed. Boston: Allyn and Bacon, 1981.

Barth, Roland. *Improving Schools from Within: Teachers, Parents, and Principals Can Make the Difference.* San Francisco: Jossey-Bass, 1990.

Benne, Kenneth D. and Sheats, Paul. "Functional Roles of Group Members." *Journal of Social Issues* 4, no. 2 (Spring 1948): 43–46.

Bennis, Warren G. "Theory and Method in Applying Behavioral Science to Planned Organizational Change." *Journal of Applied Behavioral Science* 1, no. 4 (1965).

———, Benne, Kenneth D., and Chin, Robert, eds. *The Planning of Change*, 4th ed. New York: Holt, Rinehart and Winston, 1985.

Campbell, Roald F., Cunningham, Luvern L., Nystrand, Raphael O., and Usdan, Michael D. *The Organization and Control of American Schools*, 6th ed. Columbus, Ohio: Merrill, 1990.

Delavigne, Kenneth T. and Robertson, J. Daniel. *Deming's Profound Changes: When Will the Sleeping Giant Awaken?* Englewood Cliffs, N.J.: Prentice-Hall, 1994.

Deming, W. Edwards. *Out of the Crisis: Productivity and Competitive Position.* Cambridge, Mass.: Massachusetts Institute of Technology, 1986.

Dewey, John. *How We Think*, rev. ed. Lexington: Mass.: D. C. Heath, 1933.

Doll, Ronald C. *Curriculum Improvement: Decision Making and Process*, 9th ed. Boston: Allyn and Bacon, 1996.

Drake, Thelbert L. and Roe, William H. *The Principalship*, 6th ed. Upper Saddle River, N.J.: Merrill/Prentice Hall, 2003.

Dwyer, David C., Barnett, Bruce G., and Lee, Ginny V. "The School Principal: Scapegoat or the Last Great Hope?" In Linda T. Sheive and Marian B. Schoenheit, eds., *Leadership: Examining the Elusive*. Alexandria, Va.: Association for Supervision and Curriculum Development, 1987, pp. 30–46.

Fast, Julius. *Body Language*. New York: M. Evans, 1970.

————. *The Body Language of Sex, Power, and Aggression*. New York: M. Evans, 1977.

Fiedler, Fred E. *A Theory of Leadership Effectiveness*. New York: McGraw-Hill, 1967.

Flanders, Ned A. *Analyzing Teacher Behavior*. Reading, Mass.: Addison-Wesley, 1970.

Galloway, Charles. *Silent Language in the Classroom*. Bloomington, Ind.: Phi Delta Kappa Educational Foundation, 1976.

George, Paul S. *The Theory Z School: Beyond Effectiveness*. Columbus, Ohio: National Middle School Association, 1983.

Getzels, Jacob, Lipham, James M., and Campbell, Roald F. *Educational Administration as a Social Process*. New York: Harper & Row, 1968.

Glasser, William. *The Quality School: Managing Students Without Coercion*, 2nd, expanded ed. New York: HarperPerennial, 1992.

Glatthorn, Allan A. *Curriculum Leadership: Development and Implementation*. Thousand Oaks, Calif.: SAGE Publications, 2006.

————. *The Principal as Curriculum Leader: Shaping What Is Taught and Tested*, 2nd ed. Thousand Oaks, Calif.: Corwin Press, 2000.

Gordon, Richard A., Alston, Judy A. and Snowden, Petra E. *School Leadership and Administration: Important Concepts, Case Studies, and Simulations*, 7th ed. Boston: McGraw-Hill, 2007.

Hall, Edward T. *The Silent Language*. Garden City, N.Y.: Doubleday, 1959.

Hall, Gene E. and Loucks, Susan. "Teacher Concerns as a Basis for Facilitating and Personalizing Staff Development." *Teachers College Record* 80, no. 1 (September 1978): 36–53.

————, Loucks, Susan, Rutherford, William L., and Newlove, Beaulah W. "Levels of Use in the Innovation: A Framework for Analyzing Innovation Adoption." *Journal of Teacher Education* 26, no. 1 (Spring 1975): 52–56.

————, Wallace, R. C., Jr. and Dossett, W. A. *A Developmental Conceptualization of the Adoption Process within Educational Institutions*. Austin, Tex.: Research and Development Center for Teacher Education, The University of Texas, 1973.

Hess, G. Alfred, Jr. *Empowering Teachers and Parents: School Restructuring Through the Eyes of Anthropologists*. Westport, Conn.: Bergin & Garvey, 1992.

Holt, John. *Teach Your Own: A Hopeful Path for Education*. New York: Delacorte Press/Seymour Lawrence, 1981.

Hord, Shirley M., Rutherford, William L., Huling-Austin, Leslie, and Hall, Gene E. *Taking Charge of Change*. Alexandria, Va.: Association for Supervision and Curriculum Development, 1987.

Kimbrough, Ralph B. and Nunnery, Michael Y. *Educational Administration*, 3rd ed. New York: Macmillan, 1988.

Knezevich, Stephen J. *Administration of Public Education*, 4th ed. New York: Harper & Row, 1984.

Kotkin, Joel and Kishimoto, Yoriko. "Theory F," *Inc.* 8, no. 4 (April 1986): 53–60.

Leavitt, Harold J. and Bahrami, Homa. *Managerial Psychology: Managing Behavior in Organizations*, 5th ed. Chicago: University of Chicago Press, 1988.

Lewin, Kurt. *Field Theory in Social Science: Selected Theoretical Papers*, edited by Dorwin Cartwright. New York: Harper Torchbooks, 1951.

————. "Frontiers in Group Dynamics," *Human Relations* 1 (1947): 5–41.

————, Lippitt, Ronald, and White, Ralph K. "Patterns of Aggression in Experimentally Created Social Climates." *Journal of Social Psychology* 10 (May 1939): 271–299.

Likert, Rensis. *New Patterns of Management*. New York: McGraw-Hill, 1961.

Lynd, Robert S. *Middletown: A Study in American Culture*. New York: Harcourt Brace Jovanovich, 1929.

———— and Lynd, Helen M. *Middletown in Transition: A Study in Cultural Conflicts*. New York: Harcourt Brace Jovanovich, 1937.

McCutcheon, Gail. "Curriculum Theory/Curriculum Practice: A Gap or the Grand Canyon?" In Alex Molnar, ed., *Current Thought on Curriculum*, 1985 Yearbook, 45–52. Alexandria, Va.: Association for Supervision and Curriculum Development, 1985.

McGregor, Douglas M. *The Human Side of Enterprise*. New York: McGraw-Hill, 1960.

McNeil, John D. *Contemporary Curriculum in Thought and Action*. Hoboken, N.J.: Wiley, 2006.

Maeroff, Gene I. *The Empowerment of Teachers: Overcoming the Crisis of Confidence*. New York: Teachers College Press, 1988.

Marsh, Colin J. and Willis, George. *Curriculum: Alternative Approaches, Ongoing Issues*, 3rd ed. Upper Saddle River, N.J.: Merrill/Prentice Hall, 2003.

Maslow, Abraham H. *Motivation and Personality*, 2nd ed. New York: Harper & Row, 1970.

Miel, Alice. *Changing the Curriculum: A Social Process*. New York: Appleton-Century-Crofts, 1946.

Miller, John P. and Seller, Wayne. *Curriculum: Perspectives and Practice*. White Plains, N.Y.: Longman, 1985.

Morphet, Edgar L., Johns, Roe L., and Reller, Theodore L. *Educational Organization and Administration: Concepts, Practices, and Issues*, 4th ed. Englewood Cliffs, N.J.: Prentice-Hall, 1982.

Morris, Desmond, Collett, Peter, Marsh, Peter, and O'Shaughnessy, Marie. *Gestures: Their Origin and Distribution*. New York: Stein and Day, 1979.

Ouchi, William G. *Theory Z: How American Businesses Can Meet the Japanese Challenge*. Reading, Mass.: Addison-Wesley, 1981.

Owens, Robert G. *Organizational Behavior in Education: Adoptive Leadership and School Reform*, 8th ed. Boston: Allyn and Bacon, 2004.

Palestini, Robert H. *Educational Administration: Leading with Mind and Heart*, 2nd ed. Lanham, Md.: Rowman & Littlefield Education, 2005.

Peter, Laurence J. and Hull, Raymond. *The Peter Principle: Why Things Always Go Wrong*. New York: William Morrow, 1969.

Roethlisberger, F. J. and Dickson, William J. *Management and the Worker*. Cambridge, Mass.: Harvard University Press, 1939.

Ross, Joel E. *Total Quality Management: Text, Cases, and Readings*, 2nd ed. Delray Beach, Fla.: St. Luice Press, 1995.

Sears, James T. and Marshall, J. Dan, eds. *Teaching and Thinking About Curriculum: Critical Inquiries*. New York: Teachers College Press, 1990.

Sergiovanni, Thomas J. and Carver, Fred D. *The New School Executive: A Theory of Administration*, 2nd ed. New York: Harper & Row, 1980.

Sergiovanni, Thomas J. and Starratt, Robert J. *Supervision: A Redefinition*, 8th ed. Boston: McGraw-Hill, 2007.

Short, Paula M. and Greer, John T. *Leadership in Empowered Schools: Themes from Innovative Efforts*. Upper Saddle River, N.J.: Merrill, 1997.

Snowden, Petra E. and Gorton, Richard A. *School Leadership and Administration: Important Concepts, Case Studies, and Simulations*, 6th ed. New York: McGraw-Hill, 2002.

Stufflebeam, Daniel L. et al. *Educational Evaluation and Decision Making*. Itasca, Ill.: F. E. Peacock, 1971.

Tanner, Daniel and Tanner, Laurel. *Curriculum Development: Theory into Practice*, 4th ed. Upper Saddle River, N.J.: Merrill/Prentice Hall, 2007.

Unruh, Glenys G. "Curriculum Politics." In Fenwick W. English, ed., *Fundamental Curriculum Decisions*, 1983 Yearbook, 99–111. Alexandria, Va.: Association for Supervision and Curriculum Development, 1983.

Wiles, Jon and Bondi, Joseph C. *Curriculum Development: A Guide to Practice*, 7th ed. Upper Saddle River, N.J.: Merrill/Prentice Hall, 2007.

Wiles, Kimball. *Supervision for Better Schools*, 3rd ed. Englewood Cliffs, N.J.: Prentice-Hall, 1967.

Willis, Scott. "Creating 'Total Quality' Schools." *ASCD Update* 35, no. 2 (February 1993): 1, 4–5.

Wood, George H. "Teacher as Curriculum Workers." In James T. Sears and J. Dan Marshall, eds., *Teaching and Thinking About Curriculum: Critical Inquiries*. New York: Teachers College Press, 1990, pp. 97–109.

5 Models for Curriculum Development

AFTER STUDYING THIS CHAPTER YOU SHOULD BE ABLE TO:

1. Analyze each model for curriculum development in this chapter and decide which models, if any, meet the necessary criteria for such a model.
2. Choose one model and carry out one or more of its components in your school.
3. Distinguish between deductive and inductive models for curriculum development.
4. Distinguish between linear and nonlinear models for curriculum development.
5. Distinguish between prescriptive and descriptive models for curriculum development.

SELECTING MODELS

The current literature of education is replete with discussions of modeling. Models, which are essentially patterns serving as guidelines to action, can be found for almost every form of educational activity. The profession has models of instruction, of administration, of evaluation, of supervision, and others. We can even find models of *curriculum* as opposed to models of *curriculum development*.[1]

Unfortunately, the term *model* as used in the education profession often lacks precision. It may be a tried or untried scheme. It may be a proposed solution to a piece of a problem; an attempt at a solution to a specific problem; or a microcosmic pattern for replication on a grander scale.

Some faculties have been *modeling* for years. They have been devising their own patterns for solving educational problems or establishing procedures, though they may not have labeled their activity as *modeling*.

Variation in Models

Some of the models found in the literature are simple; others are very complex. The more complex ones border on computer science, with charts that consist of squares, boxes, circles, rectangles, arrows, and so on. Within a given area of specialization (such as administration, instruction, supervision, or curriculum development), models may differ but bear great similarities. The similarities may outweigh the differences. Individual models are often refinements or revisions, frequently major, often minor, of already existing models.

Practitioners to whom a model is directed, therefore, have the heavy responsibility of selecting a model in their particular field from the often bewildering variety in the literature. If the practitioners are not disposed to apply models they discover, they may either design their own, by no means a rare event, or reject all models that prescribe order and sequence. They may thus proceed intuitively without the apparent limitations imposed by a model. After proceeding intuitively, the practitioners may then "put it all together" and come out with a working model at the end of the process instead of starting with a model at the beginning.

Four models of curriculum development are presented in this chapter, one of which is my own. I believe that using a model in such an activity as curriculum development can result in greater efficiency and productivity.

By examining models for curriculum development, we can analyze the phases their originators conceived as essential to the process. The purpose in presenting four models is to acquaint the reader with some of the thinking that has gone on or is going on in the field. Three of the chosen models were conceived by persons well known in the curriculum field: Ralph W. Tyler,[2] Hilda Taba,[3] J. Galen Saylor, William M. Alexander, and Arthur J. Lewis.[4] My own model is presented as an effort to tie together essential components in the process of curriculum development. The exercises at the end of this chapter will direct you to additional models.

Three of the models (Tyler's; Saylor, Alexander, and Lewis's; and mine) are deductive. They proceed from the general (examining the needs of society, for example) to the specific (specifying instructional objectives, for example). On the other hand, Taba's model is inductive, starting with the actual development of curriculum materials and leading to generalization.

The four models described in this chapter are linear; that is, they propose a certain order or sequence of progression through the various steps. I use the term "linear" for models whose steps proceed in a more or less sequential, straight line from beginning to end. Perhaps the term "mostly linear" would be more accurate since some doubling back to previous steps can take place even in "mostly linear" models. For simplicity's sake I'll use the term "linear." A nonlinear approach would permit planners to enter at various points of the model, skip components, reverse the order, and work on two or more components simultaneously. You might say that the ultimate in a nonlinear approach is the absence of a model when curriculum planners operate intuitively. Actually, linear models should not be perceived as immutable sequences of steps. Curriculum workers would exercise judgment as to entry points and interrelationships of components of the models.

The four models presented in this chapter are prescriptive rather than descriptive. They suggest what ought to be done (and what is done by many curriculum developers). A descriptive model takes a different approach. Proposing a descriptive model, which he termed *naturalistic*, Decker F. Walker included three major elements: platform, deliberation, and design.[5] By *platform* he meant the beliefs or principles that guided the curriculum developers. Platform principles lead to *deliberation*, the process of making decisions from among alternatives available. From the deliberation comes the curriculum *design*. Walker contrasted the naturalistic or descriptive model with the classical or prescriptive model as follows:

> This model is primarily descriptive, whereas the classical model is prescriptive. This model is basically a temporal one; it postulates a beginning (the platform), an end (the design), and a process (deliberation) by means of which the beginning progresses to the end. In contrast, the classical model is a means-end model; it postulates a desired end (the objective), a means for attaining this end (the learning experience), and a process (evaluation) for determining whether the means does indeed bring about the end. The two models differ radically in the roles they assign to objectives and to evaluation in the process of curriculum development.
>
> In the classical model objectives are essential. . . . In the naturalistic model, on the other hand, objectives are only one means among others for guiding our search for better educational programs. . . .
>
> Evaluation in the classical model is a self-corrective process for determining whether learning experiences lead to the attainment of given objectives. . . . In the naturalistic model this kind of evaluation is not *logically* necessary. Design decisions *can* be justified by reference to the platform only. . . . In the naturalistic model evaluation is a useful tool for justifying design decisions, even though it is quite possible and not nonsensical (although probably unwise) for a curriculum developer to neglect systematic formal evaluation.[6]

All of these models specify or depict major phases and a sequence for carrying out these phases. The models, including mine, show *phases* or *components*, not *people*. The various individuals and groups involved in each phase are not included in the models per se. To do so would require a most cumbersome diagram, for we would have to show the persons involved in every component. For example, if we showed the people involved in the component "specification of curriculum goals," we would need to chart a progression of steps from departmental committee to school faculty curriculum committee or extended school committee to principal to district curriculum committee to superintendent to school board. The roles of individuals and groups in the process are discussed elsewhere in this text.

MODELS OF CURRICULUM DEVELOPMENT

Curriculum development is seen here as the process for making programmatic decisions and for revising the products of those decisions on the basis of continuous and subsequent evaluation.

A model can give order to the process. As Taba stated, "If one conceives of curriculum development as a task requiring orderly thinking, one needs to examine both the order in which decisions are made and the way in which they are made to make sure that all relevant considerations are brought to bear on these decisions."[7]

The Tyler Model

Perhaps the best or one of the best known models for curriculum development with special attention to the planning phases can be found in Ralph W. Tyler's classic little book, *Basic Principles of Curriculum and Instruction*, that he wrote as a syllabus for his classes at the University of Chicago. "The Tyler rationale," a process for selecting educational objectives, is widely known and practiced in curriculum circles. Although Tyler proposed a rather comprehensive model for curriculum development, the first part of his model (selection of objectives) received the greatest attention from other educators.

Tyler recommended that curriculum planners identify general objectives by gathering data from three sources: the learners, contemporary life outside the school, and the subject matter. After identifying numerous general objectives, the planners refine them by filtering them through two screens: the educational and social philosophy of the school and the psychology of learning. The general objectives that successfully pass through the two screens become what are now popularly known as instructional objectives. In describing educational objectives Tyler referred to them as "goals," "educational ends," "educational purposes," and "behavioral objectives."[8]

Student as Source.   The curriculum worker begins his or her search for educational objectives by gathering and analyzing data relevant to student needs and interests. The total range of needs—educational, social, occupational, physical, psychological, and recreational—is studied. Tyler recommended observations by teachers, interviews with students, interviews with parents, questionnaires, and tests as techniques for collecting data about students.[9] By examining the needs and interests of students, the curriculum developer identifies a set of potential objectives.

Society as Source.   Analysis of contemporary life in both the local community and in society at large is the next step in the process of formulating general objectives. Tyler suggested that curriculum planners develop a classification scheme that divides life into various aspects such as health, family, recreation, vocation, religion, consumption, and civic roles.[10] From the needs of society flow many potential educational objectives. The curriculum worker must be something of a sociologist to make an intelligent analysis of needs of social institutions. After considering this second source, the curriculum worker has lengthened his or her set of objectives.

Subject Matter as Source.   For a third source the curriculum planner turns to the subject matter, the disciplines themselves. Many of the curricular innovations of the 1950s—the "new math," audio-lingual foreign language programs, and the plethora of science programs—came from the subject matter specialists. From the three aforementioned sources curriculum planners derive general or broad objectives that lack precision and that I would prefer to call instructional goals. These goals may be pertinent to specific disciplines or may cut across disciplines.

Mauritz Johnson, Jr., held a different perspective about these sources. He commented that the "only possible source [of the curriculum] is the total available culture" and that only organized subject matter—that is, the disciplines, not the needs and interests of learners or the values and problems of society—can be considered a source of curriculum items.[11]

Once this array of possibly applicable objectives is determined, a screening process is necessary, according to Tyler's model, to eliminate unimportant and contradictory objectives. He advised the use of the school's educational and social philosophy as the first screen for these goals.

Philosophical Screen. Tyler advised teachers of a particular school to formulate an educational and social philosophy. He urged them to outline their values and illustrated this task by emphasizing our democratic goals:

- the recognition of the importance of every individual human being regardless of race, national, social, or economic status;
- opportunity for wide participation in all phases of activities in the social groups in the society;
- encouragement of variability rather than demanding a single type of personality; and
- faith in intelligence as a method of dealing with important problems rather than depending on the authority of an autocratic or aristocratic group.[12]

In his discussion about the formulation of an educational social philosophy, Tyler personified the school. He talked about "the educational and social philosophy to which the school is committed," "when a school accepts these values," "many schools are likely to state," and "if the school believes."[13] Thus, Tyler made of the school a dynamic, living entity. The curriculum worker will review the list of general objectives and omit those that are not in keeping with the faculty's agreed-on philosophy.

Psychological Screen. The application of the psychological screen is the next step in the Tyler model. To apply the screen, teachers must clarify the principles of learning that they believe to be sound. "A psychology of learning," said Tyler, "not only includes specific and definite findings but it also involves a unified formulation of a theory of learning which helps to outline the nature of the learning process, how it takes place, under what conditions, what sort of mechanisms operate and the like."[14] Effective application of this screen presupposes adequate training in educational psychology and in human growth and development by those charged with the task of curriculum development. Tyler explained the significance of the psychological screen:

- A knowledge of the psychology of learning enables us to distinguish changes in human beings that can be expected to result from a learning process from those that cannot.

- A knowledge of the psychology of learning enables us to distinguish goals that are feasible from those that are likely to take a very long time or are almost impossible of attainment at the age level contemplated.
- Psychology of learning gives us some idea of the length of time required to attain an objective and the age levels at which the effort is most efficiently employed.[15]

After the curriculum planner has applied this second screen, his or her list of general objectives will be reduced, leaving those that are the most significant and feasible. Care is then taken to state the objectives in behavioral terms, which turns them into instructional, classroom objectives. We will return to the writing of behavioral objectives in Chapters 7, 8, and 10.

Tyler did not make use of a diagram in describing the process he recommended. However, W. James Popham and Eva L. Baker cast the model into the illustration shown in Figure 5.1.[16] In applying the Tyler rationale, Popham and Baker, advocates for the use of behavioral objectives, referred to the stage after the philosophical and psychological screenings as specification of "precise instructional objectives." Tyler saw that stage as the identification of a small number of important objectives, though general in nature, yet still specific enough to incorporate content and behavioral aspects. Tyler left room, however,

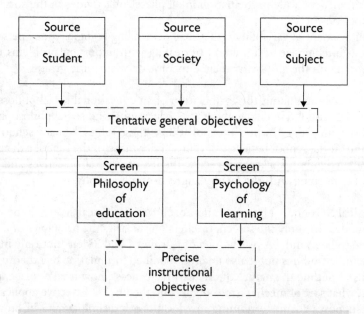

FIGURE 5.1   Tyler's Curriculum Rationale. Figure from W. James Popham and Eva L. Baker, *Establishing Instructional Goals* (Englewood Cliffs, N.J.: Prentice-Hall, 1970), p. 87. Based on the work of Ralph W. Tyler, *Basic Principles of Curriculum and Instruction* (Chicago: The University of Chicago Press, 1949), pp. 3–85. Reprinted by permission of the University of Chicago, publisher.

for curriculum workers to determine educational objectives in keeping with what they believe about learning.[17] In this respect Tyler's objectives, though behavioral in nature, may be somewhat less precise than those proposed by other behavioral objectives advocates.

For some reason, discussions of the Tyler model often stop after examining the first part of the model—the rationale for selecting educational objectives. Actually, Tyler's model goes beyond this process to describe three more steps in curriculum planning: selection, organization, and evaluation of learning experiences. He defined learning experiences as "the interaction between the learner and the external conditions in the environment to which he can react."[18] He suggested teachers give attention to learning experiences

- that will "develop skill in thinking"
- that will be "helpful in acquiring information"
- that will be "helpful in developing social attitudes"
- that will be "helpful in developing interests."[19]

He explained how to organize the experiences into units and described various evaluation procedures.[20] Although Tyler did not devote a chapter to a phase called direction of learning experiences (or implementation of instruction), we can infer that instruction must take place between the selection and organization of learning experiences and the evaluation of student achievement of these experiences.

Expanded Model.   We could, therefore, modify the diagram of Tyler's model by expanding it to include steps in the planning process after specifying instructional objectives. Figure 5.2 shows how such an expanded model might appear.

In discussing the Tyler rationale, Daniel and Laurel Tanner noted its debt to the progressive thought of John Dewey, H. H. Giles, S. P. McCutchen, and A. N. Zechiel.[21] The Tyler rationale, however, is not without its critics. As long ago as 1970, Herbert M. Kliebard took issue with Tyler's interpretation of the notions of needs, philosophical screens, selection of learning experiences, and evaluation.[22] Commenting that the Tyler rationale "has been raised almost to the status of revealed doctrine,"[23] Kliebard concluded, "But the field of curriculum . . . must recognize the Tyler rationale for what it is: Ralph Tyler's version of how a curriculum should be developed—not *the* universal model of curriculum development."[24]

Although acknowledging that "the influence of Ralph Tyler on the history of curriculum development cannot be underemphasized," Patrick Slattery took the position that "postmodern curriculum development is challenging the traditional curriculum development model of Ralph Tyler."[25] He observed that "postmodern curriculum development is concerned with biographical and autobiographical narrative . . . ."[26]

The apparent linear nature and lack of interdependence among the various components are criticisms of the Tyler rationale. If curriculum planners consider the components to be separate and fail to understand the interaction among the sources, curriculum development can become too mechanical a process. Tyler himself did not perceive the rationale as a strictly prescribed sequence of steps to be followed without fail by curriculum planners. Evidence of this can be seen in a lesser-known, but more complex, model of the rationale

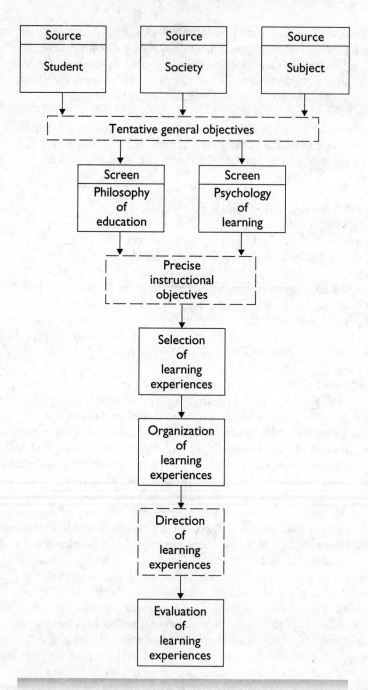

FIGURE 5.2   Tyler's Curriculum Rationale (Expanded)

presented with coauthor Mario Leyton Soto. This rendition of the rationale reveals the integration and interdependence of the various components.[27]

Referring to Tyler's *Basic Principles*, Tanner and Tanner observed that it "has been widely used in curriculum courses and widely discussed in the curriculum literature from midcentury to the present day."[28]

"Although criticisms have been offered of the Tyler rationale and competing models offered, none, in our judgment, have seriously challenged its dominance," wrote Decker F. Walker and Jonas F. Soltis.[29]

The Taba Model

Taba took what is known as a grassroots approach to curriculum development. She believed that the curriculum should be designed by the teachers rather than handed down by higher authority. Further, she felt that teachers should begin the process by creating specific teaching-learning units for their students in their schools rather than by engaging initially in creating a general curriculum design. Taba, therefore, advocated an inductive approach to curriculum development, starting with the specifics and building up to a general design as opposed to the more traditional deductive approach of starting with the general design and working down to the specifics.

Five-Step Sequence.   Eschewing graphic exposition of her model, Taba listed a five-step sequence for accomplishing curriculum change, as follows:[30]

1. *Producing pilot units* representative of the grade level or subject area. Taba saw this step as linking theory and practice. She proposed the following eight-step sequence for curriculum developers who are producing pilot units.[31]
   a. *Diagnosis of needs.* The curriculum developer begins by determining the needs of the students for whom the curriculum is being planned. Taba directed the curriculum worker to diagnose the "gaps, deficiencies, and variations in [students'] backgrounds."[32]
   b. *Formulation of objectives.* After student needs have been diagnosed, the curriculum planner specifies objectives to be accomplished. Taba used the terms "goals" and "objectives" interchangeably, a point to which we will return later.
   c. *Selection of content.* The subject matter or topics to be studied stem directly from the objectives. Taba pointed out that not only must the objectives be considered in selecting content but also the "validity and significance" of the content chosen.[33]
   d. *Organization of content.* With the selection of content goes the task of deciding at what levels and in what sequences the subject matter will be placed. Maturity of learners, their readiness to confront the subject matter, and their levels of academic achievement are factors to be considered in the appropriate placement of content.
   e. *Selection of learning experiences.* The methodologies or strategies by which the learners become involved with the content must be chosen by the curriculum planners. Pupils internalize the content through the learning activities selected by the planner-teacher.

    f. *Organization of learning activities.* The teacher decides how to package the learning activities and in what combinations and sequences they will be utilized. At this stage the teacher adapts the strategies to the particular students for whom he or she has responsibility.

    g. *Determination of what to evaluate and of the ways and means of doing it.* The planner must decide whether objectives have been accomplished. The instructor selects from a variety of techniques appropriate means for assessing achievement of students and for determining whether the objectives of the curriculum have been met.

    h. *Checking for balance and sequence.* Taba counseled curriculum workers to look for consistency among the various parts of the teaching-learning units, for proper flow of the learning experiences, and for balance in the types of learning and forms of expression.

2. *Testing experimental units.* Since the goal of this process is to create a curriculum encompassing one or more grade levels or subject areas and since teachers have written their pilot units with their own classrooms in mind, the units must now be tested "to establish their validity and teachability and to set their upper and lower limits of required abilities."[34]

3. *Revising and consolidating.* The units are modified to conform to variations in student needs and abilities, available resources, and different styles of teaching so that the curriculum may suit all types of classrooms. Taba would charge supervisors, the coordinators of curricula, and the curriculum specialists with the task of "stating the principles and theoretical considerations on which the structure of the units and the selection of content and learning activities are based and suggesting the limits within which modifications in the classroom can take place."[35] Taba recommended that such "considerations and suggestions might be assembled in a handbook explaining the use of the units."[36]

4. *Developing a framework.* After a number of units have been constructed, the curriculum planners must examine them as to adequacy of scope and appropriateness of sequence. The curriculum specialist would assume the responsibility of drafting a rationale for the curriculum that has been developed through this process.

5. *Installing and disseminating new units.* Taba called on administrators to arrange appropriate inservice training so that teachers may effectively put the teaching-learning units into operation in their classrooms.

    Taba's inductive model may not appeal to curriculum developers who prefer to consider the more global aspects of the curriculum before proceeding to specifics. Some planners might wish to see a model that includes steps in both diagnosing the needs of society and culture and in deriving needs from subject matter, philosophy, and learning theory. Taba, however, elaborated on these points in her text.[37]

    Other planners may prefer to follow a deductive approach, starting with the general—specification of philosophy, aims, and goals—and moving to the specifics—objectives, instructional techniques, and evaluation. The remaining two models described in this chapter are deductive as is Tyler's.

The Saylor, Alexander, and Lewis Model

Saylor, Alexander, and Lewis conceptualized the *curriculum planning process* in the model shown in Figure 5.3.[38] To understand this model we must first analyze their concepts of *curriculum* and *curriculum plan.* Earlier in this text you encountered their definition of curriculum: "a plan for providing sets of learning opportunities for persons to be educated."[39] However, the curriculum plan is not to be conceived as a single document but rather as "many smaller plans for particular portions of the curriculum."[40]

Goals, Objectives, and Domains.   The model indicates that the curriculum planners begin by specifying the major educational goals and specific objectives they wish to be accomplished. Saylor, Alexander, and Lewis classified sets of broad goals into four domains under which many learning experiences take place: personal development, social competence, continued learning skills, and specialization.[41] Once the goals, objectives, and domains have been established, the planners move into the process of designing the curriculum. The curriculum workers decide on the appropriate learning opportunities for each domain and how and when these opportunities will be provided. For example,

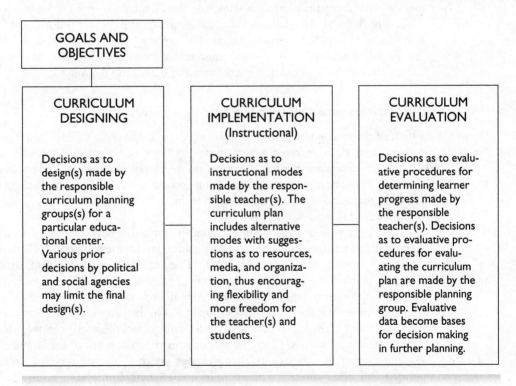

FIGURE 5.3   Saylor, Alexander, and Lewis's Conception of the Curriculum Planning Process. From J. Galen Saylor, William M. Alexander, and Arthur J. Lewis. *Curriculum Planning for Better Teaching and Learning,* 4th ed., p. 30. (New York: Holt, Rinehart and Winston, 1981). Reproduced by permission of Arthur J. Lewis.

will the curriculum be designed along the lines of academic disciplines, according to a pattern of social institutions, or in relation to student needs and interests?

Instructional Modes.   After the designs have been created—and there may be more than one—all teachers affected by a given part of the curriculum plan must create the instructional plans. They select the methods through which the curriculum will be related to the learners.[42] At this point in the model it would be helpful to introduce the term *instructional objectives.* Teachers would then specify the instructional objectives before selecting the strategies or modes of presentation.

Evaluation.   Finally, the curriculum planners and teachers engage in evaluation. They must choose from a wide variety of evaluation techniques. Saylor, Alexander, and Lewis proposed a design that would permit (1) evaluation of the total educational program, as well as (2) evaluation of the evaluation program itself.[43] The evaluation processes allow curriculum planners to determine whether or not the goals of the school and the objectives of instruction have been met.

Saylor, Alexander, and Lewis supplemented their model of the curriculum planning process with companion models depicting the elements of the curriculum system, the process of defining the goals and objectives of educational institutions, and curriculum evaluation.[44] Curriculum planners might find some synthesis of the model of the curriculum planning process with its companion models desirable. We will look at the Saylor, Alexander, and Lewis model of curriculum evaluation in Chapter 13.

Similarities and Differences among Models

The models discussed reveal both similarities and differences. Tyler and Taba outlined certain steps to be taken in curriculum development. Saylor, Alexander, and Lewis charted the components of the curriculum development process (design, implementation, and evaluation) as opposed to actions taken by the curriculum workers (diagnosis of needs, formulation of objectives, and the like). Tyler's concept of sources and screens stands out in his model.

Models are inevitably incomplete; they do not and cannot show every detail and every nuance of a process as complicated as curriculum development. In one sense the originator of a model is saying, often in graphic form, "These are the most important features." To depict every detail of the curriculum development process would require an exceedingly complex drawing or several models. One task in building a model for curriculum development is to determine what the most salient components in the process are—no easy task—and to limit the model to those components. Model builders feel themselves between the Scylla of oversimplification and the Charybdis of complexity to the point of confusion.

In looking at various models we cannot say that any one model is inherently superior to all other models. For example, some curriculum planners have followed the Tyler model for years with considerable success. On the other hand, this success does not mean that the Tyler model, for example, represents the ultimate in models for curriculum development or that any model including Tyler's is universally accepted as a basis for curriculum development.

Before choosing a model or designing a new model—certainly a viable alternative—curriculum planners might attempt to outline the criteria or characteristics they would look for in a model for curriculum improvement. They might agree that the model should show the following:

1. major components of the process, including stages of planning, implementation, and evaluation
2. customary but not inflexible "beginning" and "ending" points
3. the relationship between curriculum and instruction
4. distinctions between curriculum and instructional goals and objectives
5. reciprocal relationships among components
6. a cyclical pattern
7. feedback lines
8. the possibility of entry at any point in the cycle
9. an internal consistency and logic
10. enough simplicity to be intelligible and feasible
11. components in the form of a diagram or chart

I would agree that these are reasonable criteria to follow, and, to this end, I will now propose a model incorporating these guidelines. The model will accomplish two purposes: (1) to suggest a system that curriculum planners might wish to follow and (2) to serve as the framework for explanations of phases or components of the process for curriculum improvement.

The model is not presented as the be-all and end-all of models for curriculum development but rather as an attempt to implement the aforementioned guidelines. The proposed model may be acceptable in its present form to curriculum planners, especially those who agree with a deductive, linear, and prescriptive approach. It may, at the same time, stimulate planners to improve the model or to create another that would better reflect their goals, needs, and beliefs.

The Oliva Model

In the following pages we will look briefly at a model consisting of twelve components. The subsequent chapters of Part III elaborate on each component. This model appears in Figure 5.4.

The Twelve Components.   The model charted in Figure 5.4 illustrates a comprehensive, step-by-step process that takes the curriculum planner from the sources of the curriculum through evaluation. In Chapters 6 through 13, we will examine each part of the model. Each component (designated by Roman numerals I through XII) will be described and illustrations will be given to guide curriculum planners and their coworkers. Let us now undertake a cursory overview of the model.

You will note that both squares and circles are used in the model. The squares are used to represent planning phases; the circles, operational phases. The process starts with component I, at which time the curriculum developers state the aims of education and

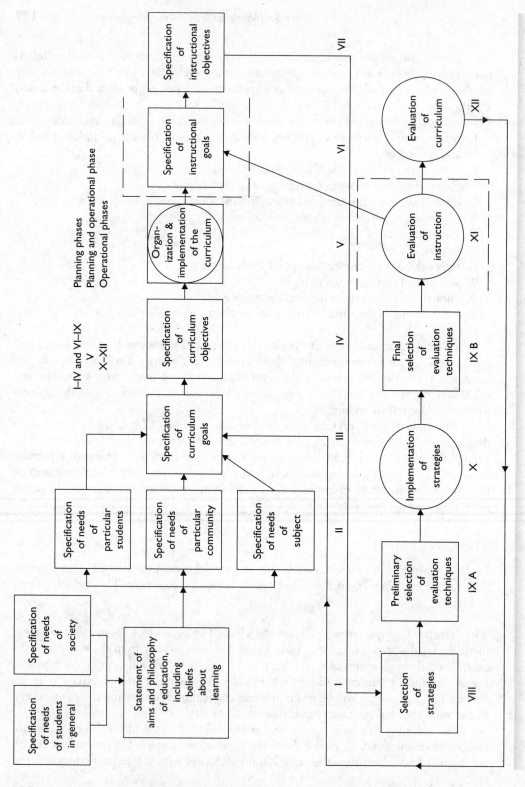

FIGURE 5.4 The Oliva Model for Curriculum Development

their philosophical and psychological principles. These aims are beliefs that are derived from the needs of our society and the needs of individuals living in our society. This component incorporates concepts similar to Tyler's "screens."

Component II requires an analysis of the needs of the community in which the school is located, the needs of students served in that community, and the exigencies of the subject matter that will be taught in the given school. Sources of the curriculum are seen as cutting across components I and II. Whereas component I treats the needs of students and society in a more general sense, component II introduces the concept of needs of particular students in particular localities, because the needs of students in particular communities are not always the same as the general needs of students throughout our society.

Components III and IV call for specifying curricular goals and objectives based on the aims, beliefs, and needs specified in components I and II. A distinction that will be clarified later with examples is drawn between goals and objectives. The tasks of component V are to organize and implement the curriculum and to formulate and establish the structure by which the curriculum will be organized.

In components VI and VII an increasing level of specification is sought. Instructional goals and objectives are stated for each level and subject. Once again we will distinguish between goals and objectives and will show by illustration how the two differ.

After specifying instructional objectives, the curriculum worker moves to component VIII, at which point he or she chooses instructional strategies for use with students in the classroom. Simultaneously, the curriculum worker initiates preliminary selection of evaluation techniques, phase A of component IX. At this stage the curriculum planner thinks ahead and begins to consider ways he or she will assess student achievement. The implementation of instructional strategies—component X—follows.

After the students have been provided appropriate opportunity to learn (component X), the planner returns to the problem of selecting techniques for evaluating student achievement and the effectiveness of the instructor. Component IX, then, is separated into two phases: the first *precedes* the actual implementation of instruction (IXA) and the second *follows* the implementation (IXB). The instructional phase component (component X) provides the planner with the opportunity to refine, add to, and complete the selection of means to evaluate pupil performance.

Component XI is the stage at which evaluating instruction is carried out. Component XII completes the cycle with evaluation not of the student or the teacher but rather of the curricular program. In this model components I–IV and VI–IX are planning phases, whereas components X–XII are operational phases. Component V is both a planning and operational phase.

Like some other models, this model combines a scheme for curriculum development (components I–V and XII) and a design for instruction (components V–XI).

Important features of the model are the feedback lines that cycle back from the evaluation of the curriculum to the curriculum goals and from the evaluation of instruction to the instructional goals. These lines indicate the necessity for continuous revision of the components of their respective subcycles.

Use of the Model.   The model can be used in a variety of ways. First, the model offers a process for the complete development of a school's curriculum. The faculty of each special area—for example, language arts—can, by following the model, fashion a plan for the curriculum of that area and design ways in which it will be carried out through instruction, or the faculty may develop schoolwide, interdisciplinary programs that cut across areas of specialization such as career education, guidance, and extraclass activities.

Second, a faculty may focus on the curricular components of the model (components I–V and XII) to make programmatic decisions. Third, a faculty may concentrate on the instructional components (VI–XI).

Two Submodels.   This twelve-phase model integrates a general model for curriculum development with a general model for instruction. Components I–V and XII constitute a curriculum development submodel which I will refer to as the curriculum submodel. Components VI–XI constitute an instructional submodel. To distinguish between the curricular and instructional components, I have enclosed the instructional submodel within broken lines.

When the curricular submodel is followed, the curriculum planners must keep in mind that the task has not been completed until the curriculum goals and objectives are subsequently translated by them or others into instruction. Furthermore, when the instructional submodel is followed, the instructional planners must be aware of the curriculum goals and objectives of the school as a whole or of a given subject area or areas.

In order to keep the model as uncluttered as possible at this point, I have not attempted to show all the nuances of the model. At several places in subsequent chapters, certain refinements and embellishments of the model will be described.

For those who prefer a model in the form of steps instead of a diagram, below is a listing of the steps shown in Figure 5.4. The model sets forth the following steps:

1. Specify the needs of students in general.
2. Specify the needs of society.
3. Write a statement of philosophy and aims of education.
4. Specify the needs of students in your school(s).
5. Specify the needs of the particular community.
6. Specify the needs of the subject matter.
7. Specify the curriculum goals of your school(s).
8. Specify the curriculum objectives of your school(s).
9. Organize and implement the curriculum.
10. Specify instructional goals.
11. Specify instructional objectives.
12. Select instructional strategies.
13. Begin selection of evaluation techniques.
14. Implement instructional strategies.
15. Make final selection of evaluation techniques.
16. Evaluate instruction and modify instructional components.
17. Evaluate the curriculum and modify curricular components.

Steps 1–9 and 17 constitute a curriculum submodel; steps 10–16, an instructional submodel.

Summary

Four models of curriculum development are presented in this chapter. Models can help us to conceptualize a process by showing certain principles and procedures. Whereas some models are in the form of diagrams, others are lists of steps that are recommended to curriculum workers. Some models are linear, step-by-step approaches; others allow for departure from a fixed sequence of steps. Some models offer an inductive approach; others follow a deductive approach. Some are prescriptive; others, descriptive.

Those who take leadership in curriculum development are encouraged to become familiar with various models, to try them out, and to select or develop the model that is most understandable and feasible for them and for the persons with whom they are working.

I have presented for consideration a model consisting of twelve components. This model is comprehensive in nature, encompassing both curricular and instructional development.

Questions for Discussion

1. On what bases would you choose a model for curriculum development?

2. Who should decide which model for curriculum development to follow?

3. In your opinion which is better: an inductive or a deductive model for curriculum development?

4. What are the strengths and limitations of a linear model for curriculum development?

5. In your opinion which is better: a prescriptive or a descriptive model for curriculum development?

Exercises

1. Define "sources" and "screens" as used by Ralph W. Tyler.

2. Explain why Tyler's model has been referred to as "linear" in nature and identify the presence or absence of linearity in each of the other models in this chapter.

3. Write a brief position paper, giving reasons for your position, on the question: "Is the Tyler rationale a suitable basis for current curriculum development?"

4. Cast Taba's steps for curriculum development into a diagrammed model.

5. Identify one or more domains in addition to the four suggested by Saylor, Alexander, and Lewis, or, alternatively, design your own pattern of domains.

6. Explain the meaning of the broken lines in the diagram of the Oliva model.

7. Explain why components X, XI, and XII of the Oliva model are shown as circles whereas the other components, except for component V, are shown as squares. Explain why component V is depicted with both a square and a circle.

8. Describe the four models of curriculum planning found in Geneva Gay's chapter in the 1980 Yearbook of the Association for Supervision and Curriculum Development (see bibliography). These models are the academic model, the experiential model, the technical model, and the pragmatic model.

9. Summarize George A. Beauchamp's concept of curriculum engineering (see bibliography).

10. Find or design a nonlinear model for curriculum development. For one example, see Mario Leyton Soto and Ralph W. Tyler, *Planeamiento Educacional* (see bibliography). This model is discussed in Peter F. Oliva, *Developing the Curriculum*, 1st ed. Little, Brown and Company, 1982, pp. 159, 161, 162.

11. Define curriculum engineering as used by Robert S. Zais (see bibliography) and report on one of the following models for curriculum engineering discussed by Zais:
    a. The Administrative (Line-Staff) Model
    b. The Grass-roots Model
    c. The Demonstration Model
    d. George Beauchamp's System
    e. Carl Rogers's Interpersonal Relations Model

12. Robert M. Gagné maintained that there is no such step in curriculum development as "selection of content" (see bibliography). State whether you agree and give reasons, citing quotations from the literature that support your position.

13. Describe the model of curricular and instructional planning and evaluation proposed by Mauritz Johnson, Jr. in *Intentionality in Education* (see bibliography).

14. Describe the Generic Curriculum Planning Model presented by Arthur W. Steller (see bibliography).

15. Describe the curriculum development models presented by Allan C. Ornstein and Francis P. Hunkins; George J. Posner and Alan N. Rudnitsky; and Decker F. Walker and Jonas F. Soltis (see bibliography).

16. Report on any model for curriculum development described by John P. Miller and Wayne Seller that is different from the models described in this chapter (see bibliography).

17. Report on the curriculum planning model described by Weldon F. Zenger and Sharon K. Zenger (see bibliography) and tell how it differs from the models described in this chapter.

18. Define the term *postmodern curriculum development* as used by some writers on curriculum (see Pinar et al., 1996 and Slattery in bibliography).

Websites

Association for Supervision and Curriculum Devlopment: http://www.ascd.org

National Staff Development Council: http://www.nsdc.org

Ralph W. Tyler: http://www.wredu.com/~wriles/Tyler.html

Tyler e Hilda Taba: Modelo Racional Normativo: http://educacion.idoneos.com/index/php/363731 (click on "Translate this page").

Endnotes

1. For a model of *curriculum*, see Mauritz Johnson, Jr., "Definitions and Models in Curriculum Theory," *Educational Theory* 17, no. 2 (April 1967): 127–140.

2. Ralph W. Tyler, *Basic Principles of Curriculum and Instruction* (Chicago: University of Chicago Press, 1949).

3. Hilda Taba, *Curriculum Development: Theory and Practice* (New York: Harcourt Brace Jovanovich, 1962).

4. J. Galen Saylor, William M. Alexander, and Arthur J. Lewis, *Curriculum Planning for Better Teaching and Learning*, 4th ed. (New York: Holt, Rinehart and Winston, 1981).

5. Decker F. Walker, "A Naturalistic Model for Curriculum Development," *School Review* 80, no. 1 (November 1971): 51–67.

6. Ibid., pp. 58–59.

7. Taba, *Curriculum Development*, pp. 11–12.

8. Tyler, *Basic Principles*, pp. 3, 37, 57.

9. Ibid., pp. 12–13.

10. Ibid., pp. 19–20.

11. Johnson, "Definitions and Models," p. 132.

12. Tyler, *Basic Principles*, p. 34.

13. Ibid., pp. 33–36.

14. Ibid., p. 41.

15. Ibid., pp. 38–39.

16. W. James Popham and Eva L. Baker, *Establishing Instructional Goals* (Englewood Cliffs, N.J.: Prentice-Hall, 1970), p. 87.

17. Tyler, *Basic Principles*, pp. 43, 50, 57

18. Ibid., p. 63

19. Ibid., Chapter 2.

20. Ibid., Chapters 3 and 4.

21. Daniel Tanner and Laurel Tanner, *Curriculum Development: Theory into Practice*, 4th ed. (Upper Saddle River, N.J.: Merrill/Prentice-Hall, 2007), p. 134.

22. Herbert M. Kliebard, "The Tyler Rationale," *School Review* 78 (February 1970): 259–272.

23. Ibid, p. 259.

24. Ibid, p. 270.

25. Patrick Slattery, *Curriculum Development in the Postmodern Era* (New York: Garland Publishing, 1995), p. 47.

26. Ibid.

27. Mario Leyton Soto and Ralph W. Tyler, *Planeamiento Educacional* (Santiago, Chile: Editorial Universitaria, 1969). See also Peter F. Oliva, *Developing the Curriculum*, 1st ed. (Boston: Little, Brown, 1982), pp. 159, 161, 162.

28. Tanner and Tanner, *Curriculum Development*, p. 134.

29. Decker F. Walker and Jonas F. Soltis, *Curriculum and Aims* (New York: Teachers College Press, 2004), p. 55.

30. Taba, *Curriculum Development*, pp. 456–459.

31. Ibid., pp. 345–379. On page 12 of her book Taba listed the first seven steps. See Chapter 11 of this text for discussion of the creation of units.

32. Ibid., p. 12.

33. Ibid.

34. Ibid., p. 458.

35. Ibid.

36. Ibid., pp. 458–459.

37. Ibid., Part 1.

38. Saylor, Alexander, and Lewis, *Curriculum Planning*, p. 30.

39. Ibid., p. 8.

40. Ibid., p. 28.

41. Ibid.

42. Ibid., Chapter 6.

43. Ibid., Chapter 7.

44. Ibid., pp. 29, 165, 334.

Bibliography

Beauchamp, George A. *Curriculum Theory*, 4th ed. Itasca, Ill.: F. E. Peacock, 1981.

Bloom, Benjamin S., ed. *Taxonomy of Educational Objectives: The Classification of Educational Goals: Handbook I: Cognitive Domain*. New York: Longman, 1956.

Gagné, Robert M. "Curriculum Research and the Promotion of Learning." *Perspectives of Curriculum Evaluation*, AERA Monograph Series on Evaluation, no. 1, 19–23. Chicago: Rand McNally, 1967.

Gay, Geneva. "Conceptual Models of the Curriculum-Planning Process." In Arthur W. Foshay, ed. In *Considered Action for Curriculum Improvement*. 1980 Yearbook, 120–143. Alexandria, Va.: Association for Supervision and Curriculum Development, 1980.

Giles, H. H., McCutchen, S. P., and Zechiel, A. N. *Exploring the Curriculum*. New York: Harper, 1942.

Jackson, Philip W., ed. *Handbook of Research on Curriculum*. New York: Macmillan, 1992.

Johnson, Mauritz, Jr. "Definitions and Models in Curriculum Theory." *Educational Theory* 17, no. 2 (April 1967): 127–140.

———. *Intentionality in Education*. Albany, N.Y. Center for Curriculum Research and Services, 1977.

Kliebard, William M. "Reappraisal: The Tyler Rationale." In William Pinar, ed. *Curriculum Theorizing: The Reconceptualists*. Berkeley, Calif.: McCutchan, 1975, pp. 70–83.

———. "The Tyler Rationale." In Arno Bellack and Herbert M. Kliebard, eds. *Curriculum and Evaluation*. Berkeley, Calif.: McCutchan, 1977, pp. 56–67.

———. "The Tyler Rationale." *School Review* 78, no. 2 (February 1970): 259–272.

Krathwohl, David R., Bloom, Benjamin S., and Masia, Bertram B. *Taxonomy of Educational Objectives: The Classification of Educational Goals: Handbook II: Affective Domain*. New York: Longman, 1964.

McNeil, John D. *Contemporary Curriculum in Thought and Action*. Hoboken, N.J.: Wiley, 2006.

McNeil, John D. *Curriculum: A Comprehensive Introduction*, 5th ed. New York: HarperCollins, 1996.

Miller, John P. and Seller, Wayne. *Curriculum: Perspectives and Practice*. White Plains, N.Y.: Longman, 1985, Chapter 9.

Oliva, Peter F. and George E. Pawlas. *Supervision for Today's Schools*, 7th ed. Part III. New York: Wiley, 2004.

Ornstein, Allan C. and Behar, Linda S., eds. *Contemporary Issues in Curriculum*. Boston: Allyn and Bacon, 1995.

_____ and Hunkins, Francis P. *Curriculum: Foundations, Principles, and Issues*, 4th ed. Boston: Allyn and Bacon, 2004.

Pinar, William, F., ed. *Contemporary Curriculum Discourses*. Scottsdale, Ariz.: Gorsuch and Scarisbrick, 1988.

————. *Curriculum Theorizing: The Reconceptualists*. Berkeley, Calif.: McCutchan, 1975.

————, Reynolds, William D., Slattery, Patrick, and Taubman, Peter M. *Understanding Curriculum: An Introduction to the Study of Historical and Contemporary Discourses*. New York: Peter Lang, 1996.

Popham, W. James. *Evaluating Instruction*. Englewood Cliffs, N.J.: Prentice-Hall, 1973.

Posner, George J. and Rudnitsky, Alan N. *Curriculum Design: A Guide to Curriculum Devlepment for Teachers*, 7th ed. Boston: Allyn and Bacon, 2006.

Saylor, J. Galen, Alexander, William M., and Lewis, Arthur J. *Curriculum Planning for Better Teaching and Learning*, 4th ed. New York: Holt, Rinehart and Winston, 1981.

Slattery, Patrick. *Curriculum Development in the Postmodern Era*. New York: Garland, 1995.

Steller, Arthur W. "Curriculum Planning." In Fenwick W. English, ed. *Fundamental Curriculum Decisions*. 1983 Yearbook. Alexandria, Va.: Association for Supervision and Curriculum Development, 1983.

Taba, Hilda. *Curriculum Development: Theory and Practice*. New York: Harcourt Brace Jovanovich, 1962.

Tanner, Daniel and Tanner, Laurel. *Curriculum Development: Theory into Practice*, 4th ed. Upper Saddle River, N.J.: Merrill/Prentice Hall, 2007.

Tyler, Ralph W. *Basic Principles of Curriculum and Instruction*. Chicago: University of Chicago Press, 1949.

———— and Leyton Soto, Mario. *Planeamiento Educacional*. Santiago, Chile: Editorial Universitaria, 1969.

Walker, Decker F. "A Naturalistic Model for Curriculum Development." *School Review* 80, no. 1 (November 1971): 51–67.

Walker, Decker F. and Soltis, Jonas F. *Curriculum and Aims*. New York: Teachers College Press, 2004.

————. *Fundamentals of Curriculum: Passion and Professionalism*, 2nd ed. Mahwah, N.J.: Lawrence Erlbaum Associates, 2003.

Wiles, Jon and Bondi, Joseph. *Curriculum Development: A Guide to Practice*, 7th ed. Upper Saddle River, N.J.: Merrill/Prentice Hall, 2007.

Zais, Robert S. *Curriculum: Principles and Foundations*. New York: Harper & Row, 1976. Chapter 19.

Zenger, Weldon F. and Zenger, Sharon K. "Planning for Curriculum Development: A Model for Administrators." *NASSP Bulletin* 68, no. 471 (April 1984): 17–28.

6

Philosophy and Aims of Education

AFTER STUDYING THIS CHAPTER YOU SHOULD BE ABLE TO:

1. Explain how aims of education are derived.

2. Cite commonly voiced statements of the aims of education.

3. Write statements of the aims of education.

4. Outline major beliefs of four well-known schools of philosophy.

5. Draft a school philosophy that could be submitted to a school faculty for discussion.

USING THE PROPOSED MODEL

A comprehensive model for the process of curriculum development, consisting of twelve phases or components, was presented in Chapter 5. For a moment, let's take another look at it (see Figure 5.4), and then I'll underscore some of its characteristics.

Examining the model reveals the following special characteristics:

1. *The model flows from the most general (aims of education) to the most specific (evaluation techniques).* Beginning here and in the remaining chapters of Part III, I will describe each component and define its terms in such a way as to show this flow.

2. *The model can be followed by curriculum planning groups (or even to some extent by individuals) in whole or in part.* The model allows for a comprehensive, holistic study of the curriculum. Given the many demands on the time of teachers, administrators, and others, it is likely that a complete look at the curriculum from the aims of education (component I) to evaluation of the curriculum (component XII) will be carried out only periodically. Although somewhat arbitrary, reassessment and revision of the various phases might be considered on the schedule shown in Box 6.1.

Faculties may wish to set their own schedules for considering the various components. Those components that are closest to the faculty, involve fewer persons, are more easily manageable, and are less costly in time and money might be reassessed with greater frequency than those components that are more remote, involve many persons, are more difficult to manage, and are more costly.

3. *A single curriculum group, like the curriculum committee of an individual school, department, or grade, will not carry out all phases of the model by itself.* Various groups, subgroups, and individuals will assume responsibility for different parts of the model. One group (for example, the school's curriculum council) may work on the first component, the aims of education. A subgroup may conduct a needs assessment and study the sources of curricular needs. The school's curriculum council may attempt to define schoolwide curriculum goals and objectives while committees within the various disciplines identify curriculum goals and objectives within particular fields. Individual faculty members and groups in various grades and departments will be engaged in specifying instructional goals and objectives. Decisions at any phase that have relevance to the entire school may be presented to the total faculty for its information and support or rejection. Throughout the process, decisions made by any of the subgroups must be presented so that relationships among the various components are clearly understood. In this respect the curriculum council of the school will serve as a coordinating body.

4. *With modifications, the model can be followed at any level or sector of curriculum planning.* Parts of the model may also be applied at the various levels and sectors that were discussed in Chapter 3.

AIMS OF EDUCATION

Proliferation of Terms

The educational literature uses a proliferation of terms, rather loosely and often interchangeably, to signify terminal expectations of education. Educators speak of "outcomes," "aims," "ends," "purposes," "functions," "goals," and "objectives." Although these terms may be used synonymously in common language, it is helpful if distinctions are made in pedagogical language.

In this book the term "outcome" applies to terminal expectations generally. "Aims" are equated with "ends," "purposes," "functions," and "universal goals." The aims of education are the very broad, general statements of the purposes of education; they are meant to give general direction to education throughout the country. Decker F. Walker and Jonas F. Soltis likened aims of education to wishes for "something desirable for people in general *that is only possible for them to have because of something they learn.*"[1]

In this text "curriculum goals," "curriculum objectives," "instructional goals," and "instructional objectives" are separate entities of special relevance to the local school or school system. Curriculum goals are defined as general, programmatic expectations without criteria of achievement or mastery, whereas curriculum objectives are specific, programmatic targets with criteria of achievement and, therefore, are measurable. The curriculum objectives stem from the curriculum goals.[2] Both curriculum goals and curriculum objectives trace their sources to the school's philosophy and the statement of aims of education.

BOX 6.1

Suggested Schedule for Reassessing Curriculum Development Components

	In Depth	Limited
Aims of education	Every 10 years	Every 5 years
Assessment of needs	Every 3 years	Every year
Curriculum goals	Every 2 years	Every year
Curriculum objectives	Every 2 years	Every year
Instructional goals	Every year	Continuously
Instructional objectives	Every year	Continuously
Organization and implementation of the curriculum	Every 10 years	Every year
Other components	Continuously	Continuously

Instructional goals are statements of instructional targets in general, nonobservable terms without criteria of achievement, whereas instructional objectives are expected learner behaviors formulated, with possible exceptions for those in the affective domain, in measurable and observable terms.[3] Instructional objectives are derived from instructional goals, and both instructional goals and instructional objectives originate from the curriculum goals and objectives.

The aims of education have special relevance to the nation as a whole. We will talk about aims of our educational system, society, and country. Presumably, in former days we could have set forth regional aims for the North, South, Midwest, and West. In the twenty-first century, however, it would seem an anachronism to promote regional aims as if the broad purposes of education in California, for example, were different from those in New York or the purposes of education in Indiana different from those of Mississippi.

Global Aims

It is possible, even desirable, to define aims of education on a global scale, and sometimes such definitions are attempted. The United Nations Educational, Scientific, and Cultural Organization (UNESCO) is the foremost exponent of attempts on a worldwide scale to state aims of education for humanity. Among the aims of education that UNESCO seeks to promote are these:

- fostering international understanding among all peoples of the world
- improving the standard of living of people in the various countries
- solving continuing problems that plague humanity, such as war, disease, hunger, and unemployment

Similar organizations, such as the Organization of American States, are also concerned with the aims of education on an international scale. The few Americans who participate in such organizations find some opportunity for expressing aims of education that can apply across national boundaries. More common are statements of aims of education by the respective nations of the world to guide the development of their own educational systems.

In any discipline, the field of curriculum notwithstanding, the specialist seeks to find or develop generalizations or rules that apply in most situations. On the other hand, the specialist must always be aware that exceptions may be found to most rules. Although we may hold to the view that curriculum development is a group process and is more effective as a result of that process, we must admit that individuals can carry out any of the components of the suggested model of curriculum development. It would seem at first sight, for example, that defining aims of education to which the entire country might subscribe would certainly be a group project. However, as we shall see, several significant statements of aims of education have been made over the years by prominent individuals. When statements are generated by individuals instead of groups, members of the social structure for which the aims are intended become, in effect, consumers and interpreters of the ideas of individuals—certainly a tenable procedure.

That statements of aims, goals, and objectives may originate from individuals rather than groups should not invalidate them. It might be said that "while individuals propose, the group will dispose." Groups should react to coherent statements in a deliberative manner. The model of curriculum development should not be construed to eliminate spontaneous, individual efforts at curriculum development. Some of the most successful innovations in schools have been effected as the result of the work of independently motivated mavericks on the school's staff.

Statements of Purposes

We are confronted with aims of education when we read statements of purposes promulgated by various societies around the world, for example:

- to inculcate family values
- to prepare youth to fit into a planned society
- to promote free enterprise
- to further the glorious revolution
- to create citizens who will serve the fatherland
- to prepare an enlightened citizenry
- to nurture the Islamic culture
- to correct social ills
- to promote the Judeo-Christian heritage

We encounter aims of education in a descriptive form when someone makes declarations like the following:

- Education is life, not preparation for life.
- Education is the molding of the young to the values of the old.

- Education is the transmission of the cultural heritage.
- Education is vocational training.
- Education is the liberal arts.
- Education is training in socialization.
- Education is intellectual development.
- Education is personal development.
- Education is socialization of groups and individuals.
- Education is the development of technological skills.

We can even find implied aims of education in slogans like these:

- If you think education is expensive, try ignorance.
- If you can read this sign, thank a teacher.
- A sound mind in a sound body.

Presumably ever since primitive peoples discovered that the flint axe was more effective for killing game than a wooden club, that animal skin protected their bodies against the elements, and that roast boar was superior to raw, they continually discussed what training they must provide their Neanderthal young so that they could cope with their environment. In their own primitive way they must have dealt with the heady topic of the purposes of education in Neanderthal Land.

Today, many thousands of years later, people still affirm coping with the environment as a central purpose of education. The common term to express this purpose is "survival skills." Instead of learning coping skills like stalking a gazelle, frightening a tiger, and spearing a fish, today's children must master the basic academic skills, learn to conserve resources, learn to live on a more densely populated planet, develop computer literacy, and know how to earn a legitimate living. Sometimes, as has been the case throughout the history of humankind, the martial arts become survival skills. Not only do the martial arts become a priority when a nation is confronted by an enemy from beyond its borders, but it is an unfortunate commentary on today's civilization that many children and adults enroll in self-defense and weapons classes so that they can protect themselves from predators on the streets of many urban areas.

Derivation of Aims

The aims of education are derived from examining the needs of children and youth in our American society, from analyzing our culture, and from studying the various needs of our society. Given the historic development of nations with their own institutions, mores, and values, and often their own language, no two countries exhibit exactly the same needs. One does not have to be an anthropologist to recognize that the needs of Japanese, Chinese, Russian, English, Mexican, or Tahitian youngsters are not identical to those of American youth. The automobile, for example, has become a "need" of American high school youth if we judge by the school parking lot crammed with vehicles of students. Nor is it a rare occurrence any more to see not only American adults in stores or cars with a cellular phone glued to their ears but also students trotting around school campuses with this "needed" application of satellite technology. Laptop computers and hand-held electronic organizers with all the bells and whistles are perceived as "needs" in today's society.

Few countries have such a heterogeneous population as the United States. A comment often heard about people in the Sunbelt cities of America, "Everybody here is from some place else," might be extended to America in toto. We are a nation of immigrants who have brought, as some say, both the best and the worst traits of the societies that we left. We cannot even claim the Native Americans, who were here first, as indigenous to America, for theory holds that they themselves migrated out of Asia across the Bering Strait.

Such heterogeneity makes it extremely difficult to reach consensus on aims of education and particularly on values central to aims. Many years ago the National Education Association attempted to identify moral and spiritual values that it believed should be taught in the public schools.[4] They listed the following ten values:

1. human personality
2. moral responsibility
3. institutions as the servants of men
4. common consent
5. devotion to truth
6. respect for excellence
7. moral equality
8. brotherhood
9. the pursuit of happiness
10. spiritual enrichment

The assumption was made that these are common values held by a majority of the people of the society at that particular time. On how many of these values could we still reach consensus? James Patterson and Peter Kim surveyed in 1991 the status of Americans' adherence to moral values and found a pronounced absence of consensus on values. Some of the beliefs and behaviors revealed by this study run counter to the more traditional conception of moral and spiritual values.[5] The specter of indoctrination has loomed so large that educators are often hesitant to identify broad-based, common, secular values to which Americans as a whole can subscribe.

We are witnessing renewed interest in character education in the schools. William J. Bennett and Michael S. Josephson, for example, have directed attention to the need for ethical values in our society. *The Book of Virtues: A Treasury of Great Moral Stories*, edited by Bennett, spoke to values such as self-discipline and faith.[6]

Josephson, founder of the Institute of Ethics, has enlisted the aid of a number of national organizations to foster character education. Input gathered from young people and adults identified six broad ethical values worthy of promoting: trustworthiness, respect, responsibility, fairness and justice, caring, and citizenship. Each of these broad values subsumes a number of related values.[7] The U.S. Congress gave added emphasis to the teaching of values when it proclaimed in 1997 a National Character Counts Week to be celebrated in October. Affirming an interest in character education, the U.S. Department of Education in the spring of 1999 awarded grants under its Partnership in Education Pilot Projects for school districts and communities in nine states (Georgia, Illinois, Kansas, New Hampshire, New Mexico, North Carolina, North Dakota, Oklahoma, and Pennsylvania) to develop programs to teach common values and ethics. Finding common ground may prove somewhat difficult considering the Gallup Organization's poll of moral views and values that revealed the gap between values held by people between 18 and 24 and people older than 65 on the morality of abortion, cloning of animals, homosexuality, and premarital sex.[8]

The extensive list of committees, educational and service organizations, and schools and school districts subscribing to the principles of Character Counts! attests to the broad public support for teaching values to young people in school and out.[9] We will return to the question of teaching values when we examine the issue of religion in the schools in Chapter 15.

Salad Bowl versus Melting Pot. As our heterogeneous population reveals plural rather than common values, the "salad bowl" concept now challenges the old "melting pot" idea. Some people argue that since few, if any, common values exist in our society, we should no longer strive to assimilate values but should collect and assemble the diverse values in a saladlike concoction that preserves the essence of each. If we make this dilemma an either/or question, we create a false dichotomy. We need the salad bowl concept to preserve the values on which Americans are divided, such as materialistic versus nonmaterialistic goals, pro-choice versus "right to life," and sectarian versus secular goals. On the other hand, we need the melting pot concept to preserve fundamental, overarching values that guide us as a nation.

In recent years the salad bowl/melting pot controversy has intensified. Whether to promote multicultural values or common values of American society is a highly charged issue both in public schools and on college campuses. We will return to this issue in Chapter 15. As we examine statements of aims of education, we soon discover that these statements are, in effect, philosophical positions based on some set of values and are derived from an analysis of society and its children and youth.

Statements by Prominent Individuals and Groups

To gain a perception of statements of educational aims, let's sample a few of the better known ones proffered by various individuals and groups over the years. In 1916 John Dewey described the functions of education in a number of ways, including its socialization of the child and its facilitation of personal growth.[10] Putting these concepts into the form of aims of education, we could say that, according to Dewey, the aims of education are (1) to socialize the young, thereby transforming both the young and society, and (2) to develop the individual in all his or her physical, mental, moral, and emotional capacities.

Dewey made it clear that the school is an agency for socializing the child:

I believe that all education proceeds by the participation of the individual in the social consciousness of the race . . . the only true education comes through the stimulation of the child's powers by the demands of the social situations in which he finds himself . . . this educational process has two sides—one psychological and one sociological—and that neither can be subordinated to the other, or neglected, without evil results following. . . . In sum, I believe that the individual who is to be educated is a social individual, and that society is an organic union of individuals. . . . I believe that the school is primarily a social institution.[11]

Dewey elaborated on his conception of education as growth in the following terms:

One net conclusion is that life is development, and that developing, growing, is life. Translated into its educational equivalents, that means (i) that the educational process has no end beyond itself; it is its own end; and that (ii) the educational process is one of continual reorganizing, reconstructing, transforming. . . . Normal child and normal adult alike, in other words, are engaged in growing. . . . Since in reality there is nothing to which growth is relative save more growth, there is nothing to which education is subordinate save more education.[12]

The National Education Association's Commission on the Reorganization of Secondary Education in 1918 spoke to the role of education in our democratic society in this way: "Education in a democracy, both within and without the school, should develop in each individual the knowledge, interests, ideals, habits, and powers whereby he will find his place and use that place to shape both himself and society toward even nobler ends."[13]

The Educational Policies Commission of the National Education Association in 1937 related the aim of education to democracy as follows:

In any realistic definition of education for the United States, therefore, must appear the whole philosophy and practice of democracy. Education cherishes and inculcates its moral values, disseminates knowledge necessary to its functioning, spreads information relevant to its institutions and economy, keeps alive the creative and sustaining spirit without which the latter is dead.[14]

In 1943—in the midst of World War II—James B. Conant, president of Harvard University, appointed a committee of professors from the fields of education and the liberal arts and sciences to examine the place of general (i.e., required, liberal) education in American society. The Harvard Committee on General Education took the position that the aim of education was "to prepare an individual to become an expert both in some particular vocation or art and in the general art of the free man and the citizen."[15] To accomplish this aim the Harvard Committee recommended a prescribed set of subjects, including English, science, mathematics, and the social studies, for all secondary school pupils.[16]

Statements of aims of education repeatedly address great themes like democracy and the progress of humanity. In 1961 the National Education Association's Educational Policies Commission elaborated on the role of education in solving the problems of humanity:

Many profound changes are occurring in the world today, but there is a fundamental force contributing to all of them. That force is the expanding role accorded in modern life to the rational powers of man. By using these powers to increase his knowledge, man is attempting to solve the riddles of life, space, and time which have long intrigued him.[17]

Before the Committee on Appropriations of the United States House of Representatives of the Eighty-Seventh Congress in 1962, Vice-Admiral Hyman G. Rickover, generally acknowledged as the father of the nuclear submarine, testified on distinctions between American and British educational systems and formulated for the committee the aims of education as he saw them:

> There is general agreement abroad that a school must accomplish three difficult tasks: First, it must transmit to the pupil a substantial body of knowledge; second, it must develop in him the necessary intellectual skill to apply this knowledge to the problems he will encounter in later life; and third, it must inculcate in him the habit of judging issues on the basis of verified fact and logical reasoning.[18]

Mortimer J. Adler expressed the aim of education and schooling as follows: "The ultimate goal of the educational process is to help human beings become educated persons. Schooling is the preparatory stage; it forms the habit of learning and provides the means for continuing to learn after all schooling is completed."[19]

John I. Goodlad addressed the themes of social purposes served by the schools, educational goals and aims, and school goals. He divided the school goals into four categories: academic, vocational, social and civic, and personal. He and his colleagues analyzed approximately a hundred goals from various sources and refined them into a list of ten categories that they saw as encompassing generally accepted goals for schooling in the United States: mastery of basic skills and fundamental processes, intellectual development, career education–vocational education, interpersonal understandings, citizenship participation, enculturation, moral and ethical character, emotional and physical well-being, creativity and aesthetic expression, and self-realization.[20]

Theodore R. Sizer, who was instrumental in the formation of the Coalition of Essential Schools in 1984, wove into his narrative of the fictitious Franklin High School the purposes of schooling and at the same time pointed out an American dilemma: ". . . some Americans do not see the schools as engines both of information and of intellectual liberation. Indeed, they find the latter—especially when so described—to be intolerable."[21]

Conflict over what education should be like dates back to ancient times as Herbert M. Kliebard pointed out in quoting from Aristotle's *Politics:*

> At present opinion is divided about the subjects of education. All do not take the same view of what should be learned by the young, either with a view to plain goodness or with a view to the best life possible; nor is opinion clear whether education should be directed mainly to understanding, or mainly to moral character. If we look at actual practice, the result is sadly confusing; it throws no light on the problem whether the proper studies to be followed are those which are useful in life, or those which make for goodness, or those which advance the bounds of knowledge. Each sort of study receives some votes in favor.[22]

This amazingly pertinent observation from ancient Greece more than 2000 years ago might well have come from the word processor of an author in the twenty-first century. In Chapter 9 you will encounter additional beliefs of individuals and groups about the aims of education when we examine some of the recommendations made in recent years for reform of the schools. You will also encounter in Chapter 15 philosophical and often conflicting positions and recommendations of other individuals and groups demanding reform and restructuring of the schools.

Statements from the Federal Government

In recent years the federal government has issued three influential statements of aims: America 2000 (1990), Goals 2000: The Educate America Act (1994), and the No Child Left Behind Act (2001).

America 2000.   In September 1989 at the University of Virginia President George H. W. Bush and the National Governors' Association developed a statement of six performance goals. The president presented this statement to the nation in his State of the Union address in January 1990 and announced in the following spring proposals for implementing the goals. Known as *America 2000*, the proposals included the creation of 535 experimental schools (one in each congressional district) for the purpose of demonstrating effective curricula and instructional techniques; voluntary national examinations in English, mathematics, science, history, and geography at the fourth-, eighth-, and twelfth-grade levels; and parental choice of school.

The six performance goals to be reached by the year 2000 were as follows:

1. All children in America will start school ready to learn.
2. The high school graduation rate will increase to at least ninety percent.
3. American students will leave grades four, eight, and twelve having demonstrated competency in challenging subject matter, including English, mathematics, science, history, and geography, and every school in America will ensure that all students learn to use their minds well, so they may be prepared for responsible citizenship, further learning, and productive employment in our modern economy.
4. U.S. students will be first in the world in science and mathematics achievement.
5. Every adult American will be literate and will possess the knowledge and skills necessary to compete in a global economy and to exercise the rights and responsibilities of citizenship.
6. Every school in America will be free of drugs and violence and will offer a disciplined environment conducive to learning.[23]

The proposals for implementing the goals were in keeping with recommendations of the 1990 Commission on the Skills of the American Workforce, which advocated national standards and national examinations.[24] The proposed goals met with varying reactions from educators around the country. Many educators welcomed realization of these noble goals but doubted very much that they could be reached in the short time to the year 2000. Educators have expressed concern about the lack of federal funding to implement the proposals, the effects of parental choice on the public schools, the expenditure of over 500 million dollars for experimental schools, and the burden of new national examinations.

Educators wondered about the need for new national examinations since the National Assessment of Educational Progress already assessed student achievement in thirty-seven states.[25] The new examinations, however, would purportedly concentrate more on thinking skills in the various disciplines than do current multiple-choice examinations.

National assessment tests, however, may lead to a national standardized curriculum, a possibility that some educators find unacceptable. These educators fear that national examinations will dictate the curriculum rather than vice versa. They also believe that a national curriculum would prevent schools from tailoring the curriculum to local needs. Some aver that national standards and assessments would penalize those students in educational and social settings where they have encountered barriers to learning.

The Congress moved to implement America 2000 by creating the National Council on Education Standards and Testing whose duty it was to oversee development of (1) national standards, beginning in the five disciplines: English, mathematics, science, history, and geography with the possibility of adding other disciplines at a later date and of (2) a voluntary system of national assessment based on the standards.

Piloting of new examinations began in seventeen states in the spring of 1992 under the direction of the New Standards Project formed by the University of Pittsburgh's Research and Development Center and the National Center on Education and the Economy. The Pew Charitable Trusts and the John D. and Catherine T. MacArthur Foundation provided substantial financial support to the New Standards Project.

That not all curriculum theorists subscribed to America 2000 can be seen in the remarks of Henry A. Giroux:

> Under the guise of attempting to revitalize the language of leadership and reform, these reports signify a dangerous attack on some of the most fundamental aspects of democratic public life and the social, moral, and political obligations of responsible, critical citizens.[26]

Goals 2000: The Educate America Act.   Following the initiative begun in the Bush administration, in the spring of 1994 the Congress passed and President Bill Clinton signed the Goals 2000: The Educate America Act authorizing federal support to the states for plans to improve the schools, reiterating in slightly edited form the six national goals earlier proposed, and adding the following two goals calling for staff development for teachers and increased parental involvement.

- The nation's teaching force will have access to programs for the continued improvement of their professional skills and the opportunity to acquire the knowledge and skills needed to instruct and prepare all American students for the next century.
- Every school will promote partnerships that will increase parental involvement and participation in promoting the social, emotional, and academic growth of children.[27]

Addressing Goals 2000: The Educate America Act, Maxine Greene saw problems with this "new national agenda for education" that called for achievement of subject-matter standards and for national assessment: the presumption that "it is realizable, poverty and inequality notwithstanding," "the implication that standards and tests can simply be imposed," and the "untapped diversity among American youth today."[28] Said Greene, "The familiar paradigms seem still to be in use; the need for alternative possibilities in the face of economic and demographic changes is repressed or ignored."[29]

Citing the family as the crucial element in raising educational standards, critics of the legislation decried the expenditure of millions of dollars, which they maintained would not guarantee improvement in the schools. They objected to involvement of the federal government in education which they believed takes autonomy away from the local schools and deprives them of their uniqueness.

It did not take a soothsayer to predict that the goals of the ambitious America 2000 and Goals 2000: The Educate America Act would not be realized by the year 2000. In fact, none of the goals had been fully achieved by that date.

No Child Left Behind Act of 2001 (NCLB).   Recognizing continuing deficiencies in education, the U.S. Congress ventured once again into the field of K–12 education, reauthorizing the Elementary and Secondary Education Act of 1965 in the form of the comprehensive PL 107-110, the No Child Left Behind Act of 2001. It was signed into law by President George W. Bush in January 2002. State educational agencies receive federal funding through grants to address the ten titles of the act, which are:

Title I: Improving the academic achievement of the disadvantaged with special attention to reading and literacy.

Title II: Preparing, training, and recruiting high quality teachers and principals.

Title III: Providing language instruction for limited English-proficient and immigrant students.

Title IV: Promoting 21st Century Schools: Safe and Drug-Free Schools and Communities.

Title V: Promoting informed parental choice and innovative programs.

Title VI: Improving academic achievement through accountability, flexibility, voluntary partnerships among the states, and the development of state assessments and standards.

Title VII: Meeting the educational and culturally related academic needs of American Indian, Native Hawaiian, and Alaska Native students.

Title VIII: Payments related to federal acquisition of real property and grants for school repairs and modernization.

Title IX: Provision regarding daily membership and attendance and definition of the terms used.

Title X: Provisions related to repeals, redesignations, and amendments to other statutes.[30]

The federal government obviously plays and will continue to play a fundamental role in identifying and promoting the aims of education in America.

You will note that the statements of aims of education cited in this chapter vary from advocacy of cognitive competencies alone to concern for the development of cognitive, affective, and psychomotor competencies. We will revisit NCLB and the issues of national standards and national assessment in Chapter 15.

PHILOSOPHIES OF EDUCATION

Greene defined philosophy as "a way of framing distinctive sorts of questions having to do with what is presupposed, perceived, intuited, believed, and known."[31] "Educational philosophy," wrote Greene, "is a matter of doing philosophy with respect to the educational enterprise as it engages the educator. . . . To do educational philosophy is to become critically conscious of what is involved in the complex business of teaching and learning."[32]

Statements of aims of education are positions taken that are based on a set of beliefs—a philosophy of education. Clearly, the authors of the illustrations of aims cited in the preceding section held certain assumptions about education, society, and how young people learn. An aim of education, then, is a statement of beliefs central to the author's philosophical creed that is directed to the mission of the school.

Four major philosophies of education have demanded the attention of educators. Only two of these philosophies appear to have large followings in today's schools. Although these philosophies are known by various names and there are schools of philosophy within schools, we shall refer to these four as *reconstructionism, progressivism, essentialism, and perennialism.*

These four schools of thought can be charted from the most liberal to the most conservative as shown in Figure 6.1. At the far left is the most liberal of these four philosophies, reconstructionism, and at the far right, the most conservative, perennialism. Although essentialism and progressivism have been widely accepted and practiced by educators, neither reconstructionism nor perennialism has found widespread endorsement in the schools. The American public appears to be far too conservative to espouse reconstructionism, and at the same time far too liberal to accept perennialism, as a prevailing philosophy. Since reconstructionism and perennialism have

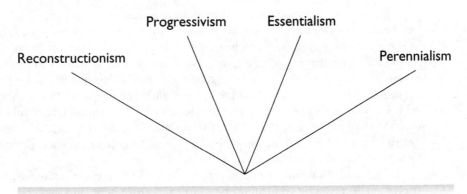

FIGURE 6.1 Four Philosophies of Education

had less impact on the schools than the two other philosophies, we will discuss them first and then come back to the two more pervasive philosophies: essentialism and progressivism.

A word of explanation about the following discussion: Although this text chooses to elaborate on *philosophies of education*, we must recognize that *philosophies of education* stem from more general *philosophies of life*. As J. Donald Butler commented, ". . . aims of education cannot just be pulled out of a hat, but must be derived from more fundamental and general thinking about value, reality, and knowledge."[33] Allan C. Ornstein and Francis P. Hunkins attributed the curriculum worker's philosophy to "his or her life experiences, common sense, social and economic background, education, and general beliefs about himself or herself and people."[34] Discussion of general philosophies is beyond the scope of this text. Numerous books describe various schools of philosophy. I would recommend two excellent, readable references:

Butler (see bibliography). Butler described naturalism, idealism, realism, and pragmatism. He included also treatments of existentialism and language analysis.

Will Durant (see bibliography). Durant described the thinking of fifteen great philosophers.

Reconstructionism

Hilda Taba pointed out that John Dewey "consistently saw the function of the school in both psychological and social terms."[35] She explained:

A flowering of the idea that education is a social process, the primary and the most effective instrument of social reconstructionism, came with the work and writings of Dewey and his followers. The main thesis of this group was that the school is not merely a residual institution to maintain things as they are; education has a creative function to play in shaping of individuals and through them in the shaping of the culture. . . . In subsequent development one fork of this dual orientation of Dewey on the function of education matured into an elaboration of the social responsibilities of the school, while the other centered more emphatically on individual development.[36]

Branching out from Dewey's philosophy, the reconstructionists followed a path that led them to propose using the school to achieve what they considered to be improvements in society. George S. Counts, in his much-discussed book, *Dare the School Build a New Social Order?*, challenged educators to reconsider the role of schools in our society.[37] In essence, reconstructionism holds that the school should not simply transmit the cultural heritage or simply study social problems but should become an agency for solving political and social problems. The subject matter to which all youngsters should be exposed consists of unsolved, often controversial, problems of the day such as unemployment, health needs, housing needs, and ethnic problems. Group consensus is the methodology by which solutions to the problems are sought.

Theodore Brameld made clear the values of the reconstructionists, referring to twelve needs including companionship, health, nourishment, and shelter.[38]

Some educators agree that young people should consider pressing social, economic, and political problems and even attempt to reach consensus on possible solutions. They do take exception, however, when teachers propose their own specific solutions which raises the specter of indoctrination, a practice unacceptable to most schools of philosophy.

With its heavy emphasis on controversial social issues and its major premise to make the school a primary agency for social change, reconstructionism has not made great inroads into the largely middle-class, centrist schools of the United States.

Perennialism

In the tradition of Plato, Aristotle, and the scholasticism of the Catholic thinker St. Thomas Aquinas, the contemporary perennialists see the aims of education as the disciplining of the mind, the development of the ability to reason, and the pursuit of truth. Unlike progressivists, who, as we shall see later, hold that truth is relative and changing, the perennialists believe that truth is eternal, everlasting, and unchanging. In their pursuit of truth, the secular perennialists joined hands with the sectarian perennialists. The secular perennialists advocated a highly academic curriculum with emphasis on grammar, rhetoric, logic, classical and modern languages, mathematics, and—at the heart of the perennialist curriculum—the great books of the Western world. In the great books of the past, one searched for truth, which in perennialist thinking is the same today as it was then and always shall be. To these academic disciplines the sectarian perennialists would add study of the Bible and theological writings.

Robert M. Hutchins, former president of the University of Chicago, was perhaps the best known exponent of the philosophy of perennialism in America. Hutchins and other perennialists eschewed immediate needs of the learners, specialized education, and vocational training. Hutchins made these points clear when he stated: "The ideal education is not an ad hoc education, not an education directed to immediate needs; it is not a specialized education, or a preprofessional education; it is not a utilitarian education. It is an education calculated to develop the mind."[39]

The perennialist agrees with the essentialist that education is preparation for life but opposes the progressivist who holds that education *is* life. If taken seriously, perennialism would afford an education suitable to that small percentage of students who possess high verbal and academic aptitude.

The perennialist looks backward for the answers to social problems. We must wonder, for example, how useful Lucretius' *De Rerum Natura* is for this and future generations in solving environmental problems. One criticism that appears to be overlooked in most critiques of perennialism is its ethnocentricity. The perennialist showcase features the great books of the Western world, considered by some as the greatest works of all humanity. Excluded are the great writings of the Eastern world, of which many of us are abysmally ignorant. An outstanding curriculum project would bring together, perhaps under the auspices of UNESCO, a group of world scholars who would draw up a set of great books of the entire world. East and West have much to say to each other.

In conclusion, perennialism has not proved an attractive philosophy for our educational system.

Essentialism

Historically, essentialism and progressivism have succeeded in commanding the allegiance of the American public. Both have been and remain potent contenders for public and professional support. Walker and Soltis highlighted the conflict between the two schools of thought when they said:

> The first half of the twentieth century witnessed a running battle between progressive educators, who saw in the ideas of Dewey and other progressives new ways to think about the curriculum, and the traditionalists, who were sure that the basic curriculum did not need change because it had proven itself essential to the education of individuals who would maintain an intellectually sound and civilized society. Many battles were fought over these opposing views, leaving a profound mark on elementary school practices especially and curriculum theory generally that is still visible today.[40]

With only slight inaccuracies, we can mark the periods of supremacy of one school over another. From 1635 with the establishment of the Boston Latin School to 1896 with the creation of John Dewey's Laboratory School at the University of Chicago—a period of 261 years—the doctrines of essentialism (with a patina of sectarian perennialism from 1635 to the advent of the English High School in 1824) held sway. Starting in 1896, moving slowly, and gathering steam in the 1930s and 1940s until 1957 (the year of *Sputnik*), progressivism emerged for a short time as the most popular educational philosophy. Its path was somewhat rocky, however, strewn as it was with the loss of the Progressive Education Association and with essentialist criticisms from sources like the Council on Basic Education, Arthur Bestor, Max Rafferty, John Keats, Albert Lynd, and Mortimer Smith. Since 1957 essentialism has reclaimed its predominant position. Since the late 1990s, however, the fostering of pupil self-esteem has been strongly emphasized; contemporary essentialist critics of education would say "overemphasized."

The aim of education according to essentialist tenets is the transmission of the cultural heritage. Unlike the reconstructionists, who would actively change society, the essentialists seek to preserve it. Again, unlike the reconstructionists, who would seek to adjust society to its populace, the essentialists seek to adjust men and women to society.

Cognitive Goals.   The goals of the essentialist are primarily cognitive and intellectual. Organized courses are the vehicles for transmitting the culture, and emphasis is placed on mental discipline. The three R's and the "hard" (i.e., academic) subjects form the core of the essentialist curriculum. In one sense the essentialist tailors the child to the curriculum, whereas the progressivist tailors the curriculum to the child.

The subject matter curriculum, which we will examine in Chapter 9, is an essentialist plan for curriculum organization, and the techniques of Assign-Study-Recite-Test are the principal methods. Erudition, the ability to reproduce that which has been learned, is highly valued, and education is perceived as preparation for some future purpose—for college, vocation, life.

In spite of the mitigating influence of Jean Jacques Rousseau, Johann Pestalozzi, and Friedrich Froebel, essentialism has for generations dominated European education and all the areas of the globe to which it has been exported. Essentialist thinking fits in well with centralized administrative structures as represented in the European and most colonial ministries of education. The ministries, following essentialist concepts, can select, proffer, and control the content to which young people are exposed. They can reward and promote the young in respect to their mastery of subject matter. They can screen youth for the universities on the basis of stringent examinations that call for recapitulation of subject matter.

William C. Bagley, one of the foremost advocates of essentialistic philosophy, strongly criticized the child-centered approach and urged teachers to follow essentialistic principles.[41] Championing emphasis on the academic disciplines, James B. Conant, in a series of reports on the junior and senior high school conducted in the late 1950s and mid-1960s, revealed an essentialistic outlook in his major recommendations.[42]

Behavioristic Principles. The essentialists found the principles of the behavioristic school of psychology to be particularly harmonious with their philosophical beliefs. V. T. Thayer called attention to the urbanization of America and immigration taking place in the late 1800s and the early 1900s in explaining the reason for the essentialists' espousal of behavioristic principles:

> The changes in American society to which we have drawn attention affected education on all levels. But the contrast between programs of education keyed, on the one hand, to the inner nature of the young person and, on the other hand, to the demands of society were most obvious on the junior high school level. Here genetic psychology was emphasizing the dynamic and distinctive potentialities of the young person, with the clear implication that nature was to be followed; whereas life outside the school, in the home and community, in business and industry, stressed the importance of education for adjustment, one that would give specific and detailed attention to the formation of desirable habits and skills and techniques. Confronted with this necessity of choice, educators turned to a psychology that would further education for adjustment.[43]

Behaviorism casts the learner in a passive role as the recipient of the many stimuli to which he or she must respond. Known in its variants as connectionism, association, S-R (stimulus-response) bond, and conditioning, behaviorism brought into the classroom drill, programmed instruction, teaching machines, standardized testing, and, of course, behavioral objectives. The movement toward specification and demonstration of competencies in both general and teacher education owes a debt to the behaviorists. Selection of content by the adult for the immature learner and reinforcement, preferably immediate and positive, are central to behavioristic thought. Noted among the behaviorists are Ivan Pavlov, the Russian scientist who performed the classic experiment in which a dog was taught to salivate at the ringing of a bell; John B. Watson, who maintained that with the right stimuli he could shape a child into whatever he wished; Edward L. Thorndike, who is considered by many to be the father of the controversial standardized test; and B. F. Skinner, who popularized teaching machines.

Teachers of the behavioristic-essentialist school fragment content into logical, sequential pieces and prescribe the pieces the learner will study. Typically, they begin instruction by giving the learners a rule, concept, or model (for example, the formula for finding the area of a rectangle) and then provide many opportunities to practice (drill) using this guide. With adequate practice the learner can presumably use the rule, concept, or model whenever he or she needs it. The learning has become a habitual part of the individual's behavior. Though human beings are prone to forget content not used regularly, the behaviorists and essentialists maintain that if the content has been thoroughly mastered, it can easily be retrieved.

Current and continuing emphasis on the basic skills and the academic disciplines clearly derives from the essentialists. Thus, present educational programs and practices maintain a strong essentialistic orientation.

Progressivism

In the late nineteenth and early twentieth centuries progressivism swept through the educational structure of America, challenging the time-honored doctrines of essentialism. Led by John Dewey, William H. Kilpatrick, John Childs, and Boyd Bode, the progressivists maintained that it was time to subordinate subject matter to the learner. Borrowing from some European philosophers like Rousseau, who advocated rearing a child in a relaxed environment without forcing learning, the progressivists created the child-centered school. Its prototype was the University of Chicago Laboratory School. Moving east from Chicago to New York, John Dewey formulated progressive beliefs in a series of publications that included *Democracy and Education*,[44] *Experience and Education*,[45] *How We Think*,[46] and *My Pedagogic Creed*.[47] By insisting that the needs and interests of learners must be considered and by recognizing that learners bring their bodies, emotions, and spirits to school along with their minds, progressivism captured the attention and allegiance of educators.

Dewey clearly stated the differences between the essential and the progressive curriculum:

> The fundamental factors in the educative process are the immature, underdeveloped being; and certain social aims, meanings, values incarnate in the matured experience of the adult. The educative process is the due interaction of these forces. . . . From these elements of conflict grow up different educational sects. One school fixes its attention upon the importance of subject matter of the curriculum as compared with the contents of the child's own experience. . . . Hence the moral: ignore and minimize the child's individual peculiarities, whims, and experiences. . . . As educators our work is precisely to substitute for these superficial and casual affairs stable and well-ordered realities; and these are found in studies and lessons.
>
> Subdivide each topic into studies; each study into lessons; each lesson into specific facts and formulae. Let each child proceed step by step to master each one of these separate parts, and at last he will have covered the entire ground. . . . Problems of instruction are problems of procuring texts giving logical parts and sequences, and of presenting these portions in class in a similar definite and graded way. Subject matter furnishes the end, and it determines method. The child is simply the immature being who is to be matured; he is the superficial being who is to be deepened; his is narrow experience which is to be widened. It is his to receive, to accept. . . .
>
> Not so, says the other sect. The child is the starting point, the center, and the end. His development, his growth, is the ideal. It alone furnishes the standard. To the growth

of the child all studies are subservient; they are instruments valued as they serve the needs of growth. Personality, character, is more than subject matter. Not knowledge or information, but self-realization, is the goal. . . . Moreover, subject matter never can be got into the child from without. Learning is active. It involves reaching out of the mind. It involves organic assimilation starting from within. . . . It is he and not the subject matter which determines both quality and quantity of learning.

The only significant method is the method of the mind as it reaches out and assimilates. Subject matter is but spiritual food, possible nutritive material. It cannot digest itself; it cannot of its own accord turn into bone and muscle and blood. The source of whatever is dead, mechanical, and formal in schools is found precisely in the subordination of the life and experience of the child to the curriculum. It is because of this that "study" has become a synonym for what is irksome, and a "lesson" identical with a task.[48]

To the progressives then, education is not a product to be learned—for example, facts and motor skills—but a process that continues as long as one lives. To their way of thinking a child learns best when actively experiencing his or her world as opposed to passively absorbing preselected content. If experiences in school are designed to meet the needs and interests of individual learners, it follows that no single pattern of subject matter can be appropriate for all learners. Brameld explained this point of view held by progessivists like Dewey and Harold Rugg:[49]

The proper subject matter of a curriculum is any experience that is educative. This means that the good school is concerned with every kind of learning that helps students, young and old, to grow. No single body of content, no system of courses, no universal method of teaching is inappropriate. For, like experience itself, the needs and interests of individuals and groups vary from place to place, from time to time, from culture to culture.[50]

The progressivist position that the child should undergo educative experiences in the here and now has led to the clichélike indicators of progressive philosophy: "education is life" and "learning by doing." The progressivists urged schools to provide for learners' individual differences in the broadest sense of the term, encompassing mental, physical, emotional, spiritual, social, and cultural differences. In both thought and practice, progressivism shows concern for the student, society, and subject matter, placing the student at the center of the learning process.

At the heart of progressive thinking is an abiding faith in democracy. Hence the progressivists see little place for authoritarian practices in the classroom and the school. They do not hold with the essentialists that the learners are immature subjects of adult preceptors and administrators but rather consider them partners in the educational process. Teachers influenced by progressive thinking see themselves as counselors to pupils and facilitators of learning rather than expounders of subject matter. Cooperation is fostered in the classroom rather than competition. Individual growth in relationship to one's ability is considered more important than growth in comparison to others.

A concern for the many unresolved problems of democracy led to a split in the progressive camp, with reconstructionists advocating that the schools become the instrument for improving society. It has been mentioned that the perennialist considers truth to be absolute, enduring, and found in the wisdom of the past; the essentialist presents the cultural heritage as truth, whereas the progressivist holds truth to be relative, changing, and in many cases as yet to be discovered. Espousing principles of pragmatism, progressivists see education as a continuing search for the truth utilizing whatever sources are needed to discover that truth.[51]

Scientific Method.   The scientific method, known also as reflective thinking, problem solving, and practical intelligence, became both a goal and a technique in the progressive school. The scientific method was both a skill to be achieved and a means of finding solutions to problems. In its simplest elements the scientific method consists of five steps:

- identifying a problem
- forming a hypothesis or hypotheses
- gathering data
- analyzing data
- drawing conclusions

The progressivists proposed the scientific method as a general method to be applied in any area of human endeavor. It is generally accepted for both unsophisticated problem solving and for sophisticated research. Taba offered a very legitimate caution about accepting this method of problem solving as complete training in the ability to think:

> But to maintain that all aspects of thinking are involved in problem solving or in the process of inquiry is one thing. To assume that following these steps also provides sufficient training in all elements of thinking is something else. For training purposes it is important both to master the various aspects of elements of thinking—such as generalizing, concept formation, analysis of assumptions, application of principle—and to use these processes in an organized sequence of problem solving. . . . If these elements are not consciously recognized and mastered, problem solving can turn into a ritualistic process of defining any kind of question, collecting any kind of data, hypothesizing any variety of solutions, and so on.
>
> Subsuming all reflective thinking under the category of problem solving has also caused certain elements of thinking to be neglected, especially those which, although involved in problem solving, are not fully attended to *while* solving problems. Among these are such mental processes as concept formation, abstracting, and various methods of induction.[52]

Experimentalist Psychology.   In behaviorism the essentialists found learning theories harmonious with their philosophy. The progressivists did not have to look far for theories of learning compatible with their views on education. They found a wealth of ideas in the experimentalist psychology of Charles S. Peirce and William James: in the field (gestalt) psychology of Max Wertheimer, Wolfgang Köhler, Kurt Koffka, and Kurt Lewin; and in the perceptual psychology of Earl Kelley, Donald Snygg, Arthur Combs, Abraham Maslow, and Carl Rogers.

The experimentalists encourage the active involvement of the learner in all his or her capacities in the educational process. Noting the influence of James throughout the twentieth century, Brameld credited James's *Principles of Psychology* as "still, in various respects, the foremost single achievement in the field by any American scholar–scientist. . . ."[53]

Gestalt Psychology.   In contrast to the behaviorists' presentation of subject matter in parts, the gestaltists concentrated on wholes, the "big picture," so to speak. They advised teachers to organize subject matter in such a way that learners could see the relationships among the various parts. This advice fit in perfectly with the progressivists' concern for "the whole child." The unit method of teaching in which content from all pertinent areas is organized into a holistic plan in order to study a particular topic or problem became a popular and enduring instructional technique. Writing unit plans is common practice among teachers today. For example, the topic of the Victorian Era provides a unifying theme for the study of the history, philosophy, government, literature, science, and fine arts of the period.

The gestaltists pointed out that the learners achieve insight when they discern relationships among elements of a given situation. The gestaltists encourage inquiry or discovery learning in order to sharpen the skill of insight. Both the experimentalists and gestaltists agree that the closer content to be mastered is to real-life situations and the closer problems are to the previous experiences of the learner, the more likelihood there is for successful mastery of the material.

Perceptual Psychology.   Of more recent vintage, perceptual psychology focused on the development of the learner's self-concept. The goal of the perceptualists is the development of the "self-actualizing" or "fully functioning" personality. Abraham H. Maslow defined self-actualization as follows:

> Self-actualization is defined in various ways, but a solid core of agreement is perceptible. All definitions accept or imply: (a) acceptance and expression of the inner core of self, i.e., actualization of these latent capacities and potentialities, "full functioning," availability of the human and personal essence; and (b) minimal presence of ill health, neurosis, psychosis, or loss or diminution of the basic human and personal capacities.[54]

The perceptualists concentrate their efforts on developing persons who feel adequate. Arthur W. Combs listed the following "four characteristics of the perceptual field which always seem to underlie the behavior of truly adequate persons":[55] (1) a positive view of the self, (2) identification with others, (3) openness to experience and acceptance, and (4) possession of a rich field of perceptions gained from both formal schooling and informal sources.[56]

According to the perceptual psychologists, teachers must help young people to develop an adequate concept of themselves and must be willing to deal with both their perceptions of the world and the world as it is. The perceptualist maintains that it is more important to know how the learner perceives the facts than what the facts of a given situation are. We all have a tendency to selectively perceive our environment. We recognize familiar faces before we pay attention to unfamiliar persons. We pick out words we know and ignore those that we do not know. We are sure that our version of the truth of any situation is the right one, for that is the way we perceive it. The perceptualists emphasize dealing with people's perceptions of the world around them.

An individual's feeling of adequacy or inadequacy can often be attributed to other people's perceptions. If a child is told by a parent that he or she is a weakling, the child may agree that it is so. If a child is told by teachers that he or she has an artistic talent, the child may seek to develop that ability. If a child is told that he or she is a poor reader, lacks aptitude for mathematics, or is short on musical talent, the child may accept these perceptions and internalize them. The child is exemplifying then what is referred to in the literature as the self-fulfilling prophecy. We are not only what we eat, as health food devotees tell us—we are what others have made us, as the perceptual psychologists maintain. Combs described how the self-concept is learned in the following passage:

> People *learn* who they are and what they are from the ways in which they have been treated by those who surround them in the process of their growing up. . . . People discover their self-concepts from the kinds of experiences they have had with life; not from telling, but from experience. People develop feelings that they are liked, wanted, acceptable, and able from *having been* liked, wanted, accepted, and from having been successful. One learns that he is these things, not from being told so, but only through the experience of *being treated as though he were so.* Here is the key to what must be done to produce more adequate people. To produce a positive self, it is necessary to provide experiences that teach individuals they are positive people.[57]

The perceptualists attacked the notion that children must experience failure. Said Combs, "Actually, the best guarantee we have that a person will be able to deal with the future effectively is that he has been successful in the past. People learn that they are able, not from failure, but from success."[58]

The progressive philosophers identified readily with the experimentalist, gestalt, and perceptual schools of psychology. Their combined efforts to humanize education captured the imagination of educators, particularly those in teacher education, flourished for a relatively brief period, peaked, but left an indelible mark on our educational system. Because of progressivism, essentialism will never be the same.

Critical Inquiry.   You will encounter in your readings discussions of *critical inquiry.* According to Kenneth A. Sirotnik,

> critical inquiry is a rigorous, time-consuming, collaborative, informed, school-based dialectic around generic questions such as: What is going on in the name of X? (X is a placeholder for things like educational goals and schooling functions; instructional practices like the use of time, tracking students, and achievement testing; organizational practices like leadership, decision making, and communication, etc.). How did it come to be that way? Whose interests are being served (and not being served) by the way things are? What information and knowledge do we have—and need to get—that bear upon the issues? . . . Is this the way we want it? . . . What are we going to *do* about all this? . . .[59]

Noting that goal statements for the public schools often differ from classroom realities, Sirotnik would view the following as more accurate statements of what goes on: "to develop in students abilities to think linearly, depend on authority, speak when spoken to, work alone, become socially apathetic, learn passively and nonexperientially, recall information, follow instructions, compartmentalize knowledge, and so on."[60]

"At the heart of critical inquiry, therefore," said Sirotnik, "is the willingness and ability of people to engage in competent discourse and communication."[61]

Constructivist Psychology. Like experimentalist, gestalt, and perceptual psychology, constructivism complements progressive philosophy. Constructivists hold that the teacher is a facilitator of learning, students must be taught to take responsibility for their own learning, learning is an active process (recall the progressives' "learning by doing"), learning must be present in ways meaningful to students, basic skills will be learned in authentic situations not by separate concentration on the skills themselves. Numerous programs and practices in schools today follow constructivist doctrine.

Nell Noddings explained:

> Constructivism—variously described as a philosophy, an epistemology, a cognitive position, or a pedagogical orientation—currently dominates mathematics and science education. One of its basic premises is that all knowledge is constructed knowledge; knowledge is not the result of passive reception. This premise is common to all forms of constructivism and is also a basic tenet of cognitive psychology. . . . Constructivists in education trace their roots . . . to [Jean] Piaget.[62]

Like other schools of psychology, constructivism does not dictate any particular program or method of instruction to accomplish its aim—the development of thinking individuals able to use knowledge effectively in society.

Constructivism is accepted by many educators, rejected by others. As examples of constructivist practices we can cite whole language, authentic assessment, guided discovery, holistic grading, and integrated curriculum. Karen H. Harris and Steve Graham pointed out that the "back-to-basics" movement was a backlash against constructivist practices.[63] The public (and many teachers) do not appear ready to fully espouse constructivist practices. As often happens, however, teachers commonly blend elements of constructivism with more traditional approaches.

The Eight-Year Study. The cause of the progressives was boosted by the Eight-Year Study, conducted by the Progressive Education Association between 1933 and 1941. Many educators recognize this study as one of the most significant pieces of educational research ever conducted in the United States. There have been few longitudinal studies that followed subjects over a period of years. Few studies have been as sweeping or have involved as many people. Students, high school teachers and administrators, curriculum consultants, researchers, and college professors all played significant roles in the study.

The Progressive Education Association was disenchanted with the typical high school college preparatory curriculum with its customary prescribed constants required for college admission. The Association wanted to see more flexibility in the secondary school curriculum but realized that such a change would not be possible as long as the colleges demanded a prescribed set of courses. It therefore enlisted the cooperation of more than 300 colleges and universities that agreed to accept graduates from a limited number of high schools without regard to the usual college entrance requirements. Obtaining the cooperation of so many colleges and universities for an experiment of this nature, which might shatter traditional notions of what is needed to succeed in college, was a feat in itself. Wilford M. Aikin, H. H. Giles, S. P. McCutchen, Ralph W. Tyler, and A. N. Zechiel were instrumental in conducting the study.[64]

The colleges and universities consented to admit graduates from thirty public and private schools regardless of their programs for a five-year period, from 1936 to 1941. Beginning in 1933 these thirty experimental schools were able to modify their programs in any way they saw fit.

Once admitted to cooperating colleges and universities, graduates of the experimental schools were matched with counterparts in the same institution who came from conventional high schools, and their performance in college was analyzed. More than 1,400 matched pairs of students were involved in this study. The findings of the Eight-Year Study are summarized as follows:

> The graduates of the experimental schools, as it turned out, did as well as or better than their counterparts in college in all subjects except foreign languages. The graduates of the experimental schools excelled their counterparts in scholastic honors, leadership positions, study habits, intellectual curiosity, and extraclass activities. The Eight-Year Study showed rather conclusively that a single pattern of required courses is not essential for success in college.[65]

The Eight-Year Study gave impetus to novel curriculum experiments like the core curriculum, which along with the progressivist experience curriculum will be discussed in Chapter 9.

Decline of Progressivism.   In spite of its contributions—placing the child at the center of the educational process, treating the whole child, appealing to children's needs and interests, providing for individual differences, and emphasizing reflective thinking—progressivism has declined in acceptance by both the public and educators. It is probably not too far from the truth to maintain that the public was never completely enamored of progressive doctrines.

It was not the Soviet Union's *Sputnik* in 1957 per se, followed by the panicky rush to the "substantive" courses—science, mathematics, and foreign languages—that caused the turn away from progressivism. Trouble had been brewing for a number of years prior to the Soviet achievement in space.

The essentialist curriculum has always been the easiest to understand and the simplest to organize and administer. It appears clear-cut and can be readily preplanned by teachers and administrators drawing on their knowledge of the adult world. We must not overlook the force that tradition plays in our society. The essentialist curriculum has been the one to which most Americans have been exposed and the one, therefore, they know best and wish to retain.

There can be no doubt that some of the so-called progressive schools went to extremes in catering to the needs and interests of children. The high school graduate who must write in block printing because he or she was not required to master cursive writing raised eyebrows among the American public. Appealing to the child's immediate needs and interests, some progressive schools seemed to sacrifice long-range needs and interests of which the immature learner was scarcely aware.

A feeling developed that the graduates of progressive schools were not learning the basic skills or the elements of the nation's cultural heritage. The public was uncomfortable with assertions from educators such as "The child should be taught to read only after he or she expresses a felt need for reading" or "There's no need to memorize the multiplication tables, you can always look them up or use a calculator."

Compared to the apparent tidiness of the essentialist curriculum and the relative ease of measuring achievement of subject matter, the progressivist curriculum appeared at times disorganized and impossible to evaluate. In attempting to deal with the whole child, the progressive school seemed to many parents to be usurping the functions of the home, and many harried teachers agreed with them.

Some of the more zealous progressivists led even Dewey to warn:

> Apart from the question of the future, continually to appeal even in childhood to the principle of interest is eternally to excite, that is, distract, the child. Continuity of activity is destroyed. Everything is made play, amusement. This means overstimulation; it means dissipation of energy. Will is never called into action. The reliance is upon external attractions and amusements. Everything is sugar-coated for the child, and he soon learns to turn everything that is not artificially surrounded with diverting circumstances.[66]

Mass education alone has contributed to the decline of progressive practices. What might work in a class of twenty-five will not necessarily work in classes of thirty-five or above. No one has yet demonstrated satisfactorily how a high school teacher of English can provide for cognitive differences among 150 students per day, let alone be effective. As long ago as 1959 James B. Conant advocated a maximum of 100 pupils per high school English teacher—a standard yet to be realized in many schools.[67]

Criticisms of progressive education by the essentialists, the behaviorists, and the scholastics converged to restore essentialism to its currently strong position. The numerous reports on educational reform in the 1970s and 1980s, some of which will be discussed in Chapter 9, revealed dissatisfaction, however, with the essentialist curriculum. Some contemporary curriculum theorists characterize the historic role of schools as an outmoded, inappropriate factory or industrial model, imposed by society on young people who are its products destined for the workforce, rewarding conformity and deemphasizing the preparation of, in the words of George H. Wood, "independent thinkers who are committed to the public good and willing to act on their own initiative."[68] Some advocates of private education portray public schools in a negative light labeling them "government schools." Linda Darling-Hammond described present school structure whose origins lie in principles of top-down organizational management, as a "conveyor belt" wherein impersonal treatment of students and rote learning predominate. Efforts at improvement like "required courses, textbooks, testing instruments, and management systems," based on a "manufacturing industries" model, according to Darling-Hammond, have been assumed to lead to student learning and have sought to produce a standard product.[69] She held that factory-model schools erect barriers to democratic education, commenting:

> Relatively few schools offer all their students a rich, active curriculum that teaches for understanding. Even fewer manage to educate a diverse set of students for constructive social

interaction and shared decision making . . . the right to learn in ways that develop both competence and community has been a myth rather than a reality for many Americans.[70]

Critical of education tied to economic goals Michael W. Apple commented, "the most powerful economic and political groups in the United States and similar nations have made it abundantly clear that for them a good education is only one that is tied to economic needs (but, of course, only as these needs are defined by the powerful)."[71] Noting that democratic ideals have long been featured in school reform Jean Anyon questioned their adequacy in the restructuring of urban schools. Anyon argued that "until the economic and political systems in which the cities are enmeshed are themselves transformed so they may be more democratic and productive for urban residents, educational reformers have little chance of effecting long-lasting educational changes in city schools."[72]

Dissatisfaction emanates also from a small group of curriculum theorists known as the reconceptualists. This group of theorists, for the most part college professors of curriculum, has expressed concern about the hidden curriculum, the values that are not directly taught but that children nevertheless experience in school. These values include the rules students live by, their relationships with peers and adults in the school, and the values embedded in the content of their studies.

The reconceptualists argue for fundamental changes in curriculum and instruction. Some view curriculum *development* as outdated and offer in its place curriculum *understanding*.[73] They draw support for their position from the humanities, especially history, philosophy, and literary criticism. William Pinar explained the interests of reconceptual theorists:

> The reconceptualists tend to concern themselves with the internal and existential experience of the public world. They tend to study not "change in behavior" or "decision making in the classroom," but matters of temporality, transcendence, consciousness, and politics. In brief, the reconceptualist attempts to understand the nature of educational experience.[74]

Pinar noted in 1975 that reconceptualists constituted 3 to 5 percent of all curriculum theorists. Another 60 to 80 percent were what Pinar called "traditionalists" whose primary mission is guiding practitioners in the schools. The others were "conceptual empiricists" whose interests lie in the behavioral sciences, of which the curriculum is one.[75] Although percentages for each of these three groups may vary somewhat today, observation of the current curriculum scene leads to the conclusion that the "traditionalists" still constitute the largest group, followed by the "conceptual empiricists," with the "reconceptualists" composing the smallest. Pinar et al. saw reconceptualization as still underemphasized in traditional curriculum textbooks.[76]

Critical Theory.   In discussing the reconceptualization of the curriculum field, Peter S. Hlebowitsh observed that "many contemporary challenges in curriculum studies have been inspired by a critical theory of education."[77] Influenced by the Institute of Social Research in Frankfort, Germany,[78] critical theorists are concerned with injustices in society and the part the school plays in sustaining those injustices, for example, in "track-ing, vocational education, special education, and teacher education."[79] Nell Noddings explained, "From the perspective of critical theorists, philosophy must be engaged with the great struggles and social movements of its times."[80]

The critical theorists offer no prescribed programs or pedagogical processes, stress-ing instead the need for empowerment of the individual with the goal of improving both the school and society. Noddings observed that "Philosophers of education have been greatly influenced by critical theory. . . ."[81]

In spite of the many conflicting philosophical views and at the risk of overgen-eralizing we might conclude the public and a majority of educators at the start of the twenty-first century endorse educational programs and practices in American schools that represent a judicious mixture of essentialist and progressive philosophy.

FORMULATING A PHILOSOPHY

In a holistic approach to curriculum development, the curriculum committee designated to lead the process examines statements of aims of education, chooses those that appear most significant, and tries its skill at fashioning its own statements.

The curriculum committee should be cognizant of the major principles of the lead-ing schools of philosophy, particularly essentialism and progressivism. They should know where they stand as individuals and as a group in the philosophical spectrum. They may discover that they have adopted, as have perhaps a majority of educators, an eclectic approach to philosophy, choosing the best from several philosophies. They may find that there is no such thing as a pure essentialist or a pure progressivist but rather, more commonly, one is an essentialist who leans toward progressive thinking (a progressive essentialist) or, conversely, a progressivist who leans toward essentialist ideas (an essen-tialistic progressivist).

Curriculum workers should take the time to think through their own philoso-phies and to formulate them into some kind of coherent statement. The formulation of philosophy is not an activity that most Americans—pragmatists as they are—engage in with either zeal or frequency. Unlike some European schools that include philosophy in their secondary school curriculum, in our high schools philosophy is conspicuous by its absence. Even on the college level philosophy professors rarely have to beat off hordes of students clamoring at their doors.

Educators should reexamine their beliefs periodically to see if they reflect changes in society and the continuous expansion of knowledge. Schools would do well to draw up a statement of philosophy, review and revise it every five years, and thoroughly reex-amine and revise it every ten years. A recommendation of this nature has been followed by schools that wish to achieve and maintain accreditation by the regional associations of colleges and schools. Whether or not a school seeks regional accreditation, it should formulate a school philosophy to establish a framework for the practices of that school.

A school's philosophy should always be the result of cooperative efforts by teachers and administrators and preferably with the additional help of parents and students. State-ments of philosophy are sometimes written and promulgated by a school administrator as the philosophy of that school. Such an activity might be engaged in to meet the terms for a report to the regional accreditation association, yet it misses the spirit of the exercise. The writing of a school philosophy should be an effort to gain consensus among divergent thinkers and to find out what aims and values the group holds in common. For this reason even a statement of philosophy drawn up by a faculty committee should be presented to the total faculty for acceptance, rejection, or modification. In a very real sense, the faculty's statement of philosophy becomes a manifesto signifying "This is what we believe" or "This is where we stand" as of now.

Value in Writing a Philosophy

Some hold that writing statements of philosophy is a waste of time, that such an effort takes too much valuable time that could be better spent in other ways, and that most efforts wind up with empty platitudes. Philosophical statements *can* become meaningless slogans, but they do not *have* to be. Should we call the following phrases of political philosophy from the Declaration of Independence—"all men are created equal"—and "they are endowed by their Creator with certain unalienable rights," including "Life, Liberty, and the Pursuit of Happiness"—empty platitudes? Why, we might ask, did our forebears not just sever relations between the motherland and the colonies instead of prattling about unalienable rights? Perhaps they recognized that they must set the stage and provide a rationale around which other like-minded persons might rally.

A school's philosophy is not of the same order or in the same class as the Declaration of Independence, yet it does set the stage and does offer a rationale that calls for the allegiance of those who proclaim it. If a statement of philosophy is to serve this purpose, it must be a truthful one and not simply platitudinous window dressing. If a school faculty believes that the major purposes of its school are to develop cognitive skills, to preserve the social status quo, or to direct the growth and development of the gifted and academically talented, it should say so. A frank statement of philosophical beliefs is much more defensible than a sanctimonious statement of platitudes that many faculty may not support and that many teachers do not translate into classroom practice.

As curriculum workers we must disabuse ourselves of the notions that it is somehow indecent to expose our beliefs and that we must feel either silly or guilty when setting forth ideals. The formulation of a school philosophy can be a valuable inservice educational experience, giving teachers and administrators a chance to exchange views and to find a common meeting ground.

A school's philosophy should include statements of belief about the purposes of education, society, the learner, and the role of the teacher. Examples of statements of philosophy written by school personnel follow. These statements are typical of philosophies written by faculties throughout the United States. They speak about democracy, the individual, and the learning process. Statements of some schools are brief; others lengthy. Some schools include goals and objectives in their statements of philosophy. Here we are concerned primarily with a school's philosophy. In Chapter 8 we will discuss the writing of curriculum goals and objectives and will provide examples of those.

These statements of philosophy reveal the schools of thought to which the faculties subscribe. In spite of the essentialistic turn in American education, progressive beliefs are still strong. Despite the current emphasis on developing the intellect, these examples show concern for the whole child. In spite of increased stress on the development of cognitive abilities, the examples provided give attention to the affect.

Ornstein and Hunkins addressed the importance of philosophy to educators in that it "helps them answer what schools are for, what subjects are of value, how students learn, and what methods and materials to use. It provides them with a framework for broad issues and tasks, such as determining the goals of education, the content and its organization, the process of teaching and learning, and in general what experiences and activities they wish to stress in schools and classrooms."[82]

Problems in Developing and Implementing a Philosophy

Before examining the examples of school philosophies, we should mention that curriculum workers often encounter two sets of problems in developing and implementing a school's philosophy. First, those who are charged with drafting a statement usually enter into the process with differing assumptions, sometimes unexpressed, about the learning process, the needs of society, and the roles of individuals in that society. The various participating individuals may well espouse differing and conflicting philosophies of life that color their beliefs about education. Somehow the differing views need to be aired and reconciled. If consensus cannot be reached, perhaps no statement of philosophy can be drafted or that which is drafted will be so inconsequential as to be useless.

A second set of problems arises from the statement of philosophical beliefs in rather general, often vague, terms that permit varying interpretations. When a statement of philosophy has been completed and presumably consensus has been reached on the *wording*, curriculum leaders will experience the continuing problem of striving to achieve consensus (sometimes even among those who drafted the statement) on *interpretations* of the wording.

EXAMPLES OF EDUCATIONAL PHILOSOPHIES

Let's look at examples of school philosophies, in this case those of a large urban school district in Iowa (Box 6.2) and of a school in a smaller community in Georgia (Box 6.3). Increasingly common in addition to statements of philosophy are statements of mission and specification of aims or goals and subgoals. Box 6.2 reproduces the statement of the educational philosophy of Des Moines, Iowa's public schools, while Box 6.3 illustrates the mission and beliefs statement of the Sallie Zetterower Elementary School in Statesboro, Georgia. You will encounter additional examples of school statements of belief in Chapter 8 where we discuss curriculum goals and objectives.

In these examples, you will notice references to democratic concepts, to respect for the individual, and to the necessity of providing programs to develop the pupil in all his or her capacities. Although some may fault the style or prose of a given school philosophy, what we have to keep in mind is the purpose of the statement—to communicate to professionals and the public the beliefs held by the personnel of a school or a school system. A philosophy serves its purpose when significant beliefs are successfully communicated.

BOX 6.2

Educational Philosophy of the Des Moines, Iowa, Public Schools

Educational Philosophy

Mission Statement. The Des Moines Public Schools equip students for life by challenging each one to achieve rigorous standards in academics, arts, and career preparation.

Belief Statement. Public education is imperative to support and sustain a diverse democratic society. To this end, we believe:

All students can and must learn.

Schools must meet the unique learning needs of each of their students.

The home, school and community must serve and support one another.

Teaching and learning require a healthy, safe and orderly environment.

Resources and services are essential for effective instruction.

All staff must continue to learn, and all schools must continue to improve.

Source: Des Moines Public Schools, *Educational Philosophy*, website: http://www.des-moines.k12.ia.us/schoolboard/6missiongoals.htm, accessed April 24, 2003. (Public domain.) Revisited March 15, 2007, at website: http://www.dmps.k12.ia.us/schoolboard/6philosophy.htm.

What amazed this author while searching the Web for examples of school and school district statements of educational philosophy is how few schools and school districts communicate their educational platforms, that is, their statements of philosophy, mission, or goals or, in the case of those school systems that have crafted such statements, how difficult it is to locate the links that lead one to those statements. One would think

BOX 6.3

Sallie Zetterower Elementary School

Mission Statement
At Sallie Zetterower, our mission is to inspire every student to think, to learn, to achieve, and to care.

Our Beliefs
Our belief is that every person:

• deserves to be treated with dignity.

• deserves to work and learn in a safe environment.
• can learn and experience success.
• is responsible for his/her own actions and words.

The attitudes and habits of teachers, students, and parents affect the quality of learning.

Source: Sallie Zetterower Elementary School, Statesboro, Georgia, *Mission Statement and Our Beliefs*, website: http://www.bulloch.k12.ga.us/szes/szes_handbook.htm, accessed March 15, 2007. Reprinted by permission.

that school systems would publish their educational platforms front-and-center to tell the world "this is what we believe."

From our beliefs about education, schooling, learning, and society, we can proceed to subsequent steps of the curriculum development process. Component I of the suggested model for curriculum development calls for a statement of educational aims and philosophy. In respect to aims of education, curriculum workers should

- be aware that educational aims are derived from and are part of one's educational philosophy
- be cognizant of national statements of aims of education made by prominent individuals and groups
- evaluate national statements and select from those statements, revising as they deem necessary, the aims of education that they find acceptable
- draw up a statement of educational aims (in keeping with pronounced statewide aims) to which they subscribe or, alternately, incorporate the aims of education they have selected into a statement of philosophy

In respect to the philosophical dimension of component I, curriculum workers should be able to

- identify principal beliefs of leading schools of educational philosophy
- analyze statements of philosophy and identify the schools to which they belong
- analyze and clarify their own educational philosophies

Summary

A holistic approach to curriculum development begins with an examination of the aims of education in society. Aims are perceived as the broad purposes of education that are national and, on occasion, international in scope.

Over the years a number of prominent individuals and groups have expressed their positions on the appropriate aims of education for America. The curriculum worker should be able not only to formulate his or her own statement of aims but should also be knowledgeable about historic and significant statements of aims.

In this chapter we examined four philosophies of education—reconstructionism, progressivism, essentialism, and perennialism—two of which, essentialism and progressivism, are deemed to have special significance for our schools.

Essentialism, with its emphasis on subject matter, has been the prevailing philosophy of education throughout most of our country's history. Progressivism, however, with its emphasis on the child's needs and interests, has had a profound impact on educational programs and practices. Curriculum workers are urged to clarify their own philosophies and to draw up a statement of their school's philosophy that can be communicated to other professionals and to the public. Samples of school philosophies are included in this chapter not as models of content—that is, statements to be borrowed—but rather as examples of process. Curriculum developers should put together their own statement of beliefs in their own words. It is very likely that their statements will be eclectic in nature, borrowing from both essentialism and progressivism.

The development of a statement of aims of education and a school philosophy is seen as the first phase or component of a comprehensive model for curriculum development.

Questions for Discussion

1. Why has the essentialistic philosophy of education been so enduring?

2. How can you keep a statement of philosophy from becoming mere verbalism?

3. If a state has adopted a statement of aims, is there any place for district or individual school statements?

4. Is truth relative or absolute? Explain with examples.

5. From what sources are aims of education derived?

Exercises

1. Compare, citing appropriate references, aims of education in a democratic society with those of a totalitarian society.

2. State at least two premises of each of the following schools of philosophy:
   a. reconstructionism
   b. perennialism
   c. essentialism
   d. progressivism

3. Write a report, using appropriate references, contrasting essentialism and progressivism.

4. Search the literature and prepare a report on the research or beliefs of one (or more) of the following people, citing quotations from one or more of that person's works:

Jean Anyon	John Dewey
Michael Apple	Friedrich Froebel
William C. Bagley	Henry A. Giroux
Louise M. Berman	Maxine Greene
Theodore Brameld	Madeleine Grumet
Deborah P. Britzman	Georg W. F. Hegel
Jerome Bruner	Johann F. Herbart
John Childs	Dwayne Huebner
Arthur Combs	Robert M. Hutchins
James B. Conant	William James
George Counts	Immanuel Kant

Earl Kelley	Philip Phenix
William H. Kilpatrick	Jean Piaget
Herbert M. Kliebard	William F. Pinar
Kurt Koffka	Hyman G. Rickover
Wolfgang Köhler	Carl Rogers
Kurt Lewin	Jean Jacques Rousseau
Sarah Lawrence	Harold Rugg
Lightfoot	Kenneth A. Sirotnik
Gail McCutchen	B. F. Skinner
James B. Macdonald	Patrick Slattery
Abraham Maslow	Donald Snygg
Alice Miel	Herbert Spencer
Maria Montessori	Florence B.
Jeanie Oakes	Stratemeyer
Ivan Pavlov	Edward L. Thorndike
Charles S. Peirce	John Watson
Johann Pestalozzi	Max Wertheimer

5. Identify several practices in the schools that follow behavioristic principles.

6. Identify several practices in the schools that follow (a) experimentalist principles, (b) gestalt principles, (c) principles of perceptual psychology, and (d) constructivist principles.

7. Demonstrate with appropriate references how particular learning theories are related to certain schools of philosophy.

8. Write a short paper with appropriate references on the place and use of memorization in the classroom.

9. Write a paper on reflective thinking and show how it can be applied in the field of specialization you know best.

10. Write a report summarizing the findings of the Eight-Year Study.

11. Search the literature for any curriculum proposals within the past five years that you would label either perennialist or reconstructionist.

12. Summarize the major beliefs of the following schools of philosophy and draw implications, if any, for the curriculum:
    a. naturalism
    b. idealism
    c. realism
    d. pragmatism
    e. existentialism
    f. scholasticism

13. Write an analysis of beliefs of the reconceptualists.

14. Write a report explaining and evaluating the beliefs of critical theorists.

15. Explain what is meant by critical inquiry.

Videos

Constructivism. 1995. Two 30- to 40-min. videos. Jacqueline Grennon Brooks explains constructivist teaching strategies. Facilitator's Guide. Book, *In Search of Understanding: The Case for Constructivist Classrooms* by Jacqueline Grennon Brooks and Martin G. Brooks.

Character Education: Application in the Classroom. 1998. 40 min., elementary (K–6) or secondary. Presents ideas for integrating character education into the curriculum. Phi Delta Kappa International, P.O. Box 789, Bloomington, Ind. 47402-0789.

Websites

Character Counts!: http://www.charactercounts.org

Character Education Partnership: http://www.character .org

Josephson Institute of Ethics: http://www.josephson institute.org

No Child Left Behind Act:
    http://www.ed.gov/nclb/landing.jhtml
    http://www.ed.gov/offices/OESE/esea/summary .html
    http://www.NoChildLeftBehind.gov

Endnotes

1. Decker F. Walker and Jonas F. Soltis, *Curriculum and Aims,* 4th ed. (New York: Teachers College Press, 2004) p. 12.

2. See Chapter 8 for discussion of curriculum goals and objectives.

3. See Chapter 10 for discussion of instructional goals and objectives.

4. Educational Policies Commission, *Moral and Spiritual Values in the Public Schools* (Washington, D.C.: National Education Association, 1951), pp. 17–34.

5. James Patterson and Peter Kim, *The Day America Told the Truth: What People Really Think About Everything That Really Matters* (New York: Prentice-Hall, 1991).

6. William J. Bennett, ed., *The Book of Virtues: A Treasury of Great Moral Stories* (New York: Simon and Schuster, 1993). See also William J. Bennett, *Our Children and Our Country: Improving America's Schools and Affirming the Common Culture* (New York: Simon and Schuster, 1988), Chapter 9 on moral literacy and character formation.

7. Michael Josephson, *Excerpts from Easier Said Than Done: A Common Sense Approach to Ethical Decision Making*, Unpublished draft. Marina del Rey, Calif.: Josephson Institute of Ethics, 1995, p. 53. Reprinted by permission.

8. 2003 Gallup Poll Social Series, *Moral Views and Values* (Princeton, N.J.: The Gallup Organization, 2003).

9. For a membership list of Character Counts! see website: http://www.charactercounts.org.

10. John Dewey, *Democracy and Education: An Introduction to the Philosophy of Education* (New York: Macmillan, 1916; New York: Free Press, 1966), Chapters 2 and 4.

11. John Dewey, *My Pedagogic Creed* (Washington, D.C.: Progressive Education Association, 1929), pp. 3–6.

12. Dewey, *Democracy and Education*, pp. 59–60.

13. Commission on the Reorganization of Secondary Education, *Cardinal Principles of Secondary Education* (Washington, D.C.: United States Office of Education, Bulletin 35, 1918), p. 9.

14. Educational Policies Commission, *The Unique Function of Education in American Democracy* (Washington, D.C.: National Education Association, 1937), p. 89.

15. Harvard Committee on General Education, *General Education in a Free Society* (Cambridge, Mass.: Harvard University Press, 1945), p. 54.

16. Ibid., pp. 99–100.

17. Educational Policies Commission, *The Central Purpose of American Education* (Washington, D.C.: National Education Association, 1961), p. 89.

18. H. G. Rickover, *Education for All Children: What We Can Learn from England: Hearings Before the Committee on Appropriations, House of Representatives, Eighty-Seventh Congress, Second Session* (Washington, D.C.: U.S. Government Printing Office, 1962), pp. 14, 17, 18.

19. Mortimer J. Adler, *The Paideia Proposal: An Educational Manifesto* (New York: Macmillan, 1982), p. 10.

20. John T. Goodlad, *A Place Called School: Prospects for the Future* (New York: McGraw-Hill, 1983), pp. 51–56.

21. Theodore R. Sizer, *Horace's School: Redesigning the American High School* (Boston: Houghton Mifflin, 1992), p. 127.

22. Herbert M. Kliebard, "The Effort to Reconstruct the Modern American Curriculum," in Landon E. Beyer and Michael W. Apple, eds., *The Curriculum: Problems, Politics, and Possibilities*, 2nd ed. (Albany, N.Y.: State University of New York Press, 1998), p. 21 as quoted from Aristotle, *Politics* (New York: Oxford University Press, 1945), p. 244.

23. U.S. Department of Education, *National Goals for Education* (Washington, D.C.: U.S. Department of Education, July 1990.

24. Commission on the Skills of the American Workforce, *America's Choice: High Skills or Low Wages* (Washington, D.C.: Commission on Skills of the American Workforce, 1991). For discussion of the 2006 New Commission on the Skills of the American Workforce see p. 473 of this textbook and National Center on Education and the Economy, *Tough Choices, Tough Times* (San Francisco: Jossey-Bass, 2006).

25. See Chapter 12 for further discussion of the National Assessment of Educational Progress and Chapter 15 on the issue of national standards.

26. Henry A. Giroux, *Living Dangerously: Multiculturalism and the Politics of Difference* (New York: Peter Lang, 1993), p. 14.

27. See Penelope M. Earley, *Goals 2000: Educate America Act: Implications for Teacher Educators* (ERIC document ED367661, 1994).

28. Maxine Greene, *Releasing the Imagination: Essays on Education, the Arts, and Social Change* (San Francisco: Jossey-Bass, 1995), p. 17.

29. Ibid.

30. See website: http://www.ed.gov/policy/elsec/leg/esea02/beginning.html#sec2.

31. Maxine Greene, *Teacher as Stranger: Educational Philosophy for the Modern Age* (Belmont, Calif.: Wadsworth, 1973), p. 7.

32. Ibid.

33. J. Donald Butler, *Four Philosophies and Their Practice in Education and Religion*, 3rd ed. (New York: Harper & Row, 1968), p. 487.

34. Allan C. Ornstein and Francis P. Hunkins, *Curriculum: Foundations, Principles, and Issues*, 4th ed. (Boston: Allyn and Bacon, 2004), p. 31.

35. Hilda Taba, *Curriculum Development: Theory and Practice* (New York: Harcourt Brace Jovanovich, 1962), p. 23.

36. Ibid.

37. George S. Counts, *Dare the School Build a New Social Order?* (New York: John Day, 1932).

38. Theodore Brameld, *Patterns of Educational Philosophy: Divergence and Convergence in Culturological Perspective* (New York: Holt, Rinehart and Winston, 1971), p. 418.

39. Robert M. Hutchins, *On Education* (Santa Barbara, Calif.: Center for the Study of Democratic Institutions, 1963), p. 18.

40. Walker and Soltis, *Curriculum and Aims*, p. 18.

41. See William C. Bagley, "An Essentialist's Platform for the Advancement of American Education," *Educational Administration and Supervision* 24, no. 4 (April 1938): 251–252.

42. See James B. Conant, *The American High School Today* (New York: McGraw-Hill, 1959); Conant, *Recom-*

mendations for Education in the Junior High School Years (Princeton, N.J.: Educational Testing Service, 1960); Conant, *The Comprehensive High School* (New York: McGraw-Hill, 1967). Also see Chapter 9 of this text for further discussion of the Conant reports.

43. V. T. Thayer, *The Role of the School in American Society* (New York: Dodd, Mead, 1960), pp. 251–252.

44. Macmillan, 1916.

45. Macmillan, 1938.

46. Macmillan, 1933.

47. Progressive Education Association, 1929.

48. John Dewey, *The Child and the Curriculum* (Chicago: University of Chicago Press, 1902), pp. 7–14.

49. Harold Rugg, et al., *Foundations for American Education* (Yonkers, N.Y.: World Book Company, 1947).

50. Brameld, *Patterns of Educational Philosophy*, p. 133.

51. For discussions of pragmatism see John L. Childs, *American Pragmatism and Education: An Interpretation and Criticism* (New York: Holt, 1956) and Edward C. Moore, *American Pragmatism: Peirce, James, and Dewey* (New York: Columbia University Press, 1961).

52. Taba, *Curriculum Development*, p. 184.

53. Brameld, *Patterns of Educational Philosophy*, pp. 96–97.

54. Abraham H. Maslow, "Some Basic Propositions of a Growth and Self-Actualization Psychology," in *Perceiving, Behaving, Becoming*, 1962 Yearbook (Alexandria, Va.: Association for Supervision and Curriculum Development, 1962), p. 36.

55. Arthur W. Combs, "A Perceptual View of the Adequate Personality," in *Perceiving, Behaving, Becoming*, 1962 Yearbook (Alexandria, Va.: Association for Supervision and Curriculum Development, 1962), p. 51.

56. Ibid., pp. 51–62.

57. Ibid., p. 53.

58. Ibid.

59. Kenneth A. Sirotnik, "What Goes on in Classrooms? Is This the Way We Want It?" in Landon E. Beyer and Michael W. Apple, eds., *The Curriculum: Problems, Politics, and Possibilities*, 2nd ed. (Albany, N.Y.: State University of New York Press, 1998), pp. 66–67.

60. Ibid., p. 64.

61. Ibid., p. 67.

62. Nell Noddings, *Philosophy of Education* (Boulder, Col.: Westview Press, 1995), p. 115.

63. Karen H. Harris and Steve Graham, "Constructivism: Principles, Paradigms, and Integration," *The Journal of Special Education* 28, no. 3 (March 1994): 240.

64. See Wilford M. Aikin, *The Story of the Eight-Year Study* (New York: Harper & Row, 1942).

65. Peter F. Oliva, *The Secondary School Today*, 2nd ed. (New York: Harper & Row, 1972), p. 120.

66. John Dewey, *Interest and Effort in Education* (Boston: Houghton Mifflin, 1913), pp. 4–5.

67. Conant, *The American High School Today*, p. 51.

68. George H. Wood, "Teachers as Curriculum Workers," in James T. Sears and J. Dan Marshall, eds., *Teaching and Thinking About Curriculum: Critical Inquiries* (New York: Teachers College Press, 1990), p. 100.

69. Linda Darling-Hammond, *The Right to Learn: A Blueprint for Creating Schools That Work* (San Francisco: Jossey-Bass, 1997), pp. 16–17.

70. Ibid., p. 7.

71. Michael W. Apple, *Cultural Politics and Education* (New York: Teachers College Press, 1996), p. 5.

72. Jean Anyon, *Ghetto Schooling: A Political Economy of Urban Educational Reform* (New York: Teachers College Press, 1997), pp. 12–13.

73. See William F. Pinar, William M. Reynolds, Patrick Slattery, and Peter M. Taubman, *Understanding Curriculum: An Introduction to the Study of Historical and Contemporary Curriculum Discourses* (New York: Peter Lang, 1996), p. 6.

74. William Pinar, ed., *Curriculum Theorizing: The Reconceptualists* (Berkeley, Calif.: McCuchan, 1975), pp. xii–xiii.

75. Ibid., p. xii.

76. Pinar et al., *Understanding Curriculum*, p. 17.

77. Peter S. Hlebowitsch, *Radical Curriculum Theory: A Historical Approach* (New York: Teachers College Press, 1993), p. 4.

78. For discussion of the Institute for Social Research see Henry A. Giroux, *Pedagogy and the Politics of Hope: Theory, Culture, and Schooling: A Critical Reader* (Boulder, Col.: Westview Press, 1997), pp. 35–70.

79. Hlebowitsch, *Radical Curriculum Theory*, p. 4.

80. Noddings, *Philosophy*, p. 67.

81. Ibid., p. 68.

82. Ornstein and Hunkins, *Curriculum*, p. 31.

Bibliography

Adler, Mortimer J. *The Paideia Proposal: An Educational Manifesto.* New York: Macmillan, 1982.

Aikin, Wilford M. *The Story of the Eight-Year Study.* New York: Harper & Row, 1942.

Anyon, Jean. *Ghetto Schooling: A Political Economy of Urban Educational Reform.* New York: Teachers College Press, 1997.

Apple, Michael W. *Cultural Politics and Education.* New York: Teachers College Press, 1996.

———. *Ideology and Curriculum,* 2nd ed. New York. Routledge, 1990.

———. "The Politics of Curriculum and Teaching." *NASSP Bulletin* 75, no. 532 (February 1991): 39–50.

Aronowitz, Stanley and Giroux, Henry A. *Education Under Siege: The Conservative, Liberal, and Radical Debate over Schooling.* South Hadley, Mass.: Bergin & Garvey, 1985.

Ayers, William C. and Miller, Janet L., eds. *A Light in Dark Times: Maxine Greene and the Unfinished Conversation.* New York: Teachers College Press, 1998.

Bagley, William C. "An Essentialist's Platform for the Advancement of American Education." *Educational Administration and Supervision* 24, no. 4 (April 1938): 241–256.

Bennett, William J., ed. *The Book of Virtues: A Treasury of Great Moral Stories.* New York: Simon and Schuster, 1993.

———. *Our Children and Our Country: Improving America's Schools and Affirming the Common Culture.* New York: Simon and Schuster, 1988.

Beyer, Landon E. and Apple, Michael W., eds. *The Curriculum: Problems, Politics, and Possibilities,* 2nd ed. Albany, New York: State University of New York Press, 1998.

Bode, Boyd H. *How We Learn.* Boston: D. C. Heath, 1940.

———. "Pragmatism in Education." *New Republic* 121, no. 16 (October 17, 1949): 15–18.

Brameld, Theodore. *Patterns of Educational Philosophy: A Democratic Interpretation.* Yonkers, N.Y.: World Book Company, 1950.

———. *Patterns of Educational Philosophy: Divergence and Convergence in Culturological Perspective.* New York: Holt, Rinehart and Winston, 1971.

Broudy, Harry S. *Building a Philosophy of Education,* 2nd ed. Englewood Cliffs, N.J.: Prentice Hall, 1961.

Brooks, Jacqueline Grennon and Brooks, Martin G. *In Search of Understanding: The Case for Constructivist Classrooms.* Alexandria, Va.: Association for Supervision and Curriculum Development, 1993.

Burrett, Kenneth and Rusnak, Timothy. *Integrated Character Education.* Bloomington, Ind.: Phi Delta Kappa, 1993.

Butler, J. Donald. *Four Philosophies and Their Practice in Education and Religion,* 3rd ed. New York: Harper & Row, 1968.

Castenell, Louis A., Jr. and Pinar, William, eds. *Understanding Curriculum as Racial Text: Representations of Identity and Difference in Education.* Albany, N.Y.: State University of New York Press, 1993.

"Character Education." *Educational Leadership* 51, no. 3 (November 1993): 6–97.

Childs, John L. *American Pragmatism and Education: An Interpretation and Criticism.* New York: Holt, 1956.

Combs, Arthur W. "A Perceptual View of the Adequate Personality." In *Perceiving, Behaving, Becoming,* 1962 Yearbook. Alexandria, Va.: Association for Supervision and Curriculum Development, 1962, pp. 50–64.

——— and Snygg, Donald. *Individual Behavior: A Perceptual Approach to Behavior,* rev. ed. New York: Harper & Row, 1959.

Commission on the Reorganization of Secondary Education. *Cardinal Principles of Secondary Education.* Washington, D.C.: United States Office of Education, Bulletin 35, 1918.

Conant, James B. *The American High School Today.* New York: McGraw-Hill, 1959.

———. *The Comprehensive High School.* New York: McGraw-Hill, 1967.

———. *Recommendations for Education in the Junior High School Years.* Princeton, N.J.: Educational Testing Service, 1960.

"The Constructivist Classroom." *Educational Leadership* 57, no. 3 (November 1999): 6–78.

Counts, George S. *Dare the School Build a New Social Order?* New York: John Day, 1932.

Cremin, Lawrence A. *The Transformation of the School: Progressivism in American Education, 1876–1975.* New York: Alfred A. Knopf, 1961.

Darling-Hammond, Linda. *The Right to Learn: A Blueprint for Creating Schools That Work.* San Francisco: Jossey-Bass, 1997.

Dewey, John. *The Child and the Curriculum.* Chicago: University of Chicago Press, 1902.

———. *Democracy and Education: An Introduction to the Philosophy of Education.* New York: Macmillan, 1916; New York: Free Press, 1966.

———. *Interest and Effort in Education.* Boston: Houghton Mifflin, 1913.

———. *My Pedagogic Creed.* Washington, D.C.: Progressive Education Association, 1929.

Durant, Will. *The Story of Philosophy: The Lives and Opinions of the World's Greatest Philosophers from Plato to John Dewey.* New York: Simon & Schuster, 1926.

Ebel, Robert L. "What Are Schools For?" *Phi Delta Kappan* 54, no. 1 (September 1972): 3–7.

Educational Policies Commission. *The Central Purpose of American Education.* Washington, D.C.: National Education Association, 1961.

———. *Moral and Spiritual Values in the Public Schools.* Washington, D.C.: National Education Association, 1951.

———. *The Unique Function of Education in American Democracy.* Washington, D.C.: National Education Association, 1937.

Eisner, Elliot W. "Curriculum Ideologies." In Philip W. Jackson, ed. *Handbook of Research on Curriculum.* New York: Macmillan, 1992, pp. 302–326.

——— and Vallance, Elizabeth, eds. *Conflicting Conceptions of Curriculum.* Berkeley, Calif.: McCutchan, 1974.

Elam, Stanley M., Rose, Lowell C., and Gallup, Alec M. "The 26th Annual Phi Delta Kappa/Gallup Poll of the Public's Attitudes Toward the Public Schools." *Phi Delta Kappan* 58, no. 1 (September 1976): 31–35.

Freire, Paulo. *Pedagogy of Hope: Reliving Pedagogy of the Oppressed.* New York: Continuum, 1992.

———. *Pedagogy of the Oppressed,* rev. 20th anniversary edition. New York: Continuum, 1993.

Giroux, Henry A. "Curriculum Planning, Public Schooling, and Democratic Struggle." *NASSP Bulletin* 75, no. 532 (February 1991): 12–25.

———. *Living Dangerously: Multiculturalism and the Politics of Difference.* New York: Peter Lang, 1993.

———. *Pedagogy and the Politics of Hope: Theory, Culture, and Schooling: A Critical Reader.* Boulder: Col.: Westview Press, 1997.

———. *Theory and Resistance in Education: A Pedagogy for the Opposition.* South Hadley, Mass.: Bergin & Garvey, 1983.

——— and Purpel, David, eds. *The Hidden Curriculum and Moral Education: Deception or Discovery?* Berkeley, Calif.: McCutchan, 1983.

Goodlad, John I. *A Place Called School: Prospects for the Future.* New York: McGraw-Hill, 1984.

Greene, Maxine. *Landscapes of Learning.* New York: Teachers College Press, 1970.

———. *The Public School and the Private Vision: A Search for America in Education and Literature.* New York: Random House, 1965.

———. *Releasing the Imagination: Essays on Education, the Arts, and Social Change.* San Francisco: Jossey-Bass, 1995.

Harris, Karen H. and Steve Graham. "Constructivism: Principles, Paradigms, and Integration." *The Journal of Special Education* 28, no. 3 (March 1994): 233–247.

Harvard Committee on General Education. *General Education in a Free Society.* Cambridge, Mass.: Harvard University Press, 1945.

Henson, Kenneth T. *Classroom Planning: Integrating Multiculturalism, Constructivism, and Education Reform,* 3rd ed. Long Grove, Ill.: Waveland Press, 2006.

Hlebowitsh, Peter S. *Radical Curriculum Theory Reconsidered: A Historical Perspective.* New York: Teachers College Press, 1993.

Hutchins, Robert M. *The Higher Learning in America.* New Haven, Conn.: Yale University Press, 1936.

———. *On Education.* Santa Barbara, Calif: Center for the Study of Democratic Institutions, 1963.

James, William. *Principles of Psychology.* New York: Henry Holt and Company, 1890.

Jelinek, James John, ed. *Improving the Human Condition: A Curricular Response to Critical Realities,* 1978 Yearbook. Alexandria, Va.: Association for Supervision and Curriculum Development, 1978.

Kilpatrick, William H., ed. *The Educational Frontier.* New York: Appleton-Century-Crofts, 1933.

Kirschenbaum, Howard. "A Comprehensive Model for Values Education and Moral Education." *Phi Delta Kappan* 73, no. 10 (June 1992): 771–776.

Kliebard, Herbert M. "The Effort to Reconstruct the Modern American Curriculum." In Landon E. Beyer and Michael W. Apple, eds. *The Curriculum: Problems, Politics, and Possibilities,* 2nd ed. Albany, N.Y.: State University of New York Press, 1998, pp. 21–33.

———. *The Struggle for the American Curriculum 1898–1958.* Boston: Routledge & Kegan Paul, 1986.

Lickona, Thomas. "The Return of Character Education." *Educational Leadership* 51, no. 3 (November 1993): 6–11.

Maslow, Abraham H. "Some Basic Propositions of a Growth and Self-Actualization Psychology." In Arthur W. Combs, ed. *Perceiving, Behaving, Becoming,* 1962 Yearbook. Alexandria, Va.: Association for Supervision and Curriculum Development, 1962.

———. *Toward a Psychology of Being,* 2nd ed. New York: Van Nostrand Reinhold, 1968.

Miller, John P. and Seller, Wayne. *Curriculum: Perspectives and Practice.* White Plains, N.Y.: Longman, 1985.

Mitchell, Richard. *The Leaning Tower of Bable and Other Affronts by the Underground Grammarian.* Boston: Little, Brown, 1984.

Molnar, Alex, ed. *Current Thought on Curriculum,* 1985 Yearbook. Alexandria, Va.: Association for Supervision and Curriculum Development, 1985.

Moore, Edward C. *American Pragmatism: Peirce, James, and Dewey.* New York: Columbia University Press, 1961.

National Education Goals Panel. *National Education Goals Report: Building a Nation of Learners.* Washington, D.C.: U.S. Government Printing Office, 1994.

———. *The National Education Goals Report. Vol. I. The National Report. Vol. II. State Reports.* Washington, D.C.: U.S. Government Printing Office, 1994.

"National Goals: Let Me Count the Ways." *The Education Digest* 56, no. 2 (October 1990): 8–26. "The National Goals—Putting Education Back on the

Road." *Phi Delta Kappan* 72, no. 4 (December 1990): 259–314.

National Governors' Association. *Educating America: State Strategies for Achieving the National Education Goals.* Washington, D.C.: National Governors' Association, 1990.

———. *Time for Results: The Governors' 1991 Report on Education.* Washington, D.C.: National Governors' Association, 1991.

Noddings, Nell. *Philosophy of Education.* Boulder, Col.: Westview Press, 1995.

Oliva, Peter F. *The Secondary School Today,* 2nd ed. New York: Harper & Row, 1972.

Ornstein, Allan C. and Behar, Linda S., eds. *Contemporary Issues in Curriculum.* Boston: Allyn and Bacon, 1995.

——— and Hunkins, Francis P. *Curriculum: Foundations, Principles, and Issues,* 4th ed. Boston: Allyn and Bacon, 2004.

Patterson, James and Kim, Peter. *The Day America Told the Truth: What People Really Believe About Everything that Really Matters.* New York: Prentice-Hall, 1991.

Piaget, Jean. *The Child's Conception of the World.* New York: Littlefield, 1975.

———. *Insights and Illusions of Philosophy.* New York: World, 1971.

Pinar, William, ed. *Curriculum Theorizing: The Reconceptualists.* Berkeley, Calif.: McCutchan, 1975.

———, Reynolds, William M., Slattery, Patrick, and Taubman, Peter M. *Understanding Curriculum: An Introduction to the Study of Historical and Contemporary Curriculum Discourses.* New York: Peter Lang, 1996.

Rickover, Hyman G. *Education for All Children: What We Can Learn from England: Hearing Before the Committee on Appropriations, House of Representatives, Eighty-Seventh Congress, Second Session.* Washington, D.C.: U.S. Government Printing Office, 1962.

Rugg, Harold et al. *The Foundations and Technique of Curriculum-Construction,* 26th Yearbook of the National Society for the Study of Education, Part 2, *The Foundations of Curriculum-Making,* ed. Guy Montrose Whipple, Bloomington, Ind.: Public School Publishing Company, 1927; New York: Arno Press and *The New York Times,* 1969.

———. *Foundations for American Education.* Yonkers, N.Y.: World Book Company, 1947.

Sears, James T. and Marshall, J. Dan. *Teaching and Thinking About Curriculum: Critical Inquiries.* New York: Teachers College Press, 1990.

Sirotnik, Kenneth A. "What Goes On in Classrooms? Is This the Way We Want It?" In Landon E. Beyer and Michael W. Apple, eds. *The Curriculum: Problems, Politics, and Possibilities,* 2nd ed. Albany, N.Y.: State University of New York Press, 1998, pp. 58–76.

Sizer, Theodore R. "Education and Assimilation: A Fresh Plea for Pluralism." *Phi Delta Kappan* 58, no. 1 (September 1976): 31–35.

———. *Horace's School: Redesigning the American High School.* Boston: Houghton Mifflin, 1992.

——— and Sizer, Nancy Faust. "Grappling," *Phi Delta Kappan* 81, no. 3 (November 1999): 184–190.

Taba, Hilda. *Curriculum Development: Theory and Practice.* New York: Harcourt Brace Jovanovich, 1962.

Tanner, Daniel and Tanner, Laurel N. *Curriculum Development: Theory into Practice,* 4th ed. Upper Saddle River, N.J.: Merrill/Prentice Hall, 2007.

———. *History of the School Curriculum.* New York: Macmillan, 1990.

Thayer, V. T. *The Role of the School in American Society.* New York: Dodd, Mead, 1960.

2003 Gallup Poll Social Series. *Moral Views and Values.* Princeton, N.J.: The Gallup Organization, 2003.

U.S. Department of Education. *America 2000: An Education Strategy.* Washington, D.C.: U.S. Government Printing Office, 1991.

———. *America 2000: Sourcebook.* Washington, D.C.: U.S. Government Printing Office, 1991.

U.S. Department of Education. *National Goals for Education.* Washington, D.C.: U.S. Department of Education, 1990.

Walker, Decker F. *Fundamentals of Curriculum: Passion and Professionalism,* 2nd ed. Mahwah, N.J.: Lawrence Erlbaum Associates, 2003.

——— and Soltis, Jonas F. *Curriculum and Aims,* 4th ed. New York: Teachers College Press, 2004.

"What Schools Should Teach." *Educational Leadership* 46, no. 1 (September 1988): 2–60.

Wiles, Jon and Bondi, Joseph C. *Curriculum Development: A Guide to Practice,* 7th ed. Upper Saddle River, N.J.: Merrill/Prentice Hall, 2007.

Wood, George H. "Teachers as Curriculum Workers." In James T. Sears and J. Dan Marshall, eds. *Teaching and Thinking About Curriculum: Critical Inquiries.* New York: Teachers College Press, 1990, pp. 97–109.

7 Needs Assessment

AFTER STUDYING THIS CHAPTER YOU SHOULD BE ABLE TO:

1. Identify and describe major sources of curriculum content.
2. Outline levels and types of needs of students.
3. Outline levels and types of needs of society.
4. Show how needs are derived from the structure of a discipline.
5. Describe the steps in conducting a needs assessment.
6. Construct an instrument for conducting a curriculum needs assessment.

CATEGORIES OF NEEDS

At the beginning of the twenty-first century the following items of content among thousands of items were being taught at specified grades somewhere in the United States:

- Kindergarten: Identification of the primary and secondary colors
- First grade: Identification of U.S. coins
- Second grade: Demonstration of ability to use period, comma, question mark, and quotation marks correctly
- Third grade: Distinguishing between a solid, liquid, and gas
- Fourth grade: Identification of common musical instruments
- Fifth grade: Demonstration of skill of administering first aid to victims of accidents
- Sixth grade: Performance of selected calisthenic skills
- Seventh grade: Demonstration of use of library reference works
- Eighth grade: Tracing historical development of own state
- Ninth grade: Using a circular saw properly
- Tenth grade: Describing preparation needed for selected careers
- Eleventh grade: Demonstrating skill in using a computer for data and word processing
- Twelfth grade: Writing a research paper

We could have listed hundreds of items that young people are called on to master in the course of their education from elementary through secondary school. For the moment these thirteen items will suffice for our purpose.

In reviewing these and other items, we could raise a number of questions. How did these particular items of content get there? What needs do the items fulfill? Have the right items been selected? What has been omitted that should have been included, and what might be eliminated from the curriculum? How do we find out whether an item is filling a need? Which needs are being met satisfactorily and which are not being met? What kinds of needs are there to which curriculum planners must pay attention?

The first section of this chapter discusses needs of students and society, classified by levels and types, and needs derived from the subject matter. The second section describes a process for conducting a curriculum needs assessment. When carrying out this process, curriculum planners study the needs of learners, society, and subject matter. With the help of the community, students, teachers, and administrators identify and place in order of priority programmatic needs that the school must address.

In the preceding chapter we saw that statements of educational aims and philosophy are based on needs of students in general and needs of society. Needs of both students and society are evident in the following examples of statements of aims and philosophy:

- to develop the attitude and practice of a sound mind in a sound body
- to promote concern for protecting the environment
- to develop a well-rounded individual
- to develop skills sufficient for competing in a global economy
- to promote the pursuit of happiness
- to enrich the spirit
- to develop the ability to use the basic skills
- to develop the ability to think
- to develop a linguistically, technologically, and culturally literate person
- to develop communication skills
- to develop respect for others
- to develop moral, spiritual, and ethical values

Statements of aims and philosophy point to common needs of students and society and set a general framework within which a school or school system will function. In formulating curriculum goals and objectives for a particular school or school system, curriculum developers must give their attention to five sources as shown by components I and II of the model for curriculum development: (1) the needs of students in general, (2) the needs of society, (3) the needs of the particular students, (4) the needs of the particular community, and (5) the needs derived from the subject matter. You will recall that Ralph Tyler, in a similar vein, listed three sources from which tentative general objectives are derived: student, society, and subject.[1]

We can expand on the needs of both students and society in a greater level of detail than is shown in the model for curriculum development by classifying the needs of students and society into two broad categories—levels and types—thereby emphasizing points that curriculum planners should keep in mind.

A CLASSIFICATION SCHEME

To focus our thinking, let's take a look at the following four-part classification scheme:

- needs of students by level
- needs of students by type
- needs of society by level
- needs of society by type

Before analyzing each category, I must stress that the needs of the student cannot be completely divorced from those of society or vice versa. The needs of one are intimately linked to those of the other. True, the two sets of needs sometimes conflict. For example, an individual's need may be contrary to society's when he or she shouts "Fire" to gain attention in a crowded theater when there is no fire. An individual's desire to keep an appointment may result in his or her speeding on the highway and thereby endangering the lives of other members of society. In these two examples, the apparent needs of the person and those of society are antithetical.

The needs of the person and the needs of society are, fortunately, often in harmony. An individual's desire to amass wealth, if carried out legally and fairly, is compatible with a democratic, productive society. The wealth may benefit society in the form of investment or taxes. An individual's need for physical fitness is congruent with society's demand for physically fit people. The literate citizen is as much a need of society as literacy is a need of the individual. A worker's need for technological proficiency contributes to our nation's economic growth. Consequently, it is sometimes difficult to categorize a particular need as specifically a need of the person or of society. That degree of refinement is not necessary. As long as the curriculum planner recognizes the need, its classification is secondary.

Lest there be a misunderstanding, the needs of the particular student do not completely differ from those of students in general but do vary from those of other students who share the same general needs. Students manifest not only their own particular needs but also the needs of young people generally in our society. The needs of a particular community do not completely vary from those of society in general but do differ in some respects from those of other communities that share the same general societal needs. The thousands of communities in the United States are, in spite of local distinctions of needs, resources, and cultural idiosyncrasies, parts of the total culture linked by transportation and mass media, including the Internet.

Interests and Wants

Before proceeding with a discussion of needs of students, we should distinguish between student *interests* and *wants* in curriculum development. *Interest* refers to attitudes of predisposition toward something (for example, auto mechanics, history, dramatics, or basketball). *Want* includes wishes, desires, or longings for something, such as the want for an automobile, spending money, or stylish clothes.

None of the models for curriculum development in Chapter 5 builds into it either the interests or wants of students. The reasons why interests and wants of students are not shown in the proposed model for curriculum development are the following:

1. Interests and wants can be immediate or long range, serious or ephemeral. Immediate and ephemeral interests and wants have less relevance than long-range and serious interests and wants.

2. Both interests and wants may actually be the bases of needs. For example, an interest in the opposite sex, which may be derived from a basic human drive, may indicate a need for curriculum responses in the areas of human and social relationships. A want may actually be a need. The want to be accepted, for example, is, in fact, the psychological need to be accepted. Alternatively, the want for a pair of expensive, designer jeans, though some may possibly argue, is not a need. If, then, interests and wants can be the bases for needs and are sometimes needs themselves, it would be redundant for them to be shown separately in a model for curriculum improvement.

3. It would be unduly complex, burdensome, and confusing for interests and wants to be shown separately in a model for curriculum development.

Curriculum workers and instructional personnel know full well, of course, that they cannot ignore interests and wants of students, for these can be powerful motivators. Certainly, as far as interests go, the literature is filled with admonitions for educators to be concerned with student needs and interests to the point where the two concepts, needs and interests, are one blended concept, needs-and-interests.

Interests and wants of students must be continuously considered and sifted in the processes of both curriculum development and instruction. Although curriculum developers cannot cater to whimsical interests and wants of students, they cannot ignore legitimate and substantial interests and wants.

NEEDS OF STUDENTS: LEVELS

The levels of student needs of concern to the curriculum planner may be identified as (1) human, (2) national, (3) state or regional, (4) community, (5) school, and (6) individual.

Human

The curriculum should reflect the needs of students as members of the human race, needs that are common to all human beings on the globe, for example, food, clothing, shelter, and good health. Franklin D. Roosevelt, in his State of the Union address to the U.S. Congress in 1941, iterated four universal needs of humanity, widely known as the Four Freedoms. These are freedom from want, freedom from fear, freedom to worship God in one's own way, and freedom of speech and expression.

The American student shares in common with his or her brothers and sisters all over the world certain fundamental human needs that the curriculum should address.

The study of anthropology could help a curriculum planner to recognize fundamental human needs.

National

At the national level, the general needs of students in American society are assessed. Chapter 6 already presented efforts to identify nationwide needs of students through statements of aims of education. We might identify as needs of students throughout the nation, development of the ability to think, mastery of basic and technological skills, preparation for a vocation or college, the ability to drive a car, consumer knowledge and skills, and a broad, general knowledge. Some of the national needs we might identify are ones held in common by inhabitants of all nations. For example, few would argue that literacy education is not essential to the development and growth of any nation. In that sense literacy education is a worldwide but not a human need because men and women do not need to read or write to exist. Human beings, however, cannot exist without food and water or with overexposure to the elements.

To become aware of nationwide needs of students, the curriculum planners should be well read, and it is helpful for them to be well traveled. The curriculum planner should recognize changing needs of our country's youth. For example, contemporary young people must learn to live with the computer, to conserve dwindling natural resources, to protect the environment, and to change some basic attitudes to survive in twenty-first century America.

State or Regional

Curriculum planners should determine whether students have needs particular to a state or region. Whereas preparing for a vocation is a common need of all students in American society, preparing for specific vocations may be more appropriate in a particular community, state, or region. General knowledge and specialized training in certain fields, such as health care, teaching, secretarial science, auto mechanics, woodworking, computer programming, and data processing, may be applied throughout the country. However, states or regions may require students to be equipped with specific knowledge and skills for their industrial and agricultural specializations. Construction workers may be needed, for example, in growing areas of the Sunbelt and not in states or regions that are losing population. Some states and regions exceed others in their need for workers in the hospitality industry.

Community

The curriculum developer studies the community served by the school or school system and asks what students' needs are in this particular community. Students growing up in a mining town in West Virginia have some demands that differ from those of students living among the cherry orchards of Michigan. In some urban communities with their melange of races, creeds, colors, and national origins, one of the greatest needs may be to learn to get along with one another. Students who finish school and choose to remain in their communities will need knowledge and skills sufficient for them to earn a livelihood in those communities.

School

The curriculum planner typically probes and excels at analyzing the needs of students in a particular school. These needs command the attention of curriculum workers to such an extent that sometimes the demands of the individual students are obscured. The need for remedial reading and mathematics is obvious in schools where test scores reveal deficiencies. The need for the English language may be pressing in a school with a large percentage of children with another native language. Recently integrated or multiethnic school populations show, as a rule, the need for opening communication among groups. Some schools (especially magnet schools specializing, for example, in science, the performing arts, health occupations, or the building trades) reflect the built-in needs of their student body.[2]

Individual

Finally, the needs of individual students in a particular school must be examined. Can it be that the needs of individual students go unattended while focus is on the needs of the many? Has the school addressed the needs of the average, the gifted, the academically talented, the physically or mentally challenged, the diabetic, the hyperactive, the withdrawn, the aggressive, the antisocial, and the creative pupil (to mention but a few categories of individual behavior)? We must ask to what extent the philosophical pledges to serve the needs of individuals are being carried out.

Each level of student needs builds on the preceding level and makes, in effect, a cumulative set. Thus, the individual student presents needs that emanate from his or her (1) individuality, (2) membership in the school, (3) residence in the community, (4) living in the state or region, (5) residing in the United States, and (6) belonging to the human race.

NEEDS OF STUDENTS: TYPES

Another dimension is added when the curriculum planner analyzes the needs of students by types. Four broad types of needs can be established: physical/biological, sociopsychological, educational, and developmental tasks.

Physical/Biological

Biologically determined, the physical needs of young people are common within the culture and generally constant across cultures. Students need movement, exercise, rest, proper nutrition, and adequate medical care. On leaving the childhood years, students need help with the transition from puberty to adolescence. In the adolescent years they must learn to cope with their developing sexuality and learn the harmful effects of alcohol, drugs, and tobacco on the human body. Providing for the disabled is a growing concern in our society. Obesity of young people is a problem calling for attention. A sound curriculum aids students to understand and meet their physical needs not only during the years of schooling but into adulthood as well.

Sociopsychological

Some curriculum developers might divide this category into social and psychological needs, yet it is often difficult to distinguish between the two. For example, an individual's need for affection is certainly a psychological need. Affection, however, is sought from other individuals and in that context becomes a social need. At first glance, self-esteem seems a purely psychological need. If we believe perceptual psychologists like Earl C. Kelley, however, the self is formed through relationships with others: "The self consists, in part at least, of the accumulated experiential background, or backlog, of the individual. . . . This self is built almost entirely, if not entirely, in relationship to others. . . . Since the self is achieved through social contact, it has to be understood in terms of others."[3]

Among the common sociopsychological needs are affection, acceptance and approval, belonging, success, and security. Furthermore, each individual, both in school and out, needs to be engaged in meaningful work. The lack of significant work may well account, at least in part, for the notorious inefficiency of some nations' bloated governmental bureaucracies.

The needs of the mentally and emotionally exceptional child fit more clearly into the psychological category. Attention must be paid to the wide range of exceptionalities: the gifted, the creative, the emotionally disturbed, the mildly retarded, and the severely retarded among others. Curriculum workers must be able to identify sociopsychological needs of students and to incorporate ways to meet these needs into the curriculum.

Educational

Curriculum planners ordinarily view their task of providing for the educational needs of students as their primary concern. The educational needs of students shift as society changes and as more is learned about the physical and sociopsychological aspects of child growth and development. Historically, schools have gone from emphasizing a classical and theocratic education to a vocational and secular education. They have sought to meet the educational needs of young people through general education, sometimes as the study of contemporary problems of students and/or society. "Life adjustment" courses and career education have been features in our educational history. The basic skills and academic disciplines are currently preferred as the curricular pièce de résistance. The curriculum worker should keep in mind that educational needs do not exist outside the context of students' other needs and society's needs.

Developmental Tasks

Robert J. Havighurst made popular the concept of a "developmental task," which he viewed as a task that had to be completed by an individual at a particular time in his or her development if that individual is to experience success with later tasks.[4] He traced the developmental tasks of individuals in our society from infancy through later maturity and described the biological, psychological, and cultural bases as well as the educational implications of each task.

Found between individual needs and societal demands, developmental tasks do not fall neatly into the schemes developed in this chapter for classifying the needs of students and the needs of society. These tasks are, in effect, personal-social needs that arise at a particular stage of life and that must be met at that stage. In middle childhood, for example, youngsters must learn to live, work, and play harmoniously with each other. In adolescence, individuals must learn to become independent, responsible citizens.

Havighurst addressed the question of the usefulness of the concept of developmental tasks in the following way:

> There are two reasons why the concept of developmental tasks is useful to educators. First, it helps in discovering and stating the purposes of education in the schools. Education may be conceived as the effort of society, through the school, to help the individual achieve . . . certain of his developmental tasks.
>
> The second use of the concept is in the timing of educational efforts. When the body is ripe, and society requires, and the self is ready to achieve a certain task, the teachable moment has come. Efforts at teaching which would have been largely wasted if they had come earlier, give gratifying results when they come at the *teachable moment*, when the task should be learned.[5]

Curriculum planners in earlier years frequently fashioned an often elaborate planning document known as a scope-and-sequence chart. This chart assigned content to be encountered at each grade level following what was known about child growth and development. Today we recognize the necessity for developmental appropriateness, that is, providing learning experiences appropriate to the age and background of the individual learner.[6] Addressing the fit between the curriculum and needs of learners, George S. Morrison saw four types of appropriateness: developmental, in terms of growth and development; individual, in terms of special needs of learners; multicultural, in terms of cultural diversity; and gender, in terms of avoiding discriminatory content or practice.[7]

NEEDS OF SOCIETY: LEVELS

The curriculum worker not only looks at the needs of students in relation to society but also at the needs of society in relation to students. These two levels of needs sometimes converge, diverge, or mirror each other. When we make the needs of students the focal point, we gain a perspective that may differ from that accorded us in studying the needs of society. In analyzing the needs of society, the curriculum worker must bring a particular set of skills to the task. Grounding in the behavioral sciences is especially important to the analysis of the needs of the individual, whereas training in the social sciences is pivotal to the analysis of the needs of society.

As we did in the case of assessing students' needs, let's construct two simple taxonomies of the needs of society: first, as to level, and second, as to type. We can classify the levels of needs of society from the broadest to the narrowest: human, international, national, state, community, and neighborhood.

Human

What needs, we might ask, do human beings throughout the world have as a result of their membership in the human race? Humans as a species possess the same needs as individual human beings—food, clothing, and shelter. Collectively, humankind has a need for freedom from want, from disease, and from fear. As a civilized society, presumably thousands of years removed from the Stone Age, human beings have the need, albeit often unrealized, to live in a state of peace. Human society, by virtue of its position at the pinnacle of evolutionary development, has a continuing need to maintain control over subordinate species of the animal kingdom. When we see the devastation wrought by earthquakes, volcanoes, hurricanes, floods, tornadoes, and drought, we are repeatedly reminded of the need to understand and control the forces of nature. Some of the needs—or demands, if you will—of society are common to the human race.

International

Curriculum developers should consider needs that cut across national boundaries and exist not so much because they are basic needs of humanity but because they arise from our loose confederation of nations. The study of foreign languages, for example, is a response to the need for peoples to communicate with each other. The nations of the world need to improve the flow of trade across their borders. They need to work out more effective means of sharing expertise and discoveries for the benefit of all nations. The more fortunate nations can assist the less fortunate to meet their developmental needs by sharing the fruits of their good fortune. The people of each nation continually need to try to understand more about the culture of other nations.

Many years ago I attempted to define a number of understandings that appeared to be essential for American youth to know about the world. Few of these understandings have changed significantly with the passing of time. With the possible exception of the last item in the following list, the same understandings are relevant to the people of every nation, not only Americans.

All American youth need to understand that

1. the world's population is rapidly outstripping its resources.
2. there is more poverty in the world than riches.
3. more than one-third of the world's population is illiterate.
4. there are more people of color in the world than white.
5. there are more non-Christians in the world than Christians.
6. our actions at home are sources of propaganda abroad.
7. nationalism is on the march as never before.
8. most of the nations of the world are struggling for technical advances.
9. you can reach by air any point on the globe within thirty-six hours. [Today I would reduce the number of hours of air journey to reflect supersonic flight and would

add "you can reach distant spots on the planet almost instantaneously via electronic mail at a miniscule cost."]

10. in spite of our problems at home, thousands of foreigners abroad want to migrate to the land of the free and the home of the brave.[8]

Surely the fact that the world's population of more than 6 billion, which is projected to reach 20 billion within two decades unless stabilized, ethnic wars such as experienced in recent years in the former Yugoslavia and Rwanda, terrorist actions, starvation in countries like Somalia, U.S.-led engagements like the war in Afghanistan, two wars with Iraq, the mistreatment of children and women in some countries, and the volatility of international financial markets provide examples of international problems that can have an impact on contemporary curriculum development.

National

The curriculum planner must be able to define the needs of the nation with some degree of lucidity. Consequently, our form of government rests on the presence of an educated and informed citizenry. Education in citizenship is to a great extent the function of the school. One means of identifying national needs is to examine the social and economic problems faced by the country. The United States has an urgent need, for example, to train or retrain persons in occupations that appear to be growing rather than declining. The curriculum planner must be cognizant of careers that are subject to growth and decline. Employment opportunities will vary from occupation to occupation. Some will experience an increase; others, a decrease.

Projecting employment opportunities between 2004 and 2014, the Bureau of Labor Statistics reported professional and related occupations (computer and mathematical occupations, health care practitioners and technical occupations, and education, training, and library occupations) will grow faster than any other major occupational group. Service occupations constitute the second largest rate of growth (health care service occupations are expected to add the most jobs among service occupations). Computer and health care occupations are expected to grow fastest whereas rail transportation, agriculture, fishing, hunting, and forestry jobs are anticipated to decrease. Employment in management, business, financial, and construction occupations is predicted to increase.[9]

A special note should be said about jobs for teachers. Employment opportunities for teachers have varied from time to time from undersupply to oversupply. In the early years of the twenty-first century school districts face an extreme shortage of teachers, let alone highly qualified teachers, to fill their classrooms. The shortage has forced school systems to add financial incentives to attract teachers especially in fields like mathematics and special education and to recruit teachers far and wide, including abroad.

Employment needs in occupations change as technology continues to develop, consumer demands change, populations shift, global competition stiffens, and outsourcing intensifies. Curriculum workers must stay attuned to changing employment needs.

Not too surprising to persons in education is the finding by the Bureau of Labor Statistics that "Among the 20 fastest growing occupations, a bachelor's or associate degree is the most significant source of postsecondary education or training for 12 of them. . . ."[10]

Schools have responded to career needs of young people through vocational education either in comprehensive high schools, vocational schools, or magnet schools. Since World War I emphasis on vocational education has waxed and waned. The Smith-Hughes Act of 1917, the George-Reed Act of 1963, the George-Dean Act of 1936, the Vocational Education Act of 1963, Charles Prosser's resolution calling for "life adjustment education" and the creation of the Commission on Life Adjustment Education in the post–World War II years, the Carl D. Perkins Act of 1984, and the School-to-Work Opportunities Act of 1994 all addressed career and life needs of youth. The Carl D. Perkins Act (Public Law 98-524, The Vocational Education Act of 1984) furnishes an interesting example of the effects of changing curricular emphases on the U.S. Congress. Amended in 1990, it became the Carl D. Perkins Vocational and Applied Technology Education Act; renewed in 1998 it appeared as the Carl D. Perkins Vocational-Technical Education Act; and reauthorized in 2006 it dropped the older and now less-popular label "vocational" and has become the Carl D. Perkins Career and Technical Improvement Act.

Renewed programs in career education from the 1970s to the present take note of deficiencies among the workforce and seek to help students gain skills necessary for successful employment. Among current means of strengthening career education are analysis of business and industrial needs of the community; specification of outcomes needed by graduates; integration of academic and career education; school-to-work transition programs; establishing partnerships with business and industry; on-the-job experiences concurrent with schooling; and guidance of students in examining a chosen set of occupations (e.g., business, health, communications), a practice known as *career clustering*.

Competition from abroad, changing consumer preferences, and continuing employee needs, such as pensions and health care in the early 2000s, have resulted in the collapse or downsizing of corporations causing the loss of thousands of jobs. As our nation strives to increase employment, it needs employees who feel secure in their work and who do not fear that the competitive free enterprise system will force them into the ranks of the unemployed.

The U.S. Congress responded to a national need—and caused the schools to respond as well—by enacting Public Law 94-192, the Education for All Handicapped Children Act of 1975. Through this and similar legislation, the Congress said that the country could not afford to waste the talents of a sizable segment of the population. The presence of programs in basic skills; citizenship; consumer, global, career, computer, and sexuality education in schools across the country is indicative of curriculum planners' responding to national needs.

The United States has many needs, from improving its educational system to solving ethnic problems to reducing crime to providing for full employment to meeting the health needs of its population to maintaining its world leadership role. The curriculum worker must be a student of history, sociology, political science, economics, and current events to perceive the needs of the nation.

We should note that some writers hold that educational policy has been too closely tied to economics with its principles of efficiency and productivity. Critical of city, state, and national efforts at reform through governmental promotion of standards, assessment, and accountability, Ernest R. House, for example, contended that "national and state leaders formulate educational policies primarily in response to national or state economic concerns without sufficient understanding or appreciation of educational institutions."[11] House observed, "Frequently, policies dedicated to efficiency and productivity in education do not result in better education or improved productivity."[12]

State

States also have special needs. When the sale of automobiles declines, the state of Michigan experiences special difficulties. When the oil industry goes into recession, Texas suffers. When drought parches the wheat belt, the producers of wheat across the Great Plains feel pain. When floods swallow valuable farm land in the Midwest, the calamity strikes producers of corn and soybean. When frost injures the citrus crop, Florida's economy is hurt. When whole industries move from the cold and expensive Northeast to sunnier climes in the United States—and even to Mexico—where labor and other costs are lower, the abandoned states feel the loss.

The continuing movement of population from the North and Midwest to the South, Southwest, and West has brought with it an array of needs not only in the states that people are deserting but also in the states whose populations are growing. Migratory waves of citizens—including those from Puerto Rico—and of noncitizens from Cuba, Vietnam, Mexico, and Haiti have had a great impact on some states in particular and, of course, on the nation as a whole. The presence of an estimated 12 million illegal immigrants already in the United States and the need for stemming the continuing stream of illegals across our porous borders raise both human and economic problems not only for the immigrants but also for the economy as a whole.

State needs become apparent when students consistently evidence inadequate academic performance. To be assured that students are demonstrating competence on state content standards, twenty-five states, as of August 2006, were requiring or getting ready to require their students to pass exit exams in order to receive a high school diploma and graduate.[13] Further, to comply with requirements of *No Child Left Behind*, states must test reading, mathematics, and science at stipulated grade levels.

Job opportunities, needs for training of specialized workers, and types of schooling needed differ from state to state and pose areas of concern for curriculum workers.

Community

Curriculum workers are more frequently able to identify the needs of a community because they are usually aware of significant changes in its major businesses and industries. They know very well, as a rule, whether the community's economy is stagnant, depressed, or booming. On the other hand, changes are sometimes so gradual that schools neglect to adapt their programs to changing community needs. For example, it is possible to find schools that offer programs in agriculture although their communities have shifted to small business and light industry long ago, or we find schools that train pupils for particular manufacturing occupations when the type of manufacturing in the area has changed or factories have been converted to automation. More subtle and more difficult to respond to are needs produced by the impersonality of large urban areas with, in too many cases, an accompanying deterioration in the quality of life. Urban dwellers need to break through the facade of impersonality and develop a sense of mutual respect. They also need to become aware of possible contributions they can make to improve life in the big city.

Shifts of population within a state create problems for communities. There may be, for example, a population movement from the city to the suburbs or farther into the country, followed later by another population shift from the country or the suburbs back to the city. During the 1970s, as disenchanted city dwellers sought a higher quality of life in the country, rural areas experienced significant growth with its accompanying problems. The U.S. Census Bureau figures showed that in the 1980s many Americans became dissatisfied with the rural areas and once again gravitated to the metropolitan areas.[14] We are currently witnessing some regrouping even *within* the metropolitan areas, as, for example, the rejuvenation and restoration of deteriorating downtown and historic areas of cities. Some suburban dwellers have been returning to the central city where properties are depressed and therefore relatively cheap (at least early on). Renovation of old homes promises to make some formerly depressed central city locations once again choice, even expensive, places to inhabit. In contrast, responding to concerns about crime, some urban dwellers have created restricted refuges with walls, gates, alarm systems, and security personnel. The twin problems of escalating costs of housing and conversion of apartments to condominiums, especially in the fast-growing areas of the country, make it difficult for low- and even middle-income workers to find single-family homes, condos, or apartments within their budgets.

Shifts in population create problems for the schools just as the tax base, on which schools rely for partial support, affects the quality of education in a community. School staffs know full well the differences in communities' abilities to raise taxes to support public education. As the *Serrano v. Priest* decision of the California Supreme Court in 1971 and the *Edgewood v. Kirby* decision of the Texas Supreme Court in 1989 clearly demonstrated, wealthier communities with the ability to raise funds through taxes on property can provide a higher quality of education than can communities with a poorer tax base.[15] In this respect community need becomes a state need because education, through the Tenth Amendment to the U.S. Constitution, is a power reserved to the states. Parenthetically we might add that community needs, including schools, become state and federal needs when communities are hit by natural disasters like 2005's Hurricane Katrina.

Schools cannot, of course, solve these societal problems by themselves. Communities must turn primarily to their state legislatures for help in equalizing educational opportunities throughout the state. On the other hand, schools can make—and cannot avoid the obligation to make—an impact on the future citizens of the community whom they are educating by making them aware of the problems and equipping them with skills and knowledge that will help them resolve some of the problems.

Neighborhood

Are there needs, the curriculum developer must ask, peculiar to the neighborhood served by the school? The answer is obvious in most urban areas. The people of the inner city have needs of which the people of the more comfortable suburbs are scarcely aware except through the press and television.

Crime and use of drugs are more common in some neighborhoods than in others. The needs of people in areas that house migrant workers are much different from those of people in areas where executives, physicians, and lawyers reside. Children in lower socioeconomic levels often achieve less in their neighborhood schools than more affluent children do in theirs. As a rule, families of children in the more fortunate schools are able to afford cultural and educational experiences that children in the less fortunate schools seldom encounter.[16]

The curriculum worker must be perceptive of changes in neighborhoods. For example, city dwellers who moved to suburbia in search of the good life are finding—after some years in a housing development, often a tract variety with a sameness of architectural design, and after countless hours of commuting—that the good life has eluded them. They have become disenchanted with wall-to-wall housing and with block after block of shopping centers. Grass, trees, and unpolluted air have given way to the bulldozer, the cement mixer, and disconcerting traffic.

Some of the suburban settlements have joined the central city in experiencing blight, decay, crime, and the host of problems that they originally ascribed to the cities. Consequently, some suburbanites have reversed direction, willing to contend with urban problems and at the same time enjoy the cultural, educational, and recreational resources of the city.

Countering the difficulty for low- and middle-income workers to find affordable housing in some sections of the country, an interesting current social development is the trend toward construction of homes larger than customary in prior years by those who can afford them and the purchase and demolition of small, older but still livable homes in middle- and upper-class neighborhoods by the more affluent, replacing those dwellings with expansive and expensive mansions. Worth watching are housing developments designed to create a congenial small-town atmosphere in a suburban-type setting. These new planned communities employ the concept of a community center surrounded by a mixture of single-family and multi-family residences and apartments. Schools and commercial and recreational facilities are planned to be within walking distance of the homes. Mass transit will link suburbs and nearby urban centers, reducing dependence on the automobile. Sites near Sacramento, California; Tacoma, Washington; Orlando and Tampa, Florida; and in Brevard County, Florida, are locales testing the small-town center concept wherein schools, shops, jobs, and services can be found within walking distance of homes. Perhaps in the twenty-first century not all of America's population will be living in the beehive dwellings predicted by some futurists.

The curriculum specialist must develop plans that show an understanding of the needs of society on all of the foregoing levels.

NEEDS OF SOCIETY: TYPES

The curriculum planner must additionally look at the needs of society from the stand-point of types. For example, each of the following types of societal needs has implications for the curriculum:

- political
- social
- economic
- educational
- environmental
- defense
- health
- moral and spiritual

A curriculum council studying the needs of society would be well advised to try to generate its own system for classifying societal needs. It might then compare its classification system with some of those found in the literature. The Seven Cardinal Principles and the Ten Imperative Needs of Youth, mentioned in Chapter 3, were efforts to identify needs of students as a function of the needs of society.

Social Processes

Numerous attempts have been made throughout the years to identify societal needs or demands under the rubrics of social processes, social functions, life activities, and social institutions. As we review several well-known efforts to specify these needs, we should recall the student-society duality of needs. "Making a home," for example, is both a societal and personal need. The person has a need for the skills of making a home while society has a need for persons who possess homemaking skills. Curriculum specialists who seek to delineate social processes or functions do so in order to identify individual needs that have social origins. It might be argued, parenthetically, that all personal needs (except purely biological ones) are social in origin.

Robert S. Zais credited Herbert Spencer for the beginning of the practice of studying society empirically.[17] In 1859 Spencer recommended that students be prepared for "the leading kinds of activity which constitute human life."[18] He classified these activities in order of importance as follows:

1. Those activities which directly minister to self-preservation
2. Those activities which, by securing the necessaries of life, indirectly minister to self-preservation
3. Those activities which have for their end the rearing and discipline of offspring
4. Those activities which are involved in the maintenance of proper social and political relations
5. Those miscellaneous activities which make up the leisure part of life, devoted to the gratification of the tastes and feelings[19]

The 1934 Virginia State Curriculum Program has been identified as one of the better-known attempts to organize a curriculum around life processes.[20] O. I. Frederick and Lucile J. Farquear reported the following nine areas of human activity that the state of Virginia incorporated into the curriculum of the schools:

1. Protecting life and health
2. Getting a living
3. Making a home
4. Expressing religious impulses
5. Satisfying the desire for beauty
6. Securing education
7. Cooperating in social and civic action
8. Engaging in recreation
9. Improving material conditions[21]

The Wisconsin State Department of Public Instruction's *Guide to Curriculum Building* has been highly regarded for its social functions approach. The Wisconsin State Department of Public Instruction listed the following social functions in its guide for a core curriculum at the junior high school level.[22]

- To keep the population healthy.
- To provide physical protection and guarantee against war.
- To conserve and wisely utilize natural resources.
- To provide opportunity for people to make a living.
- To rear and educate the young.
- To provide wholesome and adequate recreation.
- To enable the population to satisfy aesthetic and spiritual values.
- To provide sufficient social cement to guarantee social integration.
- To organize and govern in harmony with beliefs and aspirations.[23]

Florence B. Stratemeyer, Hamden L. Forkner, Margaret G. McKim, and A. Harry Passow proposed a plan for organizing curriculum experiences around activities of human beings, as shown in the following list:

Situations Calling for Growth in Individual Capacities:
Health
  A. Satisfying physiological needs
  B. Satisfying emotional and social needs
  C. Avoiding and caring for illness and injury
Intellectual power
  A. Making ideas clear
  B. Understanding the ideas of others
  C. Dealing with quantitative relationships
  D. Using effective methods of work
Moral choices
  A. Determining the nature and extent of individual freedom

    B. Determining responsibility to self and others
Aesthetic expression and appreciation
    A. Finding sources of aesthetic satisfaction in oneself
    B. Achieving aesthetic satisfactions through the environment

Situations Calling for Growth in Social Participation:
Person-to-person relationships
    A. Establishing effective social relations with others
    B. Establishing effective working relationships with others
Group membership
    A. Deciding when to join a group
    B. Participating as a group member
    C. Taking leadership responsibilities
Intergroup relationships
    A. Working with racial, religious, and national groups
    B. Working with socioeconomic groups
    C. Dealing with groups organized for specific action

*Situations Calling for Growth in Ability to Deal
with Environmental Factors and Forces:*
Natural phenomena
    A. Dealing with physical phenomena
    B. Dealing with plant, animal, and insect life
    C. Using physical and chemical forces
Technological resources
    A. Using technological resources
    B. Contributing to technological advance
Economic-social-political structures and forces
    A. Earning a living
    B. Securing goods and services
    C. Providing for social welfare
    D. Molding public opinion
    E. Participating in local and national government[24]

Taba pointed out the strength of the Stratemeyer, Forkner, McKim, and Passow scheme:

> This . . . scheme seems to be an effort to correct one deficiency of the social-process approach, the disregard for the learner. In effect, this approach combines the concepts of common activities, needs, and life situations with an awareness of the learner as a factor in curriculum design and uses both to find a unifying scheme.[25]

In sum, the curriculum worker must analyze both the needs of learners and of society. The study of both "sources," as Ralph Tyler called them, provides clues for curricular implementation and organization.

NEEDS DERIVED FROM THE SUBJECT MATTER

One major source of curriculum objectives remains for us to consider—needs as derived from the subject matter or, as Jerome S. Bruner and others would say, from the "structure of a subject."[26] Bruner refers to the structure of a subject as the "basic ideas"[27] or "fundamental principles."[28] "Grasping the structure of a subject," said Bruner, "is understanding it in such a way that permits many other things to be related to it meaningfully. To learn structure, in short, is to learn how things are related."[29]

As examples of elements of the structure of disciplines, Bruner mentioned tropism in the field of biology; commutation, distribution, and association in mathematics; and linguistic patterns in the field of language.[30] Each subject contains certain essential areas or topics (the bases for determining the scope of a course) that, if the learner is to achieve mastery of the field, must be taught at certain times and in a certain prescribed order (sequence). The sequence could be determined by increasing complexity (as in mathematics, foreign languages, English grammar, science), by logic (as in social studies programs that begin with the child's immediate environment—the home and school—and expand to the community, state, nation, and world), or by psychological means (as in career education programs that start with immediate interests of learners and proceed to more remote ones).

Changes in the Disciplines

The subject matter areas remained essentially the same (except for updating) until the 1950s with the advent of the "new math," the "new science," the "new linguistics," and the widespread development of the audio-lingual method of teaching foreign languages. The scholarly ferment of the 1950s, propelled by National Defense Education Act funds, produced such new definitions of the structures of the disciplines as the three versions of a course in biology (blue, green, and yellow) developed by the Biological Sciences Curriculum Study (BSCS). Each version presented principles of biology with a different central focus and organization. The structure of this field of science as prescribed in the green version, considered by many as the easiest of the three, centered around the topics of evolution and ecology. The blue version, considered by many as the most difficult, stressed biochemistry and physiology, and the yellow version concentrated on genetics and the development of organisms.

Two additional projects reflect the type of planning going on in the field of science in the mid-1950s and early 1960s. The Physical Sciences Study Committee (PSSC)—that began its work in 1956, just three years before the Biological Sciences Curriculum Study was initiated—unified a high school course in physics under the following four topics:

1. the universe, which includes time, space, matter, and motion
2. optics and waves, which involves a study of optical phenomena
3. mechanics, which concerns dynamics, momentum, energy, and the laws of conservation
4. electricity, which includes electricity, magnetism, and the structure of the atom[31]

In the early 1960s the Earth Science Curriculum Project developed an earth-science course with the following ten unifying themes:

1. Science as inquiry
2. Comprehension of scale
3. Prediction
4. Universality of change
5. Flow of energy in the universe
6. Adjustment to environmental change
7. Conservation of mass and energy in the universe
8. Earth systems in time and space
9. Uniformity of process
10. Historical development and presentation[32]

While scientists were overhauling the curriculum of their specialties, the foreign language curriculum workers were breaking out of the mold of the old reading-translation objectives that dominated foreign language study for generations. The following passage called attention to the change in objectives of foreign language study:

> The objectives, in order of priority, among foreign language teachers are: (a) aural comprehension, (b) speaking, (c) reading, and (d) writing. . . . The four above-mentioned linguistic objectives are integrated with the general cultural objectives, understanding of the foreign customs and foreign peoples.[33]

Foreign language study provides an excellent illustration of a sequenced structure because language students will learn a foreign language more readily when, for example, the concept of singular is presented before the concept of plural, when regular verbs are taught before irregular verbs, when the first person singular is mastered before other persons, when the present tense is perfected before other tenses, when simple tenses come before compound, and when the indicative mood is taught before the subjunctive.

Performance Objectives/Standards

Many state departments of education and/or local school districts have published syllabi, courses of study, and curriculum guides developed by teacher-specialists in particular fields.[34] These publications outline the structure of a subject, the appropriate grade level for each topic; the performance objectives, standards, skills, or minimal competencies to be accomplished; and often the order of presentation (sequence) of topics. Many cities and states and even the nation have been and continue to be engaged in the specification of performance objectives or standards in subject areas.[35]

Some education specialists criticize the movement toward adoption of performance objectives/standards. They raise objections not only to the standardizing effect but also the nature of standards that they view as imposed and contrary to pressing social needs. Although specification of subject-matter standards has been subjected to criticism, the

Boston Public Schools Standards in Chemistry

I. Content Standards
1. Properties of Matter
Broad Concept: Physical and chemical properties reflect the nature of the interactions between molecules or atoms and can be used to classify and describe matter.

1.1 Identify and explain physical properties (such as density, melting point, boiling point conductivity, and malleability) and chemical properties (such as the ability to form new substances). Distinguish between chemical and physical changes.

1.2 Explain the difference between pure substances (elements and compounds) and mixtures. Differentiate between heterogeneous and homogeneous mixtures.

1.3 Describe the three normal states of matter (solid, liquid, gas) in terms of energy, particle motion, and phase transitions.

Source: Boston Public Schools, *Chemistry High School Standards*, website: http://www.boston.k12.ma.us/teach/HSScience .pdf, accessed March 15, 2007. Reprinted by permission.

movement continues strong as we can see from the following examples from the city of Boston and the states of Arizona, California, and Massachusetts.

Boston and the Massachusetts Department of Education. Illustrative of school districts' performance standards in the various disciplines are those of the Boston Public Schools. Let's take, for example, Boston's standards for high school chemistry, shown in Box 7.1.

The Massachusetts Department of Education has created a set of prekindergarten through high school curriculum frameworks with performance standards in eight academic disciplines. Taking science as an example, the Boston performance standards parallel those of the state, which we should expect.[36]

Arizona. Extensive, detailed K–12 content standards, approved between 1996 and 2000 in nine academic disciplines, include, for example, seven standards in Comprehensive Health. Arizona classified its standards by levels: Readiness (kindergarten), Foundations (grades 1–3), Essentials (grades 4–8), Proficiency (grades 9–12), and Distinction (Honors). Each set of standards includes a rationale followed by a number of performance standards and objectives. Box 7.2 provides a sample of the Arizona taxonomy in Health from among seven standards at the Foundations level with performance objectives for the standard.

California. From content standards in seven fields, number 10.1 of the eleven content standards in the field of History and Social Science for grade 10, shown in Box 7.3, is an example of California's endeavors in curriculum development.

The purpose of the discussion of needs to this point is to direct the curriculum developers to consider three major sources of needs—the learner, the society, and the subject matter. Although, as we noted in Chapter 5, Ralph Tyler discussed these three

BOX 7.2

Arizona Department of Education Standards in Health, Foundations Level

1CH-F1 Describe relationships between personal health behavior (e.g., sleep, diet, fitness, and personal hygiene) and individual well-being.
  PO1 Explain the positive effects of a balanced, healthy lifestyle (e.g., being alert, rested, energetic, healthy)

PO2 Explain the importance of personal health-promoting behaviors (e.g., covering sneezes and coughs, proper hand washing, adequate sleep, healthy diet, physical activity).

Source: Arizona Department of Education, *Content Standards K–12,* websites: http://www.ade.state.az.us/standards/health/CompStd1.asp and http://www.ade.state.az.us/standards/contentstandards.asp, accessed March 15, 2007. Reprinted by permission.

sets of needs as sources from which tentative general objectives are derived—a sound procedure—they are examined and illustrated here as a preface to a systematic procedure for studying needs and identifying those not met by the school's curriculum. Such a procedure is usually referred to in the literature as a needs assessment.

CONDUCTING A NEEDS ASSESSMENT

In its simplest definition a *curriculum needs assessment* is a process for identifying programmatic needs that must be addressed by curriculum planners. Fenwick W. English and

BOX 7.3

California State Board of Education Content Standards in World History, Culture, and Geography: The Modern World

10.1 Students relate to the moral and ethical principles in ancient Greek and Roman philosophy, in Judaism, and in Christianity to the development of Western political thought.
  1. Analyze the similarities and differences in Judeo-Christian and Greco-Roman views of law, reason and faith, and duties of the individual.

2. Trace the development of the Western political ideas of the rule of law and illegitimacy of tyranny, using selections of Plato's *Republic* and Aristole's *Politics.*
3. Consider the influence of the U.S. Constitution on political systems in the contemporary world.

Source: Reprinted by permission, from *Content Standards in World History, Culture, and Geography: The Modern World,* websites: http://cde.ca.gov/board/pdf/history.pdf and http://www.cde.ca.gov/standards, accessed April 21, 2003. Revisited March 15, 2007, at website: http://www.cde.ca.gov/be/st/ss/hstgrade10.asp.

Roger A. Kaufman offered several interpretations of the term "needs assessment." This earlier work published by the Association for Supervision and Curriculum Development remains a thorough description of a process that school systems have been engaging in for many years. English and Kaufman described needs assessment as a process

- of defining the desired end (or outcome, product, or result) . . . of a given sequence of curriculum development
- of making specific . . . what school should be about and how it can be assessed for defining the outcomes of education . . .
- for determining the validity of behavioral objectives and if standardized and/or criterion-referenced tests are appropriate and under what conditions
- [that] is a logical problem-solving tool . . .
- [that] is a tool which formally harvests the gaps between current results . . . and required or desired results [and] places these gaps in priority . . . .[37]

The objectives of a needs assessment are twofold: (1) to identify needs of the learners not being met by the existing curriculum and (2) to form a basis for revising the curriculum in such a way as to fulfill as many unmet needs as possible. The conduct of a needs assessment is not a single, one-time operation but a continuing and periodic activity. Some curriculum workers perceive a needs assessment as a task to be accomplished at the beginning of an extensive study of the curriculum. Once the results are obtained from this initiatory needs assessment, these planners believe that further probing is unnecessary for a number of years.

Since the needs of students, society, and the subject matter change over the years and since no curriculum has reached a state of perfection in which it ministers to all the educational needs of young people, a thorough needs assessment should be conducted periodically—at least every five years—with at least minor updating annually.

A needs assessment is also not time-specific in that it takes place only at the beginning of a comprehensive study of the curriculum. A needs assessment is a continuing activity that takes place (a) before specification of curricular goals and objectives, (b) after identification of curricular goals and objectives, (c) after evaluation of instruction, and (d) after evaluation of the curriculum.[38] English and Kaufman pointed out that most school systems require six months to two years to complete a full-scale needs assessment.[39] Not all school systems, of course, conduct full-scale needs assessments. The scope of assessments varies from simple studies of perceived needs to thorough analyses using extensive data.

Perceived Needs Approach

Some schools limit the process of assessing needs to a survey of the needs of learners as perceived by (1) teachers, (2) students, and (3) parents. Instead of turning to objective data, curriculum planners in these schools pose questions that seek opinions from one or more of these groups. Parents, for example, are asked questions like these:

- How well do you feel your child is doing in school?
- Is your child experiencing any difficulty in school? If so, please explain.

- What content or programs do you believe the school should offer that are not now being offered?
- What suggestions do you have for improving the school's programs?
- Are you satisfied with the programs that the school is offering your child? If you are dissatisfied with any program, please specify which ones and your reasons.

Teachers and students may be asked to respond to similar questions in order to gain their perceptions of the school's curriculum and of needed improvements. The perceived needs approach, however, is but the first stage of the process. It is advantageous in that it is a simple process, requires relatively little time and effort, and is relatively inexpensive to conduct. It also provides an opportunity for the various groups to express their views about what is needed in the curriculum. The perceived needs approach becomes an effective public relations device when it is used with parents; it says, in effect, that the school cares to know what parents think about the school's programs and wants their suggestions. As a first step, the perceived needs approach is worthwhile.

On the other hand, the perceived needs approach is limited. By its very nature, it is concerned with perceptions rather than facts. Although the curriculum planner must learn the perceptions of various groups, he or she must also know what the facts are. The needs of learners as perceived by the various groups may be quite different from needs as shown by more objective data. Consequently, a needs assessment must be carried beyond the gathering of perception of needs.

Data Collection

Those charged with conducting a needs assessment should gather data about the school and its programs from whatever sources of data are available. Necessary data include background information about the community, the student body, and the staff. Curriculum planners will need information on programs offered and available facilities. They must have access to all test data on the achievement of students in the school. Data may be obtained from various sources, including student records; school district files; surveys of attitudes of students, teachers, and parents; classroom observations; and examination of instructional materials. English described a process for collecting data in a school through examination of appropriate documents and practices, which he referred to as a "curriculum audit."[40]

Adequate data are necessary for making decisions about the selection of fields and topics to be encountered by the students and for specifying the goals of the curriculum. The data will provide clues as to the necessity for curriculum change. All these data should be put together in a coherent fashion so that they can be analyzed and decisions can be made about revising the curriculum.[41]

A needs assessment is customarily carried out when pressure is felt by personnel in schools seeking accreditation by their regional accrediting associations. Schools desiring regional accreditation normally conduct a full-scale self-study and are visited by a full committee every ten years; they also conduct interim studies every five years. Schools applying for accreditation follow criteria established by their accrediting association, often in conjunction with materials produced by their state department of education and the National Study of School Evaluation (NSSE).[42]

STEPS IN THE NEEDS ASSESSMENT PROCESS

The needs assessment process includes the following steps:

- Setting and validating curriculum goals
- Prioritizing curriculum goals
- Converting prioritized curriculum goals to curriculum objectives[43]
- Prioritizing curriculum objectives
- Gathering data
- Identifying unmet curricular needs, i.e., gaps between desired curriculum objectives and actual curriculum objectives
- Prioritizing curricular needs
- Implementing prioritized needs
- Evaluating success of prioritized curriculum objectives[44]

These steps may look simple but in reality they are complex. They involve many people: school boards, administrators, teachers, students, parents, other members of the community. They call for an intimate knowledge of the school, school district, and community, even of the state and nation. Although leaders will be identified and charged with directing the process, needs assessment is primarily an activity requiring the participation of many groups. Those assigned leadership roles should come to the needs assessment process with a firm grounding in curriculum, sociology, and psychology.

Those conducting a needs assessment must gather extensive data about the school and community and must make use of multiple means of assessment, including opinions, empirical observation, inventories, predictive instruments, and tests. They should follow constructive techniques for involving and managing individuals and groups throughout the process, and must apply effective methods for sharing information to keep participants and the community abreast of the process. They must seek out the help of persons trained and experienced in curriculum development, instruction, staff development, budgeting, data gathering, data processing, measurement, and evaluation.

The needs assessment process is designed to inform those affected by the process as to which curriculum features should be kept as is, kept with revision, removed, and/or added.

Thus, you can see that a thorough needs assessment is more than a "quick and dirty" survey of perceived needs. When done properly, it is a time-consuming, repetitive process that requires the commitment of human and material resources sufficient to accomplish the job. A systematic process for discovering the unmet needs of learners is an essential phase of curriculum improvement.

Summary

Curriculum planners must attend to the needs of students and society. These needs may be classified as to level and type. Various attempts have been made to identify the social processes, functions, and institutions that have import for the curriculum.

Each discipline has its own unique set of elements or structure that affects decisions about scope and sequence. The structure of a subject is shown by exposition of the basic ideas, fundamental principles, broad generalizable topics, competencies, or performance objectives.

In addition to studying empirically the needs of students, society, and the disciplines, curriculum workers should conduct systematic needs assessments to identify gaps—discrepancies between desired and actual student performance. Identified unmet needs should play a major role in curriculum revision.

A curriculum needs assessment permits school systems to discover deficiencies in their curricula. In addition, it creates a vehicle for school and community cooperation, builds community understanding of the school's programs and support for the school's efforts to fill in the gaps, and forces decisions on priorities.

Questions for Discussion

1. What is the relationship between (1) needs of learners, society, and subject matter and (2) a curriculum needs assessment?

2. What is the appropriate role of the community in a curriculum needs assessment?

3. What is the appropriate role of teachers in a curriculum needs assessment?

4. What is the appropriate role of administrators and supervisors in a curriculum needs assessment?

5. What is the appropriate role of students in a curriculum needs assessment?

Exercises

1. Explain how you would go about identifying the needs of students.

2. Explain how you would go about identifying needs of society.

3. Identify several of the basic ideas (structure) of a discipline that you know well.

4. Explain how a curriculum needs assessment model could be implemented in your community.

5. Give an illustration of at least one need of students at the following levels:
   human
   national
   state or regional
   community
   school
   individual

6. Give an illustration of at least one student need of the following types:
   physical
   sociopsychological
   educational

7. Analyze Robert J. Havighurst's developmental tasks of middle childhood or adolescence (see bibliography) and judge whether you feel each task is still relevant. Give reasons for your position on each task that you feel is no longer relevant.

8. Confer with appropriate personnel in a school system you know well and see if the school system has conducted a curriculum needs assessment in recent years. Report on instrumentation and results if a needs assessment has been conducted.

9. Conduct a simple study using the Delphi Technique for predicting future development. (See Olaf Helmer reference in the bibliography.)

10. Describe the process of goal validation as explained by English and Kaufman (see bibliography).

11. Examine the report of the school-and-community committee of a school that has undergone regional accreditation and summarize the data contained therein.

12. Identify needs that the following topics or activities are supposed to fill:
    federal income tax
    Friday night football
    Jacksonian democracy
    display of children's art
    managing credit
    Beowulf
    periodic chart of the elements

adding mixed fractions
ancient Greece
building cabinets
word processing
Chinese language
Beethoven's Fifth Symphony

13. Report on ways in which schools are integrating academic and career education. Include in your report ways in which schools are easing the transition of students from school to work.

14. Read and report on Henry C. Morrison's description of social activities (see bibliography).

15. Create your own list of social processes or functions and compare this list with one found in the professional literature.

16. Read and report on Herbert Spencer's description of life activities (see bibliography).

 ## Feature Films

Stand and Deliver. 103 min. 1988. Warner Bros., Jaime Escalante teaches calculus to inner-city students in Los Angeles.

The Ron Clark Story. 96 min. 2006. Johnson & Johnson Spotlight Presentation (TV). Ron Clark teaches disadvantaged New York City students.

 ## Websites

Center on Education Policy: http://www/cep-dc.org

National Study of School Evaluation: http://www.nsse.org

Endnotes

1. See Chapter 5.
2. For discussion of magnet schools see Chapter 9.
3. Earl C. Kelley, "The Fully Functioning Self," in *Perceiving, Behaving, Becoming*, 1962 Yearbook (Alexandria, Va.: Association for Supervision and Curriculum Development, 1962), pp. 9, 13.
4. See Robert J. Havighurst, *Developmental Tasks and Education*, 3rd ed. (New York: Longman, 1972).
5. Robert J. Havighurst, *Developmental Tasks and Education*, 1st ed. (Chicago: University of Chicago Press, 1948), p. 8.
6. See Scott Willis, "Teaching Young Children: Educators Seek 'Developmental Appropriateness,'" *ASCD Curriculum Update* (November 1993): 1–8.
7. George S. Morrison, *Contemporary Curriculum K–8* (Boston: Allyn and Bacon, 1993), pp. 88–90.
8. Peter F. Oliva, "Essential Understandings for the World Citizen," *Social Education* 23, no. 6 (October 1959): 266–268.
9. U.S. Department of Labor, Bureau of Labor Statistics, *Occupational Outlook Handbook* online. Website: http://www.bls.gov/oco/oco2003.htm, accessed September 18, 2006.
10. Ibid.
11. Ernest R. House, *Schools for Sale: Why Free Market Policies Won't Improve America's Schools and What Will* (New York: Teacher College Press, 1998), p. 8.
12. Ibid., p. 10.

13. See website: http://www.cep-dc.org/pubs/hsee August2006/NewRelease8-11.pdf (Center on Education Policy), accessed September 18, 2006.

14. Donald E. Starsinic, *Patterns of Metropolitan Area and County Population Growth, 1980–1984*, Current Population Reports, Population Estimates and Projection Series P-25, No. 976, U.S. Department of Commerce, Bureau of the Census (Washington, D.C.: U.S. Government Printing Office, October 1985).

15. *Serrano v. Priest*, 5 Cal. 3rd 584, 487 P. 2nd 1241 (1971) and *Edgewood Independent School District et al. v. William Kirby et al.* S.W. Texas 777 S.S. 2d 391 (Tex. 1989).

16. For a notable and heartwarming, if dated, example of student achievement in a lower socioeconomic neighborhood, view the Warner Brothers' film *Stand and Deliver*, Burbank, Calif.: Warner Home Video, 1988, starring James Edward Olmos. The film portrays James Escalante's success in teaching calculus to inner-city students at Garfield High School in Los Angeles. View also *The Ron Clark Story* (2006), a made-for-TV Johnson & Johnson Spotlight Presentation movie starring Matthew Perry as Ron Clark who taught disadvantaged students in rural North Carolina and Harlem and currently has an academy in Atlanta.

17. Robert S. Zais, *Curriculum: Principles and Foundations* (New York: Harper & Row, 1976), p. 301.

18. Herbert Spencer, "What Knowledge Is of Most Worth?" in *Education: Intellectual, Moral, and Physical* (New York: John B. Alden, 1885). Quotations are from 1963 ed. (Paterson, N.J.: Littlefield, Adams), p. 32.

19. Ibid.

20. Hilda Taba, *Curriculum Development: Theory and Practice* (New York: Harcourt Brace Jovanovich, 1962), p. 398.

21. O. I. Frederick and Lucile J. Farquear, "Areas of Human Activity," *Journal of Educational Research* 30, no. 9 (May 1937): 672–679.

22. For discussion of the core curriculum see Chapter 9.

23. Wisconsin State Department of Public Instruction, *Guide to Curriculum Building*, Bulletin No. 8 (Madison, Wis.: State Department of Public Instruction, January 1950), p. 74.

24. Florence B. Stratemeyer, Hamden L. Forkner, Margaret G. McKim, and A. Harry Passow, Chapter 6,

"The Scope of Persistent Life Situations and Ways in Which Learners Face Them," in *Developing a Curriculum for Modern Living*, 2nd ed. (New York: Teachers College Press, 1957), pp. 146–172.

25. Taba, *Curriculum Development*, p. 399.

26. Jerome S. Bruner, *The Process of Education* (Cambridge, Mass.: Harvard University Press, 1960), p. 6.

27. Ibid., pp. 12–13.

28. Ibid., p. 25.

29. Ibid., p. 7.

30. Ibid., pp. 7–8.

31. Peter F. Oliva, *The Secondary School Today*, 2nd ed. (New York: Harper & Row, 1972), p. 151.

32. Ibid., p. 152.

33. Peter F. Oliva, *The Teaching of Foreign Languages* (Englewood Cliffs, N.J.: Prentice-Hall, 1969), p. 11.

34. For discussion of curriculum products, see Chapter 14 of this text.

35. See Chapter 15 for discussion of standards.

36. See website: http://www.doe.mass.edu/frameworks/current.html.

37. Fenwick W. English and Roger A. Kaufman, *Needs Assessment: A Focus on Curriculum Development* (Alexandria, Va.: Association for Supervision and Curriculum Development, 1975), pp. 3–4.

38. See components of the suggested model for curriculum development, Chapter 5 of this text, Figure 5.4.

39. English and Kaufman, *Needs Assessment*, p. 14.

40. Fenwick W. English, *Curriculum Auditing* (Lancaster, Penn.: Technomic Publishing Company, 1988), p. 33.

41. See Jon Wiles and Joseph C. Bondi, *Curriculum Development: A Guide to Practice*, 7th ed. (Upper Saddle River, N.J.: Merrill/Prentice Hall, 2007), p. 87 for a suggested outline of needs assessment data.

42. National Study of School Evaluation, 1699 East Woodfield Road, Suite 406, Schaumburg, Ill. 60173-4958. Website: http://www.nsse.org.

43. For discussion of Curriculum Goals and Objectives see Chapter 8 of this text.

44. For detailed steps in needs assessment and post-needs-assessment, see English and Kaufman, *Needs Assessment*, pp. 12–48.

Bibliography

Bruner, Jerome S. *The Process of Education*. Cambridge, Mass.: Harvard University Press, 1960.

Combs, Arthur W., ed. *Perceiving, Behaving, Becoming*, 1962 Yearbook. Alexandria, Va.: Association for Supervision and Curriculum Development, 1962.

English, Fenwick W. *Curriculum Auditing*. Lancaster, Penn.: Technomic Publishing Company, 1988.

——— and Kaufman, Roger A. *Needs Assessment: A Focus for Curriculum Development*. Alexandria, Va.: Association for Supervision and Curriculum Development, 1975.

Frederick, O. I. and Farquear, Lucile J. "Areas of Human Activity." *Journal of Educational Research* 30 (May 1937): 672–679.

Goodlad, John I. *Curriculum Inquiry: The Study of Curriculum Practice*. New York: McGraw-Hill, 1979.

Havighurst, Robert J. *Developmental Tasks and Education*, 3rd ed. New York: Longman, 1972.

Helmer, Olaf. "Analysis of the Future: The Delphi Method." In *Technological Forecasting for Industry and Government: Methods and Applications*, ed. James R. Bright, 116–122. Englewood Cliffs, N.J.: Prentice-Hall, 1968.

House, Ernest R. *Schools for Sale: Why Free Market Policies Won't Improve America's Schools and What Will*. New York: Teachers College Press, 1998.

Kaplan, B. A. *Needs Assessment for Education: A Planning Handbook for School Districts*. Trenton, N.J.: New Jersey Department of Education, Bureau of Planning, February 1974. ERIC: ED 089 405.

Kaufman, Roger A. "Needs Assessment." In Fenwick W. English, ed., *Fundamental Curriculum Decisions*, 1983 Yearbook. Alexandria, Va.: Association for Supervision and Curriculum Development, 1983.

——— and English, Fenwick W. *Needs Assessment: Concept and Application*. Englewood Cliffs, N.J.: Educational Technology Publications, 1979.

Kelley, Earl C. "The Fully Functioning Self." In Arthur W. Combs, ed., *Perceiving, Behaving, Becoming*, 1962 Yearbook. Alexandria, Va.: Association for Supervision and Curriculum Development, 1962, pp. 9–20.

Morrison, George S. *Contemporary Curriculum K–8*. Boston: Allyn and Bacon, 1993.

Morrison, Henry C. *The Curriculum of the Common School*. Chicago: University of Chicago Press, 1940.

National Study of School Evaluation. *Breakthrough School Improvement: An Action Guide for Greater and Faster Results*. Schaumburg, Ill.: National Study of School Evaluation, 2006.

———. *School Improvement: Focusing on Student Performance*. Schaumburg, Ill.: National Study of School Evaluation, 1997.

Oliva, Peter F. "Essential Understandings for the World Citizen." *Social Education* 23, no. 6 (October 1959): 266–268.

———. *The Secondary School Today*, 2nd ed. New York: Harper & Row, 1972.

———. *The Teaching of Foreign Languages*. Englewood Cliffs, N.J.: Prentice-Hall, 1969.

Smith, B. Othanel, Stanley, William O., and Shores, J. Harlan. *Fundamentals of Curriculum Development*, rev. ed. New York: Harcourt Brace Jovanovich, 1957.

Spencer, Herbert. *Education: Intellectual, Moral, and Physical*. New York: John B. Alden, 1885. Paterson, N.J.: Littlefield, Adams, 1963.

Stratemeyer, Florence B., Forkner, Hamden L., McKim, Margaret G., and Passow, A. Harry. *Developing a Curriculum for Modern Living*, 2nd ed. New York: Bureau of Publications, Teachers College Press, Columbia University, 1957.

Taba, Hilda. *Curriculum Development: Theory and Practice*. New York: Harcourt Brace Jovanovich, 1962.

Tyler, Ralph W. *Basic Principles of Curriculum and Instruction*. Chicago: University of Chicago Press, 1949.

Wiles, Jon and Bondi, Joseph C. *Curriculum Development: A Guide to Practice*, 7th ed. Upper Saddle River, N.J.: Merrill/Prentice Hall, 2007.

———, Bondi, Joseph, and Wiles, Michele Tillier. *The Essential Middle School*, 4th ed. Upper Saddle River, N.J.: Merrill/Prentice Hall, 2006.

Willis, Scott. "Teaching Young Children: Educators Seek 'Developmental Appropriateness.'" *ASCD Curriculum Update* (November 1993): 1–8.

Witkin, B. R. *An Analysis of Needs Assessment Techniques for Educational Planning at State, Intermediate, and District Levels*, May 1975. ERIC: ED 108 370.

Zais, Robert S. *Curriculum: Principles and Foundations*. New York: Harper & Row, 1976.

Zenger, Weldon F. and Zenger, Sharon K. *Curriculum Planning: A Ten-Step Process*. Palo Alto, Calif.: R & E Research Associates, 1982.

8 Curriculum Goals and Objectives

HIERARCHY OF OUTCOMES

Following the model for curriculum improvement suggested in Chapter 5, let's see how far we have come. We have

- analyzed needs of students in general in society
- analyzed needs of American society
- reviewed aims of education and affirmed those with which we are in agreement
- written a philosophy of education
- initiated a needs assessment by surveying needs of students in the community and school and by surveying needs of the community
- conducted a needs assessment and identified unmet needs

All of these steps are a prelude to the next phase. They provide a framework; they set the stage. They furnish data that are vital to making curricular decisions. The planning of the curriculum is now about to begin.

In Chapter 6 you encountered the terms "aims of education," "curriculum goals," "curriculum objectives," "instructional goals," and "instructional objectives" as used in this text. We discussed a hierarchy of purposes of education from the broadest to the narrowest. Let's review that hierarchy; it is essential both to this chapter on curriculum goals and objectives and to Chapter 10 on instructional goals and objectives. We might chart this hierarchy as shown in Figure 8.1.[1]

It sometimes seems that the educational literature is surfeited with discussions of goals and objectives. In spite of these many commentaries, I have included discussion of aims, goals, and objectives in three chapters of this text (Chapters 6, 8, and 10) for the following reasons:

1. They are essential components in a comprehensive model for curriculum improvement.
2. These various terms for "purpose" are used loosely and interchangeably in the literature, leading to possible confusion.
3. Some of the recommendations in the literature on the writing of goals and objectives are helpful; other recommendations seem less helpful.

Aims, Goals, and Objectives

Several problems can be found if we research the literature on aims, goals, and objectives. First, aims of education are often equated with goals, and in a lexical sense, of course, they are the same. Many years ago John W. Gardner in *Goals for Americans* was describing aims of education when he wrote:

> Our deepest convictions impel us to foster individual fulfillment. We wish each one to achieve the promise that is in him. We wish each one to be worthy of a free society, and capable of strengthening a free society. . . .

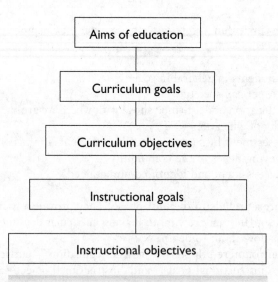

FIGURE 8.1   Hierarchy of Outcomes

Ultimately, education serves all of our purposes—liberty, justice, and all our other aims—but the one it serves most directly is equality of opportunity.

[The] . . . tasks of producing certain specially needed kinds of educated talent . . . should not crowd out the great basic goals of our educational system: to foster individual fulfillment and to nurture the free, rational and responsible men and women without whom our kind of society cannot endure. Our schools must prepare *all* young people, whatever their talents, for the serious business of being free men and women.[2]

In this case the problem of equating aims of education with goals is minor because Gardner communicates to the reader that he is consistently discussing broad goals or aims. The problem arises when discussions of aims, curriculum goals and objectives, and instructional goals and objectives are intermingled. There is little difficulty when a single meaning for a term is used in a single context or when an author clearly defines how he or she uses a term. That, however, does not always happen.

Second, the terms "educational goals" and "educational objectives" are used in the profession with varying meanings. Some use these terms in the same way other people speak of aims of education or educational aims. Some perceive educational goals as curriculum goals and educational objectives as curriculum objectives. Some substitute educational goals for instructional goals and educational objectives for instructional objectives.

Third, as we shall see in examples of school statements of goals and objectives, goals are equated with objectives, and the terms are used synonymously. However, if we believe what we read, there are two entities—one called goals and another, objectives—for numerous schools have prepared statements of both goals and objectives.

Some writers have used the terms "goals" and "objectives" interchangeably, as we can see from the writings of some early proponents of behavioral objectives. W. James Popham and Eva L. Baker wrote: "We have given considerable attention to the topic of instructional objectives because they represent one of the most important tools available to the teacher. . . . There is undoubtedly a positive relationship between a teacher's clarity of instructional goals and the quality of his teaching."[3] Robert F. Mager in his popular work on instructional objectives commented:

An instructor . . . must then select procedures, content, and methods that . . . measure or evaluate the student's performance according to the objectives or goals originally selected. . . . Another important reason for stating objectives sharply relates to the evaluation of the degree to which the learner is able to perform in the manner desired. . . . Unless goals are clearly and firmly fixed in the minds of both parties, tests are at best misleading.[4]

The widely followed taxonomies of educational objectives bear the subtitle *The Classification of Educational Goals.*[5] In some of the literature goals are objectives and vice versa. That is not the case in this textbook, as you will see.

Fourth, some curriculum specialists do not distinguish curriculum goals and objectives from instructional goals and objectives, or they use these two sets of terms synonymously. If curriculum and instruction are two different entities—the position taken in this text—curriculum goals and objectives are different from instructional goals and objectives. Only if we choose a curriculum-instruction model in which the curriculum and instruction are mirror images can curriculum goals and objectives be identical to instructional goals and objectives. This text, however, presents the view that the two are separate but related entities.

These observations are not meant to criticize the positions, definitions, or approaches of other curriculum specialists nor to hold that the definitions given in this text are the "right" or only ones. As Decker F. Walker aptly stated in an enlightened discussion of writings on curriculum:

> Curriculum clearly is an iffy subject. It belongs to Aristotle's "region of the many and variable" where certain knowledge is not possible, only opinion—multiple and various, more or less considered, more or less adequate, but never clearly true or false.[6]

Mary M. McCaslin spoke in a similar vein when she said:

> We all live in glass houses. None of us can afford glib dismissal of alternative conceptions any more than we can afford to be noncritical or nonreflective about our own work.[7]

My remarks about the differences in the use of curriculum terms convey, as mentioned in Chapter 1, that the language of curriculum is somewhat imprecise and can lead to confusion. Curriculum specialists, unfortunately, do not agree among themselves on terminology. To add to the confusion and complexity of curriculum development, curriculum planners extend the language beyond *philosophy, goals,* and *objectives* to *mission* or *vision statement; frameworks; learning, content, program,* or *performance standards; program descriptors;* and *benchmarks.* As a result, the practitioner who seeks to carry out curriculum development following principles established by the experts must first understand the contexts within which they appear.

In this text I have made distinctions between curriculum goals and objectives and instructional goals and objectives to help practitioners facilitate the natural flow of curriculum development from general aims of education to precise instructional objectives. Specifying curriculum goals and objectives, then, is viewed as an intermediate planning step between these two poles. First, let's define the terms curriculum goals and curriculum objectives, present some examples, and then develop some guidelines for writing them.

DEFINING GOALS AND OBJECTIVES

Curriculum Goals

A *curriculum goal* is a purpose or end stated in general terms without criteria of achievement. Curriculum planners wish students to accomplish the goal as a result of exposure to segments or all of a program of a particular school or school system. For example, the following statement meets this definition of a curriculum goal: "Students will demonstrate responsible behavior as citizens of our school, community, state, nation, and world."

We have already seen examples of curriculum goals in Chapter 3. The Seven Cardinal Principles—health, command of fundamental processes, worthy home membership, vocation, citizenship, worthy use of leisure, and ethical character—are examples of curriculum goals, albeit in a form of shorthand.[8] The Commission on the Reorganization of Secondary Education could have expanded these principles into forms like the following:

- The school will promote the physical and mental health of the students.
- Students will achieve a command of the fundamental processes.
- A goal of the school is to foster worthy home membership.

The Ten Imperative Needs of Youth, listed by the Educational Policies Commission, is a set of curriculum goals that, as noted earlier, included such statements as these:

- All youth need to develop salable skills.
- All youth need to develop and maintain good health, physical fitness, and mental health.
- All youth need to grow in their ability to think rationally, to express their thoughts clearly, and to read and listen with understanding.[9]

At an earlier time the Educational Policies Commission pointed to four purposes or aims of education in American democracy. It identified these aims as self-realization, human relationships, economic efficiency, and civic responsibility.[10] These purposes might be modified by a particular school or school system and turned into curricular goals, stated in a variety of ways, for example:

- The school's program provides experiences leading to self-realization.
- Our school seeks to promote human relationships.
- A goal of the school is development of skills of learners that will lead to their country's and their own economic efficiency.
- Students will develop a sense of civic responsibility.

Many variations are used for expressing these four purposes. This chapter will later present a preferred form for writing goals and objectives. For now, these four goals are shown as examples of substance, not of form.

Aims of education can become curriculum goals when applied to a particular school or school system. The distinction drawn between aims of education and curriculum goals is one of generality (or looking at it from the other end of the telescope, specificity). "To transmit the cultural heritage" and "to overcome ignorance" are aims of all school programs. No single program or school can accomplish these extremely broad purposes. A school can, of course, contribute to transmitting the cultural heritage and to overcoming ignorance; stated with those qualifications, educational aims can become curriculum goals. The expression "to contribute to the physical development of the individual" can be both an educational aim of society and a curriculum goal of a particular school or school system.

Curriculum Objectives

Curriculum goals are derived from a statement of philosophy, defined aims of education, and assessment of needs. From curriculum goals, we derive curriculum objectives. We may define a curriculum objective in the following manner: A *curriculum objective* is a purpose or end stated in specific, measurable terms. Curriculum planners wish students to accomplish it as a result of exposure to segments or all of a program of the particular school or school system.

The following example of a curriculum goal has already been presented: "Students will demonstrate responsible behavior as citizens of our school, community, state, nation, and world." From that curriculum goal the following curriculum objectives are among those which could be derived:

- Ninety percent of the student body will cast ballots during the election of student government officers.
- One hundred percent of the students will participate in the community's clean-up campaign or other community service.
- One hundred percent of the students will help raise funds and/or collect and ship supplies needed by those in the United States devastated by floods, hurricanes, tornadoes, or other calamities of nature.
- Ninety percent of the students will be able to name the candidates running for the state senate and the state assembly from their district. They will be able to identify the candidates for the principal state executive offices. They will also identify the political party affiliation of the candidates.
- Ninety percent of the students will be able to identify their current U.S. senators and their representative to the U.S. House of Representatives. They will also identify the political parties of these officeholders.
- Ninety percent of the students will participate in some project that can increase international understanding, such as contributing coins to UNICEF; writing to pen pals overseas; donating money, food, or clothing to victims of earthquakes, tsunamis, or other natural disasters abroad.

Note how the curriculum objectives refine the curriculum goal. Many curriculum objectives can emanate from the same curriculum goal. When we reach Chapter 10 you will see that some of the foregoing curriculum objectives referring to accomplishments of groups of students become instructional objectives referring to accomplishments of individual students, for example, identifying candidates for office.

LOCUS OF CURRICULUM GOALS AND OBJECTIVES

As the statements of the Seven Cardinal Principles and the Ten Imperative Needs of Youth demonstrated, curriculum goals are periodically written on a national basis by individuals and groups as proposals for consideration by schools throughout the country. However, curriculum objectives, as just defined, are too specific to emanate from national sources.

Curriculum goals and objectives are regularly written at the state, school-district, and individual school level with the expectation that they will be followed within the jurisdiction of the respective level. State pronouncements apply to all public schools in the state; school-district statements apply districtwide; and individual school specifications, schoolwide.

For the most part, curriculum goals and objectives developed at any level cut across disciplines. A school's statement of curriculum goals and objectives, for example, applies generally throughout the school. It is possible, however, for grades and departments to develop curriculum goals and objectives that do not apply generally throughout the school or subject area.

Let us suppose, by way of example, that the following statement is a curriculum goal of the school: "All children need to develop skill in working with numbers." The fourth-grade teachers could create a grade-level goal by simply reiterating the school goal as "Fourth-graders need to develop skill in working with numbers." On the other hand, the fourth-grade teachers might choose to interpret the school's curriculum goal and create a grade-level curriculum objective, as follows: "This year's fourth-graders will excel last year's by an average of five percentile points on the same math achievement test."

Another example of a schoolwide curriculum goal is "Students will improve their scores on state assessment tests." One of the school's curriculum objectives derived from this goal might be "At least eighty-five percent of the students will achieve passing scores on the statewide assessment tests." The eleventh-grade faculty might set as its objective: "Ninety percent of the juniors will pass the state assessment test this year."

We encounter a similar case with a twelfth-grade faculty when the school seeks to accomplish the following curriculum goal: "Students will develop self-discipline and self-reliance." A twelfth-grade faculty might spell out the following curriculum goal: "Seniors will demonstrate skills of independent study." The twelfth-grade teachers might be more specific by following up this curriculum goal with a curriculum objective, as follows: "At least seventy percent of the seniors will seek to improve their self-discipline, self-reliance, and self-study techniques by engaging in independent research projects at least one period (fifty-five minutes) of the school day three times a week."

Middle school teachers of physical education and health might consider the school's curriculum goal, "Students will practice healthy living habits," and draw curriculum objectives like "One hundred percent of the students will develop the ability to distinguish healthful foods," or "All students will develop the habit of customarily choosing healthful over unhealthful foods."

In all cases, the grade or departmental and school's curriculum goals and objectives must be compatible with the district's and both an individual school's and the district's curriculum goals and objectives must be coordinated with those of the state.

State Curriculum Goals and Objectives

States today, through their boards or departments of education, exert increasing leadership by promulgating statements of curriculum goals and, to a greater degree in recent years, statements of the aforementioned mission or visions, frameworks, standards or objectives, descriptors, and benchmarks. In an early document the state of Florida offered some useful advice on how to conceptualize educational goals:

> The goals of education can be conceived in terms of the life activities of human adults in modern society. These activities may generally be placed in three categories: occupational, citizenship, and self-fulfillment. By constructing such a framework, it becomes possible to state the kinds of performance which should equip adults to function effectively in society—the *objectives* of education.[11]

Reflecting changes in society; the global economy; the changing nature of the student clientele; competition public schools face from home, private, and charter schools; the issuance of vouchers to private and parochial schools; and national efforts such as America 2000, Goals 2000-The Educate America Act, and the No Child Left Behind Act of 2001 states launched reform efforts from the mid- to late-1990s to the present.

EXAMPLES OF STATE CURRICULUM GOALS

Some states have drafted statements of curriculum goals that cut across disciplines as well as within disciplines. Others have concentrated on goals within subject fields. Kentucky, for example, set forth six general learning goals, as shown in Box 8.1. Kentucky's Department of Education notes that learning goals three and four are not included in the state's academic assessment program.

Still other states accept national goals essentially as written and may or may not add to those goals. Ohio, for example, adopting national goals in 1998, added the goal "Every Ohio adult [will be] literate and able to compete in the workforce."[12]

Illinois's goals fall within subject matter fields. The Illinois State Board of Education adopted in 1997 a set of thirty goals, ninety-eight standards, and over one thousand benchmarks for seven academic disciplines plus Social and Emotional Learning. For example, mathematics comprises five of the thirty goals: #6, Number Sense; #7, Estimation and Measurement; #8, Algebra and Analytical Methods; #9, Geometry; and #10 shows Data Analysis and Probability. Box 8.2 shows the five goals in mathematics.

In Chapter 7 I spoke to the timing of needs assessment and goal specification: "A needs assessment is a continuing activity that takes place (a) before specification of curricular goals and objectives, (b) after identification of curricular goals and objectives, (c) after evaluation of instruction, and (d) after evaluation of the curriculum." To clarify the sequence of goal writing and needs assessment, we may refer to Figure 8.2.

Once curriculum goals and objectives have been spelled out, the needs assessment process proceeds to determine unmet needs. Once identified, these needs will result in the creation of more curriculum goals and objectives or a modification of those already specified.

In summary, a state may formulate both broad aims and curriculum goals (and also in some cases curriculum objectives, instructional goals, and instructional objectives as well—a depth of state planning and control decried by many curriculum workers) for all schools and all students in that state.

BOX 8.1

Kentucky's Learning Goals

1. Students are able to use basic communication and mathematic skills for purposes and situations they will encounter throughout their lives.

2. Students shall develop their abilities to apply core concepts and principles from mathematics, the sciences, the arts, the humanities, social studies, practical living studies, and vocational studies to what they will encounter throughout their lives.

3. Students shall develop their abilities to become self-sufficient individuals.

4. Students shall develop their abilities to become responsible members of a family, work group, or community, including demonstrating effectiveness in community service.

5. Students shall develop their abilities to think and solve problems in school situations and in a variety of situations they will encounter in life.

6. Students shall develop their abilities to connect and integrate experiences and new knowledge from all subject matter fields with what they have previously learned and build on past learning experiences to acquire new information through various media sources.

Source: Kentucky Department of Education, *Learning Goals and Academic Expectations.* Copyright © Kentucky Department of Education. Website: http://www.state.ky.us, accessed April 24, 2003. Used with permission of the Kentucky Department of Education, Frankfort, Kentucky 40601. Revisited March 15, 2007, at website: http://education.ky.gov/KDE/Instructional+Resources/Curriculum+Documents+and+Resources/Academic+Expectations/default.htm.

BOX 8.2

Illinois State Board of Education Goals in Mathematics

Goal 6. Demonstrate and apply a knowledge and sense of numbers, including numeration and operations (addition, subtraction, multiplication, division), patterns, ratios, and proportions.

Goal 7. Estimate, make, and use measurements of objects, quantities, and relationships and determine acceptable levels of accuracy.

Goal 8. Use algebraic and analytic methods to identify and describe patterns and relationships in data, solve problems, and predict results.

Goal 9. Use geometric methods to analyze, categorize, and draw conclusions about points, lines, planes, and space.

Goal 10. Collect, organize, and analyze data using statistical methods; predict results; and interpret uncertainty using concepts of probability.

Source: Illinois State Board of Education, *Goals for Mathematics,* website, http://www.isbe.state.il.us/ils/Default.htm, accessed April 24, 2003. Reprinted by permission. Revisited March 15, 2007, at website: http://www.isbe.state.il.us/math/standards.htm.

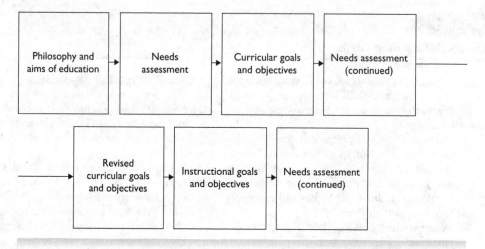

FIGURE 8.2 The Sequence of Goal Specification and Needs Assessment

School-District Curriculum Goals

In practice, school districts and individual schools may accept the state's formulation of goals and objectives verbatim or, if the state permits, may independently develop their own statements. In either case, however, the statements of the school districts and individual schools must be in harmony with the state's. The Orange County Board of Education in Orlando, Florida, a large urban school district with a multiethnic population, furnishes an example, shown in Box 8.3, of a statement of mission and goals which they refer to as "ENDS."

Individual School Curriculum Goals and Objectives

Not only do the states and school districts establish curriculum goals and objectives, but the individual schools also enter into the process by specifying their own philosophy, goals, and objectives. Box 8.4 (excerpts from *Handbook of Sequoia Middle School*, Redding, California) furnishes an example of a middle school's statement of its vision, priorities, expected competencies, and beliefs.

Although the illustrations of curriculum goals and objectives cited in this chapter follow different formats, they serve as examples of the step in the planning process that calls for the specification of curriculum goals and objectives.

CONSTRUCTING STATEMENTS OF CURRICULUM GOALS

The examples of curriculum goals demonstrate a variety of forms of expression. Some schools phrase their goals in a way that stresses the role of the curriculum or of the school, like the following examples:

- To teach students to express themselves clearly and correctly in written and oral English.

BOX 8.3

Orange County, Florida, Ends Policy

End 1: District Mission
Each student will acquire the skills, attitudes and knowledge necessary to reach full potential.

End 2: Academic Achievement
Students will achieve academically at levels commensurate with challenging and yearly individual learning goals.

2.1 Students will demonstrate the ability to think independently
Accordingly, students will
    2.1.1 Demonstrate and apply critical thinking using research, creativity, analysis, synthesis, and evaluation of information
    2.1.2 Apply their learning to real life situations appropriate to age levels
2.2 Students will master academic skills in core areas
Students will:
    2.2.1 Be literate
        2.2.1.1 Read at or above grade level by age nine
        2.2.1.2 Read a variety of texts with fluency and comprehension appropriate to the materials
        2.2.1.3 Demonstrate an aesthetic appreciation of literature
    2.2.2 Communicate effectively and fluently, both orally and in writing
    2.2.3 Use mathematical and scientific concepts to solve problems
    2.2.4 Have knowledge of current events in the context of American and world history
    2.2.5 Use the humanities and the fine arts for exploration, communication and self expression:

- Music
- Theater Arts
- Visual Arts
- Philosophy

End 3: Citizenship
Students will be productive citizens in their local, national and global communities.
Students will:
3.1 Understand and exercise the rights and responsibilities of citizenship in our democratic society
3.2 Participate productively in their communities
3.3 Appreciate both our diversity and our commonality as citizens or residents of the United States
3.4 Respect self and others by demonstrating civil behaviors
3.5 Understand the roles and expectations of U.S. citizens in the global community

End 4: Personal and Workplace Skills
Students will assume responsibility for personnel decisions and actions and will demonstrate the skills necessary for personal and workplace success.
Students will:
4.1 Practice self-discipline
4.2 Listen effectively
4.3 Set and meet deadlines
4.4 Demonstrate effective skills in team as well as individual endeavors
4.5 Effectively use technology as a necessary tool
4.6 Organize time and resources
4.7 Adjust to new situations and accept change as an opportunity for growth
4.8 Demonstrate effective interpersonal skills to develop productive working relationships

Source: Orange County Board of Education, *School Board Member Documents* (Orlando, Fla.: Orange County Board of Education, October 2001), website: http://www.ocps.net, accessed April 26, 2003. Reprinted by permission. Revisited March 15, 2007, at website: http://www.ocps.k12.fl.us/pageView.rhtml?pageID-46.

BOX 8.4

Excerpts from *Parent/Student Handbook*, Sequoia Middle School

VISION
Sequoia Middle School is a safe learning community that empowers learners with the knowledge, values, and skills to be contributing members of our society.

PRIORITIES FOR 2006–2007
    Student Achievement
    Positive School Culture
    Parent and Community Involvement

EXPECTED STUDENT COMPETENCIES
- Basic Skills—reading, writing, mathematics, listening, speaking
- Thinking Skills—creative, decision making, problem solving, visualization, reasoning, how to learn
- Personal Qualities—responsibility, self-esteem, sociability, self-management, accountability
- Resourceful—manages time, money, materials, facilities, and human resources, good work ethic
- Interpersonal—works as team member of diverse groups
- Information—acquires, evaluates, organizes, maintains, interprets, communicates, utilizes technology
- Technology—selects and applies technology for tasks

BELIEFS
- Positive relationships among students, teachers, and parents are essential for learning.
- All students can learn what is taught.
- Each of us makes a difference.
- Student growth and achievement are our primary challenges.
- Individually we are good; working together we are better.
- Students must have mastery of basic skills, have a positive work ethic, be problem solvers, work well with others, and communicate well.

Source: Sequoia Middle School, Redding, California, Excerpts from *Parent/Student Handbook*, website: http://sequoia.echalk.com/www/redding_sequoia/site/hosting/Handbook%20for%20Website%2006-07.pdf, accessed March 15, 2007. Reprinted by permission.

- To teach students to work and live together through cooperative and inclusive practices.
- To develop the students' abilities to purchase goods and services wisely.
- To help students develop respect for cultures other than their own.
- To develop potentialities of all students through authentic learning experiences.
- To provide students with learning experiences that are developmentally appropriate.

Although an expression that stresses the role of the school is common, an alternate form that focuses on the students seems preferable for a number of reasons:

1. Philosophically, this form is more in keeping with progressive doctrine, which places the pupil at the center of learning—a sound principle.

2. It is in keeping with modern instructional design, which focuses on the achievements of the learner rather than on the performance of the teacher or school.
3. It parallels common practice, as we shall see in Chapter 10, in writing instructional goals and objectives. Thus, curriculum goals may be better understood and the process of curriculum development better integrated.
4. It is easier to design evaluation processes when we know what is expected in terms of student achievement.

Writing curriculum goals in a form that starts with the students, we might revise the preceding illustrations in the following manner:

- Students will express themselves clearly and correctly in written and oral English.
- Students will demonstrate the ability to purchase goods and services wisely.
- Students will show interest in and understanding of cultures other than their own.
- Students will demonstrate the ability to work productively with others.

Characteristics of Curriculum Goals

The characteristics of curriculum goals as conceptualized in this text may be summarized as follows:

1. They relate to the educational aims and philosophy.
2. They are programmatic. Although they speak to one or more areas of the curriculum, they do not delineate the specific courses or specific items of content.
3. They refer to the accomplishment of groups (all students, students in general, most students) rather than the achievement of individual students.
4. They are broad enough to lead to specific curriculum objectives.

CONSTRUCTING STATEMENTS OF CURRICULUM OBJECTIVES

Like curriculum goals, curriculum objectives relate to the educational aims and philosophy of the school, are programmatic in nature, and refer to accomplishments of groups. Unlike curriculum goals, curriculum objectives are stated in specific terms.

Characteristics of Curriculum Objectives

Curriculum objectives are refinements of the curriculum goals. They specify performance standards for the students for whom the curriculum is designed. We can turn a curriculum goal into a curriculum objective by adding the following three elements, which we will meet again when discussing instructional objectives:

- performance or behavioral terms—that is, those skills and knowledge the students are expected to be able to demonstrate

- inferred or precise degree of mastery
- conditions under which the performance will take place, if not readily understood

To accomplish the transition from curriculum goal to curriculum objective, you may find it helpful to jot down several indicators of student performance that will serve as guides for writing the objectives. Let's take another look at the illustrative curriculum goal mentioned earlier: "Students shall demonstrate responsible behavior as citizens of our school, community, state, nation, and world." What are some indicators of learner performance that would reveal evidence of students' accomplishment of this goal? We might look for such behaviors as the following:

- care of school building and grounds
- less fighting among students
- expressions of mutual respect among ethnic groups
- orderliness in school assemblies
- participation in community youth organizations such as church groups, scout groups, and the like
- refraining from littering the school and community
- serving on committees of the school
- observing highway speed limits
- cooperation among students in inclusive classes
- taking an interest in local, state, and national elections
- engaging in discussions on ways to reduce international tensions

We can turn the first performance indicator—care of the school building and grounds—into a curriculum objective, such as "Students will demonstrate a reduction of the number of graffiti on the walls." We can add a degree of mastery to the objective and create an assessment item, with a time element and a measurement dimension, such as *By the end of April*, students will demonstrate a *ninety-five percent* reduction in the number of graffiti on the walls." From the one curriculum goal on good citizenship we can generate many curriculum objectives, and from the first performance indicator alone we can create a number of objectives.

To illustrate curriculum objectives, we'll refer to the Illinois State Board of Education's goals shown in Box 8.2 on page 219, select Goal 8, and reproduce in Box 8.5 its learning standards and benchmarks for middle and junior high school levels. You will note that the degrees of mastery and conditions are inferred ("with accuracy, whenever needed"), as is commonly done, leaving measurement to construction of items assessing achievement of specified curricular and instructional objectives.

We should take note of the fact that Theodore R. Sizer presented a different approach toward specifying curriculum objectives. At Horace's fictitious school, the "Committee's Report" cast curriculum objectives (which the "Committee" called "specific goals") into an authentic assessment framework. Said the "Committee," "We believe that our school should be driven by specific goals in the form of Exhibitions through which the students can display their grasp and use of important ideas and skills. The school's program would be to the largest practical extent the preparation for these Exhibitions."[13]

BOX 8.5

Illinois State Board of Education Standards and Benchmarks for Goal 8: Algebra and Analytic Methods

Goal 8: Use algebraic and analytic methods to identify and describe patterns and relationships in data, solve problems, and predict results

Learning Standards and Benchmarks for Middle and Junior High School
As a result of their schooling students will be able to

A. Describe numerical relationships using variables and patterns
  8A 3a Apply the basic principles of commutative, associative, distributive, transitive, inverse, identity, zero, equality and order of operations to solve problems
  8A 3b Solve problems using linear expressions, equations, and inequalities
B. Interpret and describe numerical relationships using tables, graphs, and symbols
  8B 3 Use graphic technology and algebraic methods to analyze and predict linear

relationships and make generalizations from linear patterns
C. Solve problems using systems of numbers and their properties
  8C 3 Apply the properties of numbers and operations including inverses in algebraic settings derived from economics, business, and the sciences
D. Use algebraic concepts and procedures to represent and solve problems
  8D 3a Solve problems using numeric, graphic, or symbolic representations of variables, expressions, equations, and inequalities
  8D 3b Propose and solve problems using proportions, formulas, and linear functions.
  8D 3c Apply properties of powers, perfect squares, and square roots

Source: Illinois State Board of Education, *Illinois Learning Standards for Mathematics*, Middle/Junior High School, website: http://www.isbe.state.il.us/ils/math/mag8.html, accessed April 24, 2003. Reprinted by permission. Revisited March 15, 2007, at website: http://www.isbe.state.il.us/ils/math/standards.htm.

Explanation of U.S. Supreme Court decisions, preparation of nutritious menus for the school cafeteria, preparation of a portfolio on a human emotion, completing an IRS Form 1040, drawing a map of the United States and placing a dozen states on it, and running a community service program are examples of Exhibitions possible at Horace's school.[14] In this context curriculum objectives are equated with Exhibitions, tasks by which students demonstrate achievement through performance.

Outcomes-based education, discussed in Chapter 15, is a recent movement that specifies curriculum objectives in the form of expected outcomes to be achieved by the learners. The generation of curriculum goals and objectives is a highly creative exercise. Curriculum planners will approach the specification of curriculum goals and objectives in their own style, remembering that curriculum goals and objectives set the direction for the subsequent organization and development of the curriculum and that the curriculum goals and objectives determine the activities that will take place in the many classrooms of the school.

In the discussions of statements of philosophy, aims, standards, goals, and objectives in this text, you have seen variation in styles and approaches among school systems from state to state and even within states. From inspecting examples from various school systems throughout the country we can conclude:

- First, a great deal of thought with an intimate knowledge of the students and community have gone into the statements and
- Second, because of advancements in communication and pressures from state and national levels the variations among statements are less than might be expected (or preferred by some curriculum experts).

VALIDATING AND DETERMINING PRIORITY OF GOALS AND OBJECTIVES

As stated earlier, the assessment of curriculum needs is a continuing process that starts after a school formulates its philosophy and clarifies its aims of education. The needs of society; of students in general; and of the particular students, community, and subject matter give rise to initial statements of curriculum goals and objectives. After these goals and objectives have been identified, the needs assessment process is continued to determine if any needs have not been met. When unmet needs are exposed, a revised list of curriculum goals and objectives is prepared. These goals and objectives require validation and placing in order of priority.

Validation is the process of determining whether the goals and objectives are accepted as appropriate or "right" for the school (or school system, if conducted on a systemwide level) proposing them. *Determining priority* is the placing of the goals and objectives in order of relative importance to the school. Groups concerned with the progress of the school should be enlisted to help identify suitable goals and objectives and to set priorities.

Some schools seek to validate both goals and objectives; others limit the process to validating goals on the presumption that once the goals are identified, a representative committee can handle the task of making the goals specific—that is, turning them into objectives.

Function of Curriculum Committee

The validation process, whether carried out by the state, district, or school, assumes the formation of a curriculum committee or council charged with the task. The curriculum committee will submit the goals by means of a questionnaire or opinionnaire to groups who are concerned with the progress of the school(s).

Submitting curriculum goals and any already identified curriculum objectives to a broad sampling of groups—laypersons (including parents), students, teachers, administrators, and curriculum experts (on the staffs of public school systems or on the faculties of teacher education institutions)—is good practice. The effort should be made to learn whether there is widespread acceptance of the goals formulated by the curriculum planners and what the groups' priorities are. Curriculum objectives that are developed after a broad sampling of opinion has been gathered can be submitted to either a more limited sampling of the same groups or to the curriculum committee for validation and ranking.

Data should be gathered and interpreted, preferably by a curriculum committee representative of the various groups polled. Such a committee will be called on to make judgments that will tax its collective wisdom. It cannot treat the data in a simplistic fashion, tallying responses from all groups, and simply following the majority's opinions. It needs to analyze differences of opinion, if any, among the various groups surveyed and discuss the differences among themselves and with members of the various groups.

Weighing Opinions. As a general rule, the wishes of students, for example, should not hold the same priority as the beliefs of parents and other laypeople. The opinions of groups small in number, like curriculum specialists or college professors, cannot be treated in the same light as the attitudes of large numbers of residents of the community. For that matter, the opinions of a few school administrators should not be given, simply because of their status, as great a weight as those of large numbers of teachers and parents.

Since the committee interpreting the data may not find consensus on goals and objectives among the various groups, it has the responsibility of reconciling differing positions and reaching consensus among its own members. Drawing on the opinions of the groups that have been polled, the curriculum committee must decide which goals are valid and which should be assigned priority. To set priorities is to say that some goals are more important than others and deserve more attention and emphasis in the curriculum.

It is clear that the goals of a state, district, or school should be submitted for validation and ranking by sizable numbers of educators and noneducators. It is debatable, however, whether curriculum goals and objectives of grades or departments need or should be submitted to persons beyond the school or school-district personnel. It would be somewhat impractical, redundant, expensive, and time consuming for curriculum goals and objectives of the grades and departments to be submitted to significant numbers of the school system's constituents. The faculties of the grade and department levels may satisfy their responsibilities for validation and ranking of goals and objectives by submitting their statements to the curriculum committee and to experts in the field for review and endorsement.

The process of validation and determining priorities may be repeated as often as the curriculum committee finds necessary, with modifications and repeated rankings made as a result of each survey and prior to a subsequent survey. After the curriculum goals and objectives have been validated and placed in rank order, the curriculum planners turn to the next phase in the curriculum development process—putting the goals and objectives into operation.

Summary

State school systems, school districts, and individual schools engage in the task of specifying curriculum goals and objectives. Curriculum goals and objectives are derived from the developers' philosophy and educational aims.

Curriculum goals are broad programmatic statements of expected outcomes without criteria of achievement. They apply to students as a group and are often interdisciplinary or multidisciplinary.

Curriculum objectives are specific statements of outcomes with degree of mastery and conditions either inferred or stipulated to be achieved by students as a group in the school or school system.

Curriculum goals and objectives are essential for

1. conducting a complete needs assessment to identify unmet needs
2. carrying out subsequent phases of the suggested model for curriculum improvement
3. generating instructional goals and objectives
4. providing a basis for evaluating the curriculum
5. giving direction to the program

Curriculum goals and objectives should be validated and put in order of priority by the school's curriculum committee after review by representatives of the various constituencies that the school serves.

Questions for Discussion

1. How do you go about specifying curriculum goals and objectives? Who does the specifying?

2. Which comes first: a curriculum needs assessment or the specification of curriculum goals and objectives? Why?

3. How do you turn curriculum goals into curriculum objectives?

4. Is it necessary to state curriculum goals across disciplines as well as within each discipline?

5. How do curriculum goals relate to a school's statement of philosophy and aims of education?

Exercises

1. Define and give two examples of
   a. aims of education
   b. curriculum goals
   c. curriculum objectives

2. Following definitions in this text, explain both the relationship and difference between
   a. an aim of education and a curriculum goal
   b. a curriculum goal and a curriculum objective

3. Explain the relationship of curriculum goals and objectives to needs assessment.

4. Respond to the following questions, showing your position on each:

   a. Is it necessary to write an educational philosophy in order to specify curriculum goals and objectives?
   b. Is it necessary to list educational aims in order to specify curriculum goals and objectives?

5. Locate and report on illustrations of curriculum goals either in education textbooks or in curriculum materials of any school or school system in the United States.

6. Locate and report on illustrations of curriculum objectives either in education textbooks or in curriculum materials of any school or school system in the United States.

7. Obtain and, following principles advocated in this chapter, critique the statement of
   a. curriculum goals of a school that you know well
   b. curriculum objectives of a school that you know well
   c. curriculum goals and/or objectives of a school district that you know well
   d. curriculum goals and/or objectives of one of the fifty states

8. Write as many curriculum objectives as you can for each of the following curriculum goals:
   a. Students will maintain good health and physical fitness.
   b. Students will demonstrate skill in writing.
   c. Students will develop an appreciation for the free enterprise system.
   d. Students will exhibit positive attitudes toward each other regardless of differences in gender, religion, or ethnic origin.

Small groups may wish to respond to separate parts of this exercise.

9. Describe the hierarchy of goals discussed by Ronald S. Brandt and Ralph W. Tyler (see bibliography) and give examples of each type.

10. Analyze the merits of equating Exhibitions of performance with curriculum objectives (see Sizer, bibliography).

11. Find definitions used by schools for the terms:
    framework
    mission
    program descriptors
    benchmarks

Endnotes

1. For a different hierarchy of goals see Ronald S. Brandt and Ralph W. Tyler, in Fenwick W. English, ed., *Fundamental Curriculum Decisions*, 1983 Yearbook (Alexandria, Va.: Association for Supervision and Curriculum Development, 1983), pp. 40–52.

2. John W. Gardner, "National Goals in Education," in *Goals for Americans: Programs for Action in the Sixties*, Report of the President's Commission on National Goals, Henry W. Wriston, Chairman (New York: The American Assembly, Columbia University, 1960), pp. 81, 100.

3. W. James Popham and Eva L. Baker, *Systematic Instruction* (Englewood Cliffs, N.J.: Prentice-Hall, 1970), p. 43.

4. Robert F. Mager, *Preparing Instructional Objectives* (Belmont, Calif.: Fearon, 1962), pp. 1, 3–4.

5. Benjamin S. Bloom, ed., *Taxonomy of Educational Objectives: The Classification of Educational Goals: Handbook I: Cognitive Domain* (New York: Longman, 1956) and David R. Krathwohl, Benjamin S. Bloom, and Bertram B. Masia, *Taxonomy of Educational Objectives: The Classification of Educational Goals: Handbook II: Affective Domain* (New York: Longman, 1964).

6. Decker F. Walker, "A Brainstorming Tour of Writing on Curriculum," in Arthur W. Foshay, ed., *Considered Action for Curriculum Improvement*, 1980 Yearbook (Alexandria, Va.: Association for Supervision and Curriculum Development, 1980), p. 81.

7. Mary M. McCaslin, "Commentary: Whole Language—Theory, Instruction, and Future Implementation," *The Elementary School Journal* 90, no. 2 (November 1989): 227.

8. Commission on the Reorganization of Secondary Education, *Cardinal Principles of Secondary Education* (Washington, D.C.: United States Office of Education, Bulletin No. 35, 1918).

9. Educational Policies Commission, *Education for All American Youth* (Washington, D.C.: National Education Association, 1938), pp. 225–226.

10. Educational Policies Commission, *The Purposes of Education in American Democracy* (Washington, D.C.: National Education Association, 1938).

11. Florida Department of Education, *Goals for Education in Florida* (Tallahassee, Fla.: State Department of Education, 1972), p. 4.

12. Ohio Department of Education, *Destination: Success in Education*, website: http://www.state.oh.us/goals98/goals.htm, accessed April 26, 2003.

13. Theodore R. Sizer, *Horace's School: Redesigning the American High School* (Boston: Houghton Mifflin, 1992), p. 143.

14. Ibid., pp. 8–9, 23, 48, 65, 80.

Bibliography

Bloom, Benjamin S., ed. *Taxonomy of Educational Objectives: The Classification of Educational Goals: Handbook I: Cognitive Domain.* New York: Longman, 1956.

Brandt, Ronald S. and Tyler, Ralph W. "Goals and Objectives." In Fenwick W. English, ed. *Fundamentals of Curriculum Decisions*, 1983 Yearbook. Alexandria, Va.: Association for Supervision and Curriculum Development, 1983.

Commission on the Reorganization of Secondary Education. *Cardinal Principles of Secondary Education.* Washington, D.C.: United States Office of Education, Bulletin No. 35, 1918.

Doll, Ronald C. *Curriculum Improvement: Decision Making and Process*, 9th ed. Boston: Allyn and Bacon, 1996.

Educational Policies Commission. *Education for All American Youth.* Washington, D.C.: National Education Association, 1944.

———. *The Purposes of Education in American Democracy.* Washington, D.C.: National Education Association, 1938.

Florida Department of Education. *Goals for Education in Florida.* Tallahassee, Fla.: State Department of Education, 1972.

Gardner, John W. "National Goals of Education." In *Goals for Americans: Programs for Action in the Sixties*, Report of the President's Commission on National Goals, Henry W. Wriston, Chairman. New York: The American Assembly, Columbia University, 1960.

Krathwohl, David R., Bloom, Benjamin S., and Masia, Bertram B. *Taxonomy of Educational Objectives: The Classification of Educational Goals: Handbook II: Affective Domain.* New York: Longman, 1964.

Mager, Robert F. *Preparing Instructional Objectives.* Belmont, Calif.: Fearon, 1962. 2nd ed., Belmont, Calif.: Pitman Learning, 1975.

McCaslin, Mary M. "Commentary: Whole Language-Theory, Instruction, and Future Implementation," *The Elementary School Journal* 90, no. 2 (November 1989): 227.

Popham, W. James and Baker, Eva L. *Establishing Instructional Goals.* Englewood Cliffs, N.J.: Prentice-Hall, 1970.

———. *Systematic Instruction.* Englewood Cliffs, N.J.: Prentice-Hall, 1970.

Sizer, Theodore R. *Horace's School: Redesigning the American High School.* Boston: Houghton Mifflin, 1992.

Tyler, Ralph W. *Basic Principles of Curriculum and Instruction.* Chicago: University of Chicago Press, 1949.

Walker, Decker F. "A Brainstorming Tour of Writing on Curriculum." In Arthur W. Foshay, ed. *Considered Action for Curriculum Improvement*, 1980 Yearbook. Alexandria, Va.: Association for Supervision and Curriculum Development, 1980.

Wiles, Jon and Bondi, Joseph C. *Curriculum Development: A Guide to Practice*, 7th ed. Upper Saddle River, N.J.: Merrill/Prentice Hall, 2007.

9 Organizing and Implementing the Curriculum

AFTER STUDYING THIS CHAPTER YOU SHOULD BE ABLE TO:

1. Describe and state strengths and weaknesses of various plans and proposals for organizing and implementing the curriculum.

2. Relate each organizational arrangement discussed in this chapter to (a) the psychological and sociological circumstances of the public school and (b) the achievement of one or more aims of education or curriculum goals at each of the three school levels: elementary, middle, and senior high.

3. Specify several curriculum goals for the elementary, middle, or senior high school level; choose or design and defend a curriculum organization plan that you believe will most satisfactorily result in accomplishment of these goals.

NECESSARY DECISIONS

A Hypothetical Setting

Imagine, if you will, a building complex of three schools—an elementary school of five grades plus kindergarten, a middle (formerly junior high) school of three grades, and a senior high school of four grades situated on a large tract of land. We could place this complex in a small town in any state where the three schools serve all the children of a particular school district, or we could locate it in a sector of a large urban area where the three schools are a part of the local school system.

Let's create in our own minds the administrative offices of the superintendent (or area superintendent) and school board across the street from this complex. From a second floor conference room we can look out on the children at play in the elementary school yard, we can see awkward teeny-boppers of the middle school up the street to our right, and we can observe the senior high school Harrys and Janes spinning out in their gasoline chariots from the parking lot in the background.

231

On a particular day in September a group of curriculum planners has gathered in the conference room. It is 4:00 P.M., and for the moment they stand at the window looking over the complex across the way. Activity at the elementary school has virtually ceased for the day, has just about tapered off at the middle school, and continues apace at the senior high school. Only two cars remain in the elementary school parking lot—the principal's and the custodian's.

Making up the curriculum group are the district supervisor (director of curriculum) and the chairpersons of the district curriculum steering committee and the curriculum councils of each of the three schools. In front of them—in finished form, neatly typed and packaged—are (1) the report of the needs assessment that revealed gaps in the school district's curricula and (2) a set of both district and individual school curriculum goals and objectives that they laboriously hammered out with the help of many faculty members, students, administrators, supervisors, and lay citizens.

Hypothetical Steps

The task of this curriculum group now is to decide on next steps. What do they do with the curriculum goals and objectives now that they are specified? Shall they duplicate, distribute, and then forget them? Shall they take the position that the process of defining the goals and objectives was sufficient or that the process should lead to further action? Shall they file the goals and objectives with the superintendent and principals, to be pulled out on special occasions such as visits of parent groups, accrediting committees, or others? How shall they meet the discrepancies shown by the needs assessment and the curriculum goals and objectives developed as a result of that assessment?

The curriculum planners of the district, whose leadership is represented by this committee, must decide how to put the goals and objectives into effect and how to organize the curriculum in such a way that the goals and objectives can be achieved. They must decide what structure will be most conducive to successfully accomplishing the goals and objectives and to fulfilling learner needs. They must ask themselves and their colleagues how best to go about implementing the curriculum decisions that they have made up to this point.

Assessing Curriculum Organization

The question is often posed to curriculum workers: "How shall we go about organizing the curriculum?" The literature often appears to make one of two assumptions: (1) Curriculum planners regularly have the opportunity to initiate a curriculum in a brand new school (or perhaps in a deserted old school) for which no curriculum patterns yet exist; or (2) curriculum developers automatically have the freedom to discard that which now exists and replace it with patterns of their own choosing.

Both assumptions are likely to be erroneous. Curriculum planners do not frequently experience the responsibility for developing an original curriculum for a brand new school (or more accurately, for an upcoming new school, since planning must precede construction). It is true, of course, that new schools are built to meet growths and shifts in population and to replace decrepit structures, which, like old soldiers, slowly fade away. The development of a curriculum for a brand new school does provide the opportunity for curriculum planning from the ground floor, so to speak. But even that planning must be carried out within certain boundaries, including local traditions, state and district mandates, and the curricula of other schools of the district with which they must articulate. Curriculum planners cannot expect simply to substitute as they wish new patterns of curriculum organization for old. Again, we face certain parameters: student needs, teacher preferences, administrators' values, community sentiment, physical restrictions, and financial resources.

Our fictitious curriculum group is talking about possible ways of reorganizing the curriculum to meet pupil needs and to provide the best possible structure for attaining the district's and each school's curriculum goals and objectives. The group decides that one way of approaching this task is to consider the schools' past, present, and future ideas for curriculum organization. They will identify patterns that have been tried, those currently in operation, and those that might be feasible or successful in the immediate and distant future.

At this meeting the committee decides to clarify what they mean by curriculum organization. They agree to talk with their colleagues on their schools' curriculum councils and others and come to the next meeting of this group prepared to trace the historical development of the curricular organizations of the three schools. Each will provide an overview of the more significant patterns of curriculum organization that have been studied and implemented, studied and rejected, and considered for future implementation.

Before adjourning this meeting, the committee agrees on what they will include under the rubric of curriculum organization. They define *curriculum organization as those patterns of both a curricular and administrative nature by which students encounter learning experiences and subject matter.* Thus, it includes not only broad plans for programmatic offerings, such as the subject matter curriculum, but also delivery systems, that possess an administrative dimension, such as team teaching.

Several weeks later when the committee reassembles, exhilarated by its research on the history of curriculum development in their schools, they express a newfound admiration for previous curriculum planners. Whereas the aging facades of the buildings might convey to the outside world, as the French say, that "the more things change, the more they stay the same," inside, innovation and change have been key words. The committee spends several sessions sharing their discoveries and studying what the experts say about the structures uncovered. The committee is sure that by examining past patterns, projecting future arrangements, and comparing both past practices and future possibilities with present structures, they can create more effective ways of implementing the curriculum.

This hypothetical committee's discoveries are significant enough to be shared with you. Our discussion will be organized into three major parts: the past (Where We've Been), the present (Where We Are), and the future (Where We're Going). For each period some major plans in school and curriculum organization at each of three levels—elementary, junior high/middle school, and senior high school—are described.

Remember that Axiom 3 in Chapter 2 postulates that changes do not, as a rule, start and stop abruptly but overlap. Axiom 3 applies to our hypothetical community as it does elsewhere. Consequently, when I discuss the graded school, for example, as a place where we have been, I do not imply that it has necessarily disappeared from the present or that it will not exist in the future. When I discuss the middle school, I do not suggest that its predecessor, the junior high school, no longer exists.

Nor are curricular arrangements always confined to one level. The subject matter curriculum, the graded school, the nongraded school, team teaching, and flexible scheduling exist or have existed at more than one level. By placing a curricular arrangement at a particular level, I am not saying that it could not be found or could not have been found either at the same time or at another time at other levels even in the hypothetical community used for illustrative purposes.

However, you would tire if, for example, discussion of the subject matter curriculum were repeated at each of the three levels. Therefore, I have placed the arrangements, perhaps arbitrarily, at levels where the arrangements were particularly strong, significant, or common. Unless a curricular arrangement had particular significance for more than one level and possessed distinctive characteristics for each level, as in the case of the nongraded elementary school and the nongraded high school, a particular plan is discussed at only one level.

Table 9.1 shows various curricular and organizational developments and recommendations tried in the past or present and proposals for future change. To avoid repetition many of the developments shown in the column Where We Are (Present) will continue and have not been listed in the Where We Are Going (Future) column. Their presence in the Future column does not mean that they do not exist in the present but that they are likely to become more widely adopted as years go by.

WHERE WE'VE BEEN: *CURRICULUM PAST*

THE ELEMENTARY SCHOOL

The Graded School

Historians tell us that the concept of a graded school started in Prussia, a land famed for discipline and regimentation, and migrated across the ocean to the New World.[1] The Quincy Grammar School of Boston, which opened in 1848, is credited as the first school in the United States to become completely graded. With enough youngsters for several groups, it took not a quantum leap but a simple bit of ingenuity to reason that youngsters might be taught more efficiently if they were sorted and graded. Instead of being mixed, they could be divided largely on the basis of chronological age.

The graded school has become the standard model not only for the United States but also for the world. As our country grew in population, expanded westward, and became industrialized, the number of grades provided for children by the numerous school districts of the nation increased in proportion.

By the early twentieth century twelve grades were made available and were considered sufficient for most boys and girls. School systems grew, providing the opportunity for young people to receive not ten, not eleven, but twelve years of education at public expense. For one reason or another many children and youth in early days (and to a

TABLE 9.1   Developments and Recommendations of the Past, Present, and Future

Level	Where We've Been (Past)	Where We Are (Present)	Where We're Going (Future)
Elementary	Graded school Activity curriculum Nongraded elementary school Open education and open space	Basic skills *Assessment Teaching thinking skills *Provision for students with special needs, inclusion Multiage grouping *Multicultural education *School choice *Homeschooling *Charter schools *Vouchers/tax credits *Bilingual education Cooperative learning *Whole language *Core knowledge Character education *Year-round schools	Blending of traditional and nontraditional modes Changing status of public education Increase in private education Decrease in social promotion Alternative organizational plans Differentiated classrooms Continued assessment Continued school choice
Junior high/middle	The school in between: the junior high school Conant's recommendations ASCD proposals Core curriculum	Middle school Interdisciplinary teams *Assessment	Predominance of the middle school but some reversion to K–8 schools Integrated curriculum Block/rotating schedules *Single-gender classes and schools Continued assessment
Senior high	Subject matter curriculum Conant's proposals Broad-fields curriculum Team teaching and differentiated staffing Flexible and modular scheduling Nongraded high school Ability grouping Tracking Programmed instruction Instructional television	Comprehensive high school Magnet schools Higher requirements for graduation Technological education Community service *Health education *Outcomes-based education *State and national standards *State and national assessment, exit exams Extended day and year Performance-based assessment School-to-work programs	Technology in education Continued exit exams Early-college high schools Conversion to smaller learning communities

Note: Although developments (other than assessment) on this chart are classified at only one level to avoid duplication, many are applicable at more than one level.

*See Chapter 15 for discussion of these developments.

decreasing extent today) were not able to complete the twelves grades of elementary and secondary education even in communities that offered twelve grades. We could add in passing that both public and private community junior colleges and senior institutions have been established to offer youth opportunities for further learning, but that's another story in itself.

Twelve Years as Norm. Administrators, curriculum experts, teachers, and the public have accepted the twelve years as a norm for most of our young people and have adjusted the component levels as the situation seemed to demand. Thus, until rather recently the most common organizational plan for schools across the country was the eight-four plan (eight years of elementary school and four of secondary school). Under this plan grades seven and eight were considered parts of the elementary rather than the secondary school. As the junior high school began to emerge after the first decade of the twentieth century, the six-two-four plan (six elementary, two junior high, and four senior high grades) offered a variant to the eight-four.

Communities of moderate size showed a fondness for the six-six plan (six elementary and six secondary), which clearly attaches junior high school to secondary education while at the same time burying its identity in that of the senior high school. Larger communities expressed a preference for the six-three-three plan with three years of junior high school between the elementary and senior high school. The three-year junior high school combining grades seven, eight, and nine replicated the structure of the first junior high schools that came into existence in 1909 in Columbus, Ohio, and in 1910 in Berkeley, California. Other variations have been suggested such as the six-three-five plan and the six-three-three-two plan, which would extend public secondary education through grades thirteen and fourteen. Those last two years, however, have clearly become identified with the college level. The rearrangement of the twelve years of public schooling has continued to the present, as we shall see later when we discuss the development of the middle school.

The concomitant outgrowth of the graded school was the self-contained classroom—a heterogeneous group of youngsters of approximately the same age, in multiples of twenty-five to thirty-five, under the direction of one teacher. Primary school teachers of the graded school were no longer required to master all disciplines of all grades like their counterparts in the one-room school but only to master all disciplines at the particular grade level. The group of children assigned to a teacher in a self-contained, graded elementary school spent the entire day under the watchful eye of that teacher. It has taken militant action of teacher organizations in recent years to pry loose some breathing time for elementary school teachers during the school day.

The concept of the graded school, aided by the measurement movement in education, has firmly established the principle that certain learnings should be accomplished by pupils not at certain periods of growth and development but by the end of certain grade levels. Syllabi, courses of study, and minimal competencies have been determined for each grade level. State content standards have been specified for various fields of instruction.

In the graded school, material is tailored to fit the confines of fixed times during the customary ten months of the school year. Thus, by means of a standardized test of reading, for example, we can state that a third-grade child in April (the eighth month of the school year) whose test score placed him or her at the grade norm of 3.2 (second month of the third-grade year) was reading at a level six months below the norm for that grade.

When we speak of the self-contained classroom, we normally think of the elementary school. We sometimes forget that the self-contained classroom has been the prevailing pattern in the secondary school except for a brief period of popularity of core programs, which we shall discuss later.

Like the junior and senior high schools, the elementary school adopted an organizational framework that stressed the mastery of subject matter. This framework, commonly referred to as the subject matter curriculum, will be examined shortly.

Typical Schedule. A typical week in a self-contained, subject-oriented elementary school calls for separate subjects scheduled at specific and regular times during the day. Little or no effort is made to integrate these diverse areas. Some elementary schools, of course, have never departed from this model, whereas others departed for a time and then swung back in recent years.

In the late 1920s, through the 1930s, and into the 1940s, many elementary schools, warmed by the glow of the progressive movement that championed the child over subject matter, abandoned the subject matter curriculum for the activity or experience curriculum.

The Activity Curriculum

The activity (or experience) curriculum was an attempt by educators to break away from the rigidity of the graded school. It is of historical interest that the activity curriculum was a contribution of two of the better-known laboratory schools—the Laboratory School founded by John Dewey at the University of Chicago and the University Elementary School directed by J. L. Meriam at the University of Missouri. The activity curriculum came about as an effort to translate progressive beliefs into the curriculum. As such, it captured the imaginations of elementary school educators in the first quarter of the twentieth century.

Disenchanted with the subject matter curriculum promoted by the essentialist philosophers and curriculum makers, Dewey and others sought to free the learner from the confines of a subject-centered curriculum and to create an environment that catered to the learner needs and interests.

Human Impulses. B. Othanel Smith, William O. Stanley, and J. Harlan Shores observed that Dewey's Laboratory School curriculum was based on the following four human impulses, which Dewey referred to as "uninvested capital":

> the social impulse, the constructive impulse, the impulse to investigate and experiment, and the expressive or artistic impulse.[2]

Dewey's curriculum eschewed the usual subject organizers and focused on occupations in which all men and women engaged—carpentry, cooking, and sewing.

Human Activities. The University Elementary School at the University of Missouri followed principles advocated by Junius L. Meriam and structured its program not around subjects but around human activities of observation, play, stories, and handiwork.[3] The California State Curriculum Commission outlined a daily program for an activity curriculum as shown in Table 9.2. As these two examples reveal, the content of the activity curriculum is centered on projects or experiences that are of immediate interest to the learners. The various subjects, including the basic skills, are used as a means of promoting learning rather than as ends or centers of learning for themselves.

Subject Matter from Child's World. Here the curriculum is developed by the teacher in cooperation with the pupils. The subject matter evolves from the child's world rather than from the adult world. Although the teacher can suggest activities or problems to the learners, the children's interests become the dominant factor. William H. Kilpatrick advocated pupil activities that he referred to as projects (ergo, the "project method") and took the position that the child should do his or her own thinking and planning.[4]

Problem solving—Dewey's "reflective thinking"—is the activity curriculum's instructional method par excellence. Experience in the process of problem solving is perceived by those who espouse progressive thought as more important than attaining the solutions to the problems. A great effort is made to integrate subject matter, using any and all content as needed without regard to discipline boundaries, for the solution of problems or carrying out of projects.

By its very nature, the activity curriculum cannot be fully planned in advance. Consequently, the activity curriculum can be described only after it has been completed, for the teacher cannot be sure in advance where the interests of the students will lead them.

The unit method of organizing instruction (a unit of work centered on a single topic or problem) lends itself well to the goal of problem solving. Units are designed by the teacher in cooperation with the pupils to include a sufficient variety of activities to provide for individual differences among pupils. A series of units can provide a skeletal framework for a given grade level.

Drill, if needed, is carried out in meaningful terms, not in isolated rote fashion. With the social orientation of the progressivists, the activity curriculum calls for the socialization of the learners and the use of the community as a learning laboratory.

Scheduling is flexible with time allotments variable depending on the activities under way. Pupils are grouped according to interests and abilities, obviating the need for fixed grade levels. Some schools tossed out marks, report cards, and the assumption that certain learnings have to be mastered at each grade level.

The teacher of the activity curriculum finds his or her role not as subject matter specialist and expert-in-residence but rather as a guide and facilitator of learning. Key concepts that the progressivists wove into the activity curriculum are the active rather than the passive role of the learner and the sharing of students' experiences with the teacher and each other.

The activity curriculum, like progressive education itself, left its indelible imprint on American education. Flexible scheduling, unit teaching, problem solving, project

TABLE 9.2 Schedule for an Activity Curriculum

Time	Monday	Tuesday	Wednesday	Thursday	Friday
9:00	Informal greetings, reports, observations, rhymes, music, events of current interest, informal activities designed to create a mental set conducive to a happy, profitable day.				

Arithmetical Enterprises

9:15	Playstores, banking activities, handling of school supplies, etc. Although rich in arithmetical content through which the child is trained in skills and abilities, such units also yield abundantly in group and individual situations which develop initiative, responsibility, and cooperation. The flexible period provides opportunity for individual instruction.				

Healthful Living Enterprises

10:00	Physical education enterprises, free play, the nutrition program, and adequate relief periods are provided for daily; units of work such as: "the study of milk," "a balanced meal," etc., provide enterprises which have healthful living as a center of interest but provide situations development of social and civic attitudes as well.				

Language Arts

10:50	Oral and written composition, spelling and writing develop from activities rich in opportunities for expression, as the writing of a play to be presented in the auditorium period, puppet shows, the school newspaper, etc. The period should provide opportunity for literary discrimination and original expression; the long period provides for concentration of effort and attention according to individual interest and need.				

12:00	Lunch, Rest and Directed Playground Activities				

Avocational Activities

Time	Monday	Tuesday	Wednesday	Thursday	Friday
1:00	Music; activities, music appreciation, rhythm, harmonica, band, orchestra, etc.	Nature Club, school museum, aquarium, gardens, terrarium.	Creative art and constructive activities in pottery, weaving, painting, drawing.	Use of auditorium for music, dancing, dramatics, projects, stagecraft, related to class activities.	Civics Club Committees responsible for various phases of school life.

1:50	Recreation and Rest				

Reading Groups: Library Activities

2:00	Group organization on the basis of reading ability provides opportunity for remedial work with children having reading deficiencies and library guidance to superior readers. The quiet reading period may contribute to the development of information needed in the class activities related to social science, avocational, or health or other interests.				

2:50	Recreation and Rest				

Time	Monday	Tuesday	Wednesday	Thursday	Friday
3:00	Social studies activities	Social studies activities	Free creative work period	Social studies activities	Shop enterprises

Source: Ruth Manning Hockett, ed., *Teachers' Guide to Child Development: Manual for Kindergarten and Primary Teachers* (Sacramento, Calif.: California Department of Education, 1930), pp. 355–356. Reprinted by permission.

method, nongraded schools, and open education owe a debt to the activity curriculum. Nevertheless, the activity curriculum lost popularity and died out as a viable organizational pattern for the public elementary school. There are a number of reasons for its demise.

With the activity curriculum the needs of society and the needs of the adult world took a back seat to the needs of immature youngsters. Progressive—that is, activity-oriented schools—projected an unfavorable image to the public who felt that subject-matter learning was being neglected and too much stress was being placed on the immediate interests of immature learners.

Excesses on the part of some progressive schools led to cynical jokes, such as the one in which the teacher asks, "Is the earth round or flat?" and the pupil answers, "I don't know; let's vote on it." Then there is the classic put-down of the progressive school: The teacher enters the room in the morning and asks the class, "O.K., kids, what do you want to learn today?" and the children complain, "Do we have to do what we want to do today?"

It was not commonly understood that teachers of the activity curriculum had to be more knowledgeable and *better* trained not only in subject matter but also in techniques of guiding learning. The activity curriculum also required for its success resources and facilities that exceeded those of the typical elementary school. Further, more flexible administrators and teachers were needed for successful operation of a program of this type. The secondary schools also complained when they received students, products of the activity curriculum, who had a great range of knowledge and skills but glaring gaps in their education.

The Nongraded Elementary School

The nongraded elementary school, following plans that permit continuous progress, evolved as an alternative to the graded school. The nongraded or continuous progress school was a reaction to increasing rigidity of the graded school, which was an innovation designed to provide a more efficient education for children.

Persons unfamiliar with the concept of the nongraded school are sometimes confused by the term and interpret it to signify a school without a formal marking system. When we speak of the nongraded school, we refer to schools that have abandoned grade-level designations rather than marks.

In a nongraded school, typical grade levels and standards for those levels are absent. Children are grouped for instruction according to their particular needs and progress through the program at their own speed. Effort is made to individualize—some say "personalize"—instruction. The nongraded concept has made its greatest headway at the elementary school level. However, as we shall see when we discuss developments in secondary education later in this chapter, nongradedness is possible in the high school as well.

John I. Goodlad and Robert H. Anderson, proponents of the nongraded elementary school, saw nongradedness as a reaction to the Procrustean bed of the graded school.[5] "The realities of child development defy the rigorous ordering of children's abilities and attainments into conventional graded structures," observed Goodlad and Anderson.[6]

Herbert I. Von Haden and Jean Marie King explained some of the principles underlying the nongraded school in the following way:

Nongrading is a philosophy of teaching and learning which recognizes that children learn at different rates and in different ways and allows them to progress as individuals rather than as classes. Such designations as grade one and grade three are eliminated. Flexible groupings allow the pupil to proceed from one level of work to another whenever he is ready. Thus, the children's progress is not dependent upon that of others in the room. His own readiness, interest, and capacity set the pace for each pupil. . . . Flexible grouping permits each child to move ahead with other children of approximately the same level of ability. Groupings are different for each subject area and can be changed at any time. Failure, retention, and skipping of grades are replaced by continuous progress as the pupil proceeds at his own rate. Slower children are not forced to go on with the class group before they are ready. Faster workers are not compelled to wait for the others. Individualization and continuous progress are the key elements of nongrading.[7]

Growth of Nongraded Schools. The nongraded movement began in earnest in the 1930s, grew in intensity through the 1940s and 1950s, and leveled off in the 1960s. Among the nongraded schools of the 1930s and 1940s were those in Western Springs, Illinois; Richmond, Virginia; Athens, Georgia; Youngstown, Ohio; and Milwaukee, Wisconsin.[8] In the 1950s and 1960s nongraded schools were started in Bellevue, Washington; Appleton, Wisconsin; Chicago, Illinois; and Southern Humboldt Unified School District, California.[9]

School personnel of Appleton, Wisconsin, compared the graded school with the continuous progress school, as shown in Table 9.3. The nongraded school seeks to eliminate failures and retention by permitting children to proceed through the program at their own pace. Programs of the nongraded school are organized primarily around reading levels and to a lesser extent around mathematics levels rather than around the traditional chronological age-grade levels.

Reading is used as the nucleus for grouping of youngsters in the nongraded school. Maurie H. Hillson explained:

The present-day nongraded elementary schools, for the most part, rely on levels of accomplishment in reading as the bases for advancement and assignment in a program of vertical progression through the six years of the elementary school organization. Current nongraded plans, with some rare but exciting departures, accept the format of an attempted homogeneous grouping based on factors attendant to reading achievement.[10]

To form reading groups instructors pay attention to many factors, including intelligence, achievement, motivation, readiness, and maturity. Hillson elaborated on the salient features of nongraded plans:

Briefly, then, many of the present nongraded schools are ones in which grades are replaced by levels which a child accomplishes at his own speed. No grade designators are used. These levels of experiences are clearly described and without the fear of retention or, conversely, without the fear of encroachment upon material reserved for a next higher grade, the child progresses through them as a competency is achieved. . . . The rapid learner may accomplish a three-year nongraded program in two years. . . . The slow learner may take four years to accomplish three.[11]

TABLE 9.3 Comparison of the Graded and Continuous Progress Schools

Graded Structure	Continuous Progress
1. It is assumed that all children of the same chronological age will develop to the same extent in a given period of time.	1. It is assumed that each child has his own pattern and rate of growth and that children of the same age will vary greatly in their ability and rate of growth.
2. A child who does not measure up to certain predetermined standards of what should be accomplished in nine months is called a failure.	2. No child is ever considered a failure. If he does not achieve in proportion to his ability, we study the cause and adjust his program to fit his needs and problems.
3. If a child fails, he is required to repeat the grade in which he did not meet the standards.	3. A child never repeats. He may progress more slowly than others in the group, but individual records of progress make it possible to keep his growth continuous.
4. A decision as to grade placement must be made after each nine months.	4. Decisions as to group placement can be made at any time during the three-year period (for social or emotional adjustment, an additional year if needed, etc.).
5. Grade placements are based too largely upon academic achievement.	5. Group placement is flexible, based upon physical, mental, social, and emotional maturity.
6. Fixed standards of achievement within a set time put pressures upon teachers and children which cause emotional tensions and inhibit learning.	6. Elimination of pressures produces a relaxed learning situation conducive to good mental health.

Source: Royce E. Kurtz and James N. Reston, "Continuous Progress in Appleton, Wisconsin," in David W. Beggs III, and Edward G. Buffie, eds., *Nongraded Schools in Action: Bold New Venture* (Bloomington: Indiana University Press, 1967), p. 139. Reprinted by permission.

Problems Encountered. Nongraded plans encountered problems that led to a tapering off in their popularity. Nongraded programs are much more complex than the traditional, graded organization. They require continuous flexibility, more time by the faculty, greater resources, and a style of teaching different from that in typical graded schools. Careful diagnosis must be made of the learners' needs.

Nongraded schools could become as inflexible as the graded school if teachers and administrators merely substituted reading levels for chronological grades. Continuous progress plans concentrated to a great degree on reading and to a much lesser degree on mathematics, generally leaving the other subjects in the curriculum much as they were before—traditionally organized without well-planned sequencing of levels.

Nongraded plans excelled in vertical organization of the reading curriculum and sometimes the mathematics curriculum but failed to work out relationships at any level among the various disciplines. Further, the transition from a continuous progress elementary school to a graded junior high school could be rather abrupt for the learners when the junior high school was less concerned with personalized learning.

Advocacy of the nongraded elementary school continued in the publication of the revised edition of Goodlad and Anderson (1987) and in a more recent work by Anderson and Barbara Nelson Pavan (1993).[12] Contending that "views now in ascendance are far more compatible with nongradedness, and the prospects for its implementation are therefore much better," Anderson and Pavan commented, "the time is at last ripe for a serious onslaught on literally graded practice."[13]

Open Education and Open Space

Several years ago the hypothetical elementary school created at the beginning of this chapter caught on to the tail end of a movement known as the open-space school. The interior walls between classrooms came tumbling down—or as many walls as possible in a building constructed as a graded school many years ago. The purpose in eliminating barriers between classes was to permit innovative approaches such as flexible grouping, individualized instruction, nongradedness, or, simply, the open school. In practice, the terms are often interchanged. An *open classroom*, for example, might signal a classroom operated according to principles of *open education*. At the same time, this classroom might be an *open area*, although, paradoxically, open space is not a prerequisite to open education. An *open school* might be a school that implements the open-education concept, or it might be an open-space school in which all classrooms are without walls.

C. M. Charles and others commented: "Many people think that open space and open education are synonymous. They are not. In fact they can be (but don't have to be) quite opposite."[14] Charles and others defined an open school not as an open-space school but as a school with several classrooms following principles of open education.[15] Open-space schools normally subscribe to at least some of the principles of open education, whereas open schools, as defined by Charles and coauthors, may or may not be open-space schools.

In the ensuing discussion I will use the terms "open school," "open classroom," and "open education" when speaking of the broad concept and "open space" or "open area" when talking about the architectural arrangement of classrooms without walls.[16]

Imported from Great Britain, the open-classroom concept was designed as a curriculum and organizational response to formal, traditional schools. Charles and others briefly described open education as follows:

> Open education refers to organizations and management that allow much student choice and self-direction. The teacher helps, but dominates neither the planning nor the learning activities. Instead, the teacher "facilitates" student learning. This facilitation is done through talking, exploring, suggesting options, helping find resources, and deciding on ways of working that suit the group. Emphasis falls continually on maintaining relationships, interacting positively with others, fostering a sense of personal and group worth, and providing for the development of individual potential.[17]

Louis Rubin described the philosophical basis for the open classroom as follows:

> The basic ideology is rooted in the notion that children have a natural interest and desire in learning. Thus, when there is a conducive environment, and when the learning

structure does not inhibit individuality, good education invariably will occur. What we have come to call relevance, as a result, is built into the fundamental philosophy itself; the curriculum, in short, is derived almost entirely from student interests and needs.[18]

Rubin went on to contrast the traditional and open classrooms:

The critical distinctions between open and traditional education are that the goals are different, their means of attainment vary, and different outputs are yielded by each. A traditional program, for example, requires that a prescribed course of study be followed, leaving little leeway for accommodation to individual student interests. Its chief virtue, therefore, is that we can determine in advance, to a very sizable extent, what the child will and will not learn. But in the open education climate precisely the opposite condition prevails; since the child's own intellectual interests serve as the educational point of departure, predetermined objectives must defer to individual whim and specified learning outcomes cannot be guaranteed.[19]

Common sights in the open-area schools are large expanses of classroom space, groups of a hundred or more pupils spread out and engaged in a variety of activities at many stations within the areas, and teams of teachers working with individuals, small groups, and large groups of learners.

Beliefs Underlying Open-Space Schools.   Proponents of the open classroom stress active learning and the affective domain. "The primary advantage of open space," said John H. Proctor and Kathryn Smith, "is the increased communication and interaction of teacher to teacher, teacher to student, and student to student."[20] Significant features of the open-space concept are the flexibility of grouping and the use of concrete materials that appeal to the interests and maturity level of the learners. Whereas many open elementary schools were organized into clusters or teams of a single grade level (e.g., first grade), others were nongraded and organized into multiunits.

The open-education/open-space movements crested in the early 1980s and have since dwindled to the point where they are almost nonexistent. Schools that removed walls for an open-area model have reinstalled walls or partitions to recreate small, self-contained units. What happened to this seemingly promising movement in the short space of approximately a decade?

David Pratt offered one reason for difficulties incurred by the open-space school:

The attempts to transplant the architectural aspect (of open-area schools in England) to North America has not been universally successful. Frequently, the innovation consisted of building schools with fewer interior walls, an environment into which teachers were introduced who had neither participated in, approved of, or been trained for the open environment. Continuing to teach in a conventional way, they found the absence of walls merely an audible and visible distraction. Bookcases, screens, and miniature palm trees were quickly turned into makeshift barriers between the teaching areas. Small wonder that the research evidence shows, at best, disappointing performance by students in open classrooms, not only in academic subjects but also in creativity, and an increased anxiety level.[21]

The audible and visual distractions have been, in my judgment, erroneously minimized. Visits to open classrooms rather consistently reveal a noise level that is not conducive to learning. Harried teachers must constantly elevate their voices to make themselves understood. When ardent proponents of the open classroom are questioned about the noise, their responses are often: "What noise?" or "Some noise is necessary for learning to take place." Perhaps we can attribute some of the fault for these distractions to the lack of fit between program and architecture.

Rubin pointed out that, contrary to the claims of some advocates of open education, traditional education is not necessarily as bad as some people painted it:

> In fairness, it must be acknowledged that the proponents of open education have sometimes built their case upon a straw man. Traditional education—although formalized and structured—need not be depressing nor debilitating of the learner's spirit. In point of fact, there is abundant reason to believe that some learners thrive better in a traditional setting than in an open one. To wit, children sometimes find a lack of structure uncomfortable and large doses of freedom anxiety provoking. Similarly, provisions for the affective components of education, for the emotional feelings of students, can be made in both a traditional and an open format. As a result, one cannot in good conscience claim that an unstructured, open curriculum is necessarily more "humanistic" than a structured, traditional one.
>
> Nor, to extend the point further, can one claim that an open curriculum automatically teaches the child to think more than a traditional one, or that multiage grouping cannot exist in either situation, or that prescribed programs of instruction must, inevitably, prohibit individualization. Put another way, a large number of benefits habitually claimed by champions of one approach or the other can, in reality, be used with equal effectiveness in both.[22]

In regard to the success of open-space and open-education plans, Charles and coauthors observed: "In many cases, open space has not produced the results that were hoped for. . . . There is little evidence, however, to support open education on the grounds of academic achievement."[23]

THE JUNIOR HIGH SCHOOL

The School In-Between

Educators and behavioral scientists of the late nineteenth century and early twentieth century recognized the necessity for a type of educational program and institution that would provide special attention to the needs of youngsters between childhood and adolescence. Out of this concern grew the junior high school. From its inception the junior high school was an institution in search of an identity. The early junior high schools encompassed grades seven, eight, and nine. Prior to the separation of these grades to form their own institution, grades seven and eight were normally considered an integral part of the elementary school; grades nine through twelve formed the secondary school. Early schools, if they did not house all grades in one classroom, grouped their pupils in self-contained seventh- and eighth-grade classrooms. Not until the advent of the junior high as an institution did departmentalization come to the schooling of the twelve- to fourteen-year-olds.

With the appearance of the junior high school, children entering adolescence found an institution created specifically for them. It bore the trappings of both the primary school below it and the secondary school above it. Offering both a basic general education and exploratory experiences, the junior high school spread rapidly through the first half of the twentieth century. School systems adopted either the seven-eight-nine pattern or a seven-eight model that maintained the ninth grade in the senior high school.

Educators' perceptions of the role of the junior high school have varied considerably. Is it an upward projection of the elementary school? Is it a downward extension of the senior high school? Is its purpose mainly exploratory, serving learners in a transition period between puberty and adolescence, or is it a preparatory school for the senior high? Should it be housed in the same building with the senior high school or located in a separate building?

In spite of varying perceptions of its role the junior high school serves as an example of the self-fulfilling prophecy. Established as a unique institution, the junior high school began to live up to its label "junior high." The junior high school quickly came to be identified as a part of secondary education, resulting in the kindergarten-six, seven-twelve dichotomy that to some extent still exists. Although at first it was somewhat experimental in nature with block-time scheduling and core curricula, as the years rolled by the junior high school became more and more like its higher-level companion with complete departmentalization of courses, senior-high scheduling patterns, and a subject matter curriculum.

Conant's Recommendations.   In Chapter 6 we mentioned the studies of the junior and senior high school conducted by James B. Conant. Since Conant's recommendations were so favorably received, we should be remiss not to examine some and to discern their nature. Among Conant's fourteen recommendations for the junior high school were the following:

Required Subjects for All Pupils in Grades 7 and 8
The following subjects should be required of all pupils in grades 7 and 8: English (including heavy emphasis on reading skills and composition), social studies (including emphasis on history and geography), mathematics (arithmetic except as noted . . .) and science.
     In addition, all pupils should receive instruction in home economics and all boys instruction in industrial arts. . . .

New Developments in Mathematics and Foreign Languages
A small fraction of pupils should start algebra (or one of the new brands of mathematics) in grade 8. Some, if not all, pupils should start the study of a foreign language on a conversational basis with a bilingual teacher in grade 7.

Basic Skills
Instruction in the basic skills begun in the elementary school should be continued as long as pupils can gain from the instruction. This statement applies particularly to reading and arithmetic. Pupils with average ability should read at or above grade level; superior pupils considerably above grade level. By the end of grade 9 even the poorest readers (except the mentally retarded) should read at least at the sixth-grade level.

Block-Time and Departmentalization

Provisions should be made to assure a smooth transition for the young adolescent from the elementary to the secondary school. . . . there should be a block of time set aside at least in grade 7, in which one teacher has the same pupils for two or more periods, generally in English and social studies. Otherwise, grades 7, 8, and 9 should be departmentalized. . . .[24]

Many schools reviewed, reaffirmed, or modified their curricula in light of the Conant recommendations, and our hypothetical junior high school was no exception.

ASCD Proposals. At about the same time Conant was recommending increased emphasis on the academics, the Commission on the Education of Adolescents of the Association for Supervision and Curriculum Development (ASCD) was presenting a different point of view on the function and programs of the junior high school. Writing for the ASCD, Jean D. Grambs and others, acknowledging that the junior high school was under pressure, advocated variations in lengths of class periods, programs planned explicitly for the junior high school years, ungraded programs, and a block-of-time program offered each year for three years of junior high school.[25] As we will see, a block-of-time program usually runs for two to three hours of a school day.

Whereas Conant's proposals for the school in the middle were more subject-centered, the ASCD proposals were more learner-centered. However, proponents of both points of view agreed on the necessity for adequate facilities and resources, a professionally trained staff, a moderate and manageable size of school, and ample guidance.

The Core Curriculum

Basic education, common learnings, core curriculum, and general education are terms, like goals and objectives, that are tossed about rather loosely in the profession. These terms are used by educators to describe programs that are almost at opposite poles. To some, basic education, common learnings, and general education signal a set of courses or subjects that are required of all students—the earmark of the subject matter curriculum, grounded in essentialistic philosophy. In this vein, the Harvard Committee toward the end of World War II stated its interpretation of general education:

> Clearly, general education has somewhat the meaning of liberal education [p. 52] . . . . General education, we repeat, must consciously aim at these abilities: at effective thinking, communication, the making of relevant judgments, and the discrimination of values [p. 72]. . . . It therefore remains only to draw the scheme of general education that follows from these premises. At the center of it . . . would be the three inevitable areas of man's life and knowledge . . . : the physical world, man's corporate life, his inner visions and standards [p. 98]. . . . In school, in our opinion, general education in these three areas should form a continuing core for all, taking up at least half of a student's time [p. 99]. . . . Accepting the course-unit system as established at least for the present, despite its grave weaknesses dwelt on earlier, that would amount to some eight units, preferably spaced by means of half-courses over the four years of school rather than compressed into two or three. The common and desirable divisions within these eight units would probably be three in English, three in science and mathematics, and two in the social studies. But—and this is the important point—this half

of the schoolwork to be spent on general education would seem the barest minimum, either for those not going on to college or for those who are [p. 100].[26]

James B. Conant, president of Harvard University at the time the Harvard Committee issued its report, took a similar position when he recommended general education programs consisting of required courses at both the junior and senior high school levels. In keeping with the spirit of the 1894 Report of the Committee of Ten, the 1945 Report of the Harvard Committee, and several national reports of the 1980s, high schools today designate a "core" or set of required subjects for graduation. However, in the section which follows I have used the terms "core" and "core curriculum" to describe a unique organizational structure in the secondary school, not required courses.

The essentialists championed—and still advocate—the set of required courses as their model for general education in the high school. At the other end of the spectrum, from the camps of the pragmatic and reconstructionist philosophers, come those who hold a quite different conception of general education. They frequently refer to their plans for common learnings or general education as a "core curriculum." Unlike the "continuing core for all" recommended by the Harvard Committee, the core curriculum at its inception was a radically new departure in curriculum organization. John H. Lounsbury and Gordon F. Vars noted that many curriculum specialists regarded core as a truly innovative development.[27]

What is the core curriculum? Lounsbury and Vars defined "core"—short for "core curriculum"—as follows: "Specifically, core is a form of curriculum organization, usually operating within an extended block of time in the daily schedule, in which learning experiences are focused directly on problems of significance to students."[28]

Unification of Subject Matter. The core curriculum gained momentum in the 1930s and 1940s, but its roots go back to the nineteenth century. In a presentation made by Emerson E. White to the National Department of Superintendents in 1896, White discussed one of the basic principles of core: the unification of subject matter.

> Complete unification is the blending of all subjects and branches of study into one whole, and the teaching of the same in successive groups or lessons or sections. When this union is effected by making one group or branch of study in the course the center or core, and subordinating all other subjects to it, the process is properly called the concentration of studies.[29]

Smith, Stanley, and Shores credited Ziller, founder of the Herbartian school at the University of Leipzig, and Colonel Francis W. Parker, superintendent of schools, Quincy, Massachusetts, in 1875 and later principal of the Cook County (Chicago) Normal School, as proponents of the principle of unification of subject matter.[30]

The core concept received a significant boost in the 1930s when the curriculum committees of a number of states sought to plan a curriculum around social functions of living and turned for assistance to Hollis L. Caswell, then of George Peabody College for Teachers and later of Teachers College, Columbia University. The Virginia State Curriculum Program pioneered in establishing the core curriculum—the content of which centered on societal functions.[31]

The core curriculum is in philosophy and intent the secondary school counterpart of the activity curriculum of the elementary school. Espoused as a concept for both the junior and senior high schools, the core curriculum made its greatest inroads at the junior high school level. The core concept was especially popular in the state of Maryland. However, Lounsbury and Vars pointed out that core, like many programs that are different, did not meet with universal acceptance even at the junior high school level.[32]

Characteristics of Core.   Although varying in structure and focus, core curricula, as described in this chapter, possess the following characteristics:

1. They constitute a portion of the curriculum that is required for all students.
2. They integrate, unify, or fuse subject matter, usually English and social studies.
3. Their content centers on problems that cut across the disciplines.
4. The primary method of learning is problem solving, using all applicable subject matter.
5. They are organized into blocks of time, usually two to three periods under a "core" teacher (with possible use of additional teachers and others as resource persons).
6. They encourage teachers to plan with students.
7. They provide pupil guidance.

Types of Core.   Harold B. Alberty and Elsie J. Alberty distinguished five types of core.[33] The first two are core in the sense that subjects are required of all; as such these two types fall into the classification of the subject-matter curriculum. Writing in 1962, Alberty and Alberty classified types of core as follows:

- Type 1: A set of subjects ("constants") is required for all students. Subjects are taught separately with little or no effort to relate them to each other. This type of organizational plan is predominant in high schools today.
- Type 2: Two or more subjects are correlated. Although subjects remain discrete and are taught separately, effort is made to relate one to the other. The history teacher, for example, may work with the English teacher to show students relationships between topics that they happen to be studying in the two courses.
- Type 3: Two or more subjects are fused. The majority of core programs in schools fall into this classification. English and social studies are fused or integrated and scheduled in a block of time, usually two to three periods. Not a complete departure from traditional subject matter organization, this type of core organizes content around contemporary social problems or around historic or cultural epochs. Several experimental schools of the Eight-Year Study of the Progressive Education Association used Types 2 and 3 cores.[34]
- Type 4: A block of time is established to study adolescent and/or social problems, such as school living, family life, economic problems, communication, multicultural relationships, health, international problems, conservation, and understanding the self. This type of core requires a complete departure from the typical subject matter curriculum and a thorough reorganization of the curriculum.

- Type 5: Learning activities are developed cooperatively by teachers and students, who are free to pursue whatever interests or problem areas they desire. This core program resembles the unstructured experience curriculum of the elementary school.

Core curricula tend to consume a block of time consisting of two to three periods of the school day. The remaining periods are devoted to specialized interests of students. "Block-time classes" is a term sometimes equated with "core." However, block-time classes may or may not be core classes.[35]

Reporting in 1958 on a survey of block-time classes and core programs in junior high schools, Grace S. Wright listed four types of programs in block-time classes as follows:

Type A—Each subject retains its identity in the block-time class, that is separate subjects are taught (1) with consciously planned correlation, (2) with no planned correlation.

Type B—Subjects included in the block-time class are unified or fused around a central theme or units of work or problems stemming from one or more of the subject fields in the block-time class.

Type C—Predetermined problem areas based upon the personal-social needs of adolescents—both needs that adolescents themselves have identified and needs as society sees them—determine the scope of the core program. Subject matter is brought in as needed in working on the problems. Pupils may or may not have a choice from among several of these problem areas; they will, however, have some responsibility for suggesting and choosing activities in developing units of study.

Type D—The scope of the core program is not predetermined. Pupils and teacher are free to select the problems upon which they wish to work. Subject matter content is brought in as needed to develop or to help solve the problems.[36]

Note the points of agreement between the Wright and the Alberty and Alberty classifications.

Organizational plans for a core curriculum limit blocks of time typically to a double-period throughout the junior high level or, if carried into the senior high level, decreasing blocks of time as pupils move from junior through senior high school levels.[37]

Core programs have never been fully understood by the public. "What is core?" asks the average citizen. What does an "A" in core mean to parents and to college admissions officers? Informed persons will admit that the ripples caused by the Eight-Year Study, which allowed for innovative plans like the core, generally lost their force, and colleges went back to demanding high school credit in subjects they understood.

Core teaching is a demanding task requiring skills that take special training. Teachers' colleges, by and large, neglected the preparation of core teachers. The perceived threat from the Soviet Union in 1957 renewed demand for the "hard" subjects—science, mathematics, and foreign languages—and brought about negative reactions to unusual programs like core.

Conant was less than enthusiastic about the core. Even for the block of time that he recommended for seventh grade, he held that teachers need not break down subject-matter lines.[38]

Daniel Tanner and Laurel Tanner observed that "The core idea never gained the widespread acceptance that was expected of it by progressive educators."[39]

Although core programs had largely disappeared from the scene, in recent years we have witnessed renewed interest in core-type programs. We find proposals for "integrating the curriculum" and plans in operation which emulate some of the earlier efforts at core: theme-centered instruction, block-time organization, and interdisciplinary teams.[40] Washington, D.C., public schools, for example, in 2003 were offering interdisciplinary, co-taught high school English and history courses that combined study of a period of literature with its history. Though proposals for integrated and interdisciplinary curricula are made for all levels, they are particularly in evidence at the middle school level.

Referring to an integrated curriculum with thematic units and identifying the middle school as the "natural home of integrated curriculum," James Beane named Cross Keys Middle School (Florissant, Missouri) and Marquette Middle School (Madison, Wisconsin) as examples of schools implementing what he called the "new curriculum vision."[41]

Gordon F. Vars pointed out that "the popularity of core-type integrative programs waxes and wanes from year to year, as education shifts primary attention from student concerns to subject matter acquisition to social problems and back again."[42] Continuing and renewed interest in the concept of the core curriculum is seen today in the numerous articles advocating integration of the curriculum and interdisciplinary learning.

In the mid- and late twentieth century, the junior high school underwent a metamorphosis, developing into a new institution designed to better meet the needs of the preadolescent. This innovative concept, the middle school, is discussed later in this chapter.

THE SENIOR HIGH SCHOOL

The Subject Matter Curriculum

The subject matter curriculum has been the most prevalent form of curriculum organization at all levels of American education ever since the Boston Latin School, the first Latin Grammar School in the United States, opened in 1635. The subject matter curriculum remains the most common pattern of organization throughout most of the world. Although other forms of curriculum organization have asserted themselves in the United States from time to time, the subject matter curriculum has continued strong and has gained strength in recent years with the emphasis placed on the academics and basic skills. The subject matter curriculum has existed at all levels of schooling but has been particularly entrenched at the senior high and college levels.

Smith, Stanley, and Shores pointed out that the subject matter curriculum, derived from the Seven Liberal Arts that trace their roots to ancient Greece and Rome and the Middle Ages, is the oldest and most accepted plan for organizing the curriculum. They explained:

> The Seven Liberal Arts consisted of two divisions: the trivium, which was comprised of grammar, rhetoric, and dialectic (logic); and the quadrivium, which consisted of arithmetic,

geometry, astronomy, and music. . . . In the modern period the trivium was further divided to include literature and history as distinct subjects; and the quadrivium, to include algebra, trigonometry, geography, botany, zoology, physics, and chemistry . . . the Seven Liberal Arts are still the nucleus of the subject curriculum, as a casual survey of required courses will reveal.[43]

As the name implies, the subject matter curriculum is an organizational pattern that breaks the school's program into discrete subjects or disciplines. The seventeenth century Latin Grammar School stressed classical subjects, including Greek, Latin, Hebrew, mathematics, history, and the Bible. Notably absent from this early school were English and science, which were considered too functional or too frivolous for scholars of this period. With the opening of Benjamin Franklin's Academy and Charitable School in 1751, English, science, and modern languages were added to the curriculum. Today's secondary schools offer a potpourri—some say smorgasbord—of courses.

Essentialistic in outlook, the subject matter curriculum seeks to transmit the cultural heritage. The subjects or disciplines organize knowledge from the adult world in such a way that it can be transmitted to the immature learner.

As we saw in Chapter 6 when we discussed the philosophy of essentialism, the subject matter curriculum has not been at a loss for spokespersons. Max Rafferty left no doubt of his position regarding the subject matter curriculum when he said, "What is significant for the children—what the people want for their children and mean to get—is subject matter that is systematic, organized, and disciplined and that is taught effectively and interestingly as subject matter. . . . Stress subject matter, *all* subject matter."[44]

At public school levels the subject matter curriculum has had its greatest impact at the secondary school level. Elementary and middle school faculties have been more prone to experiment and to try out new patterns of organization that depart from subject matter emphasis. Secondary school teachers and administrators have consistently tended to be more subject-centered than their counterparts at the elementary school level.

Advantages.   The subject matter curriculum presents to its followers certain distinct advantages. It is the easiest organizational pattern to structure. On the elementary school level, it is simply a matter of allocating a certain number of minutes for each subject during the course of the day. On the secondary school level, subject matter is organized into "courses" that are designated as either required subjects or electives. Every subject of the secondary school is typically scheduled for the same amount of time. The recommendations of two well-known groups helped to imprint the model of equal time for each subject in the secondary school.

At the tail end of the nineteenth century the National Education Association's Committee of Ten proposed:

Every subject which is taught at all in a secondary school should be taught in the same way and to the same extent to every pupil so long as he pursues it, no matter what the probable destination of the pupil may be, or at what point his education is to cease. Thus, for all pupils who study Latin, or history, or algebra, for example, the allotment of time and the method of instruction in a given school should be the same year by year. Not that all pupils should pursue every subject for the same number of years, but so long as they do pursue it, they should all be treated alike.[45]

A few years later, in 1906, the Carnegie Foundation for the Advancement of Teaching created the Carnegie unit, which for purposes of college admission standardized the amount of time to be spent in each subject in high school. To most people today the concept is known simply as a "unit," the Carnegie modifier having been lost over time. The Carnegie Foundation for the Advancement of Teaching defined a unit as satisfactory completion of a subject that met five days per week, a minimum of forty minutes per period, and a minimum of 120 clock hours for the school year. In addition, the Carnegie Foundation stipulated that a secondary school pupil should amass a total of sixteen units for graduation. These two recommendations were universally adopted by American secondary schools and have continued in force with infrequent modifications up to the present. In today's educational environment, states have moved well past the Carnegie Foundation's recommendation of sixteen units for high school graduation, as we shall see later in this chapter.

The content of the subject matter curriculum, unlike that of the experience curriculum, is planned in advance by the teacher or, more accurately, by the writers of the textbooks or curriculum guides that the teacher follows. The needs and interests of learners play little part in the curriculum that is organized around disciplines.

Unlike the activity or experience curriculum and the core curriculum discussed earlier in this chapter, the subject matter curriculum is well understood by the public, students, and the profession and for the most part has met with general favor. The methodology followed in the subject matter curriculum is rather straightforward. The teacher is the expert in the field and is likely to pursue a set of procedures that some instructional specialists refer to as the "assign-study-recite-test" method. William H. Burton succinctly described these procedures:

> The learning situation is organized around materials and experiences which are assigned by the teacher. The pupils then study in various ways. The results of their studying are presented and shared during a recitation period. Testing of results occurs at the conclusion of a series of assignments and may occur at stated times within the sequence.[46]

Writing in 1962, Burton stated, "The assign-study-recite-test formula will be used for many years to come."[47] What he might have said is that the assign-study-recite-test formula has been used for generations and is likely to continue for generations to come. This approach is what many people both within and without the profession call "teaching."

Cognitive Emphasis. The subject matter curriculum, which in days of old was imbedded in faculty psychology or mental discipline, has found behavioristic psychology compatible with its objectives. Student achievement is rather easily assessed, since evaluation is limited to measuring cognitive objectives by teacher-made or standardized tests. Some effort is made to measure performance in the psychomotor domain, but the perceptual motor skills are treated more or less as appendages to the cognitive domain. For example, in high schools that have separate tracks of curricula—such as general, commercial, industrial, and college preparatory—the most cognitive, the college preparatory track, is usually regarded as the most prestigious.

In the subject matter curriculum little effort is made to gauge student performance in the affective domain. Not only is evaluation of feelings and values extremely difficult, but also proponents of the subject matter curriculum, essentialists as they are, do not accept the affective domain as a primary concern of the school. Robert L. Ebel expressed this position forcefully when he said:

> Feelings are essentially unteachable.... Nor do they need to be taught.... The kind of learning on which schools should concentrate most of their efforts is cognitive competence.... Affective dispositions are important products of the human experience, but they seldom are or should be the principal targets of our educational efforts.[48]

The approach to individual differences and needs of students in the subject matter curriculum lies more in the provision of elective or special interest subjects from among which the students may choose. The breadth or scope of the subject matter curriculum and its sequence are revealed in the textbooks that are adopted for use in the classroom.

Conant's Proposals.   Conant's studies of both the American high and junior high schools strengthened advocates of the subject matter curriculum. So that you may sense the overall impact of the Conant report on the high school, which preceded the report on the junior high, let's look at several of his twenty-two recommendations.

One wonders if the titles of Conant's two reports have political significance as well as educational. His 1959 report on the high school was labeled "a first report to interested citizens," whereas his 1960 junior high school report was subtitled "a memorandum to school boards." Among Conant's proposals for the high school were the following:

Required Programs for All
A. General Education
The requirements for graduation for all students should be as follows: four years of English, three or four years of social studies—including two years of history (one of which should be American history) and a senior course in American problems or American government—one year of mathematics in the ninth grade (algebra or general mathematics), and at least one year of science in the ninth or tenth grade, which might well be biology or general physical science. By a year, I mean that a course is given five periods a week throughout the academic year or an equivalent amount of time. This academic program of general education involves nine or ten courses with homework to be taken in four years and occupies more than half the time of most students, whatever their elective programs.

B. The Elective Program
The other requirements for graduation should be successful completion of at least seven more courses, not including physical education. *All students should be urged to include art and music in their elective programs.* All students should be advised to have as the central core of their elective programs significant sequences of courses, either those leading to the development of a marketable skill or those of an academic nature.

C. Standards for Pass and Failure

The teachers of the advanced *elective* courses—foreign languages, mathematics, and science—should be urged to maintain high standards. They should be told not to hesitate to fail a student who does not meet the minimum level of performance they judge necessary for mastery of the subject in question. . . . On the other hand, for the *required* courses another standard should be applied. Since these courses are required of all, irrespective of ability, a student may be given a passing grade if he has worked to full capacity whether or not a certain level of achievement has been reached. . . .

Ability Grouping

In the required subjects and those elected by students with a wide range of ability, the students should be grouped according to ability, subject by subject. . . . This type of grouping is not to be confused with across-the-board grouping according to which a given student is placed in a particular section in *all* courses. . . .

English Composition

The time devoted to English composition during the four years should occupy about half the total time devoted to the study of English. Each student should be required to write an average of one theme a week. Themes should be corrected by the teacher. . . . No English teacher should be responsible for more than one hundred pupils.

To test the ability of each student in English composition, a schoolwide composition test should be given in every grade; in the ninth and eleventh grades, these composition tests should be graded not only by the teacher but by a committee of the entire school. Those students who do not obtain a grade on the eleventh-grade composition test commensurate with their ability as measured by an aptitude test should be required to take a special course in English composition in the twelfth grade. . . .

Diversified Programs for the Development of Marketable Skills

Programs should be available for girls interested in developing skills in typing, stenography, the use of clerical machines, home economics. . . . Distributive education should be available. . . . If the community is rural, vocational agriculture should be included. . . . For boys, depending on the community, trade and industrial programs should be available. Half a day is required in the eleventh and twelfth grades for this vocational work. . . .

Special Consideration for the Very Slow Readers

Those in the ninth grade of the school who read at a level of the sixth grade or below should be given special consideration. These pupils should be instructed in English and the required social studies by special teachers. . . . Remedial reading should be part of the work, and special types of textbooks should be provided. The elective programs of these pupils should be directed toward simple vocational work. . . .

The Programs of the Academically Talented

. . . the elective programs of academically talented boys and girls [the top 15 percent] should [include] . . . as a minimum:

Four years of mathematics, four years of one foreign language, three years of science, in addition to the required four years of English and three years of social studies, a total of eighteen courses with homework to be taken in four years. This program will require at least fifteen hours of homework each week. . . .

Highly Gifted Pupils

For the highly gifted pupils [the top 3 percent] some type of special arrangement should be made.... If enough students are available to provide a special class, these students should take in the twelfth grade one or more courses which are part of the Advanced Placement Program.

Organization of the School Day

The school day should be so organized that there are at least six periods in addition to the required physical education and driver education.... A seven- or eight-period day may be organized with periods as short as forty-five minutes.... Laboratory periods as well as industrial arts should involve double periods....[49]

The thrust of the Conant recommendations for the high school reaffirmed the subject matter curriculum and placed special emphasis on the needs of the academically talented. As such, albeit in more modern dress, it reinforced and expanded the Harvard Committee's report that had preceded it by almost fifteen years. Whereas many secondary schools rushed to implement some of Conant's recommendations, particularly those for the academically talented, they gave up on others. English teachers still wistfully hope for a maximum of one hundred pupils. School personnel still dream of a full-time counselor for every 250 to 300 pupils; the normal ratio is often one counselor to 500 or more. Conant's mid-twentieth century, gender-oriented recommendations for clerical studies and home economics for girls and trade and industrial programs for boys may well amuse us in the twenty-first century when girls enter occupations once considered the domain of boys, and vice versa. Finally, although the recommendation to group students by ability has been implemented widely in the past, its practice is generally frowned on today.

The subject matter curriculum has been popular with many curriculum planners because it lends itself well to a mechanical type of curriculum development: dropping, adding, or splitting courses, rearranging or extending sequences, updating topics, and changing textbooks. Current interest in integrating the curriculum at all levels, however, runs counter to separation of knowledge into discrete subjects. Deborah P. Britzman faulted the compartmentalization of knowledge into subjects saying:

> Compartmentalization defines the limits of relevancy, it brackets our definitions of context and content, and imposes measures of credibility that determine what we accept and reject as true and as false.[50]

A curriculum organized around separate subjects "is fragmented into instructional activities reduced to discrete blocks of time, thereby isolating subject areas and teachers, abstracting knowledge from its socio-cultural roots and political consequences, and decontextualizing knowledge and skills from their practical existence," said Britzman.[51]

Broad-Fields Curriculum

In the early part of the twentieth century a pattern of curriculum organization appeared that became—on the surface at least—a standard feature of both elementary and secondary schools. Called the broad-fields curriculum, this form of curriculum organization is a modification of the strict subject matter curriculum. Effort is made to unify and integrate content of related disciplines around broad themes or principles. For example, history A (ancient), history B (modern), and history C (American), as existed in the secondary school curriculum of New York State schools well into the 1930s, were converted into broad fields and designated simply tenth-grade social studies, eleventh-grade social studies, and twelfth-grade social studies.

"In the broad fields approach," said Tanner and Tanner, "the attempt is made to develop some degree of synthesis or unity for an entire branch of knowledge. . . . The broad fields approach may also encompass two or more branches of knowledge."[52] Smith, Stanley, and Shores noted that broad-fields courses possess varying names: survey, comprehensive, or general.[53]

Thus, we find the various elements of English (reading, writing, grammar, literature, speech, etc.) brought together under the rubric of language arts. The various social science fields (history, political science, government, economics, anthropology, sociology, etc.) were combined to become the social studies. Art, music, architecture, and literature became the humanities. Principles of physical and natural science were unified into a course in general science. The industrial arts tied together various aspects of vocational education. Physical education included health and safety. General mathematics offered knowledge and skills drawn from arithmetic, algebra, and geometry.

Robert S. Zais spoke about the advantages of the broad-fields curriculum as follows:

> Two main advantages are claimed for the broad-fields design. First, because it is ultimately based on the separate subjects, it provides for an orderly and systematic exposure to the cultural heritage. This advantage it shares with the subject curriculum. But it also integrates separate subjects, thereby enabling learners to see relationships among various elements in the curriculum. This second advantage is the special strength that the broad-fields design claims over the subject curriculum.[54]

He warned, however, "With respect to the integration claimed for the broad-fields design, it is worth noting that in practice, combining subjects into a broad field often amounts to little more than the compression of several separate subjects into a single course with little actual unification taking place."[55]

In a true broad-fields approach, teachers select certain general themes or principles to be studied at each year of the sequence of a discipline, such as social studies. Obviously, not all curricula labeled broad fields are truly of that genre.

Common criticisms of the broad-fields curriculum focus on its lack of depth as opposed to breadth, its lack of appeal to student needs and interests, and its emphasis on covering content, which excludes other important goals of education.[56]

Proponents of the broad-fields curriculum would respond to these criticisms by saying that if the curriculum were properly planned and carried out, these deficiencies would be overcome. What appears to have happened in many schools is that the rubric of broad fields has been retained but the curricula themselves have reverted to the separate disciplines of the subject matter curriculum.

The majority of boys and girls in American schools, both elementary and secondary, have been and continue to be educated under some form of the subject matter curriculum. Admittedly, some modifications have been made, but by and large the subject matter curriculum has proved to be a comfortable plan that is widely accepted in the American culture. The subject matter curriculum at the senior high school level has been favored by college admissions officers and regional accrediting associations, for it is much easier to understand and evaluate than more experimental types of curricula. We must also add that the subject matter curriculum has met with considerable success.

Team Teaching

While Conant was conducting his surveys of the American high and junior high schools, the National Association of Secondary School Principals (NASSP) in 1956 was seeking ways to cope with increased enrollments in the schools, a teacher shortage, and the introduction of new curricula in various disciplines. Under the leadership of J. Lloyd Trump, associate secretary of the NASSP, the Commission on Curriculum Planning and Development was launched to create a proposal for new ways of using staff through teaming of faculty.

Supported by the Ford Foundation's Fund for the Advancement of Education, team teaching enjoyed a brief flurry of popularity in secondary schools across the country from Newton, Massachusetts; to Evanston, Illinois; to San Diego, California. The NASSP proceeded to appoint the Commission on the Experimental Study of the Utilization of the Staff in the secondary school (with J. Lloyd Trump as its director) and to charge it with the task of promoting the cause of team teaching. Harvard University's Graduate School of Education and Claremont Graduate School (California) took a special interest in this innovative organizational plan.

J. Lloyd Trump and Delmas F. Miller defined team teaching as follows:

> The term "team teaching" applies to an arrangement in which two or more teachers and their assistants, taking advantage of their respective competencies, plan, instruct, and evaluate in one or more subject areas a group of elementary or secondary students equivalent to two or more conventional classes, using a variety of technical aids to teaching and learning through large-group instruction, small-group instruction, and independent study.[57]

Ira J. Singer described team teaching in this way:

> Team teaching may be defined as an arrangement whereby two or more teachers, with or without teacher aides, cooperatively plan, instruct, and evaluate one or more class groups in an appropriate instructional space and given length of time, so as to take advantage of the special competencies of the team members.[58]

Singer pointed out that the major factors in a team teaching plan are

- cooperative planning, instruction, and evaluation
- student grouping for special purposes (large group instruction, small group discussion, and independent study)
- flexible daily schedule
- use of teacher aides

- recognition and utilization of individual teacher talents
- use of space and media appropriate to the purpose and content of instruction[59]

The purpose of team teaching was to capitalize on the strengths of teachers, using their varying expertise in different ways. Teams were organized within subject areas and across subject fields.

A particular variant of team teaching came to be known as the Trump Plan. J. Lloyd Trump and Dorsey Baynham postulated three ingredients for an effective organizational structure that would capitalize on teacher assets and provide better opportunities for the learners. The school week, according to Trump and Baynham, should provide opportunities for pupils to attend large-group instruction, to interact in small groups, and to carry out independent study. Prophesied Trump and Baynham:

> The school of the future will schedule students in class groups an average of only 18 hours a week. The average student at the level of today's tenth grade will spend about 12 of the 18 hours in *large-group instruction and six in small-group discussion.*
>
> In addition, students will spend, on the average, 12 hours each week in school in individual *independent study.*[60]

These figures convert to forty percent of a student's time in large-group instruction, twenty percent in small-group discussion, and forty percent in independent study.

Differentiated Staffing. Team teaching offered a creative answer to the problem of using limited faculty and resources more effectively. More elaborate schoolwide staffing patterns were developed that incorporated the principle of differentiated assignment. In the early 1970s the North Miami Beach Senior High School (Florida), for example, developed a set of categories of personnel for its differentiated staffing plan. These included in addition to a principal, vice-principal, and business manager the following positions:

- *Community Relations Specialist.* Coordinates activities involving school and community.
- *Human Relations Specialist.* Seeks to create harmonious climate within the school.
- *Inservice Coordinator.* Coordinates the training and development program of the professional and paraprofessional staff.
- *Psychologist.* Counsels students on emotional problems.
- *School Social Worker.* Helps students to function adequately in school; a behavioral consultant.
- *Media Specialist.* Supervises and develops media program.
- *Media Technician.* Provides skilled technical assistance to staff and students.
- *Coordinating Librarian.* Supervises library resources.
- *Teaching Designer.* Assists teachers in improving instruction and evaluating effectiveness.
- *Teaching Prescriber.* Provides assessment, diagnosis, and prescription for each student's program through observation, testing, and individual and/or group conferences.

- *Resource Specialist.* Gathers, coordinates, and disseminates materials for helping solve specific learning situations.
- *Facilitating Teacher.* Guides students through learning; teaches specific courses.
- *Instructional Intern.* Assists a directing teacher, a college junior, senior, or graduate student who serves for a full school year in the high school.
- *Instructional Aide.* Assists by performing paraprofessional responsibilities.
- *Clerical Aide.* Performs clerical duties.[61]

In recent years secondary schools have turned away from the concepts of team teaching and differentiated staffing. However, team teaching has been a prominent aspect of plans for middle and open-space schools. Results were not always as anticipated. In some cases teachers found themselves incompatible, unable to cooperate effectively. Co-operative planning requires a high degree of interpersonal skill that some team members lacked.

Some administrators favored the large-group instruction aspect of team teaching for the convenience and economy of scheduling large numbers of students; they omit-ted the important companion features of small-group discussion and independent study. Large-group instruction by itself deprives students of interaction with the teacher and with each other. Large-group instruction, frequently coupled with instructional televi-sion, a strategy also attempted at this period, often resulted in students becoming inat-tentive and bored.

Schools experienced varying degrees of success with independent study. Plans for large-group instruction, small-group discussion, and independent study call for special facilities and resources that were missing in some schools that attempted this type of organization.

The very complexity of staffing and scheduling under team teaching patterns con-fused parents, teachers, and students. Tradition, therefore, caused them to prefer uniform blocks of time, completely supervised study, and individual assignments.

Flexible and Modular Scheduling

With but a few significant departures from traditional practice, high schools have con-tinued to schedule subjects in the conventional mode, one period per day, five days per week. The Carnegie unit, Conant's recommendations that each course meet five times a week for the academic year, and customary standards of the regional accrediting associa-tions have added to the pressure to maintain traditional scheduling.

However, it is difficult to find a logical reason why all subjects must be taught for the same period of time. Some disciplines are by their very nature more difficult to teach than others and require more time for mastery. Some courses are most effectively taught when accompanied by a laboratory that requires extra time. Some subject matter is sim-ply not as relevant as other subject matter and, therefore, should be accorded less time.

Nor is there a logical reason why equal amounts of time must be allotted to every subject every day of the week. Some days and some weeks more time is needed to explore a topic in depth. Some days it is apparent to the teacher that youngsters have not com-prehended the lesson and need to spend more time on it or undergo remedial work.

There is also not sufficient reason why the instructional mode must be standardized every period of every day. Variation should be possible for lecture, mediated instruction, laboratories, seminars, field trips, independent study, and other modes.

Efforts were made in the 1960s to break out of the mold of the standard schedule. These efforts are subsumed in a movement referred to as flexible scheduling. Donald C. Manlove and David W. Beggs III described the concept of flexible scheduling as follows:

> The flexible schedule is an organization for instruction which:
> 1. calls for classes of varying size within and between courses. (Students sometimes may meet in large assembly classes, and at other times in small inquiry classes. In addition, part of the day will be spent in individual or independent study.)
> 2. provides for instructional groups which meet at varying frequencies for varying lengths. (Some classes may meet every day of the week, others will not. Some instructional sessions will be for a short duration, others for an extended period of time.)
> 3. makes team teaching possible in any content area or for any group of students in the school. (The use of a teaching team, two or more teachers working within a given group of students on a common instructional problem, is suggested in this model.)
> 4. requires countless professional decisions by teachers about students, content, and teaching methods.[62]

Types of Schedules.   Flexible schedules have taken varying forms; some are minor departures from traditional plans, others radical changes. Among the varieties of flexible scheduling are the following:

1. Two or more periods are simply combined, as in the case of core classes.
2. Subjects are scheduled for both double and single periods in the same week. For example, some classes may meet two periods on Monday and Thursday, other classes two periods on Tuesday and Friday, but all only one period on Wednesday. Teachers can thus use the larger blocks of time in ways not permitted by the constraints of the single-period schedule.
3. Classes are rotated during the week.
4. Instead of typical forty-five minute periods, the schedule is broken into modules, which, by faculty agreement, may be multiples of fifteen, twenty, thirty, or more minutes. In an earlier text I described modular scheduling as follows:

> Modular scheduling, or flexible-modular scheduling, . . . requires complete abandonment of the division of the school schedule into equal amounts of time for each course. . . . Some subjects are scheduled for two or three modules (conceivably, even for a single module) per day. Those which require a great deal of time are scheduled in multiple modules. . . .
>
> The duration of the module is purely a matter for decision, ordinarily made by the faculty of the school at the time a modular schedule is introduced. Fifteen-minute modules are common. A school day based on fifteen-minute modules would encompass approximately twenty-five modules. Schools which follow the Stanford School Scheduling System use modules of twenty-two minutes; twenty modules make up the day. The Indiana Flexible Schedule uses fifteen modules per day of thirty minutes each. Ridgewood High School, Norridge-Harwood Heights, Illinois (as one example) has a school day

made up of twenty modules of twenty minutes plus an additional ten-minute module for homeroom period.[63]

5. Class schedules are set frequently, even daily. This "scheduling on demand" is the ultimate goal of flexible scheduling. As J. Lloyd Trump observed, it allows teachers and students the greatest possible latitude in determining their instruction and learning. Trump told how this process was accomplished at the Brookhurst Junior High School in Anaheim, California.

Individual members of teaching teams determine three days in advance what students they want to teach, in what size groups, for what length of time, in what places, and with what technological aids. Teacher job-specification forms containing this information are turned in to their team leaders. The team leaders then assemble to make a master schedule each day. The master schedule is then duplicated and made available to the students and their counselors. In a daily 20-minute meeting, with the advice and consent of their counselor (twenty minutes to a counselor), each student makes his schedule. A student noting, for example, that the schedule calls for large-group presentation on a given subject and deciding that he already knows that material, may elect rather to spend his time in independent study in the art room or library or some place else. The counselor either approves or rejects this decision. Then the student makes out his own schedule for the day in quadruplicate. One copy is for himself, one for the office, one for the counselor, and one for his parents.[64]

Traditional versus Flexible Scheduling. Flexible scheduling is an essential aspect of plans for curriculum organization such as team teaching, which calls for large-group instruction, small-group discussion, and independent study. Traditional schedules have forced teachers to use the same amounts of time for all activities.

Manlove and Beggs contrasted the traditional and the flexible schedule in Table 9.4. They summarized the advantages and disadvantages of flexible scheduling to teachers, making the comparisons shown in Table 9.5.

Trump and Miller also warned of a danger inherent in modular scheduling—or in any innovation, for that matter—"once a change is made, the new schedule can become almost as rigid as the one it replaced."[65] The complexity of operation; a structure that shifts from day to day; the high degree of planning required on the part of students, teachers, and administrators; and the decline in popularity of the team teaching concept have militated against flexible scheduling and caused some schools to return to more traditional and more commonly understood forms of scheduling.

The Nongraded High School

During the 1960s when the elementary schools were experimenting with continuous progress plans and eliminating grades as we know them, several high schools were attempting to develop ungraded patterns of organization. Prominent among these high schools were Nova High School (Broward County, Florida) and Melbourne High School (Brevard County, Florida).

In the mid-1960s Nova High School and Melbourne High School put into practice a number of innovations. Nova High School was established amid what was at that time

TABLE 9.4   Characteristics of Traditional and Flexible Schedules

Element	Traditional Schedule	Flexible Schedule
Content	Assumes each course is equivalent in requirements for mastery to all others	Assumes requirements for mastery of content vary from course to course
Facilities	Use is set by schedule	Use is determined sometimes by student needs
Groups	All class groups are nearly equal size	Class groups differ in size depending on instructional task
Scheduling unit	The day; each day in the week has the same order as every other day	The week; each day in the week has a different order
Students	Students should be in a class group or supervised study	Students may be in a class group or working independently
Teachers	All have equal numbers of classes or assignments and demands on their time	Number of classes varies from teacher to teacher and demands on time vary
Time	Usually equal for all subjects	Usually different for various subjects

Source: Donald C. Manlove and David W. Beggs III, *Flexible Scheduling: Bold New Venture* (Bloomington: Indiana University Press, 1965), p. 26. Reprinted by permission.

a semirural tract of land of now populous Broward County (Fort Lauderdale) as the first facility in a projected complex that eventually would include elementary schools, a junior high school, and a junior college as well as the high school—all publicly supported. A private institution of higher learning, Nova Southeastern University, is nearby.

TABLE 9.5   Advantages and Disadvantages of Flexible Scheduling

Advantages for Teachers	Disadvantages for Teachers
1. Provides a mean for pacing the instruction to an individual student's needs	1. Danger of not giving enough time to one subject
2. Allows teachers to make decisions about the length and frequency of learning activities	2. Requires more time and cooperative effort of teachers in making the schedule
3. Gives teachers time to work with small groups and individuals	3. Possibility of too little identification of a student with his teachers
4. Takes unnecessary repetition out of the teacher's day	4. Is difficult to schedule
5. Places increased responsibility on students for learning	5. Requires teachers to change their teaching patterns
6. Provides the opportunity to use resource experts for a large group of students in an economical way for the resource person	6. Is not understood by the public or even by all teachers

Source: Donald C. Manlove and David W. Beggs III, *Flexible Scheduling: Bold New Venture* (Bloomington: Indiana University Press, 1965), p. 67. Reprinted by permission.

Nova High School made use of teaching teams complete with clerical assistants and teacher aides. Organized on a trimester plan, Nova High School incorporated closed circuit television, a photographic laboratory, data processing equipment, and learning resource centers equipped with tape recorders, microfilm readers, and teaching machines.

A daily schedule was devised that consisted of five periods of eighty minutes each and an optional sixth period of one hour's duration. Speaking about the nongraded feature of Nova High School, Arthur B. Wolfe, director of the K–12 Center at that time, set forth the Nova Plan in these terms:

> The Nova Plan will eliminate grade designation and will establish a far wider range of learning levels through which each student may progress at a rate commensurate with his interests and abilities. Each of the established levels will be only slightly advanced over the level below, thereby enabling the student to move from one level to the next at any given time during the school year. This process will be applicable to the program of each student and to each separate subject area, thereby placing a realistic evaluation on each student's progress on an individual basis, one not entirely related to the sum total of his progress. . . .
>
> Following the enrollment of new students, records will be examined and a series of tests will be administered. The faculty will place students in an achievement group that will provide a smooth transition to a new learning environment. This process will be followed for each of the subject areas in which students may be enrolled. It will be necessary in some cases to move students forward or back until an achievement level has been found in which they will feel comfortable.[66]

Melbourne, like Nova, implemented some of the more significant innovations of the day. Situated in the stimulating setting of space-oriented Brevard County with Cape Canaveral practically in its backyard, Melbourne High School, under its principal at that time, B. Frank Brown, achieved considerable recognition for its emphasis on the academics as evidenced by its library with carrels, which resembled a college library, by its six foreign languages (including Russian and Chinese), and by its stress on independent study, particularly for the academically talented. Melbourne gained special attention, however, for its nongraded organizational plan. Melbourne grouped students not by ability as measured by tests of intelligence or scholastic aptitude but on the basis of achievement tests, subject by subject. A tenth-grade student, therefore, might be enrolled in Algebra I, Phase 2 and English II, Phase 3. Melbourne's schedule of course offerings described each of its seven phases:

- Phase 1: Subjects are designed for students who need special assistance in small classes.
- Phase 2: Subjects are designed for students who need more emphasis on the basic skills.
- Phase 3: Courses are designed for students who have an average background of achievement.
- Phase 4: Subject matter is designed for extremely well-prepared students desiring education in depth.
- Phase 5: Courses are available to students who are willing to assume responsibility for their own learning and pursue college level courses while still in high school.

- Phase Q: Students whose creative talents are well developed should give consideration to the Quest phase of the curriculum. This is an important dimension of the phased organization designed to give thrust in the direction of individual fulfillment. In this phase a student may research an area in which he is deeply and broadly curious either to develop creative powers or in quest of knowledge.
- Phase X: Subjects which do not accommodate student mobility; e.g., typing, physical education, are ungraded but unphased.[67]

Brown referred to the ungraded concept at Melbourne High School not only as the nongraded school[68] but also the multiphased school[69] and gave particular attention to the independent study or quest phase of the program. He referred to the quest phase as both "Education by Appointment"[70] because students see their teachers by appointment in a tutorial fashion and "Education by Agreement" because he recommended that schools emulate the Dalton plan by drawing up an agreement form or contract specifying the independent study that a student plans to do.[71]

Although a noble experiment in curriculum reorganization, nongradedness has not reached the goal that Brown predicted—namely, that within a few years after its inception—"every intellectually respectable high school will have some degree of nongraded education."[72]

Over the decades a number of curricular arrangements have been tried with varying degrees of success in both our hypothetical community and elsewhere. Some have been adopted; some modified; others abandoned. May we stop to wonder what innovations so highly touted today will be with us a decade, two decades, three decades from now?

WHERE WE ARE: *CURRICULUM PRESENT*[73]

THE ELEMENTARY SCHOOL

Following the so-called "Back-to-Basics" movement of the 1970s and 1980s, schools at all levels across the nation are still struggling to raise student achievement in the subject areas. Nowhere are these efforts more apparent than in the elementary school, where efforts continue to improve students' mastery of the basic skills.

Concerned about students' low achievement and public dissatisfaction, schools have taken strong and sometimes controversial measures for improving student achievement and restoring public confidence. Among the measures designed to raise student achievement during the past three decades are the following:

- Implementation of strategies based on the "effective schools" research documented by Ronald P. Edmonds, Wilbur Brookover, Lawrence Lezotte, and others.[74] This body of research has led teachers to such practices as keeping students on task, holding learners to high expectations, and monitoring pupil achievement.
- Implementation of research on instruction conducted by David C. Berliner, N. L. Gage, Donald M. Medley, Barak V. Rosenshine, and others, whose research

attributed such factors as time on task (academic engaged time) and direct instruction to effective teaching.[75]

- Emphasis—what some people would call overemphasis—on testing. Student progress is monitored by a plethora of local, state, and national tests and is measured not only by local and state criterion-referenced tests but also in some cases by national norm-referenced tests.

- Detailed planning and demand for implementation of the curriculum on a districtwide and sometimes statewide basis, sometimes referred to as "curriculum alignment." Curriculum coordinators and teachers strive for a degree of curriculum uniformity by specifying pupil performance objectives in targeted subject areas for every grade level. School personnel choose or prepare teaching materials, learning activities, and tests that fit the specified objectives. Those objectives that are tested by state and national examinations are included and coded by test. Some school systems specify objectives and administer tests for each marking period in the designated disciplines. Principals', teachers', and—ipso facto—the schools' successes are measured by pupils' mastery of the objectives. Today we find emphasis—what some people would call overemphasis—on testing. The states are currently deep into standards-based education and assessment, made more urgent by the *No Child Left Behind Act of 2001*. Consequences in the form of reduced federal funding and the enabling of parents to send their children to schools of their choice are attached to those schools whose pupils continue to show poor academic achievement.[76]

- Supplementing (some people, perhaps, would prefer the word "supplanting") traditional testing techniques, many teachers are turning to authentic or performance-based assessment in the form of individualized portfolios and projects. We will return to the use of performance-based assessment in Chapter 12.

Driven by an awareness of less than laudable student academic achievement and competitive factors like parental choice of school, vouchers, charter schools, and home-schooling, schools are continuing to seek ways to improve students' mastery of the basic skills and academics.

While struggling to fulfill essentialistic goals of subject matter achievement schools are at the same time applying progressive principles as seen in concern for enhancing the self-esteem of learners.

Teaching Thinking Skills

A good sixty years ago (1944) the Educational Policies Commission identified the ability to think as one of the Ten Imperative Needs of Youth.[77] Seventeen years later the Educational Policies Commission set forth the premise that the central purpose of American education was the development of the student's ability to think.[78] About the same time the influential National Committee of the National Education Association's Project on Instruction included among its priorities for improving the instructional program of the schools "ways of creative and disciplined thinking, including methods of inquiry and application of knowledge."[79]

In the 1980s we witnessed a resurgence of interest in the teaching of thinking skills. Prominent national organizations called for renewed and increased emphasis on the development of thinking skills. Among these associations are the National Council of Teachers of Mathematics;[80] the National Council of Teachers of English;[81] the National Science Board Commission of Pre-College Education in Mathematics, Science, and Technology;[82] and the Association for Supervision and Curriculum Development.[83]

A new body of literature defines thinking skills and suggests strategies for teaching those skills. Discussion has moved away from the general declared goal of teaching young people to think to identification of thinking skills and prescribed methods for achieving those skills.[84]

As with many other terms in education, we can find differing definitions of thinking skills. Barry K. Beyer pointed out that some people use the term "critical thinking" to signify all forms of thinking. Beyer maintained that it was a mistake to equate critical thinking with inquiry, decision making, problem solving, and other thinking skills. Said Beyer, "Critical thinking is, instead, the process of determining the authenticity, accuracy, and worth of information or knowledge claims."[85] Where the experts agree, however, is that thinking skills are fundamental, the most basic of the basic skills.

Provision for Students with Special Needs

Schools are struggling to meet the needs of many special groups—exceptionalities of all types of students, including the physically disabled, emotionally disturbed, mentally retarded, and those with behavior disorders. Bolstered by federal legislation and dollars and by state mandates and funding, special education is a fundamental part of today's curriculum. To care for the needs of many exceptionalities, special education teachers, psychometrists, and school psychologists have been in demand.

One of the groups with special needs—the so-called "students-at-risk"—has received considerable attention in recent years. Students-at-risk may be narrowly defined as those students most likely to drop out of school or broadly defined as those most likely to emerge from school with insufficient education, unprepared to play a productive role in society.

Students-at-risk tend to come from low-income environments and to perform poorly in the basic skills. Proposals for meeting the needs of students-at-risk suggest modification of instructional strategies, such as offering compensatory education and increasing student motivation; staff development to enable teachers to understand the special needs of these students; increased use of positive disciplinary practices; encouraging participation in extraclass activities; working with parents; addressing community problems; and abandonment of the graded school structure.

Increasingly, a cyclically neglected group—the gifted—is receiving attention through classes and other means that are designed for their particular intellectual capacities. Bilingual education programs are provided for those pupils for whom English is not their native language. In Chapter 15 we will examine some of the issues involved in providing for educating speakers of languages other than English and for exceptionalities.

Concentration on pupils with special needs such as the learning disabled and the gifted has provoked some objections from parents and others who perceive the schools as neglecting "woodwork children," that is, average students.

Multiage Grouping

That the concept of nongradedness is alive can be seen in the form of multiage class-rooms that can be found in elementary schools in various parts of the country. Students of different ages and abilities are grouped in a single classroom, progress at their own rate, and remain with the same teacher or teachers for two to three years.[86]

Kentucky's Primary Program, for example, follows the "cultural attributes: continuous progress, developmentally appropriate educational practices, authentic assessment, multiage and multiability classrooms, qualitative reporting methods, professional teamwork, and positive parent involvement."[87]

Cooperative Learning

The strategy of organizing people into small instructional groups with the intended purpose of helping each other is discussed in Chapter 11.

Differentiated Instruction

Over the years educators have stressed the need for individualized instruction, personalized instruction, and appealing to individual differences. In a similar vein we speak of *differentiated instruction*, teaching techniques that address the multiplicity of differences among children in today's classrooms. We will return to methods of differentiating instruction in Chapter 11.

THE MIDDLE SCHOOL

An Institution for Young Adolescents

Not too long ago our hypothetical school district maintained a traditional organizational plan for six years of senior high school. Dissatisfaction with that organizational structure had been brewing for a long time. As our school staff studied the literature and watched innovations at other school districts, they began to realize that the junior high school as they knew it was rapidly disappearing. A new institution—the middle school—was rising to the forefront, creating an organizational structure more suited to its time.

As it became clear to the personnel of our hypothetical school district that the needs of a special group of youngsters—young adolescents or, as Donald H. Eichhorn called them, "transescents"[88]—were not being met by the existing junior high school structure, they implemented dramatic and substantial changes which had an impact on all levels of the educational ladder of that district. The elementary school lost a grade, and the senior high school regained a grade that it had lost years ago to the junior high school. The junior high school was transformed into a middle school that consisted of three grades (six through eight) for preadolescents—the children in the middle.

Special Needs of Students.   Some other countries have recognized the needs of middle students for a long time, as in Germany with its *Mittelschule*. Boys and girls of the pre- and early adolescent years, ages ten to fourteen as a rule, are too mature to be treated as primary school children and too immature to be considered high schoolers. They evidence a host of physical, social, and emotional growth needs as well as educational demands. Their career and life interests are just beginning to take shape. They need time to explore, to adjust, and to socialize as well as to study.

As a result, the junior high school spun off from the other levels as a separate institution and mushroomed. From the two identified separate junior high schools with grades seven, eight, and nine in 1910, the junior highs grew to some six thousand.

Lounsbury and Vars characterized the junior high school as a significantly successful development in American education.[89] Although the seven-eight-nine pattern was the most common for the junior high school, other relatively common patterns were seven-eight, six-seven-eight, seven through ten, and eight through ten. Despite this variety, as the years passed dissatisfaction with the junior high school began to set in. It was argued that this intermediate school had become a carbon copy of the senior high school with all its trappings—interscholastic athletics, band, high school subjects, and so on.

Junior high school students were changing not only physically but also socially in response to new, unexpected social pressures and values. As a result of these changes and of society's new demands on adolescents, the program for these years was revised and updated. A new organizational pattern at the intermediate level grouped grades five or six through eight into a middle school with its own unique program, and a four-four-four system or five-three-four system began to emerge. Although the ninth grade is generally considered as "belonging" to the high school, there is some uncertainty amongst middle-school specialists as to whether the fifth grade should be attached to the elementary school or to the middle school.

Phenomenal Growth.   The middle school has experienced phenomenal growth. In 1965 the Educational Research Service of the National Education Association conducted a nationwide survey and found 65 middle schools.[90] In a 1967–1968 survey William M. Alexander reported 1,101 middle schools, and Mary Compton accounted for 3,723 middle schools in 1974.[91] Kenneth Brooks identified 4,060 middle schools operating in 1978.[92] By the mid-1980s figures showed close to 7,000 middle schools in existence.[93] A National Education Association publication in 1988 projected a figure of over 12,000 of these schools by 1992.[94] Jon Wiles, Joseph Bondi, and Michele Tillier Wiles placed the number of intermediate schools in the United States today at about 13,000.[95] Although junior high schools still exist in some communities, confirming Axiom 2 that curriculum changes of earlier periods can coexist with newer curriculum changes, their number has drastically declined as they undergo the metamorphosis from junior high school to middle school. Paul S. George, Chris Stevenson, Julia Thomason, and James Beane predicted the disappearance of the junior high school.[96]

William M. Alexander and others saw the middle school as an emerging institution and defined it in the following manner:

> To us, it is *a school providing a program planned for a range of older children, preadolescents, and early adolescents that builds upon the elementary school program for older childhood and in turn is built upon by the high school's program for adolescence.*[97]

They perceived the middle school as a distinct phase of schooling between elementary and secondary school levels.

Somewhat later Alexander in writing with Paul S. George offered the following definition:

> We define a middle school as a school *of some three to five years between elementary and high school focused on the educational needs of students in these in-between years and designed to promote continuous educational progress for all concerned.*[98]

Transformation of the junior high school into a middle school should not be perceived as a reorganization of but one level of the school system. Alexander and others observed that the change from junior high to middle school is a reorganization of the entire grade structure.[99]

Recommendations for the Middle School. Thomas E. Gatewood and Charles A. Dilg, speaking for the Association for Supervision and Curriculum Development's Working Group on the Emerging Adolescent Learner, made a series of recommendations for the middle school.[100] Let's examine a few. Speaking of the physical characteristics of transescents, they recommended:

> A program for the emerging adolescent that is adapted to the ever-changing physical needs of this learner. . . .
> Instruction related to growth of the body so that one can better understand changes in himself or herself and in others and be prepared for future changes and problems.[101]

Speaking of mental and intellectual growth, Gatewood and Dilg made the following recommendations:

> Learning experiences for transescents at their own intellectual levels, relating to immediate rather than remote academic goals.
> A wide variety of cognitive learning experiences to account for the full range of students who are at many different levels of concrete and formal operations. . . .
> Opportunities for the development of problem-solving skills, reflective-thinking processes, and awareness for the order of the student's environment.
> Cognitive learning experiences so structured that students can progress in an individualized manner. However, within the structure of an individualized learning program, students can interact with one another. . . .
> A common program in which areas of learning are combined and integrated to break down artificial and irrelevant divisions of curriculum content. . . .
> Methods of instruction involving open and individually directed learning experiences. The role of the teacher should be more that of a personal guide and facilitator of learning than of a purveyor of knowledge.[102]

Speaking of personality development characteristics, Gatewood and Dilg recommended:

Administrative arrangements to ensure that personality development has continuity both in breadth and in depth. Thus continuous, cooperative curriculum planning is essential among elementary, middle, and secondary school personnel.

A comprehensive, integrated series of learning encounters to assist learners to develop a self which they realize, accept, and approve. . . .

Classroom instruction, counseling, and extra-class activities that take into account the social-emotional needs of transescents.

An approach in working with emerging adolescents that will have consistency with basic democratic principles.[103]

Gatewood and Dilg have called attention to the broad range of physical, intellectual, and personal characteristics of middle school students. In their recommendations they have presented guidelines for meeting various needs of the emerging adolescent.

Proposed Design.   Lounsbury and Vars proposed a curriculum design for the middle school that consists of three main components: core, continuous progress (nongraded learning experiences), and variable.[104]

Core in their conception is "a problem-centered block-time program."[105] The continuous progress (nongraded) component consists of "those skills and concepts that have a genuine sequential organization."[106] Science, for example, may overlap with the core along with its placement in the nongraded component. The variable component is comprised of "the activities and programs that have proven their worth in schools . . . neither so highly sequential as to be placed exclusively in the nongraded component nor so essentially problem-centered as to fit entirely within the core."[107] The middle school curriculum as proposed by Lounsbury and Vars is shown schematically in Figure 9.1.[108] Note that this proposal incorporates some earlier principles of the core curriculum and nongradedness.

Our hypothetical junior high school has changed to a pattern that has been in successful operation throughout the United States for some forty years. The middle school in our hypothetical school district is a significant development in education for the preadolescent years.

Seeing intermediate schools as offering a "broad and personal program of general education," Wiles, Bondi, and Wiles cautioned, "standardization of the school program brought an end to the junior high school and threatens today's middle schools."[109]

THE SENIOR HIGH SCHOOL

A Comprehensive High School

The academics? Students from this school regularly achieve high scores on state tests of achievement in the subject areas and readily pass the state exit exam; graduates are placed in college and universities without difficulty; students master computer skills; science students yearly win recognition at the science fairs; foreign language students bring home prizes from state competitions in their field; many students are enrolled

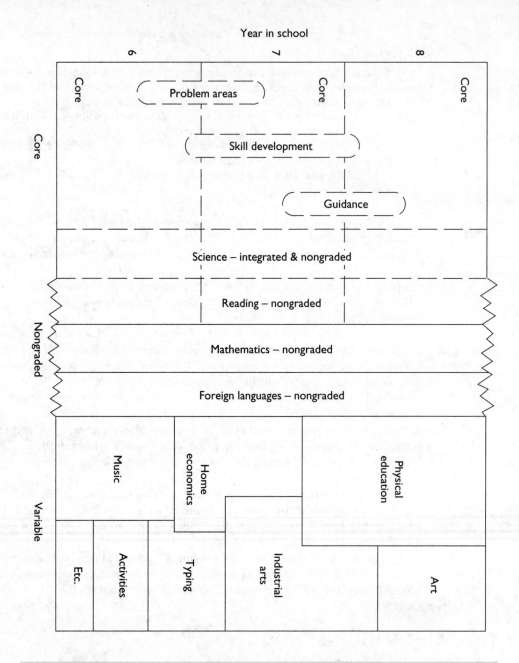

FIGURE 9.1 A Junior High/Middle School Program. Note that core classes are scheduled back-to-back in order to facilitate cross-graded grouping on a temporary basis wherever appropriate. From Gordon F. Vars, "New Knowledge of the Learner and His Cultural Milieu: Implications for Schooling in the Middle Years," Paper presented at the Conference on the Middle School Idea, College of Education, University of Toledo, November 1967. Reprinted by permission. ERIC Document No. ED016267CG901400, p. 14. See also John H. Lounsbury and Gordon F. Vars, *A Curriculum for the Middle School Years* (New York: Harper & Row, 1978), p. 45.

in advanced placement courses; the student body as a whole is well above the norm in reading and mathematics.

Marching band? They can put on a razzle-dazzle spectacular at half-time and compete with the best. They have been invited to participate in parades of the major bowls in the United States.

Football? Basketball? Try baseball, golf, and tennis. The showcase in front of the principal's office is crammed with shiny trophies won by students of this school. School officials are moving rapidly to eliminate gender discrimination in athletics and proudly display trophies won by both the boys' and girls' teams.

Business education? Students are mastering the use of computers, electronic typewriters, and fax machines. Students in all programs are encouraged to develop skill in typing and word processing.

Art? Come to the annual art show put on by the school's art students to appreciate the excellence of their work.

Vocational education? Wood shop, metal shop, electricity, and auto mechanics are all available. Each shop has ample space and is well equipped.

What we are describing here is a high-quality, traditional, comprehensive high school. As such it meets the definition of a comprehensive high school given by James B. Conant, who saw it as "a high school whose programs correspond to the educational needs of *all* youth in the community."[110] Personnel of this school concur with the Association for Supervision and Curriculum Development and with Conant as to the objectives of the school. The ASCD maintained:

> The secondary school should be a comprehensive school. If a major task of the public school in America is to develop the basic values of a free society, and mutual respect for the range of persons and groups within our diverse culture, students must have an opportunity to live and work together. The comprehensive secondary school is an essential element in the development of a common viewpoint sufficiently strong to hold our nation together.[111]

Conant cited three main objectives of a comprehensive high school:

> *First*, to provide a general education for all the future citizens; *second*, to provide good elective programs for those who wish to use their acquired skills immediately on graduation; *third*, to provide satisfactory programs for those whose vocations will depend on their subsequent education in a college or university.[112]

This school performs well on criteria suggested by both Conant and the ASCD. Conant listed the following points to be considered in evaluating a comprehensive school:

A. Adequacy of general education for all as judged by:
   1. Offerings in English and American literature and composition
   2. Social studies, including American history
   3. Ability grouping in required courses
B. Adequacy of nonacademic elective program as judged by:
   4. The vocational programs for boys and commercial programs for girls

   5. Opportunities for supervised work experience
   6. Special provisions for very slow readers
C. Special arrangements for the academically talented students:
   7. Special provisions for challenging the highly gifted
   8. Special instruction in developing reading skills
   9. Summer sessions from which able students may profit
   10. Individualized programs (absence of tracks or rigid programs)
   11. School day organized into seven or more instructional periods
D. Other features
   12. Adequacy of the guidance services
   13. Student morale
   14. Well-organized homerooms
   15. The success of the school in promoting an understanding between students with widely different academic abilities and vocational goals (effective social interaction among students)[113]

ASCD Recommendations.   Our hypothetical secondary school would meet not only the criteria set forth by Conant but also the standards recommended by the Association for Supervision and Curriculum Development. Writing for the ASCD's Commission on the Education of Adolescents, Kimball Wiles and Franklin Patterson made recommendations for the comprehensive high school, some of which are cited here:

> Certain types of growth must be promoted in all youth who attend the secondary school. Each youth should develop increased understanding of self and his responsibility in society, commitment to democratic values, economic understanding, political acumen, and ability to think. . . .
>
> The program for each individual must contain general education and specialized education. . . . One-third to one-half of each student's program should be devoted to general education . . . the required courses and activities . . . essential for competent citizenship. . . . One-half to two-thirds of each student's program should be used to develop his talents and so further his personal goals within the framework that the community is willing and able to support. . . .
>
> Choices among the various offerings of the curriculum should be made jointly by the pupil, parents, and staff members of the school in terms of the pupil's purposes, aptitude and level of achievement. . . .
>
> Each student should have one staff member who guides him throughout his high school career. . . .
>
> Each high school student should be a member of at least one home base group with which he has a continuing relationship. . . .
>
> Students should be grouped in various ways in different phases of their high school experience. . . . the general education phase of an individual's schedule should be in classes that are heterogeneously grouped. . . . In the portion of the student's program that is elective, the grouping should be homogeneous in terms of two factors: the pupil's intensity of purpose and his level of achievement.[114]

When Conant came out with his follow-up study, officials of our hypothetical senior high school were pleased that their school compared favorably with the better comprehensive high schools. They surely enrolled more than 750 pupils; they graduated at least 100 pupils every year; they offered calculus and four years of a modern foreign language (two languages, to be exact); their ratio of counselors to students was within the recommended range of 250 to 300; their students were grouped homogeneously in the elective subjects and heterogeneously in the required courses; and they offered a full range of courses in the academic disciplines, business education, homemaking, and industrial arts.[115] This school met the tests of comprehensiveness well.

Some Alternatives

The comprehensive high school was conceived as a unique American response to the needs of youth. Every young person would find in this institution programs necessary to his or her present and future success in society. The comprehensive high school was a reaction to specialized high schools that cared for specific segments of the student population. This institution would accommodate boys and girls from every social stratum and ethnic group. Students would study, work, and play together, thus breaking down barriers between them. The comprehensive high school was a democratic response to education in a democratic society.

The comprehensive high school, however, has not been free of criticism. Some felt it deemphasized the academics; others felt the opposite and claimed it deemphasized the affective domain. Some believed it was too structured; others, that is was not structured enough. Some maintained it was taking on too many responsibilities; some, that it was not assuming enough. Some accused the comprehensive high school of slighting career education; others were not satisfied with the students' achievement in the cognitive domain.

Call for Reform. Over the years we have heard repeated clarion calls for "reform" not only in secondary education but also in public education at all levels. Larry Cuban noted that efforts at reforming education have been made "again, again, and again."[116] John Henry Martin, author of *The Education of Adolescents*—the report of the National Panel on High Schools and Adolescent Education of the United States Office of Education—expressed the belief that the Seven Cardinal Principles were too inclusive and were "inflated statements of purpose."[117] He argued that the Seven Cardinal Principles were much too broad, stating, "Among the unfortunate consequences of the sweeping language of the Seven Cardinal Principles has been our assumption that the schools could reform all of society's ills. Schools have undertaken burdens that they have neither the resources nor the talents to overcome."[118] The excessive offerings and services of some high schools have caused Arthur G. Powell, Eleanor Farrar, and David K. Cohen to apply the label, "Shopping Mall High School."[119]

Richard Mitchell challenged the Seven Cardinal Principles as anti-intellectual, labeling them, "The Seven Deadly Principles" proposed by "The Gang of Twenty-Seven" (i.e., the National Education Association's Commission on the Reorganization of Secondary Education appointed in 1913). Mitchell was favorably disposed toward the NEA's Committee of Ten, which was formed in 1892 and made "largely of scholars."[120]

Martin took the position that schools cannot be responsible for all aspects of life, that goals of the school (that is, the high school) must be redefined, and that aims more modest than those of the Seven Cardinal Principles must be set. Theodore R. Sizer, however, observed that Americans have agreed for decades on the goals set forth by the Seven Cardinal Principles.[121]

Martin perceived the community as sharing responsibility for the education of youth. He advised as follows:

> Redefining the goals of schools and building new relationships between youth and adults requires that the comprehensive high school be replaced with a comprehensive program of community-based education. Such a design for the education of adolescents should delineate those purposes of education that would remain the primary responsibility of the high school, those that might better be shifted to other and new community agencies, and those that would be served by a cooperative sharing of resources.[122]

A. Harry Passow discussed proposals of five national groups looking at secondary education.[123] In addition to the reports of the National Panel on High Schools and Adolescent Education, the American public has received reports from the National Association of Secondary School Principals,[124] the National Commission on the Reform of Secondary Education (referred to as the Kettering Commission),[125] the Panel on Youth of the President's Science Advisory Committee,[126] and Educational Facilities Laboratories and IDEA.[127]

Among the proposals coming out of the national groups in the 1970s were calls for

- a reduced school day with more time being spent in work experience programs in the community
- educational options—that is, alternative forms of schooling to be selected by students and parents
- a lowering of the age of compulsory attendance to fourteen years of age
- establishment of specialized high schools in the European tradition
- an emphasis on career education
- restriction of the function of the high school to cognitive learning

It is clear that if some of these proposals were seriously considered and adopted, the comprehensive high school that was designed to bring together young people from all walks of life and offer a wide range of programs would be greatly altered or might even disappear.

Reform Efforts

Movements toward accountability, emphasis on cognitive skills and minimal competencies, expansion of content, an increase in academic engaged time, frequent testing, and the raising of marking standards have affected the high school as well as the levels below. During the 1980s and early 1990s, the high school has been examined and reexamined in a series of reports that produced numerous recommendations.[128] Schools are engaged in testing some of the proposals found in the reports.

Among the many widely discussed reports during this period were the following:

- *The Paideia Proposal: An Educational Manifesto* by Mortimer Adler for the Paideia Group (1982); one track for all, no specialized job training.[129]
- *A Nation at Risk: The Imperative for Education Reform* by David P. Gardner for the National Commission on Excellence in Education (1983); five basic subject fields for graduation, longer school day or longer school year.[130]
- *High School: A Report on Secondary Education in America* by Ernest L. Boyer, president of the Carnegie Foundation for the Advancement of Teaching (1983); required core of academic subjects, one unit of community service.[131]
- *A Place Called School: Prospects for the Future* by John I. Goodlad (1984); five domains of knowledge, common required core.[132]
- *Horace's Compromise: The Dilemma of the American High School* by Theodore R. Sizer (1984); language and math skills, no universal body of subject matter, character education.[133]
- *Essential Components of a Successful Education System* by The Business Roundtable (1990); performance-based system; assessments, rewards, and penalties for schools.[134]
- *What Work Requires of Schools: A SCANS Report for America 2000* by The Secretary's Commission on Achieving Necessary Skills; basic skills, thinking skills, personal qualities, technological competency.[135]
- *Horace's School: Redesigning the American High School* by Theodore R. Sizer (1992); competencies rather than conventional subjects, personalized teaching.[136]

Four of the studies (Adler, Business Roundtable, Gardner, and Goodlad) addressed schools at both the elementary and secondary levels.

Having reviewed past developments and evaluated present programs of the high school, our hypothetical curriculum committee—like those in other school systems throughout the country—is studying the many, sometimes conflicting recommendations for change in the high school in light of state and national legislated reform efforts.

Assessing the impact of these studies is difficult. The Conference Board reported that ten years after *A Nation at Risk*, business involvement in the schools had increased, new programs had been developed, broad-based coalitions had been formed, and the public's attention to education had been attracted and maintained.[137] Nevertheless, education reform remains very much on the agenda of nongovernmental as well as governmental organizations. The Koret Task Force on K–12 Education, comprised of resident and visiting fellows of the Hoover Institution at Stanford University, launched an effort in the fall of 2000 to address major issues in American education. Speaking of the status of K–12 education twenty years after *A Nation at Risk*, the Task Force concluded, "U.S. education outcomes in many ways show little improvement since 1970."[138]

Sizer sought to stimulate reform through the Coalition of Essential Schools, which was formed in 1984. Working with fifty-two schools Sizer attempted to combat the "shopping mall" concept of the high school by encouraging schools to reduce the amount of subject matter covered and to emphasize depth rather than breadth. Sizer's efforts encountered difficulties including financing; faculty resistance, cynicism, and inertia; parental concern over deemphasis of extracurricular activities within the context of the school day; and student objections to a more demanding, academically oriented curriculum.

Among early reported successes of the coalition schools (schools within schools) are improved reading scores, a rise in the number of graduates going on to college, and a decrease in the dropout rate. Emphasis on the academics for all students, a coaching model of instruction, smaller classes, and local faculty control are central to Sizer's efforts.

To tackle school reform more effectively the Coalition of Essential Schools entered into an alliance with the Education Commission of the States "to encourage the reform effort 'from the schoolhouse to the statehouse,'" an initiative aided by Citibank and the Danforth Foundation, labeled "Re: Learning."[139] Horace's Franklin High School, Sizer's fictitious vehicle for conveying coalition principles, pictured an "adaptation of Essential School ideas."[140] Among recommendations of the fictitious committee of Horace's school were organization of the curriculum into three areas, two stages for all, a third voluntary stage, an integrated curriculum, demonstration of mastery by Exhibition, and focus on a limited number of competencies.

Sizer, speaking of subsequent reform efforts of some of the members of the coalition, observed, "Each of these schools reports improved student academic performance, attendance, morale, and admission to college." He continued, however, ". . . comparative assessment of success or failure remains conjectural, but judgments from close observation are encouraging."[141] Currently the Coalition of Essential Schools Network comprises some 170 affiliate schools and 23 affiliate regional centers subscribing to common principles among which the affiliates opt for depth over coverage and goals applicable to all students.[142]

We have to take notice of the cyclical nature of curricular recommendations. The Committee of Ten (1894) recommended the same program for all high school students. Almost 100 years later the Paideia Group (1982) was proposing a single track for all students during their twelve years of schooling.[143] Conant (1959) recommended a year of calculus in high school, as did the Paideia Group (1982). In 1959 Conant advocated foreign languages for the academically talented (four years of one foreign language), in 1983 the National Commission on Excellence in Education recommended two years of a foreign language for the college-bound, and in that same year Boyer advocated beginning foreign language study in the elementary school and requiring two years of all high school pupils. Conant (1959) pointed to the need for more guidance counselors, as did Boyer (1983). Goodlad (1984) accepted the broad categories of human knowledge and organized experiences of the Harvard Committee on General Education (1945).

Will schools lean toward recommendations made in the 1980s and 1990s? Will they go even further back to the Committee of Ten, the Commission on the Reorganization of Secondary Education, or the Educational Policies Commission? Will they adopt other measures for reform and restructuring, such as state and national standards, state and national assessment, privatized schools, schedule revision, and smaller schools, which we examine in Chapter 15?

What we are most likely to see will be a synthesis of the many recommendations with variations determined by local school districts and the states. No single standardized model of secondary education—nor of elementary or middle schools, for that matter—is likely to be acceptable to all the school systems in the United States. Certainly, as the trend toward greater local autonomy over the school's program and toward the empowerment of teachers and parents gains momentum, diversity of models may be anticipated.

With state assessments to comply with the No Child Left Behind Act of 2001 in grades 3, 5, and 7 plus state exit exams required in many states, it has become more difficult for high school students to earn a diploma—a fact that may satisfy a long-held wish of both the public and the profession to make the high school diploma a symbol of a reasonable standard of academic achievement.

Once minimal competencies have been comfortably mastered by students, faculties can seek ways of enriching the program and responding to individual differences. Efforts to create voucher plans, proposals for tuition tax credits, and competition from private schools have contributed to forcing the public schools to reassess their programs. Although schools are now on a cognitive swing, they are not likely to abandon the psychomotor domain nor eliminate affective learnings from the curriculum. Two generations of progressive doctrine, with its concern for the whole child instead of solely the intellect, cannot be—nor should it be—lightly discarded.

During the intensity of reform efforts over the years, gains in student achievement have been less than satisfactory. Gene R. Carter, executive director of the Association for Supervision and Curriculum Development, in an online editorial, "High School Reform: What Will It Take to Engage Teens?" called attention to the fact that the high school graduation rate "hovers below 70 percent," with one-third of the dropouts doing so "without making it past 9th or 10th grade."[144] In a 1989 report, the Center for Policy Research in Education noted two waves of reform efforts. The first occurred from about 1982 to 1986 with state mandates for minimum competency standards. The second, beginning in 1986 and continuing into the present, saw efforts in some localities to restructure schooling at the local level. The Center observed that state policies were still more characteristic of first wave reform efforts than of the second wave's implementation of restructuring at the local level.[145]

Some relaxation of state mandating, however, occurred in the past decade with the movements toward empowerment of teachers and laypeople and site-based management. Note once again that change is incremental, rarely wholesale, across the board.

Donald C. Orlich in the late 1980s took a critical view of reform efforts when he observed:

> This nation has wasted billions of dollars on poorly conceived but politically popular reform movements that have sapped the energies of schoolpeople. We need a national moratorium on reforms so that educators and local policy makers can analyze their own problems. This could lead to a new concept: *local system analysis.* Each local school district would systematically study its own cultures—*yes*, cultures—*and* then implement a carefully researched, well-coordinated, and well-funded plan for specific improvements.[146]

Although state mandating had tapered off in the 1990s, reform efforts have intensified in recent years with the promulgation of national goals under three federal administrations, state and national efforts at developing standards and assessment, and individual and group recommendations. Like many efforts in education, the process of goal-setting and varying goal statements of the 1980s and 1990s has met with criticism. Kenneth A. Sirotnik found "the continual displays of lists of lofty educational goals a curious phenomenon."[147] Following the 1983 report of the National Commission on Excellence in Education (*A Nation at Risk*), George Leonard disagreed with recommendations to improve education at that time and termed them the "Great School Reform Hoax."[148] Several years later Lewis J. Perelman took a sharply critical view of reform efforts like America 2000, citing them as a failure and calling them a "hoax," and advocated nothing less than substituting a privatized system of education that makes use of the latest technology in place of public schools as we know them.[149]

Ernest R. House saw reforms of the 1980s, such as toughening of standards, testing, changes in school governance like decentralization and school choice, as low-cost efforts designed to protect middle- and upper-class interests.[150]

Addressing "the school reform enterprise," Goodlad observed, "school reforms fade and die, frequently from their own excesses."[151] Citing "apprenticeship in democracy"[152] as the primary mission of schooling, Goodlad characterized current reform efforts as "empty homilies" like "all children can learn" and "no child left behind."[153] Goodlad commented, "the current hard-and-tough era of school reform has overrun local schools like kudzu, threatening to squeeze out all else."[154]

School districts, the states, and the nation have continued pronounced efforts to improve the success and image of public education. Education held and continues to hold a top priority on the agenda of many state and national politicians of the late 1990s and early 2000s. Yet reform efforts of the 1990s in modifying goals, raising standards, assessing achievement, and promoting accountability do not satisfy some advocates of a more complete restructuring of schools and their curricula. They view recent reform efforts as promoting the so-called industrial or factory model of schooling whose goal, using standardized programs, is to prepare students for work instead of for what they believe should be the primary goal—democratic citizenship. They perceive the current model of schooling as imposed on students and teachers; viewed as perpetuating the dominance of white, male, European culture and regard it as undemocratic.[155] Renata Nummela Caine and Geoffrey Caine faulted the factory model of education for what they see as its emphasis on separate subjects, covering subject matter, memorization of facts, and lack of connectedness, averring that the model does not address "relevant skills and attributes students need for this century and the next. . . ."[156] The American public itself is ambivalent about the public schools. Forty-nine percent of the public, as surveyed by the 2006 Phi Delta Kappa/Gallup Poll of the Public's Attitudes Toward the Public Schools, would assign an A or B grade (on an A–F scale) to schools in their community but only 21 percent of the public would give similar grades to schools nationally.[157] The moral of the story: the closer the school to the general public, the higher the rating. The poorer schools are perceived as on someone else's turf.

In spite of or, perhaps we should say, because of the failure of past reform efforts, schools are making attempts to improve student achievement in responding to No Child Left Behind. Suffice it to say at this point that we are in an age of assessment and accountability. We will return to No Child Left Behind when we discuss standards and assessment in Chapter 15.

Alternative Schools.   Some of the current criticisms of public education have resulted in an increase in alternative schools at both the elementary and secondary levels. Alternative education is also known as education by choice or educational options.

Let's briefly consider the rationale for developing and supporting alternative public secondary education. Some young people, perhaps many, cannot profit from the established high school; they cannot learn effectively in a structured setting. The impact of agencies outside the school—the families, peer groups, churches, businesses, and industries—on learners is far greater than that of the school; these agencies should therefore be tapped. In a democratic society families should have a choice as to the type of education they wish their children to receive. Unless the public schools make changes from within, young people will either drop out physically, stay in and drop out mentally, or transfer to private schools.

What, we may ask, is an alternative school? The National Consortium for Options in Public Education described an alternative school as "any school (or minischool) within a community that provides alternative learning experiences to the conventional school program and is available by choice to every family within the community at no extra cost."[158]

Some school systems have established what are called "alternative schools" for young people with behavior problems who cannot function well in regular schools. However, these schools are not alternative schools in the sense described by the National Consortium because they are not available by choice. Students are assigned to these schools by the school system and must remain until their behavior improves sufficiently for them to return to their regular schools. (In the case of some alternative schools, however, choice by parents and students must necessarily be restricted by admission requirements and examinations, especially when demand for enrollment exceeds the capacity of the school.)

Free schools, street academies, storefront schools, and schools without walls are examples of alternative education. Among the better known options are the Parkway Program in Philadelphia, which dates back to 1969, and Metro High School in Chicago, which began its program in 1970. In programs of this type, the community, in effect, becomes the school. The school system enlists the cooperation of business, cultural, educational, industrial, and social institutions to serve in the education of young people. The school system draws on the talents of knowledgeable and experienced persons in the community to serve as instructors.

However, education by choice is possible in the more typical school *with* walls. Parents may be accorded the option of placing their children in open-space schools, bilingual schools, or even traditional basic skills schools. In many communities, particularly in urban centers, parents may choose to send their children to a *magnet school*, an institution that offers high-quality specialized programs around a central theme designed to attract students from all parts of the school district. Developed as a means of fostering racial integration, magnet schools offer strong academic or vocational programs in specialties that appeal to young people from all ethnic groups and that are not adequately provided, if at all, in the traditional schools.

The Boston Latin School, Detroit's Cass Technical School, the Bronx High School of Science, New York's High School for the Performing Arts, Brooklyn Tech, Stuyvestant High School in New York City, Lane Technical School in Chicago, Central High School in Philadelphia, and Lowell High School in San Francisco are examples of specialized schools that were forerunners of today's magnet schools. Since attendance at a magnet school is by choice rather than by assignment according to neighborhood boundaries, magnet schools often produce higher student motivation and achievement.

Magnet schools have grown in number in recent years.[159] Dallas, Texas, furnishes an example of the rapid growth of magnet schools. Since 1976 that community has established seven magnet schools in addition to the already existing Skyline Center: the Arts Magnet High School, the Business and Management Center, the Health Professions High School, the Human Services Center, the Law and Public Administration High School, the Transportation Institute, and the Multiple Careers for special education students. Whitney High School in Cerritos, California, has as its sole mission preparation of its academically able students for college admission.

Developments of the early 2000s and apparently the first public schools of their kind are the Puerto Rico Baseball Academy and High School with its concentration in the sport of baseball; an alternative high school in New Britain, Connecticut, offering students-at-risk training for jobs in Homeland Security; and a high school for gay, bisexual, and transgender students in New York City.

Extending the magnet school concept on a statewide basis, some states have considered or established residential public secondary schools. Opened in 1980, the prototype of such schools in the United States, the North Carolina School of Science and Mathematics in Durham, admits juniors and seniors from around the state on a competitive basis and offers them a highly intensive program.

The concept of choice in education is certainly appealing and is in the best democratic tradition. Obviously, growth in alternative schools will have an inevitable impact on the neighborhood and comprehensive schools, illustrating once again the change process in operation.

The American public—concerned that children achieve the fundamentals, that they have access to higher education, and that economy of operation is maintained—is unlikely to support radical departures from the established forms of schooling. The public is not likely to heed proposals for deschooling, that is, surrendering education of the young to businesses and other agencies in the community,[160] or for fully privatizing education.[161] On the other hand, it may well support reasonable alternatives within the existing framework. Urging parents to "demand a modern and relevant system of education," Jon Wiles and John Lundt recommended a number of alternatives to our present system of public education.[162] We will examine some of the more recent and controversial aspects of alternatives in education and school choice like charter schools and homeschooling in Chapter 15.

Requirements for Graduation

In the mid-1900s, sixteen Carnegie units were the minimum required for graduation from the four-year high school. Only the academically talented carried five or more units per year. Twenty or more units are commonly required throughout the United States, with ten or more "solid" subjects required for the regular diploma.

Since the late 1980s, states have dramatically increased the number of credits required for graduation. Idaho and Alaska, for example, require twenty-one credits for graduation; Hawaii and Missouri, twenty-two, with an increase to twenty-four by 2010; Oklahoma, twenty-three; and West Virginia, twenty-four.[163]

College-bound students exceed these minimal requirements. They are finding more of their high school program required and less elective as the number of subjects and credits that they must present for admission to college rises. States typically mandate a set (called a "core" by some people) of subjects that students must pass to earn the high school diploma. An increasing number of states have added the passing of a test to the requirements for the diploma.[164]

The movement toward raising the requirements for graduation from high school is very much in line with repeated reports that have been issued over the years. The increase in requirements brings to fruition reports of the Committee of Ten (1894), the Harvard Committee (1945), James B. Conant (1959), and several reports of the 1970s and 1980s.

We may expect school districts and states of the future that have not already strengthened high school academic requirements to follow moves to increase the number of required courses, decrease the number of electives, raise the score considered passing in the various subjects, raise grades required for eligibility in sports, deemphasize extra-class activities, cover more content, make more effective use of instructional time, set passing of local and/or state tests as a requirement for the diploma, and improve teaching techniques, including the use of computers and other forms of technology. For a move in the other direction, to *decrease* requirements for graduation, see discussion of *three-year high school* in "Scheduling" in Chapter 15.

Public education today is under great pressure to raise achievement levels of all students at all levels. It is experiencing stresses and strains, successes and failures. It faces competition for funding and from alternative forms of schooling. Further, it faces a shortage of teachers, let alone "highly qualified teachers," as required by No Child Left Behind. At one end of the continuum we find ardent champions of the public schools; at the other end, opponents who criticize what they refer to as "government schools." To present a balanced picture, Gerald W. Bracey, in annual reports on *The Condition of Public Education*, rebuts some of the criticisms of public education, presents and analyzes significant data, and cites its accomplishments.[165]

Other Modes

As we travel today's educational scene we encounter educators and laypeople who are implementing newer administrative, organizational, and curricular modes that depart from the traditional such as block scheduling, year-round schooling, and inclusion, which we will examine in Chapter 15.

To summarize Curriculum Present, we discern strong currents and countercurrents. We witness a constant tug-of-war between latter-day progressivist and essentialist educators and parents. We find champions of cooperative learning, integration of the curriculum, whole language, values education, interdisciplinary programs, inclusion and mainstreaming of exceptional children, nongradedness, multicultural education, and portfolio assessments arrayed against advocates of academic learning, separate courses, increased requirements for graduation, increased hours of the school day, increased days of the school year, phonics, traditional assessment, school choice, and national standards of achievement.

WHERE WE'RE GOING: *CURRICULUM FUTURE*

THE ELEMENTARY SCHOOL

Blending of Traditional and Nontraditional Modes

Today we find the elementary school maintaining its emphasis on the basic skills while at the same time addressing other educational, physical, social, and emotional needs of pupils. To the present time the public, through its state legislatures, has given its strong endorsement to programs of state assessment—the testing of youngsters in a number of subject areas, but especially in reading and mathematics. There is some evidence that reaction to testing is setting in. Although testing, both standardized and teacher-made, remains a feature of most schools, by parental and state support if not by educators, other forms of assessment are being incorporated into the curriculum. We will discuss newer techniques of assessment in Chapter 12.

Our hypothetical elementary school has long since restored the walls it removed in open-space days, reverting to the self-contained classroom model. The broad-fields approach will continue to predominate with more attention to integrating the curriculum through the use of units that cut across disciplines. Minimal competencies or outcomes in and across the various disciplines will be spelled out by the school, district, or state so that the direction of the school's program will be more evident. We may expect to see an increase in the practice of grading schools based on the progress made by their pupils and publication of the grades assigned. Among measures to improve pupil achievement are new instructional approaches, smaller classes, tutoring, summer sessions, and weekend classes. As never before, low-performing schools face penalties in the form of reduced funding or pupils opting to attend higher-achieving schools. The elementary school will attempt to curb the flight of pupils to private, home, and parochial schools by striving to ensure academic progress in a nurturing environment.

Mastery of the minimal competencies will be expected of all. There is the real danger that those competencies that are labeled "minimal" will become maximal as well. Teachers may be so preoccupied with helping students to achieve minimal competencies and pass the tests that measure attainment of the competencies that they will allow little time to go beyond the minimum. Current pedagogy calls for both individualized and cooperative learning experiences.

The essentialist-progressive pendulum continues to swing. The goal of the No Child Left Behind Act of 2001, that of making all pupils, including those of minorities, the disabled, and those of limited-English language ability, proficient in reading and mathematics by 2014, will keep pressure on schools for at least the next decade. Once schools have satisfied the public's desire for higher test scores and once the schools have demonstrated that pupils have mastered basic and survival skills, they may pay greater attention to the affective domain with its concern for attitudes, feelings, and values. We may find greater interest in individual students, in their learning styles, and in their special learning capacities. A growing body of research that reveals differences in learning strategies of students will affect teaching strategies.[166] We will find greater efforts on the part of administrators to match teachers' instructional styles with pupils' learning styles.[167]

Other Developments

In his State of the Union message in January 1999, President Bill Clinton issued a call for ending social promotions. Since that time a number of states and cities have ended social promotions and require students to pass state or district examinations in order to move to the next grade level. Schools seeking to reduce grade retention are substituting alternative strategies, such as those shown in Box 9.1. Concomitant with the preoccupation with testing, however, school systems more than likely will expand the ban on social promotion, increasing the number of students retained in grade.

The elementary school of the immediate future will be a sophisticated version of the school of the past, essentialistic in character but with progressive overtones. We will see continuing experimentation with varying programs and practices, for example, current efforts at looping or multiyear grouping in which teachers stay with their students for two or more years[168] and single-gender classes and schools, the latter of which is discussed in Chapter 15.

THE MIDDLE SCHOOL

Predominance of the Middle School

The junior high school has fast faded from the scene. George and others noted a wave of middle schools during the 1980s with states endorsing the middle school concept and encouraging districts to establish middle schools.[169]

Remaining junior high schools will continue to be converted into middle schools, in concept if not in name. Just as some senior high schools still cherish the historic name "academy," some newly converted middle schools may continue to call themselves "junior high schools." However, they will have all the characteristics of the modern middle school as described earlier in this chapter. New schools for transescents will continue to be specifically built as middle schools and will be referred to as "middle schools" for "middle school students."

We can anticipate further resuscitation of the core curriculum concept in the form of integrated curricula. Middle schools will continue to use interdisciplinary teams and interdisciplinary instructional units. Schools will revive earlier attempts at block and rotating scheduling. In a period of confusion on moral values and ethical behavior we may look for renewed interest in promoting character education along with the academics.

Organizations such as the National Middle School Association, the National Association of Elementary School Principals (which includes middle school principals), and the National Forum to Accelerate Middle Grades Reform are continuously seeking ways to improve the middle school programs. The National Forum, an organization composed of more than sixty educators, researchers, and officers of national associations and foundations, for example, has been identifying since 1999 "schools to watch," high-performing exemplars of middle schools.

By gathering data, making visits to schools, and applying thirty-seven criteria, the National Forum named in February 2005 fifteen middle schools as schools-to-watch in California, Georgia, Kentucky, North Carolina, Ohio, and Virginia.[170]

Strategies for Ending Social Promotion

Comprehensive approaches to ending social promotion require leadership, resources, and community support to:

Set clear objectives for students to meet performance standards at key grades.

Identify student needs early in order to apply appropriate instructional strategies.

Emphasize early childhood literacy.

Focus on providing high-quality curriculum and instruction.

Provide professional development that deepens teachers' content knowledge and improves instructional strategies to engage all children in learning.

Set out explicit expectations for all stakeholders, including families and communities, in efforts to help end social promotion.

Provide summer school for students who are not meeting high academic standards.

Extend learning time through before- and after-school programs, tutoring, homework centers, and year-round schooling.

Reduce class sizes in the primary grades.

Keep students and teachers together for more than one year and use other effective student grouping practices.

Develop transitional and dropout prevention programs for middle and high school students.

Hold schools accountable by publicly reporting school performance, rewarding school improvement, and intervening in low-performing schools.

Source: U.S. Department of Education, *Taking Responsibility for Ending Social Promotion: A Guide for Educators and State and Local Leaders, Executive Summary,* May 1999, website: http://www.ed.gov/pubs/socialpromotion/execsum.html, accessed May 4, 2003.

Innovations will, no doubt, continue to come down the pike. As an observer of curriculum developments for many years, I cannot help being awed at how rapidly some innovations flower into movements with a body of literature, recognized experts, a network of like-minded people, how-to textbooks and other media on the subject, and both preservice and inservice educational activities on the topic.

You may very well take the position that before the middle school reaches universality it may evolve into another institution, as yet undefined. Or you may well hold that middle schools will revert to earlier models of organization that combined elementary and middle schools into K–8 patterns as has happened in Baltimore, New Orleans, New York City, and Philadelphia. Hence, we can no longer predict the "universality" of the middle school but can safely say that the present middle school model will remain the predominant model throughout the country for some time to come. To support your position you can reiterate the axioms cited in Chapter 2: Change is both inevitable and necessary, for it is through change that life forms grow and develop; a school curriculum not only reflects but also is a product of its time; and curriculum changes made at an earlier period of time can exist concurrently with newer curriculum changes at a later period of time.

Earlier curriculum practices may not only exist concurrently with newer developments but also in cases where they are not currently found they may be called back into service to replace current practices.

THE SENIOR HIGH SCHOOL

Programs and Practices

Some of the present programs and practices discussed in this and later chapters will undoubtedly continue into the future, at least into the immediate future. Among these are constructivist practices and character/values education (Chapter 6), cooperative learning and recognition of multiple intelligences (Chapter 11), performance-based assessment (Chapter 12), and integration of the curriculum (Chapter 13). Schools may also become "full-service" institutions that seek to provide for intellectual, physical, vocational, cultural, and social needs of students.

If we were to fashion a mosaic of current innovative curriculum practices advocated by various groups and individuals, pupils would attend nongraded, full-service schools of choice; 220 days, year-round; following a pupil-oriented, integrated, interdisciplinary curriculum; working cooperatively; using multicultural materials; pursuing individual goals; constructively creating their own knowledge; developing their multiple intelligences; demonstrating success by exhibiting authentic performance; learning language by a whole-language approach; and deemphasizing or abandoning homework, grading, and testing as we now know it. Middle and secondary schools would feature block schedules. High schools would incorporate community service and school-to-work programs in addition to many of the practices of the other levels. Technology will permeate the curriculum.

Countertrends of national and state standards and national and state assessment make the preceding scenario somewhat unrealistic. If past is prologue, some of the current innovative practices will endure well into the twenty-first century; others will fall by the wayside. In an era of site-based management and empowerment of teachers and parents, what we are likely to see is a multitude of institutions with varying programs responding to community needs and wishes in addition to state and national standards.

Remembering Axiom 3, we can expect to find in the twenty-first century highly innovative schools (incorporating as yet-to-be-created innovations) on one hand and highly traditional schools on the other. Some of both genres will be termed effective; others, ineffective. More likely, we will find traditional schools that embody innovative practices or, put another way, innovative schools that have retained traditional practices.

TECHNOLOGY IN EDUCATION

Changes in the incorporation of technology in education are taking place rapidly, though perhaps not as rapidly as the changes in technology itself. Schools are challenged to go beyond the teaching of computer skills per se (i.e., computer literacy) to teaching computer skills as a part of education for specific careers, to using the Internet for research, to providing online lessons and courses, and to creating virtual schools. There is no stopping the technology nor should there be. Schools will learn to live with and employ technology effectively.

Two of the problems in limiting the use of technology in the classroom have been the lack of computers and the shortage of teachers with proficiency in computer skills. With the plummeting price of computers and the manufacture of $100 laptops the provision of hardware and software becomes less of a problem. Computer training today must be incorporated into the preparation program of teachers at all levels. Today's teachers must not be in the anomalous situation of possessing poorer computer skills than their students.

Access to computers and to the Internet has grown exponentially. The number of students per computer has grown from 7.3 in 1997 to 3.8 in 2002.[171] Whereas thirty-five percent of public schools in the United States had access to the Internet in 1994 by fall 2002, ninety-nine percent had access.[172]

It is common today to find school districts offering nontraditional instruction in the form of online courses, distance learning programs, and virtual high schools. In Empire High School in Vail School District, Arizona, laptops replace textbooks, creating an all-electronic school.[173] Philadelphia's School of the Future, established with support of the Microsoft Corporation,[174] and Detroit's Digital Learning Community High School with help from Apple Computer[175] offer state-of-the-art high-tech programs. We could cite examples of states and school systems from one end of the country to the other rapidly adapting their programs to developments in technology. A quick (virtual) tour would reveal Alabama's distance learning program,[176] Pennsylvania's cyber charter schools,[177] Kentucky's Virtual High School,[178] Hawaii's E- School,[179] California's Virtual Academies,[180] Montana's E-Learning Consortium,[181] Stanford University's virtual high school for gifted students,[182] and Kl2 Inc.'s virtual education program.[183] The list could be expanded as more and more school districts push their boundaries into the age of technology. Not only have the academic subjects gone high tech but also secondary students in Florida, for example, since 1999 can satisfy their physical education requirement via Florida's Virtual School.[184]

That cyberspace knows no frontiers is readily demonstrated in the teaming of the University of Texas and Mexico to enable school districts in Texas to offer mathematics and science classes from Mexican high schools[185] and in the hiring of tutors in India to help children of parents residing in the United States.[186]

The application of technology in the classroom, though enthusiastically endorsed by its proponents, has also met with criticism. Observing a diminished enthusiasm for the use of computers in education and the lack of "research unequivocally linking student technology use to improved learning," Mary Burns gave as one reason, "schools have conflated technology use with instructional quality and student engagement with improved learning and higher-order thinking. In all the excitement about new ways of teaching with technology, we educators may have neglected to pose the most fundamental question: Are students really learning?"[187] Budget cuts and No Child Left Behind mandates have further dampened enthusiasm, according to Burns. Larry Cuban depicted computers in the classroom as "oversold and underused."[188] Addressing the overdominance of computers, Lowell W. Monke saw the need to balance technology with real-life, humanizing experiences.[189] Looking to the future we may expect the movement to virtual education to fully penetrate all levels of education from pre-kindergarten to graduate schools. Schools will give witness to the fact that computer skills have become one of the basic survival skills necessary in a technologically driven society.

States will routinely require demonstration of computer skills and completion of one or more courses online in order to graduate. We will see a mixture of public, free online instruction and for-profit virtual education programs. To help meet the challenge of creating technologically literate citizens the National Educational Technology Standards Project of the International Society for Technology in Education has developed a set of standards for prekindergarten through twelfth grade.[190] Whether instruction using computer software raises student achievement is problematic. A study conducted for the National Center for Education Evaluation and Regional Assistance, Institute of Education Sciences, U.S. Department of Education found "test scores not significantly higher in classrooms using selected reading and mathematics software products."[191]

In spite of concerns about the rapid inroads of technology there's no turning back. We can't put the genie back in the bottle. Nor should we try. The challenge of the electronic age to the schools is to apply technology in such a way that it promotes the mission of the school, particularly improvement in student achievement.

Smaller Learning Communities

The elementary and middle schools are not alone in wrestling with the problems of class and school size. An interesting development that we explore in Chapter 15 is the creation of smaller schools, termed "learning communities" by some, within established schools. Detroit's aforementioned Digital Learning Community High School combines within its Crockett High School two current features—a smaller learning community and a high-tech curriculum. Should the movement to smaller high schools either within high school or separate from a larger high school gain in popularity and prove more successful in terms of student achievement, we may well be able to verify whether size of instructional units makes a difference in student achievement.

LOOKING FURTHER AHEAD

A growing number of individuals both inside and outside of the academic world are identified by the rather ambiguous label of "futurist." One of the earlier and better known persons in this group is Alvin Toffler, whose books, *Future Shock* and *The Third Wave*, provoked many of us to contemplate problems of the future and to begin considering ways to solve them.[192] High on the agenda of any futurist are problems like population control, health needs, preservation of the environment, housing needs, adequate food supplies, demands for energy, and the use and abuse of technology.

Some educational futurists view the new technology as aiding the teacher and administrator to provide a more effective education within the school setting. Others predict what amounts to a type of deschooling. More than two decades ago Peter Sleight, for example, reported on the type of deschooling that might be affected by the computer age:

> It may be that children won't attend schools at all, but attend classes in their homes, taking lessons through the computer with the teacher talking to them through a video image.
>
> Through the same network, the teacher will know whether a student is tuned in and can take "attendance" in the old-fashioned sense.
>
> Homework for the children will also be changed. No longer will they be bringing home textbooks and doing assignments on paper. Instead, they may plug into the school data base to receive their assignments, execute them on the computer screen at home and "send" it to their teacher via the computer hook-up.[193]

In the relatively few years since Sleight's prophetic comments in 1980 the use of scanning, e-mail, and faxing has become common in personal, business, and educational life. Through these techniques students can share the products of their work with each other and, in fact, with the world, if desired. Twelve years later Perelman moved beyond Sleight's predictions about deschooling and sought replacement of the traditional public school system with new techniques affected by technology, which he called "hyperlearning."[194]

As you have noted in this chapter and will note again in Chapter 15 where we discuss alternatives in education, some schools, particularly those in rural and less accessible areas, are already implementing "distance learning," instruction at home via computer networks. Computers can allow ill students to keep up with classwork and interact with their teachers and classmates. Students enrolled in distance learning courses typically complete a part of their high school program interacting with instructors by means of e-mail or, depending on their location, by personal contact.[195]

If the day comes when schools are eliminated and instruction proceeds through the medium of the computer, what will happen to the notion of face-to-face interaction between teacher and students and between student and student? We recognize the movement toward "interactive" learning by means of technology. Will interacting via a computer screen, fax, and printer enable learners to achieve the multiple goals of schooling? How will students learn to socialize with each other? What will happen to multicultural, multiethnic education? How will boys and girls learn to live in a pluralistic society? What will happen to cooperative learning? What disposition will be made of extraclass activities, driver education, and athletics formerly under the aegis of the school?

Perhaps we might wish to conceptualize computerized schooling as consuming only a portion of the day, with other forms of education in the school or community filling the remaining portion. At any rate, you may be safe in postulating that the elementary, middle, and senior high schools as we know them today and as we will know them in the immediate future may well evolve into decidedly different kinds of institutions in the distant future.

PUBLIC AND PRIVATE ENROLLMENTS

At the present time about eighty-seven percent of school-age children are enrolled in public education and approximately thirteen percent attend private and parochial schools. Figures for fall 2003 showed 48.5 million pupils in public schools. Private school enrollments were estimated at 6.3 million.[196] If the economy permits and especially if vouchers are easily obtained, we are likely to see a larger percentage of the public seeking alternatives to public education in the form of private, parochial, or charter schools or homeschooling. However, public education can survive—even flourish—by receiving adequate funding, by refining its practices, by making known its successes, and by meeting the competition head-on.

Summary

As curriculum planners proceed with their task of developing the curriculum, they must also decide on the organizational structure within which programs will be implemented. At the beginning of this chapter we visualized as illustrative examples three schools— elementary, middle, and senior high. Like their actual counterparts, our hypothetical schools have undergone numerous internal changes.

This chapter traced some of the past organizational patterns at each level, described current organizational structures, and discussed possible and probable future developments. On the elementary level we reviewed the graded school, the activity curriculum, continuous progress plans, and open-education/open-space plans. At the middle school level we looked at its predecessor, the junior high school, and at a variety of proposals for that level, including the core curriculum. We studied several organizational plans at the senior high school level, including the subject matter curriculum, the broad-fields curriculum, team teaching, differentiated staffing, flexible and modular scheduling, and the nongraded high school.

The elementary school currently emphasizes teaching basic and thinking skills and providing for students with special needs. Some schools are trying innovative departures from traditional practices. The middle school presently offers programs that have been adapted to meet the needs of preadolescents. A prevailing practice is the use of inter-disciplinary teams. The senior high school is involved in efforts to establish a quality comprehensive model, to furnish a number of alternatives both within and outside the school system, and to reinforce higher requirements for graduation.

In the near future the elementary school, if it is to retain public support must continue emphasis on the basic skills, although it will intensify some of the fundamental overtones of child-centeredness. At this level we noted cooperative learning in practice. The middle school has generally become the predominant model for the education of preadolescents. At the present time we are witnessing some reversion to the K–8, elementary-middle school model. We may expect renewed efforts at integrating the curriculum, interdisciplinary teams, and block/rotating scheduling. The comprehensive high school will share the spotlight with magnet schools and other alternatives. The high school will meet demands for reform and restructuring by adopting some of the recommendations of national studies and organizations and by incorporating some of the innovative practices found in many schools.

We can expect the ubiquitous computer, video recording devices, and other wonders of technology to literally revolutionize education at all levels. Curricula will need to respond substantively—and organizationally—to current and emerging social problems of growing concern to the American people.

Questions for Discussion

1. What are some ways of organizing and implementing the curriculum that have been repeated through American educational history?

2. Why have the graded school and the subject matter curriculum been so enduring?

3. Which of the present curriculum programs and practices do you believe are only temporary and will disappear in the future? Why?

4. How can curriculum planners reconcile conflicting proposals for reform of the high school?

5. What programs and practices would you add to the second and third sections of this chapter, "Where We Are: Curriculum Present" and "Where We're Going: Curriculum Future"?

Exercises

1. Explain what is meant by the activity curriculum. Critique this approach.

2. Describe advantages and disadvantages of the nongraded elementary school.

3. Look up the Eight-Year Study and write a report summarizing its methodology and findings.

4. Describe one or more core programs from either the professional literature or from a school with which you have firsthand experience.

5. Prepare a paper on the topic: "Shall We Group Pupils?" Whether the answer is yes or no, state reasons. If yes, explain how you would group.

6. Describe advantages and disadvantages of the nongraded elementary (continuous progress) school.

7. Describe advantages and disadvantages of the nongraded high school.

8. Describe one or more plans for team teaching and show its advantages and disadvantages.

9. Write a paper, citing at least three references, that accounts for the continuing emphasis on the basic skills.

10. Write a paper on the question of the placement of fifth grade in the educational system—in the elementary school or middle school?

11. Write a paper on the question of the placement of ninth grade in the educational system—in middle school or high school?

12. State pros and cons of specialized versus comprehensive high schools and show your position.

13. Explain what is meant by a broad-fields curriculum. Critique this approach.

14. Write a paper on the question "Why did the decade from 1955 to 1965 produce so many innovations?"

15. Read and summarize one of the national reports of the 1980s or 1990s on reform of the high school.

16. Read and summarize one of the national reports of the 1980s or 1990s on reform of the elementary school.

17. Read and summarize one of the national reports of the 2000s on reform of the elementary, middle, or high school.

18. Evaluate movements for school reform in your state as to process, substance, purpose, strengths, and weaknesses.

19. State whether you believe the school (choose any level) should limit itself to cognitive learning. Give reasons for the position taken.

20. Explain what is meant by differentiated staffing and show its advantages and disadvantages.

21. Distinguish between traditional, flexible, modular, and block scheduling and state the purposes of each.

22. Define "magnet school," state its purposes, and report on one successful example of such a school.

23. Find out if there is a residential public secondary school in your state. If there is, describe its program, its student body, its admission requirements, and its costs of operation.

24. Locate in the literature, on the Internet, or by personal contact a distance learning program for elementary, middle, or secondary school students, preferably in your state. Describe its curriculum, administration, admissions procedures, student body, teacher qualifications, promotion and retention policies, assessment practices, costs, and problems.

25. Develop a plan for using computers in the curriculum of the school that you know best.

26. Write a paper on problems a school that you know well has experienced in incorporating technology into its curriculum.

ASCD Smartbrief

Free daily educational news briefing through e-mail. Links to articles in the press. Subscribe online. Website: http://www.smartbrief.com/ascd.

Journals/Newspapers/Reports

Education Next. Quarterly. Hoover Institution, Stanford University, Stanford, Calif. 94305-6010. Website: http://www.educationnext.org.

Education Week. Editorial Projects in Education, Inc. 6935 Arlington Rd., Suite 100, Bethesda, Md. 20814-5233. Website: http://www.edweek.org.

The Futurist. Bimonthly. World Future Society, 7910 Woodmont Ave., Suite 450, Bethesda, Md. 20814. Website: http://www.wfs.org/futurist.htm.

Horace. Quarterly. Coalition of Essential Schools. CES National, 1814 Franklin St., Suite 700, Oakland, Calif. 94612. Website: http://essentialsschools.org/pub/ces_docs/resources/horace/horace.html.

Teacher Magazine. Editorial Projects in Education, Inc. 6935 Arlington Rd., Suite 100, Bethesda, Md. 20814-5233. Website: http://teachermagazine.org/tm/index.html?clean=true.

Technology Counts, an annual 50-state report on Educational Technology from *Education Week*. Website: http://www.edweek.org/rc/articles/2004/10/15/tc-archive.html.

Professional Inquiry Kit

Curriculum Integration. 1998. Eight activity folders and a videotape. Explains principles and practices of integrated curriculums. Shows how teachers can plan and execute an integrated unit, Carol Cummings, consultant. Association for Supervision and Curriculum Development, 1703 N. Beauregard St., Alexandria, Va. 22311-1714.

Videos

Available from Association for Supervision and Curriculum Development, 1703 N. Beauregard St., Alexandria, Va. 22311-1714:

The Results Video Series. 2001. Two 25-min. videos plus online Facilitator's Guide. Mike Schmoker describes reform efforts that improve pupil performance.

What Works in Schools. 2003. Three 35-min. programs on DVD disk and Facilitator's Guide. Robert J. Marzano, consultant.

What Works in Schools: Translating Research into Action. 2003. Three 30-min. videotapes and Facilitator's Guide. Robert J. Marzano explains factors that affect student achievement.

Websites

American Legislative Exchange Council: http://www.ALEC.org

Association for Supervision and Curriculum Development: http://www.ascd.org

Coalition of Essential Schools: http://www.essentialschools.org

Electronic School: http//www.electronic-school.com

Foundation and Center for Critical Thinking: http://www.criticalthinking.org

Global Schoolhouse: http://www.globalschoolnet.org/gsh

International Society for Technology in Education: http://www.iste.org

Magnet Schools of America: http://www.magnet.edu

MiddleWeb: http://www.middleweb.com

National Association of Elementary School Principals: http://www.naesp.org

National Association of Secondary School Principals: http://www.nassp.org

National Center for Education Statistics: http://www.nces.ed.gov

National Forum to Accelerate Middle Grades Reform: http://www.mgforum.org

National Middle School Association: http://www.nsma.org

NCREL, North Central Regional Educational Laboratory: http://www.ncrel.org/datause

North American Council for Online Learning: http://www.nacol.org

Endnotes

1. See William J. Shearer, *The Grading of Schools* (New York: H. P. Smith, 1898).

2. B. Othanel Smith, William O. Stanley, and J. Harlan Shores, *Fundamentals of Curriculum Development*, rev. ed. (New York: Harcourt Brace Jovanovich, 1957), p. 265.

3. See Junius L. Meriam, *Child Life and the Curriculum* (Yonkers, N.Y.: World Book Company, 1920), p. 382.

4. See William H. Kilpatrick, "The Project Method," *Teachers College Record* 19, no. 4 (September 1918): 319–335.

5. John I. Goodlad and Robert H. Anderson, *The Nongraded Elementary School*, rev. ed. (New York: Teachers College Press, 1987), p. 1.

6. Ibid., p. 3.

7. Herbert I. Von Haden and Jean Marie King, *Educational Innovator's Guide* (Worthington, Ohio: Charles A. Jones, 1974), pp. 30–31.

8. Ibid., p. 33. See also p. 38 for list of schools where nongraded plans were tried.

9. David W. Beggs III and Edward G. Buffie, eds., *Nongraded Schools in Action: Bold New Venture* (Bloomington, Ind.: Indiana University Press, 1967).

10. Maurie H. Hillson, "The Nongraded School: A Dynamic Concept," in David W. Beggs III and Edward G. Buffie, eds., *Nongraded Schools in Action: Bold New Venture* (Bloomington, Ind.: Indiana University Press, 1967), p. 34.

11. Ibid., p. 45.

12. Goodlad and Anderson, *The Nongraded Elementary School*, 1987; Robert H. Anderson and Barbara Nelson Pavan, *Nongradedness: Helping It to Happen* (Lancaster, Pa.: Technomic Publishing Co., 1993).

13. Anderson and Pavan, *Nongradedness*, pp. 13, 10.

14. From Charles, C. M. Gast, David K., Servey, Richard E., and Burnside, Houston M.: *Schooling, Teaching, and Learning: American Education*, p. 118. (St. Louis: The C. V. Mosby Co., 1978).

15. Ibid., pp. 118–119.

16. To complicate the matter further, classrooms without walls are not the same as schools without walls. Schools without walls operate from their own school buildings, sending their students wherever they need to be sent in the area to receive the education they need. Thus, the students may be studying in agencies of the community or may be enrolled in other schools.

17. From Charles, C. M., Gast, David K., Servey, Richard E., and Burnside, Houston M.: *Schooling, Teaching, and Learning: American Education*, p. 119. St Louis, 1978. The C. V. Mosby Co.

18. Louis Rubin, "Open Education: A Short Critique," in Louis Rubin, ed., *Curriculum Handbook: The Disciplines, Current Movements, and Instructional Methodology* (Boston: Allyn and Bacon, 1977), p. 375.

19. Ibid., pp. 375–376.

20. John H. Proctor and Kathryn Smith, "IGE and Open Education: Are They Compatible?" *Phi Delta Kappan* 55, no. 8 (April 1974): 565.

21. David Pratt, *Curriculum: Design and Development* (New York: Harcourt Brace Jovanovich, 1980), p. 384.

22. Rubin, "Open Education," p. 376.

23. From Charles, C. M., Gast, David K., Servey, Richard E., and Burnside, Houston M.: *Schooling, Teaching, and Learning: American Education*, pp. 118–119. St. Louis, 1978. The C. V. Mosby Co.

24. James B. Conant, *Recommendations for Education in the Junior High School Years* (Princeton, N.J.: Educational Testing Service, 1960), pp. 16–22.

25. Jean D. Grambs, Clarence G. Noyce, Franklin Patterson, and John Robertson, *The Junior High School We Need* (Alexandria, Va.: Association for Supervision and Curriculum Development, 1961).

26. Harvard Committee, *General Education in a Free Society* (Cambridge, Mass.: Harvard University Press, 1945), pp. 52–100.

27. See John H. Lounsbury and Gordon F. Vars, *A Curriculum for the Middle School Years* (New York: Harper & Row, 1978), p. 57.

28. Ibid., p. 56.

29. Emerson E. White, "Isolation and Unification as Bases of Courses of Study," *Second Yearbook of the National Herbart Society for the Scientific Study of Teaching* (now the National Society for the Study of Education) (Bloomington, Ind.: Pantograph Printing and Stationery Co., 1896), pp. 12–13.

30. Smith, Stanley, and Shores, *Fundamentals of Curriculum Development*, pp. 312–313.

31. State of Virginia, *Tentative Course of Study for the Core Curriculum of Virginia Secondary Schools* (Richmond, Va.: State Board of Education, 1934).

32. Lounsbury and Vars, *Curriculum for Middle School*, p. 57.

33. Harold B. Alberty and Elsie J. Alberty, *Reorganizing the High-School Curriculum*, 3rd ed. (New York: Macmillan, 1962), pp. 199–233. In previous editions Alberty and Alberty distinguished six types of core. They included a type of correlation related to Type 2, in which teachers of separate courses agreed on a joint theme to be taught in their respective courses.

34. See Wilford M. Aikin, *The Story of the Eight-Year Study* (New York: Harper & Row, 1942).

35. See William Van Til, Gordon F. Vars, and John H. Lounsbury, *Modern Education for the Junior High School Years*, 2nd ed. (Indianapolis: Bobbs-Merrill, 1967), pp. 181–182.

36. Grace S. Wright, *Block-Time Classes and the Core Program in the Junior High School*, Bulletin 1958, no. 6 (Washington, D.C.: U.S. Office of Education, 1958), p. 9.

37. For a widely cited theoretical model of a senior high school schedule with a "common learnings" core, see Educational Policies Commission, *Education for All American Youth* (Washington, D.C.: National Education Association, 1944), p. 244.

38. Conant, *Recommendations for Junior High*, p. 23.

39. Daniel Tanner and Laurel Tanner, *Curriculum Development: Theory into Practice*, 4th ed. (Upper Saddle River: N.J.: Merrill/Prentice Hall, 2007), p. 265.

40. See Chapter 13 of this text for further discussion of integration of the curriculum.

41. James Beane, "The Middle School: The Natural Home of Integrated Curriculum," *Educational Leadership* 49, no. 2 (October 1991): 9–13.

42. Gordon F. Vars, "Integrated Curriculum in Historical Perspective," *Educational Leadership* 49, no. 2 (October 1991): 15.

43. Smith, Stanley, and Shores, *Fundamentals of Curriculum Development*, pp. 229–230.

44. Max Rafferty, *What They Are Doing to Your Children* (New York: New American Library, 1964), pp. 43–44.

45. National Education Association, *Report of the Committee of Ten on Secondary School Studies* (New York: American Book Company, 1894), p. 17.

46. William H. Burton, *The Guidance of Learning Activities: A Summary of the Principles of Teaching Based on the Growth of the Learner*, 3rd ed. (Englewood Cliffs, N.J.: Prentice-Hall, 1962), p. 289.

47. Ibid.

48. Robert L. Ebel, "What Are Schools For?" *Phi Delta Kappan* 54, no. 1 (September 1972): 4, 7.

49. James B. Conant, *The American High School Today* (New York: McGraw-Hill, 1959), pp. 47–65.

50. Deborah P. Britzman, *Practice Makes Practice: A Critical Study of Learning to Teach* (Albany, N.Y.: State University of New York Press, 1991), p. 35.

51. Ibid.

52. Tanner and Tanner, *Curriculum Development*, p. 257.

53. Smith, Stanley, and Shores, *Fundamentals of Curriculum Development*, p. 257.

54. Robert S. Zais, *Curriculum: Principles and Foundations* (New York: Harper & Row, 1976), p. 407.

55. See Zais, pp. 407–408, for criticisms of the broad-fields curriculum.

56. Ibid.

57. J. Lloyd Trump and Delmas F. Miller, *Secondary School Curriculum Improvement: Meeting the Challenge of the Times*, 3rd ed. (Boston: Allyn and Bacon, 1979), p. 410.

58. Ira J. Singer, "What Team Teaching Really Is," in David W. Beggs III, ed., *Team Teaching: Bold New Venture* (Bloomington: Indiana University Press, 1964), p. 16.

59. Ibid.

60. J. Lloyd Trump and Dorsey Baynham, *Focus on Change: Guide to Better Schools* (Chicago: Rand McNally, 1961), p. 41.

61. North Miami Beach Senior High School, Dade County, Florida Public Schools. Reprinted by permission.

62. Donald C. Manlove and David W. Beggs III, *Flexible Scheduling: Bold New Venture* (Bloomington, Ind.: Indiana University Press, 1965), pp. 22–23.

63. Peter F. Oliva, *The Secondary School Today*, 2nd ed. (New York: Harper & Row, 1972), p. 196.

64. J. Lloyd Trump, "Flexible Scheduling—Fad or Fundamental?" *Phi Delta Kappan* 44, no. 8 (May 1963): 370.

65. J. Lloyd Trump and Delmas F. Miller, *Secondary Curriculum Improvement: Meeting the Challenges of the Times*, 3rd ed. (Boston: Allyn and Bacon, 1979), p. 398.

66. Arthur B. Wolfe, *The Nova Plan for Instruction* (Fort Lauderdale, Fla.: Broward County Board of Public Instruction, 1962), pp. 14–15.

67. Melbourne High School. Brevard County, Florida, Public Schools.

68. B. Frank Brown, *The Nongraded High School* (Englewood Cliffs, N.J.: Prentice-Hall, 1963).

69. B. Frank Brown, *The Appropriate Placement School: A Sophisticated Nongraded Curriculum* (West Nyack, N.Y.: Parker, 1965).

70. B. Frank Brown, *Education by Appointment: New Approaches to Independent Study* (West Nyack, N.Y.: Parker, 1968), p. 61.

71. For information on the Dalton (Massachusetts) Plan see Helen Parkhurst, *Education on the Dalton Plan* (New York: E. P. Dutton, 1922).

72. Brown, *Nongraded High School*, p. 44.

73. This section discusses curriculum developments that appear to be generally accepted. In addition to the programs and practices presented in this chapter we are witnessing a sizable number of rapidly spreading curriculum developments that have generated both followers and opponents. These developments are examined in other chapters, particularly in Chapter 15.

74. See *Phi Delta Kappan* 64, no. 10 (June 1983): 679–702; bibliography, p. 694. Note articles both supportive and critical of the effective schools research.

75. See Penelope L. Peterson and Herbert J. Walberg, eds., *Research on Teaching: Concepts, Findings, and Implications* (Berkeley, Calif.: McCutchan, 1979).

76. See Chapter 15 for discussion of state and national standards.

77. See Chapter 3 of this text.

78. Ibid.

79. Dorothy M. Fraser, *Deciding What to Teach* (Washington, D.C.: Project on the Instructional Program of the Public Schools, National Education Association, 1963), p. 222.

80. *An Agenda for Action* (Reston, Va.: National Council of Teachers of Mathematics, 1980).

81. *Essentials of English* (Urbana, Ill.: National Council of Teachers of English, 1982).

82. *Educating Americans for the 21st Century* (Washington, D.C.: National Science Board Commission on Pre-College Mathematics, Science, and Technology, 1983).

83. Association for Supervision and Curriculum Development, "1984 Resolutions," *ASCD Update* 26, no. 4 (May 1984), insert.

84. See Arthur L. Costa, ed., *Developing Minds: A Resource Book for Teaching Thinking*, 3rd ed. (Alexandria, Va.: Association for Supervision and Curriculum Development, 2001); Edward de Bono, "The Direct Teaching of Thinking as a Skill," *Phi Delta Kappan* 64, no. 10 (June 1983): 703–708; Jerry L. Brown, "On Teaching Thinking Skills in the Elementary and Middle School," *Phi Delta Kappan* 64, no. 10 (June 1983): 709–714; and Bruce Joyce, "Models for Teaching Thinking," *Educational Leadership* 42, no. 8 (May 1985): 4–7.

85. Barry K. Beyer, "Critical Thinking: What Is It?" *Social Education* 49, no. 4 (April 1985): 276.

86. See North Central Regional Educational Laboratory, *Critical Issues: Enhancing Learning Through Multiage Grouping*, website: http://www.ncrel.org/sdrs/areas/issues/methods/instrctn/in500.htm, accessed May 11, 2003, and Cotton, Kathleen, *Nongraded Primary Education*, at Northwest Regional Educational Laboratory, *School Improvement Research Series (SARS): Research You Can Use*, website: http://www.nwrel.org/scpd/sirs/7/cu14.html, accessed May 11, 2003.

87. Kentucky Department of Education, *Primary Program*, website: http://www.education.ky.gov/KDE/Instructional+Resources/Elementary+School/Primary+Program, accessed September 30, 2007.

88. Donald H. Eichhorn, *The Middle School* (New York: Center for Applied Research in Education, 1966), p. 3.

89. See Lounsbury and Vars, *Curriculum for the Middle School*, p. 15.

90. Ibid., pp. 22–23.

91. Ibid.

92. Kenneth Brooks, "The Middle Schools—A National Survey," *Middle School Journal* 9, no. 1 (February 1978): 6–7.

93. Valena White Plisko and Joyce D. Stern, *The Condition of Education*, 1985 edition. Statistical Report of the National Center for Education Statistics (Washington, D.C.: U.S. Government Printing Office, 1985), p. 28.

94. Sylvester Kohut, Jr., *The Middle School: A Bridge Between Elementary and High Schools*, 2nd ed. (Washington, D.C.: National Education Association, 1988), p. 7.

95. Jon Wiles, Joseph Bondi, and Michele Tillier Wiles, *The Essential Middle School*, 4th ed. (Upper Saddle River, N.J.: Merrill/Prentice Hall, 2006), p. 10.

96. Paul S. George, Chris Stevenson, Julia Thomason, and James Beane, *The Middle School—And Beyond* (Alexandria, Va.: Association for Supervision and Curriculum Development, 1992), p. 10.

97. William M. Alexander, Emmett L. Williams, Mary Compton, Vynce A. Hines, and Dan Prescott, *The Emergent Middle School*, 2nd enl. ed. (New York: Holt, Rinehart and Winston, 1969), p. 5.

98. William M. Alexander and Paul S. George, *The Exemplary Middle School* (New York: Holt, Rinehart and Winston, 1981), p. 3.

99. Alexander et al., *Emergent Middle School*, p. 4.

100. Thomas E. Gatewood and Charles A. Dilg, *The Middle School We Need* (Alexandria, Va.: Association for Supervision and Curriculum Development, 1975).

101. Ibid., p. 8.

102. Ibid., pp. 11–12.

103. Ibid., p. 16.

104. Lounsbury and Vars, *Curriculum for the Middle School*, pp. 45–48.

105. Ibid., p. 46.

106. Ibid., p. 47.

107. Ibid.

108. Gordon F. Vars, "New Knowledge of the Learner and His Cultural Milieu: Implications for Schooling in the Middle Years." Paper presented at the Conference on the Middle School Idea, College of Education, University of Toledo, November 1967, ERIC Document No. ED016267 CG 901400, p. 14. See also Lounsbury and Vars, *Curriculum for Middle School*, p. 45.

109. Wiles, Bondi, and Wiles, *The Essential Middle School*, p. 23.

110. Conant, *American High School*, p. 12.

111. Kimball Wiles and Franklin Patterson, *The High School We Need* (Alexandria, Va.: Association for Supervision and Curriculum Development, 1959), pp. 5–6.

112. Conant, *American High School*, p. 17.

113. Ibid., pp. 19–20.

114. Wiles and Patterson, *The High School We Need*, pp. 6–17.

115. See James B. Conant, *The Comprehensive High School* (New York: McGraw-Hill, 1967).

116. Larry Cuban, "Reforming Again, Again, and Again," *Educational Researcher* 19, no. 1 (January-February 1990): 3–13.

117. John Henry Martin, "Reconsidering the Goals of High School Education," *Educational Leadership* 37, no. 4 (January 1980): 280.

118. Ibid., p. 279.

119. Arthur G. Powell, Eleanor Farrar, and David K. Cohen, *The Shopping Mall High School: Winners and Losers in the Educational Marketplace* (Boston: Houghton Mifflin, 1985).

120. Richard Mitchell, *The Graves of Academe* (Boston: Little, Brown, 1981), pp. 69–70.

121. Theodore R. Sizer, *Horace's Compromise: The Dilemma of the American High School* (Boston: Houghton Mifflin, 1984), p. 78.

122. Martin, "Reconsidering Goals," p. 281. See also "High School Goals: Responses to John Henry Martin," *Educational Leadership* 37, no. 4 (January 1980): 286–298.

123. A. Harry Passow, "Reforming America's High Schools," *Phi Delta Kappan* 56, no. 9 (May 1975): 587–590.

124. National Association of Secondary School Principals, National Committee on Secondary Education, *American Youth in the Mid-Seventies* (Reston, Va.: National Association of Secondary School Principals, 1972).

125. National Commission on the Reform of Secondary Education, *The Reform of Secondary Education: A Report to the Public and the Profession* (New York: McGraw-Hill, 1973).

126. James S. Coleman, chairman, Panel on Youth of the President's Science Advisory Committee, *Youth: Transition to Adulthood* (Washington, D.C.: Superintendent of Documents, U.S. Government Printing Office, 1973; Chicago: University of Chicago Press, 1974).

127. Ruth Weinstock, *The Greening of the High School* (New York: Educational Facilities Laboratory, 1973).

128. See "A Compilation of Brief Descriptions of Study Projects," *Wingspread* (Racine, Wis.: Johnson Foundation, November 1982); *Almanac of National Reports*, wall chart (Reston, Va.: National Association of Secondary School Principals, 1983); *An Analysis of Reports of the Status of Education in America*, (Tyler, Tex.: Tyler Independent School District, 1983); A. Harry Passow, "Tackling the Reform Reports of the 1980's," *Phi Delta Kappan* 65, no. 10 (June 1984): 674–683. See also David L. Clark and Terry A. Asuto, "Redirecting Reform: Challenges to Popular Assumptions About Teachers and Students," *Phi Delta Kappan* 75, no. 7 (March 1994): 512–520 and "School Reform: What We Have Learned," *Educational Leadership* 52, no. 5 (February 1995): 4–48.

129. Mortimer J. Adler, *The Paideia Proposal: An Educational Manifesto* (New York: Macmillan, 1982).

130. National Commission on Excellence in Education, David P. Gardner, chairman, *A Nation at Risk: The Imperative for Educational Reform* (Washington, D.C.: U.S. Government Printing Office, 1983).

131. Ernest L. Boyer, *High School: A Report on Secondary Education in America* (New York: Harper & Row, 1983).

132. John I. Goodlad, *A Place Called School: Prospects for the Future* (New York: McGraw-Hill, 1984).

133. See Sizer, *Horace's Compromise*.

134. The Business Roundtable, *Essential Components of a Successful Education System* (New York: The Business Roundtable, 1990).

135. U.S. Department of Labor, Employment & Training Administration, *What Work Requires of Schools: A SCANS Report for America 2000*, website: http://wdr .doleta.gov/SCANS/whatwork/whatwork.html, accessed July 23, 2003.

136. Theodore R. Sizer, *Horace's School: Redesigning the American High School* (Boston: Houghton Mifflin, 1992).

137. Leonard Lund and Cathleen Wild, *Ten Years After A Nation at Risk* (New York: The Conference Board, 1993), p. 1.

138. Koret Task Force on K–12 Education, *Are We Still at Risk?*, website: http://www-hoover.stanford.edu/pub affairs/newsletter/00fall/kpret.html, accessed May 5, 2003.

139. Sizer, *Horace's School*, p. 209.

140. Ibid., p. 207.

141. Ibid., pp. 209–210.

142. See Coalition of Essential Schools Network websites: http://www.essentialschools.org/cs/schools/query/ q/562?x-r=runnew and http://www.essentialschools.org/ cs/schools/query/q/556?x-r=runnew, accessed October 4, 2006.

143. Do not confuse this proposal for single track, i.e., basically the same content for all students, with the single track of year-round schools, i.e, a scheduling practice. See scheduling revisions in Chapter 15.

144. See Gene R. Carter, "High School Reform: What Will It Take to Engage Teens?" *ASCD Smart Brief*, online newsletter, ascd@smartbrief.com, accessed September 19, 2006.

145. William A. Firestone, Susan H. Fuhrman, and Michael W. Kirst, *The Progress of Reform: An Appraisal of State Education Initiatives* (New Brunswick, N.J.: Center for Policy Research in Education, Eagleton Institute of Politics, Rutgers, The State University of New Jersey, 1989), p. 13.

146. Donald C. Orlich, "Educational Reforms: Mistakes, Misconceptions, Miscues," *Phi Delta Kappan* 70, no. 7 (March 1989): 517.

147. Kenneth A. Sirotnik, "What Goes on in Classrooms? Is This the Way We Want It?" in Landon E. Beyer and Michael W. Apple, eds., *The Curriculum: Problems, Politics, and Possibilities*, 2nd ed. (Albany, N.Y.: State University of New York Press, 1998) p. 65.

148. George Leonard, *Education and Ecstasy with The Great School Reform Hoax* (Berkeley, Calif.: Atlantic Books, 1987, pp. 241–263.

149. Lewis J. Perelman, *School's Out: Hyperlearning, the New Technology, and the End of Education* (New York: William Morrow, 1992).

150. Ernest R. House, *Schools for Sale: Why Free Market Policies Won't Improve America's Schools and What Will* (New York: Teachers College Press, 1998), p. 23.

151. John I. Goodlad, "Kudzu, Rabbits, and School Reform," *Phi Delta Kappan* 84, no. 1 (September 2002): 18.

152. Ibid., p. 23.

153. Ibid.

154. Ibid., p. 18

155. See, for example, James A. Banks, ed., *Multicultural Education, Transformative Knowledge, and Action: Historical and Contemporary Perspectives* (New York: Teachers College Press, 1996); Landon E. Beyer and Michael W. Apple, eds., *The Curriculum: Problems, Politics, and Possibilities*, 2nd ed. (Albany, N.Y.: State University of New York Press, 1998); Deborah P. Britzman, *Practice Makes Practice: A Critical Study of Learning to Teach* (Albany, N.Y.: State University of New York Press, 1991); William F. Pinar, William M. Reynolds, Patrick Slattery, and Peter M. Taubman, *Understanding Curriculum: An Introduction to the Study of Historical and Contemporary Curriculum Discourses* (New York: Petert Lang, 1996); and James T. Sears and J. Dan Marshall, eds., *Teaching and Thinking About Curriculum: Critical Inquiries* (New York: Teachers College Press, 1990).

156. Renate Nummela Caine and Geoffrey Caine, *Making Connections: Teaching and the Human Brain* (Alexandria, Va.: Association for Supervision and Curriculum Development, 1991), pp. 12–13.

157. Lowell C. Rose and Alec M. Gallup, "The 38th Annual Phi Delta Kappa/Gallup Poll of the Public's Attitudes Toward the Public Schools," *Phi Delta Kappan* 88, no. 1 (September 2006): 44.

158. National Consortium for Options in Public Education, *The Directory of Alternative Public Schools*, ed. Robert D. Barr (Bloomington, Ind.: Educational Alternatives Project, Indiana University, 1975), p. 2. The 1975 directory is out of print and no longer available.

159. Promoting magnet schools is the organization Magnet Schools of America. Website: http://www.magnet.edu.

160. For example, see Ivan Illich, *Deschooling Society* (New York: Harper & Row, 1971). See also Matt Hern, *Deschooling Our Lives* (Philadelphia, Pa.: New Society Publishers, 1996).

161. See Perelman, *School's Out*.

162. See Jon Wiles and John Lundt, *Leaving School, Finding Education* (St. Augustine, Fla.: Matanzas Press, 2004), pp. 15, 199–211.

163. Source: Education Commission of the States, website: http://mb2.ecs.org/reports/Report.aspx?id=908, accessed October 15, 2006.

164. For discussion of tests required for graduation, see the section on state and national standards in Chapter 15 of this text.

165. See annual Bracey Reports on "The Condition of Public Education," by Gerald W. Bracey in the *Phi Delta Kappan*, starting October 1991 and every October (except in October 1995).

166. See Ned Herrman, "The Creative Brain," *NASSP Bulletin* 66, no. 455 (September 1982): 31–46. See also "Learning Styles and the Brain," *Educational Leadership* 48, no. 2 (October 1990): 4–80 and Patricia Wolfe, *Brain Matters: Translating Research into Classroom Practice* (Alexandria, Va.: Association for Supervision and Curriculum Development, 2001).

167. See Rita S. Dunn and Kenneth J. Dunn, *Teaching Students Through Their Individual Learning Styles: A Practical Approach* (Reston, Va.: Reston Publishing Company, 1978).

168. For discussions of looping, see Lajean Shiney, *The Lawrence Looping Project*, website: http://www.teach net.com/how-to/looping, accessed October 30, 2006, and North Central Regional Educational Laboratory, *Looping*, website: http://www.ncrel.org/sdrs/areas/issues/methods/instrctn/in5lk10.htm, accessed October 30, 2006.

169. George et al., *The Middle School—And Beyond*, pp. 8, 9.

170. National Forum to Accelerate Middle Grades Reform, "Exceptional Middle-Grades 'Schools-to-Watch' Announced in Six States," website: http://www.schools towatch.org/stwnewstates.pdf, accessed October 25, 2006.

171. Source: Market Retrieval Data, *Technology in Education 2002*, "Overall School Computer Access Climbs, But Disparities Remain; Technical Education," November 1, 2002, website: http://www.schooldata.com/media1.asp, accessed October 25, 2006.

172. Source: Anne Kleiner and Laurie Lewis, *Education Statistics Quarterly*, Vol. 5, Issue 4: *Technology in Education* Vol. 5, Issue 4, "Internet Access in U.S. Public Schools and Classrooms: 1994–2002," National Center for Education Statistics website: http://nces.ed.gov/programs/quarterly/vol_5/5_4/2_2.asp, accessed October 25, 2006.

173. Empire High School website: http://www.vail .k12.az.us/principalpage.htm, accessed October 26, 2006.

174. Philadelphia School of the Future website: http://www.phila.k12.pa.us/offices, accessed October 26, 2006.

175. Detroit Digital Learning Community High School website: http://detnews.com/2205/schools/o509/30/801-328718.htm, accessed October 26, 2006.

176. Alabama Distance Learning website: http://www .mps.k12/al/us/departments/technology, accessed October 26, 2006.

177. Pennsylvania Cyber Charter Schools website: http://www.pde.state.us/charter_schools, accessed October 26, 2006.

178. Kentucky's Virtual High School website: http://www.kvhs.org, accessed October 26, 2006.

179. Hawaii's E-School website: http://www.punaridge.org/doc/teacher/eschool.Default.htm, accessed October 27, 2006.

180. California Virtual Academies website: http://ml.k12.com/mk/get/cava.osqt, accessed October 26, 2006.

181. Montana Schools E-Learning Consortium website: http://www.mselc.org, accessed October 26, 2006.

182. Stanford University Virtual High School run by the Education Program for Gifted Youth website: http://daily.stanford.edu/article/2006/10/4/onlineHighSchoolTeachesGlobal, accessed October 26, 2006.

183. K12, Inc. website: http://www.k12.com, accessed October 26, 2006.

184. Florida Virtual School website: http://www.flvs.net, accessed October 26, 2006.

185. See website: http://www.utex.edu/cee/dec/lucha/index.php?page=news, accessed October 26, 2006.

186. See Growing Stars website: http://www.growingstars.com, accessed October 26, 2006, and TutorVista website: http://www.tutorvista.com, accessed October 26, 2006.

187. Mary Burns, "Tools for the Minds," *Educational Leadership* 63, no. 4 (December 2005/January 2006): 48–53.

188. Larry Cuban, *Oversold and Underused: Computers in the Classroom* (Cambridge, Mass.: Harvard University Press, 2001).

189. Lowell W. Monke, "The Overdominance of Computers," *Educational Leadership* 63, no. 4 (December 2005/January 2006): 20–23.

190. See National Educational Technology Standards Project, International Society for Technology in Education website: http://cnets.iste.org, accessed October 26, 2006.

191. Mark Dynarski, Roberto Agodini, Sheila Heaviside, Timothy Novak, Nancy Carey, Larissa Campuzano, Barbara Means, Robert Murphy, William Penuel, Hal Javitz, Deborah Emery, and Willow Sussex, *Effectiveness of Reading and Mathematics Software Products: Findings from the First Student Cohort* (Washington, D.C.: U.S. Department of Education, Institute of Education Sciences, 2007), website: http://www.ies.ed.gov/ncee/pubs/20074005/execsumm.asp, accessed April 25, 2007.

192. Alvin Toffler, *Future Shock* (New York: Random House, 1970); *The Third Wave* (New York: William Morrow, 1980).

193. Peter Sleight, "Information Services: Possibilities Are Endless," *Fort Lauderdale News and Sun-Sentinel*, July 27, 1980, Section H, p. 3.

194. Perelman, *School's Out*.

195. See Education World, "Virtual High Schools: The High Schools of the Future?" website: http://www.education-world.com/a_curr/curr119.shtml, accessed October 27, 2006.

196. National Center for Education Statistics, "Enrollment in Elementary and Secondary Schools, by Level and Control of Institution, Selected Years, Fall 1970 to Projections for Fall 2014." See website: http://nces.ed.gov/fastfacts/display.asp?id=65, accessed October 26, 2006.

Bibliography

Adler, Mortimer J. *Paideia: Problems and Possibilities.* New York: Macmillan, 1983.

———. *The Paideia Program: An Educational Syllabus.* New York: Macmillan, 1984.

———. *The Paideia Proposal: An Educational Manifesto.* New York: Macmillan, 1982.

Aikin, Wilford M. *The Story of the Eight-Year Study.* New York: Harper & Row, 1942.

Alberty, Harold B. and Alberty, Elsie J. *Reorganizing the High-School Curriculum,* 3rd ed. New York: Macmillan, 1962.

Alexander, William M. and George, Paul S. *The Exemplary Middle School.* New York: Holt, Rinehart and Winston, 1981.

———, Williams, Emmett L., Compton, Mary, Hines, Vynce A., and Prescott, Dan. *The Emergent Middle School,* 2nd., enl. ed. New York: Holt, Rinehart and Winston, 1969.

———. "Guidelines for the Middle School We Need Now." *The National Elementary School Principal* 51, no. 3 (November 1971): 79–89.

Anderson, Robert H. and Pavan, Barbara Nelson. *Nongradedness: Helping It to Happen.* Lancaster, Pa.: Technomic, 1993.

Association for Supervision and Curriculum Development. *Effective Schools and School Improvement.* Alexandria, Va.: Association for Supervision and Curriculum Development, 1989.

————. *Teaching Thinking.* Alexandria, Va.: Association for Supervision and Curriculum Development, 1989.

Banks, James A., ed. *Multicultural Education, Transformative Knowledge, and Action: Historical and Contemporary Perspectives.* New York: Teachers College Press, 1996.

Beane, James A. *A Middle School Curriculum: From Rhetoric to Reality.* Columbus, Ohio: National Middle School Association, 1990.

Beggs, David W., III, ed. *Team Teaching: Bold New Venture.* Bloomington: Indiana University Press, 1967.

———— and Buffie, Edward G., eds. *Nongraded Schools in Action: Bold New Venture.* Bloomington: Indiana University Press, 1967.

Bell, Terrel H. "Reflections One Decade After *A Nation at Risk.*" *Phi Delta Kappan* 74, no. 8 (April 1993): 592–597.

Beyer, Barry K. "Critical Thinking: What Is It?" *Social Education* 49, no. 4 (April 1985): 276.

Beyer, Landon E. and Apple, Michael W., eds. *The Curriculum: Problems, Politics, and Possibilities,* 2nd ed. Albany, N.Y.: State University of New York Press, 1998.

Boyer, Ernest L. *High School: A Report on Secondary Education in America.* New York: Harper & Row, 1983.

Bracey, Gerald W. *Setting the Record Straight: Responses to Misconceptions About Public Education in the United States.* Alexandria, Va.: Association for Supervision and Curriculum Development, 1997.

————. "The 12th Bracey Report on the Condition of Public Education." *Phi Delta Kappan* 84, no. 2 (October 2002): 135–150. Annually in October issue.

Brandt, Ronald S., ed. *Content of the Curriculum.* 1988 Yearbook. Alexandria, Va.: Association for Supervision and Curriculum Development, 1988.

Britzman, Deborah P. *Practice Makes Practice: A Critical Study of Learning to Teach.* Albany, N.Y.: State University of New York Press, 1991.

Brooks, Kenneth. "The Middle Schools—A National Survey." *Middle School Journal* 9, no. 1 (February 1978): 6–7.

Brown, B. Frank. *The Appropriate Placement School: A Sophisticated Nongraded Curriculum.* West Nyack, N.Y.: Parker, 1965.

————. *Education by Appointment: New Approaches to Independent Study.* West Nyack, N.Y.: Parker, 1968.

————. *The Nongraded High School.* Englewood Cliffs, N.J.: Prentice-Hall, 1963.

Buffie, Edward G. and Jenkins, John M. *Curriculum Development in Nongraded Schools: Bold New Venture.* Bloomington: Indiana University Press, 1971.

Burns, Mary. "Tools for the Mind." *Educational Leadership* 63, no. 4 (December 2005/January 2006): 48–53.

Burton, William H. *The Guidance of Learning Activities: A Summary of the Principles of Teaching Based on the Growth of the Learner,* 3rd ed. Englewood Cliffs, N.J.: Prentice-Hall, 1962.

Bush, Robert N. and Allen, Dwight W. *A New Design for High School Education: Assuming a Flexible Schedule.* New York: McGraw-Hill, 1964.

Business Roundtable, The. *Essential Components of a Successful Education System.* New York: The Business Roundtable, 1990.

Caine, Renata Nummela and Caine, Geoffrey. *Making Connections: Teaching and the Human Brain.* Alexandria, Va.: Association for Supervision and Curriculum Development, 1991.

Calvin, Allen D., ed. *Programmed Instruction: Bold New Venture.* Bloomington: Indiana University Press, 1969.

Charles, C. M., Gast, David K., Servey, Richard E., and Burnside, Houston M. *Schooling, Teaching, and Learning: American Education.* St. Louis: The C. V. Mosby Company, 1978.

Coleman, James S., chairman. Panel on Youth of the President's Science Advisory Committee. *Youth: Transition to Adulthood.* Washington, D.C.: Superintendent of Documents, U.S. Government Printing Office, 1973; Chicago: University of Chicago Press, 1974.

Commission on the Reorganization of Secondary Education. *Cardinal Principles of Secondary Education.* Bulletin 35. Washington, D.C.: U.S. Office of Education, 1918.

Conant, James B. *The American High School Today.* New York: McGraw-Hill, 1959.

————. *The Comprehensive High School.* New York: McGraw-Hill, 1967.

————. *Recommendations for Education in the Junior High School Years.* Princeton, N.J.: Educational Testing Service, 1960.

Conference Board, The. *Ten Years After A Nation at Risk.* New York: The Conference Board, 1993.

Costa, Arthur L., ed. *Developing Minds: A Resource Book for Teaching Thinking.* Alexandria, Va.: Association for Supervision and Curriculum Development, 1985.

———— and Lowery, Lawrence. *Techniques for Teaching Thinking.* Pacific Grove, Calif.: Midwest Publications Critical Thinking Press, 1990.

Cuban, Larry. "At-Risk Students: What Teachers and Principals Can Do." *Educational Leadership* 70, no. 6 (February 1989): 29–32.

————. *Oversold and Underused: Computers in the Classroom.* Cambridge, Mass.: Harvard University Press, 2001.

———. "Reforming Again, Again, and Again." *Educational Researcher* 19, no. 1 (January–February 1990): 3–13.

deBono, Edward. "The Direct Teaching of Thinking as a Skill." *Phi Delta Kappan* 64, no. 10 (June 1983): 703–708.

Doyle, Denis and Levine, Marsha. "Magnet Schools: Choice and Quality in Public Education." *Phi Delta Kappan* 66, no. 4 (December 1984): 265–270.

Dunn, Rita S. and Dunn, Kenneth J. *Teaching Students Through Their Individual Learning Styles: A Practical Approach*. Reston, Va.: Reston Publishing Company, 1978.

Ebel, Robert L. "What Are Schools For?" *Phi Delta Kappan* 54, no.1 (September 1972): 3–7.

Educational Policies Commission. *Education for All American Youth*. Washington, D.C.: National Education Association, 1944.

Eichhorn, Donald H. *The Middle School*. New York: Center for Applied Research in Education, 1966.

Evers, Williamson M., ed. *What's Gone Wrong in America's Classrooms?* Stanford, Calif.: Hoover Institution Press, Stanford University, 1998.

Fantini, Mario, ed. *Alternative Education: A Source Book for Parents, Teachers, and Administrators*. Garden City, N.Y.: Anchor Books, 1976.

———. *Public Schools of Choice: Alternatives in Education*. New York: Simon and Schuster, 1973.

———. "The What, Why, and Where of the Alternatives Movement." *The National Elementary School Principal* 52, no. 6 (April 1973): 14–22.

Faunce, Roland C. and Bossing, Nelson L. *Developing the Core Curriculum*. Englewood Cliffs, N.J.: Prentice-Hall, 1951.

Firestone, William A., Furhman, Susan H., and Kirst, Michael W. *The Progress of Reform: An Appraisal of State Education Initiatives*. New Brunswick, N.J.: Center for Policy Research in Education, Eagleton Institute of Politics, Rutgers, The State University of New Jersey, 1989.

Fraser, Dorothy M. *Deciding What to Teach*. Washington, D.C.: Project on the Instructional Program of the Public Schools, National Education Association, 1963.

Fry, Edward B. *Teaching Machines and Programmed Instruction: An Introduction*. New York: McGraw-Hill, 1963.

Frymier, Jack. *A Study of Students at Risk: Collaborating to Do Research*. Bloomington, Ind.: Phi Delta Kappa, 1989.

——— and Gansneder, Bruce. "The Phi Delta Kappa Study of Students at Risk." *Phi Delta Kappan* 71, no. 2 (October 1989): 142–146.

Gatewood, Thomas E. and Dilg, Charles A. *The Middle School We Need*. Alexandria, Va.: Association for Supervision and Curriculum Development, 1975.

George, Paul S. and Lawrence, Gordon. *Handbook for Middle School Teaching*. Glenview, Ill.: Scott, Foresman, 1982.

———, Stevenson, Chris, Thompson, Julia, and Beane, James. *The Middle School—And Beyond*. Alexandria, Va.: Association for Supervision and Curriculum Development, 1992.

Glasser, William. *The Quality School: Managing Students Without Coercion*, 2nd ed. New York: HarperPerennial, 1992.

———. *Schools Without Failure*. New York: Harper & Row, 1969.

Goodlad, John I. "Kudzu, Rabbits, and School Reform." *Phi Delta Kappan* 84, no. 1 (September 2002): 16–23.

———. *A Place Called Schools: Prospects for the Future*. New York: McGraw-Hill, 1984.

——— and Anderson, Robert H. *The Nongraded Elementary School*, rev. ed. New York: Teachers College Press, 1987.

Grambs, Jean D., Noyce, Clarence G., Patterson, Franklin, and Robertson, John. *The Junior High School We Need*. Alexandria, Va.: Association for Supervision and Curriculum Development, 1961.

Hansen, John H. and Hearn, Arthur C. *The Middle School Program*. Chicago: Rand McNally, 1971.

Harrison, Charles H. *Student Service: The New Carnegie Unit*. Princeton, N.J.: The Carnegie Foundation for the Advancement of Teaching, 1987.

Harvard Committee. *General Education in a Free Society*. Cambridge, Mass.: Harvard University Press, 1945.

Hass, Glen. *Curriculum Planning: A New Approach*, 5th ed. Boston: Allyn and Bacon, 1987.

Hassett, Joseph D. and Weisberg, Arline. *Open Education: Alternatives Within Our Tradition*. Englewood Cliffs, N.J.: Prentice-Hall, 1972.

Hern, Matt. *Deschooling Our Lives*. Philadelphia, Pa.: New Society Publishers, 1996.

Herrman, Ned. "The Creative Brain." *NASSP Bulletin* 66, no. 455 (September 1982): 31–46.

Hillson, Maurie H. "The Nongraded School: A Dynamic Concept." In David W. Beggs III and Edward G. Buffie, eds. *Nongraded Schools in Action: Bold New Venture*. Bloomington: Indiana University Press, 1967.

——— and Bongo, Joseph. *Continuous-Progress Education: A Practical Approach*. Palo Alto, Calif.: Science Research Associates, 1971.

Hlebowitsh, Peter S. *Designing the School Curriculum*. Boston: Allyn and Bacon, 2005.

House, Ernest R. *Schools for Sale: Why Free Market Policies Won't Improve America's Schools and What Will.* New York: Teachers College Press, 1998.

Illich, Ivan. *Deschooling Society.* New York: Harper & Row, 1971.

"Improving Learning Conditions for Students at Risk." *Educational Leadership* 44, no. 6 (March 1987): 3–80.

"Integrating the Curriculum." *Educational Leadership* 49, no. 2 (October 1991): 4–75.

"Integrating Technology Into the Curriculum." *Educational Leadership* 56, no. 5 (February 1999): 6–91.

Jackson, Philip W., ed. *Handbook of Research on Curriculum.* New York: Macmillan, 1992.

Jacobs, Heidi Hayes, ed. *Interdisciplinary Curriculum Design and Implementation.* Alexandria, Va.: Association for Supervision and Curriculum Development, 1989.

Joyce, Bruce. "Models for Teaching Thinking." *Educational Leadership* 42, no. 8 (May 1985): 4–7.

Kilpatrick, William H. *Foundations of Method: Informal Talks on Teaching.* New York: Macmillan, 1925.

———. "The Project Method." *Teachers College Record* 19, no. 4 (September 1918): 319–335.

Kindred, Leslie W., Wolotkiewicz, Rita J., Mickelson, John M., and Coplein, Leonard E. *The Middle School Curriculum,* 2nd ed. Boston: Allyn and Bacon, 1981.

Kohl, Herbert R. *The Open Classroom: A Practical Guide to a New Way of Teaching.* New York: New York Review, distributed by Random House, 1969.

Kohut, Sylvester, Jr. *The Middle School: A Bridge Between Elementary and High Schools,* 2nd ed. Washington, D.C.: National Education Association, 1988.

Koos, Leonard V. *Junior High School,* enl. ed. Boston: Ginn and Company, 1927.

———. *Junior High School Trends.* Westport, Conn.: Greenwood Press, 1955.

"Learning in the Digital Age." *Educational Leadership* 63, no. 4 (December 2005/January 2006): 8–81.

"Learning Styles and the Brain." *Educational Leadership* 48, no. 2 (October 1990): 4–80.

Leeper, Robert R., ed. *Middle School in the Making: Readings from Educational Leadership.* Washington, D.C.: Association for Supervision and Curriculum Development, 1974.

Leonard, George. *Education and Ecstasy with The Great School Reform Hoax.* Berkeley, Calif.: North Atlantic Books, 1987, pp. 241–263.

Lightfoot, Sara Lawrence. *The Good High School.* New York: Basic Books, 1985.

Lounsbury, John H., and Vars, Gordon F. *A Curriculum for the Middle School Years.* New York: Harper & Row, 1978.

Lowery, Lawrence. *Thinking and Learning.* Pacific Grove, Calif.: Midwest Publications Critical Thinking Press, 1990.

Lund, Leonard and Wild, Cathleen. *Ten Years After A Nation at Risk.* New York: Conference Board, 1993.

Manlove, Donald C. and Beggs, David W., III. *Flexible Scheduling: Bold New Venture.* Bloomington: Indiana University Press, 1965.

Martin, John Henry. *The Education of Adolescents.* Report of the National Panel on High Schools and Adolescent Education. Washington, D.C.: United States Office of Education, 1976.

Marzano, Robert et al. *Dimensions of Thinking: A Framework for Curriculum and Instruction.* Alexandria, Va.: Association for Supervision and Curriculum Development, 1988.

Meier, Deborah. *The Power of Their Ideas: Lessons for America from a Small School in Harlem.* Boston: Beacon Press, 1995.

Meriam, Junius L. *Child Life and the Curriculum.* Yonkers, N.Y.: World Book Company, 1920.

Miller, John W. "Ten Reform Reports That Can Change Your School." *Principal* 66, no. 2 (November 1986): 26–28.

Miller, Richard I., ed. *The Nongraded School: Analysis and Study.* New York: Harper & Row, 1967.

Mitchell, Richard. *The Graves of Academe.* Boston: Little, Brown, 1981.

Monke, Lowell W. "The Overdominance of Computers." *Educational Leadership* 63, no. 4 (December 2005/January 2006): 20–23.

Morrison, George S. *Contemporary Curriculum K–8.* Boston: Allyn and Bacon, 1993.

Murray, Evelyn M. and Wilhour, Jane R. *The Flexible Elementary School: Practical Guidelines for Developing a Nongraded Program.* West Nyack, N.Y.: Parker, 1971.

National Association for Core Curriculum. *Core Today: Rationale and Implications.* Kent, Ohio: National Association for Core Curriculum, 1973.

National Center for Education Statistics. *The Condition of Education 1998.* Washington, D.C.: U.S. Department of Education, National Center for Education Statistics, 1998.

National Commission on Excellence in Education. David P. Gardner, Chairman. *A Nation at Risk: The Imperative for Educational Reform.* Washington, D.C.: U.S. Government Printing Office, 1983.

National Commission on the Reform of Secondary Education. *The Reform of Secondary Education: A Report to the Public and the Profession.* New York: McGraw-Hill, 1973.

National Education Association. *Report of the Committee of Ten on Secondary School Studies.* New York: American Book Company, 1894.

Norris, Stephen and Ennis, Robert. *Evaluating Critical Thinking.* Pacific Grove, Calif.: Midwest Publications Critical Thinking Press, 1990.

Ogden, Evelyn and Germinario, Vito. *The At-Risk Student: Answers for Educators.* Lancaster, Pa.: Technomic Publishing Company, 1988.

Oliva, Peter F. *The Secondary School Today,* 2nd ed. New York: Harper & Row, 1972.

Orlich, Donald C. "Education Reforms: Mistakes, Misconceptions, Miscues." *Phi Delta Kappan* 70, no. 7 (March 1989): 512–517.

Ornstein, Allan C. and Hunkins, Francis P. *Curriculum: Foundations, Principles, and Issues,* 2nd ed. Boston: Allyn and Bacon, 1993.

Parkhurst, Helen. *Education on the Dalton Plan.* New York: E. P. Dutton, 1922.

Passow, A. Harry, ed. *Curriculum Crossroads.* New York: Teachers College, Columbia University, 1962.

———. "Reforming America's High Schools." *Phi Delta Kappan* 56, no. 9 (May 1975): 587–596.

———. "Tackling the Reform Reports of the 1980s." *Phi Delta Kappan* 65, no. 10 (June 1984): 674–683.

Paul, Robert. *Critical Thinking: What Every Person Needs to Survive in a Rapidly Changing World.* Rohnert Park, Calif.: Center for Critical Thinking and Moral Critique. Sonoma State University, 1990.

Perelman, Lewis J. *School's Out: Hyperlearning, the New Technology, and the End of Education.* New York: William Morrow, 1992.

Peterson, Penelope L. and Walberg, Herbert J., eds. *Research on Teaching: Concepts, Findings, and Implications.* Berkeley, Calif.: McCutchan, 1979.

Phenix, Philip H. *Realms of Meaning: A Philosophy of the Curriculum for General Education.* New York: McGraw-Hill, 1964.

Pinar, William F., Reynolds, William M., Slattery, Patrick, and Taubman, Peter M. *Understanding Curriculum: An Introduction to the Study of Historical and Contemporary Curriculum Discourses.* New York: Peter Lang, 1996.

Popper, Samuel H. *The American Middle School: An Organizational Analysis.* Waltham, Mass.: Blaisdell, 1967.

Powell, Arthur G., Farrar, Eleanor, and Cohen, David K. *The Shopping Mall High School: Winners and Losers in the Educational Marketplace.* Boston: Houghton Mifflin, 1985.

Pratt, David. *Curriculum: Design and Development.* New York: Harcourt Brace Jovanovich, 1980.

Proctor, John H. and Smith, Kathryn. "IGE and Open Education: Are They Compatible?" *Phi Delta Kappan* 55, no. 8 (April 1974): 564–566.

Rafferty, Max. *What They Are Doing to Your Children.* New York: New American Library, 1964.

Ratnesar, Ramesh. "Lost in the Middle." *TIME* 152, no. 11 (September 14, 1998): 60–62.

Resnick, Lauren B. and Klopfer, Leopold E., eds. *Toward the Thinking Curriculum: Current Cognitive Research.* 1989 Yearbook. Alexandria, Va.: Association for Supervision and Curriculum Development, 1989.

"Restructuring Schools: What's Really Happening." *Educational Leadership* 48, no. 8 (May 1991): 3–76.

Roberts, Arthur D. and Cawelti, Gordon. *Redefining General Education in the American High School.* Alexandria, Va.: Association for Supervision and Curriculum Development, 1984.

Roberts, Terry and the staff of the National Paideia Center. *The Power of Paideia Schools: Defining Lives Through Learning.* Alexandria, Va.: Association for Supervision and Curriculum Development, 1998.

Rollins, Sidney P. *Developing Nongraded Schools.* Itasca, Ill.: F. E. Peacock, 1968.

Rose, Lowell C. and Gallup, Alec, M. "The 38th Annual Phi Delta Kappa/Gallup Poll of the Public's Attitudes Toward the Public Schools." 88, no. 1 (September 2006): 41–56.

Rubin, Louis, ed. *Current Movements and Instructional Technology.* Boston: Allyn and Bacon, 1977.

———. *Curriculum Handbook: The Disciplines, Current Movements, and Instructional Methodology.* Boston: Allyn and Bacon, 1977.

———. "Open Education: A Short Critique." In Louis Rubin, ed., *Curriculum Handbook: The Disciplines, Current Movements, and Instructional Methodology.* Boston: Allyn and Bacon, 1977, p. 375.

"The School in the Middle." *NASSP Bulletin* 67, no. 463 (May 1983): 1–82.

"School Reform: What We Have Learned." *Educational Leadership* 52, no. 5 (February 1995): 4–48.

Sears, James T. and Marshall, J. Dan, eds. *Teaching Thinking About Curriculum: Critical Inquiries.* New York: Teachers College Press, 1990.

Shanker, Albert. "The End of the Traditional Model of Schooling—And a Proposal for Using Incentives to Restructure Our Public Schools." *Phi Delta Kappan* 71, no. 5 (January 1990): 344–357.

Shearer, William J. *The Grading of Schools.* New York: H. P. Smith, 1898.

Singer, Ira J. "What Team Teaching Really Is." In David W. Beggs III, ed., *Team Teaching: Bold New Venture.* Bloomington: Indiana University Press, 1964, p. 16.

Sirotnik, Kenneth A. "What Goes on in Classrooms? Is This the Way We Want It?" In Landon E. Beyer and Michael W. Apple, eds. *The Curriculum: Problems, Politics, and Possibilities,* 2nd ed. Albany, N.Y.: State University of New York Press, 1998.

Sizer, Theodore R. *Horace's Compromise: The Dilemma of the American High School.* Boston: Houghton Mifflin, 1984.

———. *Horace's School: Redesigning the American High School.* Boston: Houghton Mifflin, 1992.

Slavin, Robert E., Karweit, Nancy L., and Madden, Nancy A. *Effective Programs for Students at Risk.* Needham Heights, Mass.: Allyn and Bacon, 1989.

——— and Madden, Nancy A. "What Works for Students at Risk: A Research Synthesis." *Educational Leadership* 70, no. 6 (February 1989): 4–13.

Sleight, Peter. "Information Services: Possibilities Are Endless." *Fort Lauderdale News and Sun-Sentinel,* July 27, 1980, Section H, p. 3.

Smith, B. Othanel, Stanley, William O., and Shores, J. Harlan. *Fundamentals of Curriculum Development,* rev. ed. New York: Harcourt Brace Jovanovich, 1957.

A special section on middle schools. *Phi Delta Kappan* 72, no. 10 (June 1991): 738–773.

Stephens, Lillian S. *The Teacher's Guide to Open Education.* New York: Holt, Rinehart and Winston, 1974.

Stevenson, Chris and Carr, Judy F., eds. *Integrated Studies in the Middle Grades: Dancing Through Walls.* New York: Teachers College Press, 1993.

"Students At Risk." *Educational Leadership* 50, no. 4 (December 1992/January 1993): 4–63.

Swartz, Robert and Perkins, David. *Teaching Thinking: Issues and Approaches.* Pacific Grove, Calif.: Midwest Publications Critical Thinking Press, 1990.

Tanner, Daniel and Tanner, Laurel. *Curriculum Development: Theory into Practice,* 4th ed. Upper Saddle River, N.J.: Merrill/Prentice-Hall, 2007.

"Teaching Thinking Skills in the Curriculum. *Educational Leadership* 39, no. 1 (October 1981): 6–54.

"Teaching Thinking Throughout the Curriculum." *Educational Leadership* 45, no. 7 (April 1988): 3–30.

"Thinking Skills in the Curriculum." *Educational Leadership* 42, no. 1 (September 1984): 3–87.

Timar, Thomas B. and Kirp, David L. "Education Reform in the 1980s: Lessons from the States." *Educational Leadership* 70, no. 7 (March 1989): 504–511.

Toch, Thomas. *In the Name of Excellence: The Struggle to Reform the Nation's Schools. Why It's Failing and What Should Be Done.* New York: Oxford University Press, 1991.

——— with Litton, Nancy and Cooper, Matthew. "Schools That Work." *U.S. News and World Report* 110, no. 20 (May 27, 1991): 58–66.

Toffler, Alvin. *Future Shock.* New York: Random House, 1970.

———. *The Third Wave.* New York: William Morrow, 1980.

Trump, J. Lloyd. "Flexible Scheduling—Fad or Fundamental?" *Phi Delta Kappan* 44, no. 8 (May 1963): 370.

——— and Baynham, Dorsey. *Focus on Change: Guide to Better Schools.* Chicago: Rand McNally, 1961.

——— and Miller, Delmas F. *Secondary School Curriculum Improvement: Meeting the Challenges of the Times,* 3rd ed. Boston: Allyn and Bacon, 1979.

Tyler, Ralph W. "Curriculum Development Since 1900." *Educational Leadership* 38, no. 8 (May 1981): 598–601.

Van Til, William, Vars, Gordon F., and Lounsbury, John H. *Modern Education for the Junior High School Years,* 2nd ed. Indianapolis, Ind.: Bobbs-Merrill, 1967.

Vars, Gordon F. "Integrated Curriculum in Historical Perspective." *Educational Leadership* 49, no. 2 (October 1991): 14–15.

———, Gordon F., ed. *Common Learnings: Core and Interdisciplinary Team Approaches.* Scranton, Pa.: International Textbook Company, 1969.

Virginia, State of. *Tentative Course of Study for the Core Curriculum of Virginia Secondary Schools.* Richmond Va.: State Board of Education, 1934.

Von Haden, Herbert I. and King, Jean Marie. *Educational Innovator's Guide.* Worthington, Ohio: Charles A. Jones, 1974.

Weeks, Ruth Mary. *A Correlated Curriculum: A Report of the Committee on Correlation of the National Council of Teachers of English.* New York: D. Appleton-Century, 1936.

Weinstock, Ruth. *The Greening of the High School.* New York: Educational Facilities Laboratories, 1973.

"When Teachers Tackle Thinking Skills." *Educational Leadership* 42, no. 3 (November 1984): 3–72.

White, Emerson E. "Isolation and Unification as Bases of Courses of Study," *Second Yearbook of the National Herbart Society for the Scientific Study of Teaching.* Bloomington, Ind.: Pentograph Printing and Stationery Co., 1986, pp. 12–13.

Wiles, Jon and Bondi, Joseph. *Curriculum Development: A Guide to Practice.* Upper Saddle River, N.J.: Merrill/Prentice Hall, 2007.

———, Bondi, Joseph, and Wiles, Michele Tillier. *The Essential Middle School,* 4th ed. Upper Saddle River, N.J.: Merrill/Prentice Hall, 2006.

——— and Lundt, John. *Leaving School, Finding Education.* St. Augustine, Fla.: Matanzas Press, 2004.

Wiles, Kimball. *The Changing Curriculum of the American High School.* Englewood Cliffs, N.J.: Prentice-Hall, 1963.

———— and Patterson, Franklin. *The High School We Need.* Alexandria, Va.: Association for Supervision and Curriculum Development, 1959.

Wolfe, Arthur B. *The Nova Plan for Instruction.* Fort Lauderdale, Fla.: Broward County Board of Public Instruction, 1962.

Wolfe, Patricia. *Brain Matters: Translating Research into Classroom Practice.* Alexandria, Va.: Association for Supervision and Curriculum Development, 2001.

Wright, Grace S. *Block-Time Classes and the Core Program in the Junior High School.* Bulletin 1958, no. 6. Washington, D.C.: U.S. Office of Education, 1958.

Zais, Robert S. *Curriculum: Principles and Foundations.* New York: Harper & Row, 1976.

10 Instructional Goals and Objectives

AFTER STUDYING THIS CHAPTER YOU SHOULD BE ABLE TO:

1. Identify the three major domains of learning.
2. List the major categories of learnings from one taxonomy of each of the three domains.
3. Explain the relationships between curriculum goals and objectives and instructional goals and objectives.
4. Distinguish between curriculum goals and curriculum objectives.
5. Distinguish between instructional goals and instructional objectives.
6. Be able to identify and write curriculum goals in each of the three domains.
7. Be able to identify and write curriculum objectives in each of the three domains.
8. Be able to identify and write instructional goals in each of the three domains.
9. Be able to identify and write instructional objectives in each of the three domains.

PLANNING FOR INSTRUCTION

With the curriculum decisions made, the broad territory known as instruction looms before us. In some ways it is a familiar region whose landmarks—lesson plans, teaching strategies, and tests—are recognized by administrators, teachers, students, and parents. As we enter the area of instruction, decision making remains a major responsibility, only this time the responsibility falls directly on the classroom teacher. Up to this point persons identified as curriculum planners, among whose number are classroom teachers, have been engaged in making decisions of a programmatic nature. Now classroom teachers will become occupied with making decisions of a methodological nature. They will be answering questions like these:

- What are the objectives to be accomplished as a result of instruction?

- What topics will we cover?
- What procedures are best for directing the learning?
- How do we evaluate instruction?

At this stage the teacher must decide whether to designate topics or specify competencies, whether to feature the teacher's objectives or the pupils', whether to seek mastery of content or simply exposure to the material, and whether to aim instruction at groups or at individuals.

Planning for instruction includes specifying instructional goals and objectives (discussed in this chapter), selecting instructional strategies, and choosing techniques to evaluate instruction (treated in Chapter 12).

To put our next task in perspective, let's review the steps we have taken so far. We have

- surveyed needs of students in general
- surveyed needs of society
- clarified our philosophy of education and stated general aims
- identified curriculum goals and objectives
- determined needs of students in the school, needs of the community, and needs as shown by the subject matter
- reaffirmed plans for organizing the curriculum or selected and implemented plans for reorganizing the curriculum

Having completed these steps, we are ready to undertake planning, presenting, and evaluating instruction. The instructional phases of the curriculum-instruction continuum are shown as a subset of the model for curriculum development suggested in Chapter 5.[1] The subset consists of six components (VI, VII, VIII, IX A and B, X, XI), shown in Figure 10.1. In Chapter 5, you saw diagrammed these instructional components in such a way that they could be removed from the overall model for curriculum development. However, in Chapter 1 I posited an intimate relationship between curriculum and instruction, concluding that the two could be separated for purposes of analysis but that the existence of one could not be meaningful without the other.

The Instructional Model

Figure 10.1 represents a model of instruction that, for simplicity, we will refer to as the Instructional Model. This Instructional Model is broken into two major phases: planning and operational. The operational phase is divided into two parts: the implementation or presentation of instruction and the evaluation of instruction.

The planning phase of the Instructional Model consists of four components: component VI—the identification of instructional goals; component VII—the specification of instructional objectives; component VIII—the teacher's plans for instructional strategies; and component IX—both a preliminary and a final phase of planning for the evaluation of instruction.

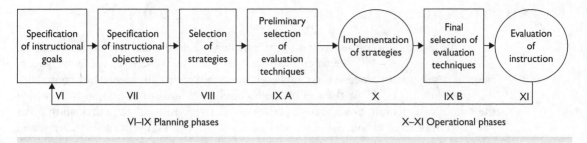

| Specification of instructional goals | | Specification of instructional objectives | | Selection of strategies | | Preliminary selection of evaluation techniques | | Implementation of strategies | | Final selection of evaluation techniques | | Evaluation of instruction |
| VI | | VII | | VIII | | IX A | | X | | IX B | | XI |

VI–IX Planning phases | X–XI Operational phases

FIGURE 10.1 The Instructional Model

Then where and how does the teacher begin to plan for instruction? Let's look at several approaches to planning for instruction. Teacher A comes into the class without a preconceived notion of what he or she will cover and pulls a theme out of the air as the spirit moves him or her. Given the profession's penchant for turning rubrics into seeming substance, some might call this approach instantaneous planning. Others, less kind, might term it nonplanning.

Teacher B takes the textbook, divides the number of chapters by the number of weeks in the school year, lists the topics of each chapter by week, and from there takes any one of a number of directions. For each topic in its turn the teacher might

- jot down some questions for class discussion
- prepare notes for a lecture
- design individual and group assignments for clarifying points in the chapters

Teacher C selects topics for study during the year, using all kinds of materials related to each topic—including the textbook—and creates a succession of units of work for the class.

Teacher B's most likely course of action is the assign-study-recite-test approach, mentioned in the preceding chapter. Teacher C will follow what is commonly called the unit method of teaching, a problem-solving approach.

All three teachers may or may not relate their plans to the predetermined curriculum goals and objectives. All three may or may not specify the instructional goals and objectives that pupils are expected to accomplish. It is my position that both of these actions should be taken by teachers.

Of course, these three illustrations of types of teachers are exaggerated. These are but three examples of an almost infinite variety of teacher models, yet the illustrations are general enough to represent a significant number of teachers. The thesis of this chapter is that, regardless of the teacher's model or style of teaching, curriculum goals and objectives are more likely to be accomplished and students more likely to demonstrate mastery of learning if instructional goals and objectives are specified before starting instruction.

INSTRUCTIONAL GOALS AND OBJECTIVES DEFINED

Before we tackle the central mission of this chapter—selecting and writing instructional goals and objectives—let's see where instructional goals and objectives come in the curriculum development process. First, however, we should review the hierarchy of outcomes discussed in Chapter 8. At the top of the hierarchy are aims of education from which the school's curriculum goals and objectives are derived. In turn, the curriculum goals and objectives serve as sources of the instructional goals and objectives. Aims are stated by prominent individuals and groups for national, and sometimes even international, consideration. Curriculum goals and objectives are formulated by individual school and school system curriculum groups. Instructional goals and objectives are specified by the classroom teacher, who is sometimes assisted by other teachers and local curriculum groups.

To put these various aims, goals, and objectives in perspective, let's look at a simple example of outcomes in their hierarchical order (Box 10.1).

From the broad aim of education, we have moved to the specific instructional objective. Now let's examine instructional goals and objectives more closely.

An *instructional goal* is a statement of performance expected of each student in a class, phrased in general terms without criteria of achievement. The term "instructional goal" is used in this text like Norman E. Gronlund's *general instructional objective*[2] and Ralph W. Tyler's term *general objective*.[3] "The student will show an understanding of the stock market" is an example of an instructional goal. It indicates the performance expected of the learner, but the performance is not stated in such a fashion that its attainment can be readily measured. As a curriculum goal points the direction to curriculum objectives, so an instructional goal points the way to instructional objectives.

An *instructional objective* is a statement of performance to be demonstrated by each student in the class, derived from an instructional goal and phrased in measurable and observable terms. We may equate the term with Gronlund's *specific learning outcome*[4] and

---

BOX 10.1

Illustration of the Hierarchy of Outcomes

- *Aim:* Students will develop knowledge and skills necessary for living in a technological society.
- *Curriculum goal:* Students will recognize the influence of the computer on our lives.
- *Curriculum objective:* By the end of the senior year, at least ninety percent of the students will have taken a computer literacy course either in this school or elsewhere.
- *Instructional goal:* The student will become familiar with personal computers.
- *Instructional objective:* The student will demonstrate skills in word processing using his or her assigned computer by writing a one-page paper with ninety percent accuracy.

Tyler's *behavioral objective*.[5] The following statement is an example of an instructional objective: "The student will convert the following fractions to percentages with 100 percent accuracy: 1/4, 1/3, 1/2, 2/3, 3/4." Instructional objectives are also known as performance objectives or competencies.

Stating Objectives

Tyler discussed four ways that instructors state objectives. Objectives as Tyler described them are:

1. things that the instructor will do. Tyler gave as examples: "to present the theory of evolution," "to demonstrate the nature of inductive proof," "to present the Romantic poets," and "to introduce four-part harmony."
2. topics, concepts, generalizations, or other elements of content that are to be dealt with in the course or courses. Tyler's examples are "The Colonial Period," and "Matter Can Be Neither Created nor Destroyed."
3. generalized patterns of behavior that fail to indicate more specifically the area of life or the content to which the behavior applies. Tyler identified illustrations of this type of objective: "to develop critical thinking," "to develop appreciation," and "to develop social attitudes."
4. terms that identify both the kind of behavior to be developed in the student and the content or area of life in which this behavior is to operate. Tyler's examples are: "to write clear and well-organized reports of social studies projects" and "to develop an appreciation of the modern novel."[6]

THE USE OF BEHAVIORAL OBJECTIVES

Whether to use behavioral objectives or not is a debate that has raged among educators for years. Supporters of behavioral objectives argue that this approach to instruction

- forces the teacher to be precise about what is to be accomplished
- enables the teacher to communicate to pupils what they must achieve
- simplifies evaluation
- makes accountability possible
- makes sequencing easier

W. James Popham, in support of behavioral objectives, wrote:

Measurable instructional objectives are designed to counteract what is to me the most serious deficit in American education today, namely, a preoccupation with the process without assessment of consequences. . . . There are at least three realms in which measurable objectives have considerable potential dividends: in curriculum (what goals are selected); in instruction (how to accomplish those goals); and in evaluation (determining whether objectives of the instructional sequences have been realized). . . . It is perhaps because I am a convert to this position that I feel viscerally, as well as believe rationally, that measurable objectives have been the most significant advance in the past 10 years.[7]

The opponents of behavioral objectives hold that writing behavioral objectives

- is a waste of time
- is dehumanizing
- restricts creativity
- leads to trivial competencies

James D. Raths voiced his opposition to behavioral objectives as follows:

> Consider the long range implications a teacher and his students must accept once it has been decided that all students are to acquire a specific instructional objective. The teacher's task becomes at once difficult and tedious. He must inform his students of the objectives to which they are expected to aspire; he must convince them of the relevance of this objective to their lives; he must give his students the opportunity to practice the behavior being taught; he must diagnose individual differences encountered by members of his group; he must make prescriptions of assignments based on his diagnosis and repeat the cycle again and again. . . . Yet even if all programs could be set up on the basis of behavioral objectives and even if strict training paradigms could be established to meet the objectives, who could argue that such a program would be other than tedious and ultimately stultifying.[8]

Among those who oppose the use of behavioral objectives are reconceptualists who view behavioral objectives as too mechanistic since they focus on observable behavior and ignore subjective behavior.[9] Some authorities have faulted the specification of instructional objectives as too narrow, too sequential, and too focused on specific, and inappropriate, content. They noted the debt of instructional objectives to behavioristic psychology and have looked instead to changes evoked by constructivist learning theories. John D. McNeil summarized these changes

> . . . as a movement to (1) higher levels of thinking as opposed to the mastery of discrete tasks or skills; (2) a concern for coherence and relationship among ideas; (3) student-initiated activities and solutions instead of recitation and prespecified correct responses; and (4) students, as opposed to the teacher or the text, as an authority for knowing, students began constructing their own understanding by working through problems and synthesizing their ideas.[10]

Although some educators would reject the use of instructional objectives, examination of instructional materials not only in the education of the young but also in the training of people in business, industry, and government demonstrates continued widespread use of this technique. Conflicting views of the value of the use of instructional objectives cannot likely be resolved on the basis of research alone. McNeil noted that the research on instructional objectives is inconclusive.[11] McNeil observed, however, "Objectives sometimes help and are almost never harmful."[12] As is the case in other issues in education decisions are often based more on philosophy than on results of research.

Problems with Behavioral Objectives

While the yea-sayers and naysayers argued with each other, the behavioral objectives camp itself added to the difficulty of convincing teachers to use behavioral objectives. Some, perhaps overenthusiastic about the behavioral objectives movement, turned off teachers by

1. assuming a rather dogmatic approach that seemed to rule out all other methods. Although I am favorably disposed toward the use of behavioral objectives and follow this approach myself, I would be hard-pressed to come up with solid experimental data to show that students exposed to a behavioral-objectives approach consistently show higher achievement than students whose instruction has been guided by other approaches.

   What some of the research reveals is that behavioral objectives can be useful in preinstructional strategies, that objectives work better if they pertain to the particular instructional task, that objectives are more effective with certain kinds of instruction than with others, that objectives are useful in accomplishing learning at higher levels of the cognitive domain, and that students of average ability, male students of high socioeconomic background, and both the more independent and less conscientious students benefit from behavioral objectives.[13]

2. resorting to formulas, which tended to make the writing of behavioral objectives mechanical rather than creative—for example, "Given the _____, the student will _____ in _____ minutes with a score of _____."

3. downplaying affective objectives—a primary concern among opponents of behavioral objectives—and sometimes implying that it is as easy to write behavioral objectives in the affective domain as in the cognitive and psychomotor domains.

Speaking of a mistake he and other proponents had made in regard to the use of behavioral objectives, Popham at a later time modified his view and advocated broader but still measureable behavioral objectives. Popham pointed to the danger of encouraging teachers to write too specific, small-scope behavioral objectives for "the resulting piles of hyperspecific instructional objectives would so overwhelm teachers that they would end up paying attention to no objectives at all."[14]

In spite of the hubbub over behavioral objectives, I believe that, with a reasoned approach, the practice of identifying and writing both instructional goals and objectives has considerable merit. Whether the regular classroom teacher specifies behavioral objectives or not, those who write individualized education programs (IEPs) for handicapped students must state both goals that students are to achieve by the end of the year and behavioral objectives for accomplishing the goals.

The writing of instructional objectives forces teachers to identify the outcomes they seek. The specification of instructional objectives simplifies the selection of instructional strategies and resources. When stated in behavioral terms, instructional objectives provide a basis for assessment, and they communicate to students, parents, and other professionals exactly what it is students are expected to demonstrate.[15] Outcome-based education of the 1990s is a direct descendant of competency- or performance-based education of the 1970s and 1980s, all three of which embody principles of behavioral objectives. We will return to outcome-based education in Chapter 15.

GUIDELINES FOR PREPARING INSTRUCTIONAL GOALS AND OBJECTIVES

To peruse the task of selecting and writing instructional goals and objectives, we will find it helpful to establish several guidelines to be followed. Instructional goals and objectives should

- relate to the already specified curriculum goals and objectives
- be specified for three domains of learning—the cognitive, affective, and psycho-motor—whenever applicable
- be identified at both low and high levels of learning with greater emphasis on the higher
- follow a few simple rules for writing

Three current emphases in instruction should also guide teachers in the specification of behavioral objectives. These emphases are (1) the development of thinking skills, (2) the integration of the curriculum through thematic interdisciplinary units, and (3) recognition of intelligence as multiple, rather than global. The conception of intellectual ability is often limited to cognitive language and mathematical skills, often interpreted in terms of a single intelligence quotient score. We have had for many years, however, tests of differential aptitudes or primary mental abilities which yield scores in such areas as language usage, verbal reasoning, numerical ability, spatial relations, abstract reasoning, and memory.[16] Howard Gardner conceptualized the existence of seven intelligences: bodily-kinesthetic, interpersonal, intrapersonal, linguistic, logical-mathematical, musical, and spatial.[17] To the seven intelligences set forth in the 1980s, Gardner, in the 1990s, added the concept of naturalist intelligence, that is, the ability to classify nature that Gardner described as "the ability to recognize and classify plants, minerals, and animals."[18]

We should add to Gardner's depiction of multiple intelligences the concepts of social intelligence as defined by Edward L. Thorndike[19] and emotional intelligence as perceived by Peter Salovey and John D. Mayer. Building on Thorndike's conception, Salovey and Mayer viewed emotional intelligence, now referred to by some people as EQ, "as a subset of social intelligence that involves the *ability to monitor one's own and others' feelings and emotions, to discriminate among them and to use this information to guide one's thinking and actions.*"[20] You will also find in some discussions of multiple intelligences a ninth intelligence—the concept of *existential intelligence*—a sensitivity to spiritual and philosophical questions about humankind's existence.[21] The concept of intelligences, in the plural, guides teachers to designing instruction that appeals to more than a single dimension of intelligence.

Relationship to Curriculum Goals and Objectives

Instructional goals and objectives should relate to curriculum goals and objectives. Unless the classroom teacher participated in drafting the curriculum goals and objectives, he or she must become familiar with them. The instructional goals and objectives are derived from the curriculum goals and objectives. Let's show this relationship by choosing a *curriculum goal* for the fifth grade: During the course of the year students will appreciably improve their skills in reading. From this general goal we may deduce the following *curriculum objectives:* (1) By the end of the eighth month, 75 percent of the students will have increased their ability to comprehend a selected set of English words by 25 percent, and (2) by the end of the academic year, all students will have met or exceeded the grade norm of 5.9 in reading comprehension.

The curriculum objectives are derived from the curriculum goals, are applied to the program and to groups of students, and are stated in measurable terms. The formulation of *instructional goals* follows and bears a direct relationship to the curriculum goals and objectives, as seen in the following examples: (1) The student will demonstrate ability to read new material silently without great difficulty, and (2) the student will demonstrate ability to read new material orally without difficulty.

Both of the foregoing statements are expectations of each pupil. The statements are couched in general terms and include no criterion of mastery. For each of the instructional goals we may create *instructional objectives.* To promote the goal of reading silently, for example, the teacher might design the following objectives: (1) The student will read silently a passage from the fifth-grade reader and then summarize orally without appreciable error in comprehension each of its four major points, and (2) the student will read silently a passage from the fifth-grade reader and then will write correct responses to eight out of ten written questions provided by the teacher.

To further the goal of reading orally, the teacher might identify the following objectives: (1) The student will read orally from a classroom library book and make no more than four mistakes in pronunciation in a passage of about 100 words, and (2) the student will read orally a passage from a classroom library book, and then orally summarize each of the three main points of the passage without appreciable error in comprehension.

Unless an instructional objective is differentiated for a particular subgroup of students—for example, bright, slow, or handicapped—it is expected that every student will master the objective. When instructional objectives are aimed at all students in a given class, they may be called *minimal competencies.*

State testing programs are designed to assess students' mastery of the minimal competencies—for example, competencies to be achieved in all or selected disciplines at the end of, say, fourth, eighth, or eleventh grade.

Some confusion may exist between curriculum and instructional goals and objectives, for in one sense they both may be designed for all students. The curriculum goals and objectives are broader in nature, are aimed at all students as a group or groups, frequently jump across grade boundaries, often cut across disciplines, and many times are relevant to more than one teacher either within a discipline or among disciplines.

There are times, however, when a curriculum objective may be congruent with an instructional objective or, put another way, an instructional objective may repeat a curriculum objective. When we as curriculum planners designate as a curriculum objective improving the scores of all students on a standardized test in mathematics by ten percentile points, we will be pleased when the mathematics curriculum (program) is functioning to that degree. When we as classroom teachers stipulate that all of our pupils score ten percentile points higher on a standardized test of mathematics, we will be pleased with each student who functions that well and may refer to our own instruction as effective if many students achieve that objective.

Though we may state them slightly differently, curriculum and instructional goals and objectives may converge. One is the alter ego of the other, so to speak. Conversely, curriculum and instructional goals and objectives may diverge. When we as curriculum planners desire that eighty percent (even one hundred percent) of the seniors with quantitative aptitude test scores at the seventy-fifth percentile elect calculus, we are talking about program, not instruction.

The distinctions between curriculum and instructional goals and objectives matter only to the extent that neither of the two sets is overlooked. If an instructional objective repeats a curriculum objective, so be it; it is a perfect fit. On the other hand, instructional objectives by their very nature tend to be more specific than the curriculum goals and objectives, focus on what takes place in the classroom, and come to pass as a result of the individual instructor's efforts. Whatever the degree of congruence, there is a direct and natural progression from curriculum goal to instructional objective.

Domains of Learning

One way of viewing learnings exists in the concepts of three domains: the cognitive, affective, and psychomotor. Within each domain we find classification systems ranking objectives in a hierarchical structure from lowest to highest level. The instructional goals and objectives should be specified for three domains of learning—the cognitive, the affective, and the psychomotor—whenever applicable. Note these three illustrations of different types of learning:

- knowledge of the system of election primaries
- enjoyment in reading
- skill in laying bricks

These examples are illustrative of the three major areas (domains) of learning. Knowledge of the primary system falls into the cognitive domain, enjoyment in reading in the affective domain, and skill in laying bricks in the psychomotor domain.

Cognitive Domain. Speaking for a committee of college and university examiners, Benjamin S. Bloom defined the cognitive domain as including objectives that "deal with the recall or recognition of knowledge and the development of intellectual abilities and skills."[22] Cognitive learnings, which involve the mental processes, range from memorization to the ability to think and solve problems.

Affective Domain. David R. Krathwohl, Benjamin S. Bloom, and Bertram B. Masia defined the affective domain as including objectives that "emphasize a feeling tone, an emotion, or a degree of acceptance or rejection."[23]

Psychomotor Domain. Robert J. Armstrong, Terry D. Cornell, Robert E. Kraner, and E. Wayne Roberson defined the psychomotor domain as including behaviors that "place primary emphasis on neuromuscular or physical skills and involve different degrees of physical dexterity."[24] Sometimes referred to as "perceptual-motor skills," psychomotor learnings include bodily movements and muscular coordination.

Ordinarily, schools assume responsibility for student achievement in all three broad areas. Although we might visualize the three horses—Cognitive, Affective, and Psychomotor—in the form of a Russian troika, racing three abreast, they are hitched more like a lead horse followed by two abreast. More often than not, Cognitive is in the forefront. On occasion, depending on the mood of the profession and the public, Cognitive is overtaken by Affective or Psychomotor.

The battle over which domain is the most important has endured for many years. With the exception of work by people like Rousseau, Froebel, Pestalozzi, and Neill (Summerhill School, England), most of the rest of the world—if we may generalize on such a vast scale—marches to the beat of the cognitive drummer. Although many fine opportunities for vocational education are provided by many countries, the cognitive domain remains the prestige category and is the entrée to institutions of higher learning. If our horses were pitted in an international race, Affective would come in a poor third.

Judging from the popularity of books critical of public education, the accountability movement in education, the flight to private schools, the development of state and national standards in the fundamental disciplines, and national and state assessments of student achievement, we might conclude that the American public is partial to the cognitive domain.

Although we find strong preferences both within and outside the profession for stressing cognitive learnings, I would encourage each teacher to identify and write instructional goals and objectives in all three domains, making allowances for the nature of the subject matter.

Normally, the domains overlap; each possesses elements of the other, even when one is obviously dominant. Thus, it is often difficult to categorize learning as falling precisely into one domain. For example, we can identify learnings that are primarily psychomotor (running a football play) and secondarily cognitive and affective. We can give examples of learnings that are primarily cognitive (civil rights legislation) and secondarily affective. We can offer examples of learnings that are primarily affective (honesty) and secondarily cognitive. We can also identify learnings that are primarily cognitive (constructing an equilateral triangle) and secondarily affective and psychomotor.

Many learnings will obviously fall into single categories. If we discount the bit of affective pleasure a student may feel in knowing the right answer, the formula for finding the area of a triangle (1/2 base × height) is pretty much a cognitive experience. Doing sit-ups, a psychomotor exercise, requires very little cognition and may evoke either a positive or negative affective response. Faith in other human beings is primarily an affective goal, secondarily cognitive, and usually not psychomotor.

The classroom teacher should identify and write instructional goals and objectives in all three domains, if indeed all three are relevant. It might be asked, "From what cloth do we cut the instructional goals and objectives?" We might respond by saying, "From the same cloth from which we cut the curriculum goals and objectives—the three sources: the needs of students, of society, and of the subject matter—with the curriculum goals and objectives themselves serving as inspiration."

In recent years critics of the three taxonomies have maintained that learnings cannot and should not be separated into domains. Others, including this author, have found the widely practiced classification of objectives into three domains a useful teaching strategy.

TAXONOMIC LEVELS

Instructional goals and objectives should be identified at both high and low levels of learning, with greater emphasis being placed on the higher levels. It is obvious that some learnings are more substantive, complex, and important than others. Note, for example, the following learning outcomes, all in the cognitive domain, to see the differences in complexity:

- The student will name the first president of the United States.
- The student will read Washington's first inaugural address and summarize the major points.
- The student will show how some of Washington's ideas apply or do not apply today.
- The student will analyze Washington's military tactics in the Battle of Yorktown.
- The student will write a biography of Washington.
- The student will evaluate Washington's role at the Continental Congress.

The knowledge and skills required for naming the first president of the United States are at a decidedly lower level than those for each of the subsequent objectives. Each succeeding item is progressively more difficult, requiring greater cognitive powers. What we have is a hierarchy of learning outcomes from lowest to highest.

Take the following illustrations from the affective domain:

- The student will listen while others express their points of view.
- The student will answer a call for volunteers to plant trees in a public park.

- The student will express appreciation for the contributions of ethnic groups other than his or her own to the development of our country.
- The student will choose nutritious food over junk food.
- The student will habitually abide by a set of legal and ethical standards.

As with examples in the cognitive domain, each objective is progressively more substantive than the preceding one.

Finally, let's look at a set of objectives from the psychomotor domain.

- The student will identify a woolen fabric by its feel.
- The student will demonstrate how to hold the reins of a horse while cantering.
- The student will imitate a right-about-face movement.
- The student will mix a batch of mortar and water.
- The student will operate a DVD player.
- The student will arrange an attractive bulletin board.
- The student will create an original game requiring physical movements.

Cognitive Taxonomy

Bloom and associates developed an extensive taxonomy for classifying educational objectives in the cognitive domain.[25] Of all classification systems the Bloom taxonomy of the cognitive domain is perhaps the best known and most widely followed. It categorizes the types of cognitive learning outcomes that are featured at all levels of the educational system.

Two new taxonomies of educational objectives appeared in 2001. Loren W. Anderson and David R. Krathwohl, editors with six contributors, published *A Taxonomy for Learning, Teaching, and Assessing: A Revision of Bloom's Taxonomy of Educational Objectives* (New York: Longman). Anderson, Krathwohl, and colleagues presented a taxonomy table with a Knowledge Dimension and a Cognitive Process Dimension. Factual, conceptual, procedural, and metacognitive knowledge constitutes the major types of the Knowledge Dimension. Major categories of the Cognitive Process Dimension seek to have the learner remember, understand, apply, analyze, evaluate, and create. Each of the major categories is divided into subtypes.

Robert J. Marzano offered a New Taxonomy that combines various types of knowledge with mental processes (*Designing a New Taxonomy of Educational Objectives*, Thousand Oaks, Calif.: Corwin Press). Marzano saw the use of degrees of difficulty to distinguish the various levels as one of the problems of the Bloom taxonomy. Marzano's New Taxonomy recognizes four types of memory, three systems of thinking, and six levels from the automatic level of retrieval processes through comprehension, analysis, and knowledge utilization processes to metacognitive and self-system processes. Each of the six levels is divided into subcategories.

Space does not permit full treatment of these taxonomies. Since the original Bloom taxonomy is well known and has been followed successfully in the profession for some fifty years, I have chosen to continue discussion of Bloom's classification system. At the same time I would recommend that teachers become familiar with and try the new taxonomies with the view to finding out whether one of the new taxonomies serves their purposes better than the original Bloom taxonomy.

Bloom and his associates classified cognitive learnings in six major categories: knowledge, comprehension, application, analysis, synthesis, and evaluation. Let's take each of these categories, refer back to the examples previously given, and place them in the appropriate categories, as follows:

- *Knowledge level:* The student will name the first president of the United States.
- *Comprehension level:* The student will read Washington's first inaugural address and summarize the major points.
- *Application level:* The student will show how some of Washington's ideas apply or do not apply today.
- *Analysis level:* The student will analyze Washington's military tactics in the Battle of Yorktown.
- *Synthesis level:* The student will write a biography of George Washington.
- *Evaluation level:* The student will evaluate Washington's role at the Continental Congress.

This taxonomy shows learning objectives as classified in a hierarchical fashion from the lowest (knowledge) to the highest (evaluation). A central premise of professional educators is that the higher levels of learning should be stressed. The ability to think, for example, is fostered not through low-level recall of knowledge alone but through application, analysis, synthesis, and evaluation.

Objectives in the cognitive domain are, of the three domains, the easiest to identify and simplest to evaluate. They are drawn primarily from the subject matter and are readily measurable, usually by written tests and exercises.

Affective Taxonomy

Shortly after the appearance of the cognitive taxonomy, Krathwohl and others, including Bloom, developed a taxonomy of objectives in the affective domain, which consists of five major categories.[26] We may categorize the affective examples given earlier in the following manner:

- *Receiving* (attending): The student will listen while others express their points of view.
- *Responding:* The student will answer a call for volunteers to plant a tree in a public park.
- *Valuing:* The student will express appreciation for the contributions of ethnic groups other than his or her own to the development of our country.
- *Organization:* The student will choose nutritious food over junk food.
- *Characterization by value or value complex:* The student will habitually abide by a set of legal and ethical standards.

The affective domain poses a difficult problem for educators. Historically, parents and educators have viewed the school's primary mission as cognitive learning. Affective learning has typically held a lesser position. As mentioned elsewhere in this text, the affective domain is still not accepted by some educators as a legitimate focus of the school. On the other hand, some educators feel that affective outcomes are more important to the individual and society than other outcomes.

The perceptual psychologist, Arthur W. Combs, stated the case for affective education, tying it to the development of adequate personalities, as follows:

> For many generations education has done an excellent job of imparting information. . . . Our greatest failures are those connected with the problems of helping people to behave differently as a result of the information we have provided them. . . . Adequate persons are, among other factors, the product of strong values. The implication seems to be clear, then, that educators must be interested in and concerned with values. Unfortunately, this is not the case in many schools and classrooms today. The emphasis is too often on the narrowly scientific and impersonally objective. . . . Education must be concerned with the values, beliefs, convictions, and doubts of students. These realities as perceived by an individual are just as important, if not more so, as the so-called objective facts.[27]

Bloom, J. Thomas Hastings, and George F. Madaus attested to the neglect of instruction for affective learning when they said:

> Throughout the years American education has maintained that among its most important ideals is the development of such attributes as interests, desirable attitudes, appreciation, values, commitment, and will power. . . . the types of outcomes which in fact receive the highest priorities in our schools, to the detriment of these affective goals, are verbal-conceptual in nature.[28]*

Bloom, Hastings, and Madaus identified these reasons for the neglect of affective learning:

> Our system of education is geared to producing people who can deal with the words, concepts, and mathematical or scientific symbols so necessary for success in our technological society.[29]
>   Standardized tests used by the schools . . . lay stress on intellectual tasks.[30]
>   Characteristics of this kind, unlike achievement competencies, are considered to be a private rather than a public matter.[31]

Some hold that affective outcomes are the province of the home and the church and that instruction in the affective domain smacks of indoctrination. "One of the reasons for the failure to give instructional emphasis to affective outcomes is related to the Orwellian overtones that attitudinal and value-oriented instruction often conjures up in the minds of teachers and the public," said Bloom and coauthors.[32]

Whose values should be taught? Are white, Anglo-Saxon, Protestant, middle-class values the ones to be promoted? Whence come the values to be selected? Although, as noted in the preceding chapter, some people believe that values cannot or should not be taught in school, others like Theodore R. Sizer held that values can and should be taught.[33]

If affective learnings should be taught and values should be among those learnings, then identifying common values is an essential task for the curriculum planner. Robert S. Gilchrist and Bernice R. Roberts urged educators to include values in the educational program:

> Somehow the notion that everyone develops and formulates his own particular value system has resulted in the educator's choice of a do-nothing position. How can we continue with this stance when the provision of experiences for the development of a value system, possibly the most important, influencing task of the educator, is hierarchically the task of the schooling process?[34]

Affective objectives are both difficult to identify and extremely difficult—often impossible—to measure, and these difficulties constitute another reason why teachers tend to shy away from the affective domain. As noted in Chapter 6, however, character education, a product of the affective domain based on common moral, spiritual, and ethical values, has been and continues to be one of the important aims of American education. In Chapter 12 we will discuss some approaches to the evaluation of student performance in the affective domain.

Psychomotor Taxonomies

For some reason difficult to fathom, the development and use of a taxonomy in the psychomotor domain have not been given as much emphasis as in the cognitive and affective domains. Taxonomies of the psychomotor domain do exist, but they seem not to be as widely known as the taxonomies of the other two domains. The examples from the psychomotor domain given earlier follow the classification system developed by Elizabeth Jane Simpson.[35] Following her taxonomy, we categorize these illustrations as follows:

- *Perception:* The student will identify a woolen fabric by its feel.
- *Set:* The student will demonstrate how to hold the reins of a horse when cantering.
- *Guided response:* The student will imitate a right-about-face movement.
- *Mechanism:* The student will mix a batch of mortar and water.
- *Complex overt response:* The student will operate a DVD player.
- *Adaptation:* The student will arrange an attractive bulletin board display.
- *Origination:* The student will create an original game requiring physical movements.

Anita J. Harrow provided a clarifying description for each of the categories of the Simpson taxonomy. She identified perception as interpreting, set as preparing, guided response as learning, mechanism as habituating, complex overt response as performing, adaptation as modifying, and origination as creating.[36] Harrow proposed her own taxonomy for classifying movement behaviors of learners. Her model consists of the following six classification levels.

1.00   Reflex Movements
      1.10   Segmental Reflexes
      1.20   Intersegmental Reflexes
      1.30   Suprasegmental Reflexes
2.00   Basic-Fundamental Movements
      2.10   Locomotor Movements
      2.20   Non-Locomotor Movements
      2.30   Manipulative Movements
3.00   Perceptual Abilities
      3.10   Kinesthetic Discrimination
      3.20   Visual Discrimination
      3.30   Auditory Discrimination
      3.40   Tactile Discrimination
      3.50   Coordinated Abilities
4.00   Physical Abilities
      4.10   Endurance
      4.20   Strength
      4.30   Flexibility
      4.40   Agility
5.00   Skilled Movements
      5.10   Simple Adaptive Skill
      5.20   Computed Adaptive Skill
      5.30   Complex Adaptive Skill
6.00   Non-Discursive Communication
      6.10   Expressive Movement
      6.20   Interpretive Movement[37]

The use of the taxonomies of the three domains as guidelines can lead to more effective instruction. The taxonomies direct attention to the three major domains of learning and to the subdivisions of each. Arranged in a hierarchical fashion, the taxonomies should serve to stimulate teachers to move their learners from the lower to the higher and more enduring levels of learning in each domain.

RULES FOR WRITING

Instructional goals and objectives should follow a few simple rules for writing. Early in this chapter we distinguished instructional goals from instructional objectives. Instructional goals defined student performance in general terms whereas instructional objectives defined it in more specific and measurable terms.

Instructional goals are often poorly stated instructional objectives. For example, "The student will know names of the first five presidents of the United States" is an instructional goal because it is not written in measurable and observable terms. We might change this instructional goal into an instructional objective by writing, "The student will name correctly and in order the first five presidents of the United States."

On the other hand, an instructional goal may serve the purpose of pointing out the direction that leads to instructional objectives. For example, the instructional goal, "The student will develop an awareness of energy needs" could lead to a multitude of instructional objectives—for example, "The student will identify the five leading oil-producing countries," "The student will identify three sources of energy that are alternatives to fossil fuels," "The student will determine how often the price of imported oil has fluctuated in the last ten years," and "The student will propose and describe three ways Americans can conserve energy."

An instructional goal may thus be written in rather broad, imprecise terms. On the other hand, it may be stated simply as a topic—for example, "The Organized Labor Movement." Implied in this topic is the instructional goal, "The student will develop an understanding of the organized labor movement."

Though variations in style of formulating instructional goals and objectives are certainly possible, there appears to be merit in starting instructional goals and objectives with "The student . . ." (in the singular) in order to (1) signal the meaning "each student" and (2) help distinguish curriculum goals and objectives from instructional goals and objectives by beginning the former with "Students . . ." (in the plural) to convey the meaning "students in general" or "groups of students." Although it is preferable for all plans to be committed to paper, it is possible for teachers to keep the instructional goals in mind and move directly to the writing of instructional objectives.

Three Elements of an Instructional Objective

The literature generally recommends that three elements or components be included in an instructional (behavioral) objective:

1. the behavior expected of the student
2. the conditions under which the behavior is to be demonstrated
3. the degree of mastery required[38]

Specifying Behavior. When specifying behavior, instructors should choose as often as possible action verbs that are subject to measurement and observation. Action words in particular distinguish instructional objectives from instructional goals. The word "understanding," for example, is unsuitable in an instructional objective because it is neither measurable nor observable. Thus, "The student will understand his or her rights under the first ten amendments to the U.S. Constitution" is an instructional goal not an instructional objective. If "understand" is changed to a performance-oriented verb, we

TABLE 10.1   Behaviorally Oriented Verbs for the Domains of Learning

Cognitive Domain (Bloom Taxonomy)	
Level	*Verbs*
Knowledge	identify, specify, state
Comprehension	explain, restate, translate
Application	apply, solve, use
Analysis	analyze, compare, contrast
Synthesis	design, develop, plan
Evaluation	assess, evaluate, judge

Affective Domain (Krathwohl Taxonomy)	
Level	*Verbs*
Receiving	accept, demonstrate awareness, listen
Responding	comply with, engage in, volunteer
Valuing	express a preference for, show appreciation by stating, show concern by stating
Organization	adhere to, defend, synthesize
Characterization by value or value complex	demonstrate empathy, express willingness to be ethical, modify behavior

Psychomotor Domain (Simpson Taxonomy)	
Level	*Verbs*
Perception	distinguish, identify, select
Set	assume a position, demonstrate, show
Guided response	attempt, imitate, try
Mechanism	make habitual, practice, repeat
Complex overt response	carry out, operate, perform
Adaptation	adapt, change, revise
Origination	create, design, originate

Note: For a useful listing of illustrative verbs see Norman E. Gronlund, *How to Write and Use Instructional Objectives* (Upper Saddle River, N.J.: Merrill, 2000), Appendices B and C. For a useful listing of verbs and direct objects applicable to the Bloom and Krathwohl taxonomies, see Newton S. Metfessel, William B. Michael, and Donald A. Kirsner, "Instrumentation of Bloom's and Krathwohl's Taxonomies for the Writing of Educational Objectives," *Psychology in the Schools* 6, no. 3 (July 1969): 227–231.

can create an instructional objective, such as "The student will write summaries of the first ten amendments to the U.S. Constitution." This cognitive objective can be raised from the comprehension level to the evaluation level by modifying the statement: "The student will write a paper listing the principal rights in the first ten amendments to the

U.S. Constitution and will evaluate the importance of each right to us today." The instructional objective, therefore, must include behavior expected of the learner as a result of exposure to instruction.

To help with the writing of instructional objectives, the teacher may wish to develop lists of behaviorally oriented verbs that can be used for each category of the three domains. Examples are shown in Table 10.1.

Specifying Conditions. The condition under which the learner demonstrates the behavior should be specified, if necessary. In the objective, "Given a list of needs of this community, the student will rank them in order of priority." "Given a list of needs of this community" is the condition under which the behavior is performed. It is an essential part of the objective. As an additional illustration, in the objective, "On the classroom wall map the student will point out the People's Republic of China." "On the classroom wall map" is the necessary condition. However, if students are to point out several countries on the same wall map, it becomes redundant and therefore unnecessary to repeat "On the classroom wall map" for each instructional objective. What the instructor should do in this case is write: "On the classroom wall map the student will point out . . . ." The instructor should then list all the geographical features to be pointed out.

To conserve the instructor's valuable time, obvious conditions need not be specified; they are simply understood. There is no need, for example, for the teacher to waste time placing before an objective "Given paper and pen" as in "Given paper and pen, the student will write an essay on the work of Joseph Conrad." Unless the use of paper and pen has some special significance and is not routine, it need not be specified. Adding routine and obvious conditions to instructional objectives can border on the ridiculous and can create an adverse reaction to the writing of instructional objectives at all. If we may exaggerate to stress the point, we do not wish to see the objective: "Given a tennis ball, a tennis racket, a tennis court, a net, a fair day, proper dress, and preferably an opponent also equipped with ball, racket, and proper dress, the student will demonstrate how to serve a tennis ball." "The student will demonstrate how to serve a tennis ball" is sufficient *ad diem*, as the lawyers say.

Specifying the Criterion. The statement of the instructional objective should include the acceptable standard or criterion of mastery of the behavior if it is not obvious. For example, a French teacher might write the following statement: "The student will translate the following sentences." There is no need to write the condition, "from French to English"; the students know that. There is no need to specify the criterion "into good English" (which should be routinely expected behavior) or "with one hundred percent accuracy," or "with no errors." Unless a criterion is specified, it can be assumed that the teacher wishes students to achieve one hundred percent accuracy.

Some objectives require more elaborate criteria than others. For example, let's go back to the illustration, "The student will write an essay on the work of Joseph Conrad." We could embellish this objective with various criteria, some of which are essential, some, not. "In legible handwriting" or "free of typographical errors" should be normal expectations and, therefore, do not have to appear in every instructional objective. On the other hand, if the instructor desires an essay with no more than three spelling errors, with no more than three grammatical errors, and with all the footnotes and bibliographical entries in correct form, that information should be conveyed to the students. The criteria are particularly important if the objective is being used as a test item. It is a necessary and sound principle of evaluation that students be informed by what standards they will be evaluated.

Robert H. Davis, Lawrence T. Alexander, and Stephen L. Yelon listed six standards and gave examples of each, as follows:

1. When mere OCCURRENCE of the behavior is sufficient, describe the behavior. Example: The knot will be tied loosely as in the photograph.
2. When ACCURACY is important, provide a statement of acceptable range or deviation. Example: The answer must be correct to the nearest whole number.
3. If the number of ERRORS is important, state the number. Example: with a maximum of one error.
4. If TIME or SPEED is important, state the minimal level. Example: within five seconds; five units per minute.
5. If a KNOWN REFERENCE provides the standard, state the reference. Example: Perform the sequence of steps in the same order as given in the text.
6. If the CONSEQUENCES of the behavior are important, describe them or provide a model. Example: Conduct the class so that all students participate in the discussion.[39]*

Novice instructors sometimes ask how the teacher decides on the criteria. How do you decide whether to permit three or four errors or whether a student should complete the task in ten rather than five minutes? These decisions are based on the teacher's past experience with students and on the teacher's professional and, if you will, arbitrary judgment. After a few years, the teacher begins to sense what is possible for students to accomplish and proceeds on that knowledge. Certain traditions may also guide the teacher. For example, 70 percent is considered by most students, teachers, and parents as so-so; 80 percent is considered not bad; 90 percent is considered good. Thus criteria in the 70 to 100 percent range often show up in statements of instructional objectives.

Although it is relatively simple to specify objectives in the cognitive and psychomotor domains, specifying criteria in the affective domain is enough to tax one's soul. We shall wrestle with the problem of establishing criteria for affective objectives in Chapter 12. At this point, however, we should mention that it is usually impossible to specify criteria for objectives in the affective domain. What criteria, for example, should we append to this objective: "The student will express a sense of pride in his or her school"?

*From *Learning System Design: An Approach to the Improvement of Instruction* by Robert H. Davis, Lawrence T. Alexander, and Stephen L. Yelon. Copyright © 1974 by McGraw-Hill. Reproduced with permission of The McGraw-Hill Companies.

Should the student's response be fervent? Passionate? The affective domain presents its unique instructional problems.

To the standards component, Davis, Alexander, and Yelon added a stability component—that is, the number of opportunities the student will be given and the number of times he or she must succeed in demonstrating the behavior.[40] We may illustrate the stability component with this example: "The student will word-process fifty words per minute on each of three successive tries." Analyzing this objective shows that "to word process" is the behavior; the conditions are understood (a central processing unit, a monitor, a keyboard, and, if printing is required, a printer, paper, ink cartridge); the performance criterion is "at least fifty words per minute"; and the stability component is "on each of three successive tries."

Generally speaking, instructional objectives should consist of at least three components: the behavior (often called the terminal behavior); the conditions; and the criterion.

VALIDATING AND DETERMINING PRIORITY OF INSTRUCTIONAL GOALS AND OBJECTIVES

Instructional goals and objectives should be validated and put in order of priority. Teachers should know whether the instructional goals and objectives are appropriate and which are the more important.

In practice, it is far simpler to validate and rank instructional goals and objectives than curriculum goals and objectives. Instructional goals and objectives are not normally submitted with any regularity to lay groups or students for this process nor to administrators. Nor do they need to be, since instructional goals and objectives are content-specific. To make a judgment on their validity and to decide which are essential require a foundation both in the subject matter being taught and in the methods for teaching that subject matter. The subject matter is often technical and beyond the knowledge and skills of lay persons and students. Instructional matters are the prerogative of persons trained in their fields of specialization.

As a result, far fewer persons need to be involved in validating and establishing priorities of instructional goals and objectives than is the case with curriculum goals and objectives.

Validating and ranking of instructional goals and objectives are usually accomplished by referring to the adopted textbooks, reference books, and curriculum guides. The authors of these materials serve as the persons who validate and set priorities. This method of validating and ordering of instructional goals and objectives is, by far, the most common.

The classroom teacher can also seek help in validating and ranking instructional goals and objectives from members of his or her team, grade level or department, other knowledgeable faculty members, curriculum consultants, and supervisors. Consultants and supervisors trained and experienced in special fields should also be able to help the classroom teacher decide which instructional goals and objectives are appropriate to the learners and which ones should be stressed. Finally, teachers may seek advice from acknowledged experts in the subject area outside the school system as well as from specialists in other school systems or in higher education institutions.

Summary

Instructional goals and objectives are directly related to the previously specified curriculum goals and objectives. Instructional goals provide direction for specifying instructional objectives.

Learning outcomes may be identified in three major domains: the cognitive, the affective, and the psychomotor. The cognitive domain is the world of the intellect; the affective, the locale of emotions, beliefs, values, and attitudes; and the psychomotor, the territory of perceptual-motor skills.

Taxonomies of each domain classify objectives in a hierarchical fashion from the lowest to the highest level of learning. Taxonomies are useful in revealing the types of learning encompassed in each domain and in guiding instructors toward placing greater emphasis on learning at the higher levels.

Instructional goals are statements written in nonbehavioral terms without criteria of mastery. With the possible exception of outcomes in the affective domain, instructional objectives should be written in measurable and observable terms.

Whenever practical and necessary, instructional objectives should consist of three components: the behavior that learners will demonstrate, the conditions under which the behavior is to be demonstrated, and the criterion to show mastery of the behavior.

Instructors validate instructional goals and objectives and place them in order of priority by referring to text materials written by experts and by seeking the judgments of knowledgeable colleagues, supervisors, and consultants from both within and outside the school system.

Questions for Discussion

1. In what ways do instructional goals and objectives differ from curriculum goals and objectives?

2. Is it necessary to specify both instructional goals and instructional objectives?

3. What are the purposes of writing instructional goals and objectives?

4. What are some alternatives to writing behavioral objectives?

5. Do instructional goals and objectives limit the creativity or artistry of the teacher? Explain.

Exercises

1. Define "cognitive," "affective," and "psychomotor."

2. Define the word "taxonomy."

3. Distinguish between a nonbehavioral goal and a behavioral objective.

4. Consult the Bloom taxonomy of the cognitive domain and prepare a list of verbs that

might be used for writing objectives in each category.

5. Consult the Krathwohl taxonomy of the affective domain and prepare a list of verbs that might be used for writing objectives in each category.

6. Consult the Simpson or Harrow taxonomies of the psychomotor domain and prepare a list of

verbs that might be used for writing objectives in each category.

7. Write one instructional objective for each of the six major categories of the Bloom taxonomy of the cognitive domain.

8. Write one instructional objective for each of the five categories of the Krathwohl taxonomy of the affective domain.

9. Write one instructional objective for each of the major categories of either the Simpson or Harrow taxonomy of the psychomotor domain.

10. State the three components of an instructional objective.

11. List and give examples of six types of performance standards that may be included in an instructional objective.

12. Describe what is meant by "stability component" and give an example.

13. Consult a reference by Howard Gardner, Thomas Armstrong, or other author and describe each of the multiple intelligences.

14. Provide illustrations of the application of the multiple intelligences in the classroom.

15. Debate the concept: The specification of instructional objectives is a desirable teaching tool.

16. Poll a group of teachers on their feelings for and their extent of use of the technique of specifying instructional objectives.

17. Choose one curriculum goal and write two curriculum objectives for it. Then write one instructional goal for one of the curriculum objectives and two instructional objectives for the instructional goal.

18. Locate (or create) an individualized education plan (IEP) and describe how it is constructed. In your explanation give examples of both annual goals and behavioral objectives derived from the goals.

 ## Videos

Armstrong, Thomas, *Multiple Intelligences: Discovering the Giftedness in All.* 1997. 44-min. videotape. National Professional Resources, publisher. Phi Delta Kappa International, P.O. Box 789, Bloomington, Ind. 47402-0789.

Books in Action: *Becoming a Multiple Intelligences School.* 2000. 15-min. videotape. Tom Hoerr explains how Howard Gardner's theory of multiple intelligences guides teachers. Association for Supervision and Curriculum Development, 1703 N. Beauregard St., Alexandria, Va. 22311-1714.

Books in Action: *The Multiple Intelligences of Reading and Writing: Making the Words Come True.* 2003. 15-min. videotape. Thomas Armstrong and others explain key concepts to help students develop literacy skills through kinesthetic, spatial, intrapersonal, and naturalist intelligences. Association for Supervision and Curriculum, 1701 N. Beauregard St., Alexandria, Va.: 22311-1714.

Goleman, Daniel, *Emotional Intelligence: A New Vision for Educators.* 1996. 40-min. videotape. National Professional Resources, publisher. Phi Delta Kappa International, P.O. Box 789, Bloomington, Ind. 47402-0789.

Websites

Accelerated Learning Network: http://www.accelerated-learning.net/multiple.htm

Endnotes

1. See Figure 5.4.

2. Norman E. Gronlund, *Writing Instructional Objectives for Teaching and Assessment*, 7th ed. (Upper Saddle River, N.J.: Merrill/Prentice Hall, 2004), pp. 17–22.

3. Ralph W. Tyler, *Basic Principles of Curriculum and Instruction* (Chicago: University of Chicago Press, 1949).

4. Gronlund, *Writing Instructional Objectives for Teaching and Assessment*, pp. 22–28.

5. Tyler, *Basic Principles of Curriculum and Instruction*, p. 57.

6. Ibid., pp. 44–47.

7. W. James Popham, "Practical Ways of Improving Curriculum via Measurable Objectives," *Bulletin of the National Association of Secondary School Principals* 55, no. 355 (May 1971): 76.

8. James D. Raths, "Teaching Without Specific Objectives," *Educational Leadership* 28, no. 7 (April 1971): 715.

9. See Peter S. Hlebowitsh, *Radical Curriculum Theory Reconsidered: A Historical Approach* (New York: Teachers College Press, 1993), pp. 11–12.

10. John D. McNeil, *Contemporary Curriculum in Thought and Action*, 6th ed. (Hoboken, N.J.: Wiley, 2006), p. 132.

11. Ibid., p. 207.

12. Ibid.

13. See James Hartley and Ivor K. Davies, "Preinstructional Strategies: The Role of Pretests, Behavioral Objectives, Overviews, and Advance Organizers," *Review of Educational Research* 46, no. 2 (Spring 1976): 239–265.

14. W. James Popham, *Classroom Assessment: What Teachers Need to Know*, 3rd ed. (Boston: Allyn and Bacon, 2002), pp. 97–98.

15. Leslie J. Briggs cited 21 reasons for writing instructional objectives in *Handbook of Procedures for the Design of Instruction* (Washington, D.C.: American Institute for Research, 1970), pp. 17-18.

16. See, for example, *Differential Aptitudes Test*, 5th ed. (New York: The Psychological Corp., 1991).

17. Howard Gardner, *Multiple Intelligences: New Horizons* (New York: Basic Books, 2006). See also Howard Gardner, *Frames of Mind: The Theory of Multiple Intelligences* (New York: Basic Books, 1983); Thomas Armstrong, *Multiple Intelligences in the Classroom*, 2nd ed. (Alexandria, Va.: Association for Supervision and Curriculum Development, 2000); Thomas Armstrong, *The Multiple Intelligences of Reading and Writing: Making the Words Come Alive* (Alexandria, Va.: Association for Supervision and Curriculum Development, 2003); Linda Campbell and Bruce Campbell, *Multiple Intelligences and Student Achievement: Success Stories from Six Schools* (Alexandria: Va.: Association for Supervision and Curriculum Development, 1999); Tom Hoerr, *Becoming a Multi Intelligences School* (Alexandria, Va.: Association for Supervision and Curriculum Development, 2000); and Harvey F. Silver, Richard W. Strong, and Matthew J. Perini, *So Each May Learn: Integrating Learning Styles and Multiple Intelligences* (Alexandria, Va.: Association for Supervision and Curriculum Development, 2000).

18. Kathy Checkley, "The First Seven . . . and the Eighth: A Conversation with Howard Gardner," *Educational Leadership* 55, no. 1 (September 1997): 8, 9.

19. Edward L. Thorndike, "Intelligence and Its Uses," *Harper's Magazine* 140 (1920): 227–235.

20. Peter Salovey and John D. Mayer, "Emotional Intelligence," *Imagination, Cognition and Personality* 9, no. 3 (1989–90): 189. See also Daniel Goleman, *Emotional Intelligence* (New York: Bantam Books, 1995) and Peter Salovey and David J. Sluyter, eds. *Emotional Development and Emotional Intelligence: Educational Implications* (New York: Bantam Books, 1997).

21. See Leslie Owen Wilson website: http://www.uswp .edu/education/wilson/learning/ninthintelligence.htm, accessed November 1, 2006.

22. Benjamin S. Bloom, ed., *Taxonomy of Educational Objectives: The Classification of Educational Goals: Handbook I: Cognitive Domain* (White Plains, N.Y.: Longman, 1956), p. 7.

23. David R. Krathwohl, Benjamin S. Bloom, and Bertram B. Masia, *Taxonomy of Educational Objectives: The Classification of Educational Goals: Handbook II: Affective Domain* (White Plains, N.Y.: Longman, 1964), p. 7.

24. Robert J. Armstrong, Terry D. Cornell, Robert E. Kraner, and E. Wayne Roberson, *The Development and Evaluation of Behavioral Objectives* (Worthington, Ohio: Charles A. Jones, 1970), p. 22.

25. Bloom, *Taxonomy: Cognitive Domain*.

26. Krathwohl et al., *Taxonomy: Affective Domain*.

27. Arthur W. Combs, ed., *Perceiving, Behaving, Becoming: A New Focus on Education*, 1962 Yearbook (Alexandria, Va.: Association for Supervision and Curriculum Development, 1962), p. 200.

28. Benjamin S. Bloom, J. Thomas Hastings, and George F. Madaus, *Handbook on Formative and Summative Evaluation of Student Learning* (New York: McGraw-Hill, 1971), p. 225.

29. Ibid.

30. Ibid., p. 226.

31. Ibid., p. 227.

32. Ibid., p. 226.

33. Theodore R. Sizer, *Horace's Compromise: The Dilemma of the American High School* (Boston: Houghton Mifflin, 1984), Chapter 6.

34. Robert S. Gilchrist and Bernice R. Roberts, *Curriculum Development: A Humanized Systems Approach* (Belmont, Calif.: Lear Siegler/Fearon, 1974), p. 13.

35. Elizabeth Jane Simpson, "The Classification of Educational Objectives in the Psychomotor Domain," *The Psychomotor Domain*, vol. 3 (Washington, D.C.: Gryphon House, 1972), pp. 43–56.

36. Anita J. Harrow, *A Taxonomy of the Psychomotor Domain: A Guide for Developing Behavioral Objectives* (White Plains, N.Y.: Longman, 1972), p. 27.

37. Ibid., pp. 1–2.

38. For helpful discussion on writing instructional objectives, see Robert F. Mager, *Preparing Instructional Objectives*, 2nd ed. (Belmont, Calif.: Fearon, 1975).

39. Robert H. Davis, Lawrence T. Alexander, and Stephen L. Yelon, *Learning System Design: An Approach to the Improvement of Instruction* (New York: McGraw-Hill, 1974), pp. 39–40.

40. Ibid., p. 41.

Bibliography

Anderson, Lorin W. and Krathwohl, David R., eds. *A Taxonomy for Learning, Teaching, and Assessing: A Revision of Bloom's Taxonomy of Educational Objectives.* New York: Longman, 2001.

Armstrong, Robert J., Cornell, Terry D., Kramer, Robert E., and Roberson, E. Wayne. *The Development and Evaluation of Behavioral Objectives.* Worthington, Ohio: Charles A. Jones, 1970.

Armstrong, Thomas. *Multiple Intelligences in the Classroom,* 2nd ed. Alexandria, Va.: Association for Supervision and Curriculum Development, 2000.

———. *The Multiple Intelligences of Reading and Writing: Making the Words Come Alive.* Alexandria, Va.: Association for Supervision and Curriculum Development, 2003.

Bernhardt, Regis, Hedley, Carolyn N., Cattaro, Gerald, and Svolopoulos, Vasilios, eds. *Curriculum Leadership: Rethinking Schools for the 21st Century.* Cresskill, N.J.: Hampton Press, 1998.

Bloom, Benjamin S., ed. *Taxonomy of Educational Objectives: The Classification of Educational Goals: Handbook I: Cognitive Domain.* White Plains, N.Y.: Longman, 1956.

———, Hastings, J. Thomas, and Madaus, George F. *Handbook on Formative and Summative Evaluation of Student Learning.* New York: McGraw-Hill, 1971.

Brandt, Ronald S. and Tyler, Ralph W. "Goals and Objectives." In Fenwick W. English, ed. *Fundamental Curriculum Decisions.* 1983 Yearbook, 40–52. Alexandria, Va.: Association for Supervision and Curriculum Development, 1983.

Briggs, Leslie J. *Handbook of Procedures for the Design of Instruction.* Washington, D.C.: American Institutes for Research, 1970.

Caine, Renate Nummela and Caine, Geoffrey. *Making Connections: Teaching and the Human Brain.* Alexandria, Va.: Association for Supervision and Curriculum Development, 1991.

Campbell, Linda. *Teaching and Learning Through Multiple Intelligences.* Boston: Allyn and Bacon, 2004.

——— and Campbell, Bruce. *Multiple Intelligences and Student Achievement: Success Stories from Six Schools.* Alexandria, Va.: Association for Supervision and Curriculum Development, 1999.

Checkley, Kathy. "The First Seven . . . and the Eighth: A Conversation with Howard Gardner." *Educational Leadership* 55, no. 1 (September 1997): 8–13.

Combs, Arthur W., ed. *Perceiving, Behaving, Becoming: A New Focus for Education.* 1962 Yearbook. Alexandria, Va.: Association for Supervision and Curriculum Development, 1962.

Davis, Robert H., Alexander, Lawrence T., and Yelon, Stephen L. *Learning System Design: An Approach to the Improvement of Instruction.* New York: McGraw-Hill, 1974.

Dick, Walter and Carey, Lou. *The Systematic Design of Instruction,* 2nd ed. Glenview, Ill.: Scott, Foresman, 1985.

Faculty of the New City School. *Celebrating Multiple Intelligences: Teaching for Success: A Practical Guide Created by the Faculty of The New City School.* St. Louis, Mo.: The New City School, Inc., 1994.

Gagné, Robert M. and Briggs, Leslie J. *Principles of Instructional Design.* New York: Holt, Rinehart and Winston, 1974.

Gardner, Howard. *Frames of Mind: The Theory of Multiple Intelligences.* New York: Basic Books, 1983.

———. *Multiple Intelligences: The Theory in Practice.* New York: Basic Books, 1993.

Goleman, Daniel. *Emotional Intelligence.* New York: Bantam Books, 1995.

Gronlund, Norman E. *Writing Instructional Objectives for Teaching and Assessment,* 7th ed. Upper Saddle River, N.J.: Merrill/Prentice Hall, 2004.

Harrow, Anita J. *A Taxonomy of the Psychomotor Domain: A Guide for Developing Behavioral Objectives.* White Plains, N.Y.: Longman, 1972.

Hartley, James and Davies, Ivor K. "Preinstructional Strategies: The Role of Pretests, Behavioral Objectives, Overviews, and Advance Organizers." *Review of Educational Research* 46, no. 2 (Spring 1976): 239–265.

Hlebowitsh, Peter S. *Radical Curriculum Theory Reconsidered: A Historical Approach.* New York: Teachers College Press, 1993.

Hoerr, Tom. *Becoming a Multiple Intelligences School.* Alexandria, Va.: Association for Supervision and Curriculum Development, 2000.

Kibler, Robert J., Barker, Larry L., and Miles, David T. *Behavioral Objectives for Instruction and Evaluation.* Boston: Allyn and Bacon, 1974.

Kim, Eugene C. and Kellough, Richard D. *A Resource Guide for Secondary School Teaching: Planning for Competence,* 6th ed. Englewood Cliffs, N.J.: Merrill, 1995.

Krathwohl, David E. "A Revision of Bloom's Taxonomy: An Overview." *Theory into Practice,* vol. 41 (Autumn 2002): 212–218.

Krathwohl, David E., Bloom, Benjamin S., and Masia, Bertram B. *Taxonomy of Educational Objectives: The Classification of Educational Goals: Handbook II: Affective Domain.* White Plains, N.Y.: Longman, 1964.

Marzano, Robert J. *Designing a New Taxonomy of Educational Objectives.* Thousand Oaks, Calif.: Corwin Press, 2001.

McAshan, H. H. *Competency-Based Education and Behavioral Objectives.* Englewood Cliffs, N.J.: Educational Technology Publications, 1979.

McNeil, John D. *Contemporary Curriculum in Thought and Action,* 6th ed. Hoboken, N.J.: Wiley, 2006.

Mager, Robert F. *Preparing Instructional Objectives,* 2nd ed. Belmont, Calif.: Fearon, 1975.

Marzano, Robert J. *Developing a New Taxonomy of Educational Objectives.* Thousand Oaks, Calif.: Corwin Press, 2001.

Nelson, Annabelle. *Curriculum Design Techniques.* Dubuque, Iowa: William C. Brown, 1990.

Popham, W. James. *Classroom Assessment: What Teachers Need to Know,* 3rd ed. Boston: Allyn and Bacon, 2002.

———. "Practical Ways of Improving Curriculum via Measurable Objectives." *Bulletin of the National Association of Secondary School Principals* 55, no. 355 (May 1971): 76–90.

———. *Systematic Instruction.* Englewood Cliffs, N.J.: Prentice-Hall, 1970.

——— and Baker, Eva L. *Establishing Instructional Goals.* Englewood Cliffs, N.J.: Prentice-Hall, 1970.

Raths, James D. "Teaching Without Specific Objectives." *Educational Leadership* 28, no. 7 (April 1971): 714–720.

Salovey, Peter and Mayer, John D. "Emotional Intelligence." *Imagination, Cognition and Personality* 9, no. 3 (1989–90): 185–211.

——— and Sluyter, David J., eds. *Emotional Development and Emotional Intelligence: Educational Implications.* New York: Bantam Books, 1997.

Silver, Harvey F., Strong, Richard W., and Perini, Matthew J. *So Each May Learn: Integrating Learning Styles and Multiple Intelligences.* Alexandria, Va.: Association for Supervision and Curriculum Development, 2000.

Simpson, Elizabeth Jane. "The Classification of Educational Objectives in the Psychomotor Domain." In *The Psychomotor Domain,* vol. 3, 43–56. Washington, D.C.: Gryphon House, 1972.

"Teaching for Multiple Intelligences." *Educational Leadership* 55, no. 1 (September 1997): 8–74.

Thorndike, Edward L. "Intelligence and Its Uses." *Harper's Magazine* 140 (1920): 227–235.

Tyler, Ralph W. *Basic Principles of Curriculum and Instruction.* Chicago: University of Chicago Press, 1949.

11 Selecting and Implementing Strategies of Instruction

AFTER STUDYING THIS CHAPTER YOU SHOULD BE ABLE TO:

1. Define style, model, method, and skills of teaching and state how each relates to the selection of instructional strategies.
2. Distinguish between generic and specific teaching skills.
3. Present a rationale for using a unit plan.
4. Relate daily lesson planning to long-range planning.

DECIDING ON INSTRUCTIONAL STRATEGIES

It's the planning period. The twelfth-grade American history teacher just left the teachers' lounge where she consumed a cup of coffee and chatted with her friends. She is seated now at a carrel in the teachers' workroom, curriculum guide and history textbook before her. The topic to be studied by the students is World War II—the European Theater. Conscientious planner that she is, she asks herself, "What is the best way to go about teaching this topic?" "What methods shall I use?" "What strategies are possible? suitable?" "How do I put together plans for instruction?" "Which suggestions from the curriculum guide should I adopt?" She jots down a number of approaches that she might use in creating a learning unit on the topic:

- Have the students read the appropriate chapters and come to class prepared to discuss them.
- Devise some key questions to give the class and let them find the answers as they read the chapter.
- Lecture to the class, adding points not covered in the text.
- Have each student write a paper on selected aspects of the war, such as the invasion of Normandy, the Battle of the Bulge, the crossing of the Rhine, and so on.

- Have students make slide presentations on selected topics, such as The Rise of Naziism, The Invasion of North Africa, D-Day, and The War on the Russian Front.
- Organize the class into small, cooperative groups with each group preparing a report to the class on a topic such as Causes of World War II; The Holocaust; The Air Force, Army, Navy, Marines, Coast Guard, or Merchant Marine in World War II.
- Have students independently search the Internet, word-process, and print a report on a topic such as Franklin Roosevelt, Winston Churchill, Adolf Hitler, Joseph Stalin, a particular battle, or a famous general on either side.
- Have each student select a related but different topic—for example, the opposing military leaders—and present an oral report to the class.
- Show a film, such as *The Longest Day* or *Saving Private Ryan*, then follow it up with small-group discussion and independent study on topics of interest to the students. Or, show parts of Ken Burns's TV film *The War* for this purpose.
- Have students draw charts of the tactics of both sides in selected major battles.
- Have students read chapters in the textbook and give them quizzes in class the next day.
- Using a large classroom wall map of Europe or a small map with an opaque projector, point out the most significant geographical features of the area.
- Write a number of objective test items that will be incorporated in the end-of-unit test and drill the students on the answers as the topic is discussed.
- Invite a combat veteran of World War II to recount his experiences.
- Have students choose books on the topic from the school or public library, read them, and present oral reports to the class, comparing what they have read in the library books with accounts in the textbook.
- Make comparisons between World War I and World War II as to causes, numbers of combatants, numbers of casualties, battle tactics, and aftermaths.

The teacher must decide how many days she will devote to the topic, whether she will use any or all of the approaches considered, which approach she will use first, and how she will put the selected approaches together.

If you refer to Figure 10.1 in the previous chapter, you will note that selecting strategies is the next step called for in the Instructional Model. In this text, "strategy" broadly encompasses the methods, procedures, and techniques the teacher uses to present the subject matter to the students and to bring about desired outcomes. A strategy ordinarily includes multiple procedures or techniques. Lecturing, for example, can include procedures such as handing out charts and calling for evaluations at the end of the lecture. It may also include techniques like set induction and closure, which are generic teaching skills.

Among the common instructional strategies are the lecture, small-group discussion, independent study, library research, mediated instruction (including PowerPoint presentations and computer-assisted instruction), repetitive drill, and laboratory work. To this list we can add coaching, tutoring, testing, and going on field trips. We could include the inquiry or discovery, inductive, and deductive methods. We could add programmed instruction, problem solving, and oral questioning. Suffice it to say that the teacher has at his or her disposal a great variety of strategies for implementing instruction.

How does the teacher decide which strategy or strategies to use? The teacher may find a curriculum guide that will detail not only strategies to be used but also objectives, suggested resources, and suggested evaluation techniques.

Unfortunately, curriculum guides do not always exist for topics that the teacher wishes to emphasize, and often when they do exist and are accessible, they do not fit the teacher's and students' purposes. Consequently, the teacher must exercise professional judgment and choose the strategies to be employed. Selecting strategies becomes a less difficult problem when the teacher recognizes that instructional strategies are derived from five major sources. Before examining each of these sources we should emphasize a point that sometimes seems to be obscured in discussions of pedagogy, particularly in days of teacher shortages when teachers are assigned out-of-field. Paulo Freire hit on this point when he said, "The fact, however, that teachers learn how to teach a particular content must not in any way mean that they should venture into teaching without the necessary competence to do it. It does not give teachers a license to teach what they do not know."[1]

SOURCES OF STRATEGIES

Objectives as Source

The choice of strategies is limited at the onset by the specified instructional objectives. Although an almost infinite number of techniques for carrying out instruction may exist, only a finite number apply to any particular objective. For example, how many alternatives does the teacher have to teach the number fact that $2 \times 2 = 4$? He or she may tell the students or give a chalk talk using the blackboard; have the students repeat again and again the $2\times$ table, or use flash cards for drill purposes; have students practice using a workbook, an abacus, or a slide rule; or let pupils use a calculator or a printed multiplication table. Of course, not all of the possible courses of action will be suitable or acceptable to the teacher or the students, which limits the range of possibilities even more.

How many techniques suggest themselves for accomplishing the following objectives? The student will

- purify water by boiling
- write an editorial
- sew a zipper into a garment
- demonstrate a high jump
- help keep his or her school clean

Sometimes the strategy is obvious. There is no practical alternative; in essence, as "the medium is the message" (to use Marshall McLuhan's words), the objective is the strategy. The student will demonstrate the high jump, for example, by performing that act. No amount of "teaching about" high jumping will permit the students to demonstrate that they can perform the high jump.

Subject Matter as Source

Subject matter provides a source of instructional strategies. With some subject matter selecting strategies is relatively simple. If we are teaching a course in servicing computers, certain operations must be mastered, such as removing and replacing a hard drive, installing programs and software, and clearing the computer of viruses.

The teacher must zero in on the subject matter and determine what principal facts, understandings, attitudes, appreciations, and skills must be mastered by the learners. Whereas some subject areas have a reputation for being harder to *learn*—for example, calculus, chemistry, and physics—others are more difficult to *teach*. Although learners may have difficulty balancing chemical equations, the strategies for teaching this content are fairly straightforward: lecture-demonstration, followed by testing. Less apparent, however, are strategies for teaching the dictum "Thou shall not cheat." What would be the most effective method for inculcating an attitude of disapproval of cheating? How would the teacher test for mastery of this affective outcome?

Teaching about a subject as opposed to *teaching* a subject is an approach that even experienced teachers must guard against. We have alluded to this practice in the instance of teaching students to high jump. We can find other illustrations as well. For example, teachers who require students to commit grammar rules to memory often test only a knowledge of these rules rather than the students' ability to apply them. Rather than use the library, students are sometimes confined to studying the Library of Congress cataloging system only in the English classroom. Again, students are permitted to verbalize what a balanced meal is but are not required to select or prepare one.

It is easy to be trapped into teaching about desired outcomes in the affective domain. Students read about democracy as a way of life but are not given the opportunity—sometimes inadvertently, sometimes deliberately—to practice democracy in the school. Students are lectured on the importance of self-discipline but are not allowed an opportunity to demonstrate it.

Teaching about content can lead to verbalism—the ability to describe a behavior but not necessarily the ability to carry it out. Verbalism is more likely to result when students are placed in a passive mode. Whenever possible, the learners should be actively involved in the instructional process; they should be placed in real situations or, barring that, in simulated ones.

These comments are not meant to rule out vicarious learning. We would be lost without it and life would be much bleaker. Pupils cannot, of course, always be involved in real situations. History for example, must be learned vicariously. Until the day when the science fiction writer's dreams become reality, we cannot project ourselves backward in time, propel ourselves physically into the future, nor project ourselves spatially into a coexistent present. For example, most of us can sail up the Amazon River only through words and pictures of someone who has performed that feat and written and photographed his or her exploits for publications like *The National Geographic Magazine* or for television. We can experience directly the here and now in our own little corner of the universe.

Vicarious experience is more efficient in cases too simple for direct experiencing by every student. Valuable time would be wasted, for example, by having each student in an automotive program demonstrate the changing of an automobile's air filter. A presentation by the instructor should suffice for learning this uncomplicated skill. Vicarious experience is the only option, however, when (1) resources are lacking, as in the case of learning to use the latest version of Windows when only earlier versions are available; (2) facilities are lacking, as in learning to inspect an automobile's brakes when a school does not have appropriate space or equipment; and (3) the experience is too complicated or expensive, as in preparing a gourmet meal of bouillabaisse, coq au vin, or moo goo gai pan.

Textbooks as Source of Subject Matter.   We can find repeated criticisms in the literature of reliance on textbooks per se. Michael W. Apple called attention to "the ubiquitous character of the textbook" when he wrote:

> Whether we like it or not, the curriculum in most American schools is not defined by courses of study or suggested programs, but by one particular artifact, the standardized, grade-level-specific text.... While the text dominates curricula at the elementary, secondary, and even college levels, very little attention has been paid to the ideological, political, economic sources of its production, distribution, and reception.[2]

Freire put what some might term a constructivist spin on his concern about the way textooks are used:

> Unfortunately, in general what has been done in schools lately is to lead students to become passive before the text.... Using their imagination is almost forbidden, a kind of sin.... They are invited neither to imaginatively relive the story told in the book nor to gradually appropriate the significance of the text.[3]

Obviously, with the wealth of knowledge surrounding learners today through print, tangible learning aids, and online data reliance on a single textbook, passively absorbed, is ineffective pedagogy.

To conclude, whether personal or vicarious in nature, instructional strategies may emerge from a variety of subject-matter sources.

Student as Source

Instructional strategies must be appropriate for the students. The teacher will not send the average third-grader to the media center to select one of Shakespeare's plays for leisure reading. Conversely, the teacher will not attempt to engage junior or senior high school boys and girls in a rousing game of London Bridge or Ring-Around-the-Rosie. Elementary Spanish is inappropriate for students ready for the intermediate level. Highly abstract verbal approaches to content do not fit the needs of the mentally retarded or slow learners. Independent study is applicable only to those with enough self-discipline and determination to profit from it.

Teachers need to capitalize on the special aptitudes or intelligences of learners. In the preceding chapter we mentioned Howard Gardner's concept of multiple intelligences.[4] An adequate school curriculum would offer experiences to develop not only linguistic and logical-mathematical intelligence but also bodily-kinesthetic, interpersonal, intrapersonal, musical, spatial, and naturalist, as well. Some would add social, emotional, and existential intelligence.[5]

Teachers who underestimate the ability of learners and talk down to them or who overestimate the aptitude of learners and talk over their heads follow approaches that do not recognize the pupil as a source of strategy. Unless the teacher is careful, one source of strategy may conflict with another. A particular methodology may relate perfectly to the objectives, and may be right on target as to the subject matter, but may be completely inappropriate from the standpoint of the learner. We may generalize, therefore, that any particular strategy must not run counter to any of the sources of strategies.

The teacher should enlist the aid of students in both long-range and short-range planning for instruction. The teacher cannot assume, for example, that his or her purposes are identical to the students' purposes in studying a subject; he or she must, therefore, make an effort to discover student purposes.

When initiating a topic, the teacher should help students identify their personal reasons, if any, for studying the material. Students should be asked to state their objectives in their own words. For example, the teacher may wish students to study the Vietnam War so (1) they can complete a section of the textbook, (2) they can fulfill a requirement of a course in history, (3) they can become familiar with that segment of our history, and (4) they might become interested enough in history to continue studying it in college. The student, on the other hand, may wish to study the Vietnam War in order to (1) understand books, television programs, and films concerned with this topic, (2) learn what friends and relatives experienced there, and (3) find out what got us into the war, why there was so much student protest, and how we can avoid getting into such a situation again.

Students may effectively participate in planning by (1) choosing among equally acceptable topics, (2) helping to identify the instructional objectives, (3) suggesting appropriate strategies, (4) choosing individual and group assignments, (5) selecting materials, and (6) structuring learning activities.

Community as Source

The desires of parents, the type of community, tradition, and convention all play a part in determining classroom strategies. Sexuality education, for example, alarms parents in many communities. Some oppose the school's venturing into this area on religious grounds; others feel it is the prerogative of the home. Consequently, examining various contraceptives might be considered by many in the community as inappropriate at any level.

A survey of drug habits among youth of a community might be rejected by some citizens who feel a negative image of the community might be the result. Counseling techniques that probe into a pupil's family life, psychological and personality tests, and values clarification may disturb parents.

Learning activities that stimulate excessive competition among students in the classroom and on the athletic field may meet with community disapproval. The use of outdated methodologies like the overuse of memorization can trouble parents as can procedures that call for behaviors either beyond the pupils' capacities or below their abilities.

Community efforts to censor materials and methods occur frequently in some localities. Although teachers may experience some difficulties with the community over their choice of techniques or content, they need not abandon a course of action for this reason alone. However, as discussed earlier in this text, involving members of the community in the process of curriculum development is desirable. Learning about community needs, beliefs, values, and mores may be necessary before the teacher can gain support for using techniques he or she believes are most effective. Through advisory committees, parent volunteer aides, parent-school organizations, and civic groups, community opinions about the school and its curricula can be gathered.

Teacher as Source

Instructional strategies must conform to (1) the teacher's personal style of teaching and (2) the model or models of instructing the teacher follows. Large-group discussion, for example, will not appeal to the teacher who prefers to work closely with students. A teacher who regularly follows an inductive model of teaching is not likely to be content with using a deductive model. Teachers should analyze the particular style of teaching they project and the models they find most suitable for their particular styles. They should seek to expand their repertoires by developing more than a single model of teaching.

Guidelines for Selecting Strategies

To help choose instructional strategies, you may wish to consider the following guidelines, which suggest that a strategy must be right for

- the learners. It must meet their needs and interests and must be in keeping with their learning styles.
- the teacher. The strategy must work for the individual teacher.
- the subject matter. Artificial respiration, for example, is taught more effectively by demonstration and practice than by lecturing.
- the time available. For example, a scientific experiment requiring an extended period of several days is not possible if sufficient time is not available.
- the resources available. Reference materials, for example, must be available if students are required to carry out research projects that necessitate their use.

- the facilities. Dividing a class into small groups for discussion purposes, for example, may be impractical if the room is small, if acoustics are poor, and if the furniture is not movable.
- the objectives. The strategy must be chosen to fulfill the instructional objectives.[6]

STYLES OF TEACHING

A style of teaching is a set of personal characteristics and traits that clearly identify the individual as a unique teacher. Personal factors that make one teacher different from another include:

- dress
- language/speech
- voice
- gestures
- energy level
- facial expressions
- motivation
- interest in people
- dramatic talent
- intellect
- scholarship

Teachers consciously or unconsciously adopt certain styles. The teacher as helper, disciplinarian, actor, friend, father or mother image, autocrat, artist, big brother or sister, or expounder of subject matter are examples of teaching styles. Barbara Bree Fischer and Louis Fischer defined teaching style as "a persuasive quality in the behavior of an individual, *a quality that persists though the content may change.*"[7] They observed that teachers differ in teaching style in much the same way that U.S. presidents varied in speaking style, famous painters differed in artistic style, or well-known tennis players demonstrated unique playing styles.

The teacher with a high, thin voice had best not rely heavily on lecture as a method. The teacher who is formal and proper in dress and manner will probably rule noisy games out of his or her repertoire. The teacher who lacks confidence in his or her management skills may not feel comfortable with a freewheeling, open-ended discussion. If a teacher of low energy level or low motivation refuses to carefully read students' assigned essays or term papers, there is little point in using such strategies.

The teacher with a penchant for scholarship will likely include among his or her methods various forms of research. The teacher with an interest in people will choose procedures in which he or she and the students are interacting not only with each other but also with people both inside and outside the school.

The teacher who is confident about his or her work will invite visitors to the classroom, use resource persons, and permit audio- and videotaping of classroom activities.

The teacher who is democratically oriented will design activities that permit students to participate in decision making. Unflappable individuals will be more inclined to try out innovative techniques that might result in failure whereas less intrepid individuals will tend to stick to the tried-and-true.

Some teachers reject the use of computers and audiovisual techniques because they do not feel competent enough to use the equipment or they harbor the attitude that the use of technology is somehow a waste of valuable time. In the judgment of these teachers, Guttenberg provided the definitive answer to instructional media—the printed page.

Fischer and Fischer identified a number of styles of teaching, including:

> *The Task-Oriented*—These teachers prescribe materials to be learned and demand specific performance on the part of the students.
>   *The Cooperative Planner*—These teachers plan the means and ends of instruction with student cooperation . . . .
>   *The Child-Centered*—This teacher provides a structure for students to pursue whatever they want to do or whatever interests them. . . .
>   *The Subject-Centered*—These teachers focus on organized content to the near exclusion of the learner.
>   *The Learning-Centered*—These teachers have equal concern for the students and for the curricular objectives, the materials to be learned.
>   *The Emotionally Exciting and Its Counterpart*—These teachers show their own intensive emotional involvement in teaching.[8]

You and I no doubt find some teaching styles more appealing and more acceptable than others. We might identify some styles as negative (e.g., undemocratic behavior) and some as positive (e.g., concern for students). Human beings that we are, we will probably give our approval to styles of teaching that emulate our own. Fischer and Fischer made their position clear:

> We do not consider all styles of teaching and learning to be equally valid. . . . Since the very idea of style is based on a commitment to individualization of instruction and the development of learner autonomy, styles that encourage undue conformity and dependence are not acceptable to us.[9]

Deborah P. Britzman took issue with the view that teaching style is "self-constructed product, mediated only by personal choice."[10] Britzman explained, "Teaching style, then, turns out to be not so much an individually determined product as a dialogic movement between the teacher, the students, the curriculum, the knowledge produced in exchange, and the discursive practices that make pedagogy intelligible."[11]

STYLES OF LEARNING

The teacher's style obviously bears some relationship to the pupils' styles of learning. Some pupils are

- eager beavers
- mules
- self-starters
- plodders
- shining stars
- skeptics

Some would add "survivors." Some learners can work under pressure; others cannot. Some need much direction; others, little. Some express themselves better orally than in written form. Some can deal with abstractions; others can learn only with concrete materials. Some learn more effectively from aural and visual techniques than through reading.

Recent research on the brain reaffirms the complexity of the functioning of the brain and at the same time reinforces differences in learners' styles. Speaking of the complex nature of the brain, Merilee Sprenger observed that if learning is to become permanent, it has to follow certain paths that she called "memory lanes," gateways to accessing the memory. She identified these lanes as semantic, episodic, procedural, automatic, and emotional.[12]

An interesting conception of functioning of the brain postulates dominance in either the left hemisphere or the right hemisphere of the brain, although both hemispheres interact. Following this conception left-hemisphere dominance appears to favor logical processes, right-hemisphere, creative. The school curriculum traditionally caters to left-hemisphere characteristics.[13] Renata Nummela Caine and Geoffrey Caine noted that the left-brain, right-brain distinction does not stand alone since, "In a healthy person, both hermispheres interact in every activity. . . . The 'two-brain' doctrine is most useful in reminding us that the brain reduces information into parts and perceives wholistically at the same time."[14]

The application of recent research on the brain to teaching and learning, according to Eric Jensen, places us on "the verge of a revolution" that "will change school start times, discipline policies, assessment methods, teaching strategies, budget priorities, classroom environments, use of technology, and even the way we think of the arts and physical education."[15] Patricia Wolfe cautioned, however, "During the past three decades, we've learned more about the brain than in all recorded history, but there is much more to learn."[16]

Pupils are as different in learning styles as teachers are in teaching styles.[17] In fact, they are more different since there are more of them. Teachers must be aware that their teaching styles can at times be at cross-purposes to their pupils'. A teaching style cannot be selected in the same way an instructional strategy can. Style is not something that can be readily switched on and off. It is not simple to change from a task-oriented to a child-centered approach. Only with considerable difficulty, if at all, can a nonemotionally exciting teacher become an emotionally exciting one. Two questions must be asked about teaching styles: Can a teacher change his or her style? Should a teacher change his or her style?

Given a willingness to change, appropriate training, counseling or therapy, if need be, a teacher can change his or her style. Contrary to ancient beliefs about the impossibility of changing a person's behavior, human beings can and do change. Sometimes personality change is modeled on the behavior of another person who is in some way important to an individual. Sometimes a crisis or trauma effects personality change. All religions share the basic premise that individuals can change their behavior. Thus, change is possible, though it may not be easy.

Perhaps a larger question is whether a teacher *should* change his or her style. Three answers are given to this question, one of which presupposes a teacher's ability to change style. First, one school of thought holds that a teacher's learning style should match the pupils'. Consequently, we would attempt to analyze the styles of the teacher and pupils respectively, then group pupils and teachers with compatible styles. The pupils and teachers would then follow their own styles.

At first glance, ignoring the complexities of analyzing styles and grouping the pupils with compatible teachers, this position seems to be very sound and logical. Rapport between teacher and pupils would most likely be high, and the classroom climate would be conducive to learning. Herbert A. Thelen supported the concept of matching teachers and students: "We remain convinced that any grouping which does not in some way attempt to 'fit' students and teachers together can have only accidental success."[18]

According to a second school of thought, there is some merit in exposing students to a great variety of personal styles during their schooling so they will learn how to interact with different types of people. Although some students might prefer the less structured, informal, relaxed approach while they are in school, a legion of high school graduates compliment their task-oriented, subject-centered teachers for having "held their feet to the fire," thereby helping them to succeed after graduation in spite of themselves.

A third response to the question of whether a teacher should change his or her style holds that a teacher should be flexible, using more than one style with the same group of students or with differing groups of students. This answer combines features of both the first and second responses. Teachers vary their styles, if they can, for particular groups of learners, and by the same token, the pupils are exposed to a variety of styles. Whatever the strategy chosen, it must conform to the teacher's inimitable style. That is why it is so important for teachers to know who they are, what they are, and what they believe. Rita S. Dunn and Kenneth J. Dunn spoke about the effect of the teacher's attitudes and beliefs on teaching style.

> The attitudes teachers hold toward various instructional programs, methods, and resources as well as the kinds of youngsters they prefer working with constitute part of their "teaching style." It is true, however that some teachers believe in specific forms of instruction that they do not practice (administrative constraints, inexperience, lack of resources, or insecurity) and that others practice methods in which they do not believe (administrative or community mandates, inability to change or to withstand pressure). It is also true that teachers may prefer students different from those they are actually teaching.[19]

"Style" and "method" are used rather loosely—and often interchangeably—in the professional literature. Fischer and Fischer cautioned, "Style is not to be identified with method, for people will infuse different methods with their own styles. For example, lecturing is not a style, in our conception, for people with distinctive styles will infuse their respective lectures with their own unique qualities."[20]

MODELS OF TEACHING

Whereas style of teaching is a personalized set of teacher behaviors, a model of teaching is a generalized set of behaviors that emphasizes a particular strategy or set of strategies. Lecturing, for example, is an instructional strategy or method. One whose predominant strategy is lecturing is fulfilling the model of lecturer. The contrast between model and style can readily be seen by a person who attends presentations given by two different lecturers.

Bruce Joyce and Marsha Weil defined a model of teaching this way: "A model for teaching is a plan or pattern that can be used to shape curriculums (long-term courses of studies) to design instructional materials, and to guide instruction in the classroom and other settings",[21] in the seventh edition of their book Joyce and Weil with Emily Calhoun noted, "Models of teaching are really models of *learning*."[22] The model or instructional role that the teacher displays guides the teacher's choice of strategies. In one sense, the model or role is the method or strategy. For example, when the teacher plays the role of questioner, questioning is the instructional strategy or method. If the teacher directs students in using computer software in a particular subject, computer-assisted instruction is the method. On the other hand, if the teacher acts as a facilitator—a much broader role—a number of instructional strategies or methods may be employed. Students may choose their own materials, make up their own questions, and critique their own work, all under the general facilitating supervision of the teacher.

Susan S. Ellis clarified the meaning of a model of teaching when she wrote:

> Models of teaching are strategies based on the theories (and often the research) of educators, psychologists, philosophers, and others who question how individuals learn. Each model consists of a rationale, a series of steps (actions, behaviors) to be taken by the teacher and the learner, a description of necessary support systems, and a method for evaluating the learner's progress. Some models are designed to help students grow in self-awareness or creativity; some foster the development of self-discipline or responsible participation in a group; some models stimulate inductive reasoning or theory-building; and others provide for mastery of subject matter.[23]

In preservice teacher education, students usually gain familiarity and some limited experience with several of the more common models of teaching, including expository teaching, group discussion, role playing, demonstration, simulation, discovery, learning laboratories, programmed instruction, tutoring, problem solving, computer-assisted instruction, and mediated instruction. The assumption teacher education institutions make is that students will gain proficiency in one or more of the models (methods) and identify those with which they will feel most comfortable. Given the limited time at their disposal, teacher education institutions can only introduce students to the many instructional models, encourage students to identify their favorites, and help students to develop a degree of skill in carrying out various models.

Bruce Joyce identified twenty-five models of teaching.[24] Joyce and Weil with Calhoun described fourteen models grouped under four categories or families: (1) information-processing, (2) social, (3) personal, and (4) behavioral systems.[25] Mary Alice Gunter, Thomas H. Estes, and Jan Schwab explained a models approach to instruction when they described some nineteen models.[26]

When we speak of models rather than methods of teaching, we convey the concept that a model is a generalized pattern of behavior that can be learned and imitated. Although teachers may develop their own enduring personal styles (which they may not be able to change easily or desire to change), they may develop skills inherent in a variety of models. Thus we might ask the same questions about models that we asked about styles: Can teachers change their models of teaching? Should they change them?

To the first question the answer must be yes. Were this not so, a significant portion of preservice and inservice teacher education would be useless. To the second question, a change of model is desirable if the teacher's stock-in-trade is limited to one particular model, no matter how successfully the teacher carries it out. Teachers should be masters of several models of teaching. Different models are necessary to reach different goals of instruction.

Need for Variety

Variety of modeling is essential to successful teaching. Constant exposure to a single model can lead to restlessness and boredom on the part of students. Let us fabricate a very unlikely situation. A teacher develops a successful model that his colleagues admire. In their search for the "right" and "best" method, they emulate their colleague to the point where every teacher in the school adopts his model. Can you imagine what school would be like if every teacher were enthusiastic about the discovery method, for example, and attempted to use it to the exclusion of other models? Life could be extremely dull for students and teachers alike.

Of course, the use of a single, consistent model by all teachers is not sound pedagogy; a model must be compatible with both the teacher's style and the students' styles of learning. Deductive thinking—in which a rule is given first, then many opportunities for applying it—is less time consuming and more efficient with some learners than inductive thinking, in which the applications are given first and the learners determine the rule from them.

Fortunately, the use of a uniform model by all teachers is unlikely. However, we can detect sentiment among some educators that there is both a "best" style and a "best" model of teaching. Grasping for surefire solutions to instructional problems, school districts throughout the country have often conducted inservice education programs designed to promote a single, supposedly universal, model of teaching.

Joyce and Weil viewed the search for the best model of teaching as a fallacy and noted that the research does not champion one model over another.[27] You will, of course, discover differences of opinion on the propriety of certain models. Some experts reject models that cast the teacher in the role of subject-matter authority and information-giver. Ernest R. House would supplant the model of teacher as information-presenter with that of teacher as tutor.[28] Caine and Caine, drawing on research on the brain, expressed the view that educators in the twenty-first century "will need to have mastered the art of facilitating self-organization by students and others. . . . They will need to have sufficiently broad cognitive horizons to be able to integrate new ideas and new information and to facilitate their introduction into ongoing and dynamic student experiences."[29]

Proficiency in a variety of models would seem to be in order for there are times when direct presentation models may be more productive than more indirect. Carl D. Glickman counseled:

> There is value in some traditional elements of schooling. For example, there is merit in reconsidering whether exchanging pencils for word processors or relying on pocket calculators instead of mental calculation have improved education. There are clear benefits to directly teaching students particular content, insisting on clear penmanship, and having students memorize certain material. Therefore, there are traditions to be retained at the same time that different configurations of time, space, methods, tools, and technology are incorporated.[30]

Yet, Glickman made clear that teachers cannot become better teachers if they repeatedly teach "the same lessons in the same manner."[31]

Much has been written attempting to describe the characteristics and traits of effective teachers. Yet, as James H. Stronge observed in considering the qualities of effective teachers, "*Effectiveness* is an elusive concept when we consider the complex task of teaching."[32] That teaching is complex is affirmed by the comment of Elizabeth Ellsworth, ". . . pedagogy is a much messier and more inconclusive affair than the vast majority of our educational theories and practices make it out to be . . . pedagogy poses problems and dilemmas that can never be settled or resolved once and for all."[33]

TEACHING SKILLS

Up to this point we have been discussing styles and models of teaching, both of which are germane to selecting particular strategies or methods. We will now add a third dimension that bears on selecting instructional strategies—teaching skills. A word is needed to signify the interrelationship between style, model, and skill of teaching. "Method" would be a tempting word to use if it did not already convey the meanings of both "strategy" and "model"—for example, the strategy of lecturing equals the model of lecturing. For want of a better term, the coining of which we will leave to others, we will use the ambiguous word "approach" to signify the interrelationship among the triumvirate of style, model, and skills. We might chart this relationship in the form of a simple diagram, shown in Figure 11.1, in which the shaded area represents the teacher's approach.

Let's take a simple illustration of this relationship. The teacher who consistently plays the role of facilitator (model) is likely to be a person who is student-centered, friendly, and relaxed, and has skill in advising, counseling, and serving as resource a person (skills). At the risk of redundancy, we might say that facilitator is the teacher's model and facilitation of learning is the teacher's instructional strategy (method).

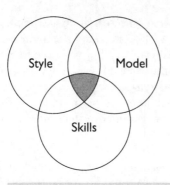

FIGURE 11.1   The Teacher's Approach

What skills are pertinent to a particular approach? For example, what skills are required for lecturing—a method used at some time or other by most teachers? We might list the following:

- ability to enunciate
- ability to project one's voice
- ability to use proper grammar and sentence structure
- ability to "read" students' facial expressions
- ability to sustain interest
- ability to relate content to past and future experiences of learners
- ability to speak to level of audience
- ability to deal with individuals causing distractions
- ability to stimulate thinking
- ability to organize thoughts

All of these abilities are generic teaching skills. We may define generic teaching skills as those instructional skills or competencies that are general in nature and can be employed by teachers in any field and at any level. The converse, special teaching skills, are specific abilities that must be demonstrated by teachers in a particular field or level. The foreign language teacher, for example, must be skilled in the generic competency of varying stimuli, while also being adept at projecting specific stimuli unique to the language being taught. Skill in translating one language into another is a special skill of a foreign language teacher, not a talent that must be evidenced by every teacher.

Generic Competencies/Skills

For many years educators have taken an interest in identifying generic teaching skills or competencies. Dwight Allen and Kevin Ryan compiled a well-known list of generic teaching skills.[34] Madeline Hunter and Douglas Russell listed seven steps—in effect, teaching skills—of planning for effective instruction.[35]

The state of Florida has identified generic teaching competencies and skills that all its teachers should possess. Florida's 2006 version of competencies/skills, which forms the basis of the Professional Education portion of the Florida Teacher Certification Examination, includes fourteen knowledge areas with two to six competencies/skills in each knowledge area. An example of one knowledge area and its competencies and skills is shown in Box 11.1. All persons seeking Florida teacher certification must pass not only the Professional Education Examination but also tests in a subject area (teaching field) and in college-level academic skills.

With appropriate training teachers can learn to master the generic teaching skills. Although generic teaching skills may be employed by all teachers at all levels, it does not follow that any teacher at any level or in any field can use any particular generic skills in just any given situation. Although every teacher should be able to ask probing questions, for example, each teacher will need to decide whether the nature of the content and the learning styles of the pupils will make probing questions appropriate.

Whether the skills are generic or specific, teachers must demonstrate a variety of instructional skills that can be adapted to their own styles and models. Research on teacher behaviors suggests that teaching skills can be imitated, learned, modified, and adopted.

The teachers' personal style, the models they follow, and the teaching competencies and skills they have mastered all affect their design for instruction. For example, teachers select strategies that match their personal styles. They follow models to which they are receptive and choose strategies for which they have the requisite teaching competencies and skills. The effective teacher implements a variety of teaching strategies as well as assessment strategies that are discussed in the following chapter.

BOX 11.1

Florida's Professional Education Competencies and Skills

Knowledge Area 10

10. Knowledge of how to plan and conduct lessons in a variety of learning environments that lead to student outcomes consistent with state and district standards (Planning).

1. Determine instructional long-term goals and short-term objectives appropriate to student needs.

2. Identify activities that support the knowledge, skills, and attitudes to be learned in a given subject area.

3. Identify materials based on instructional objectives and student learning needs and performance levels.

Source: Excerpt from *Competencies and Skills Required for Teacher Certification in Florida, Eleventh Edition,* copyrighted 2006, appears by permission of the Florida Department of Education, Assessment and School Performance Office, Tallahassee, Florida 32399-0400. Website: http://www.firn.edu/doe/sas/ftce/pdf/ftcomp00.pdf, accessed March 15, 2007.

TEACHING: ART OR SCIENCE?

The question whether teaching is an art or science has been debated almost from the time a person with the label "teacher" met with one or more disciples for the purpose of imparting some aspect of knowledge or belief. Foremost among those who view teaching as an art is Elliot W. Eisner whose widely known work, *The Educational Imagination: On the Design and Evaluation of School Programs*, perceived the teacher as artist attuned to the qualities of life in the classroom and demonstrating "connoisseurship."[36]

David Levine proposed the use of the expression "teacher as artist" to replace "teacher as technician," and "school as an experiment in democracy" in place of "school as factory."[37] Levine held that teaching for democracy "is a complex undertaking beyond the ability of teacher as technician."[38] Henry A. Giroux painted a larger role for teachers when he stated, "What classroom teachers can and must do is work in their respective roles to develop pedagogical theories and methods that link self-reflection and understanding with a commitment to change the nature of the larger society."[39]

On the other hand, those who lean toward the identification of generic teaching skills, the specification of instructional objectives, sequencing of content, national and state standards of achievement, and typical assessments would view teacher as scientist.

Successful teaching probably falls somewhere between the two poles.

ORGANIZING FOR INSTRUCTION

Planning for instruction involves selecting the following components:

- goals
- objectives
- strategies
- learning resources
- evaluation techniques

We discussed selecting instructional goals and objectives in Chapter 10 and considered selecting strategies and, indirectly, the resources needed to carry them out in this chapter. Choosing evaluation techniques is the subject of Chapter 12.

Somehow the teacher must bring all the separate components together into a cohesive plan. Both long-range and short-range planning are required. Long-range plans will be examined in Chapter 13. Let's look now at the more immediate types of plans: the short-range unit plan and the even shorter-range daily plan.

Unit Plans

The unit plan—also called a "learning unit," "teaching unit," or simply, "unit"—is a means of organizing the instructional components for teaching a particular topic or theme. Many years ago William H. Burton provided a still-serviceable definition of a unit as follows: "A unit is any combination of subject-matter content and outcomes, and thought processes, into learning experiences suited to the maturity and needs (personal and social) of the learners, all combined into a whole with internal integrity determined by immediate and ultimate goals."[40]

Although units may be written narrowly within the confines of a particular field, for example, "Changing Decimals to Fractions," current efforts to integrate the curriculum promote the creation of units that cut across the disciplines. Even with a seemingly narrow theme like "Changing Decimals to Fractions" by selecting appropriate strategies the teacher can call on multiple intelligences and incorporate other learnings including linguistic, scientific, civic, vocational, and artistic.

The unit plan ordinarily covers a period from several days to several weeks. A series of units might actually constitute a particular course. The daily plan organizes the instructional components of the day's lesson(s). A unit serves as a source of a number of daily plans. Ordinarily, instructional planning progresses from course to unit to daily plans.

The writing of unit and daily lesson plans is a key skill that teacher education institutions seek to develop in preservice teachers. Some institutions insist on a degree of meticulousness and thoroughness in writing plans that is rarely seen in practice in the classroom.

You will find considerable variation in the structure of unit plans. Burton offered a useful outline for a unit plan, as follows:

- *Title*. Attractive, brief, and unambiguous.
- *The Overview*. Brief statement of the nature and scope of the unit.
- *The Teacher's Objectives*. Understandings (generalizations), attitudes, appreciations, special abilities, skills, behavior patterns, facts.
- *The Approach*. A brief account of the most probable introduction.
- *The Pupil's Aim or Objective*. The major objective which it is hoped the learners will develop or accept.
- *The Planning and Working Period*. Learning activities with desired outcomes for each activity.
- *Evaluation Techniques*. How evidence will be gathered showing that the objectives of the unit have been developed.
- *Bibliographies*. Books useful to the teacher and books useful to the learners.
- *Audio-Visual Materials and Other Instructional Aids with Sources*.[41]

Analysis of various unit outlines shows that a unit plan should contain the title, the level or course for which it is intended, and the amount of time to be devoted to the following minimum essentials:

- instructional goals
- instructional objectives (cognitive, affective, psychomotor)
- instructional procedures (learning activities)
- evaluation techniques (preassessment, formative, summative)
- resources (human and material)

Units are written to be used; they are living documents and should be followed where helpful and augmented, reduced, revised, and discarded when inappropriate. Box 11.2 provides an illustration of a unit plan.

BOX 11.2

Illustrative Unit Plan

Title: Financing Our Community's Public Schools

Level: Senior High School—Problems of American Democracy

Time: Five Days

A. Instructional Goals

1. The student will understand that quality education is costly.
2. The student will understand that ignorance is more costly than education.
3. The student will become aware of sources of funding for the schools.
4. The student will become familiar with problems of financing education in our community.

B. Instructional Objectives

Cognitive

1. The student will describe the role and extent of local involvement in financing the schools.
2. The student will describe the role and extent of state involvement in financing the schools.
3. The student will describe the role and extent of federal involvement in financing the schools.
4. The student will explain the process by which public moneys are expended for the schools.
5. The student will explain what our public moneys buy for the schools.
6. The student will compare salaries of teachers in our community's schools with salaries paid outside of teaching.

Affective

1. The student will take a position on the property tax: necessary, too high, too low? Reasons must be stated for the position taken.
2. The student will take a position on the statement: Teachers are underpaid. Reasons must be stated for the position taken.
3. The student will take a position on federal aid to education: pro or con? Reasons must be stated for the position taken.
4. The student will take a position on the statements: The schools cost too much. There are too many frills in education. Reasons must be stated for the position taken.
5. The student will take a position on offering vouchers or tax credits to enable parents to choose the school their children will attend. Reasons must be stated for the position taken.

Psychomotor

None

C. Instructional Procedures

1. Read the district superintendent's annual report (distributed printed document or, if available, on the school district's website) and discuss the revenues and expenditures.
2. Read this year's school budget and compare with proposed budget for next year. Account for changes in the total amounts each year.
3. Draw a chart of the percentages of money spent by the locality, state, and federal government for support of the community's schools.
4. Prepare a bar graph showing the total number of dollars expended this past year by the locality, state, and federal government for the community's schools.
5. Report on your family's school tax and show how it was calculated.
6. Invite a school principal to class and interview him or her about expenditures and revenues for his or her school.
7. Invite the superintendent, a member of the superintendent's staff, or a member of the school board to class and interview him or her about expenditures and revenues for the school district.
8. Report on the costs of one federally supported program in our community's schools.
9. Consult and discuss publications of the state department of education on financing schools in the state.
10. Compare amounts of money raised throughout the state by property taxes and by sales, income, and other taxes.

11. Compare salaries of teachers in our community with salaries of (1) teachers in other communities in the state, (2) teachers in other states, and (3) persons outside of teaching.

12. Account for variations in amounts of money raised for the support of education by localities of the state and in the total amounts of money available to these localities.

13. Account for variations in amounts of money raised for the support of education by the various states.

14. Compile a list of average annual costs of selected items for which schools must pay, including instructional supplies, equipment, heat, lights, water, salaries of all personnel, insurance, and maintenance.

15. Report on the costs of vandalism in our community's schools for a one-year period.

16. Write a report advocating either greater or lesser funding for our community's schools. In your report show what is to be added or cut.

17. Suggest improved ways of funding the schools.*

D. Evaluation Techniques
   1. Preassessment
      Construct and administer a pretest to assess students' entry knowledge and skills. Sample questions might include:
      a. Estimate the total amount of money spent for the public schools of our community this past year.
      b. How is the property tax determined?
      c. Which spends more money on our community's schools: the locality, the state, or the federal government?
   2. Formative evaluation
      a. Daily oral questioning of the students by the teacher on the more difficult aspects of the lessons.
      b. Daily summaries by students and teacher at the end of each lesson.
      c. Teacher's evaluation of student products, as charts, graphs, etc.
   3. Summative evaluation
      a. Quiz on the day following conclusion of the unit. Sample test items may include questions similar to those of the pretest plus additional items. A combination of objective and essay test items may be used. Sample test items might include:
      (1) Essay: Explain the process by which our community raises money locally for the schools.
      (2) Objective: In reference to taxation, a mill is written as:
         (a) 01
         (b) 1.0
         (c) .001
         (d) .0001

E. Resources
Human
   • School principal.
   • School superintendent, member of the superintendent's staff, or member of the school board.

Instructional Aids
   • Computer, projector, and visuals.

Printed Material
   • Publications of the local school board.
   • Publications of the state department of education.
   • Publications of the U.S. Department of Education, including:

The Condition of Education: Statistical Report. Washington, D.C.: U.S. Department of Education, National Center for Education Statistics, annually.

Digest of Education Statistics. Washington, D.C.: U.S. Department of Education, National Center for Education Statistics, annually.
   • Bureau of the Census. *Statistical Abstract of the United States.* Washington, D.C.: Superintendent of Documents, U.S. Government Printing Office, annually.
   • *The World Almanac and Book of Facts.* New York: World Almanac Books, annually.

Websites
   • School district
   • State department of education
   • U.S. Department of Education, http://www.ed.gov/index.jhtml

*Students may choose to make a PowerPoint presentation on a topic listed above or a related topic of their own choice.
Note: This illustrative learning unit is based on the illustrative resource unit shown in Chapter 14.

Lesson Plans

Lesson plans chart the daily instruction. Conceivably, lesson plans could (and sometimes are) written without reference to any written unit plan. However, on strictly logical grounds, lesson plans that are higher in quality, better organized, and more complete are achieved more often with unit plans than without them. Creating units is essential to holistic planning.

Like unit planning, lesson planning is an individual exercise. According to Laurence J. Peter, "A lesson plan is simply an outline prepared in advance of teaching, so that time and materials will be used efficiently."[42] Peter pointed out that "various types of lessons require different kinds of lesson plans."[43] We might add, on a philosophical level, "Various types of teachers, various types of learners, and various types of subject matter require different types of lesson plans." On a practical level, "Various types of administrators and supervisors require different types of lesson plans."

A six-part outline for a lesson plan that can be followed subject to modification for special situations contains six components:

A. Objectives
B. Activities
C. Assignment
D. Evaluation Techniques
E. Bibliography
F. Instructional Aids and Sources[44]

A sample lesson plan based on the illustrative unit plan is shown in Box 11.3.

The less experience a teacher has, the more complete that teacher's unit and lesson plans should be. It is desirable for both experienced and inexperienced teachers to prepare rather complete unit plans to fully communicate their ideas. Experienced teachers, however, will discover ways to simplify and shorten lesson plans. Once the unit and lesson plans have been made, the teacher can pay attention to matters of teaching style, model, and skills.

PRESENTATION OF INSTRUCTION

After planning and organizing for instruction, the teacher proceeds to direct the students' learning experiences in the classroom. Entire volumes have been written on effective means of presenting instruction. Britzman commented: "Teaching is fundamentally a dialogic relation, characterized by mutual dependency, social interaction and engagement, and attention to the multiple exigencies of the unknown and the unknowable."[45]

Since this text focuses on curriculum development rather than instructional methodology, a discussion of methods of teaching will not be attempted in any detail. Instead, I would like to make a few general observations about presentation of instruction and direct you to a few sources for further study.

BOX 11.3

Illustrative Lesson Plan

First Day
Unit: Financing Our Community's Schools
Fifty minutes

A. Objectives

Cognitive

1. The student will list three sources of funding for the schools.
2. The student will describe the source(s) of local funding for the schools.
3. The student will define "property tax," "assessed valuation," and "mill."

Affective

1. The student will take positions, giving reasons whether the property tax is equitable, too high, or too low.
2. The student will express an opinion and give reasons as to whether he or she believes expenditures for schools in the community are more than adequate, adequate, or inadequate.

B. Activities

1. Set induction: Students will listen to the teacher read a recent editorial from the local newspaper on the needs of local schools. The class will discuss its perceptions of the editorial's accuracy (eight minutes).
2. Using a projector, the teacher will show charts selected from the district superintendent's annual report to the school board. Students will respond to teacher's questions about interpretation of the charts (ten minutes).
3. Using the same data, students will prepare original charts and/or graphs showing sources and amounts of funds for the community's schools this past year. Copies of the superintendent's report will also be available for students' use (ten minutes).
4. Students will listen to teacher's description of sources of local funding. Key points: property tax, assessed evaluation, tax assessor, exemptions, and millage (ten minutes).

5. Students will calculate amount of school tax to be paid on the following properties (five minutes):
   a. A house assessed at $150,000; no exemptions; millage rate of 8.5 mills.
   b. A house assessed at $250,000; homestead exemption of $5,000; millage rate of 6.52 mills.
   c. A house assessed at $350,000; homestead exemption of $25,000, plus senior citizen exemption of $5,000, and veteran's exemption of $5,000; millage rate of 7.15 mills.
6. Closure: Teacher will ask students such questions as: Which level of government spends most on the education of young people in the community? Approximately how much money was raised locally for schools last year? What percentage of funding came from the state? What percentage of funding came from the federal government? What is the current millage rate? (five minutes).

C. Assignment (two minutes)

1. See if you can find any articles in the local newspapers or on the Internet about costs of education in the community, state, or nation.
2. Ask your parents how much school tax they paid last year and, if they do not object, report to the class how much it was and how it was calculated. Also ask your parents whether they believe the property tax is too high, too low, or about right.

D. Evaluation Techniques*

1. Spot-check students' in-class work on charts and calculations of property tax.
2. Ask students to respond to teacher's oral questions at the end of the lesson.

E. Bibliography

1. Copies of the district superintendent's annual report to the school board.
2. Editorial from local newspaper.

F. Instructional Aids and Resources
   Computers
   Projector and visuals

*Teacher will schedule students who would be willing to make a PowerPoint presentation later in the week on the data prepared today in Activity B3.

Research on effective teaching in the 1970s and 1980s supported commonsense principles to the effect that students learn more if teachers expect them to learn, focus on the content to be covered, keep them on task, provide adequate practice, monitor their performance, and care about whether they succeed. There is some evidence that for certain types of learnings and for certain types of students, direct instruction of the total group by the teacher is more effective than other strategies such as small grouping, inquiry, and Socratic techniques.

Evidence also shows that coaching is an appropriate technique for some types of learnings and students. Teacher training should make prospective teachers aware of the wide range of instructional strategies possible and help them develop proficiency in the use of those strategies.

For studies on the effective teaching research you may wish to consult some of the references in the bibliography at the end of this chapter, namely works by David C. Berliner et al.; Wilbur B. Brookover et al.; Jere E. Brophy and C. M. Evertson; Jere Brophy and Thomas L. Good; N. L. Gage; Bruce Joyce and Beverly Showers; Lawrence W. Lezotte and Beverly A. Bancroft; Donald M. Medley; Barak V. Rosenshine; Jane Stallings; Herbert J. Walberg; and Merlin C. Wittrock, ed. *Handbook of Research on Teaching*, 3rd ed. (New York: Macmillan, 1986), 35 chapters on research on teaching.

The complexity of teaching is readily evident in the roles expected of the teacher. D. John McIntyre and Mary John O'Hair, for example, viewed the teacher as an organizer, communicator, motivator, manager, innovator, counselor, and ethicist as well as fulfilling professional, political, and legal roles.[46]

Although many, perhaps most, educators accept the validity of the effective teaching research on generic teaching skills, some see the generalizations on effective teaching as limited. Current research on teaching has moved in the direction of case studies of teacher performance as opposed to the "process-product" orientation of the earlier studies. Newer foci include more astute recognition and provision for individual differences in the classroom (see below and Chapter 15, "Provision for Exceptionalities.") more emphasis on social aspects of learning (e.g., cooperative learning, school as a community of learners), and realistic ("authentic") learning and performance-based ("authentic") assessment in place of standardized testing.[47]

INDIVIDUALIZED VERSUS GROUP INSTRUCTION

Controversy swirls around the respective efficacy of individualized versus group approaches to instruction. Proponents of individualization maintain that instruction must be geared toward the needs of the individual learners. Thus, we have seen strategies of programmed instruction, self-pacing, independent study, tutorials, guided independent study, and computer-assisted instruction in many classrooms. Proponents of group instruction point out that for some purposes, teaching entire groups is more efficient and practical in our mass educational system than attempting to individualize instruction. Consequently, teaching groups or subgroups in the classroom, be they heterogeneous or homogeneous, has been the time-honored approach to schooling. Research on teacher effectiveness has supported direct instruction of whole groups, at least for certain purposes.[48]

Personalized Instruction

What is clear in today's teaching is the challenge of providing for individual differences within the context of mass education. We should distinguish individualization in which the same content is presented to all students with some adaptation of methodology in order to achieve the same objectives from individualization which entails varied content and varied methodology to achieve personalized objectives.

For decades teachers have attempted to identify the most effective means of meeting the needs and interests of their students. The literature is filled with discussions and examples of ways to personalize instruction.[49] Almost every description of effective teaching includes some reference to recognizing and caring for differences in student backgrounds, abilities, personalities, learning styles, interests, and needs.

Recognizing the difficulty of attending to differences in the classroom, teachers continue to search for and try out new techniques or modifications of older approaches. Judging by the wealth of books and other media on the topic, the search for better ways to meet individual differences continues. Three instructional approaches currently command the attention of teachers. All three are interrelated, borrow from previous principles in the history of instruction, owe a debt to progressive philosophy, and give credence to time-honored principles of effective teaching. Dressed in current terminology and with the underlying principle of adapting instruction to individual learners are the philosophy and practices of:

1. **Differentiated Education,** otherwise known as "differentiated classrooms" and "differentiated instruction." The teacher who differentiates instruction creates and carries out varied, flexible learning activities designed to meet the differences among students in multiage, multiability, and multicultural classes.[50]
2. **Constructivism.** The teacher who engages in constructive techniques of instruction starts with the knowledge learners bring with them to the classroom and leads students to constructing new knowledge. Using thought-provoking questions and activities constructivist teachers provide many opportunities for students to process their learnings.[51]
3. **Scaffolding.** Using coaching techniques, pacing and sequencing the learnings, and supplying help when necessary, teachers assist pupils to progress incrementally toward achieving objectives.[52]

These approaches should be perceived as sets of practices, not specific techniques, but rather, dispositions to the use of a variety of methods to help learners achieve the instructional objectives. Fundamental and common to all three approaches are individualized instruction, active learning, the role of the teacher as facilitator, and interaction between teacher and students and among students.

Technology in Instruction

Along with the three R's, students today must—and do when they have access to the hardware and software—develop skills in using the ubiquitous computer. No one can minimize today's need for teachers to possess computer skills for instruction, word-processing, record management, presentations, distance learning, and research so that they may in turn help students to perfect these skills.

The computer, in reality, makes the world the classroom. It enables schools to offer open education in its broadest and technological sense. More and more students are using the Internet in their studies and enrolling in online courses. In acknowledging the pervasive influence of computers, teachers should not overlook in their planning other technological media like the overhead projector, television, VCR, DVD player, and digital camera. Effective teachers today combine more traditional teaching techniques using common instructional supplies and equipment with newer technological aids when creating multimedia projects.[53]

Interactive video offers a relatively new direction in individualizing instruction building onto the technology of computer-assisted instruction and combining it with features of video presentations. Gary W. Orwig and Donna J. Baumbach provided a simple definition of interactive video when they wrote: "Interactive video is a video message controlled by a computer program."[54]

Whereas typical video presentations place the learner in a passive role, interactive video permits the student to assume an active part by responding to its presentations. Orwig and Baumbach described three levels of interactive video, albeit the first level uses no computer: (1) video disc player without a computer, the least expensive setup, capable of the least interaction on the part of the student; (2) video disc player with internal computer; and (3) video disc player controlled by an external desktop computer, the most expensive arrangement, possessing the greatest capability for interaction.[55] Orwig and Baumbach saw interactive video as "a powerful instructional medium, and it has the potential to change the way people learn."[56] They commented further:

> As interactive video becomes established, it will probably have a greater impact upon individualized instruction than all the self-paced workbooks, programmed instruction, drill and practice, lap-packs, computer-assisted instruction, and other "individualized" techniques combined.[57]

With each passing year we witness increased use of the new technologies brought forth by computers, laser video discs, and interactive video. In many cases the electronic strategies are incorporated into the existing curricula; in others, they become alternatives to traditional textbook-oriented instruction.

Cooperative Learning

New versions of group instruction as well as individualized instruction have arisen. A considerable amount of research and experimentation transpired in the 1980s on presentation of instruction through cooperative learning, which is sometimes referred to as collaborative learning. Robert E. Slavin acknowledged that the concept of cooperative learning was an old idea and went on to define it in the following manner:

> Cooperative learning is a form of classroom organization in which students work in small groups to help one another learn academic material.[58]

In advancing his noncoercive lead-management control theory in the classroom William Glasser clearly supported cooperative learning, observing that "it is hard to visualize any quality school that is not deeply involved in this method of instruction."[59]

Slavin noted a key element of cooperative learning—group performance—when he said, "The term refers to classroom techniques in which students work on learning activities in small groups and receive rewards as recognition based on their group's performance."[60] Fran Lehr commented on the composition of groups, defining cooperative learning as "an instructional system that allows students of all achievement levels and backgrounds to work in teams to achieve a common goal."[61]

Cooperative learning research brings to the forefront old arguments about the relative merits of competition, cooperation, and individualization in the classroom. Competition among individuals for the teacher's approval, praise, smiling faces, grades, awards, and other forms of recognition has been a time-honored practice in our schools. We know that competition among pupils can produce negative effects, such as stifling motivation, especially when students cannot compete on an equal basis. David W. Johnson and Roger T. Johnson called attention to more than three hundred seventy-five studies conducted in the past ninety years on the effects of cooperation, competition, and individualized instruction in student achievement, and concluded that cooperative learning, furthermore, resulted in more higher-level reasoning, more frequent generation of new ideas and solutions (i.e., process gain), and greater transfer of what is learned within one situation to another (i.e., group-to-individual transfer) than did competitive or individualistic learning.[62]

Cooperative learning, as currently defined, emphasizes the positive aspects of heterogeneously grouped pupils working together to help each other. As such, it is distinguished from other cooperative methods of instruction such as small group discussion, group mastery learning, and peer tutoring, and from individualized methods such as programmed instruction, individualized mastery learning, interactive video, and independent study which retain individual achievement as the major goal. With cooperative learning, individuals are responsible to their group for the group's progress.

Cooperative learning techniques that are in practice place four to six pupils in groups, depending on the project under way. Groups are deliberately structured by the teacher to include a balance between high and low achievers, boys and girls, and ethnic backgrounds. You can easily infer that the goals of cooperative learning include but go beyond subject matter achievement into the development of group pride, self-esteem, social and emotional skills, respect for diversity, willingness to help one another, and a sense of responsibility.

Students in learning teams take responsibility for particular portions of the task, and they must share what they learn with their group in a way that group members will comprehend. Groups may be restructured from time to time depending on the tasks to be accomplished. The teacher may assign grades both for the group as a whole and for individual members of the group. In some variations of grading under cooperative learning practices, grades represent the amount of progress made by individual members of the group. Group members' dependence on each other serves as a motivator; in effect, it creates a positive form of peer pressure. Competition among teams provides a healthier climate than does competition among individuals.

In your reading or observations you will encounter specific adaptations of cooperative learning developed by individuals who have conducted research on this mode of learning. Among these are Learning Together or Circles of Learning (David W. Johnson and Roger T. Johnson), Jigsaw (Elliott Aronson et al.), Student Teams-Achievement Division or STAD (Robert E. Slavin), Team-Assisted Individualization or TAI (Robert E. Slavin et al.), and Group Investigation (Shlomo Sharan et al.).[63]

In planning, implementing, and evaluating a cooperative learning strategy teachers must take into consideration whether the facilities are conducive (or can be made conducive) to cooperative activity; whether students possess the ability to work together, sharing responsibility for the group's endeavors; or whether some training in group processes is required.

Robert J. Marzano, Debra J. Pickering, and Jane E. Pollock observed that "cooperative learning should be applied consistently and systematically, but not overused."[64] Reminding teachers that "Any strategy, in fact, can be overused and lose its effectiveness," they concluded, however, "Of all classroom grouping strategies, cooperative learning may be the most flexible and powerful."[65]

Increased emphasis today is placed on active involvement of students in their learning process not only by enabling them to work together but also by providing them with opportunities to choose learning activities and to evaluate their own performance.

Summary

Selecting instructional strategies is one of the final steps in planning for instruction. Instructional strategies are derived from a number of sources, including the objectives, the subject matter, the pupil, the community, and the teacher.

Teachers vary in their styles, models, and skills. By style we mean the unique, personal qualities that a teacher develops over the years to distinguish himself or herself from all other teachers.

When we speak of models of teaching, we mean a generalized role—a pattern of methods—such as discussion leader, online instructor, or tutor. The so-called Socratic method of stimulating thinking is a model. Jesus, for example, used both a model (preacher) and a method (sermonizing).

Skills of teaching are those generic and specific competencies necessary to design and carry out instruction. Lesson planning, for example, is a generic skill; that is, it is pertinent to all teachers at all levels. The ability to teach pupils to perform the division of whole numbers is an example of a specific skill. Both the models and skills must be compatible with the teacher's style. Instructional strategies must be appropriate to the teacher's style, model, and skill.

Instructional strategies, styles of teaching, and teaching skills are all selected, adopted, and implemented to successfully fulfill instructional goals and objectives. The ultimate purpose of all strategies, styles, models, and skills is the fostering of student achievement.

The various instructional components should be organized into, among other types of plans, short-term units and daily lesson plans. Although teachers may design their own formats for unit and lesson plans, generic outlines are suggested in this chapter. As teachers gain experience, less detail in planning is possible. However, some planning is always necessary. The reader is referred to selections from the now large body of research on effective presentation of instruction.

The chapter concluded with discussions of several strategies for presentation of instruction, called "delivery systems" by some people.[66]

Questions for Discussion

1. How do strategies, models, and styles of teaching differ from each other?

2. How would you go about matching a teacher's style and the learners' styles?

3. How do generic teaching skills differ from specific teaching skills? Give examples.

4. How do you account for the fact that specifications of generic teaching skills differ from state to state?

5. Which do you believe is most effective in promoting student achievement: individualization, competition, or cooperation?

Exercises

1. Select an instructional objective and design at least three strategies for accomplishing it.

2. Observe several teachers, describe their styles, and tell what makes each teacher unique.

3. Describe with examples how a teacher's style affects selection of instructional strategies.

4. Select one of the models of teaching described by Bruce Joyce and Marsha Weil (see bibliography) and describe it to the class.

5. Select one of the models of teaching described by Mary Alice Gunter, Thomas H. Estes, and Jan Schwab (see bibliography) and describe it in class.

6. Prepare a report on the Comparison of Teaching Models in Caine and Caine, *Making Connections* (see bibliography), p. 124.

7. Debate the issue: Teaching as an Art vs. Teaching as a Science.

8. Observe several teachers and try to identify the models they are using.

9. Select one of the generic skills described by Dwight Allen and Kevin Ryan (see bibliography); demonstrate it in class or videorecord your demonstration of the skill and critique it in class.

10. Select one of the generic skills discussed by Madeline Hunter and Douglas Russell (see bibliography); demonstrate it in class or videorecord your demonstration of the skill and critique it in class.

11. Search the literature on instruction, find several outlines for unit plans, compare them, and select or create an outline you would use, stating reasons.

12. Search the literature on instruction, find several outlines of lesson plans, compare them, and select or create an outline you would use, stating reasons.

13. List several specific teaching skills for a teaching field you know well.

14. Write an essay with appropriate references in support of or opposed to training in generic skills for all teachers.

15. Critique Florida's generic competencies and skills and decide whether you agree they are essential competencies for every teacher.

16. If your state has a required or recommended set of generic competencies, critique those competencies and decide whether you agree they are essential skills for every teacher.

17. Take a position, stating reasons, for state testing of teacher competency.

18. State your views on on-the-job assessment of beginning teachers for state certification.

19. Tell whether you believe there should be some process for national certification of teachers based on national standards. State your reasons and tell whether you believe the process should be required or voluntary.

20. Design a five- to ten-day-long unit plan appropriate for teaching toward a specific instructional goal.

21. Design a lesson plan (a daily plan) based on the unit plan that you prepared for Exercise 20.

22. Report on some of the research on effective teaching, particularly studies of time on task (academic engaged time) and direct instruction.

23. Report on the applicability and effectiveness of coaching as an instructional technique.

24. Group exercise: You are a state task force. Your task is to draw up a set of defensible generic competencies that all teachers in your state would be required to master.

25. Locate and evaluate several articles that critique the effective teaching research. (See, for example, "Beyond Effective Teaching" in the bibliography.)

26. Prepare an oral or written report on one of the following:
    a. Mastery learning
    b. Peer tutoring
    c. Differentiated instruction

d. Constructivism
e. Scaffolding

27. Conduct a demonstration of one of the following technologies adapted for classroom instruction:
    a. Computer-assisted instruction
    b. Interactive video
    c. PowerPoint presentation
    d. Online instruction

28. Prepare an oral or written report on the philosophy, purposes, procedures, and problems of cooperative learning.

29. Prepare an oral or written report on one of the following adaptations of the concept of cooperative learning:
    a. Cooperative Integrated Reading and Comprehension (Nancy A. Madden et al.)
    b. Group Investigation (Shlomo Sharan)
    c. Jigsaw (Elliott Aronson et al.)
    d. Jigsaw II (Robert E. Slavin)
    e. Jigsaw III (A. Gonzalez and M. Guerrero)
    f. Learning Together or Circles of Learning (David W. Johnson and Roger T. Johnson)
    g. Student Teams—Achievement Division (Robert E. Slavin)
    h. Team-Assisted Individualization (Robert E. Slavin et al.)
    i. Teams-Games-Tournament (David DeVries and Robert E. Slavin)

30. Report to the class on PRAXIS/Principles of Learning and Teaching/Pathwise and the Interstate New Teacher Assessment and Support Consortium (INTASC) Standards for Beginning Teacher Licensing and Development discussed in Paul R. Burden and David M. Byrd (see bibliography).

31. Describe in a written or oral report each of the five "memory lanes" identified by Marilee Sprenger (see bibliography).

Books-in-Action

Becoming a Multiple Intelligences School Package, 2000. Ten books and a 15-min. videotape. Thomas Hoerr, consultant.

Professional Inquiry Kits

Constructivism Series 2, 1999. Two 30- to 40-min. videotapes: *Putting the Learner First* and *Case Studies in Constructivist Teaching*. Facilitator's Guide. Shows constructivist principles in educational settings. Jacqueline Grennon Brooks, consultant.

Curriculum Integration, 1998. Eight activity folders plus videotape. Shows teachers how to plan and execute an integrated unit. Carol Cummings, consultant.

Learning Styles, 1996. Multimedia kit shows a learning-styles approach to instruction.

Videos

At Work in the Differentiated Classroom, 2001. Three videotapes: *Planning Curriculum and Instruction*, 48 min. *Managing the Classroom*, 33 min. *Teaching for Learner Success*, 28 min. Experienced teachers show how to manage a differentiated classroom.

A Visit to a Differentiated Classroom, 2001. Sixty-minute videotape with an Online Viewer's Guide.

The Brain and Learning, 1998. Four 25- to 45-min. videotapes. Workshop outlines, handouts, and overheads. Facilitator's Guide. Presenters: Geoffrey Caine, MariAn Diamond, Eric Jensen, Robert Sylwester, and Pat Wolfe.

The Common Sense of Differentiation: Meeting Specific Needs in the Regular Classroom, 2005. Three 35- to 45-min. programs on one DVD and a comprehensive Facilitator's Guide.

How to Scaffold Instruction for Student Success, 2002. 15- to 20-min. videotape. Teachers explain scaffolding techniques.

The Understanding by Design Video Series, 1998–2000. Three 25- to 55-min. videotapes. Grant Wiggins and Jay McTighe explain facets of understanding and the process of designing instruction.

Note: Media in Books-in-Action, Professional Inquiry Kits, and Videos can be acquired from: Association for Supervision and Curriculum Development, 1703 N. Beauregard St., Alexandria, Va. 20311-1714.

Websites

Association for Supervision and Curriculum Development: http://www.ascd.org

Community Learning Network: http://www.cln.org (on integrating technology)

Curriculum Planning Guides (Wisconsin Department of Public Instruction): http://dpi.wi.gov/pubsales/planning.html

Education World: http://www.education-world.com/a_curr/curr218.shtml (on scaffolding)

Educators' Reference Desk: http://www.eduref.org/Virtual/Lessons/index.shtml#Search)

Funderstanding: http://www.funderstanding.com/constructivism.cfm (on constructivism)

International Society for Technology in Education: http://www.iste.org

Internet Public Library: http://www.ipl.org and http://www.ipl.org/div/farq

Lesson Plan Page: http://www.lessonplanpage.com (lesson plans)

The New Curriculum: http://www.newcurriculum.com/index.php (on integrating technology into teaching)

Open Educational Resources Commons: http://www.oercommons.org (shared materials for teaching and learning K–12 through college)

Phi Delta Kappa: http://www.pdkintl.org

School Discovery: http://schooldiscovery.com (lesson plans)

TeacherspayTeachers: http://www.teacherspayteachers.com (educators buy and sell course materials)

Endnotes

1. Paulo Freire, *Teachers as Cultural Workers: Letters to Those Who Dare Teach* (Boulder, Col.: Westview Press, 1998), p. 17.

2. Michael W. Apple, "The Culture and Commerce of the Textbook," in Landon E. Beyer and Michael W. Apple, eds., *The Curriculum: Problems, Politics, and Possibilities*, 2nd

ed. (Albany, N.Y.: State University of New York Press, 1998), p. 159.

3. Freire, *Teachers as Cultural Workers*, p. 31.

4. See pp. 314–315 of this textbook.

5. Ibid.

6. See George E. Pawlas and Peter F. Oliva, *Supervision for Today's Schools*, 8th ed. Hoboken, N.J.: John Wiley & Sons, 2008, pp. 133–137.

7. Barbara Bree Fischer and Louis Fischer, "Styles in Teaching and Learning," *Educational Leadership* 36, no. 4 (January 1979): 245.

8. Ibid., p. 251.

9. Ibid., p. 246.

10. Deborah P. Britzman, *Practice Makes Practice: A Critical Study of Learning to Teach* (Albany, N.Y.: State University of New York Press, 1991), p. 232.

11. Ibid.

12. Marilee Sprenger, *Learning & Memory: The Brain in Action* (Alexandria, Va.: Association for Supervision and Curriculum Development, 1999), pp. 45–56.

13. See Lesley S. J. Farmer, "Left Brain, Right Brain, Whole Brain," *School Library Media Activities Monthly*, vol. 21, no. 2 (October 2004): 27–28, 37.

14. Renate Nummela Caine and Geoffrey Caine, *Education on the Edge of Possibility* (Alexandria, Va.: Association for Supervision and Curriculum Development, 1997), p. 106.

15. Eric Jensen, *Teaching with the Brain in Mind* (Alexandria, Va.: Association for Supervision and Curriculum Development, 1998), p. 1.

16. Patricia Wolfe, *Brain Matters: Translating Research into Classroom Practice* (Alexandria, Va.: Association for Supervision and Curriculum Development, 2001), p. 191.

17. For analysis of students' learning styles see Rita Dunn and Kenneth Dunn, *Teaching Students Through Their Individual Learning Styles: A Practical Approach* (Reston, Va.: Reston Publishing Company, 1978). See also Pat Burke Guild and Stephen Garger, *Marching to Different Drummers* (Alexandria, Va.: Association for Supervision and Curriculum Development, 1985) and "Learning Styles and the Brain," *Educational Leadership* 48, no. 2 (October 1990): 3–80.

18. Herbert A. Thelen, *Classroom Grouping for Teachability* (New York: John Wiley & Sons, 1967), p. 186.

19. Rita S. Dunn and Kenneth J. Dunn, "Learning Styles/Teaching Styles: Should They . . . Can They . . . Be Matched?" *Educational Leadership* 36, no. 4 (January 1979): 241

20. Fischer and Fischer, "Styles," p. 245.

21. Bruce Joyce and Marsha Weil, *Models of Teaching*, 2nd ed. (Englewood Cliffs, N.J.: Prentice-Hall, 1980), p. 1.

22. Bruce Joyce and Marsha Weil with Emily Calhoun, *Models of Teaching*, 7th ed. (Boston: Allyn and Bacon, 2004), p. 7.

23. Susan S. Ellis, "Models of Teaching: A Solution to the Teaching Style/Learning Style Dilemma," *Educational Leadership* 36, no. 4 (January 1979): 275.

24. Bruce Joyce, *Selecting Learning Experiences: Linking Theory and Practice* (Alexandria, Va.: Association for Supervision and Curriculum Development, 1978).

25. Joyce and Weil with Emily Calhoun, *Models of Teaching*, 7th ed.

26. Mary Alice Gunter, Thomas H. Estes, and Jan Schwab, *Instruction: A Models Approach*, 3rd ed. (Boston: Allyn and Bacon, 1999), pp. 65–315.

27. Joyce and Weil, *Models*, 2nd ed., p. 1.

28. Ernest R. House, *Schools for Sale: Why Free Market Policies Won't Improve America's Schools and What Will* (New York: Teachers College Press, 1998), p. 3.

29. Caine and Caine, *Education on the Edge of Possibility*, p. 226.

30. Carl D. Glickman, *Revolutionizing America's Schools* (San Francisco: Jossey-Bass, 1998), p. 39.

31. Carl D. Glickman, *Leadership for Learning: How to Help Teachers Succeed* (Alexandria, Va.: Association for Supervision and Curriculum Development, 2002), p. 5.

32. James H. Stronge, *Qualities of Effective Teachers* (Alexandria, Va.: Association for Supervision and Curriculum Development, 2002), p. vii.

33. Elizabeth Ellsworth, *Teaching Positions: Difference, Pedagogy, and the Power of Address* (New York: Teachers College Press, 1997), p. 8.

34. Dwight Allen and Kevin Ryan, *Microteaching* (Reading, Mass.: Addison-Wesley, 1969).

35. Madeline Hunter and Douglas Russell, "How Can I Plan More Effective Lessons?" *Instructor* 87, no. 2 (September 1977): 74–75, 88.

36. Elliot W. Eisner, *The Educational Imagination: On the Design and Evaluation of School Programs*, 2nd ed. (New York: Macmillan, 1985), p. 219.

37. David Levine, "Building a Vision of Curriculum Reform," in David Levine, Robert Lowe, Bob Peterson, and Rita Tenorio, eds., *Rethinking Schools: An Agenda for Change* (New York: The New Press, 1995), p. 53.

38. Ibid, p. 54.

39. Henry A. Giroux, *Pedagogy and the Politics of Hope: Theory, Culture, and Schooling: A Critical Reader* (Boulder, Col.: Westview Press, 1997), p. 28.

40. William H. Burton, *The Guidance of Learning Activities: A Summary of the Principles of Teaching Based on the Growth of the Learner*, 3rd ed. (Englewood Cliffs, N.J.: Prentice-Hall, Inc., 1962), p. 329.

41. Ibid., pp. 372–374.

42. Laurence J. Peter, *Competencies for Teaching: Classroom Instruction* (Belmont, Calif.: Wadsworth, 1975), p. 194.

43. Ibid.

44. Peter F. Oliva, *The Secondary School Today*, 2nd ed. (New York: Harper & Row, 1972), p. 313.

45. Britzman, *Practice Makes Practice*, p. 237.

46. D. John McIntyre and Mary John O'Hair, *The Reflective Roles of the Classroom Teacher* (Belmont, Calif.: Wadsworth, 1996).

47. See "Beyond Effective Teaching," *Educational Leadership* 49, no. 7 (April 1992): 4–73.

48. See Barak V. Rosenshine, "Academic Engaged Time, Content Covered, and Direct Instruction," *Journal of Education* 160, no. 3 (August 1978): 38–66.

49. See, for example, Dianne Ferguson, Ginevra Ralph, Gwen Meyer et al., *Designing Personalized Learning for Every Student* (Alexandria, Va.: Association for Supervision and Curriculum Development, 2001) and James M. Keefe and John M. Jenkins, *Personalized Instruction* (Bloomington, Ind.: Phi Delta Kappa Educational Foundation, 2005).

50. See, for example, Carol Ann Tomlinson, *The Differentiated Classroom: Responding to the Needs of All Learners* (Alexandria, Va.: Association for Supervision and Curriculum Development, 1999).

51. See, for example, Jacqueline Grennon Brooks and Martin Brooks, *In Search of Understanding: The Case for Constructivist Classrooms* (Alexandria, Va.: Association for Supervision and Curriculum Development, 1999). See also "The Constructivist Classroom," *Phi Delta Kappan* 57, no. 3 (November 1999): 6–78.

52. Kathleen Hogan and Michael Pressley, *Scaffolding Student Learning: Instructional Approaches and Issues* (Cambridge, Mass.: Brookline Books, 1997).

53. See Michael Simkins, Karen Cole, Fern Tavalin, and Barbara Means, *Increasing Student Learning Through Multimedia Projects* (Alexandria, Va.: Association for Supervision and Curriculum Development, 2002).

54. Gary W. Orwig and Donna J. Baumbach, *What Every Educator Needs to Know About the New Technologies: Interactive Video 1* (Orlando, Fla.: UCF/DOE Instructional Computing Resource Center, University of Central Florida, 1989).

55. Gary W. Orwig and Donna J. Baumbach, *What Every Educator Needs to Know About the New Technologies: Interactive Video 2* (Orlando, Fla: UCF/DOE Instructional Computing Resource Center, University of Central Florida, 1989).

56. Orwig and Baumbach, *Interactive Video 1.*

57. Ibid.

58. Robert E. Slavin, "Cooperative Learning and Student Achievement," in Robert E. Slavin, ed. *School and Classroom Organization* (Hillsdale, N.J.: Lawrence Erlbaum, 1989), p. 129

59. William Glasser, *The Quality School: Managing Students Without Coercion*, 2nd ed. (New York: HarperPerennial, 1992), p. 163.

60. Robert E. Slavin, "Cooperative Learning," *Review of Educational Research* 50, no. 2 (Summer 1980): 315.

61. Fran Lehr, "Cooperative Learning," *Journal of Reading* 27, no. 5 (February 1984): 458.

62. David W. Johnson and Roger T. Johnson, *Learning Together and Alone: Cooperative, Competitive, and Individualistic Learning*, 5th ed. (Boston: Allyn and Bacon, 1999), p. 203.

63. For a brief description of these techniques, see George P. Knight and Elaine Morton Bohlmeyer, "Cooperative Learning and Achievement: Methods for Assessing Causal Mechanisms," in Sharan, *Cooperative Learning*, pp. 1–7. See also Slavin, *School and Classroom Organization*, pp. 129–156 (includes extensive bibliography, pp. 151–156).

64. Robert J. Marzano, Debra J. Pickering, and Jane E. Pollock, *Classroom Instruction That Works: Research-Based Strategies for Increasing Student Achievement* (Alexandria, Va.: Association for Supervision and Curriculum Development, 2001), p. 88.

65. Ibid., p. 91.

66. For helpful reference on methods of teaching, see Paul R. Burden and David M. Byrd, *Methods for Effective Teaching*, 3rd ed. (Boston: Allyn and Bacon, 2003).

Bibliography

Allen, Dwight and Ryan, Kevin. *Microteaching*. Reading, Mass.: Addison-Wesley, 1969.

Apple, Michael W. "The Culture and Commerce of the Textbook." In Landon E. Beyer and Michael W. Apple, eds. *The Curriculum: Problems, Politics, and Possibilities*, 2nd ed. Albany, N.Y.: State University Press of New York, 1998.

Armstrong, Thomas. *Multiple Intelligences in the Classroom*, 2nd ed. Alexandria, Va.: Association for Supervision and Curriculum Development, 2000.

"Authentic Learning." *Educational Leadership* 50, no. 7 (April 1993): 4–84.

Banks, James A. *Teaching Strategies for Ethnic Studies*, 5th ed. Boston: Allyn and Bacon, 1991.

Berenson, David H., Berenson, Sally R., and Carkhuff, Robert B. *The Skills of Teaching: Content Development Skills*. Amherst, Mass.: Human Resource Development Press, 1978.

———. *The Skills of Teaching: Lesson Planning Skills*. Amherst, Mass.: Human Resource Development Press, 1978.

Berenson, Sally R., Berenson, David H., and Carkhuff, Robert R. *The Skills of Teaching: Teaching Delivery Skills*. Amherst, Mass.: Human Resource Development Press, 1979.

Berliner, David C., ed. *Phase III of the Beginning Teacher Effectiveness Study*. San Francisco: Far West Laboratory for Educational Research and Development, 1976.

Beyer, Landon E. and Apple, Michael W. *The Curriculum: Problems, Politics, and Possibilities*, 2nd ed. Albany, N.Y.: State University of New York Press, 1998.

"Beyond Effective Teaching." *Educational Leadership* 49, no. 7 (April 1992): 4–73.

Britzman, Deborah P. *Lost Subjects, Contended Objects: Toward a Psychoanalytic Analysis of Learning*. Albany, N.Y.: State University of New York Press, 1998.

———. *Practice Makes Practice: A Critical Study of Learning to Teach*. New York: State University of New York Press, 1991.

Brookover, Wilbur B. et al. *A Study of Elementary School Social Systems and School Outcomes*. East Lansing: Michigan State University, Center for Urban Affairs, 1977.

Brooks, Jacqueline Greenon and Brooks, Martin G. *In Search of Understanding: The Case for Constructivist Classrooms*, rev. ed. Alexandria, Va.: Association for Supervision and Curriculum Development, 1993.

Brophy, Jere E. and Evertson, C. M. *Process-Product Correlation in the Texas Teacher Effectiveness Study*. Austin: University of Texas, 1974.

Brophy, Jere E. and Good, Thomas L. "Teacher Behavior and Student Achievement," In Merlin C. Wittrock, ed. *Handbook of Research on Teaching*, 3rd ed. New York: Macmillan, 1986, pp. 328–375.

Bruer, John T. "In Search of . . . Brain-Based Education." *Phi Delta Kappan* 80, no. 9 (May 1999): 648–657.

Burden, Paul R. and Byrd, David M. *Methods for Effective Teaching*, 3rd ed. Boston: Allyn and Bacon, 2003.

Burton, William H. *The Guidance of Learning Activities: A Summary of the Principles of Teaching Based on the Growth of the Learner*, 3rd ed. Englewood Cliffs, N.J.: Prentice-Hall, 1962.

Caine, Renate Nummela and Caine, Geoffrey. *Education on the Edge of Possibility*. Alexandria, Va.: Association for Supervision and Curriculum Development, 1997.

———. *Making Connections: Teaching and the Human Brain*. Reading, Mass.: Addison-Wesley, 1991.

———. "Understanding a Brain-Based Approach to Learning and Teaching." *Educational Leadership* 48, no. 2 (October 1990): 66–70.

——— of Brain-Based Teaching. Alexandria, Va.: Association for Supervision and Curriculum Development, 1997.

Carkhuff, Robert R. *The Art of Helping III*. Amherst, Mass.: Human Resource Development Press, 1977.

———, Berenson, David H., and Pierce, Richard M. *The Skills of Teaching: Interpersonal Skills*. Amherst, Mass.: Human Resource Development Press, 1977.

"Collegial Learning." *Educational Leadership* 45, no. 3 (November 1987): 3–75.

Cooper, James M., ed. *Classroom Teaching Skills*, 7th ed. Boston: Houghton Mifflin, 2003.

"The Constructivist Classroom." *Educational Leadership* 57, no. 3 (November 1999): 6–78.

"Cooperative Learning." *Educational Leadership* 47, no. 4 (December 1989/January 1990): 3–66.

Dobbs, Susan. "Some Second Thoughts on the Application of Left Brain/Right Brain Research." *Roeper Review* 12 (December 1989): 119–121.

Dunn, Rita S. and Dunn, Kenneth J. "Learning Styles/Teaching Styles: Should They . . . Can They . . . Be Matched?" *Educational Leadership* 36, no. 4 (January 1979): 238–244.

———. *Teaching Students Through Their Individual Learning Styles: A Practical Approach*. Reston, Va.: Reston Publishing Company, 1978.

Eisner, Elliot W. *The Educational Imagination: On the Design and Evaluation of School Programs*, 2nd ed. New York: Macmillan, 1989.

Ellis, Susan S. "Models of Teaching: A Solution to the Teaching Style/Learning Style Dilemma." *Educational Leadership* 36, no. 4 (January 1979): 274–277.

Ellsworth, Elizabeth. *Teaching Positions: Difference, Pedagogy, and the Power of Address*. New York: Teachers College Press, 1997.

Farmer, Lesley S. J. "Left Brain, Right Brain, Whole Brain." *School Library Media Activities Monthly* vol. 21, no. 2 (October 2004): 27–28, 37.

Ferguson, Dianne L., Ginevra, Meyer, Gwen, et al. *Designing Personalized Learning for Every Student*. Alexandria, Va.: Association for Supervision and Curriculum Development, 2001.

Fischer, Barbara Bree and Fischer, Louis. "Styles in Teaching and Learning." *Educational Leadership* 36, no. 4 (January 1979): 245–254.

Floyd, Steve and Floyd, Beth with Hon, David, McEntee, Patrick, O'Bryan, Kenneth G., and Schwarz, Michael. *Handbook of Interactive Video.* White Plains, N.Y.: Knowledge Industry Publications, 1982.

Freire, Paulo. *Teachers as Cultural Workers: Letters to Those Who Dare to Teach.* Boulder, Col.: Westview Press, 1998.

Gage, N. L. *The Psychology of Teaching Methods.* 75th Yearbook of the National Society for the Study of Education, Part I. Chicago: University of Chicago Press, 1976.

———. *The Scientific Basis of the Art of Teaching.* New York: Teachers College Press, 1978.

Gardner, Howard. *Frames of Mind: The Theory of Multiple Intelligences.* New York: Basic Books, 1983.

———. *Multiple Intelligences: The Theory in Practice.* New York: Basic Books, 1993.

Giroux, Henry A. *Pedagogy and the Politics of Hope: A Critical Reader.* Boulder, Col.: Westview Press, 1997.

———. *Teachers as Intellectuals: Toward a Critical Pedagogy of Learning.* Granby, Mass.: Bergin & Garvey, 1988.

Glasser, William. *Control Theory in the Classroom.* New York: Perennial Library, 1986.

———. "The Quality School." *Phi Delta Kappan* 71, no. 6 (February 1990): 424–435.

———. *The Quality School: Managing Students Without Coercion,* 2nd ed. New York: HarperPerennial, 1992.

Glickman, Carl D. *Revolutionizing America's Schools.* San Francisco: Jossey-Bass, 1998.

———. *Leadership for Learning: How to Help Teachers Succeed.* Alexandria, Va.: Association for Supervision and Curriculum Development, 2002.

Good, Thomas L. and Brophy, Jere. *Looking in Classrooms,* 3rd ed. New York: Harper & Row, 1984.

Guild, Pat Burke and Garger, Stephen. *Marching to Different Drummers.* Alexandria, Va.: Association for Supervision and Curriculum Development, 1985.

Gunter, Mary Alice, Estes, Thomas H., and Schwab, Jan. *Instruction: A Models Approach,* 3rd ed. Boston: Allyn and Bacon, 1999.

Harmin, Merrill. *Inspiring Active Learning: A Handbook for Teachers.* Alexandria, Va.: Association for Supervision and Curriculum Development, 1994.

Henson, Kenneth T. *Methods and Strategies for Teaching in Secondary and Middle Schools,* 2nd ed. White Plains, N.Y.: Longman, 1993.

Hilke, Eileen Veronica. *Cooperative Learning.* Fastback 299. Bloomington, Ind.: Phi Delta Kappa, 1990.

Hogan, Kathleen and Pressley, Michael. *Scaffolding Student Learning: Instructional Approaches and Issues.* Cambridge, Mass.: Brookline Books, 1997.

House, Ernest R. *Schools for Sale: Why Free Market Policies Won't Improve America's Schools and What Will.* New York: Teachers College Press, 1998.

"How the Brain Learns." *Educational Leadership* 56, no. 3 (November 1998): 8–73.

"How to Differentiate Instruction." *Educational Leadership* 58, no. 1 (September 2000): 6–83.

Hunter, Madeline and Russell, Douglas. "How Can I Plan More Effective Lessons?" *Instructor* 87, no. 2 (September 1977): 74–75, 88.

Jacobs, Heidi Hayes. *Interdisciplinary Curriculum: Design and Implementation.* Alexandria, Va.: Association for Supervision and Curriculum Development, 1989.

Jensen, Eric. *Teaching with the Brain in Mind.* Alexandria, Va.: Association for Supervision and Curriculum Development, 1998.

——— and Holubec, Edythe Johnson. *Cooperative Learning in the Classroom.* Alexandria, Va.: Association for Supervision and Curriculum Development, 1994.

———. *The New Circles of Learning: Cooperation in the Classroom and School.* Alexandria, Va.: Association for Supervision and Curriculum Development, 1994.

Johnson, David W. and Johnson, Roger T. *Learning Together and Alone: Cooperative, Competitive, and Individualistic Learning,* 5th ed. Boston: Allyn and Bacon, 1999.

Jones, Beau, Palincsar, Annemarie, Ogle, Donna, and Carr, Eileen. *Strategic Teaching and Learning: Cognitive Instruction in the Content Areas.* Alexandria, Va.: Association for Supervision and Curriculum Development, 1988.

Joyce, Bruce. *Selecting Learning Experiences: Linking Theory and Practice.* Alexandria, Va.: Association for Supervision and Curriculum Development, 1978.

——— and Showers, Beverly. "The Coaching of Teaching." *Educational Leadership* 40, no. 1 (October 1982): 4–10.

——— and Weil, Marsha. *Models of Teaching,* 2nd ed. Englewood Cliffs, N.J.: Prentice-Hall, 1980.

——— and Weil, Marsha with Calhoun, Emily. *Models of Teaching,* 7th ed. Boston: Allyn and Bacon, 2004.

Keefe, James W. and Jenkins, John M. *Personalized Instruction.* Bloomington, Ind.: Phi Delta Kappa Educational Foundation, 2005.

Kellough, Richard D. and Kellough, Noreen G. *Middle School Teaching: A Guide to Methods and Resources,* 3rd ed. Upper Saddle River, N.J.: Merrill, 1999.

———. *Secondary School Teaching: A Guide to Methods and Resources: Planning for Competence.* Upper Saddle River, N.J.: Merrill, 1999.

——— and Roberts, Patricia L. *A Resource Guide for Elementary School Teaching: Planning for Competence,* 5th ed. Upper Saddle River, N.J.: Merrill/Prentice Hall, 2002.

Knight, George P. and Bohlmeyer, Elaine Morton. "Cooperative Learning and Achievement Methods for Assessing Causal Mechanisms." In Shlomo Sharan, ed. *Cooperative Learning: Theory and Research.* New York: Praeger, 1990, pp. 1–7.

"Learning Styles and the Brain." *Educational Leadership* 48, no. 2 (October 1990): 3–80.

Lehr, Fran. "Cooperative Learning." *Journal of Reading* 27, no. 5 (February 1984): 458.

Levine, David, Lowe, Robert, Peterson, Bob, and Tenorio, Rita, eds. *Rethinking Schools: An Agenda for Change.* New York: The New Press, 1995.

Lezotte, Lawrence W. and Bancroft, Beverly A. "Growing Use of the Effective Schools Model for School Improvement." *Educational Leadership* 42, no. 6 (March 1985): 23–27.

McIntyre, D. John and O'Hair, Mary John. *The Reflective Roles of the Classroom Teacher.* Belmont, Calif.: Wadsworth, 1996.

McNeil, John and Wiles, Jon. *Essentials of Teaching Decisions, Plans, Methods.* New York: Macmillan, 1989.

Marzano, Robert J. *A Different Kind of Classroom: Teaching with Dimensions of Learning.* Alexandria, Va.: Association for Supervision and Curriculum Development, 1994.

———. *What Works in Schools: Translating Research into Action.* Alexandria, Va.: Association for Supervision and Curriculum Development, 2003.

———, Pickering, Debra J., and Pollock, Jane E. *Classroom Instruction That Works: Research-Based Strategies for Increasing Student Achievement.* Alexandria, Va.: Association for Supervision and Curriculum Development, 2001.

Medley, Donald M. "The Effectiveness of Teachers." In Penelope L. Peterson and Herbert J. Walberg, eds. *Research on Teaching: Concepts, Findings, and Implications.* Berkeley, Calif.: McCutchan, 1979, pp. 1–27.

Moore, Kenneth D. *Classroom Teaching Skills,* 6th ed. Boston: McGraw-Hill, 2007.

Oakes, Jeannie. *Keeping Track: How Schools Structure Inequality.* New Haven, Conn.: Yale University Press, 1985.

Oliva, Peter F. *The Secondary School Today,* 2nd ed. New York: Harper & Row, 1972.

Orlich, Donald C. et al. *Teaching Strategies: A Guide to Better Instruction.* Lexington, Mass.: D. C. Heath, 1980.

Ornstein, Allan C., Pajak, Edward F., and Ornstein, Stacey B., eds. *Contemporary Issues in Curriculum,* 4th ed. Boston: Allyn and Bacon, 2007.

Orwig, Gary W. and Baumbach, Donna J. *What Every Educator Needs to Know About the New Technologies: Interactive Video 1.* Orlando, Fla.: UCF/DOE Instructional Computing Resource Center, University of Central Florida, 1989.

———. *What Every Educator Needs to Know About the New Technologies: Interactive Video 2.* Orlando, Fla.: UCF/DOE Instructional Computing Center, University of Central Florida, 1989.

Pawlas, George E. and Oliva, Peter F. *Supervision for Today's Schools,* 8th ed. Hoboken, N.J.: John Wiley & Sons, 2008.

"Personalized Learning." *Educational Leadership* 57, no. 1 (September 1999): 6–64.

Peter, Laurence J. *Competencies for Teaching: Classroom Instruction.* Belmont, Calif.: Wadsworth, 1975.

Peterson, Penelope L. and Walberg, Herbert J., eds. *Research on Teaching: Concepts, Findings, and Implications.* Berkeley, Calif.: McCutchan, 1979.

Rosenshine, Barak V. "Content, Time, and Direct Instruction." In Penelope L. Peterson and Herbert J. Walberg, eds. *Research on Teaching: Concepts, Findings, and Implications,* Berkeley, Calif.: McCutchan, 1979, pp. 28–56.

Sharan, Shlomo. "Cooperative Learning in Small Groups: Recent Methods and Effects on Achievement, Attitudes, and Ethnic Relations." *Review of Educational Research* 50, no. 2 (Summer 1980): 241–271.

———, ed. *Cooperative Learning: Theory and Research.* New York: Praeger, 1990.

Simkins, Michael, Cole, Karen, Tavalin, Fern, and Means, Barbara. *Increasing Student Learning Through Multimedia Projects.* Alexandria, Va.: Association for Supervision and Curriculum Development, 2002.

Slavin, Robert E. *Cooperative Learning.* White Plains, N.Y.: Longman, 1983.

———. "Cooperative Learning." *Review of Educational Research* 50, no. 2 (Summer 1980): 315–342.

———. *Cooperative Learning: Student Teams,* 2nd ed. Washington, D.C.: National Education Association, 1987.

———. *Cooperative Learning: Theory, Research, and Practice.* Englewood Cliffs, N.J.: Prentice-Hall, 1990.

———, ed. *School and Classroom Organization.* Hillsdale, N.J.: Lawrence Erlbaum Associates, 1989.

———. *Student Team Learning: An Overview and Practical Guide.* Washington, D.C.: National Education Association, 1988.

———. "Synthesis of Research on Cooperative Learning." *Educational Leadership* 48, no. 5 (February 1991): 71–77.

——— et al., eds. *Learning to Cooperate, Cooperating to Learn*. New York: Plenum, 1985. "Special Feature on Cooperative Learning." *Educational Leadership* 48, no. 5 (February 1991): 71–94.

Sprenger, Marilee. *Learning & Memory: The Brain in Action*. Alexandria, Va.: Association for Supervision and Curriculum Development, 1999.

Springer, Sally P. and Deutsch, Georg. *Left Brain, Right Brain: Perspectives on Neuroscience*, 5th ed. New York: W. H. Freeman, 1998.

Stallings, Jane. "A Study of the Implementation of Madeline Hunter's Model and Its Effects on Students." *Journal of Educational Research* 78, no. 6 (July/August 1985): 325–337.

Stronge, James H. *Qualities of Effective Teachers*. Alexandria, Va.: Association for Supervision and Curriculum Development, 2002.

Sylwester, Robert. *A Celebration of Neurons: Educator's Guide to the Human Brain*. Alexandria, Va.: Association for Supervision and Curriculum Development, 1995.

"Teaching the Information Generation." *Educational Leadership* 58, no. 2 (October 2000), 8–59.

Thelen, Herbert A. *Classroom Grouping for Teachability*. New York: John Wiley & Sons, 1967.

Tomlinson, Carol Ann. *The Differentiated Classroom: Responding to the Needs of All Learners*. Alexandria, Va.: Association for Supervision and Curriculum Development, 1999.

——— and Eidson, Caroline Cunningham. *Differentiation in Practice: A Resource Guide for Differentiating Curriculum, Grades K–5*. Alexandria, Va.: Association for Supervision and Curriculum Development, 2003.

——— and Eidson, Caroline Cunningham. *Differentiation in Practice: A Resource Guide for Differentiating Curriculum, Grades 5–9*. Alexandria, Va.: Association for Supervision and Curriculum Development, 2003.

——— and McTighe, Jay. *Integrating Differentiated Instruction and Understanding by Design: Connecting Content and Kids*. Alexandria, Va.: Association for Supervision and Curriculum Development, 2006.

——— and Strickland, Cindy A. *Differentiation in Practice: A Resource Guide for Differentiating Curriculum, Grades 9–12*. Alexandria, Va.: Association for Supervision and Curriculum Development, 2005.

Turner, Richard L. "The Value of Variety in Teaching Styles." *Educational Leadership* 36, no. 4 (January 1979): 257–258.

Vermetter, Paul J. *Making Cooperative Learning Work: Student Teams in K–12 Classrooms*. Upper Saddle River, N.J.: Merrill/Prentice Hall, 1998.

Walberg, Herbert J. "Synthesis of Research on Teaching." In Merlin C. Wittrock, ed. *Handbook of Research on Teaching*, 3rd ed. New York: Macmillan, pp. 214–229.

Weil, Marsha and Joyce, Bruce. *Information Processing Models of Teaching: Expanding Your Teaching Repertoire*. Englewood Cliffs, N.J.: Prentice-Hall, 1978.

———. *Social Models of Teaching: Expanding Your Teaching Repertoire*. Englewood Cliffs, N.J.: Prentice-Hall, 1978.

——— and Kluwin, Bridget. *Personal Models of Teaching: Expanding Your Teaching Repertoire*. Englewood Cliffs, N.J.: Prentice-Hall, 1978.

Wiggins, Grant and McTighe, Jay. *Understanding by Design*, expanded 2nd ed. Alexandria, Va.: Association for Supervision and Curriculum Development, 2005.

Willis, Scott. "Cooperative Learning Fallout?" *ASCD Update* 32, no. 8 (October 1990): 6, 8.

Wittrock, Merlin C., ed. *Handbook of Research on Teaching*, 3rd ed. New York: Macmillan, 1986.

Wolfe, Patricia. *Brain Matters: Translating Research into Classroom Practice*. Alexandria, Va.: Association for Supervision and Curriculum Development, 2001.

Evaluating Instruction

AFTER STUDYING THIS CHAPTER YOU SHOULD BE ABLE TO:

1. Define preassessment, formative evaluation, and summative evaluation, and describe the purposes of each.

2. Explain the differences between norm-referenced and criterion-referenced measurement and state the purposes for which each is intended.

3. Design test/evaluation questions in the major categories of each of the three domains of learning.

4. Define and give examples of performance-based assessment.

5. Contrast traditional assessment with performance-based assessment.

ASSESSING INSTRUCTION

Assessing Student Achievement

She holds her head in her hands, eyes transfixed on the top of the desk. She looks with displeasure at the pile of examinations in front of her, each filled with red marks indicating errors. She has administered the acid test—the examination on the unit on elections: local, state, and federal. Four weeks' work wasted! On a scale of one to one hundred and a passing grade of seventy, only twelve out of thirty-six pupils achieved the passing mark. Why? she asks herself. What went wrong? A stream of reasons floods her brain:

- The students are all blithering idiots who would fail any test no matter how simple.
- They did not pay attention when she was going over the material.
- They do not study; they are more interested in drugs and sex than in the electoral process.

- They are too careless in answering the questions.
- Their parents do not force them to do their homework.

After several moments of indulging in recrimination and blaming the poor results on the students, she begins to take a look at the situation more rationally. What are some hypotheses, she asks herself, for such a high percentage of failures? After some serious reflection, she begins to wonder:

- Were the objectives appropriate? Were they pertinent to the subject matter? Were they within the learning abilities of the pupils? Were they relevant to the students?
- Did the pupils possess the prerequisite competencies before we began the unit in which they did so poorly? How do I know?
- Did I use the right instructional techniques? Did the strategies I chose fit the learning styles of the students?
- Did I make periodic checks along the way? What did they reveal?
- Did I alert them to the type of exam?
- Did the exam questions relate to the objectives? Were they clear?
- Did the pupils have sufficient time to respond to all the questions? Were the classroom conditions suitable for exam taking?
- Were the pupils at fault for their failures? Did I fail the pupils in my role as instructor? Or was there a blending of responsibilities for the low scores?
- Did I really find out what the students did or did not learn?
- And what do I do now? How shall I treat the exam results? What effect should their scores have on the next report card? How will I explain low scores to the principal, to the pupils, to the parents?
- Did I even use the right evaluation technique?

The term "evaluation of instruction" could be expanded to read "evaluation of instruction through the assessment of student achievement." In one sense, evaluation of instruction is evaluation of the effectiveness of the instructor. For example, does the teacher choose the right delivery system? Are the instructional objectives clear? Do test items relate to objectives? Does the teacher present the material clearly? These are types of questions a supervisor asks in evaluating teacher performance. Although this book does not examine the complex and important topic of teacher performance, you will find many helpful references on this topic in the professional literature on supervision.[1] This chapter focuses on the assessment of student performance.

In another sense, evaluation of instruction is evaluation of the curriculum. It reveals the success of one dimension—how well students achieve in areas that are assessed. It may also indicate whether the content has been adequately covered. Evaluation of instruction does not answer curricular concerns such as whether the subject matter was the right choice to begin with, whether its content is relevant, whether it meets student or societal needs, whether the profession and public are satisfied with it, whether it meets the school's philosophy and aims, or whether the content has been selected wisely. These are curricular dimensions that must be evaluated in addition to assessment of student achievement. We will look at the evaluation of curriculum in the next chapter. It is easy to see, however, that evaluation of instruction, evaluation of teacher performance, and evaluation of the curriculum are all intimately interrelated.

Cycle within a Cycle

Instruction in the model for curriculum development followed in this text is a cycle within the curriculum cycle (see Figure 12.1).

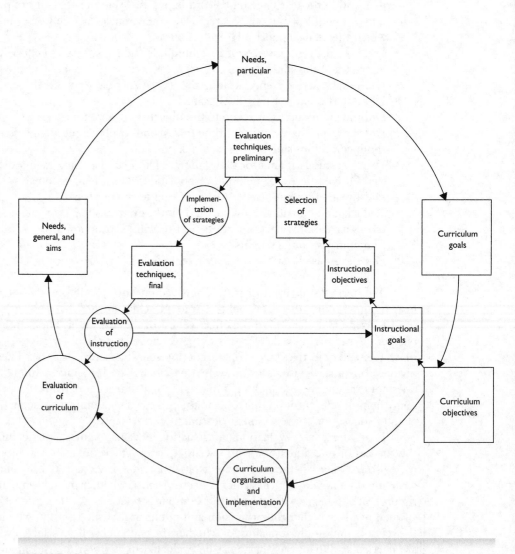

FIGURE 12.1   The Instruction and Curriculum Cycles

Let's once again pull out the instructional chain that makes up the instructional model. It is a submodel of the model for curriculum development presented in Chapter 5.

To keep the model for curriculum development uncluttered, the feedback line for this submodel was depicted simply as proceeding from the terminal component of the instructional chain—the Evaluation of instruction—directly to the beginning of the instructional model—the Specification of instructional goals.

The feedback line from the Evaluation of instruction to Specification of instructional goals demonstrates a cycle and indicates that modification in the system can be made in sequence. However, this figure would be more accurate if it showed the feedback lines to each component because evaluation results may reveal needed modifications in components anywhere in the system. The instructional submodel with all feedback lines is shown in Figure 12.2.

As we have seen, the instructional chain begins with specifying the goals. This cycle is not complete until we learn whether or not the instructional goals and objectives have been achieved. The problem before us now is one of evaluating the instruction that has taken place.

AN ERA OF ASSESSMENT

Evaluation. Assessment. Measurement. Testing. Accountability. These words are heard with great frequency today in both public and professional circles. Specialists in measurement

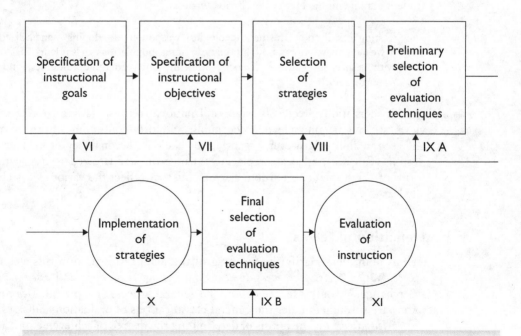

FIGURE 12.2 Instructional Model with All Feedback Lines

and evaluation are in great demand, for we are now in an era of assessment. Although this era began some time ago, its tempo began to increase considerably in the mid-1970s. In the past few years, the movement's emphasis and the sources of its impetus have changed somewhat. We are all familiar with the phenomenon of mass testing that has dominated America ever since Edward L. Thorndike conceptualized the first standardized tests. The standardized SAT and GRE tests are household words in the United States in much the same way the nonstandardized baccalaureate tests are in France.

William H. Whyte, Jr., Martin Gross, and Banesh Hoffman were all pointing to the dangers of mass testing in the late 1950s and early 1960s. Whyte and Gross were particularly concerned about personality testing, and Hoffman was critical of typical standardized multiple-choice tests.[2]

Currently, states, under No Child Left Behind (NCLB) pressure, are busily engaged in so-called "high-stakes testing," that is, examinations that can result in negative consequences in the form of retention in grade and failure to graduate from high school. Condemning test-driven school reform, Monty Neill, executive director of the National Center for Fair and Open Testing, observed, ". . . high-stakes testing . . . undermines good schools and prevents real improvement."[3]

The terms *evaluation, assessment, measurement, testing,* and *accountability* evoke strong feelings; some, pro and some, con. Some educators would banish the use of tests, both standardized and nonstandardized, because they feel the tests set an imposed, predetermined curriculum. Some view tests as measuring insignificant learnings and destructive to students' self-concepts. Faulting efforts like America 2000, which promoted testing of student achievement, Henry A. Giroux wrote:

> Testing has become the new ideological weapon in developing standardized curricula; a weapon that ignores how schools can serve populations of students that differ vastly with respect to cultural diversity, academic and economic resources, and classroom opportunities.[4]

If legislation effected by state and national representatives reflects the public's views, we might conclude that the public supports continuing efforts at assessment and accountability. However, organizations like the National Center for Fair and Open Testing (FairTest), advocate replacing reliance on standardized testing with multiple forms of "high-quality classroom assessments that reflect the various ways children really learn."[5]

Definition of Terms

At this point, let's clarify the meaning of the main terms used in this chapter. These are *evaluation, assessment, measurement,* and *testing. Evaluation* and *assessment* are used interchangeably in this text to denote the general process of appraisal. *Measurement* and *testing* are subsumed under the general classifications of evaluation and assessment.

Measurement is the means of determining the degree of achievement of a particular competency. *Testing* is the use of instruments for measuring achievement. Thus, measurement and testing are ways of gathering evaluation and assessment data. However, we have means other than testing to evaluate student performance. When we speak of evaluating a student's performance of a competency, we may or may not measure that performance. Measurement implies a degree of precision and observable behavior.

In this chapter, we will not fully explore measurement, evaluation, testing techniques, and the by-products of evaluating instruction—marking and reporting.[6] We will seek instead to develop some basic understandings about evaluating instruction, including a limited number of principles of measurement and testing.

STAGES OF PLANNING FOR EVALUATION

You will note, in referring to the proposed model for curriculum development,[7] that component IX on the selection of evaluation techniques is divided into two parts: IX A, Preliminary selection of evaluation techniques, and IX B, Final selection of evaluation techniques. This separation is made in order to convey the understanding that planning of evaluation techniques takes place both before and after instruction. However, this dual separation is an oversimplification. To be more precise, we should show planning for evaluation techniques interspersed at each stage of the Instructional Model. An expanded diagram of instruction showing the many stages of planning for evaluation is presented in Figure 12.3.

Expanded Model of Instruction

What the expanded model indicates is that the selection of evaluation techniques, including test items, is a continuous process. This concept of planning for evaluation differs from the practice of teachers who wait until the end of the instruction, then prepare and administer a test. Evaluation techniques should be jotted down at each of the five stages shown in the expanded model. Three of these stages are prior to instruction; one midinstruction; and one postinstruction. Test items should be recorded when they occur to the teacher while the content is fresh in mind. Continuous accumulation of test items and choice of other evaluation techniques can simplify end-of-instruction evaluation.

Three Phases of Evaluation

The teacher needs to be able to demonstrate skill in three phases of evaluation:

- preassessment
- formative evaluation
- summative evaluation

These terms are technical words to connote evaluation that takes place *before* instruction (preassessment), *during* instruction (formative), and *after* instruction (summative).

Preassessment. *Preassessment* possesses a dual nature. Walter Dick and Lou Carey described two types of tests that precede instruction.[8] These two types are an entry-behaviors

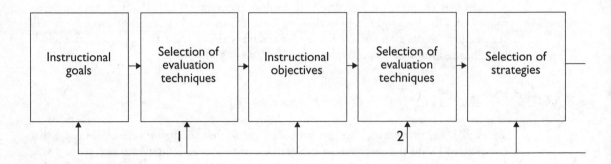

FIGURE 12.3 Stages of Planning for Evaluation

test and a pretest. The *entry-behaviors test* is "a criterion-referenced test designed to measure skills which have been identified as being critical to beginning instruction."[9] This type of preassessment is conducted to determine whether students possess the prerequisite knowledge that will enable them to proceed with the new treatment. The *pretest* is "criterion-referenced to the objectives the designer intends to teach."[10] "Criterion-referenced" tests, discussed later in this chapter, measure students' achievement not by how well they compare with their classmates but by how well they master predetermined instructional objectives.

The entry-behaviors (or entry-skills) test covers preceding (prerequisite) learnings, whereas the pretest covers subject matter to be learned. A pretest alone is not sufficient, for if students do poorly on a pretest, the instructor cannot tell whether the students did poorly because they did not know the material to come (acceptable) or did not have the prerequisite knowledge or skills (not acceptable). Some means of judging possession of prerequisite skills is essential. Lack of prerequisite skills calls for remedial instruction and repetition of instruction before proceeding to new content.

Some teachers use a pretest/posttest technique comparing scores made by pupils on a posttest with scores the pupils made on the pretest. W. James Popham warned, however, of the pitfalls of the pretest/posttest strategy. Citing the *reactive effect* of pretesting which makes it difficult for teachers to determine whether their instruction has been successful, Popham explained:

> The major problem with the traditional pretest/posttest design is that when students take a pretest, they often become sensitized to its content. As a consequence, when students receive instruction (after the pretesting is over), they tend to focus on the things they recall from the pretest.[11]

Formative Evaluation. *Formative evaluation* consists of the formal and informal techniques, including testing, that are used during the period of instruction. Progress tests

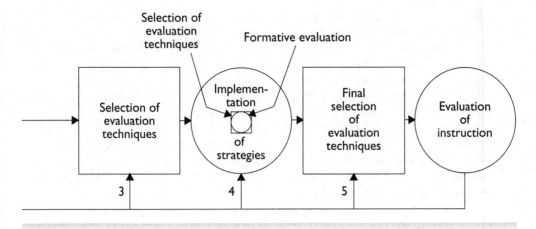

FIGURE 12.3 Continued

are an illustration of formative evaluation. Benjamin S. Bloom, J. Thomas Hastings, and George F. Madaus advised instructors to "break a course or subject into smaller units of learning" and to administer "brief diagnostic progress tests."[12]

Through formative evaluation, teachers may diagnose and take remedial action to help students overcome difficulties before they are confronted with the *terminal (summative) evaluation*. Formative evaluation enables teachers to monitor their instruction so that they may keep it on course.

Summative Evaluation. *Summative evaluation* is the assessment that takes place at the end of a course or unit. A final written examination (*posttest*) is the most frequently used means of summative evaluation of instruction. Its major purpose is to find out whether the students have mastered the preceding instruction.

Summative evaluation reveals whether or not prespecified outcomes of instruction have been achieved. In some cases, summative assessment of outcomes, particularly those in the affective and psychomotor domains, is achieved by the learner's actual demonstration of the outcomes rather than by paper-and-pencil tests, which are designed primarily for cognitive learning. Recall, however, that cognitive learning remains the primary focus of schooling.

The astute teacher uses results of summative evaluation to revise his or her program and methods for subsequent groups.

NORM-REFERENCED MEASUREMENT AND CRITERION-REFERENCED MEASUREMENT

Norm-Referenced Measurement

Two divergent concepts of measurement compete for the attention and loyalty of instructors. *Norm-referenced measurement* is the classic approach to assessment in which a student's performance on a test is compared to the performance of other students who took the test. Following this principle, standardized tests of achievement are administered and norms—standards of performance—are calculated for various groups who took the tests. The scores made by students who subsequently take the tests are compared to those made by the population on whom the test was standardized.

Classroom teachers follow the same principle whenever they measure the achievement of one student against or in relationship to that of other students in class. As a gross example of this approach to measurement, the teacher will administer a test, calculate the scores, rank the score from highest to lowest, find the middle score (which becomes a C grade), then grade all other tests in relationship to that middle grade. In this nonstandardized situation, students are rated in relationship to performance of that particular group on that particular test.

Criterion-Referenced Measurement

Since the norm-referenced approach to measurement is so common and so universally practiced, it might be asked, "What other approach is there?" *Criterion-referenced measurement* is the alternative to norm-referenced measurement. In this approach, the performance of students on a test is compared to criteria that were established in the instructional objectives. A student's success on a criterion-referenced test depends on demonstrated mastery of the objectives and not on his or her performance as related to others in the class.

Because of its long history of usage, the norm-referenced approach is reasonably well understood by teachers, students, and parents. Further, imbued with a sense of competition, many parents invite the kinds of comparisons that are made under a norm-referenced system.

Among the proponents of norm-referenced testing are standardized test makers, those who advocate competitive grading, those who have a need to screen or select persons (for example, college admissions officers), those who draw up honor rolls, admission committees of honorary societies, and those who award scholarships. Norm-referenced testing is necessary when a limited number of places are to be filled from a pool of applicants in excess of the number of places and when only a limited number of awards are to be distributed among a group of aspirants. Among the practitioners of criterion-referenced measurement are the instructional-design specialists and the district, state, and national assessment people. These persons desire to know whether students achieve mastery of specified objectives. If I may use the analogy of the smiling or frowning face, the norm-referenced tester frowns when all students pass an exam because it does not discriminate between high and low achievers. The criterion-referenced tester wears a broad smile when all students pass an exam, since students have mastered the objectives on which they were tested.

Comparison of the Two Types of Measurement

Popham identified "the most fundamental difference" between norm-referenced measurement and criterion-referenced measurement approaches to educational measurement as

. . . the nature of the interpretation that is used to make sense out of students' test performance.

With *norm-referenced* measurement, educators interpret a student's performance in relation to the performance of students who have previously taken the same examination. In contrast, a *criterion-referenced* interpretation is an *absolute* interpretation because it hinges on the extent to which the criterion assessment domain represented by the test is actually possessed by the student.[13]

On the surface, norm-referenced tests look no different from criterion-referenced tests. Popham saw differences in the construction of items for the two types of tests as a matter of "set":

The basic differences between item construction in a norm-referenced framework and item construction in a criterion-referenced framework is a matter of "set" on the part of the item writer. . . . When an individual constructs items for a norm-referenced test, he tries to produce variant scores so that individual performances can be contrasted. . . . He disdains items which are "too easy" or "too hard." He avoids multiple choice items with few alternative responses. He tries to increase the allure of wrong answer options. He does all of this to develop a test which will produce different scores for different people. . . .

The criterion-referenced item designer is guided by a different principle. His chief purpose is to make sure the item accurately reflects the criterion behavior. Difficult or easy, discriminating or indiscriminate, the item has to represent the class of behaviors delimited by the criterion.[14]

James H. McMillan offered a helpful comparison of these two approaches as shown in Table 12.1.

We should take note that the tests developed by the states to assess achievements of both students and teachers are by and large criterion-referenced.

The Instructional Model suggested in this text places the specification of instructional objectives in a central position and, therefore, leans toward a criterion-referenced approach to classroom testing. This point of view, however, does not eliminate the use of standardized tests in the school or the use of norm-referenced teacher-made tests for purposes they can fulfill. It does eliminate the use of a norm-centered approach to classroom testing that permits teachers to adopt the philosophy of the normal curve and to generate scores that result in a normal distribution of grades ranging from A through F on every test. Such a practice violates the philosophy of the normal curve, which holds that traits are distributed at random throughout the general population. No single class is a random sample of the general population. Therefore, to hold As to a mere handful, to condemn some students automatically to Fs, to grant a certain percentage of Bs and Ds, and to assign about two-thirds of a class to the so-called average or C grade is not a defensible practice.

EVALUATION IN THREE DOMAINS

Objectives, as discussed in Chapter 10, have been classified into three domains—the cognitive, the affective, and the psychomotor. Although an objective may possess elements

TABLE 12.1   Characteristics of Norm- and Criterion-Referenced (Standards-Based) Assessment

	Norm-Referenced	**Criterion-Referenced (Standards-Based)**
Interpretation	Score compared to the performances of other students	Score compared to predetermined standards and criteria
Nature of Score	Percentile rank; standard scores; grading curve	Percentage correct; descriptive performance standards
Difficulty of Test Items	Uses average to difficult items to obtain spread of scores; very easy and very difficult items not used	Uses average to easy items to result in a high percentage of correct answers
Use of Scores	To rank order and sort students	To describe the level of performance obtained
Effect on Motivation	Dependent on comparison group; competitive	Challenges students to meet specified learning target
Strenghts	Results in more difficult assessments that challenge students	Matches student performance to clearly defined learning targets; lessens competitiveness
Weaknesses	Grades determined by comparison to other students; some students are always at the bottom	Establishing clearly defined learning targets; setting standards that indicate mastery

Source: From J. H. McMillan, *Classroom Assessment: Principles and Practices for Effective Standards-Based Instruction*, 4th ed., p. 364. Published by Allyn and Bacon, Boston, MA. Copyright © 2007 by Pearson Education. Reprinted by permission of the publisher.

of more than one domain, ordinarily it will exhibit the primary characteristics of one of the three domains. The fact that objectives may not fall neatly into a single domain should not dissuade teachers from assessing pupils' performance in the various domains. Teachers may choose any of the numerous types of tests: actual performance, essay, or one or more objective tests—multiple choice, alternate response, completion, matching, or rearrangement. Table 12.2 shows seven forms of classroom assessment with the level of usefulness for various aspects of grading.[15]

Each domain presents its unique evaluation problems. Let's look at some illustrations of test items for the major categories of each domain.

Psychomotor Domain

Objectives in the psychomotor domain are best evaluated by actual performance of the skill being taught. For example, if we wish students to be able to swim 100 yards without stopping, we require that they hop into the water and show us that they can do it. The students fail, we might say, if they sink to the bottom. We may wish to qualify the per-

TABLE 12.2 Types of Assessment Items and Formats Related to Different Aspects of Grading

Aspects of Grading	Assessments						
	Forced-Choice	Essay	Short Written Response	Oral Reports	Performance Tasks	Teacher Observation	Student Self-Assessment
Informational Topics	M	H	H	H	H	M	H
Process Topics	L	M	L	M	H	H	H
Thinking and Reasoning	M	H	M	H	H	L	H
Communication	L	H	L	H	H	L	H
Nonachievement Factors	L	L	L	L	M	H	H

Key: H = high, M = medium, L = low

Source: Robert J. Marzano, *Transforming Classroom Grading.* Copyright © 2000 by McRel. (Published by Alexandria, Va.: Association for Supervision and Curriculum Development), p. 87. Reprinted by permission of McRel, Aurora, Co.

formance by requiring students to swim 100 yards in *x* number of minutes. To pass the test, students would have to satisfy that criterion.

The teacher has to make some judgmental calls when students are asked to demonstrate perceptual-motor skills. Form and grace might be considered in the 100-yard swim as well as completion or speed of completion. Evaluative judgments are made when students are asked to demonstrate the ability to make a mobile in art class, to build a bookcase in woodshop, to create a blouse in home economics, to drive a golf ball in physical education class, or to administer artificial respiration in the first-aid course.

Beyond the simple dichotomy—performance or nonperformance (pass-fail, satisfactory-unsatisfactory)—of a skill lie such factors as speed, originality, and quality. The teacher may choose to include these criteria as part of the assessment process. When judgmental criteria are to be used, they should be communicated to the students in advance. The teacher will find it helpful to identify as many indicators of the criteria as possible. For example, in the case of the mobile made in art class, indicators of quality might be durability, precision of construction, neatness, and detail.

There are times when teachers settle for a cognitive recounting of how the student would demonstrate a perceptual-motor skill. Ideally, psychomotor skills should be tested by actual performance. Because of lack of time or facilities, however, it is not always possible for every pupil to demonstrate every skill. For example, a group of students in home economics working together may have baked an apple pie. A final examination question might be, "List the steps you would take in making an apple pie." Although not altogether satisfactory from a pedagogical point of view—most of us can talk a better game than we can play—this technique may be used. We suspect, of course, that many a forlorn pie will be turned out by the inexperienced bakers before the skill is perfected.

Test Items of the Psychomotor Domain.   Here are examples of test items for each of the seven major categories of the Simpson taxonomy of the psychomotor domain:

1. *Perception:* Distinguish between an *s* and a *z* sound.
2. *Set:* Demonstrate how to hold a fishing pole.
3. *Guided response:* Make computer-generated mailing labels, following the teacher's explanation.
4. *Mechanism:* Saw a six-foot two-by-four into three pieces of equal size.
5. *Complex overt response:* Perform an auto tune-up.
6. *Adaptation:* Sketch a new arrangement for the furniture of a living room.
7. *Origination:* Paint an original landscape in watercolors.

All of these test items call for actual *performance*. Observe that all seven could equally be instructional objectives. We, therefore, have a perfect match between the objectives and the test items. On the other hand, let's take the following psychomotor objective. Is this objective at the same time a test item?

Objective for high school physical education: *The pupil will demonstrate skill in swimming*. This objective is broad, complex, and without a stipulated degree of mastery. Although it is an objective desired by the physical education instructor, it is difficult to convert into a test item as it currently stands. Establishing a series of subobjectives from which we could derive the test items would help. For example, the student will demonstrate how to

- dive into the pool
- tread water
- float face down
- float face up
- do the breaststroke
- do the crawl
- swim underwater the width of the pool

The instructor might limit appraisal of the pupils' performance in these skills to "satisfactory" or "unsatisfactory."

Cognitive Domain

Achievement in the cognitive domain is ordinarily demonstrated in school by pupil performance on written tests administered to a group—usually, but not always, an entire class. To administer individual written or oral tests on a regular basis would require an excessive amount of time. The teacher should seek to evaluate, when appropriate, student achievement in all six levels of the Bloom taxonomy of the cognitive domain, using both essay and objective test items.

Test Items of the Cognitive Domain. Whereas objective items sample knowledge of content on a broad scale, essay tests sample limited content and provide information about the student's ability to organize his or her thoughts, write coherently, and use English properly. The following test items show several ways objectives in the cognitive domain can be evaluated:

1. Knowledge
   Essay: Explain how Samuel Clemens got the name Mark Twain.
   True-False: A whale is a warm-blooded mammal.
   Completion: The United States, Russia, Great Britain, France, and _____ hold permanent seats on the UN Security Council.

2. Comprehension
   Essay: What is meant when a person says, "Now you've opened Pandora's box"?
   Multiple Choice: A catamaran is a
   a. lynx
   b. boat
   c. fish
   d. tool

3. Application
   Essay: Describe, giving at least three current illustrations, how the law of supply and demand works.
   Multiple Choice: 4 divided by 1/2 =
   a. 2
   b. 4
   c. 6
   d. 8

4. Analysis
   Essay: Analyze the school board's annual budget as to categories of funds, needs of the schools, and sources of funds.
   Multiple Choice: A survey of parents showed ninety percent believe schools are too lax in discipline; five percent too strict; and five percent undecided. We might conclude that these parents
   a. favor looser discipline
   b. favor smaller classes
   c. favor stricter teachers
   d. favor higher taxes
   e. favor all of the above

5. Synthesis
   Essay: Describe the origin and significance of the Thanksgiving Day holiday.
   (Since synthesis and the highest category of the cognitive domain—evaluation—require extensive narration, they are best evaluated through use of essay test items.)

6. Evaluation

Essay: Read the current planks from the platform of either the Democratic or Republican Party and tell whether you believe the planks fulfill current needs in the country and state your reasons. Provide evidence to support your reasons.

The types of test items selected depend on the teacher's purpose and the amount of time that can be devoted to the test. As a general rule, a combination of test items provides variety and thereby stimulates interest. If essay items are used either alone or in conjunction with objective items, sufficient time needs to be provided for students to organize their answers and to respond fully to the essay questions. The passing score should always be communicated to the learners before they take a test.

Cognitive objectives, like those for psychomotor skills, are often suitable test items. For example, if we choose the objective, "The student will be able to list the steps by which a federal bill becomes a law," the teacher has a ready-made test item, "List the steps by which a federal bill becomes a law." However, if the objective is a general competency such as "The student will be able to divide whole numbers by fractions," the teacher must create specific test items that permit students to demonstrate the competency.

Affective Domain

We should refrain from using the terms "testing" and "measurement" in reference to the affective domain. As stated earlier, student achievement in the affective domain is difficult and sometimes impossible to assess. Attitudes, values, and feelings can be deliberately concealed; learners have the right to hide personal feelings and beliefs, if they so choose. Affective learnings may not be visible in the school situation at all.

The achievement of objectives in the affective domain, therefore—though important in our educational system—cannot be measured or observed like objectives in the cognitive and psychomotor domains. For that reason, students should not be graded on an A through F or percentage system for their lack or possession of affective attributes. Except for a few affective objectives like conduct (provided it can be defined and observed), these types of learning should probably not be graded at all, even with different symbols.

We attempt to evaluate affective outcomes when we encourage students to express their feelings, attitudes, and values about the topics discussed in class. We can observe students and may find obvious evidence of some affective learnings. For example, a child who cheats has not mastered the value of honesty. The bully who picks on smaller children has not learned concern for other people. The child who expresses a desire to suppress freedom of speech has not learned what democracy means. The normal child who habitually feels that he or she cannot do the work has developed a low self-concept.

Thus, some affective behaviors are apparent. Teachers can spot them and through group or individual counseling can perhaps bring about a change in behavior. On the other hand, children are at school only six or seven hours a day. They are constantly demonstrating affective behaviors—positive and negative—outside of school, where the teacher will never have occasion to observe them. Are the students helpful at home? Are they law-abiding in the community? Do they protect the environment? Do they respect other people? Who can tell for sure without observing the behavior? Students may profess to behave in certain ways to please the teacher or others and then turn around and behave far differently outside the classroom.

Following the Krathwohl taxonomy of the affective domain, let's look at some affective objectives that contain ways for evaluating their achievement.

1. *Receiving:* The student expresses in class an awareness of friction among ethnic groups in the school.
2. *Responding:* The student volunteers to serve on a human relations committee in the school.
3. *Valuing:* The student expresses a desire to achieve a positive school climate.
4. *Organization:* The student controls his or her temper when driving.
5. *Characterization by value or value complex:* The student expresses and exemplifies in his or her behavior a positive outlook on life.

Assessment Items of the Affective Domain.   The agree-disagree attitude inventory is a frequent means used to determine achievement of affective objectives. These types of questions reveal a basic problem in teaching for affective learning. If the teacher or test maker has preconceived notions of the "correct" responses, he or she is operating in a twilight zone between achievement of affective outcomes and indoctrination. Further, remember that students can and sometimes do respond to attitudinal questions as they believe the teacher or test maker wishes them to respond rather than as they actually feel.

The attainment of affective objectives can be discerned by instruments such as opinionnaires or attitude inventories, by observation of the behavior of students, and by essay questions that ask pupils to state their beliefs, attitudes, and feelings about a given topic. Perhaps, instead of thinking of using instruments that seek to discover students' attitudes and values through an accumulation of items administered test-fashion, we should think more of asking frequent value-laden questions and listening to students' responses. Instead of leveling a continuous barrage of factual questions, teachers can interject questions like: How do you feel about . . . ? What do you believe about . . . ? Would you be interested in . . . ? Are you in agreement with . . . ?

PERFORMANCE-BASED ASSESSMENT

Although we normally equate the word "test" with "examination" and usually think of a test in a summative context at the end of the instruction, we should remember that it is really an attempt to demonstrate mastery of objectives in whatever domain. Students can demonstrate achievement both during and at the end of instruction through means other than typical examinations. For example, synthesis in the cognitive domain can be tested by means of essay items. Competency in synthesizing can also be tested by written reports during the period of instruction or by term papers at the end of instruction. A skilled instructor can tell a good deal about pupils' success just by observing their classroom performance. Individual and group oral reports may be assigned for a variety of purposes, including testing ability to speak, knowledge of the subject, and, in the case of group activities, the ability to work together. Alternative techniques of evaluation other than examinations include student logs, reports, essays, notebooks, simulations, demonstrations, construction activities, self-evaluation, and portfolios.

Employed by many teachers are practices collectively known as performance or performance-based or authentic assessment, basically a personalized approach to demonstration of prespecified outcomes. In discussing performance assessment Popham distinguished between the terms *authentic assessment* (real-life tasks) and *alternative assessment* (alternatives to traditional paper-and-pencil testing).[16]

Some advocates of performance-based assessment would substitute authentic measures for typical teacher-made and standardized tests. Others would supplement traditional testing with alternative techniques. *Horace's School* (via Theodore R. Sizer), for example, would require demonstrated "Exhibitions" of performance to earn a high school diploma.[17]

Alternative Assessment

Describing "most traditional standardized tests" as "poor predictors of how students will perform in other settings" and "unable to provide information about why students score as they do," Linda Darling-Hammond criticized standardized tests for not providing "information about how children tackle different tasks or what abilities they rely on in their problem solving."[18]

Popular on the current scene is the use of *portfolios* as an alternative assessment measure. To create a portfolio students assemble samples of their work that, in essence, show evidence of their accomplishments. Portfolios may contain creative writings, tests, artwork, exercises, reflective essays, notes on topics, and whatever other materials portray achievement. Portfolios containing a generous sampling of students' work can reduce the pressure from testing and marking. Portfolios, like Exhibitions of *Horace's School* and unlike standardized tests, are judged by qualitative rather than quantitative means.

Portfolio assessment in the classroom emulates the practice engaged in by creative artists, indeed, often by teachers. Teacher-training institutions often require student teachers to create a portfolio not only to demonstrate performance but also to carry with them as they seek employment. We should note that portfolios exemplify achievement in all three domains of learning: cognitive, affective, and psychomotor.

On the positive side portfolios tie in directly with content studied in a particular class. They offer a means of informing parents of accomplishments of their children. They provide an opportunity for students to assess their own performance. Further, they can evince a feeling of pride on the part of students whose portfolios are done well.

On the negative side are the disadvantage of the lack of reliability in grading and the time required for teachers to evaluate individual portfolios. Factors such as completeness, number of items, quality, neatness, attractiveness, effort, relevance, individuality, and creativity all enter into evaluation. Like other products that reflect achievement, standards or criteria should be set.

Alternative assessment measures may include practices that could reduce or eliminate homework and change marking practices. William Glasser, for example, joined teachers in noting that students dislike homework and often fail to complete it. Labeling compulsory homework as a coercive technique, Glasser recommended reducing required homework and allowing students to do the work in class assisted by the teacher and by their classmates.[19] Many (perhaps most) teachers and parents emphasize the positive academic benefits of homework. Recommending limitations on the amount and type of homework assigned students, Harris Cooper observed that in the case of the elementary school, research "shows little correlation between homework and test scores."[20]

Qualitative assessment, often called holistic or subjective, has appealed to many instructors in recent years. Teachers who assess students' creative efforts, like essays and portfolios, look at the product in its entirety, gaining impressions of quality, eschewing analytical treatment of grammar, style, spelling, syntax, and sentence structure. Teachers who assess holistically feel that analytical treatment of a student's work discourages further effort on the student's part.[21]

Performance-based principles of assessment may affect not only homework and grading of student work but also the marking system itself. Glasser would not place Cs, Ds, or Fs on a student's permanent transcript, in effect, eliminating symbols of failure. A+, A, and B would attest quality performance. Students who do less than quality work, designated by a temporary C, would be given the opportunity to raise the quality of their work and, therefore, their grades.[22]

Marzano took the position that "a single letter grade or a percentage score is not a good way to report achievement in any subject area, because it simply cannot present the level of detailed feedback necessary for effective learning."[23] Describing an alternative report card with no overall grade, Marzano admitted that "overall letter grades or percentage scores are so ingrained in our society that it is best not to do away with them at this time."[24] Instead, he recommended "an interim step: a report card that includes scores on standards along with overall grades."[25]

The presence of alternative assessment measures is testimony to conflicting conceptions of evaluation, indeed, of schooling. Heated debate over testing, coupled with controversy over setting of standards, centers around the issue of whether to continue to use quantifiable means of student achievement. "Why," Maxine Greene asked, "the preoccupation in a day of whole language and portfolio assessment with quantifiable measures?"[26]

Alternative assessments may supplement and reduce the use of some of the more traditional forms of classroom assessment. They are not likely for the foreseeable future at least to replace completely the use of standardized and teacher-made tests of student achievement.

Teachers should seek to develop competency in the use of a wide range of evaluative techniques. Teachers seeking to improve their classroom assessment skills might well follow the four rules of assessment outlined by Popham:

- Use only a modest number of major classroom tests, but make sure these tests measure learner outcomes of indisputable importance.
- Use diverse types of classroom assessments to clarify the nature of any learning outcome you seek.

- Make students' responses to classroom assessments central to your instructional decision making.
- Regularly assess educationally significant student affect—but only to make inferences about groups of students, not individual students.[27]

Feedback

Evaluation yields data that provide feedback about student achievement and the instructional program. It is not sufficient for evaluative data to be used solely for the purpose of measuring pupil achievement. If pupils do poorly, teachers need to find out what caused the poor showing. Teachers need to ask themselves what they must do so that subsequent groups of students—or even the same group, if repetition of the instruction appears necessary—will not encounter the same difficulties. Teachers must know what needs to be changed, and the evaluation results provide them with this evidence.

Even if pupils do extremely well, teachers should use the data to reexamine the process. The instructional goals and objectives may have been too simple; students may have been capable of achieving higher objectives. If a test was administered, the test itself may not have been valid. The questions may have been too simple, they may not have measured the essential objectives. At the implementation stage, the instructor may have omitted some crucial points and thereby left some objectives unachieved. The results of evaluation provide evidence for making changes in the instructional process.

ASSESSMENT INITIATIVES FROM BEYOND THE CLASSROOM

District Assessments

Up to this point the focus of this chapter has been on assessment of student achievement through techniques (largely testing) designed by the classroom teacher for his or her own pupils. We should not leave the topic of evaluation of instruction without giving some attention to assessment on a broader scale than the individual classroom, assessments that are of special importance to curriculum workers. Since the 1960s, an almost unbelievable amount of assessing student achievement has been going on (and continues) at the district, state, national, and international levels.

Confronted with mounting criticism over both real and perceived deficiencies as evidenced by state, national, and international test scores, many school districts in the 1980s restructured both their curricula and instructional methods. In so doing, they also restructured or introduced assessments of districtwide student achievement. Following principles of curriculum alignment, school districts created for each subject field plans that detailed objectives, activities, and resources. At the end of each marking period, students took tests developed to match the objectives in each field. Districtwide assessment has been one response to public demand for accountability.

State Assessments

In the past two decades the assessment spotlight has focused on the state level. Responding to reports such as *A Nation at Risk*,[28] states set minimum competencies for student achievement at various grade levels and for graduation from high school. Several factors motivated state legislators and departments of education to establish minimum standards of performance on tests. They were disappointed by the results of national and international assessments; they felt dissatisfied with the "products" their schools were turning out; and they heard the public clamor for concentration on subject matter and for accountability of teachers and administrators for their pupils' achievement. Assessment tests, therefore, were deemed necessary for determining whether students had achieved the competencies.

In the early years of the twenty-first century, the nation is caught up in a wave of testing aimed at school reform by holding schools accountable for their students' success in achieving state and national standards.[29] From one end of the continent to the other, we find students undergoing "high-stakes testing."

Exerting pressure on the states to develop and administer state assessments and standards, the No Child Left Behind Act of 2001 has lent impetus to the testing movement. Arizona's Instrument to Measure Standards, the California High School Exit Exam, the Georgia and Wisconsin High School Graduation Tests, the Maryland School Performance Assessment Program, the Massachusetts Comprehensive Assessment System, the North Carolina Competency Tests, South Dakota's Assessment of Content Standards, the Texas Assessment of Knowledge and Skills, and the Washington Assessment of Student Learning are but a few examples of state efforts to assess pupil achievement.

A notable exception to the movement toward single statewide assessments is the Nebraska School-based Teacher-led Assessment Reporting System (STARS) which permits the use of district-designed assessment in place of a single state test. Approved for NCLB in September 2006 by the U.S. Department of Education, Nebraska's assessment system consists of a portfolio of classroom tests, district tests, a state writing exam, and at least one nationally standardized test.[30] Pat Roschewski explained that STARS "is not based on external mandates and compliance but relies instead on the professional judgment of teachers about whether their students are learning."[31]

Assessment is, of course, an expected and necessary part of the curriculum-instructional process. Schools must determine the extent to which pupils have attained the objectives. The intensity of assessment, especially at the state level, was relatively new to the educational scene. The emphasis on assessment saw states mandating the development and administration of criterion-reference tests to measure student achievement. As the movement for educational reform continues, states are taking more seriously than ever their role as authority over the public educational system of their state. Assessment is but one phase in the exercise of that authority. States are heavily involved in developing and administering assessment programs in order to determine whether their standards are being met.

National Assessments

SAT and ACT Scores. American public education has been under repeated attack for the poor performance of students as reflected by scores on standardized tests of achievement. For whatever reasons—some say low standards in schools, social promotions, too much time off-task, poor instruction, and irrelevant content and activities—pupils' scores on certain standardized tests of verbal and quantitative reasoning skills declined between the 1950s and 1980s. The public and the critics of education took special note of the drop in the scores on the then-named Scholastic Aptitude Test (SAT), afterwards called the Scholastic Assessment Test, and the American College Testing Program (ACT). For example, scores on the verbal portion of the SAT dropped between 1952 and 1982[32] and then stabilized for almost a decade.[33] Scores on the mathematics portion showed a decline before 1991. Since that time, scores on both the verbal and math portions rose, with verbal scores, according to Gaston Caperton, President of the College Board, at their highest average score in more than a decade and math scores stabilized at a thirty-year high.[34] In 2003 SAT verbal scores were the highest in sixteen years while math scores were the highest since 1967.[35] The rise in SAT test scores during that time may be attributed in part to improvements in curriculum (advanced math and science) and in instruction, including the use of technology.

In early 2005 the SAT (now known as the SAT Reasoning Test or simply SAT) was lengthened. Analogy questions were dropped and a writing test was included. Math and critical reading scores decreased somewhat in 2006, possibly because of the newness of the examination.[36]

The proportion of high school graduates who took the SAT rose from thirty-four percent in 1972 to forty-eight percent in 2006.[37] Thirty-eight percent of those who took the test in 2006 were minority students.[38]

Though widely used, the SAT is not without criticism. The National Center for Fair and Open Testing (FairTest), for example, cites inaccuracy, bias, and susceptibility to coaching as fundamental flaws.[39]

Some forty percent of all seniors graduating in 2006 took the American College Testing Program (ACT) test at some point in their high school years. Thirty-six percent of these graduates elected to take the optional writing test that was initiated in February 2005.[40]

Between 1970 and 1982, ACT scores suffered a downward trend.[41] ACT scores rose between 1984 and 1996, reversing the downward trend and except for a slight dip in 1989 the average ACT composite score remained relatively stable through 2002,[42] then increased from 2003 to 2004, remained at 2004 level in 2005, and rose again in 2006, the largest increase since 1991.[43]

Composite scores for both males and females rose in 2006 as did the scores of minorities, although those of Hispanics remained stable. Average scores of males on math and science exceeded those of females whereas females achieved higher average scores in English and reading.[44]

National Assessment of Educational Progress (NAEP). Since 1969 when the National Assessment of Educational Progress (NAEP), known as "The Nation's Report

Card," came into existence, it has operated with federal funding. Since 1988 the National Assessment Governing Board (NAGB), now composed of twenty-six members appointed by the U.S. Secretary of Education, sets policies for the NAEP. The Commissioner of Education Statistics, head of the National Center for Education Statistics of the U.S. Department of Education, serves as administrator of the assessment program.[45]

In 1964, with the backing of the Carnegie Corporation, Ralph W. Tyler and the Committee on Assessing the Progress of Education began to develop criterion-referenced tests for nationwide assessment.

Testing, which began in 1969, now encompasses the following areas: the arts (theatre, music, visual arts), civics, geography, U.S. history, mathematics, reading, science, and writing. In 1985–1986 NAEP undertook the first national assessment of third-, seventh-, and eleventh-grade students in their knowledge and skills in using the computer.[46] An NAEP assessment in foreign language is under development. In the fall of 2003 NAEP piloted an assessment of twelfth-grade students in Spanish.[47] NAEP administered its first economics assessment to high school seniors in winter 2006.[48] Twelfth-graders will take the first assessment in world history in 2012.[49]

NAEP tests from 40,000 to 150,000 students, in some 900 to 2,500 schools depending on the number of disciplines to be tested.[50] Reassessments are conducted periodically[51] and a "report card" showing national and state results is issued to the public after each assessment. NAEP reports national scores of students in grades four, eight, and twelve.[52] Data are reported by gender, race/ethnicity, region of the country, parents' highest level of education, type of school, type of location, and eligibility for free/reduced-price school lunch program.[53] In addition to reporting data on a nationwide basis, NAEP conducts and reports state-assessment data for those states participating in the program.

A sampling of findings from some of the NAEP reports includes:

- Both mathematics and reading scores of fourth- and eighth-graders in 2007 showed improvement.[54]
- For the NAEP science assessment conducted in 2005 the percentage of fourth-graders performing at or above the Basic achievement level increased from sixty-three percent in 1996 to sixty-eight percent in 2005; eighth-graders 59 percent in 2005 at or above the Basic level represented no overall improvement; the 54 percent at or above Basic level achieved by twelfth-graders remained below scores in 1996.[55]
- The average reading score for students in grade twelve was lower in 2005 than in 1992 but about the same as in 2002.[56]
- Both fourth-graders and eighth-graders recorded significantly higher performance at or above both the Basic and Proficient levels in mathematics between 1990 and 2005.[57]
- White, black, and Hispanic students in all three grades (grades four, eight, and twelve) tested in U.S. history in 2006 scored higher than in 1994; whites scored higher than in 2001; there was no significant change in test scores of black and Hispanic students from scores made in 2001.[58]
- "Average geography scores for fourth- and eighth-graders were higher in 2001 than in 1994 (the last geography testing), while the performance of twelfth-graders

was not significantly different . . . twenty-one percent of fourth-graders, thirty percent of eighth-graders, and twenty-five percent of twelfth-graders performed at or above the Proficient level."[59]

- Fourth-graders achieved a higher average score in civics in 2006 than in the previous testing in 1998.[60]

- On the first ever national assessment of knowledge of economics, administered in 2006 at grade twelve, 79 percent of students performed at Basic level or higher.[61]

Scores on the NAEP assessments have been inconsistent since NAEP began testing in 1969, sometimes up, sometimes down, sometimes stable. Progress has been made but improvements are still in order. Gaps between scores made by whites and by other racial/ethnic groups have narrowed over the past twenty years but more remains to be done to close the gaps.

From analysis of these national studies, curriculum workers can make comparisons of their local and state assessment data against national and state norms and can make inferences about areas in need of remediation.

When NAEP was under formation, some educators expressed great concern that the data would identify and possibly embarrass specific schools. NAEP has allayed those concerns, reporting data only for groups and not identifying schools. On the other hand, localities and states often release the assessment data that they have gathered on individual schools so that the public and profession can make comparisons among schools within the district and state.

Dissatisfaction with our educational system runs so deep that many educators, business people, parents, and others advocate national assessment, an undertaking that runs counter to historic objections to a national curriculum and to revealing test scores of individuals and schools. The 26th Annual Phi Delta Kappa/Gallup Poll of the public's attitudes toward public schools found strong support for a standardized national curriculum (83 percent) and standardized national examinations that students must pass for promotion and graduation (73 percent).[62] Lest these beliefs appear transitory, 68 percent of the public (72 percent of public school parents) polled in the 34th Phi Delta Kappa/Gallup Poll would require all fifty states to use a single nationally standardized test.[63]

Advocates of national assessment argue that national testing will require schools throughout the nation to examine their instructional techniques and curricula (particularly the basic disciplines) and to take action to correct deficiencies revealed by the tests. Those who oppose national assessment argue that national testing will result in a national, common curriculum that cannot adequately provide for differences that exist among schools and among students in various communities.

NAEP may be fulfilling a hitherto unforeseen role of auditor as a result of the No Child Left Behind Act, which requires states to administer their state-developed tests of math and reading annually in grades three through eight while NAEP assesses fourth- and eighth-graders in these same subjects every two years. Comparison of state scores with those of NAEP with its extensive assessment experience can result in reflecting negatively on educational progress or the quality of state assessment in those states where students do well on the state tests but poorly on NAEP. We will return to the issues of national curriculum and national standards in Chapter 15.

International Assessments

Since the 1960s the United States has participated in international assessments of student achievement. Two of the major American associations conducting surveys have been the International Assessment of Educational Progress (IAEP) and the International Association for the Evaluation of Educational Achievement (IEA).

International Assessment of Educational Progress (IAEP). Benefitting from its experience directing the National Assessment of Educational Progress, the Educational Testing Service—with funding from the U.S. Department of Education and the National Science Foundation—cooperated with representatives of five countries in 1988 to initiate the first International Assessment of Educational Progress (IAEP). IAEP assessed mathematics and science proficiency of thirteen-year-olds in five countries (Ireland, Korea, Spain, the United Kingdom, and the United States) and four Canadian provinces (British Columbia, New Brunswick, Ontario, and Quebec). The U.S. average was below others in both mathematics and science.[64] Scores of U.S. students on international assessments reinforce scores made on national assessments, demonstrating that the achievement of our students remains less than desirable.

In IAEP's second international assessment, conducted in 1991, fourteen countries assessed science and mathematics achievement of nine-year-olds and twenty countries assessed the achievement of thirteen-year-olds. In both science and mathematics Korea and Taiwan rated at the top of the larger countries with the United States coming in third for nine-year-olds and seventh for thirteen-year-olds, a not too dismal picture.[65]

If perceptions of college instructors are valid indicators, a Carnegie Foundation for the Advancement of Teaching survey of some 20,000 college faculty members in thirteen countries plus Hong Kong revealed that only fifteen percent of the American instructors felt that their high school graduates were adequately prepared in mathematics; only twenty percent in writing and speaking. Hong Kong faculty topped the math survey (forty percent satisfied). South Korea faculty headed the writing and speaking list (sixty percent satisfied).[66]

International Association for the Evaluation of Educational Achievement (IEA). Funded by the U.S. Office of Education and the Ford Foundation, the International Association for the Evaluation of Educational Achievement (IEA) has conducted cross-national studies of student achievement in mathematics, science, literature, reading comprehension, foreign languages (English and French), and civic education.[67] Carried out on a grand scale, the study surveyed some 250,000 students and 50,000 teachers in twenty-two countries. In 1964, the First International Mathematics Study alone surveyed more than 130,000 students taught by over 13,000 teachers in more than 5,000 schools in twelve countries.[68] The Second International Mathematics Study, funded by the National

Science Foundation and the U.S. Department of Education in 1981–1982, followed up the First International Mathematics Study by assessing and comparing achievement of 12,000 eighth- and twelfth-grade students enrolled in college-preparatory mathematics classes in some twenty countries.[69]

Third International Mathematics and Science Study (TIMSS).   Conducted by IEA at the TIMSS & PIRLS International Study Group in Boston College's Lynch School of Education and funded by the National Science Foundation and the National Center for Education Statistics of the U.S. Department of Education, the Third International Mathematics and Science Study (TIMSS), the most comprehensive study of its kind, conducted in 1995, tested over a half million students in forty-one countries, including some 33,000 in public and private schools in the United States at the fourth-, eighth-, and twelfth-grade levels. The study compared scores made by students in mathematics and science.[70] To cite a few of the findings of TIMSS in 1995:

> U.S. fourth graders score above the international average in science and are outperformed only by students in Korea. U.S. fourth graders score above the international average in mathematics.[71]
>
> U.S. eighth graders score above the international average in science. U.S. eighth graders score below the international average in mathematics. U.S. eighth graders are out-performed in *both* subjects by Austria, Bulgaria, Czech Republic, Hungary, Japan, Korea, Netherlands, Singapore, and Slovenia.[72]
>
> U.S. twelfth graders scored below the international average and among the lowest of the 21 TIMSS nations in both mathematics and science general knowledge in the final year of secondary school.[73]

Third International Mathematics and Science Study-Repeat (TIMSS-R).   Continu-ing a cycle of international assessments in mathematics and science, TIMSS-R in 1999 tested the achievement of eighth-graders in thirty-eight countries. The 1999 study found:

- In mathematics U.S. eighth-graders outperformed their peers in seventeen nations and performed lower than their peers in fourteen nations.
- In science U.S. eighth-graders outperformed their peers in eighteen nations and performed lower than their peers in fourteen nations.
- The mathematics and science performance of U.S. eighth-graders relative to all countries in this testing was lower in 1999 than in the previous testing in 1995.
- The achievement of U.S. eighth-graders in mathematics and science showed no change between 1995 and 1999.[74]

Third International Mathematics and Science Study (TIMSS 2003).   On its regu-lar four-year cycle the third assessment of the IEA series surveyed in 2003 students in fourth- and eighth-grade mathematics and science in over forty countries.[75] Following are among the findings in mathematics:

- U.S. students showed improvement between 1995 and 2003.

- Singapore students excelled those in all other participating countries in both fourth and eighth grades.
- At fourth grade Hong Kong SAR, Japan, and Taipei student achievement followed that of Singapore.
- Korea, Hong Kong SAR, and Taipei trailed Singapore at the eighth-grade level.[76]

The same Asian countries topped the science achievement list with Singapore ahead of Taipei, Japan, and Hong Kong SAR at the fourth-grade level and again at the eighth-grade level with Taipei, Hong Kong SAR, and Korea next.[77] At the time of writing of this text IEA was readying its next four-year assessment in 2007. Efforts are being undertaken to link NAEP results with TIMSS results in order to make possible comparisons between participating states and countries.[78]

Comparing test results of American students on TIMSS 2003 (fourth- and eighth-graders) and PISA (Programme for International Student Assessment, mostly tenth-graders) with scores of peers in eleven other industrialized countries, the American Institutes for Research concluded that U.S. students, rating eighth or ninth at all three levels, "consistently performed below average." PISA, a project of the Organisation for Economic Cooperation and Development, headquartered in Paris, assesses achievement of 4,500 to 10,000 fifteen-year-olds in each participating country on a three-year cycle. Forty-one countries participated in 2003 and some fifty-eight countries in 2006.[79] The conclusion of the American Institutes for Research regarding the performance of American students reinforces the observation made by *Science Daily* to the effect that, although U.S. students took the TIMSS science assessment score above the international average, their performance is just average when judged against those of students in comparable countries.

Progress in International Reading Literacy Studies (PIRLS). Two studies, one in 1991 and another ten years later in 2001, revealed the following data about the reading literacy skills of U.S. students:

- (1991) U.S. nine-year-olds rated at the top of the list of larger countries on the International Association for the Evaluation of Educational Achievement study during the school year 1991–1992 on reading literacy in thirty-two countries. U.S. fourteen-year-olds came in second, just below France.[80]
- (2001) Assessing fourth-graders in thirty-four participating countries, the Progress in International Reading Literacy Study of 2001 (PIRLS), a follow-up of the 1991 study and the first in a projected five-year cycle, reported U.S. fourth-graders in ninth place, performing significantly above the international average on the combined literacy scale and outperforming their peers in twenty-three of the thirty-four countries. Of the top performers, Sweden, the Netherlands, and England, in that order, headed the list, scoring significantly higher than their U.S. counterparts.[81]
- (2006) American high school students won top Intel Foundation Young Scientist Awards in the Intel Science and Engineering Fairs, administered by Science Service.[82]

- (2007) Since 1999 the U.S. team has come in first in consecutive biennial competitions of the National Geographic World Championship, formerly known as the International Geographic Olympiad, sponsored by the National Geographic Society. The U.S. team took second place in the eighth competition losing out to the Mexican team.[83] In spite of the successes of the U.S. teams in these competitions a 2005–2006 survey conducted by Roper Public Affairs for the National Geographic Society found young American adults lacking in geographic literacy.[84]

Some American students did well on the tests; others, poorly. Interpretation of test scores is always a problem, especially so with transnational studies. Those who interpret the data can fault the philosophy, the process, and the findings. They can single out positive or negative aspects to emphasize. In spite of difficulties in interpreting the data we are, of course, interested in how well American students do on international assessments, particularly in the light of the previously proclaimed *America 2000* goal of having our students rank first in the world in mathematics and science—a goal that NCLB clearly shows still eludes us.

Will our students reach NCLB's performance goal of proficiency level or above in reading/language arts and mathematics by 2013–2014?[85]

Gerald W. Bracey cautioned against comparing results students made on assessments conducted by one organization with those of another organization's assessment results. In particular, he singled out the National Assessment for Educational Progress, whose test results he held to be invalid and not according with test results of other organizations. Giving examples, he stated:

> . . . American 9-year-olds finished second in the world in reading among 27 nations in *How in the World Do Students Read?* [IEA study, 1991] Yet only 32% of fourth-graders were judged proficient or better in the 2000 NAEP reading assessment. Similarly, American fourth-graders were third in the world on the TIMSS science test [1995], but only 13% were judged proficient or better on the 1996 NAEP science assessment.[86]

Bracey later pointed to the gains made by American eighth-graders shown by TIMSS between 1995 and 2003. He noted that where scores of students in thirteen out of twenty-two nations had declined in mathematics only three small countries (Latvia, Lithuania, and Hong Kong) made greater gains than the much larger United States, which serves so many more students. Further, where scores of students in twelve of the nations declined in science, those of American eighth-graders rose.[87]

In his first report on the condition of public education Gerald W. Bracey speaking of "the big lie about public education" commented, "[international] comparisons have generated much heat, but very little light."[88]

International assessments reveal how difficult it is to make comparisons of student achievement across cultures and to account for variations. Differences among nations that may affect scores include curricula, instructional strategies, political and social conditions, length of school year, time allocated to studies in school and at home, proportion of young people in school, number of pupils per teacher, motivation of students, dedication of parents to education, and traditions.[89]

Whether from international or other assessments, test scores do signal strengths and weaknesses. Low test scores demand that curriculum workers determine whether the subject matter tested is essential and, if so, what measures must be taken for students to achieve mastery.

Summary

Although evaluating instruction is generally perceived as an activity taking place at the end of the instructional process, teachers should begin selecting evaluation techniques as soon as they identify their instructional goals. Two types of preassessment are suggested: one to evaluate the pupils' possession of prerequisite knowledge and/or skills to begin study of the new subject matter, the other to determine whether pupils have already mastered the subject matter to be presented.

Evaluation that takes place during the process of instruction is referred to as formative evaluation and is necessary to monitor both pupil progress and the ongoing success of the instructional program. Summative evaluation is evaluation that comes at the end of instruction, as represented in a final examination.

Distinction is made between norm-referenced measurement in which a student's achievement on tests is compared to other students' achievement and criterion-referenced measurement in which a student's achievement is compared to a predetermined criterion of mastery. Norm-referenced tests are used when selection must be made from among a group of persons. Criterion-referenced tests are used to determine whether students achieved the objectives specified in advance.

The major purpose of evaluating instruction is to determine whether or not students accomplished the objectives. Instructors should design means of evaluating pupil performance in the three domains of learning—cognitive, psychomotor, and affective—whenever possible. Tests in the cognitive domain are normally written essay or objective tests administered to an entire class. Discovery of psychomotor outcomes is best carried out by means of actual performance tests of the skill being taught. Although we may speak of measurement and testing in the cognitive and psychomotor domains, we should use the more general term evaluation in reference to the affective domain. Though evaluating affective achievement is difficult and normally imprecise, teachers should engage in this activity. At times, evaluation of affective objectives will not be apparent at all. Nevertheless, affective learning is an important dimension of education, and instructors should strive to determine the best way they can the extent to which students have achieved the desired objectives.

Instructors should keep in mind that there are numerous techniques other than testing for evaluating pupil performance. Good pedagogy calls for a diversity of evaluation techniques, as appropriate.

Feedback is an important feature of the Instructional Model. On the basis of evaluative data, instructors revise the preceding components of the model for subsequent instruction. Evaluation is perceived as a continuous, cyclical process.

A great deal of assessment of student achievement is planned and administered by educators and measurement specialists from outside the individual classroom. District- and state-level assessments are designed and carried out to spot both strengths and deficiencies in the curricula of the schools. National and international assessments lend a broader perspective to student achievement.

Questions for Discussion

1. Are schools overemphasizing testing? Explain.

2. Are schools overemphasizing the use of objective tests? Explain.

3. Should schools use more norm-referenced tests or more criterion-referenced tests?

4. How would you recommend evaluating accomplishment of affective objectives? Give examples.

5. How would you rate American students' performance on international assessments?

Exercises

1. Distinguish between evaluation, measurement, and testing.

2. Select a unit you will teach and prepare a pretest for it.

3. Search the literature on tests and measurement and prepare a set of guidelines for writing (a) essay, (b) multiple-choice, (c) alternate-response, (d) matching, (e) rearrangement, (f) completion items.

4. State the purposes for which essay test items are designed; state the purposes for objective test items.

5. Write a report on the use of test results.

6. Write an essay-test item and an objective-test item for each of the major categories of the cognitive domain.

7. Write a test item for each of the major categories of one of the taxonomies of the psychomotor domain.

8. Design some techniques for evaluating objectives in each of the major categories of the affective domain.

9. Deliver an oral report to the class on whether affective objectives can and should be evaluated.

10. Define formative evaluation and give some examples for a unit you are teaching or will teach.

11. Define summative evaluation and describe how you will conduct the summative evaluation for a unit that you are teaching or will teach.

12. Distinguish between quantitative and qualitative assessment.

13. Describe procedures you would use to evaluate
    a. oral reports
    b. group work
    c. products created by students (give examples)
    d. term papers
    e. dramatic presentations
    f. physical exercises (give examples)
    g. PowerPoint presentations

14. Write a paper on the strengths and limitations of performance-based assessment.

15. Provide examples of authentic assessment in any subject field.

16. Read Theodore R. Sizer's book *Horace's School* (see bibliography), define, and cite examples of "Exhibitions."

17. Give an example of holistic assessment.

18. Debate the issue: Teachers should eliminate homework.

19. Debate the issue: Failing grades should be eliminated from a marking system.

20. Report to the class on changes in SAT and ACT scores in the last ten years.

21. Report on the district-level plan for assessing student achievement in a school district that you know well.

22. Report on results of a recent school district assessment in a particular subject area.

23. Report on your state's or another state's plans for assessing student achievement.

24. Report on results of a recent state assessment in a particular subject area.

25. Choose one of the areas in which the National Assessment of Educational Progress has conducted periodic assessments and describe trends.

26. Prepare an oral or written analysis of one of the following works from the late 1980s (see bibliography):
    a. Paul Gagnon, ed. and the Bradley Commission on History in Schools. *Historical Literacy: The Case for History in American Education.*
    b. Diane Ravitch and Chester E. Finn, Jr., *What Do Our 17-Year-Olds Know? A Report on the First National Assessment of History and Literature.*

27. Prepare a position paper on national assessment, national academic standards, and national curriculum.

28. Describe findings of a recent international study of student achievement involving American students.

29. Prepare a position paper on whether or not NAEP scores should be compared with state assessment scores.

30. Prepare a position paper on whether or not NAEP scores should be compared with international assessment scores.

 ## Action Tool

Guide for Instructional Leaders, Guide 2: An ASCD Action Tool. Grant Wiggins, John L. Brown, and Ken O'Connor, consultants. Binder with materials on steps to improve assessments, grading, and reporting. Alexandria, Va.: Association for Supervision and Curriculum Development, 2003.

 ## Professional Inquiry Kits

Balanced Assessment: Enhancing Learning with Evidence Centered Teaching. Eight activity folders and a CD-ROM. Joseph Ciofalo, ETS, consultant. Alexandria, Va.: Association for Supervision and Curriculum Development, 2005.

Grading and Reporting Student Learning. Robert J. Marzano and Tom Guskey, developers. Eight activity folders and a videotape on grading and reporting purpose and principles to assure quality assessment. Alexandria, Va.: Association for Supervision and Curriculum Development, 2002.

Videos

Using Classroom Assessment to Guide Instruction. Three 30-min. videotapes. Explains how to modify instruction based on classroom assessments. Alexandria, Va.: Association for Supervision and Curriculum Development, 2002.

What Works in Schools. Three 35-min. programs on DVD with Facilitator's Guide. Robert J. Marzano discusses school-level, teacher-level, and student-level factors affecting student achievement. Alexandria, Va.: Association for Supervision and Curriculum Development, 2003.

 ## Websites

American Federation of Teachers: http://www.aft.org

American Institutes for Research: http://ww.air.org

Gerald R. Bracey: http://www.america-tomorrow.com/bracey

College Board: http://www.collegeboard.com

Educational Testing Service: http://www.ets.com

Intel Foundation: http://www.intel.com/education/index.htm

International Association for the Evaluation of Educational Achievement: http://iea.nl

National Assessment of Educational Progress: http://nces.ed.gov/nationsreportcard and http://nationsreportcard.gov

National Center for Education Statistics: http://nces.ed.gov

National Center for Fair and Open Testing: http://www.fairtest.org

National Education Association: http://www.nea.org/index.html

Progress in International Reading Literacy Study: http://www.pirls.org

Science Service: http://www.sciserve.org

Third International Mathematics and Science Study: http://timss.bc.edu/index.html

Endnotes

1. For a discussion of teacher evaluation see George E. Pawlas and Peter F. Oliva, *Supervision for Today's Schools*, 8th ed. (Hoboken, N.J.: John Wiley & Sons, 2008), Chapters 10, 12, and 13.

2. William H. Whyte, Jr., *The Organization Man* (New York: Simon and Schuster, 1956); Martin L. Gross, *The Brain Watchers* (New York: Random House, 1962); Banesh Hoffman, *The Tyranny of Testing* (New York: Crowell-Collier, 1962).

3. Monty Neill, "The Dangers of Testing," *Educational Leadership* 60, no. 5 (February 2003): 45.

4. Henry A. Giroux, *Living Dangerously: Multiculturalism and the Politics of Difference* (New York: Peter Lang, 1993), p. 16.

5. Lisa Guisbond and Monty Neill, "Failing Our Children: No Child Left Behind Undermines Quality and Equity in Education," eds. Forrest W. Parkay, Eric J. Anctil, and Glen Hass, *Curriculum Planning: A Contemporary Approach*, 8th ed. (Boston: Allyn and Bacon, 2006), p. 78.

6. See Cecil R. Reynolds, Robert B. Livingston, and Victor Willson, *Measurement and Assessment in Education* (Boston: Allyn and Bacon, 2006). See also Tom Kubiszyn and Gary Borich, *Educational Measurement and Testing: Classroom Application and Practice*, 7th ed. (Hoboken, N.J.: John Wiley & Sons, 2003).

7. See Figure 5.4 of this textbook.

8. Walter Dick and Lou Carey, *The Systematic Design of Instruction*, 2nd ed. (Glenview, Ill.: Scott, Foresman, 1985), p. 109.

9. Ibid. Reprinted with permission.

10. Ibid.

11. W. James Popham, *The Truth About Testing: An Educator's Call to Action* (Alexandria, Va.: Association for Supervision and Curriculum Development, 2001), p. 129.

12. From *Handbook on Formative and Summative Evaluation of Student Learning*, p. 53, by Benjamin S. Bloom, J. Thomas Hastings, and George F. Madaus. Copyright © 1971 by McGraw-Hill. Reproduced with permission of The McGraw-Hill Companies. See also Benjamin S. Bloom, George F. Madaus, and J. Thomas Hastings, *Evaluation to Improve Learning* (New York: McGraw-Hill, 1981), a revision of Part I of the *Handbook*.

13. W. James Popham, *Classroom Assessment: What Teachers Need to Know*, 3rd ed. (Boston: Allyn and Bacon, 2002), pp. 110–111.

14. W. James Popham, *Evaluating Instruction*, p. 30. Reprinted by permission of Prentice-Hall, Inc., Englewood Cliffs, New Jersey.

15. For examples of various types of assessment items, see Robert J. Marzano, *Transforming Classroom Grading* (Alexandria, Va.: Association for Supervision and Curriculum Development, 2000), pp. 86–105.

16. W. James Popham, *Assessment for Educational Leaders* (Boston: Allyn and Bacon, 2006), p. 234.

17. Theodore R. Sizer, *Horace's School: Redesigning the American High School* (Boston: Houghton Mifflin, 1992).

18. Linda Darling-Hammond, Jacqueline Ancess, and Beverly Falk, *Authentic Assessment in Action: Studies of Schools and Students at Work* (New York: Teachers College Press, 1995), p. 7

19. William Glasser, *The Quality School: Managing Students Without Coercion*, 2nd ed. (New York: HarperPerennial, 1992), pp. 115–117.

20. See American Federation of Teachers website: http://www.aft.org/parents/k5homework, accessed November 26, 2006.

21. For discussion of holistic assessment, see Elizabeth Daly, ed. *Monitoring Children's Language Development: Holistic Assessment in the Classroom* (Portsmouth, N.H.: Heinemann, 1991).

22. Glasser, *Quality School*, pp. 104–111.

23. Marzano, *Transforming Classroom Grading*, p. 106.

24. Ibid., p. 109.

25. Ibid.

26. Maxine Greene, *Releasing the Imagination: Essays on Education, the Arts, and Social Change* (San Francisco: Jossey-Bass, 1995), p. 170.

27. Popham, *The Truth About Testing*, p. 104

28. National Commission on Excellence in Education, David P. Gardner, chairman. *A Nation at Risk: The Imperative for Educational Reform* (Washington, D.C.: U.S. Government Printing Office, 1983).

29. See Chapter 15 for further discussion of state and national standards.

30. See website: http://www.nde.state.ne.us/focusstars/index.htm, accessed November 27, 2006.

31. Pat Roschewski, "Nebraska STARS Line Up," *Phi Delta Kappan* 84, no. 7 (March 2003): p. 517.

32. Ernest L. Boyer, *High School: A Report on Secondary Education in America* (New York: Harper & Row, 1983), pp. 22–26.

33. U.S. Department of Education, National Center for Education Statistics, *The Condition of Education 1996*, NCES 96-304, by Thomas M. Smith (Washington, D.C.:

U.S. Government Printing Office, 1996), p. 86. See also John Cloud, "Should SATs Matter?" *Time* 157, no. 10 (March 12, 2001): 62–76.

34. Press release, College Board, *2001 College Bound Seniors Are the Largest, Most Diverse Group in History: More Than a Third Are Minority, but Gap Remains*, website: http://www.collegeboard.com/sat/cbsenior/yr2001/pdf/CompleteCBSReport.pdf, accessed May 24, 2003.

35. See press reports August 27, 2003.

36. *2001 College Board Senior* and "College Board Announces Scores for New SAT® with Writing Section," August 29, 2006, website: http://www.collegeboard.com/press/releases/150054.html, accessed November 27, 2006.

37. "College Board Announces" and website: http://www.collegeboard.com/prod_downloads/aboutnews_info/cbsenior/yr2006/cbs-2006_release.pdf, accessed November 27, 2006.

38. "College Board Announces."

39. Website: http://www.fairtest.org/univ/newsatfact.htm, accessed November 27, 2006.

40. "2006 ACT National Score Report News Release," August 16, 2006. Website: http://www.act.org/news/releases/2006/ndr.html, accessed November 28, 2006.

41. Boyer, *High School*, pp. 22–26.

42. 2002 ACT National and State Scores, *Five-Year History of College-Bound Students' Scores*, website: http://www.act.org/news/data/02/tsum.html, accessed May 24, 2003.

43. "2006 ACT National Score Report."

44. Ibid.

45. National Center for Education Statistics, U.S. Department of Education, *"What Is NAEP?,"* website: http://nces.ed.gov/nationsreportcard/about, accessed May 25, 2003.

46. See Michael E. Martinez and Nancy A. Mead, *Computer Competence: The First National Assessment* (Princeton, N.J.: National Assessment of Educational Progress, Educational Testing Service, 1988).

47. Website: http://nces.ed.gov/nationsreportcard/foreignlanguages, accessed November 28, 2006.

48. Website: http://nces.ed.gov/nationsreportcard/economics, accessed November 28, 2006.

49. Website: http://nces.ed.gov/nationsreportcard/worldhistory, accessed November 28, 2006.

50. National Center for Education Statistics, website: http://nces.ed.go/nationsreportcard/about/nationalwho.asp, accessed November 28, 2006.

51. For NAEP assessment schedule projected through 2017, see website: http://nces.ed.gov/nationsreportcard/about/assessmentsched.asp, accessed December 6, 2006.

52. Website: http://nces.ed.gov/nationsreportcard/about, accessed November 28, 2005.

53. National Center for Education Statistics, website: http://nces.ed.gov/nationsreportcard/about, accessed November 28, 2006.

54. Websites: http://nationsreportcard.gov/math_2007, http://nationsreportcard.gov/reading_2007, accessed October 2, 2007.

55. Website: http://nces.ed.gov/nationsreportcard/pubs/main2005/2006466.asp, accessed November 28, 2006.

56. Website: http://nationsreportcard.gov/reading_math_grade12_2005/s0201.asp, accessed August 16, 2007.

57. Website: http://nces.ed.gov/nationsreportcard/nrc/reading_math_2005/s0017.asp?printver=, accessed August 16, 2007.

58. J. Lee and A. Weiss, *The Nation's Report Card: U.S. History* (NCES 2007-474), U.S. Department of Education, National Center for Education Statistics (Washington, D.C.: U.S. Government Printing Office). Website: http://nces.ed.gov/nationsreportcard/pubs/main 2006/2007474.asp, accessed May 17, 2007.

59. Andrew R. Weiss, Lutkus, Anthony D., Hildebrant, Barbara S., and Johnson, Matthew S., *The Nation's Report Card: Geography, 2001*, National Center for Education Statistics, June 2002, website: http:nces.ed.gov/nationsreportcard/pubs/main2001/2002484.asp, accessed May 25, 2003.

60. Website: http://nationsreportcard.gov/civics_2006/c0101.asp, accessed August 10, 2007.

61. Website: http://nces.ed.gov/nationsreportcard/pubs/main2006/2007475.asp, accessed August 10, 2007.

62. Stanley M. Elam, Lowell C. Rose, and Alec M. Gallup, "The 26th Annual Phi Delta Kappa/Gallup Poll of the Public's Attitudes Toward the Public Schools," *Phi Delta Kappan* 76, no. 1 (September 1994): 48.

63. Lowell C. Rose and Alec M. Gallup, "The 34th Annual Phi Delta Kappa/Gallup Poll on the Public's Attitudes Toward the Public Schools," *Phi Delta Kappan* 84, no. 1 (September 2002): 45.

64. See Archie E. Lapointe, Nancy A. Mead, and Gary W. Phillips, *A World of Difference: An International Assessment of Mathematics and Science* (Princeton, N.J.: Center for the Assessment of Educational Progress, Educational Testing Service, 1989).

65. Educational Testing Service, International Assessment of Educational Progress, 1992, as reported in National Center for Education Statistics, *The Condition of Education 1994*, 1994, p. 62.

66. Ernest L. Boyer, Philip G. Altbach, and Mary Jean Whitlaw, *The Academic Profession: An International Perspective* (Princeton, N.J.: The Carnegie Foundation for the Advancement of Teaching, 1994), pp. 40–41.

67. See T. Neville Posthlethwaite, "International Educational Surveys," *Contemporary Education* 42, no. 2 (November 1970): 61–68. Joseph Featherstone, "Measuring

What Schools Achieve: Learning and Testing," *The New Republic* 169, no. 2 (December 6, 1973): 19–21. "International Study Brings Coleman Report into Question," *Phi Delta Kappan* 55, no. 5 (January 1974): 358. See also L. C. Comber and John P. Keeves, *Science Education in Nineteen Countries* (New York: John Wiley & Sons, 1973); Alan C. Purves, *Literature Education in Ten Countries* (New York: John Wiley & Sons, 1973); Robert L. Thorndike, *Reading Comprehension Education in Fifteen Countries* (New York: John Wiley & Sons, 1973); International Association for the Evaluation of Educational Achievement, *Science Achievement in Seventeen Countries: A Preliminary Report* (Oxford, England: Pergamon, 1988).

68. See Torsten Husén, ed., *International Study of Achievement in Mathematics*, vols. 1 and 2 (New York: John Wiley & Sons, 1967).

69. See Curtis C. McKnight et al., *The Underachieving Curriculum: Assessing U.S. School Mathematics from an International Perspective* (Champaign, Ill.: Stipes Publishing Company, 1987). See also National Center for Education Statistics, *Second International Mathematics Study: Summary Report for the United States* (Washington, D.C.: National Center for Education Statistics, 1985).

70. U.S. Department of Education, *Attaining Excellence: A TIMSS Resource Kit* (Washington, D.C.: Office of Reform and Dissemination, Office of Educational Research and Improvement, 1997), p. 11. ERIC document 410 122. See also National Center for Education Statistics, *The Condition of Education 1998*, op. cit. and references to three reports *Pursuing Excellence* in bibliography. See also website: http://timss.bc.edu/timss1995.html, accessed November 28, 2006.

71. *Attaining Excellence*, p. 56.

72. Ibid., p. 52.

73. Sayuri Takahira, Patrick Gonzalez, Mary Frase, and Laura Hersh Salganik, *Pursuing Excellence: A Study of U.S. Twelfth-Grade Mathematics and Science Achievement in International Context: Initial Findings from the Third International Mathematics and Science Study* (Washington, D.C.: National Center for Education Statistics, 1997), p. 28. ERIC document 419 717.

74. *Trends in International Mathematics and Science Study: Highlights from the Third International Mathematics and Science Study-Repeat (TIMSS-R)*, National Center for Education Statistics, U.S. Department of Education, website: http://nces.ed.gov/timss/highlights.asp, accessed May 26, 2003. See also website: http://timss.bc.edu/timss1999.html, accessed November 28, 2006. For information on TIMSS testing beyond 1999, see the website of the International Study Center, Boston College, Lynch School of Education: http://timss.bc.edu/index.html, accessed May 26, 2003.

75. I. V. S. Mullis, M. O. Martin, E. J. Gonzalez, and S. J. Chrostowski, "TIMSS 2003 International Mathematics Report," *Findings from IEA's Trends in International Mathematics and Science Study at the Fourth and Eighth Grades, TIMSS 2003* (Chestnut Hill, Mass.: TIMSS & PIRLS International Study Group, Lynch School of Education, Boston College, 2004). Website: http://timss .bc.edu/timss2003/mathD.html. M. O. Martin, I. V. S. Mullis, E. J. Gonzalez, and S. J. Chrostowski, "TIMSS 2003 International Science Report," *Findings from IEA's Trends in International Mathematics and Science Study at Fourth and Eighth Grades, TIMSS 2003* (Boston: Chestnut Hill, Mass.: TIMSS & PIRLS International Study Group, Lynch School of Education, Boston College, 2004). Website: http://timss.bc.edu/timss2003/scienceD.html, accessed November 28, 2006. See also website: http://timss .bc.edu/timss2003.html.

76. Website: http://timss.bc.edu/PDF/t03_download/ T03_M_ExecSum.pdf, accessed November 28, 2006.

77. Website: http://timss.bc.edu/PDF/t03_download/ T03_S_ExecSum.pdf, accessed November 28, 2006.

78. National Center for Education Statistics, "Linking the National Assessment of Education Progress (NAEP) and the Third International Mathematics and Science Study (TIMSS): A Technical Report," website: http:// nces.gov/pubsearch/pubsinfo.asp?pubid=98499, accessed December 1, 2006.

79. American Institutes for Research website: http:// www.air/org/news/documents/Release200511math.htm. See also http://www.pisa.oecd.org/pages/0,2966,en_3225 2351_32235907_1_1_1_1_1,00.html.

80. International Association for the Evaluation of Educational Achievement, Study of Reading Literacy, *How in the World Do Students Read? 1992*, as cited in National Center for Education Statistics, U.S. Department of Education, *The Condition of Education, 1994*, p. 58.

81. National Center for Education Statistics, U.S. Department of Education, website: http://nvces.ed.gov/ pubs2003/2003073.pdf, accessed May 26, 2003.

82. See Intel Foundation website: http://www.intel .com/education/isef/winners.htm, accessed April 9, 2007.

See also Science Service website: http://www.sciserve.org/ isef/results/INYSAW.asp, accessed April 9, 2007.

83. National Geographic Press Release, August 9, 2007, "Mexico Takes Gold at National Geographic World Championship," website: http://press.nationalgeographic .com/pressroom/index.jsp?pageID=pressReleases_detail& siteID=1&cid=1186682141587, accessed August 10, 2007.

84. See *National Geographic News* website: http://news .nationalgeographic.com/news/2006/05/0502_060502_ geographic.html, accessed February 17, 2007.

85. Website: http://www.bisd.us/nclb/Performance% 20Goals.htm, accessed August 20, 2007.

86. Gerald W. Bracey, "The 12th Bracey Report on the Condition of Public Education," *Phi Delta Kappan* 84, no. 2 (October 2002): 143.

87. Gerald W. Bracey, "The 16th Bracey Report on the Condition of Public Education," *Phi Delta Kappan* 88, no. 2 (October 2006): 156.

88. Gerald W. Bracey, "Why Can't We Be Like We Were?" *Phi Delta Kappan* 73, no. 2 (October 1991): 113.

89. For discussion of the "hoaxes and myths that mar the public perception of American education" see Gerald W. Bracey, "The Fourth Bracey Report on the Condition of Public Education," *Phi Delta Kappan* 76, no. 2 (October 1994): 115–127. See also first three Bracey reports, *Phi Delta Kappan*, October 1991, 1992, 1993.

See also Gerald W. Bracey, "Tinkering with TIMSS," *Phi Delta Kappan* 80, no. 1 (September 1998): 36. See also Gerald W. Bracey, *Setting the Record Straight: Responses to Misconceptions About Public Education in the United States* (Alexandria, Va.: Association for Supervision and Curriculum Development, 1997): 75–111.

For differing interpretations of the ranking of American students on international assessments see Lawrence C. Stedman, "The New Mythology About the Status of U.S. Schools," *Educational Leadership* 52, no. 5 (February 1995): 80–85; Gerald W. Bracey, "Stedman's Myths Miss the Mark," *Educational Leadership* 52, no. 6 (March 1995): 75–80; and Lawrence C. Stedman, "Let's Look Again at the Evidence," *Educational Leadership* 52, no. 6 (March 1995): 78–79.

Bibliography

Alexander, Lamar. *The Nation's Report Card: Improving the Assessment of Student Achievement.* Cambridge, Mass.: National Academy of Education, 1987.

Allen, Russell et al. *The Geography Learning of High-School Seniors.* Princeton, N.J.: National Assessment of Educational Progress, Educational Testing Service, 1990.

Applebee, Arthur N., Langer, Judith A., and Mullis, Ina V. S. *Crossroads in American Education: A Summary of Findings.* Princeton, N.J.: National Assessment of Educational Progress, Educational Testing Service, 1989.

———. *Literature and History: The Instructional Experience and Factual Knowledge of High-School Juniors.*

Princeton, N.J.: National Assessment of Educational Progress, Educational Testing Service, 1987.

———. *The Writing Report Card: Writing Achievement in American Schools.* Princeton, N.J.: National Assessment of Educational Progress, Educational Testing Service, 1986.

———. *Writing Trends Across the Decade 1974–1984.* Princeton, N.J.: National Assessment of Educational Progress, Educational Testing Service, 1986.

Applebee, Arthur N., Langer, Judith A., Jenkins, Lynn B., Mullis, Ina V. S., and Foertsch, Mary A. *Learning to Write in Our Nation's Schools: Instruction and Achievement in 1988 at Grades 4, 8, and 12.* Princeton, N.J.: National Assessment of Educational Progress, Educational Testing Service, 1990.

Ausubel, David P. *The Acquisition and Retention of Knowledge: A Cognitive View.* Boston: Kluwer Academic Publishers, 2000.

Beatty, Alexandra S. *NEAP 1994 U.S. History Report Card: Findings from the National Assessment of Educational Progress.* Washington, D.C.: U.S. Department of Education, Office of Educational Research and Improvement, 1996.

Beyer, Barry. *How to Conduct a Formative Evaluation.* Alexandria, Va.: Association for Supervision and Curriculum Development, 1995.

Bloom, Benjamin S., ed. *Taxonomy of Educational Objectives: The Classification of Educational Goals: Handbook I: Cognitive Domain.* White Plains, N.Y.: Longman, 1956.

Bloom, Benjamin S., Hastings, J. Thomas, and Madaus, George F. *Handbook of Formative and Summative Evaluation of Student Learning.* New York: Mc-Graw-Hill, 1971.

———, Madaus, George F., and Hastings, J. Thomas. *Evaluation to Improve Instruction.* New York: Mc-Graw-Hill, 1981.

Boyer, Ernest L. *High School: A Report on Secondary Education in America.* New York: Harper & Row, 1983.

———, Altbach, Philip G., and Whitlaw, Mary Jean. *The Academic Profession: An International Perspective.* Princeton, N.J.: The Carnegie Foundation for the Advancement of Teaching, 1994.

Bracey, Gerald W. "American Students Hold Their Own." *Educational Leadership* 50, no. 5 (February 1993): 66–67.

———. *Setting the Record Straight: Responses to Misconceptions About Public Education.* Alexandria, Va.: Association for Supervision and Curriculum Development, 1997.

———. "Stedman's Myths Miss the Mark." *Educational Leadership* 52, no. 6 (March 1995): 75–80.

———. "TIMSS: The Message and the Myths." *Principal* 77, no. 3 (June 1998): 18–22.

———. "The 12th Bracey Report on the Condition of Public Education." *Phi Delta Kappan* 84, no. 2 (October 2002): 135–150. Bracey Reports on the Condition of Public Education, *Phi Delta Kappan*, annually, usually in October.

———. "The 16th Bracey Report on the Condition of Public Education," *Phi Delta Kappan* 88, no. 2 (October 2006): 151–166.

———. "Why Can't They Be Like We Were?" *Phi Delta Kappan* 73, no. 2 (October 1991): 104–117.

Caine, Renate Nummela and Caine, Geoffrey. *Making Connections: Teaching and the Human Brain.* Alexandria, Va.: Association for Supervision and Curriculum Development, 1991.

Celis, William, 3rd. "International Report Card Shows U.S. Schools Work." *New York Times* (December 9, 1993) Section A, 1, 126.

Comber, L. C. and Keeves, John P. *Science Education in Nineteen Countries.* New York: John Wiley & Sons, 1973.

Daly, Elizabeth, ed. *Monitoring Children's Language Development: Holistic Assessment in the Classroom.* Portsmouth, N.H.: Heinemann, 1991.

Danielson, Charlotte and Abrutyn, Leslye. *An Introduction to Using Portfolios in the Classroom.* Association for Supervision and Curriculum Development, 1997.

Darling-Hammond, Linda, Ancess, Jacqueline, and Falk, Beverly. *Authentic Assessment in Action: Studies of Schools and Students at Work.* New York: Teachers College Press, 1995.

Davis, Robert H., Alexander, Lawrence T., and Yelon, Stephen L. *Learning System Design.* New York: Mc-Graw-Hill, 1974.

Dick, Walter and Carey, Lou. *The Systematic Design of Instruction,* 2nd ed. Glenview, Ill.: Scott, Foresman, 1985.

Donohue, Patricia L., Voelkl, Kristin E., Campbell, Jay R., and Mazzeo, John. *NAEP 1998 Reading Report Card for the Nation.* Washington, D.C.: National Center for Education Statistics, Office of Educational Research and Improvement, 1999.

Dossey, John A. et al. *The Mathematics Report Card: Are We Measuring Up? Trends and Achievement Based on the 1986 National Assessment.* Princeton, N.J.: National Assessment of Educational Progress, Educational Testing Service, 1988.

Elam, Stanley M., Rose, Lowell C., and Gallup, Alec M. "The 23rd Annual Gallup Poll of the Public's Attitudes Toward the Public Schools." *Phi Delta Kappan* 73, no. 1 (September 1991): 41–56.

———. "The 26th Annual Phi Delta Kappa/Gallup Poll of the Public's Attitudes Toward the Public Schools." *Phi Delta Kappan* 76, no. 1 (September 1994): 41–56.

Elley, Warwick B. *How in the World Do Students Read?* IEA Study of Reading Literacy. Hamburg: International Association for the Evaluation of Educational Achievement, 1992.

Featherstone, Joseph. "Measuring What Schools Achieve: Learning and Testing." *The New Republic* 169, no. 2 (November 1970): 19–21.

Frase, Mary. *Pursuing Excellence: A Study of U.S. Fourth-Grade Mathematics and Science Teaching, Learning, Curriculum, and Achievement in International Context: Initial Findings from the Third International Mathematics and Science Study.* Washington, D.C.: U.S. Department of Education, National Center for Education Statistics, 1997.

Gagnon, Paul, ed. and the Bradley Commission on History in Schools. *Historical Literacy: The Case for History in American Education.* New York: Macmillan, 1989.

Gay, L. R. *Educational Evaluation and Measurement: Competencies for Analysis and Application,* 2nd ed. Columbus, Ohio: Charles E. Merrill, 1985.

Giroux, Henry A. *Living Dangerously: Multiculturalism and the Politics of Difference.* New York: Peter Lang, 1993.

Glasser, William. *The Quality School: Managing Students Without Coercion,* 2nd ed. New York: HarperPerennial, 1992.

Goodlad, John I. *A Place Called School: Prospects for the Future.* New York: McGraw-Hill, 1984.

Greene, Maxine. *Releasing the Imagination: Essays on Education, the Arts, and Social Change.* San Francisco: Jossey-Bass, 1995.

Gronlund, Norman E. *How to Construct Achievement Tests,* 4th ed. Englewood Cliffs, N.J.: Prentice-Hall, 1988.

Gross, Martin L. *The Brain Watchers.* New York: Random House, 1962.

Guisbond, Lisa and Neill, Monty. "Failing Our Children: No Child Left Behind Undermines Quality and Equity in Education," eds. Forrest W. Parkay, Eric J. Anctil, and Glen Hass, *Curriculum Planning: A Contemporary Approach,* 8th ed. Boston: Allyn and Bacon, 2006.

Guskey, Thomas R. "What You Assess May *Not* Be What You Get." *Educational Leadership* 51, no. 6 (March 1994): 51–54.

Hammack, David C. et al. *The U.S. History Report Card: The Achievement of Fourth-, Eighth-, and Twelfth-Grade Students in 1988 and Trends from 1986 to 1988 in the Factual Knowledge of High-School Juniors.* Princeton, N.J.: National Assessment of Educational Progress, Educational Testing Service, 1990.

Harrow, Anita J. *A Taxonomy of the Psychomotor Domain: A Guide for Developing Behavioral Objectives.* White Plains, N.Y.: Longman, 1972.

Herman, Joan, Aschbacher, Pamela, and Winters, Lynn. *A Practical Guide to Alternative Assessment.* Alexandria, Va.: Association for Supervision and Curriculum Development, 1992.

Hill, Clifford and Larsen, Eric. *Testing and Assessment in Secondary Education: A Critical Review of Emerging Practice.* ERIC document ED353445, 1992.

Hirsch, E. D., Jr. *The Schools We Need: Why We Don't Have Them.* New York: Doubleday, 1996.

Hoffman, Banesh. *The Tyranny of Testing.* New York: Crowell-Collier, 1962.

Husén, Torsten, ed. *International Study of Achievement in Mathematics,* vols. 1 and 2. New York: John Wiley & Sons, 1967.

International Association for the Evaluation of Educational Achievement. *Science Achievement in Seventeen Countries: A Preliminary Report.* Oxford, England: Pergamon, 1988.

Jaeger, Richard M. "World Class Standards, Choice, and Privatization: Weak Measurement Serving Presumptive Policy," *Phi Delta Kappan* 74, no. 2 (October 1992): 118–128.

Kibler, Robert J., Cegala, Donald J., Miles, David T., and Barker, Larry L. *Objectives for Instruction and Evaluation.* Boston: Allyn and Bacon, 1974.

Krathwohl, David R., Bloom, Benjamin S., and Masia, Bertram B. *Taxonomy of Educational Objectives: The Classification of Educational Goals: Handbook II: Affective Domain.* White Plains, N.Y.: Longman, 1964.

Kubiszyn, Tom and Borich, Gary. *Educational Measurement and Testing: Classroom Application and Practice,* 7th ed. Hoboken, N.J.: John Wiley & Sons, 2003.

Langer, Judith A., Applebee, Arthur N., Mullis, Ina V. S., and Foertsch, Mary A. *Learning to Read in Our Nation's Schools.* Princeton, N.J.: National Assessment of Educational Progress, Educational Testing Service, 1990.

Lapointe, Archie E., Mead, Nancy A., and Phillips, Gary W. *A World of Differences: An International Assessment of Mathematics and Science.* Princeton, N.J.: Center for the Assessment of Educational Progress, Educational Testing Service, 1989.

Linn, Robert L. and Dunbar, Stephen B. "The Nation's Report Card Goes Home: Good News and Bad About Trends in Achievement." *Phi Delta Kappan* 72, no. 2 (October 1990): 127–133.

McDonald, Joseph, Barton, Eileen, Smith, Sidney, Turner, Dorothy, and Finney, Maria. *Graduation by Exhibition: Assessing Genuine Achievement.* Alexandria, Va.: Association for Supervision and Curriculum Development, 1993.

McKnight, Curtis C. et al. *The Underachieving Curriculum: Assessing U.S. School Mathematics from an International Perspective.* Champaign, Ill.: Stipes Publishing Company, 1987.

McMillan, James H. *Classroom Assessment: Principles and Practices for Effective Instruction*, 3rd ed. Boston: Allyn and Bacon, 2004.

Mager, Robert F. *Preparing Instructional Objectives*, 2nd ed. Belmont, Calif.: Fearon, 1975.

Marchesani, Robert J. *Using Portfolios for More Authentic Assessment of Writing Ability.* ERIC document ED347555, 1992.

Martin, Michael O., Beaton, Albert E., Gonzalez, Eugenio J., Kelly, Dana L., and Smith, Teresa A. *Mathematics and Science Achievement in IEA's Third International Mathematics and Science Study (TIMSS).* Chestnut Hill, Mass.: Center for the Study of Testing, Evaluating, and Educational Policy, School of Education, Boston College, 1998.

———, M. O., Mullis, I. V. S., Gonzalez, E. J., and Chrostowski, S. J. "Findings from IEA's Trends in International Mathematics and Science at the Fourth and Eighth Grades." *TIMSS 2003 International Science Report.* Chestnut Hill, Mass.: TIMSS and PIRLS International Study Center, Lynch School of Education, Boston College, 2004.

Martinez, Michael E. and Mead, Nancy A. *Computer Competence: The First National Assessment.* Princeton, N.J.: National Assessment of Educational Progress, Educational Testing Service, 1988.

Marzano, Robert J. *Transforming Classroom Grading.* Alexandria, Va.: Association for Supervision and Curriculum Development. 2000.

———. *What Works in Schools: Translating Research into Action.* Alexandria, Va.: Association for Supervision and Curriculum Development, 2003.

———, Pickering, Debra, and McTighe, Jay. *Assessing Student Outcomes: Performance Assessment Using the Dimension of Learning Model.* Alexandria, Va.: Association for Supervision and Curriculum Development, 1993.

———, Pickering, Debra, and Pollock, Jane E. *Classroom Instruction That Works: Research-Based Strategies for Increasing Student Achievement.* Alexandria, Va.: Association for Supervision and Curriculum Development, 2001.

Mullis, I. V. S., Martin, M. O., Gonzalez, E. J., and Chrostowski, S. J. "Findings from IEA's Trends in International Mathematics and Science at the Fourth and Eighth Grades." *TIMSS 2003 International Mathematics Report.* Chestnut Hill, Mass.: TIMSS and PIRLS International Study Center, Lynch School of Education, Boston College, 2004.

National Alliance of Business. *Achieving World Class Standards in Math and Science.* Washington, D.C.: National Alliance of Business, 1997.

National Assessment of Educational Progress. *The 1990 Science Report Card.* Princeton, N.J.: Educational Testing Service, 1992.

———. *Trends in Academic Progress.* Princeton, N.J.: Educational Testing Service, 1992.

National Center for Education Statistics. *The Condition of Education.* Washington, D.C.: U.S. Department of Education, National Center for Education Statistics, annually.

National Commission on Excellence in Education, David P. Gardner, chairman. *A Nation at Risk: The Imperative for Educational Reform.* Washington, D.C.: U.S. Government Printing Office, 1983.

Neill, Monty. "The Dangers of Testing." *Educational Leadership* 60, no. 5 (February 2003): 45.

O'Connell, Pat, Peak, Lois, Dorfman, Cynthis Hern, Azzam, Rima, Chacon, Ruth, and colleagues. *Introduction to TIMSS: The Third International Mathematics and Science Study.* Washington, D.C.: U.S. Department of Education, Office of Educational Research and Improvement, 1997.

Ogle, Laurence T. and Alsalam, Nabeel. *The Condition of Education 1990*, vol. 1. *Elementary and Secondary Education.* Washington, D.C.: U.S. Department of Education, 1990.

Oliva, Peter F. *The Secondary School Today*, 2nd ed. New York: Harper & Row, 1972.

——— and Pawlas, George E. *Supervision for Today's Schools*, 7th ed. New York: John Wiley & Sons, 2004.

Paulson, F. Leon, Paulson, Pearl R., and Meyer, Carol A. "What Makes a Portfolio a Portfolio?" *Educational Leadership* 48, no. 5 (February 1991): 60–63.

Peak, Lois. *Pursuing Excellence: A Study of U.S. Eighth-Grade Mathematics and Science Teaching, Learning, Curriculum, and Achievement in International Context: Initial Findings from the Third International Mathematics and Science Study.* Washington, D.C.: U.S. Department of Education, National Center for Education Statistics, 1996.

Persky, Hilary R., Rees, Clyde M., O'Sullivan, Christine Y., Lazer, Stephen, Moore, Jerry, and Shrakami, Sharif. *NAEP 1994 U.S. Geography Report Card: Findings from the National Assessment of Educational Progress.* Washington, D.C.: U.S. Department of

Education, Office of Educational Research and Improvement, 1996.

————, Sandene, Brent A., and Askew, Janice M. *The NAEP 1997 Arts Report Card: Eighth-Grade Findings from the National Assessment of Educational Progress.* Washington, D.C.: National Center for Education Statistics, Office of Educational Research and Improvement, 1998.

Plisko, Valena White and Stern, Joyce D. *The Condition of Education 1985.* Washington, D.C.: U.S. Department of Education, National Center for Education Statistics, 1985.

Popham, W. James. *Assessment for Educational Leaders.* Boston: Allyn and Bacon, 2006.

————. *Classroom Assessment: What Teachers Need to Know,* 3rd ed. Boston: Allyn and Bacon, 2002.

————. *Evaluating Instruction.* Englewood Cliffs, N.J.: Prentice-Hall, 1973.

————. *The Truth About Testing: An Educator's Call to Action.* Alexandria, Va.: Association for Supervision and Curriculum Development, 2001.

Posthlethwaite, T. Neville. "International Educational Surveys." *Contemporary Education* 42, no. 2 (November 1970): 61–68.

Pratt, Chastity. "U.S. Math Team: Perfect: Md. Student, 5 Others Ace World Competition." *The Washington Post* (July 20, 1994), Section A, 1,9.

Purves, Alan C. *Literature Education in Ten Countries.* New York: John Wiley & Sons, 1973.

Ravitch, Diane. *National Standards in American Education: A Citizen's Guide.* Washington, D.C.: The Brookings Institution, 1995.

———— and Finn, Chester E., Jr. *What Do Our 17-Year-Olds Know? A Report on the First National Assessment of History and Literature.* New York: Harper & Row, 1987.

Reynolds, Cecil R., Livingston, Robert B., and Willson, Victor. *Measurement and Assessment in Education.* Boston: Allyn and Bacon, 2006.

Roschewski, Pat. "Nebraska STARS Line Up." *Phi Delta Kappan* 84, no. 7 (March 2003): 517–520.

Rose, Lowell C. and Gallup, Alec M. "The 34th Annual Phi Delta Kappa/Gallup Poll on the Public's Attitudes Toward the Public Schools." *Phi Delta Kappan* 84, no. 1 (September 2002): 45. Phi Delta Kappa/Gallup Polls on the Public's Attitudes Toward the Public Schools, annually, usually September.

Rotberg, Iris C. *Balancing Change and Tradition in Global Education.* Lanham, Md: Scarecrow Press, 2005.

Simpson, Elizabeth Jane. "The Classification of Educational Objectives in the Psychomotor Domain." In *The Psychomotor Domain,* vol. 3, 43–56. Washington, D.C.: Gryphon House, 1972.

Sizer, Theodore R. *Horace's School: Redesigning the American High School.* Boston: Houghton Mifflin, 1992.

Smith, Thomas M. *The Condition of Education 1996.* Washington, D.C.: U.S. Department of Education, National Center for Education Statistics, 1996.

Smythe, Mary-Jeanette, Kibler, Robert J., and Hutchings, Patricia W. "A Comparison of Norm-Referenced and Criterion-Referenced Measurement with Implications for Communication Instruction." *The Speech Teacher* 22, no. 1 (January 1973): 1–17.

Stedman, Lawrence C. "Let's Look Again at the Evidence." *Educational Leadership* 52, no. 6 (March 1995): 78–79.

————. "The New Mythology About the Status of U.S. Schools." *Educational Leadership* 52, no. 5 (February 1995): 80–85.

Strenio, Andrew, Jr. *The Testing Trap.* New York: Rawson, Wade, 1981.

Takahira, Sayuri, Gonzalez, Patrick, Frase, Mary, and Salganik, Laura Hersh. *Pursuing Excellence: A Study of U.S. Twelfth-Grade Mathematics and Study: Initial Findings from the Third International Mathematics and Science Study.* Washington, D.C.: U.S. Department of Education, National Center for Education Statistics, 1998.

Whyte, William H., Jr. *The Organization Man.* New York: Simon and Schuster, 1956.

Wiggins, Grant. "Teaching to the (Authentic) Test." *Educational Leadership* 46, no. 7 (April 1989): 41–47.

Wirt, John, Snyder, Tom, Sable, Jennifer, Choy, Susan P., Bae, Yupin, Stennett, Janis, Gruner, Allison, and Perie, Marianne. *The Condition of Education 1998.* Washington, D.C.: U.S. Department of Education, National Center for Education Statistics, 1998.

13 *Evaluating the Curriculum*

AFTER STUDYING THIS CHAPTER YOU SHOULD BE ABLE TO:

1. Describe several processes for evaluating the curriculum.
2. Explain the major features of at least two models of curriculum evaluation.
3. Describe how one or more models of curriculum evaluation can be used by curriculum planners.
4. Select and apply a model of curriculum evaluation.
5. Describe eight principles of curriculum construction and explain their significance to curriculum planners.

PURPOSES AND PROBLEMS OF CURRICULUM EVALUATION

Years ago in a college foreign language class, the instructor lured his students into a grammatical frame of mind by promising to reveal to them "the secrets of the subjunctive." In this chapter some of the secrets of curriculum evaluation will be disclosed. I'll make this revelation right now. The secrets of evaluation are

- to ask questions
- to ask the *right* questions
- to ask the *right* questions of the *right* people

Depending on the problems, questions might be addressed to teachers, administrators, pupils, laypeople, parents, other school personnel, or experts in various fields, including curriculum.

As is often necessary in pedagogical discourse, we must first clarify terms before we can talk about them. We find numerous articles and textbooks on educational, instructional, and curriculum evaluation. The broadest of these terms—*educational evaluation*—is used in this text to encompass all kinds of evaluations that come under the aegis of the school. It includes evaluation not only of curriculum and instruction but also of the grounds, buildings, administration, supervision, personnel, transportation, and so on.

Instructional evaluation, discussed in the preceding chapter, is an assessment of (1) pupils' achievement, (2) the instructor's performance, and (3) the effectiveness of a particular approach or methodology. *Curriculum evaluation* includes instructional evaluation. Recall that the Instructional Model is a submodel of the comprehensive curriculum development model. Curriculum evaluation also goes well beyond the purposes of instructional evaluation into assessment of the program and related areas. Albert I. Oliver listed five areas of concern that call for evaluation. "The five Ps," as he termed them, are program, provisions, procedures, products, and processes.[1]

The axiom that change is inevitable not only in education but also outside of education was advanced early in this text. As curriculum planners, we wish changes in education to take place for the better. Because the creations of mortals are always less than perfect, we can always seek improvement. Evaluation is the means for determining what needs improvement and for providing a basis for effecting that improvement.

You have already encountered in Chapter 7 one dimension of curriculum evaluation—the needs assessment, a process by which you can identify gaps in the curriculum. In this chapter we are concerned with the evaluation of curricula that are or have been in operation.

Problems in Evaluation

Many concede that one place where we are vulnerable in education is in evaluating the programs we have instituted. Our evaluation is often spotty and frequently inconclusive. We should be able to demonstrate, for example, whether

- Interdisciplinary teamwork results in higher student achievement than the self-contained classroom.
- Integrated curricula result in higher student achievement than discrete disciplines.
- The learning of a second language helps in learning one's native language.
- Nongraded schools are more effective than graded.
- Modern materials to teach reading are better tools than *The McGuffey Reader*.
- The specification of minimal competencies improves student performance.
- One series of biology texts results in greater student achievement in biology than another series.
- An inductive or deductive approach is more effective in teaching grammar.
- Cooperative learning is more effective than either didactic or individualized learning.
- Class size makes a difference in pupil achievement.

- A whole-language approach to teaching language arts is more effective than a phonics approach.
- Student achievement is higher in single-sex classrooms.
- Computer-assisted math courses result in student achievement higher than that in courses taught without computers.
- Achievement of students in virtual schools is as high as achievement of students in traditional schools.

Many of the conclusions reached about the success of educational innovations have been based on very limited evidence. The lack of systematic evaluation may be attributed to a number of causes. Careful evaluation can be very complicated. It requires know-how on the part of the evaluators and, therefore, training in evaluation. Further, it is time and energy consuming and often expensive. We could say that schools generally do not do a thorough job of evaluation and what they do is often not too helpful.

Daniel L. Stufflebeam and others observed that evaluation was ill and suffered from the following symptoms:

1. The avoidance symptom. Because evaluation seems to be a painful process, everyone avoids it unless absolutely necessary. . . .
2. The anxiety symptom. . . . Anxiety stems primarily from the ambiguities of the evaluation process. . . .
3. The immobilization symptom. . . . Schools have not responded to evaluation in any meaningful way. . . .
4. The skepticism symptom. . . . Many persons seem to argue that there is little point in planning for evaluation because "it can't be done anyway." . . .
5. The lack-of-guidelines symptom. . . . Among professional evaluators . . . is the notable lack of meaningful and operational guidelines. . . .
6. The misadvice symptom. Evaluation consultants, many of whom are methodological specialists in educational research, continue to give bad advice to practitioners. . . .
7. The no-significant-difference symptom. . . . Evaluation . . . is so often incapable of uncovering any significant information. . . .
8. The missing-elements symptom. [There] is a lack of certain crucial elements needed if evaluation is to make significant forward strides. The most obvious missing element is the lack of adequate theory. . . .[2]

Revising the Curriculum Model

As in our analysis of evaluating instruction, we will develop some general understandings about curriculum evaluation and will discuss a limited number of evaluation procedures. Let's begin by taking a look at the Curriculum Model shown in Figure 13.1, which is a submodel of the proposed model for curriculum improvement.

The Curriculum Model is conceptualized as consisting of four components—Curriculum goals, Curriculum objectives, Organization and implementation of the cur-

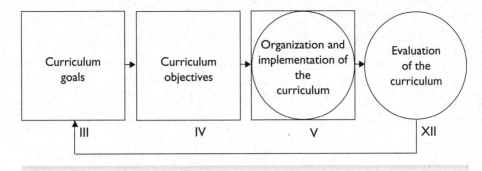

FIGURE 13.1 Curriculum Model with One Feedback Line

riculum, and Evaluation of the curriculum. A feedback line connects the Evaluation component with the Goals component, making the model cyclical in nature. We should refine the Curriculum Model in two ways. First, as with the Instructional Model, we should show the feedback line as affecting more than just the Curriculum goals. Although the impact on Curriculum goals is felt through all subsequent components, evaluative data should feed back to each of the components of the Curriculum Model. A more precise rendering of the feedback concept would show lines from Evaluation of the curriculum not only to Curriculum goals but also to Curriculum objectives and to Organization and implementation of the curriculum, as shown in Figure 13.2.

Second, let's make clear that evaluation of the curriculum is not something done solely at the end of a program's implementation but is an operation that takes place before, during, and at the end of the implementation. Figure 13.3 shows the continuous nature of curriculum evaluation in a manner similar to the way in which the continuous nature of instructional evaluation was shown. Circles within the squares of Figure 13.3 indicate that curriculum evaluation is going on while evaluation procedures are being planned.

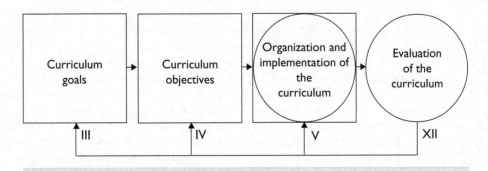

FIGURE 13.2 Curriculum Model with All Feedback Lines

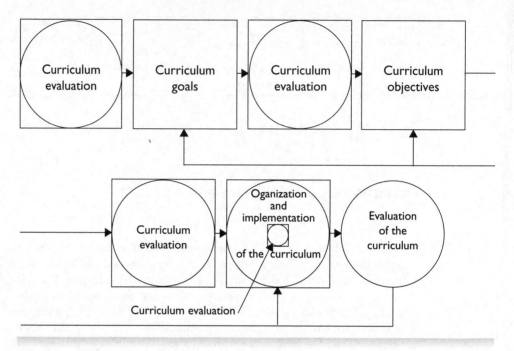

FIGURE 13.3 Continuous Nature of Curriculum Evaluation

DELIMITING EVALUATION

Difference between Instructional and Curriculum Evaluation

Some instructors and curriculum planners believe that assessing the achievement of *instructional* objectives constitutes *curriculum* evaluation. Thus, if students achieve the cognitive, affective, and psychomotor learnings, the curriculum is considered effective. To follow that line of reasoning, we would add all the evaluations of instruction together in a one-plus-one fashion presumably to determine the success of the curriculum. This position makes the mistake of equating curriculum with instruction. If this were the case, separate components for the Evaluation of instruction and Evaluation of the curriculum would not be shown in the Curriculum Development Model (Figure 5.4).

However, instruction and curriculum are not the same. The instructional process may be very effective whereas the curriculum, like the times, may be out of joint. In Aldous Huxley's *Brave New World*, the society runs very efficiently, but few would opt to live there. Instructional evaluation may reveal that pupils are achieving the instructional objectives. On the other hand, unless we evaluate the curriculum—the programs—we may be effectively teaching all the wrong things. If I may exaggerate to make this point, we could do a beautiful job of teaching young people that:

- The earth is flat.
- The earth is the center of the solar system.
- One ethnic group is inherently superior to another.
- All children can be doctors and lawyers.
- White-collar workers always earn more money than blue-collar workers.
- There will always be plenty of cheap energy.
- All scientific advancements are the result of American ingenuity.
- Illnesses are caused by the evil eye.

The primary purpose of curriculum evaluation is, of course, to determine whether the curriculum goals and objectives are being carried out. However, we want to answer other questions as well. We want to know if the goals and objectives are right to begin with. We want to learn whether the curriculum is functioning while in operation. We want to find out if we are using the best materials and following the best methods. We must learn whether the products of our schools are successful in higher education and in jobs, whether they can function in daily life and contribute to society. We must also determine whether our programs are cost-effective—whether we are getting the most for our money.

Difference between Evaluation and Research

Discussion of evaluation inevitably leads us into the area of research. Evaluation is the process of making judgments, research is the process of gathering data to make those judgments. Whenever we gather data to answer problems, we are engaged in research. However, the complexity and quality of research differ from problem to problem. We may engage in research ranging from simple descriptive research to complex experimental research. As an example of the former: How many books does the school media center possess per child? As an example of the latter: Do children with learning disabilities perform more effectively when they are in segregated classes or when they are mainstreamed? Most ambitious of all—and very rare—are longitudinal studies like the Eight-Year Study that compared the success in college of graduates from traditional high schools to that of graduates from experimental high schools.[3]

The field of evaluation often calls for the services of specialists in evaluation and research. Some large school systems are able to employ personnel to direct, conduct, and supervise curriculum evaluation for their school systems. These people bring to the task a degree of expertise not shared by most teachers and curriculum planners. Some school systems, which do not hire their own evaluation personnel, invite in outside consultants to help with particular curriculum problems and research. However, most evaluative studies must be and are conducted by the local curriculum planners and the teachers. The shortage of trained personnel and the costs of employing specialists are prohibitive for many school systems. Even in large systems that employ curriculum evaluators, many curriculum evaluation tasks are performed by teachers and curriculum planners.

EVALUATION MODELS

Models have been developed showing types of evaluation that schools should carry out and the processes they should follow. As in the case of models of instruction and of curriculum development, evaluation models differ in detail and the points which their creators choose to include.

Those who direct curriculum evaluations, whether from inside or outside the school system, must possess a high level of expertise and be well grounded in both curriculum and assessment. They must be familiar with common approaches to evaluation. Indicative of the level of complexity in curriculum evaluation is the number of approaches. Stufflebeam, for example, discussed twenty-two evaluation approaches in his book *Evaluation Models*.[4] John D. McNeil affirmed that "the field of evaluation is full of different views about its purposes and how it is to be carried out."[5]

This chapter is designed to sensitize the reader to the complexities of curriculum or program evaluation, to describe a few selected models of curriculum evaluation, and to direct your attention to other sources of information and models.[6]

For our purposes let's look first at two rather simple approaches to curriculum evaluation that we will label, for want of a better term, *Limited Models*. Then let's turn to two frequently cited, well-known *Comprehensive Models*—that of J. Galen Saylor, William M. Alexander, and Arthur J. Lewis,[7] a rather easily understood model that shows the scope and nature of curriculum evaluation, and the model of the Phi Delta Kappa National Study Committee on Evaluation, a more complex model written in rather technical terms.[8]

Limited Models

Assessment of Curriculum Objectives. Recall that Chapter 8 described curriculum goals and objectives and distinguished them from instructional goals and objectives. Recall also that we defined curriculum objectives as "specific, measurable, programmatic statements of outcomes to be achieved by students as a group in the school or school system."[9]

We ascribed the following characteristics to curriculum objectives, paralleling characteristics of instructional objectives:

- they specify performance or behavior to be demonstrated
- they include a degree of mastery
- they state conditions under which the performance will take place, if not readily understood

Drawing on previously specified nonmeasurable curriculum goals, curriculum objectives pertain to programs, not specific content, and refer to accomplishments of groups of students (all students, students in general, most students, groups of students) rather than the achievement of individual students. Curriculum evaluation assesses programs directly and individual student performance indirectly. Instructional evaluation assesses individual students directly and programs indirectly.

The most fundamental approach to curriculum evaluation—one that must be taken regardless of other supporting approaches—is the assessment of achievement of the specified curriculum objectives. Observation surveys, portfolios, and test results are all means by which to gather evaluative data. Let's take a few examples of curriculum objectives for a given year and mention a corresponding technique for evaluating.

- The number of incidents of conflict among members of diverse ethnic groups will be reduced by fifty percent (statistics).
- All students will demonstrate proficiency in performing without error a selected number of computer skills (samples of work, observation).
- The high school dropout rate will be decreased by ten percent (statistics).
- Pupils will increase their leisure-time reading by ten percent (book reports, school media center circulation figures).
- Eighth-graders will raise their scores on a standardized test of mathematics by ten percentile points (test results).
- An increased twenty percent of both boys and girls will elect participation in interscholastic, intramural, or individualized athletic activities (statistics).
- Ten percent more high school students will enroll in elective music or art courses (statistics).
- All students will demonstrate knowledge of the seriousness and facts of AIDS and what they must do to protect themselves from the disease (class discussions, counseling, portfolios, quizzes).
- Students will evidence responsible citizenship by demonstrating knowledge of our political system (class discussion, portfolios, quizzes).
- Students will describe ethical behavior in a given number of problem situations (class discussions, reflective papers, observation).

Curriculum planners must determine whether the programmatic (i.e., curricular) objectives have been achieved. If the curriculum objectives have been reached, planners would then identify next steps by specifying new curriculum objectives and establishing new priorities. If the curriculum objectives have not been met, planners must decide whether the objectives still merit pursuing and if so, what measures must be taken to achieve them.

The Evaluation of School Improvement Plan of the Goldsboro Elementary School for Math, Science, and Technology in Sanford, Florida, furnishes an example of identification of a school's success in achieving stated curriculum priorities and objectives. Reproduced in Box 13.1 is the school's second of six priorities with data on the achievement or nonachievement of the goal's three objectives as determined by results on the Florida Comprehensive Assessment Test.

Assessment of Guiding Principles of Curriculum Construction and Organization.
Certain principles are inherent in constructing and organizing the curriculum. In one sense these principles are characteristics of curriculum construction and organization. In another sense they are continuing problems for curriculum developers.

Supplementing assessment of the curriculum objectives, curriculum workers should assess the degree to which they implement basic principles of curriculum construction and organization. In this chapter we will describe eight perennial problems of curriculum construction and organization: scope, relevance, balance, integration, sequence, continuity, articulation, and transferability.

An evaluation process cognizant of these problems would provide answers to such questions as:

- Is the scope of the curriculum adequate? Realistic?
- Is the curriculum relevant?
- Is there balance in the curriculum?
- Is curriculum integration desirable?
- Is the curriculum properly sequenced?
- Is there continuity of programs?
- Are curricula well articulated between levels?
- Are learnings transferable?

To answer questions like these curriculum planners must understand the nature of the principles. The assessing of principles of curriculum construction and evaluation not only calls for gathering of considerable data but also for intelligent reflection on the part of the evaluators.

EIGHT CONCEPTS OF CURRICULUM CONSTRUCTION

Although a model for curriculum improvement may show us a process, it does not reveal the whole picture. It does not show us, for example, how we go about choosing from competing content, what we do about conflicting philosophies, how we assure articulation between levels, how we learn to live with change, how dependent we are on effective leadership, what incentives motivate people to try out new ideas, how to go about finding the information we need to make intelligent decisions, and how we release human and material resources to do the job.

We already examined in Chapter 4 several major problems of curriculum development, including effecting change, group dynamics, interpersonal relationships, decision making, curriculum leadership, and communication skills. The eight guiding principles to be discussed are not only perennial problems for curriculum developers but, in essence, are also concepts that lead to the formulation of principles of curriculum development. The creation of a well-functioning sequence, for example, is a continuing problem for the curriculum developer. At the same time, the curriculum planner must understand the concept of sequencing, which is essential to an effective curriculum. Bringing the two elements, curriculum and sequencing, together we formulate the principle: An effective curriculum is one that is properly sequenced. We will, therefore, refer to these eight guiding factors as problems, concepts, or, by inference, principles.

BOX 13.1

Evaluation of School Improvement Plan, 2004–2005 Goldsboro Elementary Magnet School for Math, Science, and Technology State Priority 2: Student Performance

STATE PRIORITY 2: 2 of 3 objectives met:

Objective 2: Increase by 3% (from 69% to 72%) the average percentage of students (all curriculum groups) scoring at or above Level 3 in Reading with a portion of the gain at each grade level.

Objective met: FCAT Reading scores show the following data for all curriculum groups: 79% of all 3rd grade students at or above Level 3; 78% of all 4th grade students at or above Level 3; 71% of all 5th grade students at or above Level 3. This shows an average increase of 7% (from 69% to 76%) with a portion of the gain at each grade level.

Objective 3: Increase by 3% (from 64% to 67%) the average percentage of students (all curriculum groups) scoring at or above Level 3 in Math with a portion of the gain at each grade level.

Objective not met: FCAT Math scores show the following data for all curriculum groups: 72% of

all 3rd grade students at or above Level 3; 55% of all 4th grade students at or above Level 3; 62% of all 5th grade students at or above Level 3. This shows an average decrease of 1% (from 64% to 63%) Gains were made in 3rd and 5th with a decrease at 4th. During the 2004 FCAT testing, 98% of all students met AYP in math. Minority students did not meet this goal. Review of 2005 FCAT testing shows that AYP was not met by minority students in the area of Mathematics.

Objective 4: Establish a baseline of cardio-vascular fitness for 100% of the students enrolled in physical education classes at Goldsboro Elementary Magnet School.

Objective met: Baseline data was established for second through fifth graders through formal pre and post testing. Informal data was gathered on all Kindergarten and first graders.

Source: Goldsboro Elementary Magnet School for Math, Science, and Technology, *Evaluation of School Improvement Plan, 2004–2005*, Sanford, Florida. Website: http://goldsboro.scpc.k12.us/main/2005_2006_SIP.pdf, accessed March 16, 2007. Reprinted by permission.

All eight concepts are interrelated. We shall first examine four concepts closely related to each other: scope, relevance, balance, and integration. The last three are dimensions of scope; all four relate to the choice of goals and objectives. We shall then consider three other closely interrelated concepts: sequence (or sequencing), continuity, and articulation. The last two are dimensions of sequencing. Finally, we shall look at the concept of transferability.

Scope

Scope is usually defined as "the breadth" of the curriculum. The content of any course or grade level—identified as topics, learning experiences, activities, organizing threads or elements,[10] integrative threads,[11] or organizing centers,[12]—constitutes the scope of the curriculum for that course or grade level. The summed content of the several courses or grade levels makes up the scope of the school curriculum. J. Galen Saylor and William M. Alexander in an earlier work defined scope in the following way: "By scope is meant the breadth, variety, and types of educational experiences that are to be provided pupils as they progress through the school program. Scope represents the latitudinal axis for selecting curriculum experiences."[13]

When teachers select the content that will be dealt with during the year, they are making decisions on scope. When curriculum planners at the district or state level set the minimum requirements for graduation from high school, they are responding to the question of scope.

We encounter a problem when we equate the activities or learning experiences with scope. It is true that the sum of all activities or learning experiences reveals the scope of the curriculum. However, the activities or learning experiences are the operational phases of the topics. For example, to present the topic of the Renaissance, we can design many activities or learning experiences to teach that topic, including viewing photographs of works of art of the period, writing biographies of famous artists, reading novels about the period, reading histories of the period, writing reports on the roles of the church and state during this time, and so on.

Organizing Centers or Threads.   John I. Goodlad defined the elements of scope as "the actual focal points for learning through which the school's objectives are to be attained."[14] He wanted to convey the meaning of these elements as one term for the following reason:

> Nowhere in the educational literature is there a term that conveys satisfactorily what is intended in these focal points. The words *activities and learning experiences* are used most frequently but are somewhat misleading. Under the circumstances there is virtue in using the technical term *organizing centers*. Although somewhat awkward, the term does permit the inclusion of such widely divergent focal points for learning as units of work, cultural epochs, historical events, a poem, a film on soil erosion, and a trip to the zoo. The *organizing center* for teaching and learning may be as specific as a book on trees or as general as press censorship in the twentieth century. *Organizing centers determine the essential character of the curriculum.*[15]

In a similar vein, Tyler advised those who are organizing the curriculum to identify the organizing threads or elements—that is, the basic concepts and skills to be taught.[16] Thus, curriculum planners must choose the focal points, the basic concepts and skills, and the knowledge that will be included in the curriculum. A central problem of this horizontal organization that we call scope is the delimitation of the concepts, skills, knowledge, and attitudes to be included.

Explosion of Knowledge.   Teachers must continuously wrestle with the problem of limiting subject matter. Knowledge, spurred on by constantly evolving technology, increases at a fantastic—and often alarming—rate. Have you tried to keep up with the mind-boggling amount of information on the Internet? Have you ridden the learning curves of every new technological invention from DVD recorders to digital cameras to high-definition television to multi-function cell phones and ever-increasingly complex software that requires more and more computer memory?

Humankind has no sooner begun to live more or less comfortably with the computer than it has become involved in cloning, in vitro fertilization, stem-cell research, and splicing genes to create new life forms. Humankind has journeyed through space but now worries about the debris floating around in our solar system. Humankind has harnessed the atom but has not learned to dispose of radioactive waste safely.

Aims Procedure.   Somehow, someway, curriculum workers must select the concepts, skills, and knowledge to be incorporated into the curriculum. Many years ago Hollis L. Caswell and Doak S. Campbell suggested a procedure for determining the scope of the curriculum. Referring to the process as the "aims procedure," they outlined the steps as follows:

> First, a general all-inclusive aim of education is stated. Second, this all-inclusive statement is broken up into a small number of highly generalized statements. Third, the statement of a small number of aims is divided to suit the administrative organization of the school [for the elementary, junior high, or senior high school divisions]. . . . Fourth, the aims of each division are further broken up by stating the objectives to be achieved by each subject. Fifth, the general objectives for the subjects in each division are analyzed into specific objectives for the several grades; that is, statements in as specific terms as possible are made of the part of the subject objectives to be achieved in each grade. The specific objectives for all the subjects in each grade represent the work to be carried forward in the respective grades and indicate the scope of work for the grades.[17]

Caswell and Campbell perceived the specific objectives—not learning experiences, focal points, topics, or organizing threads—as indicating the scope of the curriculum.

Necessary Decisions.   With time so precious and the content burden so great, every organizing center included in the curriculum must be demonstrably superior to those not included. Decisions as to the superiority of the selected elements are reached by group consensus, by expertise, or by both. Curriculum planners must answer questions to which there are no easy answers, like these:

- What do young people need to succeed in our society?
- What are the needs of our locality, state, nation, and world?
- What are the essentials of each discipline?

Decisions on the scope of the curriculum are multiple and relate to the curriculum as a whole, the various disciplines, courses or content within the disciplines, units, and individual lessons.

Curriculum workers must make decisions on scope not only within each of the three domains of learning but also from among the domains. Within the domains they must raise questions such as the following:

- Shall we include a course in geology as well as biology (cognitive)?

- Shall we include development of charity as a value as well as the attitude of cooperation (affective)?
- Shall we teach auto mechanics as well as driver education (psychomotor)?

Curriculum planners and teachers may find the determination of scope within a domain, albeit taxing, easier to resolve than making decisions between domains. Which domain, it must be asked, is most important? This question resurrects philosophical arguments about the nature of knowledge, the nature and needs of learners and of society. The question brings us back to Herbert Spencer's classic query, "What knowledge is of most worth?"[18] Arno Bellack addressed the same question and concluded that schools should enable teachers to develop students' knowledge in the major disciplines.[19]

Others have stressed the domain of knowledge—the cognitive domain. Jerome S. Bruner wrote: "The structure of knowledge—its connectedness and its derivations that make one idea follow another—is the proper emphasis in education";[20] Robert L. Ebel championed cognitive learning;[21] and Philip H. Phenix said: "My thesis, briefly, is that all curriculum content should be drawn from the disciplines, or to put it another way, that only knowledge contained in the disciplines is appropriate to the curriculum."[22]

Arthur W. Combs, Abraham H. Maslow, and others, on the other hand, looked beyond the realm of knowledge to the development of values and the self-concept as central to the educational process.[23] We shall not reopen the great debate between cognitive and affective learning, but we should point out that the issue looms large in determining the scope of the curriculum.

Many teachers and curriculum planners, refusing to rely on their own judgment, leave decisions on scope to others—to curriculum consultants, to writers of curriculum guides, and to the authors and publishers of textbooks. Thus, the scope consists, for example, of many pages of one or more texts, and the determination is made simply by dividing the number of pages by the number of days' schooling or by dividing the number of topics and learning activities in a course of study by the number of days or weeks. Although this simplistic planning is better than none, the curriculum would be far more pertinent if, through a systematic, cooperative process, planners exercised their own combined professional judgment and selected from the entire field only those concepts, skills, and knowledge they deemed appropriate to their school, learners, society, state, region, and country.

On today's scene it seems as if the scope of the curriculum is all laid out for teachers in the form of state or national standards and assessments, that all teachers have to do is assure that the curriculum is aligned with the standards and assessments and then teach to those standards and tests. Though standards-based education does impose limitations on curriculum decision making, it does not eliminate the many daily decisions that teachers must make in planning, organizing, presenting, and evaluating their lessons. We will return to standards-based education in Chapter 15.

Relevance

To assert that the curriculum must be relevant is to champion Mom's blueberry pie. For who can disagree that Mom's blueberry pie is one of the tastiest dishes ever concocted and is in the great American tradition? No one will stand up and argue for an irrelevant curriculum. However, the repeated demand for relevance in the curriculum—unless it is a strawman—must indicate a lack of this essential characteristic in the curriculum.

Varying Interpretations. The difficulty of determining relevance lies in the multitude of interpretations of the word. What is considered relevant education for suburbia may not be for the inner city. What is considered relevant for the Anglo may not be for the Hispanic. What is relevant to the essentialists may not be to the progressivists. Relevance, like beauty, is in the eyes of the beholder. "Like the words 'relation' and 'relating,' " said Harry S. Broudy, " 'relevance' excludes virtually nothing, for everything mentionable is relevant in some sense to everything else that is mentionable."[24]

We should stress the word *considered* in "what is considered relevant." Whether the curriculum is relevant or not may be beside the point. The consumers of curriculum—the constituents and patrons of the school—will form attitudes toward relevance. Curriculum planners must deal first with perceptions of relevance before they can deal with the question of relevance itself. William Glasser attributed students' perceptions of their lessons as "boring" to the fact that they could not relate what they were studying to their lives.[25]

Arguments about relevance swirl around immediate (as opposed to remote) needs and interests of learners. College and work, for examples, are psychologically if not chronologically far into the future for most children. They feel a need for certain knowledge *now*. Like Scarlett O'Hara, they'll worry about remote needs tomorrow.

Disagreements arise over contemporary as opposed to historic content. There is some question as to how many students would enroll in history courses—with the possible exception of American history—if the classes were not required. History teachers constantly have trouble showing young people the value of history, and the more ancient the history, the more difficulty they have.

Conflicts come about between the academic studies and the career-technical, that is, vocational curriculum. Preparation for careers is of extreme importance to young people. They can see the value in skill courses but often do not realize that the academic areas may (1) provide a grounding needed in every curriculum and (2) open new vistas toward other careers. English teachers, for example, must feel an increasing despair that, in spite of their best efforts, the American population—arguably a more or less literate public in one of the most highly developed countries on earth—is not really a reading public. Furthermore, what is read is not of the highest quality. We can attribute the lack of reading in part to difficulties young people experience when learning to read in school. Children acquire early a like or dislike for reading.

We can also attribute the lack of reading to the American frontier mentality that equated reading with effete living and not with the macho men and pioneer women who tamed the West. Finally, television has delivered a significant blow to the printed word. Watching television is easier and more enjoyable to many, though perhaps less imaginative than reading. Will the computer, perhaps, by combining the printed word and technology, lead to increased reading, if not of great literature (who wants to sit at a monitor and read Shakespeare's plays?), then of the plethora of material careering down the information superhighway?

Disagreements over relevance arise from conceptions of what exists in society and what should be. The question becomes: Should curriculum planners educate young people for life as it is or as they think it should be? Should the curriculum develop the desire of citizens to read nonfiction, to subscribe to scholarly journals, to listen to classical music, and to frequent art galleries? Should the curriculum encourage young people to make money, to prefer pop fiction, to enjoy rock music, and to artistically liven up their own homes? Should the curriculum remain neutral and abstain from all such value-laden content, or, conversely, should it expose the learners to both "highbrow" and "lowbrow" content?

Arguments arise over the relative merits of the concrete versus the abstract. Some prefer to concentrate on content that can be experienced with the senses whereas others prefer to concentrate on developing the intellect through high-level generalizations.

An Explanation of Relevance. B. Othanel Smith clearly explained relevance when he wrote:

> The teacher is constantly asked "Why should I learn that?" "What is the use of studying history?" "Why should I be required to take biology?" If the intent of these questions is to ask what use can one make of them in everyday activities, only general answers are possible. We can and do talk about the relevance of subject matter to the decisions and activities that pupils will have to make. We know, among other things, that they must:
> - choose and follow a vocation,
> - exercise the tasks of citizenship,
> - engage in personal relationships,
> - take part in culture-carrying activities . . .
> . . . the question of relevance boils down to the question of what is most assuredly useful.[26]

Smith admitted that it is difficult to show the utility of abstract subject matter:

> Unfortunately, the utility of this form of subject matter is much more difficult to demonstrate. . . . Perhaps the chief reason utility of abstract knowledge cannot be demonstrated to the skeptic is that a great deal of it functions as a second-order utility. A first-order utility is illustrated in the skills that we use in everyday behavior such as handwriting and reading. The second-order utility consists of a learning that shapes behavior, but which is not itself directly observable in behavior.[27]

Uses of Knowledge. Smith classified the uses of knowledge that are not directly observable as associative, interpretive, and applicative.[28] By associative Smith meant the learner's ability to relate knowledge freely, sometimes bringing about solutions to problems. Abstract knowledge helps individuals to interpret their environment, which they cannot do without fundamental knowledge. Abstract subject matter enables learners to apply concepts to solve new problems.

Curriculum workers must, with considerable help from students and others, decide what is meant by relevance and then proceed to make the curriculum as relevant as possible.

Balance

Balance is an unusual curriculum concept that on the surface seems obvious but with some probing becomes somewhat cloudy. Nailing down a precise definition of balance is difficult. Many—perhaps most—educators feel that somehow the curriculum is in a state of imbalance. Years ago Paul M. Halverson made an observation that we could well repeat today, "Curriculum balance will probably always be lacking because institutions of all kinds are slow in adapting to new needs and demands of the culture except when social change is rapid and urgent in its implications for these institutions."[29]

Balance, then, is something that schools may not have but apparently should. How would we know a balanced curriculum if we saw one? This is the key question for us to examine.

The search for a definition is complicated by differing interpretations of the word "balance" as it applies to the curriculum. Halverson spoke of balancing ends and means, as follows: "A balanced curriculum implies structure and order in its scope and sequence (means) leading to the achievement of educational objectives (ends)."[30]

Goodlad would bring the learner-centered curriculum and the subject-centered curriculum into balance, commenting:

> Much recent and current controversy over the curriculum centers on the question of what kind and how much attention to give learners and subject matter, respectively. The prospect of stressing one to the exclusion of the other appears scarcely worthy of consideration. Nonetheless, the interested observer has little difficulty finding school practices emphasizing one component to the impoverishment of the other.[31]

Ronald C. Doll looked at balance from the learner's standpoint and described it as follows:

> A balanced curriculum for a given learner at a given time would completely fit the learner in terms of his or her particular educational needs at that time. It would contain just enough of each kind of subject matter to serve the individual's purposes and to speed his or her development. . . . Perhaps the best that can be done in working toward balance is to be clearer about what is valued for the growth of individual learners and then to apply these values in selecting curriculum content, grouping pupils for instruction, providing for articulation, and furthering guidance programs.[32]

In the foregoing comments Goodlad stressed the need for balance between the learner and the subject-centered curriculum whereas Doll emphasized the need for a curriculum that fits individuals through a judicious balance of group and individual experiences.

Sets of Variables. We can apply the principle of balance in a number of ways. Given the typical elementary school, middle or junior high school, and a comprehensive senior high school, curriculum planners should seek balance between the following sets of variables. You will note below that some of the sets of variables call for proportions or splits other than a fifty-fifty distribution. When we speak of proportions, we distort the mathematical concept of balance as equilibrium. In reference to the curriculum, however, we cannot and probably should not always seek to achieve a fifty-fifty balance. There are times when a "balance" of one-third/two-thirds is defensible.

1. *The child-centered and the subject-centered curriculum.* This variable presupposes a balance between the conflicting philosophies of progressivism and essentialism.
2. *The needs of society and of the learner.* The curriculum must be not only socially but also personally oriented.
3. *General and specialized education.* While the curriculum of a comprehensive high school consists of at least fifty percent general education courses, electives must be available for learners in specialized fields. School systems in various parts of the country offer alternatives to the general-specialized-education balance in the same school by providing separate high schools for specialized education, by allowing dual registration in both the regular high school and a vocational secondary school or community college, or by joining forces with other public schools to operate an area career-technical center.
4. *Breadth and depth.* The curriculum can be so broad as to be superficial or conversely so profound as to limit learning. In either extreme learning is restricted.
5. *The three domains, if we may create a three-way balance.* We cannot ignore the cognitive or affective or psychomotor domain. Youngsters cannot find their own balance when learning is limited to one domain.
6. *Individualization and mass education.* We must find some way to individualize or personalize instruction within the context of a mass educational system. Many recommendations have been made to achieve individualization—from programmed instruction to individually prescribed instruction to diagnostic-prescriptive teaching to independent study. However, of necessity, education remains largely a group process. We must discover effective ways of combining grouping techniques like cooperative learning, subgroupings both small and large, and instruction of the total class with personalized techniques.
7. *Innovation and tradition.* Tradition provides for stability and finds favor with the public. Constant innovation, often for its own sake, keeps faculties, students, and parents in a state of perpetual turmoil. We must pace innovations as to frequency and quantity in order to digest and evaluate changes taking place.
8. *The logical and psychological.* These variables are equated in a philosophical context with the differences between essentialism and progressivism. Some content must be organized according to the logic of the subject matter; some to the logic of the learner.
9. *The needs of the exceptional and the nonexceptional child.* If intelligence is distributed at random among the population, some two-thirds of the students are in the "average" range. Curriculum planners must be careful that attention to the needs of special groups does not far outstrip attention to the needs of the more numerous average student who are sometimes referred to as "woodwork children."[33]
10. *The needs of the academically talented or gifted and the slow.* In recent times if we have stressed either group, we have catered to the needs of slow learners. Per-

haps we assumed that the academically talented and the gifted will teach themselves in spite of school. Or perhaps we were guided by statistics; there are more slower students than academically talented (the top fifteen percent) and gifted (the top three percent). Schools must address the needs of both rapid and slow learners.

11. *Methods, experiences, and strategies.* Teachers should use a mixture of techniques, including audio and visual media. Some schools rely almost exclusively on the printed word, which runs counter to the public's addiction to mediated learning—films, recordings, television, and the computer with its access to the Internet.

12. *The immediate and the remote in both time and space.* Some people would omit the study of ancient history (too remote) or the study of the non-Western world (too distant or irrelevant). In fact, some discount the value of history per se. They would design only sparkling, new, contemporary, "with-it" curricula. In an era of globalization, people of the twenty-first century need a sense of the roots of civilization combined with an understanding of the many present-day diverse cultures on our shrunken planet, indeed, among us.

13. *Work and play.* At all levels youngsters need some balance, though certainly not fifty-fifty, between academic work and leisure or physical activities. Play in the form of games, sports, and personal pursuits not only helps alleviate incipient boredom but can be an education in itself. Some of the avocations pursued by young people may become vocations or lifelong interests.

14. *The school and the community as educational forces.* Teachers sometimes forget that there is much to be learned outside the walls of the classroom. In fact, in many important areas of life more is learned of both a positive and negative nature outside of school than in school. Curriculum planners should build ways of using the community as an educational laboratory. If the world can be one's oyster, the community can be one's pearl.

15. *Between disciplines.* Disciplines, especially elective ones in the secondary school, vie with each other for student enrollment. Occasionally, a school becomes known for an exceptionally strong department in some discipline. Although excellence is to be encouraged, this situation may imply less than excellence in other disciplines. Curriculum planners should seek to foster excellence in all fields.

16. *Between programs.* The college preparatory program of the secondary school often dwarfs other curricula. Curriculum planners must ensure that the general, career-technical, business, and other curricula have their place in the sun as well as the college preparatory curriculum.

17. *Within disciplines.* The natural and social sciences, as examples, should offer a mixture of didactics and inquiry learning. The foreign language curriculum should seek achievement in comprehension, speaking, and writing as well as reading. No single phase of a particular discipline should be permitted to crowd out other important phases.

Striving for balance in the curriculum is an essential responsibility of the curriculum planner.

Integration

Curriculum workers should concern themselves with the problem of integrating subject matter. Integration, in the context of a curriculum construction concept, means the blending, fusion, or unification of disciplines, a concept visited in Chapter 9 when we discussed the activity and core curricula. A fully integrated curriculum tears down barriers between disciplines and fuses disciplines under overarching themes or topics. Unlike determination of scope and sequence, which must be accomplished, the integration of disciplines is an optional and controversial undertaking. Whether to integrate the curriculum is an issue which divides educators.

Whether curriculum planners choose to integrate subject matter hinges upon their philosophy of the nature of knowledge, the nature of learners, and the purposes of education. Many educators support the integration of subject matter based on their analyses of studies pointing to successes with interdisciplinary curricular plans. Tyler defined integration as "the horizontal relationship of curriculum experiences" and went on to say, "The organization of these experiences should be such that they help the student increasingly to get a unified view and to unify his behavior in relation to the elements dealt with."[34] Hilda Taba commented, "It is recognized that learning is more effective when facts and principles from one field can be related to another, especially when applying this knowledge."[35]

However, our schools have typically and traditionally behaved as if the integration of subject matter were not too important or even detrimental to student achievement. The tenacity of the subject matter curriculum, which organizes subject matter into discrete disciplines, has been shaken only briefly by experiments like the activity curriculum and the core curriculum. The activity curriculum on the elementary school level and the core curriculum on the secondary school level sought to break down the disciplinary barriers and to organize education around problems to be solved, using whatever subject matter was applicable. The popularity of integrated curricula has waxed and waned over the years. We are witnessing a renewed interest in curriculum integration, particularly at the middle school level where interdisciplinary programs are a common feature.

Subject matter may be organized on the basis of separate disciplines with their own time blocks. Another approach is to integrate it either on a schoolwide basis (as with the core curriculum) or on the classroom level (as with certain types of unit plans) without regard for disciplines.

Not all educators, of course, are advocates of integrating subject matter. Some believe that the various disciplines should be taught separately. Thus, they reject the broad-fields approach to curriculum organization and recommend that teachers and students concentrate on the separate disciplines.

The progressives feel with considerable logic that understanding is enhanced when the artificial barriers between disciplines are removed. It is true that human beings solve their problems by judiciously selecting whatever subject matter is needed. However, whether a program to educate the immature learner must consist of integrated disciplines is debatable. Two responses have been made over the years to reduce the separateness of disciplines. Subject matter has been both correlated and integrated. Curriculum planners have positioned themselves somewhere on a continuum that appears as follows:

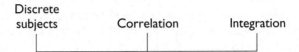

Correlation of Subject Matter.   Correlation is the relating of subjects to one another while still maintaining their separateness. Relationships between subjects taught at a particular school level are shown to pupils, as in the cases of history and literature; math and science; art, music, and literature.

Subjects may be correlated horizontally across one grade level or vertically across two or more. As an example of the latter, ancient history, taught in the sophomore or junior year of high school, may be correlated with Latin, taught in the junior or senior year. The study of Latin is therefore enriched by this progression. If the courses are taken concurrently, the study of both disciplines is enhanced.

Correlation becomes integration when the subjects lose their identities. In the cultural-epoch core approach to curriculum organization, epochs of humankind's history provide the framework; the subjects—English, social studies, science, mathematics, art, music—illuminate the cultural epochs. In the case of either correlation or integration, cooperative planning by all teachers affected is necessary.

Two Views of Curriculum Integration.   Taba offered two views of curriculum integration. The first view is the one we have been discussing: the horizontal relationship of subjects. In addition, said Taba, "Integration is also defined as something that happens to an individual."[36] If we follow the second view, "The problem, then, is that of developing ways of helping individuals in this process of creating a unity of knowledge. This interpretation of integration throws the emphasis from integrating subjects to locating the integrative threads."[37]

Regardless of whether the subject matter is presented to the learner in an integrated fashion by the teacher, the learner must integrate the knowledge into his or her own behavior. The distinction between an educated and an erudite person lies in the degree to which knowledge is integrated in the person.

Taba remarked:

> Unification of subjects has been a theme in education ever since the Herbartians. By far the greatest number of experimental curriculum schemes have revolved around the problem of unifying learning. At the same time we are far from achieving unification, partly because of fear of loss of disciplined learning if the study of specialized subjects is discarded, and partly because as yet no effective basis has been found for unifying school subjects.[38]

You have seen and will see a number of references to interdisciplinary/multidisciplinary integrated curricula in this text. Although many schools seek to employ an interdisciplinary approach to curriculum and instruction at more than one level, integration of the curriculum was, in the days of the core curriculum, found more frequently in the junior high school and is at present a noticeable feature of most middle schools.

Integrated curricula challenge the time-honored organization of curricula into separate disciplines. James A. Beane pointed to the difficulty of implementing an integrated curriculum when he said, "To resist the powerful push for a prescribed, separate subject curriculum and related tests is no easy thing to do."[39] Curriculum planners must decide whether they will make a conscious effort either to correlate or to integrate subject matter and, if they plan to do either, what organizational structure they will create to do so.[40] Scope, relevance, balance, and integration are interrelated principles to which curriculum workers must give attention.

Sequence

Sequence is the order in which the organizing elements or centers are arranged by the curriculum planners. Whereas scope is referred to as "the what" of curriculum organization, sequence is referred to as "the when." Sequence answers the questions of when and where the focal points will be placed. Some time ago Saylor and Alexander defined sequence as

> the order in which educational experiences are developed with pupils. Sequence refers to the "when" in curriculum planning. Determination of the sequence of educational experiences is a decision as to the most propitious time in which to develop those educational experiences suggested by the scope. If we think of scope as the latitudinal aspect of curriculum planning, sequence becomes the longitudinal axis.[41]

Once we identify the scope of the curriculum, we must put the elements into some kind of meaningful order. Let's take a simplified illustration from the reading curriculum. Suppose as reading teachers we wish students to be able to

- read novels
- read words
- read paragraphs
- read sentences
- recognize letters of the alphabet

Is there some particular order in which pupils learn those elements? The answer is obvious here. The student should recognize letters of the alphabet first, then proceed to reading words, sentences, paragraphs, and novels. Unless one is a Mozart-like prodigy, one does not normally begin to demonstrate reading skills by reading adult tomes.

But take the following organizational threads in economics:

- insurance
- real estate
- banking

- stock market
- inflation
- recession
- foreign exchange

What is the sequence in this case? Is there a preferred sequence? What makes it preferred? As another example, in what order should we study the American Revolution, the War of 1812, the Korean War, World War I, the Civil War, the Vietnam War, World War II, the Persian Gulf War, the War in Iraq, and the Spanish-American War? The answer in this case is simple, you say. Simply place the wars in chronological order. But could there be any other defensible way of sequencing these items?

The problem of sequencing produces questions about

- the maturity of the learners
- the interests of the learners
- the readiness of the learners
- the relative difficulty of the items to be learned
- the relationship between items
- the prerequisite skills needed in each case

Ways of Sequencing.   How do curriculum workers decide which content comes first? Sequencing is accomplished in a variety of ways, including arranging the content.

1. From the simplest to the most complex. We must deal with tens, for example, before we work with hundreds.
2. In chronological order. History is most often taught in this fashion.
3. In reverse chronological order. Occasionally, a history teacher will start with the most recent events and work backward to the most ancient under the assumption that pupils' attention can be grasped quicker with more recent and therefore more familiar events. Themes that exist in the present may be seen repeated as they go backward in time.
4. From the geographically near to the geographically far. Some argue that it makes more sense to study phenomena and conditions close to home and to gradually expand the learner's horizons ultimately to the world and even the universe.
5. From the far to the near. This procedure focuses on distant lands and reserves study of the home environment—the pièce de résistance—until the end.
6. From the concrete to the abstract. The pupil learns to count blocks by first manipulating them physically and only later manipulating them mentally.
7. From the general to the particular. This approach starts with the principle and proceeds to examples.
8. From the particular to the general. This approach starts with examples and proceeds to the principle.

When we are determining sequencing, we will find that there are times when the order of the units of content does not matter. When we are studying the works of twentieth-century American authors, we might want to group writers of drama, short stories, novels, and nonfiction, but it is not likely to make a great deal of difference which grouping or which author within the grouping we study first.

There are times when we will deliberately violate a sequence. The class may be studying the political structure of ancient Rome, for example, when a landmark case affecting the country's political and social system is decided by the U.S. Supreme Court. This immediate and significant case is permitted to alter the planned sequence.

Prerequisite Skills.   As a rule, pupils cannot engage in a unit of content until they have mastered the preceding skills. The student of algebra is hard pressed unless he or she has mastered arithmetic skills. The student cannot succeed in a second-year foreign language class without mastering the skills developed in the first year. For this reason the assessment of prerequisite skills is sound pedagogy. Teachers must know whether the students have mastered the skills needed to proceed with the tasks before them.

Dubious Sequencing.   Some curriculum planners in the past, following their own notions of what constitutes prerequisite skills, have instituted sequencing that is hard to defend on any solid grounds. For years, high school students were required, for example, to take general science, biology, chemistry, and physics in that order. Actually, none is necessarily dependent on the other. Each science depends more on mastery of reading and mathematics than on mastery of other sciences. We can find evidence of dubious sequencing in mathematics with the prescribed order of algebra I, geometry, algebra II, trigonometry, and calculus. Although it may be wise planning to start with algebra I and hold calculus for the end, there is little reason to hold algebra II until after the completion of geometry. Why is *Macbeth* invariably taught after *Julius Caesar*? Why does American history often come after world history? From a chauvinist point of view, we could argue that American history ought to come first in the senior high school sequence.

Conceptions of Sequencing.   Donald E. Orlosky and B. Othanel Smith discussed three conceptions of sequencing: (1) sequencing according to need, (2) macrosequencing, and (3) microsequencing. According to the first conception,

> the learner orders his own learning as he deals with a situation from moment to moment. He selects what he wants to know as the need arises. If he makes a mistake in the selection he simply goes through the process again until he finds that which satisfies his present need. This is an opportunistic notion of sequencing but those who advocate it maintain that it is psychologically sound.[42]

This perception of sequencing fits the views of some progressive educators and proponents of open education.

Macrosequencing follows principles of child development expounded by persons like Arnold Gesell, Frances L. Ilg, and Jean Piaget. Macrosequencing, said Orlosky and Smith, is the organization of knowledge and the formulation of instruction to coincide with the different stages of the individual's development. For a long time teachers have arranged the knowledge of instruction roughly in accordance with the development of the child. Examining the existing program of studies of almost any school proves that it corresponds roughly to the child's development.[43]

Microsequencing is the ordering of subject matter according to the prerequisite knowledge required of each unit of content. "This assumes," said Orlosky and Smith, "that for any learning task there is a hierarchy extending from the very simple to the more abstract and complex elements which lead to the attainment of a specified objective."[44]

Curriculum planners are called on to make decisions on placement of content at the appropriate grade levels. Using the terms "sequence" and "grade placement" together, B. Othanel Smith, William O. Stanley, and J. Harlan Shores observed:

> There are only two possible approaches to the solution of problems of grade placement and sequence. *The first* accepts the child as he is and adjusts the experience to his level of development while holding the instructional goals constant. . . . *The second approach* assumes curriculum experiences to be located at a given grade level and provides learnings to adjust the child to these experiences—that is, to get him ready for the learning.[45]

Where to Begin.   Disagreements over the process of sequencing center on whether curriculum planners should start with learners or subject matter. The first demands choosing emphases in keeping with the learners' actual growth and development, or, when learning experiences are, in current terminology, "developmentally appropriate"; the second, placing subject matter at the grade level at which it is assumed learners will be able to master it. The latter approach to sequencing has been the historic approach.

Smith, Stanley, and Shores advocated a blending of the two approaches, holding it unrealistic to subscribe wholeheartedly to either approach.[46]

They counseled curriculum workers to take into account the maturation, experiential background, mental age, and interests of the learners and the usefulness and difficulty of the subject matter when developing a sequence.[47] The ordering of the organizing elements of the curriculum is one of the major tasks of the curriculum developer.

Continuity

Continuity is the planned repetition of content at successive levels, each time at an increased level of complexity. Tyler described continuity as follows:

> Continuity refers to the vertical reiteration of major curriculum elements. For example, if in the social studies the development of skills in reading social studies is an important objective, it is necessary to see that there is recurring and continuing opportunity for these skills to be practiced and developed. This means that over time the same kinds of skills will be brought into continuing operation. In similar fashion, if an objective in science is to develop a meaningful concept of energy, it is important that this concept be dealt with

again and again in various parts of the science course. Continuity is thus seen to be a major factor in effective vertical organization.[48]

Spiral Curriculum. The principle of continuity is represented in what has been called the spiral curriculum.[49] Concepts, skills, and knowledge are introduced and reintroduced—for example, the repetition of addition, study of democracy, writing, personal health, and conservation, each reintroduction enhancing the earlier exposures.

Expertise Needed. Planning a curriculum for continuity requires a high degree of expertise, which demands both knowledge of the subject field and of the learners. For example, to plan a mathematics sequence for twelve grades with appropriate scope, sequence, and continuity requires the combined skills of subject matter specialists and teachers. Continuity is not simply repetition of content but also repetition with increasing levels of complexity and sophistication. Whereas elementary school youngsters, for example, may learn that democracy means government of the people, by the people, and for the people, secondary students may wrestle with controversial and unresolved problems of democracy.

Experience will reveal to curriculum developers which units of content must be reintroduced and at what point. Preassessment, if only of the most rudimentary kind, is essential before each new organizing element is broached. Preassessment will uncover whether the learners are ready for (1) new content based on prior content and (2) prior content that will be repeated at a more complex level.

Articulation

If we view continuity as the spiraling of content upward through the grades of a particular school, we should view articulation as the meshing of organizing elements across school levels—that is, across elementary and middle or junior high schools, across junior high or middle and senior high schools, and across senior high school and college. Like continuity, articulation is a dimension of sequencing.

Horizontal and Vertical. Oliver used the term "articulation" synonymously with "horizontal articulation" or "correlation." He equated the concept of "continuity" with "vertical articulation."[50] Regarding correlation as a halfway move toward integration, I would agree with calling correlation horizontal articulation. Sequence, continuity, and articulation are all interrelated. I would separate continuity from vertical articulation and define continuity as a reintroduction of content at progressively more complex levels and articulation as the meshing of the curriculum of the various levels of the educational ladder to provide for smooth transition on the part of the learners. This meshing may or may not involve reintroduction of units of content, progressively more difficult. When speaking of articulation, I am addressing the problem of vertical articulation.

Unfortunately, efforts at articulation between levels are in many cases feeble and ineffective. Cooperative efforts are necessary among curriculum workers if articulated sequences are to be planned from kindergarten through twelfth grade and beyond.

We find considerable unplanned repetition of content among levels. This is neither articulation nor continuity but a laissez-faire attitude that permits curriculum workers to develop their own programs without knowledge of what instructors at preceding and succeeding levels are teaching.

With our decentralized system of education, lack of articulation occurs frequently. Articulation is particularly difficult in some states where separate school districts managing different levels of schooling exist side by side under separate administrators and separate school boards. Even when all levels of schooling are centralized under a single administrator and school board, articulation remains a problem.

Gaps between Levels.   We often find great gaps between levels. The seventh-grade teacher (failing or refusing to preassess) assumes certain levels of mastery of knowledge when children enter from the elementary school; the senior high school teacher expects certain entry skills from youngsters who are promoted from the middle or junior high school. Repeatedly, college instructors decry high school students' lack of skills that assure success in college.

Personal Articulation.   There is not only a need for planned articulation of subject matter but also for pupils' personal articulation. Schools look for ways to respond to students' varied capabilities. Some junior high/middle school pupils, for example, are able to tackle senior high school subjects. Some senior high school pupils can perform ably in advanced placement courses given in the high school and in junior or senior college courses in their area of residence. Some students can skip a year of high school and enter college early or can skip the lower division of college and enroll in the upper division.

Improved articulation eases the movement of pupils from one level to the next, which can be a traumatic experience for most young people. With all the problems of social adjustment as they enter a higher level, they have little need for suffering either needless repetition, exposure to subject matter that is too easy for them, or, worse yet, grasping for learnings beyond their abilities and skills. Thus, curriculum planners cannot avoid the problem of articulation.

Let's recap what has been said about sequencing, continuity, and articulation. Continuity and articulation are dimensions of sequencing. Sequencing is the logical or psychological arrangement of units of content within lessons, units, courses, and grades. Continuity is the planned introduction and reintroduction of the same units of content through the grades of a school system at ever-increasing levels of complexity. Articulation is the planned sequencing of units of content across grade levels—that is, from one grade level to the next to ensure that the next grade level takes up where the previous grade level left off.

The three principles—sequence, continuity, and articulation—are interrelated and complement each other. Material must be appropriately sequenced at whatever level. Articulation must be observed to ensure that there are no gaps in a sequence from one grade level to the next, whereas continuity must be sought to permit students to achieve greater depth in a subject.

Although this text presents sequencing and related principles in a favorable light as useful concepts in planning, organizing, and evaluating the curriculum, as we have noted many times in this text, views on many concepts and practices in education differ. The concepts of sequencing and the spiral curriculum are no exception. Holding that "there is little interest today in sequencing,"[51] John D. McNeil wrote, "Current research casts doubt on rigid conceptions of skill hierarchies and spiraled curriculum. Although there may be some valid skill hierarchies such as teaching addition before multiplication, little evidence supports hierarchies such as those in Bloom's taxonomy."[52]

Transferability

Whatever is taught in school should in some way possess transfer value, that is, learning in school should have applicability in either a broad or narrow sense outside of school and after school years. Education for education's sake—the mark of the learned person—is simply not sufficient as a goal of education. Education should in some way enrich the life of the individual.

The transfer of learning or transfer of training, as it is sometimes called, has been discussed at some length in the literature of educational psychology.[53] Transfer gives a permanence to learning beyond the moment of its first introduction into the classroom.

Career-technical education possesses a built-in one-upmanship in transferability. You can see the transfer; it's apparent. Skills learned in industrial arts and career education classes can be transferred to life situations. Teachers of psychomotor skills are particularly fortunate because pupils have no difficulty seeing the transfer value of these areas of study. Students can and will use the skills they learn in such areas as music, art, physical education, typing, word-processing, and homemaking. Transfer is paramount with most teachers of perceptual-motor skills. Physical educators tout the carry-over value of their activities—that is, transfer.

Transfer in the affective and cognitive areas is more difficult to discern. Of course, we wish students to carry over ethical values and positive attitudes into their daily living. We would like a student who demonstrates democratic principles in the classroom to retain that behavior all his or her life. Transfer of cognitive learning is most often visible in student performance on assessment and standardized tests, in admission to and success in college, and in the evaluations employers give of the intellectual competence of their employees.

Proponents of faculty psychology (mental or formal discipline) maintained that rigorous subjects disciplined the mind; thus, such education was generally transferable. Some of the essentialists have held that education is the storing of data—computer fashion—for use at a later date when the occasion arises. Unfortunately, disuse sets in; we forget, and when we need to retrieve the supposedly stored data, we find that they have slipped away. Unlike the cases of bicycling and swimming, skills never forgotten, we can but cite the difficulty of retrieving locations and steps in using computer applications after a period of disuse.

It has generally been believed by many—a holdover of the formal discipline days—that certain subjects lead to transfer more than other subjects. After an exhaustive study of more than 8,000 students, Thorndike concluded:

> The expectation of any large difference in general improvement of the mind from one study rather than another seems doomed to disappointment. The chief reason why good thinkers seem superficially to have been made such by having taken certain school studies is that good thinkers have taken such studies, becoming better by the inherent tendency of the good to gain more than the poor from any study.[54]

Daniel Tanner and Laurel Tanner pointed out that the Eight-Year Study disproved the notion that a high school student must complete a prescribed sequence of subjects in order to be successful in college.[55]

Taba, however, explained the more current view on transfer as follows: "The recent ideas on transfer have returned to earlier assumptions of the possibility of fairly wide transfer, depending on the level of generalizing that takes place regarding either the content or the method of approach."[56] Thus, if teachers wish to encourage transfer, they must stress general principles.

Current Beliefs.   Let's summarize some of the current beliefs about transfer.

- Transfer is at the heart of education: it is a—if not the—goal of education.
- Transfer is possible.
- The closer the classroom situation is to the out-of-classroom situations, the greater is the transfer.
- Transfer can be increased and improved if teachers consciously teach for transfer.
- Transfer is greater when teachers help pupils to derive underlying generalizations and to make applications of those generalizations.
- Generally speaking, when the learner discovers knowledge for himself or herself, transfer is enhanced.

Bruner provided an example of children in a fifth-grade class learning "a way of thinking about geography" as opposed to being dished out selected, unconnected geographical facts.[57] Bruner encouraged teachers to use a discovery approach, justifying it on the grounds of "increased intellectual potency, intrinsic rewards, useful learning techniques, and better memory processes."[58]

Guided Discovery.   The jury is still out on the question of the extent of use of inquiry or discovery methods. David Ausubel pointed out that some discovery techniques can be an inefficient use of time.[59] Renate Nummela Caine and Geoffrey Caine were critical of discovery learning when they said, "Unfortunately, even this often fails to work because discovery learning is used as a trick or device to get students to remember the facts that the teacher wants them to remember."[60] Some authorities prefer to speak of guided discovery rather than discovery per se. Whatever the process used—discovery or other—enhancement of meaning during the process of instruction should increase the degree of transfer.

Transferability is a principle of both instruction and the curriculum. When we talk about methods of teaching for transferability, we are referring to the instructional process. When we analyze what the learner has transferred, we are in the area of curriculum. Curriculum developers should specify objectives, select content, and choose instructional strategies that will lead to maximum transfer. Furthermore, plans for evaluating the curriculum should include means of judging the degree of the transfer of the many segments of the curriculum.

Implications of the Continuing Curriculum Concepts

Given the range and the many facets of the curriculum concepts covered, it is useful to briefly redefine them in the light of the curriculum worker's responsibilities. Curriculum workers attend to

- *scope* when they select topics to be studied and specify the instructional objectives
- *relevance* when they "effect a congruence between the entire school system and the social order in which the young of today will spend their adult lives"[61]
- *balance* when they maintain certain sets of elements proportionately
- *integration* when they make an effort to unify subject matter
- *sequence* when they determine the order in which subject matter will be made available to the students
- *continuity* when they examine the curriculum of each course and grade level to discover where units of content may fruitfully be repeated at increased levels of complexity
- *articulation* when they examine the curriculum of each discipline at each grade level to be sure the subject matter flows sequentially across grade-level boundaries
- *transferability* when they seek ways to achieve maximum transfer of learning

In identifying the eight guiding principles of curriculum development, we give structure to a philosophy of curriculum development, saying that we believe a functional curriculum is one that attends to scope, relevance, balance, integration, sequence, continuity, articulation, and transferability.

COMPREHENSIVE MODELS

The foregoing limited models focus on specific aspects of the curriculum: accomplishment of the curriculum objectives and the presence or absence of selected guiding factors in curriculum construction. Let's examine now two models which ask us to evaluate the entire curriculum development process.

The Saylor, Alexander, and Lewis Model

Figure 13.4 shows how J. Galen Saylor, William M. Alexander, and Arthur J. Lewis charted a model of curriculum evaluation.[62] The Saylor, Alexander, and Lewis model calls for evaluating five components:

1. the goals, subgoals, and objectives
2. the program of education as a totality
3. the specific segments of the education program
4. instruction
5. evaluation program

The first, third, and fourth components contribute to the second—evaluating the program of education as a totality—by, among other ways, providing data that bear on the total program. In the figure, these relationships are shown by the three arrows between the boxes, which point toward the second component. By including the fifth component—evaluation program—in their model, Saylor, Alexander, and Lewis suggested that it is necessary to evaluate the evaluation program itself. No arrow is shown from the box labeled "evaluation program" because the evaluation of the evaluation program is perceived as an independent operation that has implications for the entire evaluation process. Perhaps we could embellish the Saylor, Alexander, and Lewis model by drawing four curved arrows leading out of the right-hand side of the Evaluation Program box to the right-hand side of each of the four boxes above it.

Once again, as we look at the model, we encounter the terms "formative evaluation" (evaluation that takes place during a component) and "summative evaluation" (evaluation that takes place at the end of a component). Saylor, Alexander, and Lewis's model calls attention to both formative and summative aspects of evaluation of each component.

Evaluation of Goals, Subgoals, and Objectives. Goals, subgoals, and objectives are evaluated (validated) in their formative stages by

1. analysis of the needs of society
2. analysis of the needs of the individual
3. referring the goals, subgoals, and objectives to various groups
4. referring the goals, subgoals, and objectives to subject matter specialists
5. use of previous summative data

Curriculum planners must make their own analyses of whether a given goal, subgoal, or objective meets the needs of society and of the learners. They should seek the judgments of students (if they are mature enough), teachers, parents, and other laypeople and should further consult subject matter specialists to determine whether a given goal, subgoal, or objective is appropriate to the particular discipline. Data gained from previous tryouts of the program should be used to revise goals, subgoals, and objectives prior to the next trial. For practical purposes, instead of referring every goal, subgoal, and

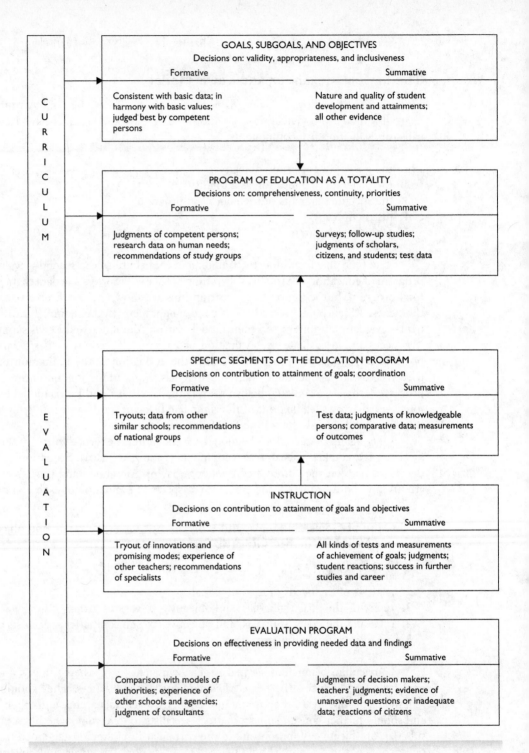

FIGURE 13.4 The Saylor, Alexander, and Lewis Evaluation Model. From J. Galen Saylor, William M. Alexander, and Arthur J. Lewis, *Curriculum Planning for Better Teaching and Learning,* 4th ed. (New York: Holt, Rinehart and Winston, 1981), p. 334. Reproduced by permission of Arthur J. Lewis.

objective to all the groups mentioned, the curriculum planner may elect to refer the goals for validation to all groups and the subgoals and objectives for validation to just the teachers, subject matter specialists, and other curriculum specialists.

To clarify this validation process, let's take as an example the prosaic objective in the psychomotor domain—the baking of bread loaves in homemaking class. Although we can certainly teach young people to bake bread loaves and can evaluate their performance in this psychomotor skill, a more fundamental question must be answered: Should the baking of bread loaves be included in the homemaking curriculum?

The question is not so simple to answer as it might first appear. A number of questions must be raised before this particular item of content can be validated. Some of these questions are as follows:

- Does society (the community, the home, the family) have any need for breadbakers?
- Is the skill of baking bread necessary or helpful to the individual?
- Does teaching the skill make sense in the light of comparison of costs of the home-baked bread versus store-bought bread?
- Does it require more energy to bake a loaf of bread at home or for commercial bakers to produce loaves for sale?
- Is there some overriding aesthetic or personal satisfaction in baking bread as opposed to purchasing it?
- Is home-baked bread more nutritious than store-bought bread?
- If baking bread is a content item, what other items were left out of the curriculum so that it could be included? Which items are the most important?
- Would experts in homemaking assert that this content item is essential to the homemaking curriculum?
- What percentage of families today bake their own bread?
- Is this skill something that can and should be taught in the home rather than in school?
- What has the success or failure of previous groups of students been in respect to this particular skill?

As we have seen, goals, subgoals, and objectives are established for the total program of the school. They are also established for specific program segments and for instruction. The accomplishment of curricular goals, subgoals, and objectives is revealed through an evaluation of the total program, the specific segments, and instruction.

Although Saylor, Alexander, and Lewis make the evaluation of the program of education as a totality the second component of their model of curriculum development, I would prefer to vary the sequence. Let's comment first on the two other components that impinge on the total educational program—the evaluation of instruction and of the specific segments of the program. We will return to the evaluation of the total program in a moment.

Evaluation of Instruction.   We examined procedures for evaluating instruction in Chapter 12. Saylor, Alexander, and Lewis recommended that after instructional goals and objectives are specified and validated as part of the formative evaluation process, the antecedent conditions should be examined—a process referred to by some evaluators as *context evaluation*. The learners' total educational environment, the characteristics of the learners and the teachers, classroom interaction, and the curriculum design are all evaluated and may affect the choice of instructional goals and objectives.[63] The use of criterion-referenced and norm-referenced tests and other evaluative techniques provides formative and summative data on the success of instruction.

Evaluation of Specific Segments.   The specific segments of the program require evaluation. Saylor, Alexander, and Lewis included within their concept of specific segments the following: "the plan for organizing curriculum domains, the design or designs of the curriculum for each domain, courses offered, other kinds of sets of learning opportunities provided, extrainstructional activities sponsored, services provided students, and the kinds of informal relations that characterize the institutional climate."[64]

Assessment data from district, state, and national sources should be gathered by the curriculum planners for purposes of formative evaluation of the specific program segments. At this stage data from the National Assessment of Educational Progress, for instance, can prove helpful. If, for example, the NAEP data revealed that nine-year-old children in urban areas of the southeast United States are more deficient in reading skills than children in comparable urban areas elsewhere in the country, intensive examination of the reading program of the particular school system is essential. SAT and ACT scores will provide clues. International assessments like TIMSS may also provide helpful data.[65] State and district assessments, focusing as they do on children of the state and locality, will be even more meaningful in this respect.

Evaluative Instruments.   At this stage, too, the evaluation instruments of the National Study of School Evaluation (NSSE) may be used to gather empirical data about specific areas of study and other segments of the program.[66] This particular set of standards is often used by schools as part of a self-study process for regional accreditation. These instruments permit faculties to analyze the principles related to the particular program, the evaluation techniques used, plans for improvement, and the current status.

Fenwick W. English proposed a way of looking at specific segments of the curriculum through a technique referred to as "curriculum mapping."[67] Following this technique, teachers analyze the content they present and the amount of time spent on each topic. Advocating calendar-based curriculum mapping as a means of integrating the curriculum and assessment, Heidi Hayes Jacobs likened a curriculum map to

> . . . a school's manuscript. It tells the story of the operational curriculum. With this map in hand, staff members can play the role of manuscript editors, examining the curriculum for needed revision and validation.[68]

Jacobs saw the technique in which each teacher creates a map showing processes, skills, concepts, topics, and assessments to be incorporated in his or her teaching over the course of a year as more effective than lists of goals, objectives, skills, and concepts prepared by usual curriculum committees.[69]

In a later work Jacobs explained, "Primarily, mapping enables teachers to identify gaps, redundancies, and misalignments in the curriculum and instructional program and to foster dialog among teachers about their work."[70]

Curriculum planners must design summative measures to determine whether the curriculum goals and objectives of the specific segments have been achieved. If it were desired, for example, that seventy-five percent of the students in a senior high school be involved in at least one extraclass activity, a simple head count would reveal whether this objective has been realized. As is the case when evaluating instruction, sometimes the objective itself is the evaluation item. On the other hand, if it is desired to know whether a fourth-grade class whose members average two months below grade level in mathematics at the beginning of the year raised its scores to grade level by the end of the year, pretesting and posttesting will be necessary.

Evaluation of the Total Program.   The functioning of the curriculum as a whole must be evaluated. The curriculum planners want to learn whether the goals and objectives of the total curriculum have been realized.

The aforementioned National Study of School Evaluation enables schools to gather opinions of constituencies of the school by making available inventories for teachers, students, and parents to register their perceptions about the school and its programs. English adapted the concept of a management audit to curriculum evaluation, defining an audit as "an objective, external review of a record, event, process, product, act, belief, or motivation to commit an act."[71] English went on to describe a curriculum audit as "a process of examining documents and practices that exist within a peculiar institution normally called a 'school' in a given time, culture, and society."[72] From documents, interviews, and on-site visits, the auditor, sometimes an external agent, seeks to determine how well programs are functioning and whether they are cost-effective. English pointed out that the curriculum audit is both a process and a product in that the auditor engages in collecting and analyzing data and prepares a report delineating the results. Standards applied by English to a school district's curriculum audit include district control over its people, program, and resources; clear program objectives; documentation about its programs; use of district assessments; and program improvements.[73]

Studies of the needs of society and of young people speak to the question of the school's total program. Unless one limits the school's program to purely cognitive goals, some response should be made to some of the pressing problems of the day. These studies provide formative data for the curriculum planners. Surely problems like abuse of the environment, waste of natural resources, discrimination of all types, and the misuse of chemical substances should be examined by young people.

Saylor, Alexander, and Lewis recommended formative evaluation of the program of education as a totality by means of "judgments of competent persons, research data on human needs, recommendations of study groups." They recommended summative evaluation of the educational program through "surveys; follow-up studies; judgments of scholars, citizens, and students; test data."[74]

Summative evaluation of the total program is conducted in several ways. Empirical data are gathered to determine if curriculum objectives have been accomplished. Schoolwide test data are analyzed. Follow-up studies reveal the success or lack of success of young people after leaving the school. Finally, surveys ask teachers, parents, students, and others to evaluate the school's program.

Evaluation of the Evaluation Program.   The program for evaluating the curriculum should be continuously assessed. Judgments about how evaluation will be conducted should be made before an innovation or change is put into practice. The techniques for ongoing evaluation and final evaluation must be carefully planned and followed.

Sometimes it is beneficial to enlist the services of an evaluation specialist to review the evaluation techniques proposed by the curriculum planners. Questions must be answered as to whether the instruments to be used are reliable and valid; whether the evaluation program is comprehensive, covering all the dimensions of the curriculum to be evaluated; and whether the procedures are appropriate and possible. Reactions and suggestions about the evaluation procedures should be obtained from those who are most intimately exposed to them—the students and teachers.

If research studies are to be conducted, specialists inside or outside the system should review the proposed research techniques to determine whether they meet the standards of acceptable research.

When data are ultimately gathered, the planners may feel the need to request the help of evaluation specialists to treat and interpret the data. It must now be determined whether all the variables have been considered and appropriately controlled and whether the evaluation measures are designed to assess the appropriate objectives. For example, a cognitive test of American history will not assess student performance of citizenship skills. The ability to recite rules of grammar does not guarantee skill in writing.

When flaws are discovered in the evaluation program, changes should be made. Conclusions reached as a result of research and evaluation are often attacked, not on their substance, but on the evaluation processes by which they were reached.

For example, why is it that we can find skeptics for almost every curricular innovation ever tried? You name it—core curriculum; competency-based education; open education; team teaching; nongradedness; the once new, now old math; and so on—and we can find criticisms of it. Some who object do so because they are not convinced that the evaluation techniques purported to have been used actually proved the superiority of an innovation. Students of curriculum might well examine the processes for evaluating almost any program, change of program, or innovation in their school system—past or present—and at any level to find out if curricula were evaluated rigorously. Students are also likely to discover many innovations evaluated on the basis of perceived opinion of success (without adequate data), participants' feelings about the program (like/dislike), change of pace (variety as a spice), pleasure of being involved (Hawthorne effect), administrative assertion ("I say it works"), cost (if it was an expensive undertaking, it has to be good), public relations ("Look what we've done for your/our young people"), and perceived leadership ("We're in the vanguard," also known as "on the cutting edge").

To conclude, Saylor, Alexander, and Lewis have illuminated the major evaluation components that confront curriculum planners in the process of curriculum development. Less technical than some models, the Saylor, Alexander, and Lewis model offers a comprehensive view of curriculum evaluation.

The CIPP Model

The Phi Delta Kappa National Study Committee on Evaluation, chaired by Daniel L. Stufflebeam, produced and disseminated a widely cited model of evaluation known as the CIPP (context, input, process, product) model.[75] Reference has already been made in Chapter 4 to two of the major features of the CIPP model: stages of decision making and types of decisions required in education.[76]

Comprehensive in nature, the model reveals types of evaluation, of decision-making settings, of decisions, and of change. Defining evaluation in the following way, "Evaluation is the process of delineating, obtaining, and providing useful information for judging decision alternatives," Stufflebeam clarified what was meant by each of the parts of the definition:

1. *Process.* A particular, continuing and cyclical activity subsuming many methods and involving a number of steps or operations.
2. *Delineating.* Focusing information requirements to be served by evaluation through such steps as specifying, defining, and explicating.
3. *Obtaining.* Making available through such processes as collecting, organizing, and analyzing, and through such formal means as statistics and measurement.
4. *Providing.* Fitting together into systems or subsystems that best serve the needs or purposes of the evaluation.
5. *Useful.* Appropriate to predetermined criteria evolved through the interaction of the evaluator and the client.
6. *Information.* Descriptive or interpretive data about entities (tangible or intangible) and their relationships.
7. *Judging.* Assigning weights in accordance with a specified value framework, criteria derived therefrom, and information that relates criteria to each entity being judged.
8. *Decision Alternatives.* A set of optional responses to a specified decision question.[77]

"The evaluation process," said Stufflebeam, "includes the three main steps of delineating, obtaining, and providing. These steps provide the basis for a methodology of evaluation."[78] Before we begin to examine the various elements of the CIPP model, let's look at a figure of the entire model, shown in Figure 13.5.

In flowchart form, the model consists of rectangles (with small loops attached), hexagons, ovals, a circle, a fancy *E*, solid and broken lines with arrows, and three types of shading. Shaded dark, the hexagons show types of decisions; hatched, the ovals, the circle, and the big *E* depict activities performed; and lightly shaded, the rectangles stand for types of evaluation.

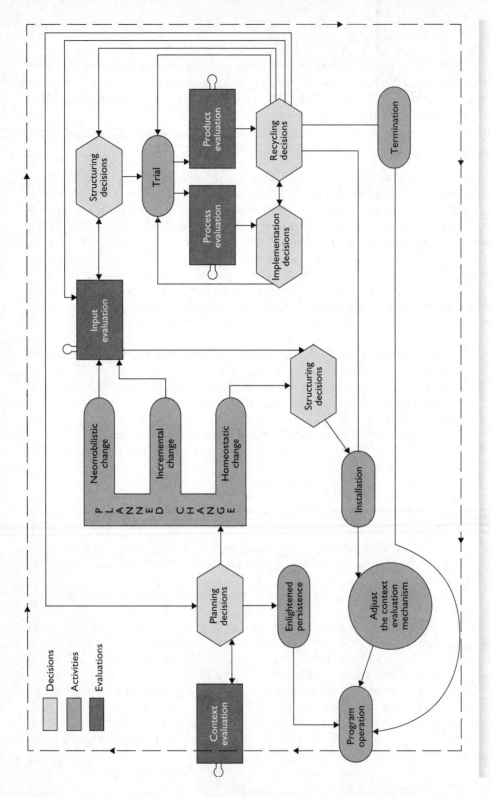

FIGURE 13.5 The CIPP Evaluation Model. From Daniel L. Shufflebeam et al., *Educational Evaluation and Decision Making* (Itasca, Ill.: F. E. Peacock, 1971), p. 236. Reprinted by permission.

Four Types of Evaluation. The Phi Delta Kappa Committee pointed to four types of evaluation—context, input, process, and product—hence, the name of the model CIPP. Context evaluation is "the most basic kind of evaluation," said Stufflebeam. "Its purpose is to provide a rationale for determination of objectives."[79] At this point in the model, curriculum planner-evaluators define the environment of the curriculum and determine unmet needs and reasons why the needs are not being met. Goals and objectives are specified on the basis of context evaluation.

Input evaluation has as its purpose "to provide information for determining how to utilize resources to achieve project objectives."[80] The resources of the school and various designs for carrying out the curriculum are considered. At this stage, the planner-evaluators decide on procedures to be used. Stufflebeam observed, "Methods for input evaluation are lacking in education. The prevalent practices include committee deliberations, appeal to the professional literature, the employment of consultants, and pilot experimental projects."[81]

Process evaluation is the provision of periodic feedback while the curriculum is being implemented. Stufflebeam noted, "Process evaluation has three main objectives—the first is to detect or predict defects in the procedural design or its implementation during the implementation stages, the second is to provide information for programmed decisions, and the third is to maintain a record of the procedure as it occurs."[82]

Product evaluation, the final type, has as its purpose

> . . . to measure and interpret attainments not only at the end of a project cycle, but as often as necessary during the project term. The general method of product evaluation includes devising operational definitions of objectives, measuring criteria associated with the objectives of the activity, comparing these measurements with predetermined absolute or relative standards, and making rational interpretations of the outcomes using the recorded context, input, and process information.[83]

Stufflebeam outlined the types of evaluation in respect to objectives, methods, and in relation to decision making in the change process as shown in Table 13.1.

Four Types of Decisions. The hexagons in Figure 13.5 represent four types of decisions, which were mentioned in Chapter 4: Planning, Structuring, Implementing, and Recycling. Note in the figure that the hexagon Planning decisions follows Context evaluation; Structuring decisions follows Input evaluation; Implementation decisions follows Process evaluation; and Recycling decisions follows Product evaluation.[84]

Decision making, according to the Phi Delta Kappa Committee, occurs in four different settings:[85]

a. small change with high information
b. small change with low information
c. large change with high information
d. large change with low information

Four Types of Changes. In these settings, four types of changes may result: neomobilistic, incremental, homeostatic, and metamorphic. *Neomobilistic change* occurs in

TABLE 13.1   Four Types of Evaluation

	Context Evaluation	**Input Evaluation**	**Process Evaluation**	**Product Evaluation**
Objective	To define the *operating context*, to identify and assess *needs* and *opportunities* in the context, and to diagnose *problems* underlying the *needs* and *opportunities*.	To identify and assess *system capabilities*, available input *strategies*, and designs for implementing the strategies.	To identify or predict, in process, *defects* in the procedural design or its implementation, to provide information for the preprogrammed decisions, and to maintain a record of *procedural events* and activities.	To relate *outcome information* to objectives and to context, input, and process information.
Method	By describing the context; by comparing actual and intended inputs and outputs; by comparing probable and possible system performance; and by analyzing possible causes of discrepancies between actualities and intentions.	By describing and analyzing available human and material resources, solution strategies, and procedural designs for relevance, feasibility and economy in the course of action to be taken.	By monitoring the activity's potential procedural barriers and remaining alert to unanticipated ones, by obtaining specified information for programmed decisions, and describing the actual process.	By defining operationally and measuring criteria associated with the objectives, by comparing these measurements with predetermined standards or comparative bases, and by interpreting the outcomes in terms of recorded context, input and process information.
Relation to decision making in the change process	For deciding on the *setting* to be served, the *goal* associated with meeting needs or using opportunities, and the *objectives* associated with solving problems, i.e., for *planning* needed changes.	For electing *sources of support*, solution *strategies*, and procedural designs, i.e., for *structuring* change activities.	For *implementing* and *refining the program design and procedure*, i.e., for effecting process control.	For deciding to *continue, terminate, modify,* or *refocus* a change activity, and for linking the activity to other major phases of the change process, i.e., for recycling change activities.

Source: Daniel L. Stufflebeam, an address given at the Eleventh Annual Phi Delta Kappa Symposium on Educational Research, Ohio State University, June 24, 1970. Quoted in Blaine R. Worthen and James R. Sanders, *Educational Evaluation: Theory and Practice* (Worthington, Ohio: Charles A. Jones, 1973), p. 139. Reprinted by permission.

a setting in which a large change is sought on the basis of low information. These changes are innovative solutions based on little evidence. *Incremental changes* are series of small changes based on low information. *Homeostatic change*, which is the most common in education, is a small change based on high information. Finally, *metamorphic change*, a large change based on high information, is so rare that it is not shown on the CIPP model.

The model plots the sequence of evaluation and decision making from context evaluation to recycling decisions. The committee has touched up the model with small loops that look like lightbulbs on the evaluation blocks to indicate that the general process of delineating, obtaining, and providing information is cyclical and applies to each type of evaluation.

The ovals, the circle, and the *E* in the model represent types of activities, types of change, and adjustment as a result of the evaluations made and decisions taken. The CIPP model presents a comprehensive view of the evaluation process. Like Saylor, Alexander, and Lewis, Stufflebeam and his associates also called for evaluation of the evaluation program. Said the Phi Delta Kappa Committee: "To maximize the effectiveness and efficiency of evaluation, evaluation itself should be evaluated. . . . The criteria for this include internal validity, external validity, reliability, objectivity, relevance, importance, credibility, scope, pervasiveness, timeliness, and efficiency."[86]

THE CURRICULUM MODEL WITH TYPES OF EVALUATION

To refine our concept of the necessary types of evaluation and to show what types are carried out at specific stages, I have rediagrammed the Curriculum Model in Figure 13.6. In this submodel of the model for curriculum development, the types of evaluation are now numbered for easy reference.

Let's review each of the numbered elements:

1. As a part of context evaluation, needs are assessed.
2. Curriculum goals are validated.
3. Curriculum objectives are validated.
4. Context evaluation begins with the needs assessment and continues up to the implementation stage.
5. Input evaluation takes place between specification of curriculum objectives and implementation of the curriculum.
6. Process evaluation is carried out during the implementation stage. Michael Scriven described three types of process research: noninferential studies, investigations of causal claims about the process, and formative evaluation.[87] Noninferential studies are those observations and investigations of what is actually happening in the classroom. Investigation of causal claims is referred to by some educators as "action research."[88] This type of research is a less than rigorous attempt to establish

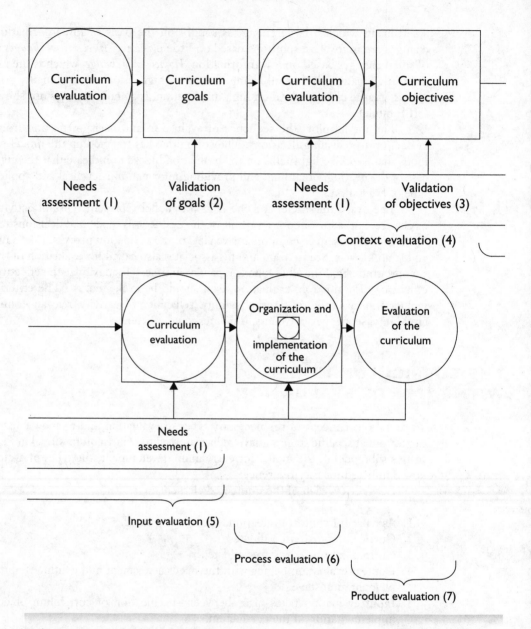

FIGURE 13.6 Sequence and Types of Evaluation

whether one teaching technique is better than another. Formative evaluation is assessment during the course of a study or program. To these three types of process research we might add the term "descriptive research," of which noninferential studies of teacher and student classroom behavior represent one form. The use of survey instruments and the application of the instrument standards also fall into the category of descriptive research.

7. Product evaluation is summative evaluation of the entire process. This type of evaluation is sometimes referred to as outcome evaluation or program evaluation. Program evaluation, however, is used not only in the sense of summative evaluation but also as a synonym for the entire process of curriculum evaluation. Thus, a model for curriculum evaluation might also be called a model for program evaluation.

The Saylor, Alexander, and Lewis and CIPP models provide us with two different ways of viewing the process of curriculum evaluation. The models are similar to the extent that they urge a comprehensive approach to evaluation. They are different in the terminology they use and the level of detail they depict. The Saylor, Alexander, and Lewis model is somewhat less complex than the CIPP model and may perhaps be more readily understood by curriculum workers in general. The CIPP model may be more appealing to specialists in curriculum evaluation. Some dissatisfaction has been expressed for so-called process-product research. McNeil discussed what he perceived as the continuing methodological and theoretical problems of this form of research. He cautioned of overemphasis on generalization of results.[89]

STANDARDS FOR EVALUATION

The use of any evaluation model will be more effective and proper if the evaluators follow some agreed-on standards. The Joint Committee on Standards for Educational Evaluation, chaired by James R. Sanders, identified four attributes of an evaluation: utility, feasibility, propriety, and accuracy.[90] This committee proposed seven utility standards "to ensure that an evaluation will serve the information needs of intended users."[91] They offered three feasibility standards "to ensure that an evaluation will be realistic, prudent, diplomatic, and frugal."[92] Eight propriety standards were advanced "to ensure that an evaluation will be conducted legally, ethically, and with due regard for the welfare of those involved in the evaluation, as well as those affected by its results."[93] Twelve accuracy standards were suggested "to ensure that an evaluation will reveal and convey technically adequate information about the features that determine worth or merit of the program being evaluated."[94]

With evaluation of the curriculum, we conclude the model for curriculum development proposed in this text. However, I must stress that there is really no fixed end to the model; it is cyclical. Results of evaluation produce data for modifying earlier components. Without evaluation there can be no considered modifications and, therefore, little likelihood in improvement.

Summary

Evaluation is a continuous process by which data are gathered and judgments made for the purpose of improving a system. Thorough evaluation is essential to curriculum development. Evaluation is perceived as a process of making judgments, whereas research is perceived as the process of gathering data as bases for judgments.

Eight concepts that present perennial or continuing problems were considered. Each was presented as a guiding principle to which curriculum workers must give attention.

Scope is the breadth of the curriculum—the "what." The major task in planning the scope of the curriculum is selection of content, organizing elements, organizing centers, or integrative threads from the wealth of possible choices.

Relevance is the usefulness of content to the learner. What makes determining the relevance of a curriculum difficult is the variety of perceptions of what is relevant. A consensus of the opinions of the various constituencies and patrons of the school should be sought by curriculum workers to determine what is of sufficient relevance to be included in the curriculum.

Curriculum planners should strive for balance among a number of variables. When a curriculum gives excessive attention to one dimension or to one group and ignores or minimizes attention to others, the curriculum may be said to be out of balance and in need of being brought into balance.

Integration is the unification of disciplines—the weakening or abandoning of boundaries between discrete subjects. Many educators feel that integrated content helps students in the task of problem solving. Relevance, balance, and integration are perceived as dimensions of scope.

Sequence is the "when"—the ordering of the units of content. Attention must be paid to prerequisite learning requirements.

Continuity is the planned introduction and reintroduction of content at subsequent grade levels and at ever-increasing levels of complexity. This concept is at the heart of the "spiral curriculum."

Articulation is the meshing of subject matter and skills between successive levels of schooling to provide a smooth transition for boys and girls from a lower to higher level. Sequence, continuity, and articulation are all related concepts. Continuity and articulation are perceived as dimensions of sequencing.

Transferability is that characteristic of learning which when realized in one setting permits it to be carried over into another setting. Although there is no proof that certain subjects per se enhance the transfer of learning, there is some evidence to support the thesis that teaching basic principles of a discipline and stressing their application increase transfer. Transfer is a much-desired goal of education.

Curriculum planners engage in various types of evaluation and research. Among the types of evaluation are context, input, process, and product. Among the types of research are action, descriptive, historical, and experimental. In another vein, curriculum planners engage in both formative (process or progress) evaluation and in summative (outcome or product) evaluation.

Two limited models of curriculum evaluation (assessment of curriculum objectives and assessment of guiding principles of curriculum organization and construction) and two comprehensive models of curriculum evaluation (the Saylor, Alexander, and Lewis model and the CIPP model) were discussed. The Saylor, Alexander, and Lewis model seeks evaluation of five components: the goals, subgoals, and objectives; the program of education as a totality; the specific segments of the education program; instruction; and the evaluation program. The CIPP model was designed by the Phi Delta Kappa National Study Committee on Evaluation, which was chaired by Daniel L. Stufflebeam. It is more complex and technical than the Saylor, Alexander, and Lewis model. The CIPP model combines "three major steps in the evaluation process (delineating, obtaining, and providing), . . . three classes of change settings (homeostasis, incrementalism, and neomobilism), . . . four types of evaluation (context, input, process, and product), and . . . four types of decisions (planning, structuring, implementing, and recycling)."[95] The creators of both these models also urged an evaluation of the evaluation program. The limited and comprehensive models may be used independently or in conjunction with each other.

Curriculum evaluators from both inside and outside are employed by school systems. Much of the burden for curriculum evaluation falls on teachers as they work in the area of curriculum development. Following a set of agreed-on standards improves the evaluation process. Attention should be given to utility, feasibility, propriety, and accuracy standards.

Evaluation of the curriculum is the culmination of the model for curriculum development proposed in this textbook. Though placed at the end of the diagrammed model, evaluation connotes the end of one cycle and the beginning of the next. Improvements in the subsequent cycle are made as a result of evaluation.

 ## Questions for Discussion

1. What are several signs other than test scores that reveal a curriculum is not working?

2. What is the role of the teacher in curriculum evaluation?

3. What are the pros and cons of employing a curriculum evaluator from outside the school system?

4. What are the pros and cons of action research?

5. How does the Hawthorne effect enter into curriculum evaluation? Cite examples from your experience or from the literature.

Exercises

1. Outline the scope of a course you have taught or plan to teach.

2. Poll a number of teachers, students, and parents to find out what they feel is relevant in the curriculum and what relevant topics they think have been left out.

3. Determine in what ways a curriculum you know well appears to be in or out of balance. If you believe that the curriculum is out of balance, recommend ways to bring it into balance.

4. Report on any planned efforts you can find to correlate or integrate subject matter.

5. Outline and explain the rationale of the sequence of the topics or elements of a course you have taught or plan to teach.

6. Determine whether a school you know well has planned the curriculum keeping in mind the principle of continuity. Recommend improvements in continuity, if necessary.

7. Determine whether a school system you know well has planned the curriculum keeping in mind the principle of articulation. Recommend improvements in articulation, if necessary.

8. Show the transfer value of a discipline that you are certified or becoming certified to teach.

9. Define context, input, process, and product evaluation.

10. Report on evidence of any of the types of evaluation in exercise 9 carried out in a school system you know well.

11. Look up and explain to the class what is meant by internal validity, external validity, reliability, objectivity, relevance, importance, credibility, scope, pervasiveness, timeliness, and efficiency as they relate to the evaluation of evaluation programs.

12. Define empirical data, descriptive research, action research, historical research, experimental research, and dynamic hypotheses.

13. Draw up a list of skills needed by a curriculum evaluator.

14. Show with appropriate evidence that a school system you know well has used evaluative data to modify a curriculum.

15. Determine and provide evidence as to whether curriculum evaluation in a school system you know well suffers from any of the eight symptoms listed by the Phi Delta Kappa National Study Committee on Evaluation.

16. Explain the difference between goal-based evaluation and goal-free evaluation. Compare these two approaches and state under what conditions each is appropriate.

17. This assignment is for four students. Refer to the publication of the Joint Committee of Standards for Educational Evaluation (see bibliography). Each student should select one of the four attributes (utility, feasibility, propriety, and accuracy) of an evaluation and describe to the class the standards suggested for it. Critique the standards as to applicability and appropriateness.

18. Describe any curriculum changes that have come about as a result of district or state assessments.

19. For those currently teaching: Carry out a curriculum mapping in the grade or course you teach.

20. Report on the process and product of a curriculum audit conducted in any school system you know or reported in the literature. (See the Fenwick W. English reference on curriculum auditing for case studies.)

21. Prepare a written or oral report on the process and results of any piece of action research that you have done or can locate in a school system or in the literature.

22. Look up and prepare a written or oral report on one of the following:

    Center for the Study of Evaluation CSE Model
    Malcolm Provus on Discrepancy Evaluation
    Michael Scriven on Goal-Free Evaluation
    Robert E. Stake on Case Study Research

    See bibliography for sources. Other sources for these models or models not listed are acceptable for this exercise.

23. Look up and report on the principles and process of the Accelerated Schools Project. (See Finnan et al. in bibliography.)

24. Read and evaluate the twelve emerging trends or issues that Worthen, Sanders, and Fitzpatrick believe likely to influence significantly the future of program evaluation (see bibliography).

25. Prepare a written or oral report on the Effective Schools Process. (See "Effective Schools," *Phi Delta Kappan* in the bibliography.)

Professional Inquiry Kit

Curriculum Integration. Eight activity folders and a videotape. Carol Cummings, developer. Alexandria, Va.: Association for Supervision and Curriculum Development, 1998.

Videos

Curriculum Mapping: Charting the Course for Content. Two 30-min. videotapes. Facilitator's Guide. Heidi Hayes Jacobs, consultant. Grade-level and subject-level teams create and use curriculum maps. Alexandria, Va.: Association for Supervision and Curriculum Development, 1999.

Getting Results with Curriculum Mapping. One 30-min. videotape. Facilitator's Guide. DVD also available. Alexandria, Va.: Association for Supervision and Curriculum Development, 2006.

Websites

Educational Resources Information Center (ERIC): http://www.eric.ed.gov

Effective Schools Process: http://www.pdkintl.org/prof dev/esp/esphome.htm

National Center for Accelerated Schools: http://www .acceleratedschools.net

National Study of School Evaluation: http://www.nsse .org

UMI ProQuest Digital Dissertations: http://il.proquest .com/brand/umi.shtml

Endnotes

1. Albert I. Oliver, *Curriculum Improvement: A Guide to Problems, Principles, and Process,* 2nd ed. (New York: Harper & Row, 1965), p. 306.

2. Daniel L. Stufflebeam et al., *Educational Evaluation and Decision Making* (Itasca, Ill.: F. E. Peacock, 1971), pp. 4–9.

3. For an account of the Eight-Year Study see Wilford M. Aikin, *The Story of the Eight-Year Study* (New York: Harper & Row, 1942).

4. Daniel L. Stufflebeam, *Evaluation Models* (San Francisco, Calif.: Jossey-Bass, 2001).

5. John D. McNeil, *Contemporary Curriculum in Thought and Action,* 6th ed. (Hoboken, N.J.: Wiley, 2006), p. 199.

6. For references to additional evaluation models see exercise 29 and bibliography at the end of this chapter.

7. See J. Galen Saylor, William M. Alexander, and Arthur J. Lewis, *Curriculum Planning for Better Teaching and Learning,* 4th ed. (New York: Holt, Rinehart and Winston, 1981).

8. See Stufflebeam et al., *Educational Evaluation.*

9. See Chapter 8.

10. Ralph W. Tyler, *Basic Principles of Curriculum and Instruction* (Chicago: University of Chicago Press, 1949), p. 86.

11. Benjamin S. Bloom, "Ideas, Problems, and Methods of Inquiry," in *The Integration of Educational Experiences,* 57th Yearbook, National Society for the Study of Education, Part 3 (Chicago: University of Chicago Press, 1958), pp. 84–85.

12. John I. Goodlad, *Planning and Organizing for Teaching* (Washington, D.C.: National Education Association, 1963), Chapter 2.

13. J. Galen Saylor and William M. Alexander, *Curriculum Planning for Better Teaching and Learning* (New York: Holt, Rinehart and Winston, Inc., 1954), p. 284.

14. Goodlad, *Planning and Organizing,* p. 28.

15. Ibid.

16. Tyler, *Basic Principles,* p. 86.

17. Hollis L. Caswell and Doak K. Campbell, *Curriculum Development* (New York: American Book Company, 1935), p. 152.

18. See p. 197 of this textbook.

19. See Arno A. Bellack, "What Knowledge Is of Most Worth?" *The High School Journal* 48 (February 1965): 318–322.

20. Jerome S. Bruner, *On Knowing* (Cambridge, Mass.: Harvard University Press, 1962), p. 120.

21. See Robert L. Ebel, "What Schools Are For," *Phi Delta Kappan* 54, no. 1 (September 1972): 3–7.

22. Philip H. Phenix, "The Disciplines as Curriculum Content," in *Curriculum Crossroads,* ed. A. Harry Passow (New York: Teachers College Press, Columbia University, 1962), p. 57.

23. See Arthur W. Combs, ed. *Perceiving, Behaving, Becoming,* 1962 Yearbook (Alexandria, Va.: Association for Supervision and Curriculum Development, 1962).

24. Harry S. Broudy, *The Real World of the Public Schools,* (New York: Harcourt Brace Jovanovich, 1972), p. 179.

25. William Glasser, *The Quality School: Managing Students Without Coercion*, 2nd ed. (New York: HarperPerennial, 1992), p. 7.

26. B. Othanel Smith et al., *Teachers for the Real World* (Washington, D.C.: American Association of Colleges for Teacher Education, 1969), pp. 130–131. Reprinted with permission. See also Harry S. Broudy, B. Othanel Smith, and Joe R. Burnett, *Democracy and Excellence in American Secondary Education* (Chicago: Rand McNally, 1964), Chapter 3. Broudy, Smith, and Burnett discuss four uses of knowledge: replicative (repetition of a skill), associative, applicative, and interpretive.

27. Smith et al., *Teachers*, p. 131.

28. Ibid, pp. 131–133.

29. Paul M. Halverson, "The Meaning of Balance," *Balance in the Curriculum*, 1961 Yearbook (Alexandria, Va.: Association for Supervision and Curriculum Development, 1961), p. 7.

30. Ibid., p. 4.

31. Goodlad, *Planning and Organizing*, p. 29.

32. Ronald C. Doll, *Curriculum Improvement: Decision Making and Process*, 9th ed. (Boston: Allyn and Bacon, 1996), pp. 186–187.

33. Romesh Ratnesar, "Lost in the Middle," *Time* 152, no. 11 (September 14, 1998): 60–64.

34. Tyler, *Basic Principles*, p. 85.

35. Hilda Taba, *Curriculum Improvement: Theory and Practice* (New York: Harcourt Brace Jovanovich, 1962), p. 298.

36. Ibid., p. 299.

37. Ibid.

38. Ibid., pp. 298–299.

39. James A. Beane, in Chris Stevenson and Judy F. Carr, eds., *Integrated Studies in the Middle Grades: Dancing Through Walls* (New York: Teachers College Press, 1993), p. x. The Stevenson and Carr book describes the experiences of Vermont teachers who created and implemented integrated teaching plans.

40. For discussion of types of integrated curricula see Gordon F. Vars, ed. *Common Learnings: Core and Interdisciplinary Team Approaches* (Scranton, Pa.: International Textbook Company, 1969).

41. J. Galen Saylor and William M. Alexander, *Curriculum Planning for Better Teaching and Learning* (New York: Holt, Rinehart and Winston, 1954), p. 249.

42. Donald E. Orlosky and B. Othanel Smith, *Curriculum Development: Issues and Insights* (Chicago: Rand McNally College Publishing Company, 1978), p. 267.

43. Ibid., p. 251.

44. Ibid., p. 267.

45. B. Othanel Smith, William O. Stanley, and J. Harlan Shores, *Fundamentals of Curriculum Development*, rev. ed. (New York: Harcourt Brace Jovanovich, 1957), p. 171.

46. Ibid.

47. Ibid., pp. 174–186.

48. Tyler, *Basic Principles*, pp. 84–85.

49. See Jerome S. Bruner, *The Process of Education* (Cambridge, Mass.: Harvard University Press, 1960), pp. 13, 52–54.

50. Oliver, *Curriculum Improvement*, p. 222. Some authors also refer to scope as a horizontal dimension of curriculum organization and sequence as a vertical dimension.

51. McNeil, *Contemporary Curriculum*, p. 332.

52. Ibid.

53. See Edward L. Thorndike, "Mental Discipline in High School Studies," *Journal of Educational Psychology* 15, no. 1 (January 1924): 1–22; continued in 15, no. 2 (February 1924): 83–98. See also Edward L. Thorndike, *The Principles of Teaching* (New York: Seiler, 1906) and Sidney L. Pressey and Francis P. Robinson, *Psychology and the New Education*, rev. ed. (New York: Harper & Row, 1944).

54. Thorndike, "Mental Discipline," (February 1924), p. 98.

55. Daniel Tanner and Laurel Tanner, *Curriculum Development: Theory into Practice*, 4th ed. (Upper Saddle River, N.J.: Merrill/Prentice Hall, 2007), p. 87.

56. Hilda Taba, *Curriculum Development*, p. 124.

57. Jerome S. Bruner, "Structures in Learning," *Today's Education* 52, no. 3 (March 1963): 26.

58. Ibid., p. 27.

59. See David P. Ausubel, *Educational Psychology: A Cognitive View* (New York: Holt, Rinehart and Winston, 1968).

60. Renate Nummela Caine and Geoffrey Caine, *Making Connections: Teaching and the Human Brain* (Alexandria, Va.: Association for Supervision and Curriculum Development, 1991), p. 47.

61. Broudy, *Real World*, p. 193.

62. Saylor, Alexander, and Lewis, p. 334.

63. Ibid., pp. 350–352.

64. Ibid., p. 344.

65. See Chapter 12 for discussion of national and international assessments.

66. See Chapter 7 of this textbook regarding NSSE instruments.

67. Fenwick W. English, "Curriculum Mapping," *Educational Leadership* 37, no. 7 (April 1980): 558–559. See also Donald F. Weinstein, *Administrator's Guide to Curriculum Mapping: A Step-by-Step Manual* (Englewood Cliffs, N.J.: Prentice-Hall, 1988).

68. Heidi Hayes Jacobs, *Mapping the Big Picture: Integrating Curriculum and Assessment K–12* (Alexandria, Va.: Association for Supervision and Curriculum Development, 1997), p. 17.

69. Ibid., pp. 4, 8.

70. Heidi Hayes Jacobs, ed., *Getting Results with Curriculum Mapping* (Alexandria, Va.: Association for Supervision and Curriculum Development, 2004), p. vi.

71. Fenwick W. English, *Curriculum Auditing* (Lancaster, Pa.: Technomic Publishing Company, 1988), p. 3.

72. Ibid., p. 33.

73. Ibid., pp. 33–34.

74. Saylor, Alexander, and Lewis, *Curriculum Planning*, p. 334.

75. Stufflebeam et al., *Educational Evaluation*, pp. 218–235.

76. See pp. 99–100 of this textbook.

77. Daniel L. Stufflebeam, an address given at the Eleventh Annual Phi Delta Kappa Symposium on Educational Research, Ohio State University, June 24, 1970. Quoted in Blaine R. Worthen and James R. Sanders, *Educational Evaluation: Theory and Practice* (Worthington, Ohio: Charles A. Jones, 1971), p. 129.

78. Ibid.

79. Ibid., p. 136.

80. Ibid.

81. Ibid., p. 137.

82. Ibid.

83. Ibid., p. 138.

84. Stufflebeam et al., *Educational Evaluation*, pp. 79–84.

85. Ibid., pp. 61–69.

86. Ibid., p. 239.

87. See Michael Scriven, "The Methodology of Evaluation," *Perspectives of Curriculum Evaluation*, AERA Monograph Series on Curriculum Evaluation No. 1 (Chicago: Rand McNally, 1967), pp. 49–51.

88. For discussions of action research see Jean McNiff with Jack Whitehead, *Action Research: Principles and Practices* (New York: RoutledgeFalmer, 2002) and Richard Sagor, *Guiding School Improvement with Action Research* (Alexandria, Va.: Association for Supervision and Curriculum Improvement, 2000).

89. McNeil, *Contemporary Curriculum*, p. 333.

90. The Joint Committee on Standards for Educational Evaluation, James R. Sanders, Chair, *The Program Evaluation Standards: How to Assess Evaluations of Educational Programs*, 2nd ed. (Thousand Oaks, Calif.: Sage Publications, 1994). See also The Joint Committee on Standards for Educational Evaluation, Daniel L. Stufflebeam, Chair, *Standards for Evaluations of Educational Programs, Projects, and Materials* (New York: McGraw-Hill, 1981), pp. 19, 51, 63, 97.

91. The Joint Committee, *The Program Evaluation Standards*, p. 23.

92. Ibid., p. 63.

93. Ibid., p. 81.

94. Ibid., p. 125.

95. Stufflebeam et al., *Educational Evaluation*, p. 238.

Bibliography

Aikin, Wilford M. *The Story of the Eight-Year Study.* New York: Harper & Row, 1942.

Armstrong, David G. *Developing and Documenting the Curriculum.* Boston: Allyn and Bacon, 1989.

Association for Supervision and Curriculum Development. *Balance in the Curriculum.* 1961 Yearbook. Alexandria, Va.: Association for Supervision and Curriculum Development, 1961.

Beane, James A. "Foreword: Teachers of Uncommon Courage." In Chris Stevenson and Judy F. Carr, eds. *Integrated Studies in the Middle Grades: Dancing Through Walls.* New York: Teachers College Press, 1993.

Bellack, Arno. "What Knowledge Is of Most Worth?" *High School Journal* 48, no. 5 (February 1965): 318–332.

Bloom, Benjamin S. "Ideas, Problems, and Methods of Inquiry." In *The Integration of Educational Experiences.* 57th Yearbook. National Society for the Study of Education, Part 3, pp. 84–85. Chicago: University of Chicago Press, 1958.

Broudy, Harry S. *The Real World of the Public Schools.* New York: Harcourt Brace Jovanovich, 1972.

Bruner, Jerome S. *On Knowing: Essays for the Left Hand.* Cambridge, Mass.: Harvard University Press, 1962.

———. *The Process of Education.* Cambridge, Mass.: Harvard University Press, 1960.

———. *The Relevance of Education.* New York: Norton, 1973.

———. "Structures in Learning." *Today's Education* 52, no. 3 (March 1963): 26–27.

Caine, Renate Nummela and Caine, Geoffrey. *Making Connections: Teaching and the Human Brain.* Alexandria, Va.: Association for Supervision and Curriculum Development, 1991.

Caswell, Hollis L. and Campbell, Doak S. *Curriculum Development.* New York: American Book Company, 1935.

Center for the Study of Evaluation. *Evaluation Workshop I: An Orientation.* Del Monte Research Park, Monterey, Calif.: CTB/McGraw-Hill, 1971. Participant's Notebook and Leader's Manual.

Combs, Arthur W., ed. *Perceiving, Behaving, Becoming.* 1962 Yearbook. Alexandria, Va.: Association for Supervision and Curriculum Development, 1962.

"Curriculum Evaluation: Uses, Misuses, and Nonuses." *Educational Leadership* 35, no. 4 (January 1978): 243–297.

Doll, Ronald C. *Curriculum Improvement: Decision Making and Process*, 9th ed. Boston: Allyn and Bacon, 1996.

Drake, Susan. *Planning Integrated Curriculum: The Call to Adventure*. Alexandria, Va.: Association for Supervision and Curriculum Development, 1993.

Ebel, Robert L. "What Schools Are For." *Phi Delta Kappan* 54, no. 1 (September 1972): 3–7.

"Effective Schools." *Phi Delta Kappan* 83, no. 5 (January 2002): 375–387.

Eisner, Elliot W. *The Educational Imagination: On the Design and Evaluation of School Programs*, 2nd ed. New York: Macmillan, 1985.

———. "Educational Connoisseurship and Criticism: Their Form and Functions in Educational Evaluation." *Journal of Aesthetic Education* 10, numbers 3–4 (July–October, 1976): 13–150.

English, Fenwick W. *Curriculum Auditing*. Lancaster, Pa.: Technomic Publishing Company, 1988.

———. "Curriculum Mapping." *Educational Leadership* 37, no. 7 (April 1980): 558–559.

——— and Steffy, Betty E., *Deep Curriculum Alignment: Creating a Level Playing Field for All Children on High-Stakes Tests of Educational Accountability*. Lanham, Md.: Scarecrow Press, 2001.

Finnan, Christine, St. John, Edward P., McCarthy, Jane, and Slovacek, Simeon P. *Accelerated Schools: Lessons from the Field*. Thousand Oaks, Calif.: Corwin Press, 1996.

Glasser, William. *The Quality School: Managing Students Without Coercion*, 2nd ed. New York: HarperPerennial, 1992.

Goodlad, John I. *Planning and Organizing for Teaching*. Washington, D.C.: National Education Association, 1963.

Guba, Egon, and Lincoln, Yvonna S. *Effective Evaluation: Improving the Usefulness of Evaluation Results Through Responsive and Naturalistic Approaches*. San Francisco: Jossey-Bass, 1981.

Halverson, Paul M. "The Meaning of Balance." In *Balance in the Curriculum*. 1961 Yearbook, 3–16. Alexandria, Va.: Association for Supervision and Curriculum Development, 1961.

"Integrating the Curriculum." *Educational Leadership* 49, no. 2 (October 1991): 4–75.

Jacobs, Heidi Hayes. *Getting Results with Curriculum Mapping*. Alexandria, Va.: Association for Supervision and Curriculum Development, 2004.

———, ed. *Interdisciplinary Curriculum: Design and Implementation*. Alexandria, Va.: Association for Supervision and Curriculum Development, 1989.

———. *Mapping the Big Picture: Integrating Curriculum and Assessment K–12*. Alexandria, Va.: Association for Supervision and Curriculum Development, 1997.

Johnson, Mauritz, Jr. *Intentionality in Education: A Conceptual Model of Curricular and Instructional Planning and Evaluation*. Albany, N.Y.: Center for Curriculum Research and Services, 1977.

Joint Committee on Standards for Educational Evaluation, James R. Sanders, Chair. *The Program Evaluation Standards: How to Assess Evaluations of Educational Programs*, 2nd ed. Thousand Oaks, Calif.: Sage Publications, 1994.

———, Daniel L. Stufflebeam, Chair. *Standards for Evaluations of Educational Programs, Projects, and Materials*. New York: McGraw-Hill, 1981.

Lindvall, C. M., and Cox, Richard C., with Bolvin, John O. *Evaluation as a Tool in Curriculum Development: The IPI Evaluation Program*. American Educational Research Association Monograph, no. 5. Chicago: Rand McNally, 1970.

McNeil, John D. *Contemporary Curriculum in Thought and Action*, 6th ed. Hoboken, N.J.: Wiley, 2006.

McNiff, Jean with Jack Whitehead. *Action Research in Organisations*. London: Routledge, 2000.

Marsh, Colin J. and Willis, George. *Curriculum: Alternative Approaches, Ongoing Issues*, 4th ed. Upper Saddle River, N.J.: Merrill/Prentice Hall, 2007.

National Study of School Evaluation. *Breakthrough School Improvement: An Action Guide for Greater and Faster Results*. Schaumburg, Ill.: National Study of School Evaluation, 2005.

Oliver, Albert I. *Curriculum Improvement: A Guide to Problems, Principles, and Processes*, 2nd ed. New York: Harper & Row, 1977.

Orlosky, Donald and Smith, B. Othanel, eds. *Curriculum Development: Issues and Insights*. Chicago: Rand McNally, 1978, Part 5.

Owen, John M. and Rogers, Patricia J. *Program Evaluation: Forms and Approaches*. Thousand Oaks, Calif.: Sage Publications, 1999.

Phenix, Philip H. "The Disciplines as Curriculum Content." In *Curriculum Crossroads*, ed. A. Harry Passow, 57–65. New York: Teachers College Press, Columbia University, 1962.

The Phi Delta Kappa/Gallup Polls of the Public's Attitudes Toward the Public Schools. *Phi Delta Kappan*. Annually, usually September.

Pressey, Sidney L. and Robinson, Francis P. *Psychology and the New Education*, rev. ed. New York: Harper & Row, 1944.

Provus, Malcolm. *Discrepancy Evaluation for Educational Program Improvement and Assessment*. Berkeley, Calif.: McCutchan, 1971.

Ratnesar, Romesh. "Lost in the Middle." *Time* 152, no. 11 (September 14, 1998): 60–64.

Rogers, Frederick A. "Curriculum Research and Evaluation." In Fenwick W. English, ed. *Fundamental Curriculum Decisions*, 1983 Yearbook, 142–153. Alexandria, Va.: Association for Supervision and Curriculum Development, 1983.

Sagor, Richard. *Guiding School Improvement with Action Research.* Alexandria, Va.: Association for Supervision and Curriculum Development, 2000.

Saylor, J. Galen and Alexander, William M. *Curriculum Planning for Better Teaching and Learning.* New York: Holt, Rinehart and Winston, 1954.

———, Alexander, William M., and Lewis, Arthur J. *Curriculum Planning for Better Teaching and Learning*, 4th ed. New York: Holt, Rinehart and Winston, 1981.

Scriven, Michael. "Goal-Free Evaluation" In E. R. House, ed. *School Evaluation: The Politics and Process.* Berkeley, Calif.: McCutchan, 1973.

———. "The Methodology of Evaluation." *Perspectives of Curriculum Evaluation.* AERA Monograph Series on Curriculum Evaluation, no. 1, 39–83. Chicago: Rand McNally, 1967.

Shaw, Ian F. *Qualitative Evaluation.* Thousand Oaks, Calif.: Sage Publications, 1999.

Smith, B. Othanel et al. *Teachers for the Real World.* Washington, D.C.: American Association of Colleges for Teacher Education, 1969.

Smith, B. Othanel, Stanley, William O., and Shores, J. Harlan. *Fundamentals of Curriculum Development*, rev. ed. New York: Harcourt Brace Jovanovich, 1957.

Stake, Robert E. *The Art of Case Study Research.* Thousand Oaks, Calif.: Sage Publications, 1995.

———. "Language, Rationality, and Assessment." In *Improving Educational Assessment and an Inventory of Measures of Affective Behavior*, ed. Walcott H. Beatty. Alexandria, Va.: Commission on Assessment of Educational Outcomes, Association for Supervision and Curriculum Development, 1969.

Stevenson, Chris and Carr, Judy F., eds. *Integrated Studies in the Middle Grades: Dancing Through Walls.* New York: Teachers College Press, 1993.

Stufflebeam, Daniel L. *Evaluation Models.* San Francisco: Jossey-Bass, 2001.

——— et al. *Educational Evaluation and Decision Making.* Itasca, Ill.: F. E. Peacock, 1971.

Taba, Hilda. *Curriculum Development: Theory and Practice.* New York: Harcourt Brace Jovanovich, 1962.

Tanner, Daniel and Tanner, Laurel. *Curriculum Development: Theory into Practice*, 4th ed. Upper Saddle River, N.J.: Merrill/Prentice Hall, 2007.

Thorndike, Edward L. "Mental Discipline in High School Studies." *Journal of Educational Psychology* 15, no. 1 (January 1924): 1–22, continued in vol. l5, no. 2 (February 1924): 83–98.

Tyler, Ralph W. *Basic Principles of Curriculum and Instruction.* Chicago: University of Chicago Press, 1949.

——— ed. *Educational Evaluation: New Roles, New Means.* 68th Yearbook of the National Society for the Study of Education. Chicago: University of Chicago Press, 1969.

Tyler, Ralph W., Gagné, Robert M., and Scriven, Michael. *Perspectives of Curriculum Evaluation.* AERA Monograph Series on Curriculum Evaluation, no. 1. Chicago: Rand McNally, 1967.

Vars, Gordon F., ed. *Common Learnings: Core and Interdisciplinary Team Approaches.* Scranton, Pa.: International Textbook Company, 1969.

———. "Integrated Curriculum in Historical Perspective." *Educational Leadership* 49, no. 2 (October 1991): 14–15.

Weinstein, Donald F. *Administrator's Guide to Curriculum Mapping: A Step-by-Step Manual.* Englewood Cliffs, N.J.: Prentice-Hall, 1988.

Worthen, Blaine R., Sanders, James R., and Fitzpatrick, Jody L. *Educational Evaluation: Alternative Approaches and Practical Guidelines*, 2nd ed. New York: Longman, 1997.

14 *Curriculum Products*

AFTER STUDYING THIS CHAPTER YOU SHOULD BE ABLE TO:

1. Construct a curriculum guide.
2. Construct a resource unit.
3. Identify sources of curriculum materials.

TANGIBLE PRODUCTS

The Biblical expression "By their fruits ye shall know them" can certainly be applied to curriculum workers. Walk into the curriculum laboratory of any public school or university and you may be surprised, perhaps even overwhelmed, by the evidence of the productivity of curriculum development workers. The products of their efforts are there for all to see—tangible, printed, and often packaged in eye-catching style.

Curriculum workers have been turning out products for many years. Unfortunately, some curriculum developers view the creation of products as the final rather than the intermediate phase of curriculum improvement. The products are meant to be put into practice, tried out, revised, tried again, revised again, and so on.

Creating curriculum products not only has a functional value—the production of a plan or tool for implementing or evaluating the curriculum—but also gives the planners a great psychological boost. In producing tangible materials, they are able to feel some sense of accomplishment.

Throughout this text we have already seen a number of kinds of curriculum products. Chapter 6 contained examples of statements of philosophy and aims of education.

Chapter 7 included needs assessment surveys and reports, sections of courses of study and curriculum guides, and portions of a state's statement of minimal standards. In Chapter 8 we saw statements of curriculum goals and objectives. Statements of instructional goals and objectives formed a part of Chapter 10. Unit and lesson plans were outlined in Chapter 11. Chapter 12 discussed instruments for evaluating instruction, and Chapter 13, instruments for evaluating the curriculum.

Judging from the tasks that curriculum coordinators, consultants, directors, and other workers are called on to do in the schools, there is a healthy demand for training in the production of curriculum materials. In this chapter we will discuss the creation and use of several of the more common products found in the schools.

The content, the form, and the names by which curriculum materials are known are almost as varied as the number of groups that author them. Curriculum bulletins, curriculum guides, courses of study, syllabi, resource units, and source units can be found in the curriculum libraries of school systems.

Because curriculum materials are impermanent—nonstandardized products made primarily for local use—the variations among them are considerable. To put the creation of curriculum products into perspective, we must visualize curriculum committees and individuals in thousands of school districts all over the United States constructing materials that they feel will be of most help to their teachers. Terms for these types of curriculum materials may signal quite different products or may be used synonymously. A curriculum guide, for example, may be quite different from a course of study. On the other hand, what is called a curriculum guide in one locality may be called a course of study in another. For this reason it is difficult to predict what will be discovered in any particular curriculum product until it is examined.

The curriculum products that we will consider in this chapter are

1. curriculum guides, courses of study, and syllabi
2. resource units

We will not discuss curriculum materials that have been discussed in preceding chapters, such as unit plans, lesson plans, and tests. All curriculum materials share the common purpose of serving as aids to teachers and planners in organizing, implementing, and evaluating curriculum and instruction. Although state and national standards have impacted the creation of curriculum guides and other curriculum materials, necessitating the incorporation of objectives and learning activities designed to meet required standards, the production of curriculum products remains a viable part of the teaching process.

CURRICULUM GUIDES, COURSES OF STUDY, AND SYLLABI

Three kinds of curriculum products are clearly related. These are (1) curriculum guides, (2) courses of study, and (3) syllabi. As already noted, some curriculum workers make no distinction among the three types. The following are definitions of the terms used in this chapter:

1. A *curriculum guide* is the most general of the three types of materials. It may cover a single course or subject area at a particular grade level (e.g., ninth-grade English); all subjects at a particular grade level (e.g., ninth grade); a sequence in a discipline (e.g., language arts); or an area of interest applicable to two or more courses or grade levels (e.g., occupational safety). When a curriculum guide covers a single course, it may also be called a course of study. However, a curriculum guide is a teaching aid with helpful suggestions rather than a complete course of study in itself.
2. A *course of study* is a detailed plan for a single course, including text materials (content). A well-known example of a curriculum product of this nature is *Man: A Course of Study*, which has been widely used in the schools and seen on television.[1] A course of study includes both what is to be taught (content)—in summary or in complete text—and suggestions for how to teach the course.
3. A *syllabus* is an outline of topics to be covered in a single course or grade level.

Curriculum Guide Formats

Let's look more closely at the creation of a curriculum guide. What is its purpose? Who should be included in the task? Curriculum guides are used in at least two ways. In less structured situations where teachers have a great deal of flexibility in planning, a curriculum guide provides many suggestions to teachers who wish to use it. In that case the curriculum guide is one source from which teachers may derive ideas for developing their own resource units, learning units, and lesson plans. In more structured situations a curriculum guide specifies minimal objectives that students must master in the discipline. It may spell out objectives for each marking period. The guide may identify teaching materials and suggest learning activities. It may be accompanied by pretests and posttests for each unit or marking period.

A curriculum guide may be written by a group of teachers or planners or by an individual. In the latter case, the guide is often reviewed by other specialists before it is disseminated within the school system. For those who write a curriculum guide, the process is almost as important as the product. The task of constructing a guide forces the writers to clarify their ideas, to gather data, to demonstrate creativity, to select content, to determine sequence, and to organize their thoughts.

Examination of curriculum guides from various school districts will reveal a variety of formats. Some school systems that develop curriculum guides follow a single format. Because the substance of guides varies from format to format, some school districts find it useful to prepare more than one type of guide. Many curriculum guides are lengthy documents, so I will not attempt to reproduce examples in this text. Instead we will look at the formats that are often employed.

From the many formats for curriculum guides we may select three that we will call, for lack of better labels, the comprehensive, sequencing, and test-coding formats.

The Comprehensive Format.   Curriculum planners following a comprehensive format would include the following components in a curriculum guide for a particular level of a discipline—for example, ninth-grade social studies.

1. *Introduction.* The introduction includes the title or topic of the guide, the subject and grade level for which the guide is designated, and any suggestions that might help users. Some statement should be included as to how the curriculum guide relates to prespecified statements of philosophy and aims and curriculum goals and objectives

2. *Instructional goals.* In this section, instructional goals (called general objectives by some planners) are stated in nonbehavioral terms. Instructional goals should relate to the schools' curriculum goals and objectives.

3. *Instructional objectives.* Instructional objectives (called specific, performance, or behavioral objectives by some planners) for the particular grade level of the subject should be stated in behavioral terms and should encompass all three domains of learning, if all are applicable.

4. *Learning activities.* Learning experiences that might be used by the teacher with pupils should be suggested and placed in preferred sequence.

5. *Evaluation techniques.* Suggestions should be given to teachers on how to evaluate student achievement. This section of the guide could include general suggestions on evaluating, sample test items, or even complete tests.

6. *Resources.* Attention should be given to human resources—persons who might be called on to assist with the content of the guide—and to material resources, including books, audiovisual aids, equipment, and facilities.

An illustration of a comprehensive curriculum guide format is shown in Figure 14.1.

Some writers of comprehensive guides also include a topical outline of the content. No effort is made to separate the goals and objectives into time periods, nor are the components sequenced for the teacher. This format is not prescriptive. Guides of this nature

TOPIC	GOALS	OBJECTIVES	ACTIVITIES	EVALUATION TECHNIQUES	RESOURCES

FIGURE 14.1   Comprehensive Curriculum Guide Format

are supplementary aids for the professional teacher. They offer the maximum flexibility to the teacher, who may choose or reject any of the suggested goals, objectives, activities, evaluation techniques, or resources. You will note this format is similar to a unit plan, which we discussed in Chapter 11.[2] The curriculum guide, however, is broader in scope than the unit plan and offers more alternatives.

Some curriculum planners prefer to cast their comprehensive guides in the following format:

The Sequencing Format. Georgia's list of thinking skills (Table 14.1), developed in the 1980s and keyed to the Bloom taxonomy, furnishes an example of this type of curriculum product.[3] Guides of this nature

1. specify behavioral objectives for each competency area
2. indicate at what grade level(s), K–12, each competency will be taught
3. code objectives at each grade level, for example, as to whether they are introduced (I), developed (D), mastered (M), reinforced (R), or extended (E) at that level

This format provides an overall view of the sequencing of the objectives of the discipline. Teachers retain the opportunity for making decisions on when and how the objectives will be taught at each grade level.

The Test-Coding Format. Offering teachers the least flexibility is the test-coding format, which

1. lists objectives to be mastered by the learners at each marking period of each grade level of a given discipline.
2. codes each objective to district, state, and national criterion-referenced and/or norm-referenced tests that are administered by the school district.

Let's say, for example, a district has developed a set of ten instructional objectives to be accomplished in Health at the second-grade level. The district has further developed tests at the end of each marking period (sometimes as well as comprehensive tests at the end of the year) to determine whether these objectives have been achieved by pupils. Following a test-coding format teachers would specify which objectives were to be pursued during which marking period. Teachers may follow a similar procedure in dealing with state standards and state assessment tests.

Though teachers may exercise choice of learning activities and supplementary resources, they are held accountable for student achievement every marking period. Locally written tests to assess student mastery of the objectives are administered at the end of each marking period.

The three formats can, of course, be combined and expanded. Test-coding can be added to the comprehensive format. Behavioral or performance indicators may be included to refine the behavioral or performance objectives. For example, one indicator for the instructional objective "The student will describe the effects of freon released in the environment" might be "The student will specify principal uses of freon." Reference

TABLE 14.1 Georgia's List of Thinking Skills

Topic	Concept/Skill	K–4	5–8	9–12
A. Recall	The learner will			
	recognize information previously encountered such as facts, concepts or specific elements in a subject area.	ID	DR	R
1. Identification	ascertain the origin, nature or definitive characteristics of an item.	ID	DR	R
2. Observation	obtain information by noting, perceiving, noticing and describing. Observation may involve looking, listening, touching, feeling, smelling or tasting.	ID	DR	R
3. Perception	become aware of objects through using the senses, especially seeing or hearing.	ID	DR	R
B. Comprehension	The learner will			
	understand information that has been communicated.	ID	D	R
1. Translation	change information from one form to another, maintaining accuracy of the original communication.	ID	DR	DR
2. Analogy Recognition	infer that if two things are known to be alike in some respects then they may be alike in others.	ID	DR	DR
C. Hypothesizing	The learner will assume, making a tentative explanation.	I	DR	DR
1. Prediction	tell or declare beforehand.	I	DR	DR
2. Imagination	form a mental image of, represent or picture to oneself.	I	DR	DR
D. Application	The learner will put information to use.	I	DR	DR
1. Clarification	make something easier to understand.		ID	DR
2. Hypothesis Testing	try out ideas for possible solutions.	I	ID	DR
3. Operational Definition	order ideas into a step by step plan.		ID	DR
4. Decision Making	choose the best or most desirable alternative.	I	ID	DR
5. Consequence Projection	define further steps toward probable solutions or identify cause/effect relationships.	I	ID	DR
E. Analysis	The learner will			
	break down a concept, problem, pattern or whole into its component parts, systematically or sequentially, so that the relations between parts are expressed explicitly.	ID	DR	
1. Comparison	determine similarities and differences on the basis of given criteria.	ID	DR	R
2. Classification	place elements into arbitrarily established systems of groupings and subgroupings on the basis of common characteristics.	ID	DR	R

(continued)

TABLE 14.1 Continued

Topic	Concept/Skill	K–4	5–8	9–12
3. Selection	choose an element from a set of elements on the basis of given criteria.	ID	DR	R
4. Association	relate elements either given or as they come to mind.	ID	DR	R
5. Inference	draw a conclusion based on facts or evidence.	I	ID	DR
6. Interpretation	express meaning of or reaction to an experience.	I	ID	DR
7. Qualification	describe by enumerating characteristics.	I	ID	R
F. Synthesis	The learner will			
	arrange and combine elements to form a structure, pattern or product.	I	ID	DR
1. Summarization	express a brief or concise restatement.	I	ID	DR
2. Generalization	formulate or derive from specifics (to make universally applicable) a class, form or statement.	I	ID	DR
3. Formulation of Concepts	originate or express ideas.		ID	DR
4. Integration	form into a whole and unite information.		ID	DR
G. Evaluation	The learner will			
	make judgments regarding quantity and quality on the basis of given criteria.		ID	DR
1. Justification	show adequate reason(s) for something done.	I	ID	DR
2. Imposition of Standards	assure equal comparison with established criteria.		ID	DR
3. Judgment	form an idea or opinion about any matter.		ID	DR
4. Internal Consistency	understand that all the parts of a process fit together.		ID	DR
5. Value	establish worth or esteem.	I	ID	DR

Source: Georgia Department of Education, *Essential Skills for Georgia Schools* (Atlanta: Division of Curriculum Services, Georgia Department of Education, 1980), pp. 87–88. Reprinted by permission.

is made to criteria for instructional objectives discussed in Chapter 10. Criticizing the lack of specificity of "typical instructions" (that is, objectives) found in curriculum guides, E. D. Hirsch, Jr. mused, "It might be wondered how it is possible for states and localities to produce lengthy curriculum guides that, for all their bulk, fail to define specific knowledge for specific grade levels."[4]

No matter what format is followed by a school system, curriculum guides should be used and revised periodically. It is an open secret that curriculum guides are often written to satisfy a local or state mandate. Having completed the task of writing the documents, teachers set them aside and allow them to accumulate dust. Teachers' failure to use the curriculum guides demonstrates once again that commitment to the process is an essential ingredient. Curriculum guides that are handed down, for example, generate little commitment. They may be followed out of necessity but without enthusiasm. Even those guides that are written by teachers rather than by curriculum consultants will be accepted only if teachers perceive the task as useful to them rather than as a response to directives from superordinates.[5]

RESOURCE UNIT

A resource unit, called a source unit by some curriculum workers, is "an arrangement of materials and activities around a particular topic or problem."[6] The resource unit is a curriculum product that falls somewhere between a teacher's learning unit and a course of study or curriculum guide. I explained elsewhere:

> The resource unit is a source of information and ideas for teachers to use. . . . The major purpose of the resource unit is to provide ideas for a teacher who wishes to create [a] learning unit on the same topic. . . . The resource unit contains a wealth of suggestions and information which will aid the teacher in supplementing material found in the basic textbook. The resource unit shortens the busy teacher's planning time and simplifies [the] work [of constructing] learning units . . .[7]

In essence, the resource unit serves the same general purpose as a course of study or curriculum guide. The major distinction between these types of products is that the resource unit is much narrower in scope, focusing on a particular topic rather than on an entire year, course, subject area, or sequence. Although we may encounter a course of study or curriculum guide for eleventh-grade American history, for example, we may also find resource units on topics within American history, such as the Age of Jackson, the Great Depression, or the War on Terrorism.

The same outline that was suggested for a comprehensive curriculum guide applies to the resource unit. An example of a resource unit is given in Box 14.1. Note the relationship between this illustrative resource unit and the illustrative learning unit plan in Chapter 11.

SOURCES OF CURRICULUM MATERIALS

These illustrations of curriculum products barely suggest the types that are already available or can be constructed. In every state of the union, curriculum committees have created a wide variety of useful materials. Curriculum developers and others who are searching for curriculum materials beyond the textbooks and accompanying teachers' manuals may locate examples in several places: curriculum libraries of colleges and universities, particularly those of schools and departments of education; curriculum centers of the public school systems; state and national professional education associations; the

BOX 14.1

A Resource Unit

Grade Level/Course:
Senior High School/Problems
of American Democracy
Topic: Education in the United States

A. Introduction

The enterprise of education in the United States consumes over 800 billion dollars per year, close to 500 billion of which are spent on public elementary and secondary schools. About twenty-five percent of the population is enrolled in schools from nursery through graduate level. In some way, schooling touches the lives of every person in the country, yet schooling itself is rarely studied in the schools. Although most people have their own ideas about education, their database is often limited or lacking. The purpose of this resource unit is to provide students with facts, insights, and understandings about the American educational system.

B. Instructional Goals
   1. Cognitive
      The student will become familiar with
      a. the purposes of education in the United States
      b. the general structure of education in the United States
      c. the ways in which education in the United States is administered and financed
      d. major differences between the U.S. system of education and systems of other countries
   2. Affective
      The student will appreciate
      a. the complexity of the U.S. educational system
      b. our decentralized system of education
      c. the extent and complexity of problems facing education in the United States
      d. the achievements of American schools
C. Instructional Objectives
   1. Cognitive
      The student will be able to
      a. identify sources of funding for education

   b. explain local, state, and federal responsibilities for education
   c. state purposes of levels of education: elementary, middle, junior high, senior high, community college, senior college, and university
   d. tell the strengths and weaknesses of our decentralized system of education
   e. explain how teachers are prepared and hired
   f. describe how the educational dollar is spent
   g. account for differences in the support of education by the various states
   h. identify problems facing the schools and tell what efforts are being made to solve them
   i. account for the growth of private schools, charter schools, and home-schooling
   j. compare the American system of education with the system in another country
   2. Affective
      The student will
      a. write a statement of purposes of education as he or she sees them
      b. state what he or she feels constitutes a good education
      c. state with reasons whether he or she believes compulsory education is desirable
      d. describe how he or she feels education should be funded
      e. take a position on whether public school education or private school education is better
      f. take a position on whether American education or European (or Asian) education is better
      g. show his or her position by written reports on some controversial issues such as prayer in the schools, the teaching of the theory of evolution, censorship of textbooks and library books, busing of students for purposes of integrating the races, and bilingual education
   3. Psychomotor
      None

D. Learning Activities

1. Read provisions of the United States Constitution regarding education, especially the First, Tenth, and Fourteenth Amendments.
2. Read provisions of the state constitution regarding education.
3. Examine recent state and federal legislation on education.
4. Prepare a chart showing the percentages of funding for education from local, state, and federal sources.
5. Prepare a diagram showing overall dollars spent in any one year for education by local, state, and federal sources in the student's home state.
6. Observe an elementary, middle/junior high, and secondary class in action, and afterward compare such aspects as objectives, materials, methods of teaching, and student conduct.
7. Visit a community college and interview one of the administrators on the purposes and programs of the community college.
8. Invite a private and/or parochial school administrator to come to class to talk on purposes and programs of his or her school.
9. Invite a panel of public school principals at elementary, middle/junior high, and secondary levels to come to class to talk on problems they face in administering their schools.
10. Critique the requirements for a teacher's certificate in the student's home state.
11. Gather and present data on the funding of higher education in both the United States and in the student's home state.
12. Read and evaluate several statements of purposes of education.
13. Read and evaluate a book or article critical of American public education.
14. Report on pressure groups that influence education.
15. Critique the awarding of vouchers or tax credits that enable parents to send their children to schools of their choice.
16. Find out how teachers are trained, certified, and employed in the student's home state.
17. Find out how school administrators are trained, certified, and employed in the student's home state.
18. Attend a school board meeting and discuss it in class.
19. Visit the superintendent's office and hear the superintendent (or his or her deputy) explain the role of the superintendent.
20. Find out what the school tax rate is in the student's home community, how moneys are raised for the schools, and how much money is expended in the community for schools.
21. Find out how much teachers and administrators are paid in the student's home community and what fringe benefits they receive.
22. Examine the staffing patterns of an elementary, middle, or secondary school and determine types of employees needed to run the school.
23. Find out how serious the dropout problem is in the student's home community and what is being done to solve it.
24. Determine whether or not student achievement in schools of the student's home district is satisfactory. If not, account for reasons for unsatisfactory achievement and report on measures that are being taken to improve the situation.
25. Explain the pros and cons of private management of public schools as opposed to public administration.
26. Choose a controversial educational issue and write a paper showing positions of several prominent persons or groups and the student's own position.
27. Research and prepare a report on the public's attitudes toward public schools.
28. Find out requirements for graduation from high school and promotion from grade to grade in your state.
29. Go to your state Department of Education website and find out your state's standards of learning.
30. Explain what is meant by "high-stakes testing" and show your position on it.

Note: Many of the topics under Learning Activities may be researched on the Internet. Students may make reports individually or as group panels at the teacher's determination. Some students may wish to make their reports as PowerPoint presentations.

BOX 14.1

Continued

E. Evaluation Techniques
   1. Give a pretest consisting of objective test items to survey student's factual knowledge about education in the United States. Sample test items:
      a. Responsibility for state control of education in the United States is derived from the U.S. Constitution's
         (1) First Amendment
         (2) Fifth Amendment
         (3) Tenth Amendment
         (4) Fourteenth Amendment
      b. Policies for local school districts are promulgated by
         (1) advisory councils
         (2) school boards
         (3) teachers' unions
         (4) school principals
   2. Evaluate student's oral reports.
   3. Evaluate student's written work—reports, charts, etc.
   4. Observe student's reactions and comments in class discussion.
   5. Give a posttest of objective items similar to those of the pretest.
F. Resources
Educational Leadership. Alexandria, Va.: Association for Supervision and Curriculum Development, monthly.
National Assessment of Educational Progress, *The Nation's Report Card.* Washington, D.C.: U.S. Government Printing Office, periodically.

National Center for Education Statistics, *The Condition of Education.* Washington, D.C.: U.S. Government Printing Office, annually.
———. *Digest of Education Statistics.* Washington, D.C.: U.S. Government Printing Office, annually.
———. *The Nation's Report Card* (reports on the National Assessment of Educational Progress). Washington, D.C.: U.S. Government Printing Office, periodically.
———. *Projections of Education Statistics.* Washington, D.C.: U.S. Government Printing Office, periodically.
Phi Delta Kappan. Bloomington, Ind., monthly.
U.S. Bureau of the Census, *Statistical Abstract of the United States.* Washington, D.C.: U.S. Government Printing Office, annually.
Websites
   National Assessment of Educational Progress. http://nces.ed.gov/nationsreportcard/
   National Center for Education Statistics. http://nces.ed.gov
   School district
   State department of education
   U.S. Census Bureau. http://www.census.gov
   U.S. Department of Education. http://www.ed.gov/index.jhtml
World Almanac and Book of Facts. New York: World Almanac Books, annually.

offices of curriculum consultants; state departments of education; regional educational laboratories; ERIC; and the Internet.

Great variation can be found in both the format of printed curriculum materials and in the types of available materials. Beyond typical curriculum guides, we can find curriculum materials packaged into multimedia kits consisting of films, filmstrips, charts, audiotapes, videotapes, CDs, CD-ROMs, DVDs, and so on.

Summary

Curriculum planners and teachers frequently engage in developing curriculum products that will be of use to teachers in their school systems. In this chapter we looked at these types of products: curriculum guides, courses of study, syllabi, and resource units.

Curriculum guides should provide many suggestions to teachers for teaching a single course, a subject area at a particular grade level, an entire sequence, or an area of interest. Curriculum guides should include instructional goals, instructional objectives, activities, evaluation techniques, and resources. Sometimes curriculum planners incorporate an outline of the content. Courses of study cover single courses and often contain a considerable amount of content material. Syllabi list topics to be covered.

Resource units are, in essence, minicurriculum guides for teaching particular topics or problems. Limited to single topics or problems, resource units offer types of suggestions similar to those found in curriculum guides.

In the creation of curriculum materials, both the process and product are important. Examples of curriculum materials can be acquired from a number of sources.

Questions for Discussion

1. Should writing curriculum guides be the job of the curriculum director or coordinator? Explain.

2. Should schools borrow curriculum guides from each other?

3. How do curriculum guides, resource units, and teaching units differ from each other?

4. Where would you place the production of curriculum guides, courses of study, resource units, and the like in the model for curriculum development presented by the author of this text?

5. How can you integrate state and national standards and assessments into the construction of curriculum products?

 ## Exercises

1. List various curriculum products and state values you see in each.

2. List various curriculum products and state problems you see in each.

3. Locate and critique samples of curriculum guides, courses of study, syllabi, and resource units.

4. Survey opinions of teachers on the value of curriculum guides and other products listed in exercise 3.

5. Determine to what extent teachers in a school system you know well use their curriculum products. Account for their use or lack of use.

6. Locate and report on a curriculum product called a "scope and sequence chart."

7. Locate and list sources of curriculum materials available (1) in the school system, (2) in nearby colleges or universities, (3) from state departments of education, (4) from regional educational service agencies, (5) from professional associations, and (6) from business and industry.

8. Report on Fenwick W. English's alternative to the conventional curriculum guide. (See bibliography.)

9. Analyze a curriculum guide and determine whether it allows teachers enough flexibility or too much flexibility.

10. Analyze a curriculum guide and determine whether it is linked to state and national standards.

11. Create a resource unit on a topic that you will at some point be teaching.

12. (Group exercise) Construct a curriculum guide for a subject area at a grade level of your choice.

 ## Videos

Understanding by Design Video Series. Three 25- to 55-min. videotapes. Grant Wiggins and Jay McTighe, consultants. Shows process for designing curricular units. Alexandria, Va.: Association for Supervision and Curriculum Development, 2000.

Websites

Association for Supervision and Curriculum Development: http://www.ascd.org

Evergreen Curriculum Guides & Resources (Canada): http://www.sasked.gov.ed.ca/branches/curr/evergreen/index.shtml

Memphis City Schools: Curriculum and Instruction: http://mcsk12.net/admin/tlapages/curriculumguides/index.asp

National Assessment of Educational Progress: http://nces.ed.gov/nationsreportcard and http://nationsreportcard.gov

National Center for Education Statistics: http://nces.ed.gov

Endnotes

1. See Jerome S. Bruner, *Man: A Course of Study* (Cambridge, Mass.: Educational Services, 1965). See also website: http://www.coe.ufl.edu/CT/Projects/MACOS.html, accessed December 11, 2006.

2. See pp. 350–353 of this textbook.

3. See Chapter 10 for discussion of the Bloom taxonomy.

4. E. D. Hirsch, Jr., *The Schools We Need: And Why We Don't Have Them* (New York: Doubleday, 1996): 28.

5. For a critical view of conventional curriculum guides see Fenwick W. English, "It's Time to Abolish Conventional Curriculum Guides," *Educational Leadership* 44, no. 4 (December 1986–January 1987): 50–52.

6. Peter F. Oliva, *The Secondary School Today*, 1st ed. (Scranton, Pa.: International Textbook Company, 1967), p. 176.

7. Ibid.

 ## Bibliography

Carr, Judy F., and Harris, Douglas E. *Succeeding with Standards: Linking Curriculum, Assessment, and Action Planning.* Alexandria, Va.: Association for Supervision and Curriculum Development, 2001.

English, Fenwick W. "It's Time to Abolish Conventional Curriculum Guides." *Educational Leadership* 44, no. 4 (December 1986–January 1987): 50–52.

Glatthorn, Allan A., Boschee, Floyd, and Whitehead, Bruce M. *Curriculum Leadership: Development and Implementation.* Thousand Oaks, Calif.: Sage Publications, 2006.

Hirsch, E. D., Jr. *The Schools We Need: And Why We Don't Have Them.* New York: Doubleday, 1996.

Oliva, Peter F. *The Secondary School Today*, 1st ed. Scranton, Pa.: International Textbook Company, 1967.

Issues in Curriculum Development

AFTER STUDYING THIS CHAPTER YOU SHOULD BE ABLE TO:

1. Identify current and continuing curriculum issues that are brought about by social and political forces and explain their significance for curriculum development.

CURRENT CURRICULUM ISSUES

Curriculum planners are buffeted by strong educational, social, and political forces affecting the curriculum decisions they must make. Movements have emanated from networks of like-minded professional educators, from the public in general, and from individuals and pressure groups from outside of the teacher education profession. In this chapter we explore the effects of some of these pressures in shaping the school curriculum.

Some of the desires of both pressure groups and the public generally and, even on occasion, of professional educators have been enacted into law, for example, the formulation and testing of state standards. No state or federal law, however, has mandated the strong movement of cooperative learning and the rise and fall of open-space education. Those nonmandated movements that have become practices in the schools have done so by gathering enough voluntary support among the *teacher education* and *public school professionals* to translate them into action. Conversely, when a nonmandated practice no longer maintains support, like open-space education, for example, it becomes diminished or disappears.

Borrowing the rubric of Chapter 9 where we examined a number of curriculum innovations and programs by periods of history, ending with Curriculum Future, this chapter returns to Curriculum Present. In the following pages we will explore some of the significant contemporary curriculum developments set forth as responses to some of the problems plaguing schools. Some of the issues and their related developments are not new but remain highly controversial, for example, the place of religion in public education. Others are relatively new attempts at solving perennial problems.

For purposes of discussion the issues and related developments are divided into twelve categories, as follows:

1. Academic area initiatives
2. Alternative schooling arrangements
3. Bilingual/bicultural education
4. Censorship
5. Gender
6. Health education
7. Multiculturalism/diversity
8. Privatization
9. Provision for exceptionalities
10. Religion in public education
11. Scheduling arrangements
12. Standards/assessment

It can easily be recognized that discrete separation of these twelve categories, or rubrics, which I'll refer to as issues, cannot be made. In one sense, they are all interrelated. Some bear close relationship with each other. For example, you cannot divorce academic initiatives (i.e., programs) from standards and testing. You cannot discuss bilingual/bicultural education without relating to multiculturalism and diversity. You cannot separate problems of censorship from religion. As curriculum and instruction cannot be truly separated except for purposes of discussion so the twelve categories cannot be completely separated except for purposes of clarification.

In the following pages of this chapter we discuss differences of opinion, controversies, and developments emanating from these issues.

1. Academic Area Initiatives

By academic area initiatives we mean curriculum developments that have been undertaken to correct perceived lacks in the schools' course offerings. Initiatives may apply to changes in programmatic responses to satisfy current curriculum goals or may be dramatic revisions of those goals, changing the academic programs radically. In this section we will look generally at forces effecting academic changes. Many modifications of traditional school curricula can be readily identified. Throughout the discussion of the remaining eleven categories we will identify and explore specific academic areas other than those presented in this first category.

Reform—constant reform—remains a central theme of American education. All agree that our public schools are not doing as well as we'd like but all do not agree on what to do about perceived problems. Some, espousing essentialist thought, recommend focusing narrowly on reading and mathematics, with perhaps science thrown in, while others, following progressive doctrine, maintain that attention must be paid to the whole child, not just the child's intellect. Among the goals of current proposals for reform are increasing the number of students graduating from high school with the regular diploma, preparation of students for success in college and the workforce, and the preservation (some would say resurrection) of America's standing as an economic power and world leader.

Necessary Skills.   Representative of contemporary thinking about the status of American education and recommendations for correcting its deficiencies is the 2006 report of the National Center on Education and the Economy's New Commission on the Skills of the American Workforce funded by the Annie E. Casey Foundation, Bill and Melinda Gates Foundation, William and Flora Hewlett Foundation, and Lumina Foundation for Education.[1] The Commission in its report, *Tough Choices, Tough Times*, admitted about America that "we never dreamed that we would end up competing with countries that could offer large numbers of highly educated workers willing to work for low wages,"[2] namely, China, India, and elsewhere.

Affirming that America can no longer claim to have the best educated workforce in the world, the Commission called attention to the fact that the percentage of the world's population of college students has declined in America from thirty percent to fourteen percent over the past thirty years.[3] Like Thomas L. Friedman, who addressed the movements of globalization and outsourcing,[4] the Commission noted that the global economy has gone digital. To cope, America must adapt to the new economic era restructuring its educational system so its students will graduate with skills that will permit them to compete in the global marketplace. Specifically, the Commission report recommended a broad-based education that goes beyond mastery of the traditional content areas and into the development of personal traits like creativity, self-discipline, flexibility, and adaptability.[5]

Strengthening the Academic Programs.   In addition to following mandates of NCLB for specification of state standards and subsequent testing, discussed later in this chapter, school systems are adding subject requirements and credits for graduation. Kentucky, for example, will increase the number of mathematics credits from three to four, effective with the class of 2012.[6] Within its requirement of twenty-one credits, Maryland will call for tests in English, algebra/data analysis, biology, and government for graduation in 2009.[7] Interestingly, in spite of current movements to increase offerings in math and science, a recent survey by Public Agenda found that neither parents nor students were overly concerned about the amount of math and science in their schools' curricula.[8]

Core Knowledge.   Concentrating on overcoming American students' deficiencies in cultural literacy (i.e., basic knowledge), the core knowledge schools, conceptualized in the 1980s by E. D. Hirsch, Jr., professor (now emeritus) of English, University of Virginia, offer a core of academic subjects in grades K–8 comprising fifty percent of their school curriculum. The Core Knowledge Foundation conducts research, publishes materials, conducts workshops for teachers, and promotes core knowledge schools.[9]

Hirsch perceived core knowledge (initially called *cultural literacy*) as broad general knowledge that ideally should be possessed by all members of our democratic society. This knowledge, in Hirsch's view, should be the major goal of schooling in America.[10]

A core knowledge curriculum starts in the elementary school and imparts that knowledge deemed by scholars, educators, and laypeople to be important information about American culture. A culturally literate person is one who possesses a store of knowledge about the culture—people, places, facts, vocabulary, and historic and current events. Although elements of this knowledge may change from time to time, most items remain the same or change slowly. Advocates of core knowledge see cultural literacy as enabling citizens of our society to read with understanding, to communicate thoughts to others within our society, to contribute to the development of our society, and to open doors that lead to success in our nation. Some people would view core knowledge as basically traditional education.

Hirsch called for knowledgeable people to join him in developing a list of cultural items sufficiently important for incorporating in the curriculum, especially at the elementary school level.[11] Cultural literacy would not require in-depth knowledge of all items; in many cases an imprecise—even superficial knowledge—enough for a reader or listener to comprehend what a writer or speaker means—would suffice. For example, one does not need to understand the concepts of Mendel's laws or nuclear fission to understand references to those terms in a book, magazine, newspaper article written for the general reader, or, we might add, in a conversation or speech to a general audience.

Cultural literacy gives precedence to an overriding American culture and the English language, rejecting the concept of pluralism espoused by some in which aspects of all subcultures in the nation are studied with equal concentration. Supporters of cultural literacy view the fragmentation of the culture and the populace's lack of commonly shared information as serious problems that schools face in their attempts to develop literate citizens.

Opponents of cultural literacy view lists of cultural items as superficial learning, considering them memorized trivia that can be looked up rather than stored in the brain. They also hold it presumptuous for any individual or group to deign to draw up a list of items that all pupils in America must know. However, Hirsch and his colleagues began with a tentative list, urged study and review of the list by others, and made clear that their list was *descriptive*—not *prescriptive*—of information possessed by culturally literate Americans.[12]

That Hirsch's proposals have proved appealing to many curriculum planners is evidenced by the rapid growth of Core Knowledge Schools since their conception in the 1980s. Starting with Three Oaks Elementary School in Fort Myers, Florida, and P.S. 67 in South Bronx, New York, credited as the first and second schools of this type,[13] schools—public, charter, parochial, and private—following core knowledge curricula to varying degrees in 2006 numbered close to 1,000.[14]

Diversification of Programs.   Many of the students who drop out do so because the curriculum is of little interest to them. With the overall national graduation rate around sixty-eight percent (but lower for disadvantaged minorities),[15] school districts are resorting to a variety of plans to encourage students to remain in school and earn the regular diploma. Whereas some school districts are intensifying emphasis on the traditional subjects, other school systems are experimenting with adding content to the academic program that may be more appealing to some students.

With Congress's 2006 reauthorization of the Carl D. Perkins Act initially passed in 1990, Vocational Education, now called Career and Technical Education (CTE), has become a desired alternative to the college preparatory program, leading to growing enrollments. No longer is CTE limited to the former concepts of "industrial arts," "shop," and "ag" (agriculture). Kenneth Gray noted that most CTE students are now enrolled in business, healthcare, trade/industry, and information technology.[16] A search through the activities and course lists of high schools and to some degree middle schools throughout the country will reveal engineering-oriented activities like robotics and agriculturally oriented courses like aquaculture and biotechnology.

Aiming at offering academic programs that would encourage students to stay in school and graduate, Florida made national news in late 2006 by designating 440 high school major areas of interest. In addition to earning sixteen credits in a common academic core students would choose within the remaining eight elective courses a sequential major of four credits. Majors range from College Studies to Digital Arts to Music-Orchestra to Sports Medicine to Television Production. School districts would select from the 440 approved majors those which would be most feasible and applicable to their schools, student body, and community.[17]

Other Personalizing of the Curriculum. As we noted in Chapter 9, James B. Conant as long ago as 1959 was urging special attention to the needs of the academically talented (top fifteen percent) and the highly gifted (top three percent).[18] Along with efforts of schools to meet the needs of low achievers and minority populations through special classes and tutoring, for example, increased attention is now returning to the needs of the academically talented and gifted students. The National Center for Education Statistics, for example, reported that about thirty percent of American high school students in 2003–2004 completed courses in the Advanced Placement or the International Baccalaureat programs.[19] Nevada, in cooperation with the University of Nevada-Reno (UNR), has opened Davidson Academy, a public school for exceptionally gifted middle and high school students.[20] At Davidson Academy students follow individualized learning plans, are taught by both Davidson teachers and professors from UNR, and have the opportunity to take college-level courses. Dual enrollment wherein high school students earn credit in college courses are relatively common offerings for the college bound.[21]

In recounting examples of current curricular and instructional initiative across the nation we cannot but note the diversity of efforts schools are making to enable students to succeed in college and the global workplace.

2. Alternative Schooling Arrangements

In the 1960s and 1970s school districts were engaged in efforts to accommodate students who could not fare well in the established public schools by offering options either within or outside the school. Among the more common alternatives outside the established schools were the so-called free schools, storefront schools, and schools without walls in which individuals, organizations, and businesses in the community participated in the education of youth. School systems took advantage of the human and material resources available in the community and offered students practical instruction in a setting less structured than the established school. A common plan was the assignment of students to these learning stations for a portion of the day with the remainder of the day spent at the established school. This type of alternative, posing numerous problems of quality of instruction, administration, and accountability, has diminished in popularity to the point where we rarely hear of this kind of experimental offering.

Still popular, however, are alternatives within the school systems themselves, particularly magnet schools with their special foci. Among well-known magnet schools seeking to meet current needs are Alexandria, Virginia's, Thomas Jefferson High School of Science and Technology; Indianapolis's Crispus Attucks Medical Magnet School emphasizing health care; Maryland's Joppatowne High School with its unique emphasis on homeland security; and high school residential magnets Natchitoches, Louisiana's School for Math, Science, and the Arts, and Durham, North Carolina's School of Science and Mathematics.

On the scene are schools not meant to serve as magnets but rather as models to be emulated such as Philadelphia's School of the Future, a high-tech, state-of-the-art public school designed by the Microsoft Corporation in cooperation with the school district.

In calling these structures options we should mention that, although parents and students may opt to attend a magnet or model school, admission depends on availability and students' meeting entrance requirements, often in the form of a test or, as in the case of Philadelphia's School of the Future, by lottery.

In passing we should mention that some school systems maintain alternative schools where students posing behavior problems are assigned for varying periods of time. Assignment to the alternative school for students with behavior problems is at the option of school personnel.

Most of the foregoing types of alternative schools have been perceived as strengthening the public school system.

Parental Choice.   In recent years, pressure has been building for the state to support parental choice of schools whether public or private. Wrapped up in the concept of school choice are movements toward school vouchers, tax credits, charter schools, and homeschooling, all strong and growing. These movements represent efforts at *privatization*, that is, the management of public school systems by private corporations, a topic to be discussed later in this chapter.

Historically, parents who had children in a school district with more than one school at the same level were required to send their children to schools within the assigned subdistrict of their local school district. Parents could send their children to schools outside their assigned subdistricts only in special cases, such as to attend a magnet school or another school that offered programs that were not available within the child's assigned subdistrict. Also parents have encountered difficulty when they wished to send their children to public schools across school-district lines; this type of move, if permitted, could result in parents paying tuition to the school district of choice. Since 1985, however, Minnesota's School District Enrollment Options Program (Open Enrollment) has allowed parents to choose for their children to attend a public school or program outside the district in which they live. State funding follows the students.

Choice within school districts has become increasingly more common. In 1995 Berkeley, California, for example, divided its district into three zones and permitted choice of elementary schools within a resident's zone. In the fall of 1998, Seattle ceased arbitrary assignment of students to schools and permitted parents to select the public school they would like their children to attend. Plans cannot, of course, guarantee that parents and students will receive their first choice. Factors such as demand, facilities, and racial balance affect whether choices can be honored. Choice of school within the public system, although resisted by some school administrators and school boards, is a less contentious issue than the larger issue of provision of public funds for parental choice of school from among private and parochial schools. Working with schools to help parents become informed, the GreatSchools Network engages parents in evaluating and improving schools and shares information about understanding standards, learning activities, state tests and scores, understanding report cards, and best practices.[22]

School Vouchers/Tax Credits. Growing since the early 1900s is the practice of issuing taxpayer-funded vouchers to enable public school students to attend private and parochial schools.[23] Milton Friedman, Nobel Prize–winning economist, is credited with proposing in 1955 the use of vouchers to enable parents to send their children to schools of their choice. The requirements for participation in voucher programs vary from state to state and community to community. Some states provide vouchers only to low-income families. Some state or community plans permit use of vouchers in religious schools, as in Milwaukee and Cleveland, whereas others do not, as is the case in Maine and Vermont.

Funding of vouchers varies. Arizona and Pennsylvania have opted for income tax credits—in Arizona, to taxpayers, and in Pennsylvania, to corporations that support vouchers. Voucher/tuition plans of one type or another have been on the scene many years. Maine's and Vermont's plans date back to the late 1800s. In these two states tuition is issued to "tuition towns" where no public school exists. Maine and Vermont towns share the funding with the state.

Ever since the U.S. Supreme Court rendered its decision in the case of *Pierce v. Society of Sisters* in 1925, parents have had the choice of sending their children to private schools, at their own expense, of course.[24] Litigation over vouchers has erupted, however, particularly over allowing use of the vouchers in religious schools, which opponents of voucher plans hold as an unconstitutional infringement on the First Amendment.

Wisconsin in 1990 became the first state to offer parents in low-income brackets payments up to $2,500 per pupil so that their children might attend Milwaukee's private/nonsectarian schools. Targeted at low-income families, the Milwaukee Parental Choice Program offered vouchers in 2006–2007 at a maximum of $6,351 per student to families with income at 1.75 times the established poverty level. Legislation passed in 2006 considerably expanded the Milwaukee program.

In 1995 the Wisconsin legislature permitted use of the vouchers in religious schools. Overturning a 1997 decision by the state appeals court, the Wisconsin Supreme Court in June 1998 ruled the Milwaukee voucher program constitutional. The U.S. Supreme Court, by an 8–1 vote in December 1998, refused to hear an appeal from Wisconsin, thereby affirming the action of the Wisconsin Supreme Court.

Initiated in 1996–1997, Cleveland's voucher program allows use of the vouchers in religious schools. Challenges to the plan took the case to the Sixth U.S. Circuit Court of Appeals, which in December 2001 held the Cleveland plan unconstitutional. The following June, by a 5–4 decision, the U.S. Supreme Court reversed the decision and declared that the Cleveland plan, which allowed the use of vouchers in religious schools, was not an infringement on the First Amendment, thus allowing Cleveland's program to continue.

In 1999 Florida became the first state to offer statewide vouchers, known as Opportunity Scholarships, to students in schools that were graded as failing two years in a row. Additionally, McKay Scholarships provided for children with special needs. Florida's plan, like those in Milwaukee and Cleveland, permits use of the vouchers in religious schools. In August 2002 a circuit judge ruled Florida's Opportunity Scholarships plan unconstitutional but allowed it to continue while the state appealed the decision to the First District Court of Appeals. The Florida Supreme Court in January 2006 declared the Opportunity Scholarship Program unconstitutional on the grounds that it violated a 1998 constitutional amendment that required a statewide uniform system of public schools. In the spring of 2007 the Florida legislature had under consideration granting tax credits to businesses that donated money for scholarships. Georgia that same spring enacted legislation providing state funds for parents of public school children in special education to attend private school.

The sides in this controversy are sharply drawn. Supporters of voucher systems include private and parochial schools, the religious right, parents who are dissatisfied with public schools for one reason or another, parents and politicians who do not subscribe philosophically to a public education system, and organizations such as the Alliance for School Choice, Center for Education Reform, Children's Scholarship Fund, and the Milton and Rose D. Friedman Foundation. Numbered among opponents of voucher systems are the National Education Association, teachers' unions, parents who are satisfied with their public schools, parents and politicians who believe in a unifying public school system, the American Civil Liberties Union, Americans United for Separation of Church and State, and People for the American Way.

Advocates of voucher programs argue that provision of choice will, in the long run, strengthen the public schools by forcing them, for economic reasons, to overcome those problems that have provoked parental dissention. Opponents view vouchers as breaking the Jeffersonian wall of separation of church and state. Brian Gill and colleagues noted the predominance of religious schools in voucher programs.[25]

An analysis of the Cleveland voucher program by Amy Hanauser reported in January 2002 that 99.4 percent of the students in the program were enrolled in religious schools.[26]

Advocating a federally funded voucher program, President George W. Bush in 2005 proposed federal funding of vouchers for students who had been attending private schools when displaced by Hurricane Katrina to enable them to attend private schools in other parts of the nation. Then again, in 2006, President Bush proposed a national voucher plan for low-income families whose children are in low-performing schools.

Ambivalence regarding voucher programs exists throughout the country. Whereas Wisconsin, Ohio, and Florida embraced vouchers, California and Michigan have rejected such measures.

Public opinion on vouchers fluctuated during the 1990s.[27] The public's uncertainty clearly continues as revealed by Phi Delta Kappa/Gallup polls. A large majority supported improving public schools in place of awarding vouchers in 1999,[28] favored vouchers in 2002,[29] and again approved choice of private school at public expense in 2006.[30] Georgia furnished an example of support for school choice through its law in 2007 providing state funds for parents to send special-education students to private schools.

Even though private schools possess advantages over public schools in that they can select their students and have smaller classes, the jury is out as to whether shifting funds from public schools to private and parochial schools actually improves student achievement.[31] Critics of vouchers argue that parental choice of school is not the answer to the social ills that impede learning.

What is remarkable is the small percentage of students who take advantage of the school choice option. Speaking at a school choice forum in 2006, U.S. Secretary of Education Margaret Spellings remarked that out of 4 million students eligible for school choice only 38,000—less than 1 percent—actually transferred to a higher-performing school.[32]

Charter Schools.   Rapidly developing in the late 1990s and continuing into the 2000s, charter schools have added another dimension to the element of school choice.

Based on a free-market, neoliberal concept derived from the economic theory of Adam Smith,[33] charter schools, supported by tax moneys, are freed of some of the regulations of their local school district and state. These schools may be housed within a school system or operated outside of the school system, they may or may not use public school personnel, and they may be run for or without profit.

Minnesota is credited with establishing the first American charter school in 1991. Charter schools have grown exponentially since that date, with Arizona, California, and Michigan leading the nation in the development of charter schools. Figures on the growth of charter schools between 1999 and 2006 reveal a rapid growth of the charter school movement. Whereas 1999 statistics showed close to 1,500 charter schools operating in thirty-one states and the District of Columbia and serving over 250,000 students,[34] in 2006 the Center for Education Reform reported 4,000 charter schools serving over 1 million students in forty states and the District of Columbia.[35]

Charter schools gain their status through the issuing of a charter by the local school board or the state department of education. Teachers, laypeople, and organizations may apply for charters, which will grant them, as Donna Harrington-Lueker explained, "waivers exempting them from the state education code, local school board policies, and provisions of the union contract,"[36] leaving in place provisions pertaining to disclosure of finances, health, safety, and civil rights.

States vary in their procedures for granting a charter. Michigan, for example, has allowed local school boards, boards of intermediate service districts, and boards of community and senior colleges and universities to grant charters. Whereas charters in

Massachusetts are issued by its state department of education, charters in Georgia must be approved by both the local school board and the state department of education.[37]

In Arizona a state charter board, local school boards, and the Arizona Board of Education have the power to grant school charters. New York State has empowered the State University of New York (SUNY) as well as the New York State Board of Regents to authorize charters and, in the case of New York City, the Chancellor of the New York City school system.[38]

Paralleling Britain's grant-maintained schools, U.S. charter schools are supported by tax moneys. They put into practice principles of site-based management, placing responsibility for student success squarely on the shoulders of the schools' personnel. Unlike contractual schools managed by corporations with a profit motive, charter schools may be operated by either for-profit business organizations or by individuals or groups not for profit.

Charter schools come in all shapes and sizes. Some operate making use of school personnel, although management rests in the hands of the founders of the school, not the local school board. New Jersey sets no limit to the number of charter schools. Idaho limits the number of charter schools in each school district whereas Nevada and New York limit the number of charter schools in the state. California allows existing schools as well as new schools established by individuals and groups to apply for a charter; 50 percent of the teachers at an existing school must favor a charter before it can be granted. California grants charters to homeschools whereas Colorado does not. Arizona permits religious schools to hold a charter if their program is not sectarian. Legislation in Florida would prohibit charters to sectarian institutions. Initial charters may run for a varying length of time, typically three to five years.

What of the programs of the charter schools? All charter schools promote achievement in the basic skills. Many seek to prepare students for college admission. Some charter schools are established for students who are experiencing difficulty in the public schools (e.g., those with learning disabilities, those at risk, and those demonstrating behavior problems). Others aim not only to develop traditional skills but also offer a particular focus as, for example, Advanced Math and Science Academy, Marlborough, Massachusetts (Russian curriculum model); Cesar Chavez Public Charter for Public Policy, Washington, D.C.; Conservation Corps Charter School, San Jose, California (work-study); Fast Forward, Logan, Utah (students-at-risk); Marlton Charter School for the Deaf, Los Angeles; Media Technology Charter High School, Boston; Medical Center Charter School, Houston, Texas (healthcare); Odyssey-Magellan Charter School, Appleton, Wisconsin (gifted); and Promise Academy, Harlem, New York City (educationally deprived). Coming into service as well as the place-bound schools are the distance-learning online charter schools. These few examples reveal the great differences in charter school programs. Although all seek to improve achievement of students in basic skills, they depart in their educational focus and programs. Helping promote the cause of charter schools is the $30 million grant in 2006 from the Bill and Melinda Gates Foundation to the New Schools Venture Fund for creation of 200 charter schools in low-income sections of Chicago, Los Angeles, New York, Oakland, and Washington, D.C.[39]

Although numbers of charter schools continue to increase, the movement is not in one direction. Boston, for example, with help from the Boston Foundation, the Boston Teachers Union, the Boston School Committee, and the mayor, has established within its public school system seventeen pilot schools that have been granted considerable autonomy.[40]

That the public is generally favorable toward charter schools is demonstrated by the 38th Annual Phi Delta Kappa/Gallup Poll of the Public's Attitudes Toward the Public Schools, which showed approval of charter schools by the public, especially by public school parents, rising sharply between 2000 and 2006.[41]

Dissatisfaction with student achievement in the public schools motivates many, if not most, of the parents who opt for charter schools. Seeking an alternative to the public schools, some parents embrace charter schools as a more acceptable alternative than vouchers. Parents who perceive the public schools as promoting values unacceptable to them join with the free marketers in supporting charter schools.

Those who oppose charter schools object to the use of tax moneys for private and parochial schools while public schools suffer from inadequate funding. Supporters argue that competition from the charter schools will force public schools to improve.

Charter schools manifest the problems of church–state relations when public tax moneys flow to sectarian schools. Proponents of vouchers for religious schools argue that there is no inherent violation of the principle of separation of church and state inasmuch as the funds go to the student, not to the school.

Coming onto the scene, raising issues of bilingual education, diversity, and religion, are publicly funded, language-oriented charter schools such as Ben Gamla Charter School, a Kindergarten–8 English-Hebrew school in Hollywood, Florida,[42] and the Khalil Gibran International Academy, an English-Arabic middle school, in Brooklyn, New York.[43] Although proponents of public schools of this type maintain that instruction in religious doctrine can be excluded, critics question whether teaching religious beliefs can be avoided. Like public schools, generally, success of charter schools varies from school to school. We can find charter schools meeting parental expectations. We can find charter schools that have opened with fanfare and have folded for one reason or another, often financial. A 2007 four-part report by *The Orlando* [Florida] *Sentinel* on the some 300 charter schools supported by tax moneys in Florida revealed significant problems of both an academic and administrative nature.[44] The research comparing success of students in charter schools with that of students in public schools is inconclusive. Some studies point to success of students in charter schools[45] while others point to success of students in public schools.[46] Parents do, however, appreciate the smaller classes of the charter schools and the relatively more secure environment.

Failure to fulfill expectations will result in nonrenewal of charters. Existing public schools are attempting to counteract demands for charter schools by restructuring their programs, by working more closely with parents and community advisory groups, by offering appealing in-system alternatives such as magnet schools or pilot schools, and, of course, by evaluating the success of charter schools. Further, they have themselves established charter-like schools, that is, schools that remain an integral part of the school system but have been granted a degree of autonomy by the school board.

In addition to charter schools we may see the concept of chartering applied to the school district. Three county school systems in Florida, for example, in late 1999 secured dispensation from some state regulations in order to create pilot charter districts.

Homeschools/Unschooling. An increasingly popular option that also discomforts public school personnel is homeschooling and its variant of *unschooling* as an alternative to public education. Estimates of children homeschooled range from 850,000 found in 1999 by the Parent Survey of the National Household Surveys Program (NHES), a data-collection agency of the National Center for Education Statistics,[47] to 1.1 million reported in the NHES survey of 2003, a twenty-nine percent jump between 1999 and 2003, representing an increase from 1.7 percent of the U.S. student population to 2.2 percent.[48] Compared with the 48.5 million public school students and 6.3 million private school students in the United States[49] in more than 95,000 public schools and over 28,000 private schools[50] homeschooling remains a relatively small, though expanding and significant, portion of the enterprise of education in America. Whereas in earlier years public schools sought to provide alternative education under their supervision and control, homeschools seek to provide alternative education outside of the control of public school administrators and faculty.

The education of children in the home dates back to the "dame" or "kitchen" schools of colonial days where parents or other educated adults would tutor individuals or instruct small groups in private homes. John Holt, one of the leading exponents of homeschooling, has encouraged parents to take their children out of the public schools and provide for their education at home.[51]

Homeschooling has threatened the time-honored tradition of compulsory education. In the early 1980s Mississippi was reportedly the only state in the nation that gave legal sanction to homeschooling. Today, however, homeschooling is permitted in all fifty states. One of the more serious blows against state compulsory attendance laws was the U.S. Supreme Court's decision in *Wisconsin v. Yoder*, the First Amendment religious liberty case in which the Supreme Court ruled that Amish parents could not be required to send their children to school beyond the eighth grade.[52]

Advocates of homeschooling may be found among conservatives on the right and liberals on the left. The same disillusionment with the public schools that led parents to establish private and parochial schools has also led to the increase in home education. Parents may choose homeschooling for their children because they are dissatisfied with, among other factors, the secular orientation of the public schools, poor academic achievement, lack of safety in the schools, drug use among students, lack of discipline and bullying, violence, large classes, peer pressures, and the forced socialization of their children with others whom they deem undesirable. On the other hand, those parents who reject the option of homeschooling see value in their children's participation in the many extra-class activities offered in the public schools and their socializing with their classmates.

The statistics of homeschooling are imprecise and difficult to obtain, in part because of the nebulous definition of homeschool. In some cases, a homeschool consists of parents instructing only their own children in their own home. In other cases groups of parents band together to form a school for their children in someone's home, in their church, or at another location.

The curricula vary from the use of structured lessons and textbooks from educational publishers; to online instruction; to private tutoring, including the hiring of online tutors in India and elsewhere,[53] to *unschooling*, a variation of homeschooling that permits students to tailor their own education.[54] Unschooling should be distinguished from *deschooling* as recommended by Ivan Illich in which boys and girls find their education in the community at large.[55]

Restrictions on homeschools vary from state to state. Some states require homeschools to obtain approval of their curricula and to accept varying degrees of monitoring by the boards of education of their local school districts. For example, homeschool instructors may have to furnish to the local school board copies of their curriculum materials, lists of textbooks, information on number of days and hours of instruction, attendance data, and test results. Some may be required to administer standardized tests. Some groups of homeschoolers have bypassed local school districts by conducting their programs under the aegis of an established private school.

Advocates of homeschools will most likely continue to challenge both the constitutionality of compulsory attendance laws per se and the state restrictions on homeschooling. The U.S. Congress took note of the popularity of homeschooling by exempting homeschools from provisions of the 1994 reauthorization of the Elementary and Secondary Education Act concerning the licensing of homeschool teachers.

Success of pupils in homeschooling is difficult to measure as monitoring of homeschooling is spotty and results vary from school to school. Lawrence M. Rudner of the ERIC Clearinghouse on Assessment and Evaluation reported some positive data gathered on a 1998 assessment of achievement of more than 20,000 homeschooled K–12 students in almost 12,000 families. Median test scores of homeschooled students were found to be above scores made by students in public, parochial, and private schools. In addition, demographic data revealed that parents of homeschoolers had a higher level of education and higher median income than parents generally across the nation.[56]

Although secular public schools can never satisfy those who prefer a sectarian education, renewed academic excellence in the public schools—a result of restructuring and reform—may make the public school more attractive to some of those now involved in homeschooling.

Magnet schools, charter schools, pilot schools, vouchers, and homeschooling offer alternatives to traditional public schools.

Speaking of the various forms of alternative schooling a number of years ago, David S. Hurst observed:

> Like it or not the ultimate adoption of some of these alternatives appears inevitable. . . . Schools in the United States will not become victims of a single alternative to traditional structures; instead we will wind up with levels of alternatives, ranging from our most traditional schools today to avant-garde institutions on the fringes of society.[57]

Gerald W. Bracey, in his analysis of successes, criticisms, and the privatization of public schools, however, saw current alternatives to public education as a war being waged to destroy the public schools.[58]

3. Bilingual/Bicultural Education

The 2005 American Community Survey of the U.S. Bureau of the Census numbered almost 52 million people from the age of five and older, 19.4 percent of the U.S. population as speakers of languages other than English at home.[59] As ethnic groups whose first language is other than English grow in size and power, more and more curriculum workers find themselves charged with the task of developing bilingual education programs. In 1967 amendments to the Elementary and Secondary Education Act, the U.S. Congress provided support for bilingual education programs.

Second-language instruction is not limited to the most widely spoken languages. As a result of state legislation requiring second-language studies in the public schools, some children of Native Americans in Oklahoma starting in 1993–1994 were learning Cherokee, Chickasaw, Choctaw, Creek, and Seminole languages. Although bilingual education programs are offered in a number of languages, the largest number of students in bilingual programs are Hispanic. The U.S. Bureau of the Census estimated the Hispanic population in the United States in 2006 at 44.3 million, 14.8 percent of the total (300 million) population. The Hispanic populations of both California and Texas are now a "minority-majority," exceeding fifty percent.[60]

The U.S. Supreme Court's decision in the *Lau v. Nichols* case in 1974, which required San Francisco to provide English language instruction for the Chinese-speaking students, advanced the cause of bilingual education.[61] The efforts of Hispanic groups have largely brought about the current emphasis on bilingual (and, in addition, bicultural) education.

Bilingual education is an educational, linguistic, social, cultural, political, and economic issue. As such, it has become highly controversial. Dade County (Florida) provides an example of continuing public discord over this issue. In April 1973, after a large number of Spanish-speaking refugees had immigrated from Cuba, Dade County was declared a bilingual community. Many "Anglos" took issue with the designation of the county as bilingual. This sentiment came to a head in 1980 when county voters approved an ordinance prohibiting the conduct of government business in any language other than English except in the cases of emergencies and elections. Thirteen years later with almost fifty percent of the population of Dade County Hispanic and with more than fifty percent speaking languages other than English the Dade County Commission repealed the English-only ordinance. In 1994 the Third District Court of Appeals rejected a challenge to the authority of the county commission to repeal the English-only ordinance and upheld the commission's right to do so.

The English-only/Spanish-only argument flared again the summer of 1999 in Texas. With most of its population speaking Spanish, the small town of El Cenizo attracted attention and controversy by passing an ordinance to conduct local government business in Spanish, with provision for translation in English. A Texas pizza chain met with strong criticism in early 2007 when it announced it would accept Mexican pesos in payment.

Bilingual education in the schools, the designation of English as an official language, and the mandating of the use of only English in schools and government offices are related issues that continue to generate considerable controversy. Voters have spoken on both sides of the issue. The National Association for Bilingual Education promotes the cause of bilingual education whereas the Center for Equal Opportunity opposes it. Championing the cause of English as the official national language are English First and U.S. English, Inc., whereas the American Civil Liberties Union stands opposed.

English-only legislation at the state level has met with mixed results. In the spring of 1990, Alabama voters overwhelmingly adopted an amendment to their state constitution recognizing English as the official language of their state government. In the spring of 1991 Puerto Rico passed a law that designated Spanish as the only official language of the commonwealth, rescinding a 1902 law that had designated both Spanish and English as official languages. In 1995 Puerto Rico passed and the governor signed the English-also law declaring both English and Spanish as official languages. The language issue has heated up periodically in Puerto Rico. One of the reasons for Puerto Ricans rejecting statehood has been the effort of some members of the U.S. Congress to make English the official language if Puerto Rico becomes a state.

Arizona and California provide cases that demonstrate the divisiveness of the English-as-official-language issue. In 1988 Arizona passed by voter initiative a law making English the official language. Two years later the federal district court in Phoenix declared the law unconstitutional. An advocacy group, Arizonans for Official English, appealed the district court decision. In 1996, the Ninth Circuit Court of Appeals upheld the decision of the federal district court. With an appeal to the Arizona Supreme Court on hold, in 1997 the U.S. Supreme Court vacated the decisions of the district and circuit courts. The following year the Arizona Supreme Court agreed with the district and appeals courts and ruled the law unconstitutional. In 1999 the U.S. Supreme Court refused to consider the Arizona voter initiative, thus allowing the decision of the Arizona Supreme Court to stand. However, on its eighth attempt, voters in Arizona in November 2006 approved Proposition 103 adopting English as the official language, making it the twenty-eighth state to do so.[62]

Since the late 1960s, California with its polyglot population has offered programs of bilingual education in its schools. In June 1998 California voters overwhelmingly endorsed Proposition 227 that scuttled bilingual education and in its place mandated an English-language immersion program for students of limited language ability. Although some school districts have threatened not to abide by the law, a federal judge ruled that the law did not violate the rights of minorities. Proposition 227 left some room for schools to offer English-language instruction part of the time and for parents through waivers to continue their children in bilingual education programs. Although bilingual education is championed by language minorities, some members of minority groups supported the banning of bilingual education programs because they perceived fluency in English as essential for career opportunities for their children.

From as far back as 1811, states have passed a law or constitutional amendment that specifies English as the official language of their state governments. Hawaii, however, has designated both English and Hawaiian as official languages of the state and teaches both English and Hawaiian in its schools. That the English-as-official language controversy continues to arise periodically is seen by the enactment of a measure by the Nashville,

Tennessee, Metro Council in February 2007 making English the official language, a move that the mayor subsequently vetoed.

The controversy over bilingual education brings into sharp focus the opposing philosophies of acculturation versus pluralism. The resurgence of the melting-pot concept, with its emphasis on blending, has challenged the salad-bowl concept of pluralism. Proposals from both Democrats and Republicans to establish English as the official language of the federal government have surfaced from time to time in both the Senate and the House of Representatives. This issue, intensified by public pressures for immigration reform, resulted in a bill passed by the U.S. Senate in spring 2006 declaring English the official national language.

Those who support making English the official language note that throughout our nation's history immigrants have learned English. Proponents of bilingual education, however, believe that curtailment of bilingual education and designation of English as the official language are discriminatory. They maintain that an English-only instructional approach impedes the learning of children who are not native speakers of English. Critics, on the other hand, argue that bilingual education segregates students, exacerbates problems posed by diversity, and has proved ineffective.

Curriculum planners as well as the public are also divided as to the exact definitions of "bilingual" and "bicultural." To some, bilingual education may simply mean setting up English classes for students who are not native speakers of English. Others often extend bilingual education to include additional dimensions, including teaching courses in the native language. Fitchburg High School (Massachusetts), for example, offers courses in Spanish for Native Speakers to enable native speakers of Spanish to improve their use of their own language.[63]

Educators are in disagreement as to whether programs designed to promote mastery of English should allow for instruction of students in their native language until they achieve English language skills or should immerse students in English from the start. The U.S. Department of Education has usually required schools that wished to receive bilingual education funds to provide instruction in the native language. When the U.S. Department of Education sought to force Fairfax County, Virginia, to offer instruction to all students in their native language, Fairfax County brought suit on the grounds that its program of intensive English for speakers of other languages was successful, as shown by their test scores. In late 1980, the U.S. Department of Education, on the strength of the success of Fairfax County students, decided not to force Fairfax County to provide instruction in the native language.

Immersion in English has been an alternative to bilingual education. Results of English-immersion programs, though not conclusive, show some indications of improvement in English-language learning by nonnative speakers of English. Although California and Arizona, for example, have both used language-immersion techniques, exemptions and waivers are possible under certain circumstances. Responding to Proposition 227, Oceanside, California, however, ceased all non-English instruction and reported in the summer of 1999 that its English-immersion program resulted in significant improvement in English and other subjects by non-English-speaking students.

The U.S. House of Representatives has jumped into the fray on more than one occasion since passage of the 1968 Bilingual Education Act, as seen, for example, in its proposals for an English-Language Empowerment Act (1996) and its English Language Fluency Act (1998) that offered funding to the states in the form of block grants and set a maximum of three years for student participation in federally funded bilingual education programs. The English Language Acquisition, Language Enhancement, and Academic Achievement Act replaced the Bilingual Education Act that expired in 2002. The thrust of the English Language Acquisition Act is on the development of English-language skills rather than on bilingual education.

Terminology has contributed to the public's negative views about bilingual education. An early term for an instructional program known as "English as a second language" has encountered strong objections on the part of champions of English who misinterpret the term to imply relegating English to second place. "English for Speakers of Other Languages," referred to as ESOL, and English Language Learners (ELL) have reduced the misunderstanding. The public's continuing ambivalence toward bilingual education is readily documented. While Arizona and California, for example, were curtailing bilingual education, Colorado voters in 2002 refused to ban bilingual education.

To overcome some of the objections to typical bilingual education schools in some states, such as California and Washington, have been attempting dual-language classes with half the class composed of native speakers of English and half composed of native speakers of Spanish. In addition to mastery of the subject matter, objectives of dual-language include the development of fluency in two languages and increased understanding between cultures.

Both the existence of bilingual education and its methodology remain sensitive and controversial issues. An alternative school in Kansas City, Kansas, for example, ran into difficulty with its English-only policy in 2005 when it suspended and later rescinded the suspension of a boy who was speaking Spanish in the hall. How best to improve the achievement of nonnative speakers not only in mastering English but also other subjects that require mastery of English, plus how to raise their success rate on state standardized tests, are issues yet to be resolved.

Intertwined with bilingual/bicultural education are the issues of multiculturalism and multicultural education, which are discussed later in this chapter.

4. Censorship

Schools in many communities throughout the United States find themselves enmeshed in a seemingly endless struggle with individuals and groups in the community seeking to censor textbooks and library books and to prohibit certain types of instruction or, conversely, to promote certain types of instruction. Attempts to remove library books, textbooks, and other teaching materials from the schools are frequent and widespread. Dissension over this issue and over religion, as we shall see again later in this chapter, stems from differing interpretations of the First Amendment to the U.S. Constitution, which says:

> Congress shall make no law respecting an establishment of religion, or prohibiting the free exercise thereof; or abridging the freedom of speech, or of the press; or the right of the people peaceably to assemble, and to petition the government for a redress of grievances.

Seven books of a phenomenal series have sold more than 300 million copies in over sixty languages and have made a heretofore obscure British author, J. K. Rowling, one of the best-selling authors of all time. The books are the adventures of Harry Potter. Although these imaginative books have delighted children around the world and have turned many children on to reading, they are not without challenge. In fact, the Harry Potter series in 2005 was ranked as the most challenged book of the twenty-first century.[64]

Endorsed by the Vatican on one hand for their theme of the triumph of good over evil, the Harry Potter books have brought challenge from parents and pastors of some religious sects as perceiving lack of family values and containing witchcraft and occultism. Some school districts have required written permission from parents before allowing pupils to check out the Harry Potter books. When the Cedarville, Arkansas, school board placed the Harry Potter books on restricted shelves, a circuit judge ruled in 2003 against the school board and ordered the books returned to the open shelves. In a similar vein the Georgia Board of Education in 2006 supported the refusal of the suburban Atlanta Gwinnett School Board to remove the Harry Potter books from its schools.

The Harry Potter books, of course, are not the only books challenged or banned from schools and public libraries. Between 1990 and 2000 the Office of Intellectual Freedom of the American Library Association (ALA) recorded 6,364 challenges to books, most of which were unsuccessful.[65] The ALA numbered more than 3,000 challenges between 2000 and 2005.[66]

Protest over schoolbooks has been a big problem in some communities. Schoolbook protestors have made their appearance in communities from one end of the United States to the other. Protests against certain schoolbooks include charges that they

- portray too much sex or violence
- use profanity
- use poor English
- promote "secular humanism," are irreligious, anti-Christian
- are un-American, lacking in patriotism
- promote one-worldism and globalization
- are racist
- depict the "wrong" values
- teach the theory of evolution instead of scientific creationism
- are too graphic
- are antifamily
- condone gay lifestyle

Books have been challenged on political grounds as well, for example, in the case of the Miami-Dade School Board's decision in 2006 to ban *Vamos a Cuba* and its English translation, *A Visit to Cuba*, as an inaccurate portrayal of life in Cuba. Pressures can arise for material to be *included* as well as excluded, as in the case of the Texas Board of Education in 2004 requiring the publisher of health textbooks to define marriage as between a man and a woman.

Efforts to censor topics of public discussion, reading matter, films, videorecordings, drama, television, music, and artwork recur in the schools—and in society at large—with great frequency, testing First Amendment rights to free speech and press. In recent years, charges of obscenity, for example, have produced vigorous challenges to art exhibitions, novels, films, and lyrics to musical compositions.

The definition of obscenity has proved to be elusive. The U.S. Supreme Court has let local communities determine what printed and visual matter violates their community standards and possesses "no redeeming value." Many people consider the sufficient standard to be U.S. Supreme Court Justice Potter Stewart's famous statement about obscenity, "I know it when I see it."

Schools have both engaged in self-censorship and responded to pressures for censorship from outside forces. A sampling of targets of those who protest their use reveals a wide range. Some of the works attacked in various parts of the country between 1990 and 2006 (not necessarily the first time they were targeted) and the purported reasons claimed by those objecting were:

Little Red Riding Hood, violence (1990–1991)

My Friend Flicka by Mary O'Hara, certain words (1990–1991)

Snow White, violence (1992)

The Dead Zone and *The Tommyknockers* by Stephen King, rape and language (1992)

Daddy's Roommate by Michael Willhoite, homosexuality (1992)

A Light in the Attic, by Shel Silverstein, manipulation of parents by children (1993)

The Autobiography of Malcolm X, antiwhite, pro-Islam (1994)

Peter Pan, portrayal of Native Americans (1994)

Roselily by Alice Walker, antireligious and *Am I Blue?* antimeat-eating (1994)

An American Childhood by Anne Dillard, violent snowball fight (1994)

Tex by S. E. Hinton, language (1995)

The Light in the Forest by Conrad Richter, too graphic (1996)

Beloved by Toni Morrison, racial content (1998)

Roll of Thunder, Hear My Cry by Mildred D. Taylor, language (2002)

What My Mother Doesn't Know by Sonya Sones, sexual content and language (2004)

And Tango Makes Three by J. Richardson and P. Parnell, homosexuality (2006)

Repeated candidates for banning are J. D. Salinger's *Catcher in the Rye* and Mark Twain's *The Adventures of Huckleberry Finn*; John Steinbeck's *The Grapes of Wrath* and *Of Mice and Men*; Maya Angelou's *I Know Why the Caged Bird Sings*; Katherine Paterson's *A Bridge to Terebithia*; Judy Blume's *Forever*; Maurice Sendak's *In the Night Kitchen*; Robie Harris's *It's Perfectly Normal*; Robert Cormier's *The Chocolate War*; Hans Christian Andersen's *The Little Mermaid*; and the Grimm brothers' *Fairy Tales* appear on some lists. Richard Wright's *Black Boy* and *Native Son* have both evoked challenges. Books dealing with racial themes whether written by a white author (Twain) or black (Morrison, Wright) can provoke controversy.

Efforts have been made to remove or revise textbooks in the field of health because of material on sexuality education and in historical treatments of Columbus's discovery of the New World and contributions of European Western civilization. You will note that efforts to censor materials come from both the right (*My Friend Flicka, Catcher in the Rye*) and the left (*Peter Pan, Huckleberry Finn*).

Any work dealing with homosexuality stirs considerable protests as in the case of Michael Willhoite's *Daddy's Roommate* (1992). Even suggestions that it is all right to be different, as is the case of Todd Tuttle's *Spot* (2001), can become controversial. Not only is literature concerning homosexuality an issue but also related is the controversy over gay-supported or gay-straight clubs meeting on school campuses.

The teaching of values has come under attack by protesters who hold that some of the schoolbooks undermine traditional American values. Protesters have taken special exception to the book *Values Clarification*, ostensibly because the program that it proposes allows students to express their own views on personal problems.[67]

The teaching of the Darwinian theory of the evolution of humankind has long been a cause of concern to those espousing intelligent design or scientific creationists, who champion the biblical account of creation in *Genesis*. Mentioned in Chapter 3, the *Scopes* trial in Tennessee in the 1920s reflected the sentiments of the creationists. In 1968 in the case of *Epperson v. Arkansas* the U.S. Supreme Court ruled that the theory of evolution may be taught.[68]

The evolution–creationism issue rose frequently in the 1980s and 1990s. In 1982 the federal district court holding that scientific creationism was a religious doctrine struck down an Alabama statute that would have required instruction in scientific creationism in addition to the theory of evolution. In June 1987 the U.S. Supreme Court ruled unconstitutional Louisiana's Balanced Treatment for Creation Science and Evolution Science Act of 1981, which would have required that scientific creationism be given equal instructional time with the theory of evolution. In October 1990, more than twenty years after *Epperson*, the Texas Education Agency's approval of state-adopted textbooks that taught the theory of evolution made national news.

The New Mexico State Board of Education in October 1999 barred the study of creationism in the public school science curriculum while retaining the study of the theory of evolution. Illinois lent yet another dimension to the issue when also in October 1999 its state Board of Education eliminated the word "evolution" from its state standards, using the expression "change in time." Challenges to the teaching of evolution continue up to the present as we will see later in this chapter when we discuss the companion issue of religion in education.[69]

Often protests over schoolbooks are not intended to force the schools to eliminate certain material but to adopt textbooks that incorporate particular topics, such as scientific creationism. Although the Supreme Court has ruled that reading the Bible and prayers for devotional purposes in the school are unconstitutional, many groups are still attempting to reintroduce or introduce these sectarian practices into the public schools' curriculum.

Underlying some of the protests over textbooks is the perennial conflict of differing secular and religious values in a pluralistic society and the interpretation of the Jeffersonian doctrine of separation of church and state, an issue explored later in this chapter.

First Amendment cases have cropped up in the arena of student expression. Schools, establishing dress codes, have sought to ban T-shirts, which they deemed to carry disruptive, offensive, vulgar, profane, or lewd language. In the face of a possible lawsuit, the Roswell, New Mexico, school board, for example, in the fall of 1999 rescinded a decision banning student displays of pentagrams, a symbol of the Wiccan religion. A Minnesota high school disallowed a student from wearing a sweatshirt with the words "Straight Pride." The U.S. District Court in St. Paul in the spring of 2001 held the school's ban on the sweatshirt unconstitutional. Likewise, when a student was suspended at a New Jersey high school for wearing a T-shirt with the word "redneck" on it, he and his brothers contested the action. Although the district court supported the school, the Third Circuit Court of Appeal in October 2002 ruled that the student was within his First Amendment rights to wear the shirt. A middle school student in Pennsylvania in 2006 won his case against his school district that had expelled him for writing violent rap lyrics. Principals have had to decide whether to allow an elementary school student to sing a song critical of the U.S. president (Florida), a high school student wearing clothing with a Confederate flag (South Carolina), a high school student wearing an antigay T-shirt (California), and a high school student bearing a banner with the words "Bong Hits 4 Jesus" (Alaska). The courts must consistently weigh First Amendment rights to free speech against the potential for disruption of the ongoing educational program.

The student press has run afoul of internal censorship by school administrators who frequently or regularly review and restrict student articles, stories, and photographs prior to publication. Administrators tend to expunge materials that are critical of the school, appear racist and are offensive or obscene.

The U.S. Supreme Court in a 5–3 decision in *Hazelwood v. Kuhlmeier* (1988) affirmed school officials' authority to censor student publications. Reversing an appellate court decision, the Supreme Court ruled that school officials may exercise prior review and restraint of student publications if such action serves any valid educational purpose.[70] *Hazelwood* erupted in 1983 when the principal of a high school suppressed articles in the school newspaper on student pregnancy and divorce. The Supreme Court decision permits administrators to censor various forms of student expression, although nondisruptive expression as determined in *Tinker v. Des Moines Independent Community School District* (1969) still stands. In the latter case the Supreme Court ruled that students had the right to protest the Vietnam War by wearing black armbands.[71]

Hazelwood, in effect, permits censoring of articles that may reflect unfavorably on the school, as in the case of articles on religion, sex, drugs, alcohol, and even partisan political statements. Administrators have chastised teachers directing class writing projects and those serving as sponsors of student newspapers and yearbooks when they have allowed text and photographs to be printed that officials felt objectionable. Such cases transpired in Tennessee in 2005 when the school confiscated copies of the student newspaper that discussed birth control and condoms and in Rhode Island in 2006 when a parent sued the school board for refusing to allow the yearbook photo of her son posed in chain mail and carrying a sword. As a rule, administrative decisions to censor student publications are not frequently challenged, especially in the light of *Hazelwood*. However, the state of Oregon saw fit to enact legislation in July 2007 protecting the First Amendment rights of student journalists in public high schools and public institutions of higher learning.[72]

To respond to various social and political pressures, curriculum planners need not only professional knowledge and skills but also skills in public relations and working with community groups. When dealing with controversial issues in the curriculum, they should have channels through which they may determine the seriousness of problems, the strength of community feelings, and the ways in which issues might be resolved before they become magnified and disproportionate. They need established procedures by which parents can register objections to materials and at the same time secure broad-based review of those objections. Some objections may prove valid, necessitating removal of the materials; some may prove valid at certain levels; some may prove invalid. Community mores, state and national law, national educational needs, learners' maturity level, and children's right to learn must all be taken into consideration when making decisions on suppressing or, conversely, including materials. School officials must avoid the extremes of everything goes, on one hand, and nothing controversial may be published on the other hand.

Before leaving our discussion of censorship, we should not neglect to note a less recognized form, that is, self-censorship by the publishing industry. Diane Ravitch candidly described how publishers of textbooks and tests, in order to gain state adoptions via their guidelines on bias, advise their editors and authors to guard against choices of words, topics, and locations that might in any way be taken exception to by any group or subgroup of our society.[73] Thus, pressure groups both directly and indirectly can influence what is taught in schools. To reduce or eliminate controversy some school systems appoint committees consisting of teachers, laypersons, and, in some cases, students to make recommendations to school authorities on whether or not to keep or remove challenged books and other media. Another means by which schools seek to reduce parental objections to literature assigned to be read by students is granting parents the right to request substitute titles for their children.

5. Gender

Madeleine R. Grumet highlighted the significance of gender not only in education but universally as well when she wrote, "What is most fundamental to our lives as men and women sharing a moment on this planet is the process and experience of reproducing ourselves."[74] Gender as an issue in the schools revolves around practices in instruction, curriculum, and administration that result in one gender demonstrating higher achievement or having greater opportunities in certain fields and activities than the other, leading to inequity or discrimination.

Gender inequity has been a perennial problem in education. Title IX of the Educational Amendments of 1972 passed by the U.S. Congress caused school personnel to examine programs and to remove practices that discriminate between the sexes.

Restricting homemaking to girls and industrial arts to boys, for example, is a sexist practice. Funding of interscholastic athletics, with the lion's share traditionally going to boys' athletics, has been challenged as sexist. The integration of females into male athletic teams and males into female teams has stirred controversy within the profession and outside.

We can find considerable argument as to what degree, if any, sex stereotypes and gender discrimination in school actually exist. In the mid-1980s Myra and David Sadker studied over 100 fourth-, sixth-, and eighth-graders in four states and the District of Columbia, observing language arts, English, mathematics, and science classes. The Sadkers held that, regardless of the subject or grade level, boys dominated classroom interaction and received more attention from the teacher than did girls.[75]

A 1992 study commissioned by the American Association of University Women (AAUW) and researched by the Wellesley College Center for Research on Women reported data on gender discrimination and concluded that schools were shortchanging girls.[76] In the winter of 1994 the American Civil Liberties Union filed a complaint with the U.S. Department of Education against the Educational Testing Service (ETS) and the College Entrance Examination Board on behalf of the National Center for Fair and Open Testing (FairTest) charging discrimination against females on the Preliminary Scholastic Achievement Test (PSAT) and the National Merit Scholarship Qualifying Test (NMSQT) citing the fact that more males than females were National Merit Scholarship semifinalists and winners.[77] ETS and the College Board responded by consenting to add a writing portion to the PSAT/NMSQT under the presumption that females would do well on writing.[78]

For years the theme has prevailed that our educational system discriminates against girls. We see evidence of the fact that girls have moved educationally to the forefront and boys may now be the ones experiencing inequity.

- The National Center for Education Statistics' study, *Trends in Educational Equity of Girls & Women: 2004*, found females in elementary and secondary school "now doing as well as or better than males on many indicators of achievement and educational attainment, and that large gaps that once existed between males and females have been eliminated in most cases and have significantly decreased in other cases. Women are still underrepresented in some fields of study, as well as more generally in doctoral and first-professional degree programs, although they have made substantial gains in the past 30 years."[79]
- Surveying gender gaps in 2006 for white, black, and Hispanic students, the Manhattan Institute for Policy Research found for each ethnic group females leading males in high school graduation rates in each case.[80]
- Michael Gurian and Kathy Stevens reported that less than forty-four percent of college students are male.[81]

While Janice Weinman described barriers girls face in school, Judith Kleinfeld noted the bias that exists is against boys, especially those of minority groups.[82] Although boys continue to excel girls in mathematics, science, engineering, and technology, girls demonstrate higher achievement in other fields and the gap between girls and boys in traditional male areas has narrowed.

The AAUW in a 1998 follow-up study conducted for it by the American Institutes for Research reflected the progress made by females in education, noting, however, males' continued dominance in technology.[83] Historically, more boys have enrolled in mathematics and science courses than girls, whereas more girls have gravitated to language and the humanities. The 1998 AAUW study found girls closing the gap in some mathematics and science courses while boys continued to lead in participation in computer science and in higher-level courses in mathematics and science. Greater numbers of girls continue to participate in the language arts, foreign languages, fine arts, sociology, and psychology. Although the gender gap in studies may be narrowing in some respects, a plus for the girls, the study concluded, "In fact, course-taking patterns, when viewed as a whole, suggest that girls may be getting a broader education than boys by deepening their exposure to math and science and by enrolling in more courses in other subject areas."[84] The Horatio Alger Association provided further evidence that girls' attention to studies, academic achievement, and career goals surpass those of boys.[85] Sara Mead made note of the fact that more boys drop out of school, are held back a grade, or are suspended than girls. However, she concluded that boys' overall achievement and attainment of certificates and degrees are not in decline, that the plight of boys is exaggerated, and that the racial and economic gaps are more serious than the gender gap.[86]

Children's attitudes about gender roles are shaped early and, like many attitudes and values, are strongly influenced by the children's significant others—parents, relatives, close friends, teachers, coaches, role models, and other persons whom they respect. A study by Jacquelynne S. Eccles and Rena D. Harold at the University of Michigan found that "already by the first grade, girls have a more negative assessment of their general athletic ability than do boys."[87] Athletic skills at early ages are virtually comparable regardless of gender. Not until puberty can physiological differences between boys and girls account for differences in athletic abilities. Sex roles are to a large extent culturally determined; the school often perpetuates those social determiners, either through the intentional or the hidden curriculum. One has only to look at the subordinate role in which females are cast and the superordinate role accorded males by some societies on this globe to provide evidence of the impact of culture in shaping male and female behavior. If culture is a determining factor, as most people believe, we should perhaps be concerned about some of the changes in the culture itself since, on the flip side, as observed by Lynn Phillips, girls are beginning to exhibit some of the lesser admired traits demonstrated more often by males, such as aggressive antisocial behavior and use of tobacco, alcohol, and drugs.[88] Although we can cite countless cases of discrimination against girls, the rash of schoolhouse shootings in the late 1990s and early 2000s carried out by boys, boys' higher dropout rate, the fact that boys are subjected to torment and bullying more often than girls, and the percentage of boys who commit suicide all suggest that boys may now be the neglected gender. Addressing the education of boys, psychologists Dan Kindlon and Michael Thompson viewed the traditional gender stereotypes about masculinity held by parents, teachers, and others as destructive of boys' emotional lives.[89]

As mentioned earlier in this text, as long ago as 1972, Robert J. Havighurst perceived the achievement of a masculine or feminine social role as one of the developmental tasks of adolescence.[90] The accomplishment of these roles is no longer simple, if it ever was. Though traditional attitudes toward the roles of men and women are still held by sizable segments of the public—especially among certain ethnic groups and nationalities, in certain areas of the country, and by certain religious groups—the distinctions in roles have been changing rapidly. Cultural and family attitudes may well shape perceptions of sex roles and contribute to gender discrimination to a much greater extent than schools. What once appeared to be male occupations, like truck driving, construction work, firefighting, police work, and fighter pilot, are no longer the exclusive province of the male. With females now assigned to naval vessels we may expect the term *seaman* to go into oblivion along with *mankind, mailman,* and *Dear Sirs.* Conversely, a "house husband" is no longer unheard of, and the female can be the family "breadwinner." Men can pursue careers and avocations that were formerly considered only for women, such as nursing, elementary school teaching, and secretarial work. Schools today are counseling girls to take science, mathematics, and industrial arts, courses formerly viewed as more appropriate for boys. On the other hand, boys are advised to elect the fine arts, language, and home economics subjects often considered particularly suitable for girls. The unisex philosophy has shaken, if not toppled, some of the stereotypes of men and women.

In response to changing attitudes about gender-based stereotypes, authors have had to "de-sex" their textbooks. They may no longer use the single generic pronoun "he" to refer to both sexes. Just as authors may no longer portray all persons in their textbooks as Caucasian, so also they may no longer depict males and females as performing only socially or culturally predetermined occupations.

There is an awareness that women have been discriminated against in the workplace. Such discrimination includes fewer opportunities for women to gain executive positions in some occupations and the fact that women continue to earn lower salaries than men do in comparable positions.

Efforts are being made to eradicate vestiges of gender discrimination and to equalize opportunity between males and females. Senate Bill 1463, for example, introduced in 1993 by Senator Barbara Mikulski as amendments to the Elementary and Secondary Education Act of 1965, comprising two titles: Gender Equity in Mathematics and Science and Elimination of Sexual Harrassment and Abuse, became the Gender Equity in Education Act in 1994. Looking back at the need for Title IX, sexist stereotypes and discriminatory practices when found are being eradicated. Curriculum workers are proceeding to design curricula that will help to eliminate bias, based not only on race, creed, and national origin, but if it exists also on gender.

School systems have sought to answer criticisms of gender discrimination through careful attention to curriculum and instruction, counseling, and staff development. Borrowing a leaf from private schools and the concept of all-male black schools, some school systems have attempted classes and schools segregated by gender on the assumption that student achievement and behavior are improved when the sexes are separated and cannot distract each other. Single-sex classes and single-sex schools have been cropping up all around the country. Noting just three single-sex public schools in the United States in 1995, the National Association for Single Sex Public Education (NASSPE) reported at least 262 public schools offering gender-separate education in March 2007; fifty-two were completely single-sex plans, but most, however, were coeducational schools with some single-sex classrooms.[91] Several public school districts including Austin and Dallas, Texas; Chicago, Philadelphia, and New York have established all-girl leadership academies. At the time of writing this textbook Austin was considering opening an all-boys leadership academy.[92] The federal government gave its blessing to single-sex education in late 2006 when it amended antidiscrimination regulations of Title IX permitting single-sex classes and single-sex schools as long as they are voluntary and the school district provides equal coeducational classes in the same subject. Since "separate but equal" did not hold in the case of race, some people wonder if "separate but equal" will endure in the case of gender.

The research is not clear whether segregating classes or schools by gender results in the positive aspects attributed to it. Patricia B. Campbell and Jo Sanders commented in 2002, "There is no national comprehensive controlled study of academic performance for U.S. students in public and private K–12 single-sex and coed schooling."[93] That same year, speaking of private, single-sex schools (as opposed to single-sex classes within otherwise coed schools), Cornelius Riordan argued, ". . . the research is 'exceedingly persuasive' in demonstrating that single-sex schools are effective in terms of providing both greater equality and greater achievement, especially for low-income and working-class students, most particularly for African-American and Hispanic-American boys *and* girls."[94] Addressing what has been referred to as the "boy crisis," Caryl Rivers and Rosalind Chait Barnett in 2006 maintained that only rural and inner-city boys were experiencing problems and they saw no need for single-sex education.[95]

Debate continues on the effectiveness of single-sex education. Proponents maintain that distractions are reduced and instruction can be tailored to the differing manner in which girls and boys behave, respond mentally and physically to instruction, and process information. Critics, on the other hand, view single-sex classes and schools as unnecessary segregation since differences in achievement are not all that great. Ambivalence toward single-sex education was demonstrated in results obtained when the Association for Supervision and Curriculum Development asked readers of its online newsletter whether they believed children benefit from single-sex education. Forty-nine percent were unsure; thirty-five percent said "yes," and sixteen percent replied "no."[96]

We cannot leave the issue of gender as it affects schooling without mention of the impact of sexual diversity on the curriculum. The public's views on such topics as understanding sexual orientation and the historical contributions of gays, lesbians, bisexuals, and transsexuals range from demands for silence to support of discussion. Controversy also swirls around students holding meetings of gay and gay-straight organizations on the school campus, raising First Amendment issues and sometimes evoking litigation.[97]

6. Health Education

No better example of the convergence of needs of students and needs of society can be found than the health-related problems experienced by today's young people. In addition to offering long-standing programs of physical fitness, hygiene, and nutrition education, many of which are now being revised, the schools are confronted with a number of health problems that demand the close attention of curriculum planners. Specifically, the schools are seeking ways to respond to the use and abuse of alcohol, drugs, and tobacco, to the high incidence of teen pregnancies, and to the prevalence of sexually transmitted diseases, including acquired immune deficiency syndrome (AIDS).

Let's briefly look at the dimensions of these problems and schools' responses to them.

Drugs, Alcohol, Tobacco.   Several annual national surveys shed light on children's and adolescents' use of illicit drugs, alcohol, and tobacco. Among these are studies conducted by the Substance Abuse and Mental Health Services Administration (SAMHSA) of the U.S. Department of Health and Human Services, the Institute for Social Research at the University of Michigan, Parents' Resource Institute for Drug Education (PRIDE),[98] and American Legacy Foundation.[99]

SAMHSA's *National Survey on Drug Use and Health* (NSDUH), formerly National Household Survey on Drug Abuse (NHSDA), is a primary source of information on the use of illicit drugs, alcohol, and tobacco among the general, noninstitutionalized population twelve years of age and older. NSDUH annually interviews some 67,500 Americans ages twelve and older every year. Data for 2005 released in the fall of 2006 indicated rather widespread use of illicit drugs, alcohol, and tobacco. Surveying nine categories of illicit drug use, NSDUH estimated 8.1 percent of the population aged twelve and older (19.7 million) used illicit drugs at some time during the month preceding the survey. However, the overall rate between 2002 and 2005 remained constant. Marijuana topped the list of the most commonly used illicit drugs.[100] Troubling are the findings that girls have caught up with boys in illicit drug use, now exceed boys in the use of cigarettes and prescription drugs, and are new users of substances more frequently than boys.[101]

The *National Survey* recorded 57.8 percent of the population twelve or older as current drinkers (at least one drink in the past thirty days) and 22.7 percent of the same population as binge drinkers (five or more drinks at the same time or within a couple of hours of each other). Consumption of alcohol, up slightly from 2004, was highest among the population aged twenty-one to twenty-five. Although alcohol consumption was heaviest among males in the twelve years or older group, in the twelve to seventeen group females exceeded males.[102] The tragic use of alcohol by young people is underscored by the 2002 statistic revealing the fact that 29 percent of Americans ages fifteen to twenty killed in motor vehicle crashes had been drinking.[103]

While the current use of all tobacco products by Americans age twelve and older in the last month dipped from 2002 to 2003 and stayed the same from 2003 to 2005, the current use of cigarettes declined somewhat from 2002 to 2005.[104]

Since 1975, the Institute for Social Research at the University of Michigan, with funds from the National Institute on Adolescent Drug Abuse, has annually surveyed the use of tobacco, alcohol, and illicit drugs by high school seniors, college students, and young adults. In 1991 the Institute began collecting data from eighth- and tenth-graders. The Institute for Social Research reports its annual findings in *Monitoring the Future*.

Drawing from findings of the 2006 survey of some 50,000 eighth-, tenth-, and twelfth-grade students in 400 secondary schools nationwide, the Institute for Social Research reported:

- Adolescents' decade-long drop in illicit drug and alcohol use continued to decline in 2006.
- Methamphetamine and cocaine use has generally declined since the late 1990s.
- Ecstasy registered an insignificant increase among twelfth-graders.
- OxyContin use showed decline from 2005.
- Although cigarette smoking among secondary school students had declined since the mid-1990s, 2006 saw eighth- and tenth-graders experiencing no further decline in daily smoking while twelfth-graders showed a small decline.[105]

Encouraging are the negative attitudes teenagers are manifesting today about the use of drugs, alcohol, and tobacco. The concerted effort of parents, schools, media, and government to combat drug use may account for the turnaround.

The University of Michigan studies show that although a clear majority of teenagers disapprove of the use of drugs and abuse of alcohol, too many students still do not perceive the risks involved in use of drugs, alcohol, and tobacco. Obviously, the struggle against use of illicit drugs, consumption of alcohol, and addiction to tobacco is far from over.

The public is obviously concerned about the drug problem in the schools but ranks other problems higher. Annual Phi Delta Kappa/Gallup Polls from 1998 through 2007 reveal that the public ranks the use of drugs fourth or lower in the list of problems facing the schools of their communities. Lack of discipline, which headed the poll lists for many years, held second place below violence in the 1998 poll, rose to first place again in the 1999 poll, fell to second place in 2000 through 2002, came third in 2003 through 2006, and second in 2007. Lack of financial support, which had been in third place in 1998 and 1999, rose to the top of the list in 2000 through 2007.[106]

Teenage Pregnancies, Live Births, and Abortions.   Along with the decline in the use of illicit drugs, alcohol, and tobacco, the frequency with which teenagers engage in sexual activity and the number of teenage pregnancies, births, and abortions have steadily dropped.[107] The National Center for Health Statistics of the Centers for Disease Control and Prevention (CDC) estimated 757,000 pregnancies among teenagers ages fifteen to nineteen in 2002, about one-fourth fewer than estimated in 1990.[108] The rate of pregnancies of all races dropped from a high of 116.8 per thousand females in 1990 to 76.4 in 2002. The more than 700,000 pregnancies resulted in some 425,000 live births, 215,000 induced abortions, and 117,000 fetal losses.[109] The birthrate for the same period declined from 59.9 in 1990 to 43.0 in 2002.[110] Significantly, three out of four teens reported using a method of contraception at their first intercourse; ninety-one percent of males and eighty-three percent females at their most recent intercourse. Although American females ages fifteen to nineteen registered a decline in birthrates, comparison with other developed countries shows Canada with twenty births per thousand, Germany with ten, and France with eight.[111] Statistics for this same demographic group disclosed a dramatic almost fifty percent drop in the number of induced abortions: 40.3 in 1990 to 21.7 in 2002.[112] More than 200,000 induced abortions in the ages fifteen to nineteen group, as well as the over 1 million abortions annually among the general female population, however, remain cause for concern.

As disturbing as the figures on teenage pregnancies, births, and abortions are, of particular interest is the change in attitudes among teenagers. In spite of the omnipresence of sexual stimuli through movies, television, and the Internet as well as much-publicized peccadillos of public figures, the Centers for Disease Control and Prevention noted that several studies have shown that the proportion of teenagers who are sexually experienced declined in the 1990s. At the same time, the use of condoms and injectable and implant contraceptives has increased.[113] Not only did fewer high school students report having had sexual intercourse (51 percent in 1991, 47 percent in 2005) but 63 percent reported in 2005 using a condom during last sexual intercourse as opposed to 46 percent in 1991.[114] Apparently, a fortuitous combination of factors has led to a reversal of student attitudes.

Sexual intercourse is not always the in-thing. Programs calling for abstinence; fear of AIDS and other sexually transmitted diseases; distribution of sexuality information and condoms; provision of organized after-school recreation; willingness of more and more parents to discuss sexual topics with their children and to support sexuality education programs in the schools; and efforts by teachers, churches, social agencies, government, and foundations have combined to reverse attitudes of the permissive so-called sexual revolution of the sixties through the eighties.

Sexually Transmitted Diseases.   How to reduce the lower, but continuing high, incidence of sexually transmitted diseases (STDs) is of paramount concern not only to public health workers but also to curriculum planners. How serious the problem is can be seen from the figures for notifiable diseases. The National Institute of Allergy and Infectious Diseases recorded the existence of more than twenty sexually transmitted diseases (STDs) in the United States in 1999.[115] H. Weinstock, S. Berman, and W. Cates estimated that each year 19 million Americans become newly infected with a sexually transmitted disease, about half of whom are between ages fifteen and twenty-four.[116] Americans with genital herpes, for example, number some 45 million with about a million people infected each year.[117]

Still of concern to health workers, educators, and the public is acquired immuno-deficiency syndrome (AIDS), although the incidence and number of deaths from AIDS has dropped dramatically since the late 1990s. Historically, the pace of HIV/AIDS spread has been startling. The United Nations' *Global Summary of the AIDS Epidemic* reported for the year 2006 estimates of 39.5 million people worldwide living with HIV, 4.3 million newly infected, and 2.9 million deaths from AIDs; 360,000 of the deaths were children under fifteen.[118] First diagnosed in the United States in 1981, cases of HIV rose rapidly, peaked at some 150,000 infections per year in the mid-1980s, and declined to approximately 40,000 per year in 2000.[119] More than 1 million people were living with HIV/AIDS in the United States in 2006 with 40,000 new HIV infections anticipated during that time. Of the 22 million who have died from HIV/AIDS worldwide since its diagnosis more than 500,000 were Americans.[120]

Schools, churches, social agencies, and parents all have roles to play in combatting teenage pregnancies, births, abortions, and sexually transmitted diseases. Sexuality education is one response to these problems that affect the well-being not only of children and youth but also of society.

Sexuality Education and School Clinics.   Health-related problems pose the classic question to curriculum planners. To what extent must the schools respond to problems of society? What can the schools do about these overwhelming problems? If educators agree that the schools can make some response, how will that response be made?

The public appears to be in rather general agreement about the schools' efforts to educate young people about the hazards of using alcohol, drugs (both prescription and nonprescription), and tobacco. State legislatures, reflecting public opinion, have in some cases mandated instruction on the use and abuse of these substances. In spite of the schools' concerted attack on the use of alcohol, drugs, and tobacco, however, usage among young people continues to cause concern.

In the area of sexuality or sex education, however, parents and other citizens of the community are in sharp disagreement. Attitudes range from support for strong sexuality education programs in the schools to avoidance of the topic. Attitudes of the various religious and ethnic groups differ considerably on responses schools should take toward sexual problems. Since sexuality education is value-laden, some people believe the schools' program should be confined to the academics, leaving moral education to the home and church.

Unlike Sweden where sexuality education has for years been compulsory in elementary through high school and has presented a frank treatment of the multiple aspects of the topic, American schools differ widely in their approaches.[121] Although all states have some form of sexuality education, their programs range from abstinence only (abstinence only until marriage) to abstinence plus, a broad sexuality curriculum teaching not only abstinence but also some of the most controversial aspects of human sexual behavior, including discussion of anatomy, birth control, masturbation, use of condoms, risky behaviors, and homosexuality. Whereas only seven percent of Americans were found to object to sexuality education in schools, some, often on religious grounds, would ban sexuality education in its entirety.[122] A 1998 Kaiser Family Foundation and ABC Television poll found that only eighteen percent of adults favored teaching abstinence only.[123] Nevertheless, the federal government has historically funded abstinence-only programs.[124] That a change of attitude toward the abstinence-only approach is seen in the fact that several states in 2007 elected to opt out of the U.S. Department of Health and Human Services' State Abstinence Education Grant.

Deeming abstinence-only education as ineffective, the U.S. House of Representatives at the end of June 2007 allowed funding of Title V Abstinence Education Program grants to the states to expire.

That sexuality education can be a sensitive issue is demonstrated in the experiences of two U.S. surgeons general. Responding in 1986 to the AIDS crisis, C. Everett Koop, former surgeon general of the United States, strongly endorsed sex education, recommending that it begin in the third grade. Koop was severely criticized for his positions on sex education, AIDS education, use of condoms, and abortion. In July 1989, after eight years as surgeon general, Koop resigned. Attitudes toward sexual issues brought down a second surgeon general, Joycelyn Elders. Appointed by President Clinton in 1992, Elders, a pediatrician from Arkansas, was asked to resign in December 1994, just two years after her appointment reportedly as a result of announced positions she had taken publicly on sexuality topics such as distribution of condoms, abortion, and masturbation. Individuals and groups like the American Coalition for Traditional Values called for her resignation after she responded to a question at the United Nations World AIDS Day to the effect that masturbation is a part of human sexuality and perhaps should be a topic of study.

Critics of sexuality education believe that exposure of young people to sex education leads to promiscuity and threatens traditional family values. They are also concerned about the lack of well-trained instructors. Opponents are worried that the current curricula stress the physical aspects rather than the moral issues of sexuality education. They claim that sexuality education has not been able to solve the problem of teenage pregnancies and sexually transmitted diseases. They argue instead for no sexuality education in school or a sexuality education curriculum that promotes abstinence.

Part of the controversy over sexuality education lies in the fact that people define it in different ways. Reflecting the range of positions held about sexuality education from the most conservative to the most liberal are those who opt for abstinence-only-until-marriage to abstinence-plus/comprehensive programs. The new rubric of "marriage education" has entered our pedagogical vocabulary to take its place alongside other specialized educations. Those who advocate abstinence only allow for no sexuality topics beyond abstinence. They decry so-called "safe sex" approaches. Organizations included in the abstinence-only column are Choosing the Best, the Family Research Council, and the Medical Institute for Sexual Health.

Included in an abstinence-plus/comprehensive approach is the basic position of abstinence combined with study of other factors that encourage safe sex and reduction of risky behaviors. Proponents of abstinence plus/comprehensive programs include the American Alliance for Health, Physical Education, Recreation and Dance; the American Public Health Association; the American School Health Association; the National Coalition to Support Sexuality Education; and the Sexuality Information and Education Council of the United States.

Although some critics argue that education about sex should be the parents' responsibility, repeated polls confirm that a sizable majority of the public look to the schools for imparting both sexuality information and values to American children and young adults.

Curriculum planners are likely to encounter controversy whatever position they take with regard to sexuality education. If they put sexuality education in the schools, some communities will object to its presence in the curriculum. If they ignore sexuality education, critics say the schools are neglecting their responsibilities and not meeting the needs of learners or society. If they establish a purely biological approach to sexuality education or try to teach sexual content in a value-free context, criticism arises because the school has omitted the moral aspects of the subject, and many people contend that the moral dimension is more important than the biological. If they introduce moral education—that is, values—which values will be taught? For example, shall the school condemn, condone, or ignore artificial birth control measures?

Schools have been challenged for including discussion of homosexual behavior in their curricula and conversely for omitting or poorly treating the topic of homosexuality. Some schools have tried to find a middle ground by allowing teachers to discuss controversial topics if they are raised by the students but not permitting introducing and teaching of the topic.

School-Based Health Clinics.   Examples of controversies over school health services exist in the presence of school-based health clinics and distribution of condoms, measures designed to cope with the problems of teenage pregnancies, births, abortions, and sexually transmitted diseases. Viewing school-based primary health centers as "one of the building blocks of full-service schools," Joy G. Dryfoos defined a full-service school as a school that "integrates education, medical, social, and/or human services that are beneficial to meeting the needs of children and youth."[125] Dryfoos saw the full-service school as a "seamless institution" providing quality education and services through school and community collaboration.[126] School-based clinics or health centers are a fundamental manifestation of the full-service school. Whereas Dryfoos made note of only ten school-based clinics in 1983,[127] the National Assembly on School-Based Health Care affirmed more than 1,700 school-based health clinics in forty-four states in 2006 serving approximately 2 million children.[128] A proposal in the U.S. Senate in 2006 sought to provide federal funding for school-based health clinics.[129] Not all of these, however, distribute condoms or advise students on sexuality problems.

Part-time and full-time physicians and other health personnel provide physical examinations and much-needed information and counseling about health problems and family planning. Clinics have been established at elementary, middle, and secondary school levels. The dispensing of contraceptives or prescriptions for contraceptives and pertinent counseling to middle and high school students are particular points of conflict between the school and community. Some religious, political, and ethnic groups have strongly protested contraceptive services. The National Conference of Catholic Bishops, for example, has repeatedly protested the distribution of contraceptives in the public schools and is against abortion.

School systems in the United States and Canada have provided both contraceptives and counseling through their school clinics. In the winter of 1999 the French government authorized school nurses to distribute morning-after pills to teenage girls. In the fall of 1990 Baltimore became one of the first cities in the United States to distribute both birth control pills and condoms in its middle and high schools. In the spring of 1991, the New York City Board of Education, in spite of objections from religious groups, approved a plan to distribute condoms in its high schools beginning in the fall of 1991. The Philadelphia school board took a similar action in the summer of 1991. Among some forty urban school systems that make condoms available to youth are

Chicago, Los Angeles, Miami, and Washington. The New York Supreme Court may have set a precedent for other areas in its decision that students did not have to obtain parental consent to receive condoms.[130] That ligitation does not cease is demonstrated by the 2005 court ruling that caused suspension of Montgomery County, Maryland's sexuality education program.

In spite of the controversial nature of condom distribution, as long ago as 1993 forty-one percent of the public surveyed by the 25th Annual Phi Delta Kappa/Gallup Poll supported distribution of condoms to all students who want them while another nineteen percent approved distribution with parental consent.[131] Follow-up studies of high school boys who had access to condoms found no increase in sexual activity.[132]

Educators and the public, by and large, agree that the school has some responsibility for helping young people develop the knowledge and attitudes necessary to preserve and improve their own and the nation's health. Thus, exemplifying the principle of adaptation of the curriculum to the needs of the learners, society, the times, and the subject matter, schools have modified their curricula of health education, science, and the social studies to incorporate study of critical health and social problems.

Curriculum planners can make a convincing argument that the preservation of the health and well-being of the American people (and, therefore, the nation) is the most basic survival skill of all. In urgency, it surpasses thinking skills, reading, writing, and arithmetic. In spite of challenges sexuality education has become a staple of today's curriculum. One strategy in handling complaints by parents about the sexuality curriculum is to allow students to opt out of the course or the part of the course that deals with sexual topics. Schools face a continuing struggle in imparting sexuality education given the pervasive sexual imagery throughout society and the sexual content of movies, television, and music. For reasons basic to their cultures Western European nations demonstrate more acceptance of teen sex, distribution of contraceptives, and sexuality education.

Deborah P. Britzman posed a thoughtful question about sexuality education: "Shall we admit that nothing about sex education is easy and that, if the direction is to make a curriculum that both forgets the difficulty of knowledge and does not incite curiosity, sex education will continue to signify 'our passion for ignorance'?"[133]

While we examine the highly contentious issue of sexuality education we must not ignore other issues in health and physical education. To combat the modern malady of obesity schools are paying closer attention to food and drinks served in the school cafeteria, offered as classroom treats, and available in vending machines. A grant from the Robert Wood Johnson Foundation to the Alliance for a Healthier Generation, a joint endeavor of the American Heart Association and the William J. Clinton Foundation, provided funds in 2006 for some 300 schools in twelve states to improve nutrition, physical activity, and healthy lifestyles.[134]

Of concern, too, is the reduction or absence of physical education in the schools, including the limitation or outright elimination of the time-honored practice of recess in elementary school. Not only is time for play and recess giving way to current efforts to improve student academic achievement but also traditional childhood games like tag are being abandoned for fear of injuries. Hence, although public sentiment generally supports incorporating into health education efforts to safeguard and improve the physical and mental well-being of students, controversy in this area of the curriculum seems never to be completely dispelled.

7. Multiculturalism/Diversity

Among the more polarizing issues in education, ranking right along with religion, is the issue most commonly referred to as multiculturalism or diversity. The 2006 U.S. Census data cited previously reveal the rapid growth of minority populations. More than one-third (100.7 million) of the U.S. population of some 300 million were minority populations. Of the largest minority groups Hispanics, the fastest growing minority, numbered as already noted more than 44 million (close to 15 percent of the total population). Blacks were the next largest ethnic group at 40.2 million (over 13 percent). Asians, the second fastest growing minority, accounted for 14.9 million (about 5 percent).

Racial/Ethnic Integration. Ever since the decision in the case of *Brown v. Board of Education of Topeka, Kansas,*[135] more than fifty years ago in which the U.S. Supreme Court invalidated the "separate-but-equal" practices permitted by the 1896 *Plessy v. Ferguson* decision[136] and ruled segregation of the races unconstitutional, efforts have been under way to racially integrate the schools. Problem areas have included curriculum materials that were slanted toward white, middle-class culture to teaching methods, testing, and administrative practices such as busing, desegregation of faculties, and methods of discipline.

Over four decades ago sociologist James S. Coleman surveyed some 4,000 elementary and secondary schools, 60,000 teachers, and 600,000 students to determine the extent and sources of inequality of educational opportunity among ethnic groups.[137] Authorized by the 1964 Civil Rights Act, the Coleman Report, which was issued in 1966, supported the desegregation of schools. Coleman concluded that achievement of students is influenced first by their social environment (families and peers); second, by their teachers; and third, by nonpersonal resources such as per pupil expenditures on education. A dozen years later, after observing the operation of schools that had been integrated, Coleman concluded that integration per se does not necessarily increase the achievement of black students. He remained committed to integration but maintained that parents should choose whether black students attend integrated schools.

That not all black parents have been satisfied with progress made by their children in the public schools is evidenced by the suit brought in 1986 by eight families, including Linda Brown Smith (of the 1954 *Brown v. Board of Education* decision), once again against the board of education of Topeka, Kansas. At issue was the contention by the black families that Topeka had not done enough to desegregate its schools. U.S. District Court Judge Richard D. Rogers ruled in the spring of 1987 against the plaintiffs, a decision that was reversed by a three-judge panel of the Tenth U.S. Circuit Court of Appeals in December 1989, in effect holding that segregation still existed in the Topeka schools.

Busing, primarily of black children to predominantly white schools, has been a frequent court-ordered remedy since the U.S. Supreme Court's 1971 decision in the North Carolina case of *Swann v. Charlotte-Mecklenburg Board of Education*, which required desegregation "with all deliberate speed."[138] The trend, however, is clearly away from court-ordered busing for purposes of integrating the schools. Busing plans to desegregate have been or are being ended in communities across the country from Seattle to Boston, a center of angry protest over the desegregation plan mandated by the U.S. District Court in 1974. In the pivotal case of the Charlotte-Mecklenburg schools after thirty years of court-ordered busing to achieve racial balance the Fourth Circuit Court of Appeal in 2001 ordered the school system to discontinue busing. The following year the U.S. Supreme Court refused to hear the appeal from the circuit court, in effect, allowing the circuit court decision to stand.

Ruling on the Little Rock, Arkansas, desegregation plan, a federal judge of the U.S. District Court of Eastern Arkansas in February 2007 released from federal supervision the Little Rock, Arkansas, school-district scene of President Dwight Eisenhower's 1957 order for troops to escort nine black students into Central High School. Although federal oversight to ensure that school districts become "unitary" (i.e., without traces of segregation) has diminished, school systems are still grappling with the problem of integrating schools. In 2006, the U.S. Supreme Court had before it two cases from Seattle and Louisville, Kentucky, contesting the constitutionality of their use of race as a factor in assigning or denying students the school of their choice.

Examining national data for the year 2000–2001 researchers for Harvard's Civil Rights Project concluded that as the courts ended desegregation plans the public schools were becoming more resegregated. The researchers discovered that nearly forty percent of public school enrollments were minority students; the white students were most segregated; Latinos, the most segregated minority; and Asians the most integrated minority.[139]

In spite of efforts to integrate the schools racially, segregation continues especially in urban areas where whites are opting to send their children to high-performing public, charter, private, or parochial schools or school their children at home. Adding a subtitle to his book, *The Shame of the Nation*, Jonathan Kozol labeled the existence of segregated and resegregated schools in inner-city neighborhoods as *The Restoration of Apartheid Schooling in America*.[140] On the horizon are efforts of some schools to narrow the achievement gap among ethnic groups through socioeconomic rather than racial integration.[141] Using sociometric rather than racial criteria has gained currency in the light of the U.S. Supreme Court decision of June 2007, which prevented school districts not still under court order to desegregate from using race as a factor in assigning students in order to achieve diversity in their schools.

The magnet school, which was discussed in Chapter 9, has provided a partial solution to the problem of multicultural student bodies in urban settings. The laudable concept of the magnet school, however, has itself been attacked for splitting the community. To reduce racial conflict and prevent racial problems from arising, many school systems have established multiracial committees whose task it is to recommend solutions to tensions and incidents of conflict among racial groups. Multiracial committees and entire faculties find that, in order to eliminate negative attitudes and conflicts, they must analyze all aspects of the school, including the "hidden curriculum"—the school climate, social relationships among individuals and groups, values and attitudes held by both students and faculty, rules on student conduct, unspoken expectations, and unwritten codes of conduct.

New Curriculum Responses. The thrust of desegregation efforts is shifting from the physical movement of pupils to securing racial balance in the schools to reconstruction of the curriculum. Demands are increasing for the institution of "Afrocentric" curricula that would feature contributions made by early African civilizations before colonial powers expanded into the continent. Proponents of Afrocentric programs feel that the schools have placed too much emphasis on European achievements and culture. They point to Africa as the birthplace of humankind, cite African achievements in the fine arts, mathematics, and science, and take the position that the school curriculum ignores or minimizes the contributions of African civilizations. An ostensible purpose of Afrocentric curricula is to enhance black students' pride in their ethnic origins.

Like bilingual education, other-centric curricula—which some people call a "curriculum of inclusion"—are an issue that goes to the heart of the debate over cultural pluralism versus the melting pot of acculturation. Should the curriculum reflect and equate all cultures, maintaining their separate identities and creating a mosaic or fruit salad as some people term it, or should schools seek to develop citizens who manifest values of a common, national American culture? For example, the Portland, Oregon, school system has promoted multiculturalism through its *African-American Baseline Essays*, which present contributions attributed to African civilizations.[142] Black and white educators are found on both the supporting and the opposing sides of the debate over ethnocentric curricula.

Among recent plans to address the needs of black students and to develop nonblack students' understanding of black culture and history is Philadelphia's course in African American history required of all high school students. More extensive overhaul of both the curriculum and school organization is the plan of Omaha to divide its school district into three along ethnic lines—black, Hispanic, and white. Questions have been raised, however, about the historical interpretation of some of the content presented in some of the Afrocentric curricula. In addition, some educators are concerned about the extent to which ethnocentric curricula will further fragment the curriculum. Will there need to be Latino-centric, Asian-centric, Islamic-centric, and many additional other-centric curricula to reflect every culture represented in the public schools?

Cultural Diversity. Like so many concepts in education, multiculturalism can be and is interpreted in a variety ways from students' learning to work together and appreciate each other's culture or as Kenneth T. Henson defined it

> *Multiculturalism* refers to establishing and maintaining a classroom climate where students with many differences in background, potential, and challenges learn to work with all of their classmates and learn to appreciate their uniqueness.[143]

to the title of Christine E. Sleeter's book *Multicultural Education as Social Activism*,[144] or as James A. Banks expressed the goal of multicultural education: "to reform schools, colleges, and universities so that students from diverse racial, ethnic, and social-class groups will experience educational equality."[145]

The core issue in multiculturalism or cultural diversity is the struggle for predominance between the melting-pot and salad-bowl concepts. Those who champion a melting-pot concept point to the eventual assimilation of early immigrant groups—the Irish, the Italians, the Poles, the Germans, the Scandinavians, Asians, and others—into the American culture. Lilian and Oscar Handlin viewed the social reforms of the Great Society of the 1960s as resulting in supplanting equality of opportunity with equality of results, a breakdown in traditional family and social values, a splintering of homogeneity in America into numerous subgroups, the rejection of responsibility for one's actions and the portrayal of self as victim, the identification of success in terms of group affiliation instead of individual achievement, and the reinterpretation of American history.[146] Speaking of multiculturalism, the Handlins said:

> By denigrating the very core of traditional American middle-class education, in favor of the mores of the social margins, multiculturists effectively robbed students of the few tools useful for their future that schools could impart.[147]

Less accepting of the melting-pot concept are Hispanics and blacks. Typical of challenges to the melting-pot concept is the comment by Hugh B. Price:

> The trouble is that the melting pot works only at the margins and only in some aspects of life. It seldom works socially and has succeeded in education and the labor market only under duress. It took decades of political, judicial, and legislative pressure to include some, and only some, minorities and women in the melting pot.[148]

Jeannie Oakes saw melting as "almost entirely in one direction"—Americanization of immigrants "in the sense of conformity to white Anglo-Saxon mores."[149]

Advocates of cultural diversity feel multicultural education should permeate the curriculum, not just in English and social studies, the more common fields for study of diverse cultures. Most educators concede that the public schools have done a poor job of teaching about the contributions of ethnic groups. Educators generally endorse and promote inclusion of information about the contributions of males and females of all races, creeds, ethnic groups, and national origins. Responding to the belief that our curriculum is too European-centered, the Miami-Dade school system provided in 2002 a K–12 African American Values curriculum and the state of Massachusetts mandated the study of non-Western civilizations in its history curriculum. However, some educators state that just adding ethnocentric and multicultural content to achieve this purpose is not sufficient because it simply superimposes this content on a traditional, white, male, Anglo, middle-class curriculum structure.

Addressing selection of content in the schools, Deborah P. Britzman concluded:

> The liberal arts canon, or the body of knowledge deemed "sacred and great," valorizes the worldviews of white male writers to the extent of significantly excluding all other views. The presentation of European and North American white male authors as the faithful

transmitters of universal experience obscures their cultural specificity, socio-historical context, and political interests served and perpetuated by the canon's selective biases.[150]

Skirmishes over content of the English literature courses at the college level pit the traditionalists who favor the classic authors ("dead white men," to their critics) with the postmodernists who prefer contemporary authors who reflect cultural diversity and changes in modern society. Geneva Gay in an earlier writing advocated *curriculum deseg-regation* as a means of achieving educational equality.[151] Gay classified efforts to construct curricula for culturally diverse populations as first-, second-, and third-generation curriculum desegregation. According to Gay's classification, the first generation introduced the study of the contributions of ethnic personalities, revision of textbooks to eliminate bias against and stereotypes of minorities and women, and programs such as compensatory education, Head Start, Upward Bound, and cultural enrichment. The second generation incorporated bilingual education, multicultural education, provisions for the handicapped, and efforts to eliminate sex discrimination. Gay noted that neither the first- nor the second-generation curriculum desegregation efforts changed the basic structure of the curriculum. The third and current generation of curriculum desegregation must, according to Gay, subscribe to the principle that "a pluralistic ideology must replace an assimilationist orientation" and work toward the goal of "ultimately making American society more genuinely egalitarian."[152] Gay set forth a difficult task for the schools:

> anything short of total instructional reform is likely to be ineffective . . . educational equality for diverse learners cannot be achieved within the existing curriculum structures and with present assumptions about what are valuable educational outcomes. At their very core these structures and assumptions are ethnocentric and discriminatory . . . the foundations of curriculum . . . must become culturally pluralistic . . . information taught about various cultures and groups must be presented as having equal value and . . . expected outcomes must be deliberately taught. Knowledge of facts about cultural pluralism, values that promote human diversity, and skills in social activism to combat oppression and create a more egalitarian society and world should all be included in efforts to achieve curriculum desegregation.
>
> Multiculturalism should be the driving force of subsequent efforts to desegregate school curricula. It is a reconstructive and transformative principle. Its application necessitates changing the fundamental value assumptions, substantive content, operational strategies, and evaluation procedures of all instructional programs that are planned and implemented for all students.[153]

The implementation of multicultural curricula has not always come easily as evidenced by New York City's experience with the initial draft of its *Children of the Rainbow* curriculum guides, the first of which appeared in 1990. Opponents charged that multicultural curricula conflicted with parental rights, featured unacceptable lifestyles, inappropriately dealt with social issues, and departed from the basic skills.[154] In a much different vein the Oakland, California, school board created a furor at the tail end of the 1990s with its decision to declare Black English, otherwise known as Ebonics, as a second language, a move widely condemned by both prominent blacks and whites, as an impediment to black students' learning Standard English. Language specialists have held Black English to be a dialect of American English and not a foreign language. The Oakland board clarified the intent of its decision as creation of a path toward learning Standard English, not incorporation of Black English into the curriculum as a foreign language to be taught and learned. Hawaii, too, faces its own linguistic difficulties as it wrestles with the use of Pidgin English, which some hold as detrimental to learning Standard English.

All-Male, Primarily Black Schools. Alternative education took on a new aspect in 1990 with Milwaukee's plans to create within the public school system two African American Immersion Schools (one elementary and one middle school). New York City drew up plans for the Ujamaa Institute, which would also focus on programs for black male students. To counter objections to the planned schools, proponents argued that the schools, located in the inner city, already have an entirely African American student body. Opponents point out that the schools may still violate Title IX of the Educational Amendments of 1972, which outlawed discrimination based on gender. In fact, Detroit had planned to open in the fall of 1991 three schools, open to males of all races, with an African American curricular emphasis. The American Civil Liberties Union (ACLU) and the National Organization for Women (NOW) brought suit, objecting to the exclusion of girls. In August 1991 U.S. District Court Judge George Woods ruled that the schools could not open unless females were also admitted. So that the schools might open, the Detroit school board agreed to admit girls. Currently, as noted earlier in this chapter, school systems still have at varying levels of creation both single-sex classrooms and schools and schools or curricula exclusively or predominantly black oriented.

Dealing with Cultural Diversity. Determining what responses the schools should make to the cultural diversity of our population is one of the greatest challenges for curriculum workers. The issue of multiculturalism and plural values versus cultural mainstreaming and common values has grown in intensity on both public school and college campuses. The issue is entangled in a myriad of social, political, economic, educational, philosophical, secular, and religious values. Banks advocated the teaching of social justice issues in addition to the basic skills.[155]

On the positive side, all the recent efforts to empower ethnic minorities and women prove that educators are searching for ways to educate all children and raise the achievement level of those individuals and groups who are not now succeeding in the schools. Banks commented, however, that "the United States is still a long way from realizing the ideals expressed in the Declaration of Independence in 1776."[156]

Citing George Washington's concept of *e pluribus unum*, that is, the creation of a unified people through assimilation of immigrants in American customs, Arthur M. Schlesinger, Jr. observed:

> Our task is to combine due appreciation of the splendid diversity of the nation with due emphasis on the great unifying Western ideas of individual freedom, political democracy, and human rights.[157]

Commented Schlesinger in 1992, "If the republic now turns away from Washington's old goal of 'one people,' what is its future?—disintegration of the national community, apartheid, Balkanization, tribalization?"[158] In widely quoted remarks made before the Knights of Columbus in New York City in 1915, Theodore Roosevelt asserted in strong terms his belief that "there is no room in this country for hyphenated Americans. . . . The one absolutely certain way of bringing this nation to ruin . . . would be to permit it to become a tangle of squabbling nationalities." In a similar vein, Patrick J. Buchanan in 2006 held that our nation was risking Balkanization.[159]

Promoting cultural diversity by increasing minority participation in education, business, and government has been the controversial practice of affirmative action. The issue of cultural diversity on university campuses loomed large in three landmark affirmative-action cases brought to the U.S. Supreme Court by white plaintiffs. In the case of the *Regents of the University of California v. Bakke*,[160] the Supreme Court in 1978 ruled that race could be considered in admitting students, in this case to the medical school at Davis, in order to achieve campus diversity, but quotas could not be used. In two cases (*Grutter v. Bollinger et al.* and *Gratz et al. v. Bollinger et al.*)[161] before them in 2003 from the University of Michigan, the Supreme Court reaffirmed the *Bakke* decision allowing race to be considered for admission, in these cases to the law and undergraduate schools, respectively, but without allocating points or quotas to minorities.

Speaking to the question of affirmative action a proposed amendment to the State of Michigan constitution before the voters in November 2006, though prohibiting discrimination, would

> ban public institutions from using affirmative action programs that give preferential treatment to groups or individuals based on their race, gender, color, ethnicity or national origin for public employment, education or contracting purposes.[162]

A partial solution to minority entrance into colleges and universities is a guarantee by some states to admit students who rank in the top percentage of their high school class. The College Board has weighed in on the problem of cultural factors that some minorities experience when taking tests by creating SAT II, tests in particular subjects and in the test takers' languages.

Yet to be resolved, however, is the question of whether affirmative action should be abandoned entirely or continue to apply primarily to African Americans for reasons of historic discrimination or whether it should apply across the board to all minorities that are experiencing discrimination.

As the minority populations increase through domestic births and immigration, we may expect to see increased attention to multicultural education. Paul R. Burden and David M. Byrd offered precautionary advice when they wrote, "As you consider individual differences produced by cultural diversity, you should examine your own values and beliefs for evidences of bias and stereotyping."[163]

Banks would have the school teach about both American ideals and American realities, saying, "In a democratic curriculum, students need to be taught about and have opportunities to acquire American democratic values at the same time learning about

American realities that challenge these ideals, such as discrimination based on race, gender, and social class."[164]

Perhaps we need to think about multiculturalism today as not only a domestic but also a global issue, especially when, as mentioned earlier in this chapter, Americans are outsourcing education for their children by turning to online tutors across the globe. We can certainly find both support for and antagonism to the globalization and outsourcing of our American industries. Some people feel that we need to learn to live with the development; others would curtail the movement of our industries abroad, protecting American labor. According to some opponents of the contemporary world culture even the label of "international," as in "International Baccalaureate," smacks of anti-Americanism. Nevertheless, many educators realize that schools must equip students with skills needed to compete and survive in the developing global economy. Foreign language instruction, as one manifestation of twenty-first century needs, is intensifying across the country. Although Spanish by necessity remains a high priority, we find enrollments jumping in elementary school through high school across the country in the nontraditional languages (i.e, those not ordinarily taught in American schools—Arabic, Farsi, Hindi, Mandarin, and Russian). Presumably, the judgment has been made by educators and the public that skill in the nontraditional languages will help students compete in the global marketplace. In 2006 President George W. Bush took note of the shortage of speakers of nontraditional foreign languages such as Arabic, Chinese, Japanese, and Korean by launching the National Security Language Initiative, designed to educate students, teachers, and government workers in critically needed foreign languages.[165]

Opinions differ not only on definitions of multiculturalism but also what the schools' responses to this issue should be. Turner County (Georgia) High School seniors in April 2007 made national news with their response to multiculturalism: holding for the first time an integrated school-sponsored prom.

8. Privatization

Privatization as applied to education in its essence is the shift from public to private control of schools. To some the ideal form of education is a free-market system that allows parents to choose the schools their children will attend. Gerald W. Bracey, however, viewed privatization as the commercializing of education, a "war against America's public schools."[166]

Privatization presumes that educational management organizations (EMOs), following free-market business principles, released from restrictions imposed by state and locality, can be more successful in terms of student achievement than the present governmental system of school administration and supervision. Further, EMOs are a response to the public's desire for school choice. Dissatisfaction with public schools, disenchantment with government generally, calls for educational reform, and adherence to a business philosophy have fostered the movement toward privatization. Danny Weil noted that privatization now goes beyond the realm of schools into the management of prisons; corporate sponsorship of heretofore public art, science, and technology exhibits; endorsement of products by local governments; and governmental efforts to privatize Social Security and Medicare.[167]

Contracting.   Reminiscent of performance contracting in the late 1960s as exemplified by the Texarkana, Texas, schools,[168] public schools in the 1990s began turning noticeably to private organizations to manage their schools.

Dade County (Florida) and Baltimore, among other communities in the early 1990s, experimented with private educational management by contracting with Educational Alternatives, Inc. (later known as the TesseracT Group), which viewed its arrangement with schools as a "public-private partnership" rather than privatization.[169] Education Alternatives offered an instructional program called "TesseracT," encompassing a number of practices, including a constructivist approach to learning, whole language, use of technology, and inservice training of teachers.[170] The TesseracT Group ceased operating in 2000. Today one TesseracT school, purchased by the students' parents and operated as a nonprofit school, remains in Eagan, Minnesota.

The largest of the private managers of public schools, Whittle Communications' Edison Project, was founded in 1992 and began operation with four schools in 1995. Although statistics vary depending on contracts gained and lost in any year and sources of data, in the school year 2006–2007 the Edison Schools, a for-profit EMO, comprised of six divisions, reported serving approximately 285,000 students in nineteen states and the District of Columbia, including approximately 23,000 in the United Kingdom. Among Edison Schools' responsibilities are management of charter schools, and after-school and summer school programs.[171] In 2002 Edison Schools entered into a contract with Philadelphia to manage twenty low-performing schools. Characteristic of not only Edison's schools but also of other EMO schools are longer school days and longer school years.

Started in 1994 by Mike Feinberg and Dave Levin in a fifth-grade inner-city program in Houston and followed a year later with a middle school in South Bronx, Knowledge Is Power Program (KIPP), a nonprofit EMO, offers a tuition-free, open enrollment college-prep public schools program in low-income settings. The KIPP schools feature long days, required Saturday classes, required summer school, and homework. In 2006 KIPP reported management of fifty-two public schools in sixteen states and the District of Columbia, enrolling more than 12,000. Forty-nine of the fifty-two were charter schools; forty-five, middle schools.[172]

Other organizations in educational management are Chancellor Beacon Academies, the Leona Group, Mosaica (which took over the EMO Advantage Schools), National Heritage Academies, and SABIS Educational System.

Contractual plans normally call for management of existing schools with existing faculty with ultimate control retained by the school board. Contractual schools, unlike many charter schools, remain public schools albeit with private management whereas independent for-profit charter schools of the EMOs hire their own faculty and provide their own curricula. In its annual report on for-profit EMOs for the year 2005–2006 the Commercialism in Education Research Unit at Arizona State University reported fifty-one EMOs operating in twenty-eight states and the District of Columbia, enrolling more than 237,000 students.[173] The number of schools managed by these fifty-one dropped from 535 in 2004–2005 to 521. The large EMOs accounted for 15 percent of U.S. charter schools and 21 percent of U.S. charter school students.[174]

Private entrepreneurs maintain that they can offer more efficient administration and improve student achievement at less cost than under public school management. Private operation of public schools has reaped both praise and criticism. Teachers have praised those schools where student achievement has risen and where teachers have experienced advantages of training in new techniques and help in the form of materials, equipment, and aides. Criticism has emanated from teachers, including their unions, who fault use of tax moneys in for-profit operations and differentials in funding. Controversy centers around results of student achievement, costs of operation, quality of facilities and teaching staff, and quality and quantity of materials and supplies.

Accountability will play a fundamental role in the cases of both the contractual and charter schools. Whether student achievement is enhanced under private management and to what extent and whether contracting is cost-effective must be clearly demonstrated over a period of time if this relationship with private enterprise is to continue. Private management must translate its goals into reality if it is to obtain and retain contracts or charters. In passing we should note that many school systems have already privatized food, custodial, and transportation services.

9. Provision for Exceptionalities

One of the earmarks of restructured schools is the effort to include as many pupils as possible who evidence special needs within the framework of the regular class. In this category are students with learning difficulties, emotional disorders, educational deficiencies, and physical and mental impairment. Although *special education* often takes on the connotation of programs for students with disabilities of one type or another, the broader concept of special needs today encompasses the gifted.

Early one-room schools functioned on a multiage, multigrade principle. As schools grew larger and graded, they cared for the needs of pupils in heterogeneous groups retaining age of students as the primary form of grouping.

Through the mid-twentieth century, ability or homogeneous grouping became popular. Schools grouped students by intelligence and, in isolated cases, by achievement. Proponents of ability grouping, also known as tracking, claimed advantages for the teacher in handling groups where the range of abilities was narrowed. They felt brighter students would not be held back by slower students and each group could move at its own pace. Critics maintained that ability grouping denies students the opportunity to associate with all kinds of students and leads to lowering of self-esteem of those placed in the slower sections. Whether we call the lower groups Section A or The Bluebirds, students know that they have been placed in those groups because they are less able academically than pupils in the higher groups. Nor were the academic achievement results of ability grouping so superior to heterogeneous grouping as to merit this form of curriculum organization.

Ability grouping has been debated for many years. Today tracking of students is generally frowned on for both philosophical and pedagogical reasons. Many schools that had been tracking students have derailed those tracks in favor of heterogeneous models. This movement had often applied to gifted students who formerly were placed in separate classes for all or part of a day or even in separate schools. However, dual high school/college classes, enrollments in Advanced Placement and the International Baccalaureate, and even a separate school for gifted students, mentioned earlier in this chapter, now offer separate paths for the gifted. In one respect magnet schools continue a form of homogeneous grouping, not based on ability, of course, but on academic and vocational interests.

Key concepts in the handling of students with special needs are *mainstreaming* and *inclusion*. What curriculum worker has not yet encountered Public Law 94-192? This enactment of the U.S. Congress, the Education for All Handicapped Children Act of 1975, supplementing Section 504 of the Rehabilitation Act of 1973, was structured to eliminate discrimination against the physically or mentally challenged including those with behavior disorders. Celebrating the thirtieth anniversary of the 1975 enactment of the Education for All Handicapped Children Act that was retitled in 1990 as the Individuals with Disabilities Education Act (IDEA) and reauthorized again in 2004, the House of Representative in November 2005 reaffirmed the success of the act in aiding children with disabilities. Currently, IDEA serves some 269,000 infants and toddlers, 679,000 preschoolers, and 6,000,000 children and youth ages six to twenty-one.[175]

Conforming to P.L. 94-192, schools must make special provisions to ensure that all handicapped children receive a "free and appropriate" education. To accomplish this goal, schools must develop an individualized educational plan (IEP) for every handicapped child. IEPs, which contain annual performance objectives for each child and must be reviewed each year, require a considerable amount of the faculty's time. Determining the appropriate educational program and the best placement for each child requires difficult judgments by teachers and administrators.

Until *Education for All Handicapped,* the common plan for treating students with special needs was pulling them out of classes or segregating them in their own classes. *Education for All Handicapped* called for placement of students in "the least restrictive environment." One manifestation of that principle is "mainstreaming"—that is, placement of students in regular classrooms with nonhandicapped children—unless their handicaps require special treatment or equipment or are so severe that they cannot be taught effectively in the regular classroom.

Educators still disagree, however, as to whether handicapped youngsters are best taught by placement in regular or special classes, in regular or special schools. At the present time the popular means of organizing the curriculum for students with special needs is *inclusion* or full inclusion, which broadens the concept of *mainstreaming*.

Ann T. Halvorsen and Thomas Neary defined *inclusion* in terms of *inclusive education* and distinguished it from *mainstreaming*:

> Inclusive education, according to its most basic definition, means that students with disabilities are supported and receive the specialized instruction delineated by their individualized education programs (IEPs) within the context of the core curriculum and general class activities. Mainstreaming, in contrast, confers a sort of "dual citizenship" on students who move between general and special education settings. . . .[176]

Although the literature on inclusion often refers to "students with disabilities," Suzanne E. Wade and Judy Zone made clear that, "When focusing on individuals with disabilities, advocates of inclusion seek to change the philosophy and structure of schools so that *all* students, despite differences in language, culture, ethnicity, economic status, gender, and ability, can be educated with their peers in the regular classroom in their neighborhood schools."[177] "Inclusion means," wrote Carol A. Kochhar, Lynda L. West and Juliana M. Taymans, "children learning side by side although they may have different educational goals."[178]

Students in inclusive classrooms may be working on different materials and at a different rate, teachers may make use of resource specialists to help them, and pulling students out of class is still an option if a student is unmanageable or needs special treatment that cannot be provided in the regular class setting. Where we find agreement on the desirability for creating inclusive classes we can also often find disagreement on methods of implementation. Inclusive programs vary from placement of all students with disabilities in regular classes full time, to including students with special needs in regular classes part time, to admitting to regular classes those exceptional students whom the school deems able to profit from being included. In the last case the school system may retain special classes or even special schools for those who are not included. James McLeskey and Nancy L. Waldron saw "add-on programs" called "inclusion," as "superficial change," explaining, "This approach amounts to simply replicating special education services in the general education classroom, while keeping students with disabilities and their teacher substantially segregated from the learning community of the general education classroom. . . . This approach to 'inclusion' is reminiscent of the mainstreaming movement."[179] Some advocates of inclusion accept as their goal nothing less than full inclusion, embracing diversity of all types.

Accompanying inclusion are the concomitant concepts and practices of differentiated curriculum and differentiated instruction. Carol Ann Tomlinson and Jay McTighe speak of "Understanding by Design," which "focuses on what we teach and what assessment evidence we need to collect" and "Differentiated Instruction," which focuses on "whom we teach, where we teach, and how we teach."[180] In an earlier work Tomlinson contrasted the differences in approaches between traditional and differentiated classrooms, presenting in the differentiated classroom column a pedagogy designed to meet the needs of varying types and levels of learners (Box 15.1). Some educators are concerned that parents of students who are not handicapped might charge that their children are being discriminated against by not having individualized educational programs designed for them. Perhaps, at some distant time when all class sizes are more manageable and student achievement in reading, mathematics, and science meets state and national standards, schools might reach the admirable goal of individualizing education plans for all students.

Mainstreaming and inclusion have met with mixed reviews from educators. Teachers accept the premise that students with special needs can learn from each other—a premise of another restructuring program, cooperative learning.[181] On the other hand, teachers point out the difficulties in differentiating instruction in the light of class loads, lack of help, and lack of time. The move to inclusive practices, as with most major changes, is not without objections from those responsible for implementing the change.

BOX 15.1

Comparing Classrooms

Traditional Classroom
- Student differences are masked or acted upon when problematic
- Assessment is most common at the end of learning to see "who got it"
- A relatively narrow sense of intelligence prevails
- A single definition of excellence exists
- Student interest is infrequently tapped
- Relatively few learning profile options are taken into account
- Whole-class instruction dominates
- Coverage of texts and curriculum guides drives instruction
- Mastery of facts and skills out-of-context are the focus of learning
- Single option assignments are the norm
- Time is relatively inflexible
- A single text prevails
- Single interpretations of ideas and events may be sought
- The teacher directs student behavior
- The teacher solves problems
- The teacher provides whole-class standards for grading
- A single form of assessment is often used

Differentiated Classroom
- Student differences are studied as a basis for planning
- Assessment is ongoing and diagnostic to understand how to make instruction more responsive to learner need

- Focus on multiple forms of intelligences is evident
- Excellence is defined in large measure by individual growth from a starting point
- Students are frequently guided in making interest-based learning choices
- Many learning profile options are provided for
- Many instructional arrangements are used
- Student readiness, interest, and learning profile shape instruction
- Use of essential skills to make sense of and understand key concepts and principles is the focus of learning
- Multi-option assignments are frequently used
- Time is used flexibly in accordance with student need
- Multiple materials are provided
- Multiple perspectives on ideas and events are routinely sought
- The teacher facilitates students' skills at becoming more self-reliant learners
- Students help other students and the teacher solve problems
- Students work with the teacher to establish both whole-class and individual learning goals
- Students are assessed in multiple ways

Source: From *The Differentiated Classroom: Responding to the Needs of All Learners* by Carol Ann Tomlinson (Alexandria, Va.: ASCD, 1999). Used with permission. The Association for Supervision and Curriculum Development is a worldwide community of educators advocating sound policies and sharing best practices to achieve the success of each learner. To learn more, visit ASCD at www.ascd.org.

McLeskey and Waldron attributed teachers' and principals' resistance to the substantive nature of the changes required. They pointed out that sometimes those teachers who are regarded as most effective and successful in terms of student achievement resist efforts at inclusion for fear that their class's level of achievement would be lowered by admitting students with disabilities.[182]

It is apparent that shifting to an inclusive model of instruction necessitates fundamental modifications in school philosophy and practices. Legislation may well speed the move toward inclusive education. Laws providing for special needs of students furnish a clear illustration of the impact that federal legislation can have on the curriculum planner.

10. Religion in the Schools

In colonial America religion and education were symbiotic. The Latin grammar school prepared young men to teach and to preach. Protestants of various creeds settled in most of the colonies, and Roman Catholics settled in Maryland; clashes over Christian religious beliefs among the early colonists were inevitable. Conflicts were exacerbated over the years as immigrants of all faiths came to the New World, adding beliefs such as Judaism, Islam, Confucianism, Buddhism, Bahaism, and Shinto to those of the Native Americans and the early arriving Christians.

There are so many varieties of Christians in the United States that it is difficult to count them. They include Baptists, Christian Scientists, Episcopalians, Greek Orthodox, Jehovah's Witnesses, Lutherans, Methodists, Mormons, Presbyterians, Roman Catholics, and Seventh-Day Adventists. Other religions also contain divisions: Judaism has Orthodox, Reform, Hasidic, and Sephardic groups. Sunni Moslem doctrine conflicts with Shiite doctrine. The Christian denominations have divided even further. For example, Lutherans of the Missouri Synod hold differing beliefs from the Evangelical Lutherans. The Free Will, Missionary, and Southern Baptists are but three segments of that large denomination. America also is home to agnostics, deists, humanists, Unitarians, and atheists.

Forty-five simple words, written in 1791, have generated hundreds of disputes over their meaning. Disagreements over these words continue to this day and may very well continue as long as the republic of the United States lasts. The words referred to are as follows:

> Congress shall make no law respecting an establishment of religion, or prohibiting the free exercise thereof, or abridging the freedom of speech, or of the press, or the right of the people peaceably to assemble, and to petition the Government for a redress of grievances.

These powerful words, known as the First Amendment to the U.S. Constitution, are the center of conflicts over freedom of religion, speech, press, and assembly. Almost daily there is news of a lawsuit that contends infringement of one or more of these freedoms. The question of whether religion should be included in the public schools has evoked fiery debates over the years. Time and again the U.S. Supreme Court has reaffirmed the doctrine of separation of church and state. This doctrine has been attributed to Thomas Jefferson and James Madison in particular; it was Thomas Jefferson who wrote of the "wall of separation between church and state."

The question of how high and how impregnable that wall should be has yet to be completely resolved. Decisions of the U.S. Supreme Court, the ultimate arbiter of constitutional issues, have kept that wall relatively high—much to the chagrin of those Americans who would like to see it fall and those who would fortify it even more. Those practices with religious connotations in the school that have most often necessitated court adjudication are prayer or reading of Bible passages in the classroom and at school-sponsored events, Bible study, use of public moneys to aid sectarian schools, released time for religious instruction off school grounds, celebration of religious holidays, teaching of evolution, values education, pledging allegiance to the American flag, permitting religious groups to meet in the school, posting of the Ten Commandments, and extracurricular activities that require a religious test for participation.

Decisions on the constitutionality of religious practices in the schools have frequently invoked the Fourteenth Amendment (due process), which has made the First Amendment binding on the states and had figured so prominently in early racial discrimination cases. From the wealth of U.S. Supreme Court decisions, in addition to those previously mentioned earlier in this chapter and in Chapter 3's discussion of censorship, the following appear to have special relevance for the public school curriculum. (The state of origin of each case is indicated in parentheses.)

- *West Virginia Board of Education v. Barnette*, 319 U.S. 624 (1943) (West Virginia). Ruled that Jehovah's Witnesses would not be required to salute the American flag.
- *People of the State of Illinois ex rel. McCollum v. Board of Education of School District No. 71, Champaign, Ill.*, 333 U.S. 203 (1948) (Illinois). Ruled that released time for religious instruction in the school was unconstitutional.
- *Zorach v. Clauson*, 343 U.S. 306 (1952) (New York). Ruled that released time for religious instruction off school grounds was permissible.
- *Engle v. Vitale*, 370 U.S. 421 (1962) (New York). Ruled that the prayer that originated with the New York State Board of Regents for use in the schools violated the principle of separation of church and state.
- *School District of Abington Township v. Schempp*, (Pennsylvania) and *Murray v. Curlett* (Maryland), 374 U.S. 203 (1963). Ruled that readings from the Bible and recitation of the Lord's Prayer in the school were unconstitutional.
- *Wallace v. Jaffree*, 472 U.S. 38 (1985) (Alabama). The U.S. Supreme Court affirmed the decision of the U.S. Court of Appeals, which had reversed an earlier ruling by the U.S. District Court that had allowed Alabama schools to hold a period of silence for meditation or voluntary prayer.
- *Bender v. Williamsport Area School District*, 475 U.S. 534 (1986) (Pennsylvania). The U.S. Supreme Court let stand the federal district court's decision that under

P.L. 98-377, the Equal Access Act of 1984, religious groups made up of students in the high school could meet at that school if other student groups also had access to the school's facilities. The Supreme Court in June 1993 ruled in *Lamb's Chapel v. Center Moriches Union Free School District*, 124 L Ed 2d 352 (1993) (Long Island, New York), that religious groups could meet after school hours if the schools were open to other groups from the community.

Prayer, Bible reading, and Bible study, held unconstitutional practices, remained volatile issues in the mid- and late 1990s. In June 1992 the U.S. Supreme Court in *Lee v. Weisman*, 505 U.S. 577 (1992) (Rhode Island) upheld an appellate court ban on school-sponsored, clergy-delivered prayer at graduation, even though the prayer was nonsectarian and attendance was voluntary. Hailing the decision were the American Civil Liberties Union and Americans United for Separation of Church and State. Critical of the decision were the Christian Coalition and Liberty Counsel. A flurry of court cases followed *Lee v. Weisman*. In early June 1993 the Supreme Court refused to hear the Texas case *Jones v. Clear Creek Independent School District*, 977 F 2d 963 (5th Circuit, 1992), in which the appellate court had ruled in favor of student-led school prayer. Later that same month a federal district judge in New Jersey allowed student-led prayer. The ACLU immediately appealed to the Third Circuit Court in Philadelphia, which blocked student-led prayer at two high schools in Camden County, New Jersey.

In one form or another, the issue of prayer in the school has been raised repeatedly in the courts. In *Santa Fe Independent School District v. Doe* (2000) (Texas) the U.S. Supreme Court ruled against student-led prayer at football games. On the other hand, after the Eleventh Circuit Court of Appeals had ruled in the case of *Adler v. Duval County School Board*, 206 F3d 1070 (11th Cir. 2000) (Florida) that a student chosen by his or her peers could include prayer in a talk at graduation, the U.S. Supreme Court in December 2002 sent the case back to the Circuit Court of Appeals for reconsideration in light of *Santa Fe Independent School District v. Doe*.

Members of the U.S. Congress, mainly Republicans, in 1995 and again in 1999 considered launching an amendment to the U.S. Constitution that would sanction prayer in the public schools, a move opposed by the American Bar Association among others. Efforts by states and localities to find substitutes for organized, school-sanctioned prayer are a moment of silence for reflection or silent prayer; voluntary, student-planned, student-led prayer at nonmandatory events; prayer and Bible reading before or after school in the school building or around the flagpole, and permission for religious clubs to meet on campus. Released time for religious instruction off campus remains a viable option in some states.

Carl D. Glickman contrasted the protagonists in the battles over religion in the schools:

> One group, identified as the secular humanists, says that public education and religion should never be mixed. . . . The other group, identified as religious fundamentalists, argue that America is a Christian nation and that Christian values are essential for a moral, ethical, and responsible society.[183]

Warmly contested in the early years of the twenty-first century are inclusion of the phrase "under God" during the recitation of the Pledge of Allegiance and the posting of the Ten Commandments and "In God We Trust" plaques throughout the school. The Ninth U.S. Circuit Court of Appeals in 2002 ruled that "under God," two words inserted in the Pledge of Allegiance in 1954, violated the principle of separation of church and state and ordered discontinuance of the pledge in schools. The Circuit Court, however, held implementation of the decision in abeyance pending appeals.

Although the U.S. Supreme Court ruled in *Stone et al. v. Graham* 449 U.S. 39 (1980) the Kentucky statute to post copies of the Ten Commandments in public school classrooms unconstitutional, the U.S. House of Representatives in 1999 passed legislation (later rejected by the Senate) permitting display of the Ten Commandments in public schools and public buildings. In a similar vein, two years later Maryland legislators rejected a proposal to post "In God We Trust" signs in school classrooms, yet Mississippi mandated their posting and Virginia permitted schools to do so. Proponents of prayer and Bible reading in the public schools find it difficult to understand why a government founded on religious principles would declare religious practices in the schools unconstitutional. They maintain that the founding fathers had no antagonism toward religion, but rather sought to prevent the federal government from establishing a national religion. They point out that state and national legislatures make references to God, the Declaration of Independence addresses "Divine Providence," our currency contains the phrase "In God We Trust." Those who argue for religious practices in the schools, however, often assume a largely Protestant ethic. They downplay the pluralistic nature of our society and the fact that many beliefs—including non-Christian religions—are now represented in the public schools. Jewish parents and children find the New Testament unacceptable. Catholics read from Catholic versions of the Bible, such as the Vulgate or Douay-Rheims, rather than the Protestant King James Version or one of the many other revised versions. Moslems' holy book is the Koran.

Advocates of the separation of church and state note that *Pierce v. Society of Sisters* gave believers the right to send their children to private parochial schools where a religiously homogeneous student population can be instructed in the beliefs of that particular sect. Furthermore, they maintain that the wall of separation between church and state protects not only the freedom of religion but also the freedom from religion.

Conflicts over the separation of church and state abound. Argument swirls around the use of taxpayer moneys to provide vouchers for use in religious schools. For example, whereas the Wisconsin Supreme Court in 1998 sanctioned the use of taxpayer money to allow Milwaukee children through its Parent Choice Program to attend religious schools, overturning a ruling of the Fourth District Court of Appeals, the Maine Supreme Judicial Court in the spring of 2006 held that Maine's law against use of public moneys to fund tuition to religious private schools was constitutional. The following fall the U.S. Supreme Court declined to hear an appeal of the Maine case, thereby letting stand the decision of the Maine court.

We can cite additional examples of continuing controversies over religion in education in the early part of the twenty-first century:

- The Virginia Senate approved a bill in February 2000 requiring a minute of silent meditation daily in its schools in place of reading a prayer.
- Virginia's House of Delegates proposed a constitutional amendment in 2005 that would permit prayer on all public property including schools.
- A Brevard County, Florida, school faced suit in 2005 when it scheduled graduation ceremonies at a Christian church that refused to cover its cross. Although the judge permitted the ceremonies because of the short timing, he indicated a church location was not appropriate and should not be used in the future.
- The Ohio legislature passed a law in 2006 requiring public schools to post donated copies of the national motto "In God We Trust" and the state motto "With God All Things Are Possible."
- A high school in Nevada made news and incurred a lawsuit in 2006 when the commencement address of the school valedictorian was cut off on her insertion of religious content into her speech.
- The Southern Baptist Convention in summer 2006 rejected a resolution urging parents to withdraw their children from public schools and send them to private schools or school them at home.
- A federal district judge in 2007 ruled that a fourth-grader's constitutional rights in a New York State elementary school had been violated when the school denied her permission to distribute a religious message during noninstructional time.

The use of the Bible in the curriculum can create dissension. The objectives in offering a course in the Bible or readings therefrom for purposes other than prayer range from studying the Bible as the word of God, as an important historical document, or as a great work of literature. Some of those who would ban the use of the Bible in the curriculum perceive its study as proselytizing.

Whenever religious instruction arises in public education it faces protests unless it takes into consideration the fact that today's classes are (1) multicultural with students holding a wide range of beliefs about religion and (2) taught objectively not from a sectarian point of view nor from a claim to historical accuracy, with the Bible as a piece of literature that has affected the lives of people both Christians and non-Christians. Even the distribution of Bibles in school, as by Gideons International, has been held unconstitutional.

Increasingly, educators and others are expressing concern over the schools' failure to include instruction about the contributions and effects of religion throughout the history of the United States and the world. Some teachers and authors of textbooks are fearful that they may offend people's sensitivities, veer away from religion entirely. Many students, therefore, are to a large extent ignorant of the importance of religion in the development of this country. Glickman expressed the concern that "we haven't acknowledged that there is a common core of virtue for American education, routed in religious, spiritual, and private conscience."[184] Noting the deplorable lack of knowledge about fundamentals of religion and its importance in our society, Stephen Prothero stressed the need for classes in religious literacy.[185]

A relevant curriculum would incorporate the study of both Bible literacy and comparative religions as a part of the general education of every student. Such a curriculum would focus on teaching about religion, not the teaching of religion. A person cannot fully appreciate the arts, literature, history, psychology, philosophy, or sociology—or even science, with which religion is often at odds—without studying the influence of religion on these areas of human endeavor. Certainly, students should gain familiarity with the world's great masterpieces of religious literature. A knowledge about religion is one attribute of the culturally literate person. Christians who promote the use of the Bible in the curriculum for sectarian purposes are not enamored with comparative religion or world religion courses that place the Bible on an equal footing with other sectarian texts.

A 2005 Gallup survey for the Bible Literacy Project revealed students' lack of knowledge of the Bible and English teachers' beliefs that such knowledge was important to them.[186] Mindful of the contribution of the Bible to civilization and literature, high schools are offering elective courses in biblical literacy and history. The Georgia Board of Education made news in 2007 when it enabled Georgia to become the first state to both approve and fund elective courses in the Literature and History of the Old and New Testaments,[187] authorizing local school districts to offer nondevotional Bible electives. Controversy can arise, however, over Bible courses even if they are elective.[188]

Curriculum planners must be mindful, however, that many people claim that the schools advocate "secular humanism" and would not be satisfied with nonsectarian teaching about religion. Secular humanism implies faith in humankind and subscription to social and moral values that are not necessarily derived from belief in a divine being. Though the public schools do not, in reality, promote a doctrine of secular humanism, the absence of sectarian practices in itself provokes some people to accuse the schools of promoting secular humanism.

At this point in time it appears as if the movement to elective courses in religious literacy is growing. It is difficult to know exactly how many schools offer classes on the Bible. As of early 2007 the National Council on Bible Curriculum in Public Schools numbered 373 schools in thirty-seven states using the Bible as primary textbook supplemented by unit and lesson plans.[189] Since initiating its program in 2006, the aforementioned Bible Literacy Project reported eighty-three schools in thirty states using along with the Bible its book, *The Bible and Its Influence*.[190]

The controversy over religion in education brings us once again to the issues of curriculum content and censorship. Since the *Scopes* trial in 1927,[191] controversy has centered on the issue of teaching the Darwinian theory of evolution versus the biblical interpretation of the origin of the human species that proponents label "scientific creationism," "creation science," or, simply, "creationism." The more recent terminology in place of "creationism" is "intelligent design," which holds that the universe is so complex that there must be an intelligent power behind it. Organizations are aligned on either side of the issue. The Discovery Institute's Center for Science and Culture seeks to promote the teaching of intelligent design[192] while the National Center for Science Education defends the teaching of evolution.[193]

Proposals to incorporate study of intelligent design as a counterbalance to study of theory of evolution surfaced among members of the Ohio Board of Education (2002) and in the Missouri House of Representatives (2004). Intelligent design has appeared on the agendas of state legislators and local school boards in many states, including Alabama, California, Georgia, Louisiana, Michigan, Ohio, Pennsylvania, and Tennessee. A 2001 survey found creationist activity in twenty-eight states.[194]

Proponents of intelligent design maintain that evolution is but an unproved theory whereas opponents of intelligent design hold that scientific evidence supports evolution. A bill in the Utah legislature in 2005 would require informing students that not all scientists accept the theory of evolution. Attempting to counter the teaching of the theory of evolution, Ohio's Board of Education mandated critical analysis of the theory of evolution in biology classes but then in 2006 dropped its mandate. South Carolina's Education Oversight Committee also in 2006 took the opposite position proposing discussion and analysis of scientific data related to the theory of evolution.

Cobb County, Georgia, and Dover, Pennsylvania, both ran into troubles over the evolution/intelligent design issue. Responding to stickers that had been placed in biology textbooks stating that evolution is a theory, not a fact, parents in Cobb County in 2004 brought suit to remove the stickers. The district court judge ruled in their favor, holding the stickers were an endorsement of religion. Although the Eleventh Circuit Court of Appeals ordered the district court to conduct a new trial or hold more hearings, the Cobb County school board at the end of 2006 ceased the practice.

Dover schools in 2004 went a step further than applying stickers to textbooks. They mandated teaching intelligent design. Ruling on the subsequent lawsuit brought by Dover parents opposed to the school board's action, the district court judge in December 2005 held for the parents declaring intelligent design a violation of the First Amendment. Just prior to the decision, school board members who had endorsed the intelligent design mandate were voted out of office.

Demonstrating the seemingly endless struggle in the religious war over evolution versus intelligent design is the experience in Kansas. The Kansas State Board of Education delivered a blow against the theory of evolution, not by banning its teaching from Kansas schools, but by disallowing questions on the theory of evolution on the state's science assessment examinations. The Kansas action met with such protest, both within and outside of Kansas, that in 2000 Kansas citizens voted out of the state board office two of the three state board members who had sanctioned removal of evolution questions. The state board in 2001 reversed its 1999 action and voted to incorporate evolution questions on the state science tests. However, Kansas revisited the issue in 2004 when proponents of intelligent design gained positions on the state school board. Following their election new standards in science questioned the theory of evolution. Changing again, the Kansas state board issued its 2007 science standards with a more balanced treatment of evolution.

Like so many political, social, and educational issues, positions on creationism versus evolution range broadly from rejection of evolution outright to complete rejection of creationism or intelligent design. A frequent approach of those who advocate teaching intelligent design is their call for teaching intelligent design along with the theory of evolution. Bill Frist, senator from Tennessee and cardiology surgeon, for example, in addressing the Rotary Club in summer 2005 encouraged teaching of both faith-based theory and evolution. Within the circle of supporters of the theory of evolution are religious believers who hold that the ages-long process of evolution is credible within the context of religious doctrine. Refraining from endorsing either creationism or intelligent design, Pope Benedict XVI gave credit to scientific progress but observed that evolution has not been completely proved.[195]

What does the American public think about the evolution/intelligent design issue? Two polls, one conducted in 2004 by CBS and one in 2005 by the Pew Research Center for the People & the Press in cooperation with the Pew Forum on Religion and Public Life, found Americans divided on the origins of life but over two-thirds support teaching of both evolution and intelligent design in the public schools. Among the respondents a sizable minority would substitute the teaching of intelligent design for the theory of evolution.[196] And what does the American public think about the place of character and values education and religion in the public school? Although some people fear that values that run counter to their own may be imposed on young people, Nel Noddings argued for critical examination of values and discovery of shared values and individual commitments, concluding that "teaching in the domain of values need not be dogmatic."[197]

President Clinton, responding to the public's generally religious orientation, in a move to derail efforts to amend the Constitution to permit prayer in the schools, in the summer of 1995 ordered the Department of Education to compile and transmit to the nation's schools a list of religious practices that are already legally permitted by the Constitution and judicial decisions. Guidelines recommended to the local schools by the Department of Education would allow students to (1) pray individually or in informal groups if they do not cause disruption, (2) carry and read the Bible or other religious literature, (3) distribute religious literature, and (4) wear religious clothing. The recommendations would not allow prayer in classes or assemblies conducted by students or school personnel.

A more detailed set of governing principles was promulgated by Secretary Rod Paige, U.S. Department of Education, in February 2003. Among the guidelines were the following:

- students may pray when not engaged in school activities or instruction . . . may read their Bibles or other scriptures, say grace before meals, and pray or study religious materials during recess, the lunch hour, or other noninstructional time . . .
- students may organize prayer groups, religious clubs, and "see you at the pole" gatherings before school . . . such groups must be given the same access to school facilities for assembling as is given to other non-curricular groups . . .
- when acting in their official capacities as representatives of the state, teachers, school administrators, and other school employees are prohibited by the Establishment Clause from encouraging or discouraging prayer, and from actively participating in such activity with students . . .
- schools have the discretion to dismiss students to off-premises religious instruction . . .
- students may express their beliefs about religion in homework, artwork, and other written and oral assignments free from discrimination based on the religious content of their submissions . . .

- student speakers at student assemblies and extracurricular activities such as sporting events may not be selected on a basis that either favors or disfavors religious speech . . . where school officials determine or substantially control the content of what is expressed, such speech is attributable to the school and may not include prayer or other specifically religious (or anti-religious) content . . .
- school officials may not mandate or organize prayer at graduation . . . where students or other private graduation speakers are selected on the basis of genuinely neutral, evenhanded criteria and retain primary control over the content of their expression, however, that expression is not attributable to the school and therefore may not be restricted because of its religious (or anti-religious) content . . .
- school officials may not mandate or organize religious ceremonies. However, if a school makes its facilities and related services available to other private groups, it must make its facilities and services available on the same terms to organizers of privately sponsored religious baccalaureate ceremonies.[198]

The guidelines are not law, are not binding on the schools nor, if implemented, are they free of legal challenge.

Charles C. Haynes observed that avoidance of religion in the curriculum is far from neutral. Editing a thoughtful guide from the Freedom Forum First Amendment Center at Vanderbilt University with legal editor Oliver Thomas, Haynes commented, "Students need to learn that religious and philosophical beliefs and practices are central to lives of many people."[199] In a more recent guide on incorporating First Amendment principles in the public schools Haynes and others spoke of the Association for Supervision and Curriculum Development–First Amendment Center initiative, which has four primary goals:

1. To create consensus guidelines for a school interested in creating and sustaining First Amendment principles in the school community.
2. To establish project schools at which First Amendment principles are understood and applied throughout the school community.
3. To encourage and develop curriculum reforms that reinvigorate and deepen teaching about the First Amendment across the curriculum.
4. To educate school leaders, teachers, school board members and attorneys, and other key stakeholders about the meaning and significance of First Amendment principles and ideals.[200]

Both guides, addressed to school leaders and parents, contain useful material for dealing with the thorny issue of religion in the schools. Addressing both religious and existential issues in both the curriculum and the preparation of teachers, Noddings advocated teaching *about* religion and discussion of the beliefs of the various religions.[201] Noddings took the position that "Professional programs must make it clear to teachers that the study and discussion of religious and existential questions is legitimate."[202] She commented, "The best teachers will be prepared to present not only the full spectrum of belief but also the variety of plausible ways in which people have tried to reconcile their religious and scientific beliefs."[203]

That other countries cope with the issue of religion in the schools can be seen by the diametrically opposed actions taken by France and Spain in late 2003. While France was adhering to a strictly secular society, forbidding students from wearing religious symbols in school, Spain was mandating Catholic religious instruction every year for Catholic children, taught by nuns in religious dress and whose salaries are paid by the government.

The debate over secular versus sectarian curricula for the public schools will be difficult to resolve because strong emotions, values, and fundamental beliefs about life and death underscore the controversy. Addressing the issue in our country, Haynes wrote that the Freedom Forum guide was based on the conviction that finding common ground on many of the issues that divide us is possible within the civic framework provided by the Religious Liberty clauses of the First Amendment to the U.S. Constitution. The key is for all sides to step back from the debate and to give fresh consideration to the democratic first principles that bind us together as a people.[204]

11. Scheduling

Can you remember when the school year started in late August or right after Labor Day and ended in early or late June? Can you remember when children had two weeks off in the winter and spring and almost three months of what the French call "les grandes vacances"? During vacation periods the schools sat like silent sentinels. Was it only yesterday that children attended school 180 days a year, about six hours a day, five days a week, following the same class schedule every day? Do you remember when you encountered school-age children out of school on a school day they were either sick or truant? Not so any more. They may be on the blue track while those in school are on the green track.

Remember when gleeful children greeted the long summer holiday with the doggerel, "no more pencils, no more books, no more teacher's sassy looks"?; when the nuclear WASP family (Mom, Dad, brother, sister, and Rover) piled into the station wagon (few SUVs then) and took off for an experience in family togetherness at the seashore or in the mountains or just motoring (gasoline was cheaper then)? No longer. Reforms of the mid- and late 1990s wrought a restructuring of many schools' instructional time schedules. No dimensions of time have been left untouched, not the hour, not the day, not the week, not the year.

School Hours, Day, and Week.   Changes in the daily hourly schedule have affected primarily the secondary school. Look at the bell schedule of many high schools today and you'll fast discover that periods have been lengthened and courses no longer meet five days a week for equal amounts of time according to the time-honored Carnegie unit.

Alternative Daily Schedules.   Where secondary school classes formerly met for a customary 50 to 55 minutes daily, they now may meet in alternative time frames from some 85 to 120 minutes per day for only one semester. Throughout the country you can find creative variations in high schools' allocation of time. While some schools are implementing longer periods, longer days, and longer school years, others are operating longer days but shorter school weeks.

In 1983 Joseph M. Carroll proposed what he called the Copernican Plan, a system-wide approach to school reform. Named after the famed astronomer of the late fifteenth and early sixteenth centuries who, contrary to church teachings, held that the earth revolved around the sun rather than vice versa, fomented a revolution in how the heavens were perceived. The Copernican Plan comprised a number of reform features among which is "block scheduling." Carroll stated, "no research supports continuing with the Carnegie unit; it actually impairs effective instruction."[205] Reminiscent of scheduling innovations of the 1950s, extended periods meeting less than five days per week became increasingly more common. Longer periods meeting fewer times a week permitted teachers to work with fewer students in a day and allowed more time for confronting content in greater depth.

Floyd Boschee and Mark A. Baron described the Copernican Plan as a major restructuring of high school organization in which students are given the option of either enrolling in one four-hour class each day for a period of thirty days or enrolling in two two-hour classes each day for sixty days. Under the first option, each student would enroll in six of these four-hour classes each year, while the second option requires students to enroll in three two-course trimesters each year (totalling 180 instructional days per year for both options). In both options, the remainder of the day is composed of a seminar, an elective class, and a lunch period.[206]

Carroll observed that the Copernican Plan can have different formats structured to the needs of the school. A common plan, however, is the 4 × 4 schedule consisting of blocks of four 90- or 120-minute classes each day, either alternating from day to day or alternating from semester to semester. That block scheduling offers a viable plan is seen in the manner in which time is scheduled at Waunakee (Wisconsin) High School (Table 15.1). At Waunakee High four 90-minute classes meet each day. The A

TABLE 15.1   Block Schedule, Waunakee High School, Waunakee, Wisconsin, 2007–2008

8:05 a.m.	1st Warning Bell
8:12 a.m.	2nd Warning Bell
8:15 a.m.–9:50 a.m.	1A/1B
10:00 a.m.–11:30 a.m.	2A/2B
11:30 a.m.–12:10 p.m.	"Early" Lunch (40 minutes)
11:40 a.m.–1:10 p.m.	3A/3B hour *Early Class*
12:10 p.m.–1:40 p.m.	3A/3B hour *Late Class*
1:10 p.m.–1:50 p.m.	"Late" Lunch (40 minutes)
1:50 p.m.–3:25 p.m.	4A/4B hour

Source: Reprinted by permission.

and B schedules alternate throughout the week. One week classes on the A schedule meet three times, the B schedule classes meet twice. The following week classes on the B schedule meet three times, A, twice. Some classes meet one semester; other classes, two semesters.

The Center for Education Reform estimated that by the end of 1996 some ten to twenty-five percent of schools throughout the United States had adopted some form of block scheduling.[207] The popularity of block scheduling, however, waxes and wanes. Whereas the Utah public schools in the fall of 2003 were following block schedules, the Dallas public schools were reverting from a class schedule of 90 minutes every other day to traditional seven- or eight-period days. The National Education Commission on Time and Learning recommended that those schools that stay on the existing traditional schedule devote that time exclusively to core academic subjects and to lengthen the school day if they wish to maintain clubs, athletics, and other activities. The Commission on Time and Learning saw value in flexible and block scheduling.[208]

Among the perceived advantages of block scheduling are the devotion of more time to instruction and the capability of exploring subjects in depth. Difficulty in maintaining student interest in lengthy periods and trading breadth for depth are regarded as problems by some critics of block scheduling. Hard data on the benefits of shifting from traditional to block schedules are scarce. The Center for Education Reform found the benefits of block scheduling unclear.[209]

School Year.　Dissatisfaction with student achievement has resulted in calls for alterations in schools' schedules through extending the school year and/or year-round education. Behind the rationale for the lengthened school year was the perception that student achievement would rise given additional exposure to the subject matter.

Lengthening the School Year.　Children in the United States average six hours per day in school whereas children in some other countries average as many as eight hours. In the United States 180 days per year is the norm for students (although we find some minor variations in several states) whereas the school year in China, Germany, and Japan exceeds two hundred days.[210] American pupils meet an average of five and one-half hours for instruction, including physical education and electives. It is little wonder that the National Commission on Excellence in Education in its 1983 publication *A Nation at Risk* recommended schools schedule a seven-hour day 200 to 220 days per year.[211]

Don Glines noted that as early as 1840 urban schools were open 240 to 250 days, although few students attended that length of time.[212] To the present time schools have not moved in a wholesale fashion into imitating European or Asiatic patterns of a longer school year. As is the case with some school systems that tried block scheduling, some school systems that adopted and tested a longer school year for a variety of financial, instructional, and administrative reasons shifted back to the traditional mode. Charter schools and those under educational management organizations have found it easier to extend instruction beyond the traditional 180 days. For example, the school year for students in Edison schools is 198 days.[213] KIPP schools, although operating 180 days, extend the school year with sessions on Saturdays and during the summer.[214] In some cases school districts have extended the school year in conjunction with year-round schooling.

Regarding a lengthened school year, Sizer's fictitious Franklin Middle and High Schools would extend the school year from 36 to 42 weeks, divide the year into four terms with each term preceded by one week for varied activities, and would lengthen the school day from 8 A.M. to 4 P.M.[215] Interest in and discussion of lengthening the school year to 210 days, although not necessarily implemented, continue to surface as, for example, in Florida in 1999. Complementary to the school year is the lengthening of the school day as in the case of Edison schools' seven to eight hours[216] and KIPP schools' 7:30 A.M. to 5 P.M. schedule.[217]

Year-Round Education (YRE).   More subject to debate than lengthening the school period, day, or year is the movement toward year-round education, a further reaction to the traditional schedule. Most proponents of YRE point out that the traditional calendar is a product of an agrarian society that required young people to work on farms in the summers. Consequently, advocates claim new responses must be made in an industrial, technological age. Charles Ballinger made clear his opinion of the traditional nine-month schedule: "The traditional school calendar is not educational now, has never been, and never will be."[218]

The concept of year-round education is not brand new. Bluffton, Indiana, is credited with operating a year-round school as early as 1904. Several other schools systems conducted year-round programs in the early 1900s, among them Aliquippa, Pennsylvania; Minot, North Dakota; Nashville, Tennessee; Newark, New Jersey; and Omaha, Nebraska. The Christa McAuliffe Elementary School at Oxnard, California, opened in 1987, is named as the first school built specifically with year-round education.[219]

Vicki T. Howell pointed out that year-round education died out before World War II but was reborn in the late 1960s and early 1970s.[220] Citing the rapid growth of year-round schools, primarily public, Ballinger reported 1,350,000 children in 1,688 schools in 23 states enrolled in year-round schools in 1992.[221] Figures for the year 1998–1999 showed 2,040,611 students being educated in 2,986 year-round schools in the United States, Canada, and the Pacific Region; 98 percent of these schools were in the United States.[222] Year-round education remains an attractive option for close to 3,000 schools in 46 states and the District of Columbia in 2005–2006. California accounts for the largest number of schools on year-round schedules.[223]

Single and Multitrack.   When speakers discuss year-round schooling, they should be questioned as to whether they refer to single-track or multitrack plans. The difference is significant. Single-track plans divide the number of attendance days into learning periods with vacation periods spread throughout the year or with optional intervals called intersessions (often three weeks, of which one is vacation time) between the learning periods. Programs during the intersession may be either for enrichment or remediation, most commonly, the latter. Teachers may opt to be off during the intersessions or work and receive extra pay.

Multitrack systems were a response to overcrowded schools. Francis Howell School District in St. Charles, Missouri, is credited with creating the first multitrack program in the United States in 1969.[224] Students are divided into tracks (A, B, C, D; red, green, blue, yellow). By staggering the school year for each group and having one group out at all times, schools can increase the capacity accommodated in the same school by 20 to 25 percent. Multitracking year-round education has proved a suitable alternative for financially strapped communities that do not wish to enter into constructing new schools.

Single-track schools constitute the majority of year-round plans. Many schools have implemented and maintained plans for year-round schooling. Oxnard, California, Elementary School District, for example, lists twenty year-round elementary and middle schools on single track or multitrack in addition to its Christa McAuliffe Elementary School.[225] Others have experimented with year-round plans and abandoned them. A significant number of school systems that experimented with year-round schedules have reverted to traditional schedules, including Albuquerque, Los Angeles, San Diego, and several districts in central Florida. Advocates maintain, however, that schools coming on line will replace the ones that have dropped out.

It is difficult to generalize on YRE until we know what type of plan is in operation. There are almost as many permutations and combinations as creative minds can conceive. We will not tax the reader with a description of the many existing plans which include 45–15 (four 9-week periods, 45 days each, 180 days total plus four 3-week optional intersessions, 15 days each), 60–20, 60–15, 90–30, quarter system, quinmesters, Concept 6, and others.[226]

What are the purported advantages and disadvantages of year-round schooling? Among the many reported advantages are improved retention of learning since breaks are shorter with improved attendance of both students and teachers, fewer dropouts, chance for remediation (single track), increased capacity (multitrack), financial savings (multitrack, but single track can cost more), reduced vandalism, accommodation to parental jobs that provide short vacation periods; and diminished teacher burnout. Those who object to year-round education cite disruption of family vacation schedules, especially if parents have children in schools on different tracks, ineffective intersessions (single track), increased teacher stress, and problems of organizing and administering.

The jury is out on teacher burnout and stress with tracking plans. Burnout may diminish because of more frequent breaks but if teachers contract year-round, stress and burnout may increase. Whether year-round education enhances learning is problematic. In reviewing a number of studies of year-round education in the 1990s, Blaine R. Worthen supported some of the claims of proponents of YRE like better attitudes of students, fewer dropouts, better teacher attitudes, decreased vandalism, and better student attendance.[227] Regarding the effect of YRE on academic learning, Worthen commented, "Overall, there appears to be a slight but not overwhelming advantage for YRE students in learning basic content. What is clear is that well-implemented YRE programs do not result in any lessening of learning."[228] In a similar vein Elizaebth A. Palmer and Amy E. Bemis commented, "It is reasonable to conclude that students attending YRS are likely to perform as well as if not better than their peers in traditional nine-month programs, especially at the upper elementary school level."[229] Howell cautioned, however, "In actuality there are no long-range studies to prove the superiority of traditional or YRE calendars in relation to knowledge retention or achievement."[230]

While educators are making their beliefs known, what is the public's attitude toward an extended school year and YRE? An earlier survey provides some clues about public sentiment. The 24th Annual Phi Delta Kappa/Gallup Poll found fifty-five percent of the public favoring an increase of thirty days, making a school year of ten months or 210 days, a majority favoring four or five segments with three-week vacation breaks.[231] Most experts reaffirm the necessity in the case of year-round education as with any innovation to build consensus among the constituencies of the school in advance of implementation.

Three-Year High School Programs.   In June 2003 Florida lawmakers provided the opportunity for high school students to complete their high school education a year early with eighteen credits instead of twenty-four. The legislation created two tracks for the three-year high school program, college preparatory and career, the sole difference between the two programs being the lack of a requirement for mathematics higher than algebra 1 for those on the career track. Students on the three-year program would forgo physical education requirements and electives beyond three required in the eighteen credits. Students in the three-year program would still have to pass the state assessment tests. Some educators believe students may find admission to college more difficult if they choose the three-year program as they will present fewer courses for consideration.

Dual Enrollment/Early-College Schools.   Perhaps in place of three-year high school programs we may expect to see more linkings between high schools and colleges in the form of dual high school/community college enrollment and in the creation of early-college schools, such as Bard High School in New York City where students take college courses in their last two years of high school.

Class and School Size.   Both class size and school size are subjects of considerable disagreement. Some educators take the position that what goes on in the classroom is more important than class size. Many express the belief that classes can become too large in a time when teachers are charged with meeting the individual interests and needs of a diverse student population. The Hoover Institution would remove the blanket restrictions on class size,[232] while People for the American Way support limitation on class size.[233]

The people of Florida have made it clear that they believe class size does make a difference. Florida voters created a dilemma for the state in November 2002 when, in spite of financial implications and over opposition from many in the state power structure including the governor, they approved by a 52.9 percent majority an amendment to the state constitution mandating reductions in class size to 18 students per grades K–3, 22 per grades 4–8, and 25 per high school class, to be phased in at an average of two students per year in each class until taking effect in 2010. Coming at a time of diminished revenues, state legislators wrestled with budgeting problems and means of carrying out the wishes of the electorate. Some take the position that highly qualified teachers can successfully teach large classes, thereby reducing the number of teachers needed, which would allow schools to pay the expert teachers higher salaries. Success of reduction in class size appears mixed and depends on variables that include the makeup of the class and the teacher's skills. At the present time the governor and legislature are bound to implement the voters' wishes. However, efforts are being made for repeal of the amendment. In whatever manner the problem is resolved, the class-size amendment is an example of the public taking on the role of curriculum developers—by revising the state constitution no less—with the hope of improving student achievement.

School size presents an additional area of controversy. Some educators as well as parents defend the construction and operation of large schools for the broad curricular and extraclass programs they can offer. On the other hand, the movement to small schools and small learning communities has become decidedly pronounced in the first decade of the twenty-first century, especially in the light of grants provided by the Bill and Melinda Gates Foundation for the establishment of smaller high schools. Instead of constructing new schools, many are organized within the confines of a larger school, each with its own group of students and cadre of teachers and administrators. Atlanta, Chicago, Miami-Dade, and New York City are among locations throughout the country attempting to improve student achievement, attendance rates, and graduation rates by creating smaller high schools. The Institute for Student Achievement partners with school districts in several states to develop small learning communities.[234] Although we might like to have more data on the effects of small learning communities on student academic achievement, several studies from the late 1990s to the present indicate a number of positive results.[235]

While we follow the progress or retrogression of changes in scheduling patterns, class and school size, and organizational plans, we'll want to keep track of the success or failure of the return to the old K–8 organizational plan that eliminates the separate middle school, as in New Orleans, New York, and Philadelphia.

12. Standards

Perhaps the most pervasive and contentious issue discussed in this chapter is standards-based education. In spite of a backlash in some states against the consequences of standards-based assessment the movement toward setting standards, making schools and teachers accountable, and assessing student achievement continues strong.

The origin of this wave of reform movement of standards is attributed to the 1983 report *A Nation at Risk*, with the movement beginning in earnest as a result of the promulgation of the America 2000 under President George H. W. Bush, Goals 2000 Education America Act under President Bill Clinton, and No Child Left Behind Act under President George W. Bush.

Schools have, of course, followed standards throughout their history. Historically, these standards have been locally developed. What characterizes this tide of standards is their point of origin, the state level, and the detailed specifications in the content areas, literally prescriptions, that all students in the state are expected to achieve. At the present time the country is awash in standards—local, state, and national. In past years, local school districts on their own initiative specified standards they wished their students to achieve, aligned the curriculum with the local standards, and tested to learn whether students had achieved the standards. If students were not successful, schools devised their own remedial procedures.

Where the present standards movement differs from other efforts is in the creation of state and national standards coupled with state-created standardized tests of students' achievement of the standards, under pressure from the federal level currently in the form of the No Child Left Behind Act (NCLB). It is on the basis of standardized assessment, referred to as *high-stakes testing*, that students, teachers, and schools are rewarded or punished. Rewards include favorable publicity, students' promotion, and increased funding. Punishments include unfavorable reports to the public, students' retention in grade, withholding the high school diploma, and permitting parental choice of private or parochial school through taxpayer-paid vouchers or tax credits.

What we have at present, in effect, is a *national* system of *state* standards, the intent of which is the improvement of public education. In spite of widespread dissatisfaction with public education that evoked the standards movement, a number of researchers and writers, including Gerald W. Bracey[236] and Deborah Meier,[237] have contested the premise that American schools have failed.

The standards movement evokes strong opinions on both sides of the issue. Dissenters object to the entire direction education has taken toward specifying uniform standards and assessment, whether national or state, whether voluntary or mandated, holding that schools should be more concerned about curricula that foster student self-esteem and bringing about improvements in American society. Critical of the adoption of content standards as a means of reform, Ernest R. House wrote, "Such an approach overestimates the degree to which teachers will adopt standards and miscalculates how teachers will react if their students' test scores are made public. The history of such attempts is rampant with teachers' teaching the test items under conditions of strong accountability and manipulating or distorting the scores."[238] Critical of the repeated call for "tougher standards," Alfie Kohn noted, "the Tougher Standards movement usually consists of *imposing specific requirements and trying to coerce improvement* by specifying exactly what must be taught and learned—that is, by mandating a particular kind of education."[239] Opponents of standards-based education attribute the standards movement to conservative desires to preserve a business-oriented, efficiency model of traditional education, root out "progressive education," and supplant public education with private. Kohn commented, "the Tougher Standards movement tends to favor *Old-School teaching*, the sort of instruction that treats kids as though they were inert objects, that prepares a concoction called 'basic skills' or 'core knowledge' and then tries to pour it down children's throats."[240]

Marion Brady referred to the standards movement as a "juggernaut."[241] Applying Susan Ohanian's term "Standardisto,"[242] meaning an advocate of standards-based education, Brady observed, "From the Standardisto perspective, all that is necessary is to determine what most 'well-educated' people know, organize it, distribute it to the schools, and demand that teachers teach it and students learn it. In the name of reform, the Standardistos are freezing in bureaucratic place the worst aspects of traditional education."[243] Many of those who reject nationwide or statewide standards for all students would champion individualized standards for each student.

Although objections have been leveled at the standards movement, the specification of state and national standards remains popular with the public, the business community, and those whom the public has elected to office. High-stakes exit exams that determine high school graduation have become a common manifestation of the state-standards movement. For example, in action similar to that taken in a growing number of states, during the fall of 2003, Maryland made passing its High School Assessments a requirement for graduation and receipt of a regular diploma, to become effective in 2009. Starting with the 2006–2007 freshman high school class, Florida includes the passing of the writing portion of its Florida Comprehensive Achievement Test for students to graduate. Schools are rapidly increasing the requirements in mathematics and science.

Although opponents of standards-based education would undoubtedly like to see the whole movement just go away, Judy F. Carr and Douglas E. Harris advised, "National, state, and local standards are important resources for teachers, but these standards have little meaning until teachers and administrators take true ownership of them."[244] On the positive side, Carr and Harris viewed standards as reinforcing teacher practices, bringing focus to assessments, and substituting focused strategies based on standards for piecemeal efforts.[245] Those who find they can work with standards seek to adapt the use of the standards to their instruction and supplement standardized assessment with performance evaluations. In discussing the process of aligning the curriculum, Fenwick W. English and Betty E. Steffy recommended "using national and international standards as qualitative benchmarks for the simple reason that such comparative indicators enable educators to engage in evaluative activities that speak to such matters as curriculum rigor and quality, which are open and public and do not depend on a secretive content domain that is nobody's specific curriculum."[246] Rejecting the use of norm-referenced standardized tests that compare students, English and Steffy proposed aligning the curriculum with "public and specific curriculum benchmarks."[247]

Concomitant with the development of standards-based education was the movement known as *outcome-* or *outcomes-based education* (OBE) that seeks specification of learning "outputs," sometimes referred to as "exit outcomes," accompanied by "authentic" performance assessment of student mastery of the outcomes. William G. Spady defined outcome as "a culminating demonstration of learning."[248]

More acute in the battle over standards is the possibility of the creation of a single set of national standards and a single set of assessments. Among those who espouse state standards, subscribing to the belief of the state's responsibility for education, are those who oppose national standards, a national curriculum, and national assessment. In spite of objections to national efforts in this direction, however, in actuality we already have elements of national standards, curriculum, and assessment.

The current debate over the issues of a national curriculum, national standards, and national assessment is reminiscent of the argument over the creation of the National Assessment of Educational Progress (NAEP) in the 1960s when educators predicted dire results if NAEP were allowed to conduct nationwide tests. Some forty-plus years have passed and NAEP has taken a valued place in the educational spectrum not only because of its technical competence but also because it has zealously guarded results so individuals and schools could not be identified. Its results are reported for regions, age groups, and ethnic groups, which lessens its impact on the curriculum of individual schools. We noted in Chapter 12, however, that as a result of the No Child Left Behind Act NAEP scores may reflect on state assessments when comparisons are made between the two.

A national curriculum would mean some uniformity of standards across the country. In effect, we already have earmarks of a rather loose national curriculum at the moment.

The same textbooks are adopted in many states, bringing a semblance of uniformity at least to content. Professional associations have produced and disseminated curriculum materials widely, further standardizing the curriculum. Standards spelled out by the states are not all that different from state to state.

Among the arguments against implementing national standards are that they will limit the creativity of local schools, they are likely to be minimal standards, it is impossible to establish a common set of standards in a country so diverse, they will fail without sufficient funding, and they will be limited to core disciplines. Proponents of federal and state standards argue that we need to be competitive educationally with other countries, national standards will encourage school improvement, national standards are necessary in an age of mobility of population, and present standards are too loose. The naysayers contend that national standards will not promote equality of opportunity for all children including minorities while the yea-sayers claim that the opposite is true. Our two major educational associations have taken different sides of the fence with the National Education Association opposing national standards and assessment whereas the American Federation of Teachers endorsed their development and use. Noting that "there are attractive arguments for federal and state control over curricula—to ensure a set of academic outcomes for all students in America," Glickman joined those opposed to federal and state control, saying:

> the underlying assumption is that local schools lack either the inclination or the capacity to develop and hold themselves to rigorous curricular goals and assessments . . . federal and state controls over local curricula is clearly a statement of skepticism about participatory democracy. . . . Developing curricula and standards "away" from local schools and communities rules out the very flexibility that state and federal policymakers claim to support in their schizophrenic exhortations of "empowerment."[249]

Hirsch, however, faulted the argument for local control, commenting on the "curricular chaos of the American elementary school":

> we assume, quite reasonably, that agreement has been reached locally regarding what shall be taught to children at each grade level—if not within the whole district, then certainly within an individual school. . . . But despite the democratic virtue of that principle, the idea that there exists a coherent plan for teaching content within the local district, or even within the individual school, is a gravely misleading myth.[250]

More than a decade ago Diane Ravitch made a comment still true when she said, "Discussions of standards tend to turn at once into debates and about testing."[251] Basically, the issue centers around quantitative (i.e., traditional and standardized tests) versus qualitative (i.e., authentic) performance techniques and the use of portfolios. Historically and up to the present moment, schools have employed quantitative techniques to assess student achievement. It is not too much of an exaggeration to say that is the way the American public wants it.

Whether educators favor a national curriculum, national standards and national assessments, the public clearly supports the idea as they have demonstrated on repeated Phi Delta Kappa/Gallup Polls. The 26th Annual Phi Delta Kappa/Gallup Poll of the

Public's Attitudes Toward the Public Schools (1994), for example, found that an overwhelming majority of those surveyed believed standardized national examinations based on a national curriculum that students must pass for promotion or graduation (as some people say, "with consequences") were either very important or quite important.[252] Arguments for local determination of standards appear to run counter to opinions of a large segment of the public.

However, the public is uncertain about the testing that goes with standards. For example, the 39th Annual Phi Delta Kappa/Gallup Poll of the Public's Attitudes Toward the Public Schools revealed in 2007 that the public was divided over whether there was too much achievement testing in the public schools, and well over half felt increased testing either hurt or made no difference.[253]

Advocating a "standards-based education" Peter W. Hill and Carmel A. Crevola of the University of Melbourne concluded, "all students should have a right to an education system that ensures high standards for all."[254] Addressing the issues of national standards and assessments Ravitch provided some thoughtful remarks:

> Do we really want higher standards? Do we want schools where students work hard and take their education seriously? Do we want a society in which everyone is well educated and knowledgeable about history, literature, science, mathematics, and the arts? Or do we want schools where academic studies are no more important, perhaps less important, than athletics and social activities? . . . Finally, a system of standards and assessments, no matter how reliable, will not solve all the problems of American education. It will not substitute for the protection of a loving family, it will not guard children against violence in the streets, it will not alleviate poverty, and it will not turn off the television at night. But a system of standards and assessments might help to focus the priorities of the educational system on teaching and learning, which is no small matter in a world where what you are and what you can aspire to depends increasingly on what you know. As a society our goal must be to see that knowledge is broadly democratized, that *all* children in America have equal educational opportunity, that the work of teachers is valued and respected, that the brainpower of this nation is treated as its most precious resource, and that we do not waste the educational potential of even one of our citizens.[255]

Weighing the use of standards and caveats in their use, Beverly Falk concluded:

> Standards and standards-based assessments *can* ultimately support better learning if they are used to direct teaching toward worthy goals, to promote teaching that is responsive to how students learn, to examine students in multiple ways that can be used to inform instruction, to keep students and parents apprised of progress, to trigger special supports for students who need them, and to evaluate school practices. If all these aspects of the standards, assessment, and accountability picture are addressed, standards and standards-based assessments have the potential to be of enormous benefit to teaching and learning.[256]

Historically, following the Tenth Amendment to the U.S. Constitution, education was considered the province of the states. Federal aid to education and, therefore, interference with states' prerogatives were limited to exceptions such as vocation education. Today, federal involvement in education, particularly through P.L. 107-110, the

No Child Left Behind Act of 2001, a reauthorization of the Elementary and Secondary Education Act of 1965, is pervasive. Marc R. O'Shea made clear the transition of authority from local to state to federal authority:

> The sudden transfer of power from the local school districts and to state authorities was surprising short-lived. Before states could even formulate policies and procedures to use the power of their standards, their influence over the curriculum was trumped by the federal government through the reauthorization of the Elementary and Secondary Education Act, now known as No Child Left Behind.
>
> The new law requires states to use academic content standards to benchmark federally mandated "adequate yearly progress" . . . Despite continuing controversy, state content standards have emerged as the most powerful manifestation of the school reform that began with *A Nation at Risk* more than 20 years ago.[257]

Among the many requirements of NCLB, now in its fifth year, are:

- states must specify academic content standards
- there must be a single statewide accountability system
- all students must make adequate yearly progress, meeting proficient level of achievement by 2013–2014
- states must assess student achievement in mathematics and reading at least once in grades 3–5, once in grades 6–9, and once in 10–12
- beginning in the school year 2007–2008 states must add assessment in science at least one time in grades 3–5, once in grades 6–9, and once in 10–12
- states must issue an annual state report card
- all teachers teaching core academic subjects must be highly qualified not later than the end of the 2005–2006[258]
- children in Title I schools, primarily the lowest achieving students from low-income families, may transfer to a public school or public charter school in their district when their school has failed to make adequate yearly progress for two consecutive years or more
- children from low-income families in Title I schools that have failed to make adequate yearly progress for at least three consecutive years are eligible for supplemental educational services such as tutoring and after-school instruction.[259]

Obviously, as in other cases of federal pronouncements on education, many of the goals have not been met. Since becoming law (2002) NCLB has been both praised and criticized. It has met with both successes and failures. Its attention to the basic skills of reading and mathematics has received both public approval and disapproval; approval because the basic skills are the essential foundations to further learning; disapproval because excessive attention to reading and math provides less time for the arts and physical education, let alone recess. Providing for school choice and the aim for highly qualified teachers are viewed as positives whereas the excessive emphasis on standardized teaching forces teachers into teaching to the tests, excluding other content and use of procedures that evaluate other types of learning and behaviors.

Other criticisms of NCLB are inadequate funding by the federal government, reputed cultural bias in the tests, and the measures for judging school performance. States are agitating for a change in the system of evaluating the schools from reporting percentage of students who pass the state tests to a growth model by which schools are rated according to the progress of each student. Other problems center around testing and reporting progress of special education students, those with disabilities, and others with limited English proficiency. Critics fault NCLB's intense concentration on reading and mathematics to the limitation or exclusion of physical education in an era of child obesity, poor nutrition habits, and lack of physical exercise. The National Association for Sport and Physical Education, one of five national associations that make up the American Alliance for Health, Physical Education, Recreation & Dance, for example, cited the lack of a requirement for physical education in the elementary and middle schools of approximately thirty percent of the states.[260]

Reflecting the need for students to perform "vigorous daily physical activity," in 2007 Texas required school districts to annually assess the physical fitness of students in grades K–12 in addition to stipulating minimal periods of daily physical activity for students in grades K–8.[261]

Debate continues as to whether student achievement is higher since NCLB was enacted. It is probably an understatement to say that the states have been restive under NCLB. Many oppose NCLB for its inadequate funding and what many educators perceive as an unconstitutional encroachment of the federal government on the states' responsibilities for education. Utah's action in 2005 rejecting provisions of NCLB that conflict with Utah's educational goals or that require state funding shows the intensity of opposition. The federal government's power, however, rests on its control of the purse strings for grants to educational programs.

A sampling of the public's attitudes toward NCLB revealed a number of objections, such as including the test scores of special education students with scores of all other students, and judging a school successful or failing by the percentage of students who pass a test as opposed to improvement shown by students.[262]

As with so many educational assessments, achievement results under NCLB are mixed. Kansas, for example, reported ninety-one percent of its schools making adequate yearly progress in 2004–2005.[263] However, twelfth-grade test scores in 2005 by the National Assessment of Educational Progress were not as rosy. From its analysis of over 21,000 high school seniors NAEP reported "reading performance declines for all but top performers" and "less that one-quarter performing at or above Proficient in mathematics."[264] Bracey pointed to a fundamental problem, the gap between state and NAEP-determined proficiency. He explained:

> Both state standards and NAEP achievement levels for determining proficiency are wholly arbitrary—both lack any connection to external criteria for validation—and the NAEP levels are far too high.[265]

Drawing on reports on the gap between state-defined and NAEP-defined proficiency, Bracey made note that state levels of proficiency were much higher than NAEP levels and that the gap ranged from ten percent in Massachusetts to 55 percent in Texas, with the average gap at 38 percent.[266] *U.S. News & World Report*'s chart, *Falling Short*, clearly shows state test scores exceeding NAEP's national test scores, causing some people to wonder about differing definitions of proficiency levels between state and national tests.[267]

Gauging the public's attitude toward NCLB under half of the public, according to the 39th Annual Phi Delta Kappa/Gallup Poll, has somewhat favorable or very favorable opinions toward the No Child Left Behind Act.[268] Some organizations and leaders view the maintenance of high expectations as a key to enhancing student achievement. Reminiscent of calls of the Effective Schools Research of the 1980s for holding students to high expectations, the Education Trust similarly advocates high expectations of students and presents "Dispelling the Myth" awards to schools that have achieved exceptional success with students from low-income and minority families.[269] Bill Gates, too, addressing a U.S. Senate Committee, projected a high goal for American education: "Every child in America should graduate from high school ready for college, career and life."[270]

Although identifying the problems of testing and accountability requirements for students with disabilities and those learning English, Jack Jennings and Diane Stark Rentner saw NCLB as

> clearly having a major impact on American education. There is more testing and account-ability. Greater attention is being paid to what is being taught and how it is being taught. Low-performing schools are also receiving greater attention. The qualifications of teachers are coming under greater scrutiny. Concurrently, with NCLB, scores on state reading and mathematics tests have risen.[271]

At the time of writing of this textbook the U.S. Congress had NCLB under study for reauthorization, revision, or revocation.

In the first years of the twenty-first century we see a pronounced movement toward the specification of content standards and the assessment of those standards, including the use of high-stakes tests to determine grade retention and high school graduation.

IMPROVEMENTS NEEDED FOR CURRICULUM REFORM

Consensus Building

Looking at the plethora of proposals for reform and restructuring of the schools, even educators, let alone the public, from time to time must express bewilderment. Shall states, prodded by the federal government, administer standardized high-stakes tests to assess student achievement of state content standards? Shall schools go in the direction of core knowledge or constructivism?

Shall we mainstream the gifted? Shall we create national standards? Shall we change the school calendar? Is the effective teaching research passé? Shall we introduce character, values, and ethics education? Shall we cut the arts, career, and physical education, spending most of the time on reading, mathematics, and science? Shall we privatize education? Or are charter schools and homeschooling the answers to public school problems?

We find individuals and like-minded groups advocating their own measures to reform and restructure schools. Whom should administrators, teachers, and parents heed? Which educational organization has the "right" solution or can we buy all solutions? Which approach to teaching English is better: phonics or whole language? Is the curriculum for the twenty-first century found in a full-service school with a standards-based education and an integrated, interdisciplinary curriculum; its pupils in inclusive classrooms learning cooperatively, using multicultural materials; without common academic standards; employing authentic assessment?

With the empowerment of teachers and parents the building of consensus becomes a paramount concern. Inadequate funding, overcrowded schools, discipline, and drug use head the list of the public's concerns.[272] Borrowing a leaf from the perceptual psychologists, reformers must deal first with perceptions of the public and gain commitment before they can effect lasting change.

Our informed public is well aware of repeated efforts at reforming the public schools. Curriculum workers cannot express impatience if the public asks why we have had to engage repeatedly in reform efforts. When, they ask, will we come up with solutions that will be both effective and reasonably permanent? Curriculum workers today must demonstrate the interpersonal and technical skills necessary to building consensus among constituencies of the school. They must lay a groundwork, experiment, and demonstrate results to gain acceptance. Assertions to the effect that "research shows" when, indeed, that research may or may not show, will not satisfy a tradition-oriented public, nor for that matter, tradition-oriented teachers and administrators. Researchers and pioneers must encourage teachers and administrators to try out new ways without making them feel that everything they have been doing, possibly for many years, is wrong. In fact, innovators have a heavy responsibility for demonstrating that the newer programs they advocate are, indeed, superior to the ones they would replace.

Research

Not only do the results of research need to be disseminated, but also both quantity and quality of educational research need to be expanded. The school systems need to be close partners with institutions of higher learning in the conduct of research. For instance, the National Council for the Accreditation of Teacher Education (NCATE)—the voluntary accrediting agency to which schools of education may belong—promotes cooperative research between school systems and schools and colleges of education.[273]

The profession is in particular need of more experimental research and more longitudinal studies. We have many status studies and surveys of opinions and practices (favored by doctoral candidates in education) but not enough controlled research or, for that matter, less controlled action research. Curriculum planners should encourage teachers to participate in controlled research studies and to engage in their own unsophisticated action research to determine answers to simple problems that may be applicable only in their own classrooms. Diane Ravitch cautioned:

> Massive changes in curricula and pedagogy should be based on solid research and careful field-tested demonstration before they are imposed on entire school districts and states.

There has been no shortage of innovation in American education; what is needed before broad implementation of any innovation is clear evidence of its effectiveness.[274]

Dissemination

The curriculum workers' efforts would be greatly enhanced if we had better ways of disseminating results of research and experience with innovative programs. Though we have the Educational Resources Information Center (ERIC), regional educational laboratories, national research and development centers, national centers within the Institute of Education Sciences of the U.S. Department of Education, and many curriculum journals, the results of research and experimentation do not reach the classroom teacher to the degree they should.[275]

The rapid spread of concepts, programs, and practices such as mastery learning, critical thinking, cooperative learning, community service, and whole language would seem to refute the premise that dissemination of curriculum innovations is slow. However, speed is a relative concept. Forty-five miles per hour may be too slow on a four-lane interstate highway but too fast on a country road. Innovations still take a considerable amount of time to find their way to thousands of public school districts and millions of elementary and secondary school teachers.

Curriculum decisions are still made on the basis of limited information and without all currently available data. Curriculum leaders must take special responsibility to stay informed of current research so that they can channel essential information to the classroom teacher and other curriculum workers.

Since so many agencies and associations now have websites and the computer has become a way of life, we may anticipate more rapid dissemination of research and ideas on every aspect of life, including education.

Preparation

Better programs are needed to prepare curriculum leaders and planners. To gain some perception of the preparation needed by curriculum developers, we might refer to Chapter 1 on the areas of learning from which the field of curriculum is derived, to Chapter 3 on the multiple levels and sectors of curriculum planning, and to Chapter 4 on the roles of various personnel in curriculum development. States might reasonably institute certificates in curriculum development. Such certificates would parallel those now offered in administration, supervision, guidance, and other specialties. Such a certificate would go a long way toward establishing curriculum as a field of specialization in its own right. Furthermore, teacher education institutions should assure that their graduates gain what might be called "curriculum literacy"—that is, knowledge about the curriculum field and basic skills in curriculum development.

Role of Teacher Organizations

We could cite the many contributions to curriculum development, research and study of such professional organizations as the American Association of School Administrators, the American Educational Research Association, the American Federation of Teachers, the Association for Supervision and Curriculum Development, the Association of Teacher Educators, the National Education Association, the national associations of elementary, middle, and secondary school principals, and associations in the specific disciplines.

The two most powerful organizations that represent the interests of teachers are the National Education Association (NEA) and the American Federation of Teachers (AFT), which is affiliated with the AFL-CIO. Although the NEA is not a union in the sense of being affiliated with organized labor, the missions of the NEA and the AFT often coincide. In fact, the two organizations on more than one occasion have talked seriously of merger.

Teachers' organizations influence the curriculum both directly and indirectly. Some curriculum decisions are made not at the customary curriculum council table but at the bargaining table in negotiations between teachers (labor) and the school district (management). Ordinarily, these negotiations are concerned with working conditions, rights of teachers, salary, benefits, and the like. Some items of negotiation are clearly curricular in nature. In communities in which school management and a teachers' organization have effected a contract, the process of curriculum planning will likely need to be modified from that of school systems without formal contracts. Regardless of their personal desires, school administrators are bound by the terms of a negotiated contract. Teacher unions are not without their critics as can be seen in remarks made by Steve Jobs, CEO of Apple at an education reform conference, in 2007.[276]

Ways need to be established to integrate efforts of the teachers' organizations into the school district model for curriculum development. As members of the teachers' organizations themselves, curriculum planners can strive to enlist the teachers' organizations in the cause of continuous curriculum improvement.

Curriculum Future—An Afterthought

Among the various issues discussed in this chapter are a number of current curricular practices and programs. Some of these will remain with us for many years. If past is prologue, however, some will become universal practice, some will continue to exist in certain localities and certain schools, some will be modified, some will be abandoned, and some newer developments will take the place of some of the older.

Curriculum development today is a blend of many practices and programs both innovative and time-honored. As we proceed in the twenty-first century, our schools will be buoyed up by a judicious mixture of the old and the new.

Summary

This chapter is, in effect, a continuation of Curriculum Present, a theme that we began in Chapter 9 where we discussed some generally accepted curricular programs and practices. In this chapter we have examined twelve current issues of direct concern to curriculum planners. These issues, brought about by social and political forces, are academic area initiative, alternative schooling arrangements, bilingual education, censorship, gender, health education, multiculturalism/diversity, privatization, provision for exceptionalities, religion in public education, scheduling arrangements, and standards/assessment. Curriculum workers must be aware of the dimensions of these and other current issues as they attempt to develop curricula.

The chapter concluded with a brief discussion of professional issues that have an impact on the curriculum: the need for improved consensus building, the need for more and better research, the need for better means of disseminating the results of curriculum research and experimentation, the need for improved training programs for curriculum developers, and the need to clarify the role of teacher organizations in curriculum improvement.

Commenting on the "river of ink that was spilled in the education disputes of the twentieth century," Ravitch observed:

> What American education most needs is not more nostrums and enthusiasms but more attention to time-tested truths. It is a fundamental truth that children need well-educated teachers who are eclectic in their methods and willing to use different strategies depending on what works best for which children. It is another fundamental truth that adults must take responsibility for children and help them develop as good persons with worthy ideals.[277]

Questions for Discussion

1. What general guidelines would you recommend for curriculum planners to follow in dealing with controversial curriculum issues?

2. What current curriculum developments do you predict will be universally accepted ten years from now?

3. What are some current controversial curriculum issues not included in this chapter?

4. How do you account for repeated efforts to reform the public schools?

5. What measures would you recommend for reforming and restructuring the public schools?

Exercises

1. Select one of the current curriculum issues, search the literature, review local practices, and document with references the degree to which it appears to be an issue both locally and nationally. Show your position on the issue and suggest ways for solving it.

2. Select any current curriculum program, locate one or more research studies on this program, and draw conclusions on its effectiveness.

3. Document any instances of the following curriculum problems within the past three years in the school district you know best:
   a. racial conflicts.
   b. religious conflicts
   c. gender inequity
   d. textbook or library book protests

4. Research the literature on core knowledge schools and critique their curriculum.

5. Prepare a position paper on one of the following topics:
   a. the movement to establish public charter schools
   b. the movement to provide taxpayer-paid vouchers for students to attend the school of their choice
   c. the use of taxpayer-paid vouchers at parochial schools

6. Write a report on the extent and effectiveness of homeschooling in the United States.

7. Report on the purposes and effectiveness of any bilingual education program in your region.

8. Tell how a school system you know well handles protests about books and other materials.

9. Prepare a report showing your position on the question whether gender inequity exists in the schools and, if so, whether one gender or the other suffers disproportionately.

10. Show with appropriate supporting data your position on single-sex classes.

11. Find in your state's or local district's guidelines curricula and/or policies regarding sexuality education.

12. Prepare a report describing policies and practices for handling diversity in the classroom.

13. Explain your positive or negative opinion on whether public schools should be managed under contracts with educational management organizations.

14. Prepare a position paper on whether to include the following students in regular classes:
   a. children with disabilities
   b. children with behavior disorders
   c. gifted children

15. Prepare a report showing your position of one of the following topics:
   a. prayer in the public schools
   b. reciting the phrase "under God" in the Pledge of Allegiance
   c. teaching the Bible

   d. teaching intelligent design or evolution
   e. holding religious extraclass activities in the schools
   f. distribution of Bibles in the schools

16. Prepare a report contrasting the advantages and disadvantages of smallish schools/smaller learning communities as opposed to large high schools. Show your position on which you feel provides a better education.

17. Prepare a position paper on one of the following:
   a. lengthened school year
   b. year-round schools (single track)
   c. year-round schools (multitrack)

18. Report on any departures from traditional scheduling that you are familiar with or that you can find in your region or in the literature.

19. Make a comparison of the set of curriculum content standards for any discipline in your state and that of another state.

20. Show your position on whether public schools should have a set of curriculum content standards that is universally mandated throughout the United States.

21. Prepare a report showing your position on enforcing "high-stakes" testing that sets consequences for low achievers.

22. Propose ways to decrease the number of high school dropouts.

23. Define characteristics and skills of a "highly qualified" teacher.

24. Support or oppose the role of teacher unions.

25. Support or oppose the role of the federal government in education.

26. Tell, citing evidence, whether you feel that the *No Child Left Behind Act* has helped or hurt public education.

CD-ROM

Standards ToolKit, 2nd ed., TeachMaster Technologies, 2000. A resource for searching state standards and benchmarks, designing standard-based curriculum, and linking to websites that provide standards-based lesson plans. Association for Supervision and Curriculum Development, 1703 N. Beauregard Street, Alexandria, Virginia 22311-1714.

 ## Feature Film

Inherit the Wind. 127 min. Black and white. United Artists, 1960. Based on the *Scopes* trial in Tennessee in 1925 on the teaching of the theory of evolution. Stars Frederic March, Spencer Tracy, and Gene Kelly.

 ## Online Resources

Association for Supervision and Curriculum Development
ASCD SmartBrief (weekdays) To register: http://www.smartbrief.com/ascd.
Phi Delta Kappa International
    Classroom Tips (bimonthly, five times)

EdgeMagazine (bimonthly)
PDK Connection (three times a year)
Topics and Trends (monthly)
Phi Delta Kappa/Gallup Poll archive: all polls since 1969
To register: http://www.pdkintl.org

 ## Professional Inquiry Kits

Differentiating Instruction for Mixed-Ability Classrooms, 1996. Carol Ann Tomlinson explains how to adapt curriculum and instruction to students' interests and learning profiles. Association for Supervision and Curriculum Development, 1703 N. Beauregard Street, Alexandria, Virginia 22311-1714.

Educating Culturally and Linguistically Diverse Students, 1998. Shows ways to educate a diverse student population. Northeast and Islands Regional Educational Laboratory at Brown University. Belinda Williams, Senior Developer. Association for Supervision and Curriculum Development, 1703 N. Beauregard Street, Alexandria, Virginia 22311-1714.

 ## Videos

At Work in the Differentiated Classroom, 2001. Three 25- to 45-min. videotapes. Classroom scenes demonstrating the key elements of planning, and managing differentiated classrooms. Facilitator's Guide. Also available on DVD. Association for Supervision and Curriculum Development, 1703 N. Beauregard Street, Alexandria, Virginia 22311-1714.

Beyond the Standards Movement: Defending Quality Education in an Age of Test Scores, 2000. 30 min. Alfie Kohn argues against current obsession with raising standards and standardized tests. National Professional Resources, Inc., 25 S. Regent Street, Port Chester, New York 10573.

Using Standards to Improve Teaching and Learning, 2000. Three 30-min. videotapes. Shows teachers and principals implementing standards in their schools and classrooms. Association for Supervision and Curriculum Development, 1703 N. Beauregard Street, Alexandria, Virginia 22311-1714.

Websites

Accelerated Schools Project: http://www.acceleratedschools.net

Advocates for Youth: http://www.advocatesforyouth.org

The Alan Guttmacher Institute: http://www.agi-usa.org

Alliance for School Choice: http://www.allianceforschoolchoice.org

American Alliance for Health, Physical Education, Recreation, and Dance: http://www.aahperd.org

American Association of Colleges for Teacher Education: http://aacte.org

American Association of University Women: http://www.aauw.org

American Booksellers Foundation for Free Expression: http://www.abffe.com

American Civil Liberties Union: http://www.aclu.org

American Family Association: http://www.afa.net

American Federation of Teachers: http://www.aft.org

American Legacy Foundation: http://americanlegacy.org

American Legislative Exchange Council: http://www.alec.org

American Library Association: http://www.ala.org

American Library Association Office of Intellectual Freedom: http://www.ala/org/alaorg/oif

American Public Health Association: http://www.apha.org

Americans for Religious Liberty: http://www.arlinc.org

American School Health Association: http://www.ashaweb.org

Americans United for Separation of Church and State: http://www.au.org

Association for Supervision and Curriculum Development: http://www.ascd.org

Annie E. Casey Foundation: http://www.aecf.org

Bible Literacy Project: http://www.bibleliteracyproject.org

Cato Institute: http://www.cato.org

Center for American Progress: http://www.americanprogress.com

Center for Education Reform: http://www.edreform.com

The Center for Health and Health Care in Schools: http://healthinschools.org/home.asp

Center for Individual Rights: http://www.cir-usa.org

Center for Science and Culture: http://www.discovery.org/csc

The Center for Scientific Creation: http://creationscience.com

Centers for Disease Control and Prevention: http://www.cdc.gov

Centers for Equal Opportunity: http://www.ceusa.org

Choosing the Best: http://www.choosingthebest.org

Christian Coalition: http://www.cc.org

The Civil Rights Project at Harvard University: http://www.civilrightsprojectharvard.edu

William J. Clinton Foundation: http://www.clintonfoundation.org

Coalition of Essential Schools: http://www.essentialschools.org

College Board: http://www.collegeboard.com

Commission on the Skills of the American Workforce: http://www.ncrel.org/sdrs/areas/issues/envrnmnt/stw/sw0.htm.

Core Knowledge Foundation: http://www.coreknowledge.org

Corporation for National and Community Service: http://www.nationalservice.org

Council for American Private Education: http://www.capenet.org

Discovery Institute: http://www.discovery.org

Economic Policy Institute: http://www.epinet.org

Edison Schools: http://www.edisonschools.com

Education Disinformation Detection and Reporting Agency: http://america-tomorrow.com/bracey/EDDRA

Education Policy Institute: http://www.educationpolicy.org

Education Sector: http://www.educationsector.org

The Education Trust: http://www2.edtrust.org/edtrust

Educational Excellence Network: http://www.edexcellence.net

Educational Resources Information Center: (ERIC): http://www.eric.ed..gov

Effective Schools Research: http://www.effectiveschools.com

English First: http://www.englishfirst.org

Family Research Council: http://www.frc.org

First Amendment Center: http://www.firstamendmentcenter.org

First Amendment Schools: http://www.firstamendmentschools.org

Focus on the Family: http://www.family.org

Free Expression Network: http://www.freexpression.org

Freedom Forum: http://www.freedomforum.org

Milton and Rose D. Friedman Foundation: http://www.friedmanfoundation.org

Bill and Melinda Gates Foundation: http://www.gatesfoundation.org

GreatSchools: http://www.greatschools.net

Gurian Institute: http://www.gurianinstitute.com

Alan Guttmacher Institute: http://www.guttmacher.org

Hoover Institution: http://www.hoover.org

Hudson Institute: http://www.hudson.org/hudson

The Inclusion Network: http://www.inclusion.org

Institute for American Values: http://www.americanvalues.org

Institute of Education Sciences: http://www.ed.gov/about/offices/list/ies/index.html

Institute for Student Achievement: http://www.student-achievement.org

International Association for the Evaluation of Educational Achievement: http://www.iea.nl

International Reading Association: http://www.reading.org

Thomas Jefferson Center for the Protection of Free Expression: http://www.tjcenter.org

Robert Wood Johnson Foundation: http://www.rwjf.org

Kaiser Family Foundation: http://www.kff.org

Knowledge Is Power Program: http://www.kipp.org

Leona Group: http://www.leonagroup.com

Learning First Alliance: http://www.learningfirst.org

Making the Grade: http://www.gwu.edu/~mtg

Manhattan Institute: http://www.manhattan-institute.org

Mayerson Foundation: http://www.mayersonfoundation.org

Medical Institute for Sexual Health: http://www.medinstitute.org

Mid-Continent Regional Educational Laboratory: http://www.mcrel.org/standards

Monitoring the Future: National Institute on Drug Abuse: http://www.MonitoringtheFuture.org

National Academy of Education: http//www.naeducation.org

National Alliance for Public Charter Schools: http://www.publiccharters.org

National Assembly on School-Based Health Clinics: http://www.nasbhc.org

National Assessment of Educational Progress: http://nces.gov/nationsreportcard

National Association for Bilingual Education: http://www.nabe.org

National Association for Single Sex Public Education: http://www.singlesexschools.org/schools.html and http://www.singlesexschools.org/classrooms.htm

National Association for Sport & Physical Education: http://www.aahperd.org/naspe

National Association for Year-Round Education: http://www.nayre.org

National Campaign to Prevent Teen Pregnancy: http://www.teenpregnancy.org

National Center on Education and the Economy: http://nces.org

National Center for Education Statistics: http://nces.ed.gov

National Center for Fair & Open Testing: http://www.fairtest.org

National Center for Health Statistics: http://www.cdc.gov/ncgswww/default.htm

National Center for Home Education: http://www.nche.hslda.org

National Center for Learning and Citizenship: http://ecs.org

National Center for Learning Disabilities: http://www.ncld.org

National Center for Policy Analysis: http://www.ncpa.org

National Center for Science Education: http://www.natcenscied.org

National Center for the Study of Privatization in Education: http://www.ncspe.org

National Clearinghouse for Alcohol and Drug Information: http://www.health.org/pubs/nhsda

National Coalition Against Censorship: http://ncac.org

National Coalition to Support Sexuality Education: http://www.advocatesforyouth.org/rrr/ncsse.htm

National Condom Availability Clearinghouse://http://www.advocatesforyouth.org

National Consortium for Specialized Secondary Schools of Mathematics, Science, and Technology: http://www.ncsssmst.org

National Council for the Accreditation of Teacher Education: http://www.ncate.org

National Council on Bible Curriculum in Public Schools: http://www/bibleinschools.net

National Council on Economic Education: http://econedlink.org

National Council for Teachers of English: http://www.ncte.org

National Education Association: http://www.nea.org

National Guideline Clearinghouse: http://www.guideline.gov

National Home Education Research Institute: http://www.nheri.org

National Household Education Surveys Program: http://nces.ed.gov/nhes

National Institute of Child Health and Human Development: http://www.nichd.nih.gov

National Institute on Drug Abuse: http://www.nida.nih.gov/NIDAhome.html

National Reading Panel: http://www.nationalreadingpanel.org

National Research Center for the Gifted and Talented: http://www.gifted.uconn.edu/NRCGT.html

National Service-Learning Clearinghouse: http://www.servicelearning.org

The New Commission on the Skills of the American Workforce: http://www.skillscommission.org

New Schools Venture Fund: http://www.newschools.org

North American Council for Online Learning: http://www.nacol.org

Parents Advocating School Accountability: http://www
.pasaorg.tripod.com

Parents' Resource Institute for Drug Education: http://
www.pridesurveys.com

People for the American Way: http://www.pfaw.org

Pew Forum on Religion and Public Life: http://www.pew
forum.org

Phi Delta Kappa: http://www.pdkintl.org

Phi Delta Kappa Members: http://www.pdkmembers.org

The Profoundly Gifted Institute: http://www.highlygifted
.org

Public Agenda: http://www.publicagenda.org

Regional Education Laboratories: http://ies.ed.gov/ncee/
edlabs/regions

Renaissance Group: http://www.uni.edu/coe/inclusion/
contact.html

Rethinking Schools: http://www.rethinkingschools.org

SABIS: http://www.sabis.net

School Choices: http://www.schoolchoices.org

Charles and Helen Schwab Foundation: http://www
.schwabfoundation.org

Sex Information and Education Council of the United
States: http://www.siecus.org

State Standards: http://www.statestandards.com

Substance Abuse and Mental Health Services Administration: http://www/samhsa.gov

TesseracT: http://www.tesseract.pvt.k12.mn.us

Texas Freedom Network: http://www.tfn.org

U.S. Charter: http://www.uscharterschools.org

U.S. Department of Education: http://www.ed.gov

U.S. Department of Health and Human Services: http://
www.hhs.gov

U.S. English: http://www.us-english.org/inc

Urban Institute: http://www.urban.org

Endnotes

1. National Center on Education and the Economy, *Tough Choices, Tough Times: A Report of the New Commission on Skills of the American Workforce* (San Francisco: Jossey-Bass, 2006).

2. National Center on Education and the Economy, *Tough Choices, Tough Times: Executive Summary*, website: http://www.skillscommission.org/pdf/exec_sum/ToughChoices_EXECSUM.pdf, accessed January 2, 2007.

3. Ibid.

4. Thomas L. Friedman, *The World Is Flat* (New York: Farrar, Strauss and Giroux, 2005).

5. National Center on Education and the Economy, *Executive Summary*, op. cit.

6. See Kentucky Board of Education website: http://www.education.ky.gov/cgi-bin/MsmFind.exe?Query=math+2012&submit+Search, accessed January 2, 2007.

7. See Maryland Department of Education, *Summary of Requirements for the Graduating Class of 2009 and Beyond*, website: http://www.marylandpublicschools.org/MSDE/testing/hsa, accessed January 2, 2007.

8. See "What, Me Worry? New Survey Shows American Parents and Students Satisfied with Current Math/Science Education," February 15, 2006, Public Agenda website: http://www.publicagenda.org/press-release_detail_cfm?list=67, accessed January 2, 2007.

9. See Core Knowledge Foundation website: http://coreknowledge.org/CK, accessed January 3, 2007.

10. E. D. Hirsch, Jr., "Cultural Literacy," *The American Scholar* 52, no. 2 (Spring 1963): 159–169 and E. D.

Hirsch, Jr., *Cultural Literacy: What Every American Needs to Know* (Boston: Houghton Mifflin, 1987).

11. See, for example, E. D. Hirsch, Jr. and William G. Rowland, *A First Dictionary of Cultural Literacy: What Our Children Need to Know* (Boston: Houghton Mifflin, 1998) and E. D. Hirsch, Jr., Joseph F. Kett, and James S. Trefil, *The New Dictionary of Cultural Literacy: What Every American Needs to Know* (Boston: Houghton Mifflin, 2002).

12. Hirsch, Jr., *Cultural Literacy*, p. xiv.

13. E. D. Hirsch, Jr., "Core Knowledge," *Newsweek* 120, no. 12 (September 21, 1992): A8–9.

14. See Core Knowledge Foundation website: http://www.coreknowledge.org/CK/schools/schools_list.htm, accessed January 3, 2007.

15. See Christopher B. Swanson, "Graduation Rates: Real Kids, Real Numbers," December 1, 2–4, Urban Institute website: http://www.urban.org/publications/311114.html, accessed January 2, 2007.

16. See Kenneth Gray, "Is High School Career and Technical Education Obsolete?" November 3, 2004, *Phi Delta Kappan* website: http://www.pdkintl.org/kappan/k_v86/K0410gra.htm, accessed January 2, 2007.

17. See "Florida's 440 Major Areas of Interest for Students Entering High School in 2007–2008," Florida Department of Education website: http://www/fldoe.org/news/2006/2006_12_11/MjorAreasofInterest.pdf, accessed January 3, 2007.

18. See pp. 255–256 of this textbook.

19. See National Center for Education Statistics, *Academic Pathways, Preparation, and Performance: A Descriptive*

Overview of the Transcripts from the High School Graduating Class of 2003–2004, November 2006, *Selected Findings*, p. 7, website: nttp://nces.ed.gov/pubs2007/2007316.pdf, accessed January 3, 2007.

20. See Davidson Academy website: http://davidson academy.unr.edu/Articles,aspx?ArticleID=134, accessed January 3, 2007.

21. See National Center for Education Statistics, "Dual Enrollment of High School Students at Postsecondary Institutions: 2002–2003," website: http://nces.ed.gov/surveys/peqis/publications/2005008, accessed January 3, 2007.

22. See Great Schools Network website: http://www.greatschools.net.

23. Milton and Rose D. Friedman Foundation, *The ABCs of School Choice*, 2006–2007 edition (Indianapolis, Ind.: Milton and Rose D. Friedman Foundation, 2006). To read online see website: http://64.71.179.146/friedman/downloadFile.do?id=102, accessed April 13, 2007.

24. *Pierce v. Society of Sisters*, 268 U.S. 510 (1925).

25. Brian P. Gill, P. Michael Trimpane, Karen E. Ross, and Dominic J. Brewer, *Rhetoric Versus Reality: What We Know and What We Need to Know About Vouchers and Charter Schools* (Santa Monica, Calif.: RAND, 2001), p. 64.

26. Policy Matters Ohio, *Cleveland School Vouchers: Where the Students Come From*, website: http://www.policymattersohio.org/voucherintro.html, accessed June 14, 2003.

27. See Stanley M. Elam, Lowell C. Rose, and Alec M. Gallup, "The 23rd Annual Gallup Poll of the Public's Attitudes Toward the Public Schools," *Phi Delta Kappan* 73, no. 1 (September 1991): 47. Stanley M. Elam, Lowell C. Rose, and Alec M. Gallup, "The 26th Annual Phi Delta Kappa/Gallup Poll of the Public's Attitudes Toward the Public Schools," *Phi Delta Kappan* 76, no. 1 (September 1994): 48–49. Lowell C. Rose and Alec M. Gallup, "The 30th Annual Phi Delta Kappa/Gallup Poll of the Public's Attitudes Toward the Public Schools," *Phi Delta Kappan* 80, no. 1 (September 1998): 44.

28. Lowell C. Rose and Alec M. Gallup, "The 31st Annual Phi Delta Kappa/Gallup Poll of the Public's Attitudes Toward the Public Schools," *Phi Delta Kappan* 81, no. 1 (September 1999): 44.

29. Lowell C. Rose and Alec M. Gallup, "The 34th Annual Phi Delta Kappa/Gallup Poll of the Public's Attitude Toward the Public Schools," *Phi Delta Kappan* 84, no. 1 (September 2002): 46.

30. Lowell C. Rose and Alec M. Gallup, "The 38th Annual Phi Delta Kappa/Gallup Poll of the Public's Attitudes Toward the Public Schools," *Phi Delta Kappan* 88, no. 1 (September 2006): 44.

31. For differing views regarding vouchers see Martin Carnot, *School Vouchers: Examining the Evidence* (Washington, D.C.: Economic Policy Institute, 2001), website: http://www.epinet.org/studies/vouchers-full.pdf, accessed January 14, 2007 and Milton and Rose D. Friedman, *The ABCs of School Choice*, op. cit. For examples of differing results of research comparing achievement of students in private schools with those in public schools see Paul E. Peterson and Elena Llaudet, *On the Public-Private School Achievement Debate* (Cambridge, Mass.: Kennedy School of Government, Harvard University, 2006) and Craig Chamberlain, *Public Schools Equal or Better in Math Than Private or Charter Schools*, 2006 (News Bureau, University of Illinois at Urbana-Champaign). Article on study of NAEP math data conducted by researchers Sarah and Christopher Lubienski, website: http://www.news.uiuc.edu/NEWS/06/0123lubienski, accessed January 15, 2007.

32. U.S. Secretary of Education, Margaret Spellings, press release, April 5, 2006, U.S. Department of Education website: http://www.ed.gov/news/press releases/2006/04/04052006.html, accessed January 16, 2007.

33. For discussion of neoliberalism see Weil, *School Vouchers and Privatization*, Chapter One.

34. U.S. Department of Education, *The State of Charter Schools 2000-Fourth-Year Report, January 2000, Executive Summary*. Website: http://www.ed.gov/pubs/charter4th year/es_html, accessed March 4, 2000, and June 14, 2003.

35. See Center for Education Reform website: http://www.edreform.com/index.cfm?fuseAction=stateStats&p SectionID=15&cSectionID=44, accessed April 7, 2007.

36. Donna Harrington-Lueker, "Charter Schools," *The American School Board Journal* 181, no. 9 (September 1994): 22.

37. See Donna Harrington-Lueker, "Charter 'Profit,'" *The American School Board Journal* 181, no. 9 (September 1994): 27–28.

38. See April Gresham, Frederick Hess, Robert Maranto, and Scott Williams, "Desert Bloom: Arizona's Free Market in Education," *Phi Delta Kappan* 81, no. 10 (June 2000): 751–757. See also Carol Ascher and Arthur R. Greenberg, "Charter Reform and the Education Bureaucracy: Lessons from New York State," *Phi Delta Kappan* 83, no. 7 (March 2002): 513–517.

39. See New Schools Venture Fund website: http://www.newschools.org/viewpoints/gatesrelease2006.html, accessed January 20, 2007.

40. See The Boston Foundation website: http://www.tbf.org/About/about-L2.asp?ID=97, accessed January 20, 2007.

41. Lowell C. Rose and Alec M. Gallup, "The 38th Annual Phi Delta Kappa/Gallup Poll of the Public's Attitudes Toward the Public Schools," p. 44.

42. Website: http://www.bengamlacharter.org, accessed August 13, 2007.

43. Website: http://schools.nyc.gov/doefacts/factfinder/ServiceDetails.aspx?id=135, accessed August 13, 2007.

44. See *The Orlando Sentinel*, Section A, March 25 through 28, 2007.

45. See Matthew Carr and Samuel R. Staley, *Using the Ohio Proficiency Test to Analyze the Academic Achievement of Charter School Students: 2002–2004*, Buckeye Institute website: http://www.buckeyeinstitute.org/docs/Policy_Brief_Charter_Achievement.pdf, accessed January 20, 2007. See also U.S. Department of Education, *Charter High Schools Closing the Achievement Gap* (Washington, D.C.: U.S. Government Printing Office, 2006).

46. National Education Association, *Charter Schools Show No Gains Over Public Schools*, National Education Association website: http://www.nea.org/charter/naepstudy.html, accessed January 20, 2007.

47. National Center for Education Statistics, "Home Schooling in the United States: 1999," website: http://nces.ed.gov/pubs2001/HomeSchool, accessed June 15, 2003. For additional information on homeschooling see National Education Research Institute website: http://www.nheri.org and NHERI journal *Home School Research*.

48. National Center for Education Statistics website: http://nces.ed.gov/nheri/homeschool, accessed January 20, 2007.

49. National Center for Education Statistics website: http://nces.ed.gov/fastfacts/display.asp?id=65, accessed January 20, 2007.

50. National Center for Education Statistics website: http://nces.ed.gov/programs/digest/d05/tables/dt05_084.asp, accessed January 20, 2007.

51. John Holt, *Teach Your Own: A Hopeful Path for Education* (New York: Delacorte Press/Seymour Lawrence, 1981). See also John Holt, *How Children Fail* (New York: Dell, 1964).

52. *Wisconsin v. Yoder* 406 U.S. 205 (1972).

53. See, for example, Growing Stars website: http://growingstars.com, accessed January 20, 2007 and Tutor Vista website: http://www.tutorvista.com, accessed January 20, 2007.

54. See, for example, *Unschooling Is a Type of Homeschooling*, website: http://geocities.com/Heartland/Pointe/2073/article.html, accessed January 20, 2007.

55. Ivan Illich, *Deschooling Society* (New York: Harper & Row, 1971).

56. Lawrence M. Rudner, "Student Achievement and Demographic Characteristics of Home School Students in 1998," *Education Policy Analysis Archives* 7, no. 8, March 21, 1999, Gene V. Glass, ed., College of Education, Arizona State University, website: http://epaa.asu.edu/epaa/vtn8, accessed June 15, 2003. See Lawrence M. Rudner, "The Scholastic Achievement of Home School Students," *ERIC/AE Digest*, ERIC Clearinghouse on Assessment

and Evaluation, 1999, website: http://ericfacility.net/ericdigests/ed435709.html, accessed June 15, 2003.

57. Dave S. Hurst, "We Cannot Ignore the Alternatives," *Educational Leadership* 52, no. 1 (September 1994): 78.

58. Gerald W. Bracey, *What You Should Know About the War Against America's Public Schools* (Boston: Allyn and Bacon, 2003).

59. American Community Survey, U.S. Bureau of the Census website: http://www.factfinder.census.gov/servlet/ACSSAFFFacts?_event=geo_id=0100, accessed January 22, 2007.

60. U.S. Bureau of the Census, Robert Bernstein, Public Information Office, website: http://census.gov/Press-Release/www/releases/archives/population/010048.html, accessed May 17, 2007.

61. *Lau v. Nichols*, 414 U.S. 563 (1974).

62. See U.S. English, Inc. website: http://www.us-english.org, January 22, 2007, accessed January 22, 2007.

63. See Fitchburg High School website: http://www.fitchburg.k12.ma.us/fhs/index.php, accessed January 22, 2007.

64. American Library Association, "Most Challenged Books of the 21st Century (2002–2005)" website: http://www.ala.org/ala/oif/bannedbooksweek/bbwlinks/topten2000to2005.htm, accessed January 2, 2007.

65. American Library Association, "Challenged and Banned Books," website: http://www.ala.org, accessed June 17, 2003. See also Office of Intellectual Freedom website: http://www.ala.org.alaorg/oif and The Online Books Page, "Banned Books on Line," for lists of books suppressed or censored by legal authorities from historic times to the present, website: http://onlinebooks.library.upenn.edu/banned-books.html.

66. American Library Association, *Most Challenged Books*, op. cit.

67. Sidney B. Simon, Leland W. Howe, and Howard Kirschenbaum, *Values Clarification* (New York: Hart, 1972). For a grammarian's criticism of values clarification see Richard Mitchell, *Less Than Words Can Say* (Boston: Little Brown, 1979). pp. 79–95.

68. *Epperson v. Arkansas*, 393 U.S. 97 (1968).

69. See pp. 522–524 of this textbook for discussion of more recent cases.

70. *Hazelwood School District v Kuhlmeier*, No. 86-836 (1994).

71. *Tinker v. Des Moines Independent Community School District*, 393 (U.S. 503), 89 Cup. Ct. 733 (1969).

72. See http://landru.leg.state.or.us/07reg/measures/hb3200.dir/hb3279.en.html, accessed July 28, 2007.

73. Diane Ravitch, *The Language Police: How Pressure Groups Restrict What Students Learn* (New York: Alfred Knopf, 2003).

74. Madeline Grumet, *Bitter Milk: Women and Teaching* (Amherst, Mass.: The University of Massachusetts Press, 1988), p. 4.

75. Myra and David Sadker, "Sexism in the Schoolroom of the 80's," *Psychology Today* 19, no. 3 (March 1985): 54–57.

76. American Association of University Women and Wellesley College Center for Research on Women, *How Schools Shortchange Girls: The AAUW Report: A Study of the Major Findings on Girls and Education* (Washington, D.C.: AAUW Educational Foundation, 1992).

77. See Marcia Thurmond, *Civil Liberties: The National Newsletter of the ACLU 380, spring 1994*, website: http://www.skepticfiles.org/aclu/thurmond.htm, accessed January 27, 2007.

78. See *FairTest Examiner,* "Test-Makers to Revise Nat.Merit Exam to Address Gender Bias: FairTest Complaint Will Lead to Millions More for Girls, Fall 1996," website: http://www.fairtest.org/examarts/fall96/natmerit .htm, accessed January 27, 2007.

79. National Center for Education Statistics, U.S. Department of Education, *Trends in Educational Equity of Girls & Women: 2004,* website: http://nces.ed.gov/pubs2005/equity, accessed January 27, 2007.

80. Jay P. Greene and Marcus A. Winters, *Leaving Boys Behind: Public High School Graduation Rates,* Civic Report 48, Manhattan Institute for Policy Research, April 2006, website: http://manhattan-institute.org/html/cr_48.htm, accessed January 27, 2007.

81. Michael Gurian and Kathy Stevens, *The Minds of Boys: Saving Our Sons from Falling Behind in School and Life* (San Francisco: Jossey-Bass, 2005), p. 22.

82. Janice Weinman and Judith Kleinfeld, "Do Public Schools Shortchange Girls on Educational Opportunities?" *Insight* 14, no. 4 (December 14, 1998). See also Judith Kleinfeld, "Student Performance: Males versus Females," *The Public Interest* 134 (1999).

83. American Association of University Women and American Institutes for Research, *Gender Gap: Where Schools Fail Our Children* (New York: Marlowe & Co., 1999).

84. Ibid, p. 12.

85. Horatio Alger Association, *The State of Our Nation's Youth* (Alexandria, Va.: Horatio Alger Association, 1997).

86. Sara Mead, "The Truth About Boys and Girls," Education Sector, June 27, 2006, website: http://www .educationsector.org/analysis/analysis_show.htm?doc_ id=378305, accessed January 28, 2007.

87. Jacquelynne C. Eccles and Rena D. Harold, *Gender Differences in Sport Involvement: Applying the Eccles' Expectancy-Value Model* (Ann Arbor, Mich.: University Press, n.d.), pp. 28–29.

88. Lynn Phillips, *The Girls Report* (New York: National Council for Research on Women, 1998).

89. Dan Kindlon and Michael Thompson, *Raising Cain: Protecting the Emotional Life of Boys* (New York: Ballantine Books, 1999).

90. Robert J. Havighurst, *Developmental Tasks and Education,* 1st ed. (Chicago: University of Chicago Press, 1972).

91. National Association for Single-Sex Public Education, website: http://www.singlesexschools.org/schools .html, accessed January 28, 2007.

92. Austin Independent School District website: http://www.austin.isd.tenet.edu/schools/annrichards/ research.phtml, accessed April 22, 2007.

93. Patricia B. Campbell and Jo Sanders, "Challenging the System: Assumptions and Data Behind the Push for Single-Sex Schooling," in Amanda Datnow and Lea Hubbard, eds., Gender Policy and Practice (New York: Routledge Falmer, 2002), p. 32.

94. Cornelius Riordan, "What Do We Know About the Effects of Single-Sex Schools in the Private Sector?: Implications for Public Schools," in Datnow and Hubbard, eds., Gender Policy and Practice (New York: Routledge Falmer, 2002), p. 11.

95. Caryl Rivers and Rosalind Chait Barnett, "Don't Believe in 'Boy Crisis.'" April 10, 2006, Brandeis University website: http://www.brandeis.edu?news/item?newsitem_id= 104601&show_release_date=1, accessed January 28, 2007.

96. Association for Supervision and Curriculum Development, *SmartBrief,* December 14, 2006, website: http://www.smartbrief.com/ascd, accessed January 28, 2007.

97. See American Civil Liberties Union, "Federal Judge Rules Okeechobee, FL Students Can Form Gay-Straight Alliance Club," April 6, 2007, website: http:// www.aclu.org/lgbt/youth/29283prs20070406.html, accessed April 22, 2007.

98. Parents Resource Institute for Drug Education (PRIDE) website: http://www.pridesurveys.com/Reports/ index.html#national.

99. American Legacy Foundation website: http:// americanlegacy.org.

100. *National Survey on Drug Use and Health,* U.S. Department of Health and Human Services, September 2006, website: http://oas.samhsa.gov/nsduh/2k5nsduh/ 2k5Results.htm#High, accessed April 10, 2007.

101. Office of National Drug Control Policy Media Campaign, National Youth Anti-Drug Media Campaign, *New Report on Alarming Trends in Girls' Use of Drugs, Alcohol, Cigarettes, and Prescription Drugs,* February 9, 2006, website: http://www.mediacampaign.org/newsroom/press 06/020906.html, accessed January 31, 2007.

102. *National Survey,* op. cit.

103. See The NSDUH Report, *Driving Under the Influence (DUI) Among Young Persons*, December 31, 2004, website: http://oas.samhsa.gov/2k4/youthDUI/youth DUI.pdf, accessed January 31, 2007.

104. *National Survey*, op. cit.

105. University of Michigan, Institute for Social Research, press release December 21, 2006, Study website: http://www.monitoringthefuture.org, accessed January 31, 2007.

106. See the annual Phi Delta Kappa/Gallup Poll of the Public's Attitudes Toward the Public Schools, *Phi Delta Kappan*, usually in September issue.

107. National Center for Health Statistics, Centers for Disease Control and Prevention, "U.S. Pregnancy Rates in the United States Lowest in Two Decades," September 11, 2000, website: http://www.cdc.gov/nchs/releases/00facts/trends.htm, accessed June 27, 2003.

108. Stephanie J. Ventura, Joyce C. Abma, William D. Mosher, and Stanley K. Henshaw, National Center for Health Statistics, Centers for Disease Control and Prevention, *Recent Trends in Teenage Pregnancy in the United States, 1990–2002*, January 11, 2007, website: http://www.cdc.gov/nchs/products/pubs/pubd/hestats/teenpreg 1990-2002/teenpreg1990–2002.htm, accessed February 2, 2007.

109. Centers for Disease Control and Prevention, *Teenpreg 1990–2002*, tables on pregnancy, live births, abortions, and fetal losses, website: http://www.cdc.gov/nchs/data/hestat/teenpreg1990-2002_tables.pdf, accessed February 3, 2007.

110. Ibid.

111. Joyce V. Abma, Gladys M. Martinez, Dr. William Mosher, and Brittany S. Dawson, Centers for Disease Control and Prevention, *Teenagers in the United States: Sexual Activity, Contraception, and Childbearing: 2002*, website: http://www.cdc.gov/nchs/data/series/sr_23/sr23_024 .pdf, accessed February 2, 2007.

112. Centers for Disease Control and Prevention, *Teenpreg 1990–2002* tables, op. cit.

113. National Center for Health Statistics, Centers for Disease Control and Prevention, "U.S. Pregnancy Rates Lowest in Two Decades," op. cit.

114. National Interagency Forum on Child and Health Statistics, *America's Children: Key National Indicators of Well-Being, 2007*, website: http://www.childstats .gov/americaschildren/beh4.asp, accessed July 14, 2007.

115. National Institute of Allergy and Infectious Diseases, "An Introduction to Sexually Transmitted Diseases," July 1999, website: http://www.niaid.nih.gov/factsheets/stdinfo.htm, accessed June 28, 2003.

116. H. Weinstock, S. Berman, and W. Cates, "Sexually Transmitted Diseases Among American Youth: Incidence and Prevalence Estimation, 2000," Alan Guttmacher Institute, *Perspectives on Sexual and Reproductive Health 2004*

36 (1): 6–10 at Centers for Disease Control and Prevention website: http://cdc.gov/std/stats04/trends2004.htm, accessed February 3, 2007.

117. U.S. Department of Education, *Genital Herpes*, May 2005, website: http://www.4woman.gov/faq/std herpe.htm#2, accessed February 3, 2007.

118. United Nations, *Global Summary of the AIDS Epidemic*, December 2006, website: http://data.unaids.org/pub/EpiReport/2006/02-Global_Summary_2006_Epi Update_eng.pdf, accessed February 3, 2007.

119. Centers for Disease Control and Prevention, *Morbidity and Mortality Weekly Report*, June 1, 2001, website: http://www.cdc.gov/mmwr/PDF/wk/mm5021.pdf, accessed June 27, 2003.

120. Centers for Disease Control and Prevention, CDC, *Morbidity and Mortality Weekly Report*, June 2, 2006, "Twenty-Five Years of HIV/AIDS—United States, 1981–2006," website: http://www.cdc.gov/MMWR/preview/MMWRhtml/mm5521a1.htm, accessed February 3, 2007.

121. See RFSU (the Swedish association for sexuality education), *Knowledge, Reflection, and Dialogue: Swedish Sexuality Education in Brief*, website: http://www.rfsu .org/swedish_sexuality_education.asp, accessed April 15, 2007.

122. See "Sex Education in America," *An NPR/Kaiser/Kennedy School Poll*, 2007, website: http://www.npr.org/templates/story/story/php?storyID=1622610, accessed February 3, 2007.

123. Heather Boonstra, "Legislators Craft Alternate Vision of Sex Education to Counter Abstinence-Only Drive," *The Guttmacher Report on Public Policy*, May 2002, Vol. 5, No. 2, an analysis of a 1998 poll by the Kaiser Family Foundation and ABC Television, website: http://www .guttmacher.org/pubs/tgr/05/2/gr050201.html, accessed February 3, 2007.

124. See Sexuality Information and Education Council of the United States (SIECUS), *Sexuality Education and Abstinence-Only-Until-Marriage Programs in the States: An Overview*, 2005, website: http://siecus.org/policy/states/2005/analysis.html, accessed February 2, 2007.

125. Joy C. Dryfoos, "Full-Service Schools: What They Are and How to Get to Be One," *NASSP Bulletin* 77, no. 557 (December 1993): 1–3.

126. Joy C. Dryfoos, *Full-Service Schools: A Revolution in Health and Social Services for Children, Youth, and Families* (San Francisco: Jossey-Bass, 1994), p. 12.

127. Dryfoos, "Full-Service Schools, What They Are," op. cit.

128. National Assembly on School-Based Health Care, *School-Based Health Care Establishment Act of 2006*, website: http://www.nasbhc.org/APP/2006_SBHC_Legislation_ Summary.pdf, accessed February 3, 2007.

129. Ibid.

130. 584 N.Y.S. 2d (N.Y. Sup. Ct., 1992).

131. Stanley M. Elam, Lowell C. Rose, and Alec M. Gallup, "The 25th Annual Phi Delta Kappa/Gallup Poll," *Phi Delta Kappan* 75, no. 2 (October 1993): 152.

132. National Condom Availability Clearinghouse, *The Facts: School Condom Availability*, July 30, 2007, website: http://www.advocatesforyouth.org/publications/fact sheet/fsschcon.htm, accessed July 31, 2007.

133. Deborah P. Britzman, *Lost Subjects, Contested Objects: Toward a Psychoanalytical Inquiry of Learning* (Albany, N.Y.: State University of New York Press, 1998), p. 76.

134. Robert Wood Johnson Foundation, *American Heart Asociation, Clinton Foundation, Robert Wood Johnson Foundation to Help Schools Create Healthier Environment for Nation's Schools*, February 13, 2006, website: http://www.rwjf.org/newsroom/newsreleasesdetail.jsp?id=10395, accessed February 3, 2007.

135. *Brown v. Board of Education of Topeka, Kansas*, 347 U.S. 483, 74 Sup. Ct. 686 (1954).

136. *Plessy v. Ferguson*, 163 U.S. 537, 16 S. Ct. 1138 (1896).

137. See James S. Coleman et al., *Equality of Educational Opportunity* (Washington, D.C.: U.S. Office of Education, 1966).

138. *Swann v. Charlotte-Mecklenburg Board of Education*, 402 U.S. 1 (1971).

139. Erica Frankenberg, Chungmei Lee, and Gary Orfield, "A Multiracial Society with Segregated Schools: Are We Losing the Dream?" The Civil Rights Project, Harvard University, January 2003, website: http://www.greaterdiversity.com/education-resources/ed_articles03/AreWeLosingtheDream.pdf, accessed April 11, 2007.

140. Jonathan Kozol, *The Shame of the Nation: The Restoration of Apartheid Schooling in America* (New York: Crown Publishers, 2005).

141. See Richard D. Kahlenberg, "The New Integration," *Educational Leadership* 63, no. 8 (May 2006): 22–26.

142. Portland Public Schools, *African-American Baseline Essays* (Portland, Ore.: Portland Public Schools, 1989). See also Portland Public Schools, *Multicultural/Multiethnic Education in Portland Public Schools*, 1988).

143. Kenneth T. Henson, *Curriculum Planning: Integrating Multiculturalism, Constructivism, and Education Reform* (Long Grove, Ill.: Waveland Press, 2006), p. 5.

144. Christine E. Sleeter, *Multicultural Education as Social Activism* (Albany, N.Y.: State University of New York Press, 1996).

145. James A. Banks, *Cultural Diversity and Education: Foundations, Curriculum, and Teaching*, 5th ed. (Boston: Allyn and Bacon, 2006), p. 3.

146. Lilian and Oscar Handlin, "America and Its Discontents: A Great Society Legacy," *The American Scholar* 64, no. 1 (Winter 1995): 15–37.

147. Ibid., p. 36.

148. Hugh B. Price, "Multiculturalism: Myths and Realities," *Phi Delta Kappan* 74, no. 3 (November 1992): 212.

149. Jeannie Oakes, *Keeping Track: How Schools Structure Inequality* (New Haven: Yale University Press, 1985), p. 26.

150. Deborah P. Britzman, *Practice Makes Practice: A Critical Study of Learning to Teach* (Albany, N.Y.: State University of New York Press, 1991), p. 41.

151. Geneva Gay, "Achieving Educational Equality Through Curriculum Desegregation," *Phi Delta Kappan* 72, no. 1 (September 1990): 56–62.

152. Ibid., p. 60.

153. Ibid., p. 62.

154. See Leslie Agard-Jones, "Implementing Multicultural Education," *Multicultural Education* 1, no. 1 (Summer 1993): 13–15, 38.

155. James A. Banks and Cherry McGee Banks, eds. *Multicultural Education: Issues and Perspectives*, 5th ed. (Hoboken, N.J.: Wiley, 2004), p. 5.

156. Ibid., p. 9.

157. Arthur M. Schlesinger, Jr., *The Disuniting of America: Reflections on a Multicultural Society* (Knoxville, Tenn.: Whittle Direct Books, 1991), pp. 82–83.

158. Ibid., p. 67.

159. Patrick J. Buchanan, *State of Emergency: The Third World Invasion and Conquest of America* (New York: Thomas Dunne Books, St. Martin's Press, 2006), p. 13.

160. *Regents of the University of California v. Bakke*, 438 U.S. 265 (1978).

161. *Grutter v. Bollinger et al.* [N. 02-241, 539 U.S. (June 23, 2003)] and *Gratz et al. v. Bollinger et al.* 539 U.S. [N. 02-516 (June 23, 2003)].

162. State of Michigan, State Ballot Proposal Status, website: http://www.michigan.gov/documents/Statewide_Bal_Prop_Status_145801_7.pdf, accessed February 6, 2007.

163. Paul R. Burden and David M. Byrd, *Methods for Effective Teaching: Promoting K–12 Student Understanding*, 4th ed. (Boston: Allyn and Bacon, 2007), p. 96.

164. James A. Banks, *Educating Citizens in a Multicultural Society* (New York: Teachers College Press, 1997), p. 9.

165. U.S. Department of Education, *Teaching Language for National Security and American Competitiveness*, January 2006, website: http://www.ed.gov/teachers/how/academic/foreign-language/teaching-language.html, accessed August 1, 2007.

166. Gerald W. Bracey, *The War Against America's Public Schools: Privatizing Schools, Commercializing Education* (Needham Heights, Mass.: Allyn and Bacon, 2001). See also Gerald W. Bracey, *What You Should Know About the War Against America's Public Schools* (Boston: Allyn and Bacon, 2003).

167. Danny Weil, *School Vouchers and Privatization: A Reference Handbook* (Santa Barbara, Calif.: ABC-CLIO, 2002).

168. See "Performance Contracting as Catalysts for Reform," *Educational Technology* 9, no. 8 (August 1969): 5–9. See also Charles Blaschke, "Performance Contracting Costs, Management Reform and John Q. Citizen," *Phi Delta Kappan* 53, no. 4 (December 1971): 245–247. See also Daniel J. Dieterich, "Performance Contracting: Pot of Gold? Or Pandora's Box?" *The English Journal* 61, no. 4 (April 1972): 606–614.

169. Scott Willis, "Public Schools, Private Managers," *ASCD Update* 36, no. 3 (March 1994): 1.

170. Ibid.

171. Edison Schools website: http://www.edison schools.com/edison-school/about-us, accessed February 9, 2007. See also website: http://edisonschools/edison-schools/about-us, accessed February 9, 2007. See also website: http://www.edisonschools/edison-schools/faqs, accessed February 9, 2007.

172. See Knowledge Is Power Program websites: http://www.kipp.org, http://www.kipp.org/01, and http://www.kipp.org/01/whatisakippschool.cfm, accessed February 9, 2007.

173. Alex Molnar, David R. Garcia, Margaret Bartlett, and Adrienne O'Neill, *EMO Annual Report: Profiles of For-Profit Education Management Organizations 2005–2006*, Commercialism in Education Research Unit, Arizona State University, May 2006, website: http://epsl .asu.edu/ceru/CERU_2006_emo.htm, accessed February 9, 2007.

174. Educational Policies Studies Laboratory, Commercialism in Education Research Unit, Arizona State University, *EMO Industry Consolidating, Reconfiguring to Meet Demand for Supplemental Education Services*, website: http://epsl.asu.edu/ceru/Documents/EPSL-0605-104-CERU-press.pdf, accessed February 9, 2007.

175. Library of Congress, Thomas, 109th Congress, 1st session, H. Con. Res. 288, Concurrent Resolution, website: http://thomas.loc.gov/cgi-bin/query/D?c109:2:/temp/~c109HhuX09, accessed February 10, 2007.

176. Ann T. Halverson and Thomas Neary, *Building Inclusive Schools: Tools and Strategies for Success* (Boston: Allyn and Bacon, 2001), p. 1.

177. Suzanne E. Wade and Judy Zone, "Creating Inclusive Classrooms: An Overview," in Suzanne E. Wade, ed. *Inclusive Education: A Casebook and Readings for Prospective and Practicing Teachers* (Mahwah, N.J.: Lawrence Erlbaum Associated, 2002), p. 7.

178. Carol A. Kochar, Lynda L. West, and Juliana M. Taymans, *Successful Inclusion: Practical Strategies for a Shared Responsibility* (Upper Saddle River, N.J.: Merrill, 2000), p. 9.

179. James McLesky and Nancy L. Waldron, *Inclusive Schools in America: Making Differences Ordinary* (Alexandria, Va.: Association for Supervision and Curriculum Development, 2000), p. 13.

180. Carol Ann Tomlinson and Jay McTighe, *Integrating Differentiated Instruction + Understanding by Design* (Alexandria, Va.: Association for Supervision and Curriculum Development, 2006), pp. 2–3. See also Grant Wiggins and Jay McTighe, *Understanding by Design* (Alexandria, Va.: Association for Supervision and Curriculum Development, 1998).

181. See pp. 358–360 of this text.

182. McLeskey and Waldron, *Inclusive Schools in America*, p. 21.

183. Carl D. Glickman, *Revolutionizing America's Schools* (San Francisco: Jossey-Bass, 1998), p. 93.

184. Ibid., p. 98.

185. Stephen Prothero, *Religious Literacy: What Every American Needs to Know—And Doesn't* (San Francisco: HarperSanFrancisco, 2007). See also David Van Biema, "The Case for Teaching the Bible," *Time* 169, no. 14 (April 2, 2007): 40–46.

186. Bible Literacy Project, *Bible Literacy Report: Executive Summary*, website: http://www.bibleliteracy.org/Site/PressRoom/press_execsum.htm, accessed February 15, 2007.

187. Georgia Department of Education, *Georgia Performance Standards for Literature and History of the Old Testament Era* and *Georgia Performance Standards for Literature and History of the New Testament Era*, websites: http://www .doe.k12.ga.us/DMGetDocument,aspx/Literature%20and %20History%20of%20Old%20Testament%29Course .pdf?p=6CC6799F8C1371F60835F40DAB1B1FB27867 ED909BA92F3B9B541E3C48706D48&Type=D, accessed April 21, 2007 and http://www.doe.k12.ga.us/DMGet Document.aspx/Literature%20and%20History%20of% 20New%20Testament%20Course.pdf?p=6CC6799F8C 1371F6FD10AA52C2BCFC3D96C726B7ABF94BEB949 55CB55C734AB7&Type=D, accessed April 21, 2007.

188. See Texas Freedom Network, *The Bible and the Public Schools: Report on the National Council on Bible Curriculum in Public Schools*, website: http://www.tfn.org/religiousfreedom/biblecurriculum/execsummary, accessed February 16, 2007.

189. National Council on Bible Curriculum in Public Schools website: http://www.bibleinschools.net/sdm .asp?pg=implemented, accessed April 21, 2007.

190. The Bible Literacy Project website: http://www .bibleliteracy.org/site/news/bibl_newsOpEd060414.htm, accessed April 21, 2007. See also Cullen Schippe and Chuck Stetson, eds., *The Bible and Its Influence* (New York/Fairfield, Va.: BLP Publishing, 2006). For limited preview of *The Bible and Its Influence* go to website: http://books

.google.com, accessed April 21, 2007, and type in Search box: *The Bible and Its Influence*.

191. See p. 67 of this text.

192. See Center for Science and Culture, Discovery Institute, *A Scientific Dissent from Darwinism*, website: http://www.dissentfromdarwin.org, accessed February 16, 2007.

193. See National Center for Science Education, *Defending the Teaching of Evolution in the Public Schools*, website: http://www.ncseweb.org, accessed February 16, 2007.

194. University of Missouri Kansas City Law School, *Creationism in 2001: A State-by-State Report*, website: http://www.law.umkc.edu/faculty/projects/ftrials/conlaw/creationismreport.pdf, accessed February 16, 2007.

195. See National Center for Science Education, *The Latest on Evolution from the Pope*, April 12, 2007, website: http://www.ncseweb.org/resources/news/2007/XX/721_the_latest_on_evolution_from_t_4_12_2007.asp, accessed April 21, 2007.

196. See CBS News website: http://www.cbsnews.com/stories/2004/11/22/opinion/polls/main657083.shtml and the Pew Forum on Religion & Public Life, *Public Divided on Origins of Life: Religion, A Strength and Weakness of Both Parties*, August 25, 1995, website: http://pewforum/surveys/origins#1, accessed February 16, 2007.

197. Nel Noddings, *Educating for Intelligent Belief and Unbelief* (New York: Teachers College Press, 1993), p. 139.

198. U.S. Department of Education, "Guidance on Constitutionally Protected Prayer in Public Elementary and Secondary Schools," February 7, 2003, website: http://www.ed.gov/policy/gen/guid/religionandschools/prayer_guidance.html, accessed July 10, 2003.

199. Charles C. Haynes and Oliver Thomas, eds., *Finding Common Ground: A First Amendment Guide to Religion and Public Education* (Nashville, Tenn.: The Freedom Forum First Amendment Center, 1994), p. 1.3.

200. Charles C. Haynes, Sam Chaltain, John E. Ferguson, Jr., David L. Hudson, Jr., and Oliver Thomas, *The First Amendment in Schools: A Guide from the First Amendment Center* (Alexandria, Va.: Association for Supervision and Curriculum Development, 2003), p. 17.

201. Noddings, *Education for Intelligent Belief and Unbelief*, p. xv.

202. Ibid., p. 137.

203. Ibid., p. 144.

204. Haynes and Thomas, *Finding Common Ground*, p. 1.1.

205. Joseph M. Carroll, "Organizing Time to Support Learning," *The School Administrator* 51, no. 3 (March 1994): 26–28, 30–32. See also Joseph M. Carroll, "The Coperni-can Plan Evaluated: The Evolution of a Revolution," *Phi Delta Kappan* 76, no. 2 (October 1994): 104–113.

206. Floyd Boschee and Mark A. Baron, *Outcome-Based Education: Developing Programs Through Strategic Planning* (Lancaster, Pa.: Technomic Publishing Co., 1993), p. 133.

207. The Center for Education Reform, "Scheduling On the Block," November 1996, website: http://www.edreform.com/pubs/block.htm, accessed July 13, 2003. See also Andrea Brumbaugh, "The Copernican Plan: Changing the School Schedule," School Renewal Discussion Forum, June 2001, website: http://www.schoolrenewal.org/strategies/i-4X4-ab.html, accessed July 13, 2003.

208. National Education Commission on Time and Learning, *Prisoners of Time* (Washington, D.C.: National Education Commission on Time and Learning, April 1994). ERIC document ED366115 (1994).

209. The Center for Education Reform, "Scheduling On the Block," op. cit.

210. PBS, *School-by-School Reform*, Courtenay Singer, "Making Time to Learn," September 2005, website: http://www.pbs.org/makingschoolswork/sbs/kipp/time.html, accessed February 17, 2007.

211. National Commission on Excellence in Education, *A Nation at Risk: The Imperative for Educational Reform* (Washington, D.C.: U.S. Government Printing Office, 1983), p. 29.

212. Don Glines, *Philosophical Rationale for Year-Round Education*. ERIC document ED368075 (1994).

213. Metropolitan School District of Perry Township, Indiana, website: http://msdpt.k12.in.us/html/documents/Edison_schools.pdf, accessed July 29, 2007.

214. PBS, *School-by-School Reform*, Courtenay Singer, "Making the Time to Learn," op. cit.

215. Sizer, *Horace's School*, p. 146.

216. Metropolitan School District of Perry Township, Indiana, op. cit.

217. Making Schools Work with Hedrick Smith, *School-by-School Reform*, "KIPP: Knowledge Is Power Program," September 2005, website: http://www.pbs.org/makingschoolswork/sbs/kipp/index.html, accessed July 29, 2007.

218. Charles Ballinger, *Annual Report to the Association on the Status of Year-Round Education*. ERIC document ED358551 (1993).

219. Vicki T. Howell, *An Examination of Year-Round Education: Pros and Cons That Challenge Schooling in America*. ERIC document ED298602 (1988).

220. Ibid.

221. Ballinger, *Annual Report*.

222. Elizabeth A. Palmer and Amy E. Bemis, "Year-Round Education," University of Minnesota Extension

Service, 1999, website: http://www.extension.umn.edu/distribution/familydevelopment/components/7286-09.html, accessed July 13, 2003.

223. National Association for Year-Round Education, *Number of Public, Charter, and Private Schools with Year-Round Programs, 2005–2006*, website: http://www.nayre.org/SchoolsbyState.html, accessed February 17, 2007.

224. National Association for Year-Round Education, *Year-Round Education Web Sites* website: http://www.nayre.org/related.html, accessed July 13, 2003.

225. California Department of Education, *2005–2006 Oxnard Elementary Year-Round Schools*, website: http://www.cde.gov/ls/fa/yr/oxnardyreschls05.asp, accessed February 17, 2007.

226. See Howell, *An Examination of Year-Round Education*, for description of various plans. See also David J. Musatti, *Year-Round Education: Calendar Options*. ERIC document ED343278 (1992).

227. Blaine R. Worthen, *What Twenty Years of Educational Studies Reveal about Year-Round Education*. ERIC document ED373413 (1994), p. 21.

228. Ibid., pp. 11, 23.

229. Palmer and Bemis, "Year-Round Education," op. cit.

230. Howell, *An Examination of Year-Round Education*, p. 25.

231. Stanley M. Elam, Lowell C. Rose, and Alec M. Gallup, "The 24th Annual Gallup/Phi Delta Kappa Poll of the Public's Attitudes Toward the Public Schools," *Phi Delta Kappan* 74, no. 1 (September 1992): 49.

232. Edward Paul Lazear, *Smaller-Class Size No Magic Bullet*, Hoover Institution, 2000, website: http://www.hoover.org/publications/digest/3476106.html, accessed February 18, 2007.

233. People for the American Way, *Class-Size Reduction vs. Vouchers*, 2003, website: http://www.pfaw/general/default.aspx?oid=9682, accessed February 18, 2007.

234. Institute for Student Achievement, *Partners Schools*, website: http://www.studentachievement.oe/schoolpartners.html, accessed February 18, 2007.

235. See U.S. Department of Education, Smaller Learning Communities Program, website: http://www.ed.gov/programs/skp/research.html, accessed April 22, 2007; U.S. Department of Education, Office of Vocational and Adult Education, website: http://www.ed.gov/about/offices/list/ovae/pi/hs/schoolsize.html, accessed April 22, 2007; and Phi Delta Kappa, "The Impact of School Size: Large Schools vs. Small Ones," *Topics & Trends*, February 2007, website: http://www.pdkmembers.org/TNT/V6-07.pdf, accessed February 28, 2007.

236. Gerald W. Bracey, *Setting the Record Straight: Responses to Misconceptions About Public Education in the United States* (Alexandria, Va.: Association for Supervision and Curriculum Development, 1997). See also annual reports by Bracey on the condition of public education since 1992 in fall issues (usually October) of *Phi Delta Kappan*.

237. Deborah Meier, *Will Standards Save Public Education?* (Boston: Beacon Press, 2000).

238. Ernest R. House, *Schools for Sale: Why Free Market Policies Won't Improve America's Schools and What Will* (New York: Teachers College Press, 1998), p. 91.

239. Alfie Kohn, *The Schools Our Children Deserve: Moving Beyond Traditional Classrooms and "Tougher Standards"* (Boston: Houghton Mifflin, 1999), p. 22.

240. Ibid., p. 14.

241. Marion Brady, "The Standards Juggernaut," *Phi Delta Kappan* 81, no. 9 (May 2000): 649–651.

242. Susan Ohanian, *One Size Fits Few: The Folly of Educational Standards* (Portsmouth, N.H.: Heinemann, 1999): pp. ix–x.

243. Brady, "The Standards Juggernaut," p. 649.

244. Judy F. Carr and Douglas E. Harris, *Succeeding with Standards: Linking Curriculum, Assessment, and Action Planning* (Alexandria, Va.: Association for Supervision and Curriculum Development, 2001), p. 2.

245. Ibid., pp. 5, 14, and 145.

246. Fenwick W. English and Betty E. Steffy, *Deep Curriculum Alignment: Creating a Level Playing Field for All Children on High-Stakes Tests of Educational Accountability* (Lanham, Md.: The Scarecrow Press, 2001), p. 63.

247. Ibid., pp. 63–74.

248. Ron Brandt, "On Outcome-Based Education: A Conversation with Bill Spady," *Educational Leadership* 50, no. 4 (December 1992/January 1993): 66.

249. Glickman, *Revolutionizing America's Schools*, p. 43.

250. Hirsch, *The Schools We Need*, p. 26.

251. Diane Ravitsch, *National Standards in American Education: A Citizen's Guide* (Washington, D.C.: The Brookings Institution, 1995), p. 11.

252. Elam et al., "The 26th Annual Phi Delta Kappa/Gallup Poll," p. 48.

253. Lowell C. Rose and Alec M. Gallup, "The 39th Annual Phi Delta Kappa/Gallup Poll of the Public's Attitudes Toward the Public Schools," *Phi Delta Kappan* 89, no. 1 (September 2006): 36–37.

254. Peter W. Hill and Carmel A. Crevola, "The Role of Standards in Educational Reform for the 21st Century," in David D. Marsh, ed., *Preparing Our Schools for the 21st Century*, 1999 Yearbook (Alexandria, Va.: Association for Supervision and Curriculum Development, 1959), p. 139.

255. Ravitsch, *National Standards in American Education*, pp. 178, 186.

256. Beverly Falk, *The Heart of the Matter: Using Standards and Assessment to Learn* (Portsmouth, N.H.: Heinemann, 2000), p. 102.

257. Marc R. O'Shea, *From Standards to Success: A Guide for School Leaders* (Alexandria, Va.: Association for Supervision and Curriculum Development, 2005), pp. 1–2.

258. U.S. Department of Education website: http://www.ed.gov/policy/elsec/leg/esea02/index.html, accessed February 24, 2007.

259. U.S. Department of Education, *No Child Left Behind: A Parent's Guide, 2003*, website: http://www.ed.gov/parents/academic/involve/nclbguide/parentsguide.pdf, accessed February 24, 2007.

260. American Alliance for Health, Physical Education, Recreation & Dance, "Most States Receive a Failing Grade on Physical Education Requirements," *State of the Nation Report*, website: http://www.aahperd.org/naspe/ShapeOfTheNation/template.cfm?template=pressRelease.html, accessed April 23, 2007.

261. Division of Governmental Relations, Texas Education Agency, *Briefing Book on Public Education 80th Texas Legislative Session*, July 2007, website: http://www.tea.state.tx.us/tea/LegBreBooJul07.pdf, accessed July 20, 2007.

262. Rose and Gallup, "The 38th Annual Phi Delta Kappa/Gallup Poll," pp. 51–52.

263. Kansas Department of Education, *Accountability Report, 2004–2005*, website: http://www3.ksde.org/accountability/accountability_report_2004_2005.pdf, accessed February 24, 2007.

264. Wendy Grigg, Patrick Donahue, and Gloria Dion, *The Nation's Report Card: 12th Grade Reading and Mathematics 2005*, Institute of Education Sciences, National Center for Education Statistics, National Assessment of Educational Progress, February 2007, website: http://nces.ed.gov/nationsreportcard/pubs/main2005/2007468.asp, accessed February 24, 2007.

265. Gerald W. Bracey, "The 16th Bracey Report on the Condition of Public Education, *Phi Delta Kappan* 88, no. 2 (October 2006): 152.

266. Ibid.

267. Elizabeth Weiss Green, "Local Success, Federal Failure," *U.S. News & World Report* 142, no. 8 (March 5, 2007): 44–45.

268. Rose and Gallup, "The 39th Annual Phi Delta Kappa/Gallup Poll," p. 34.

269. Claire Campbell, contact, "The Education Trust Honors Five 'Dispelling the Myth' Schools," October 30, 2006, website: http://www2.edtrust.org/EDTrust/Press+Room/DTM+Winners+2006.htm, accessed April 23, 2007.

270. Bill Gates co-chair, "U.S. Senate Committee Hearing," March 7, 2007, website: http://www.gatesfoundation.org/MediaCenter/Speeches/Co-ChairSpeeches/Billg Speeches/BGSpeechesHELP-070307.htm, accessed April 23, 2007.

271. Jack Jennings and Diane Stark Rentner, "Ten Big Effects of the No Child Left Behind Act on Public Schools," *Phi Delta Kappan* 88, no. 2 (October 2006): 113.

272. See Rose and Gallup, "The 39th Annual Phi Delta Kappa/Gallup Poll," p. 44.

273. National Council for the Accreditation of Teacher Education, *NCATE 101: A Primer on Accreditation* (Washington, D.C.: National Council on the Accreditation of Teacher Education, 2006).

274. Diane Ravitsch, *Left Back: A Century of Failed School Reform* (New York: Simon and Schuster, 2000), p. 453.

275. See Appendix for websites of centers, institutes, journals, and laboratories.

276. Steve Jobs, *Steve Jobs Criticizes Teacher Unions*, MacMinute website: http://www.macminute.com/2007/02/18/jobs-teacher-unions, accessed February 25, 2007.

277. Ravitsch, *Left Back: A Century of Failed School Reforms*, p. 453.

Bibliography

In order to assist those who wish to do research on a given topic discussed in this chapter, this bibliography includes a number in parentheses to indicate the number to be found in the list of twelve contemporary issues discussed in this chapter. A (G) after the reference signifies General.

Agard-Jones, Leslie. "Implementing Multicultural Education." *Multicultural Education* 1, no. 1 (Summer 1993): 13–15, 38. (7)

Alan Guttmacher Institute. *Sex and America's Teenagers.* New York: The Alan Guttmacher Institute, 1994. (6)

American Association of University Women and American Institutes for Research. *Gender Gaps: Where Schools Fail Our Children.* New York: Marlowe & Co., 1999. (5)

American Association of University Women Educational Foundation. *Separated by Sex: A Critical Look at Single-Sex Education for Girls.* Washington, D.C.: AAUW Educational Foundation, 1998. (5)

American Library Association, Office of Intellectual Freedom. *Intellectual Freedom Manual*, 6th ed. Chicago: American Library Association, 2002. (4)

Ballinger, Charles. *Annual Report to the Association on the Status of Year-Round Education, 1993*. ERIC document ED358551. (11)

Banks, James A. *An Introduction to Multicultural Education*. Boston: Allyn and Bacon, 2002. (7)

———. *Cultural Diversity and Education: Foundations, Curriculum, and Teaching*. Boston: Allyn and Bacon, 2006. (7)

———. *Educating Citizens in a Multicultural Society*. New York: Teachers College Press 1997. (7)

———, and Banks, Cherry A. *Multicultural Education: Issues and Perspectives*, 5th ed. Hoboken, N.J.: Wiley, 2004. (7)

Barnes, Julian. "Unequal Education." *U.S. News & World Report* 136, no. 19 (March 29, 2004): 66–75. (7)

Berger, Allen. "Performance Contracting and Educational Accountability Elements." *Theory Into Practice* 3, no. 8 (April 1972): 4–8. (8)

Biema, David Van. "The Case for Teaching the Bible." *TIME* 169, no. 14 (April 2, 2007): 40–46. (10)

Blaschke, Charles. "Performance Contracting Costs, Management Reform, and John Q. Citizen." *Phi Delta Kappan* 53, no. 4 (December 1971): 245–247. (8)

Boschee, Floyd, and Baron, Mark A. *Outcome-Based Education: Developing Programs Through Strategic Planning*. Lancaster, Pa.: Technomic Publishing Co., 1993. (11, 12)

Bracey, Gerald W. *Setting the Record Straight: Responses to Misconception About Public Education in the United States*. Alexandria, Va.: Association for Supervision and Curriculum Development, 1997. (G)

———. "The 16th Bracey Report on the Condition of Public Education." *Phi Delta Kappan* 88, no. 2 (October 2006): 151–166. (12)

———. *The War against America's Public Schools: Privatizing Schools, Commercializing Education*. Boston: Allyn and Bacon, 2002. (8)

———. *What You Should Know about the War Against America's Public Schools*. Boston: Allyn and Bacon, 2003. (G)

Brady, Marion. "The Standards Juggernaut." *Phi Delta Kappan* 81, no. 9 (May 2000): 649–651. (12)

Brisk, Maria Estela. *Bilingual Education from Compensation to Quality Schooling*. Mahwah, N.J.: Lawrence Erlbaum Associates, 2006. (3)

Britzman, Deborah P. *Lost Subjects: Contested Objects: Toward a Psychoanalytic Inquiry of Learning*. Albany, N.Y.: State University of New York Press, 1998. (7)

———. *Practice Makes Practice: A Critical Study of Learning to Teach*. Albany, N.Y.: State University of New York Press, 1991. (7)

Burden, Paul R., and Byrd, David M. *Methods for Effective Teaching*, 3rd ed. Boston: Allyn and Bacon, 2003. (7)

Campbell, Patricia B., and Sanders, Jo. "Challenging the System: Assumptions and Data Behind the Push for Single-Sex Schooling." In Amanda Datnow and Lea Hubbard, eds. *Gender in Policy and Practice*. New York: RoutledgeFalmer, 2002. (5)

Carr, Judy F., and Harris, Douglas E. *Succeeding with Standards: Linking Curriculum, Assessment, and Action Planning*. Alexandria, Va.: Association for Supervision and Curriculum Development, 2001. (12)

Carroll, Joseph M. "The Copernican Plan Evaluated: The Evolution of a Revolution." *Phi Delta Kappan* 76, no. 2 (October 1994): 104–113. (11)

———. "Organizing Time to Support Learning." *The School Administrator* 51, no. 3 (March 1994): 26–28, 30–33. (11)

"The Charter Schools Movement." *Phi Delta Kappan* 79, no. 7 (March 1998): 488–511. (2)

Coleman, James S., et al. *Equality of Educational Opportunity*. U.S. Office of Education, 1966.

Dryfoos, Joy G. *Full-Service Schools: A Revolution in Health and Social Services for Children, Youth, and Families*. San Francisco: Jossey-Bass, 1994. (6)

———. "Full Service Schools: What They Are and How to Get to Be One." *NASSP Bulletin* 77, no. 557 (December 1993): 1–3. (6)

Eccles, Jacquelynne S., and Harold, Rena D. *Gender Differences in Sport Involvement: Applying the Eccles' Expectancy-Value Model*. Ann Arbor, Mich.: University Press, n.d. (5)

Elam, Stanley M., Rose, Lowell C., and Gallup, Alec M. "The 23rd Annual Gallup Poll of the Public's Attitudes Toward the Public Schools. *Phi Delta Kappan* 73, no. 1 (September 1991): 47. (2)

———. "The 24th Annual Phi Delta Kappa/Gallup Poll of the Public's Attitudes Toward the Public Schools." *Phi Delta Kappan* 74, no. 1 (September 1992): 49. (6, 11)

———. "The 25th Annual Phi Delta Kappa/Gallup Poll of the Public's Attitudes Toward the Public Schools." *Phi Delta Kappan* 75, no. 2 (October 1993): 146. (3)

———. "The 26th Annual Phi Delta Kappa/Gallup Poll of the Public's Attitudes Toward the Public Schools." *Phi Delta Kappan* 76, no. 1 (September 1994): 48–49. (2, 12)

English, Fenwick W., and Steffy, Betty E. *Deep Curriculum Alignment: Creating a Level Playing Field for All*

Children on High-Stakes Tests of Educational Account-ability. Lanham, Md.: Scarecrow Press, 2001. (12)

Ewers, Justin. "Making History." *U.S. News & World Report* 136, no. 10 (March 29, 2004): 76–80. (7)

Falk, Beverly. *The Heart of the Matter: Using Standards and Assessment to Learn.* Portsmouth, N.H.: Heinemann, 2000. (12)

Feinberg, Rosa Castro. *Bilingual Education: A Reference Handbook.* Santa Barbara, Calif.: ABC-CLIO, 2002. (3)

Finnan, Christine, St. John, Edward P., McCarthy, Jane, and Slovacek, Simeon. *Accelerated Schools in Action: Lessons from the Field.* Thousand Oaks, Calif.: Corwin Press, 1996. (12)

Friedman, Thomas L. *The World Is Flat: A Brief History of the Twenty-First Century.* New York: Farrar, Strauss and Giroux, 2005. (1)

Flygare, Thomas J. "The Case of Seagraves v. State of California." *Phi Delta Kappan* 63, no. 2 (October 1981): 98–101. (10)

Gay, Geneva. "Achieving Educational Equality Through Curriculum Desegregation." *Phi Delta Kappan* 72, no. 1 (September 1990): 56–62. (7)

———. *At the Essence of Learning: Multicultural Education.* West Lafayette, Ind.: Kappa Delta Pi, 1994. (7)

———. *Culturally Responsive Teaching: Theory, Research & Practice.* New York: Teachers College Press, 2000. (7)

Gill, Brian P., Timpane, Michael, Ross, Karen E., and Brewer, Dominic J. *Rhetoric Versus Reality: What We Know and What We Need to Know About Vouchers and Charter Schools.* Santa Monica, Calif.: RAND, 2001. (2)

Glickman, Carl D. *Revolutionizing America's Schools.* San Francisco: Jossey-Bass, 1998. (10, 12)

Glines, Don. *YRE Basics: History, Methods, Concerns, Future.* ERIC document, 1994. ED369144. (11)

Green, Elizabeth Weiss. "Local Success, Federal Failure." *U.S. News & World Report* 142, no. 2 (March 5, 2007): 44–45. (12)

Gresham, April, Hess, Frederick, Maranto, Robert, and Milliman, Scott. "Desert Bloom: Arizona's Free Market in Education." *Phi Delta Kappan* 81, no. 10 (June 2000): 751–757. (2)

Grumet, Madeleine R. *Bitter Milk: Women and Teaching.* Amherst, Mass.: University of Massachusetts Press, 1988. (5)

Gurian, Michael, and Stevens, Kelly. *The Minds of Boys: Saving Our Sons from Falling Behind in School and Life.* San Francisco: Jossey-Bass, 2005. (5)

Halvorsen, Ann T., and Neary, Thomas. *Building Inclusive Schools: Tools and Strategies for Success.* Boston: Allyn and Bacon, 2001. (9)

Handlin, Lilian, and Handlin, Oscar. "America and Its Discontents: A Great Society Legacy." *The American Scholar* 64, no. 1 (Winter 1995): 15–37. (7)

Harrington-Lueker, Donna. "Charter 'Profit.'" *The American School Board Journal* 181, no. 9 (September 1994): 27–28. (2)

———. "Charter Schools." *The American School Board Journal* 181, no. 9 (September 1994): 22–26. (2)

Haynes, Charles C., and Thomas, Oliver. *Finding Common Ground.* Nashville, Tenn.: The Freedom Forum First Amendment Center at Vanderbilt University, 1994. (10)

Haynes, Charles C., Chaltain, Sam, Ferguson, John E., Jr., Hudson, David L., Jr., and Thomas, Oliver. *The First Amendment in Schools: A Guide from the First Amendment Center.* Alexandria, Va.: Association for Supervision and Curriculum Development, 2003. (4, 10)

Henson, Kenneth T. *Curriculum Planning: Integrating Multiculturalism, Constructionism, and Education Reform.* Long Grove, Ill.: Waveland Press, 2006.

Hill, Peter W., and Crevola, Carmel A. "The Role of Standards in Educational Reform for the 21st Century." In David D. Marsh, ed. *Preparing Our Schools for the 21st Century.* 1999 Yearbook. Alexandria, Va.: Association for Supervision and Curriculum Development, 1999, pp. 117–142. (12)

Hirsch, E. D., Jr. *Cultural Literacy: What Every American Needs to Know.* Boston: Houghton Mifflin, 1987. (1)

———, Kett, Joseph F., and Trefil, James S. *The New Dictionary of Cultural Literacy: What Every American Needs to Know,* 2nd ed. Boston: Houghton Mifflin, 2002. (1)

———, and Rowland, William G. *A First Dictionary of Cultural Literacy: What Our Children Need to Know.* Boston: Houghton Mifflin, 1998. (1)

Holt, John. *How Children Fail.* New York: Dell, 1964. (2)

———. *Teach Your Own: A Hopeful Path for Education.* New York: Delacorte Press/Seymour Lawrence, 1981. (2)

Horatio Alger Association. *The State of Our Nation's Youth.* Alexandria, Va.: Horatio Alger Association, 1997. (5)

House, Ernest R. *Schools for Sale: Why Free Market Policies Won't Improve America's Schools and What Will.* New York: Teachers College Press, 1998. (8)

Howell, Vicki T. *An Examination of Year-Round Education: Pros and Cons That Challenge Schooling in America.* ERIC document ED298602 (1998). (11)

Hurst, David S. "We Cannot Ignore the Alternatives." *Educational Leadership* 52, no. 1 (September 1994): 78. (2)

Illich, Ivan. *Deschooling Society*. New York: Harper & Row, 1971. (2)

"Improving Instruction for Students with Learning Needs." *Educational Leadership* 64, no. 5 (February 2007): 8–66. (9)

Jennings, Jack, and Rentner, Diane Stark. "Ten Big Effects of the No Child Left Behind Act on Public Schools," *Phi Delta Kappan* 88, no. 2 (October 2006): 110–113. (12)

Johnston, L. D., O'Malley, P. M., and Bachman, J. G. *Monitoring the Future Study, 1975–2002. Volume 1: Secondary School Students*. Bethesda, Md.: National Institute on Drug Abuse, 2003. (6)

———. *Monitoring the Future National Survey on Drug Use, 1975–2002. Volume II: College Students and Adults Ages 19–40*. Bethesda, Md.: National Institute on Drug Abuse, 2003. (6)

———, and Schulenberg, J. E. (2007). *Monitoring the Future: National Results on Adolescent Drug Use: Overview of Key Findings: 2006*. Bethesda, Md.: National Institute on Drug Abuse. (6)

Kochhar, Carol A., West, Linda L., Taymans, Juliana M., and others. *Successful Inclusion: Practical Strategies for a Shared Responsibility*. Upper Saddle River, N.J.: Merrill, 2000. (11)

Kohn, Alfie. *The Schools Our Children Deserve: Moving Beyond Traditional Classrooms and "Tougher Standards."* Boston: Houghton Mifflin, 1999. (1, 12)

Kozol, Jonathan. *The Shame of the Nation: The Restoration of Apartheid Schooling in America*. New York: Crown Publishers, 2005. (7)

McLesky, James, and Waldron, Nancy L. *Inclusive Schools in Action: Making Differences Ordinary*. Alexandria, Va.: Association for Supervision and Curriculum Development, 2000. (9)

Meehan, Diana M. *Learning Like a Girl: Educating Our Daughters in Schools of Their Own*. New York: Public Affairs, 2007. (5)

Meier, Deborah. *Will Standards Save Public Education?* Boston: Beacon Press, 2000. (12)

National Commission on Excellence in Education. *A Nation at Risk: The Imperative for Educational Reform*. Washington, D.C.: U.S. Government Printing Office, 1983. (G)

Noddings, Nell. *Educating for Intelligent Belief or Unbelief*. New York: Teachers College Press, 1993. (10)

Oakes, Jeannie. *Keeping Track: How Schools Structure Inequality*. New Haven, Conn.: Yale University Press, 1985. (7)

Ohanian, Susan. *One Size Fits Few: The Folly of Educational Standards*. Portsmouth, N.H.: Heinemann, 1999. (12)

O'Shea, Marc R. *From Standards to Success: A Guide for School Leaders*. Alexandria, Va.: Association for Supervision and Curriculum Development, 2005. (12)

Phillips, Lynn. *The Girls Report*. New York: National Council for Research on Women, 1998. (5)

Popham, W. James. *The Truth About Testing: An Educator's Call to Action*. Alexandria, Va.: Association for Supervision and Curriculum Development, 2001. (12)

Prothero, Stephen. *Religious Literacy: What Every American Needs to Know and Doesn't*. San Francisco: Harper SanFrancisco, 2007. (10)

Ravitch, Diane. *The Language Police: How Pressure Groups Restrict What Students Learn*. New York: Alfred Knopf, 2003. (4)

———. *Left Back: A Century of Failed School Reform*. New York: Simon and Schuster, 2000. (12)

———. *National Standards in American Education: A Citizen's Guide*. Washington, D.C.: The Brookings Institution, 1995. (12)

Riordan, Cornelius. "What Do We Know About the Effects of Single-Sex Schools in the Private Sector?" In Amanda Datnow and Lea Hubbard, eds. *Gender Policy and Practice*. New York: RoutledgeFalmer, 2002. (5)

Roberts, Raymond R. *Whose Kids Are They Anyway?: Religion and Morality in America's Public Schools*. Cleveland: The Pilgrim Press, 2002. (10)

Rose, Lowell C., and Gallup, Alec M. "The 30th Annual Phi Delta Kappa/Gallup Poll of the Public's Attitudes Toward the Public Schools." *Phi Delta Kappan* 80, no. 1 (September 1998): 44. (2)

———. "The 31st Annual Phi Delta Kappa/Gallup Poll of the Public's Attitudes Toward the Public Schools." *Phi Delta Kappan* 81, no. 1 (September 1999): 44. (2)

———. "The 34th Annual Phi Delta Kappa/Gallup Poll of the Public's Attitudes Toward the Public Schools." *Phi Delta Kappan* 84, no. 1 (September 2002): 46. (2)

———. "The 38th Annual Phi Delta Kappa/Gallup Poll of the Public's Attitudes Toward the Public Schools." *Phi Delta Kappan* 88, no. 1 (September 2006): 41–56. (G)

Rotberg, Iris C. *Balancing Change and Tradition in Global Education Reform*. Lanham, Md: Scarecrow Press, 2005. (7)

Schippe, Cullen, and Stetson, Chuck, eds. *The Bible and Its Influence*. New York: BLP Pub., 2006. (10)

Schlesinger, Arthur M., Jr. *The Disuniting of America: Reflections on a Multicultural Society*. New York: W. W. Norton, 1992. (7)

Siegel, Harvey. "Evolution vs. Creationism." *Phi Delta Kappan* 63, no. 2 (October 1981): 95–98. (10)

Sizer, Theodore R. *Horace's School: Redesigning the American High School.* Boston: Houghton Mifflin, 1992. (G)

Sleeter, Christine E. *Multicultural Education as Social Activism.* Albany, N.Y.: State University of New York Press, 1996. (7)

Sommers, Christina Hoff. *The War Against Boys: How Misguided Feminism Is Harming Our Young Men.* New York: Simon and Schuster, 2000. (5)

Stewart, Vivien. "Citizens of the World." *Educational Leadership* 64, no. 7 (April 2007): 8–14. (7)

U.S. Department of Education, *Building on Results: A Blueprint for Strengthening the No Child Left Behind Act.* Washington, D.C.: U.S. Department of Education, 2007. (12)

———. *Charter High Schools: Closing the Achievement Gap.* Washington, D.C.: U.S. Government Printing Office, 2006. (2)

Wade, Suzanne E., ed. *Inclusive Education: A Casebook and Readings for Prospective and Practicing Teachers.* Mahwah, N.J.: Lawrence Erlbaum Associates, 2000. (9)

Weil, Danny. *School Vouchers and Privatization.* Santa Barbara, Calif.: ABC-CLIO, 2002. (2, 8)

Weinman, Janice, and Kleinfeld, Judith. "Do Public Schools Shortchange Girls on Educational Opportunities?" *Insight* 14, no. 46 (December 14, 1998). (5)

Willis, Claudia, and Steptoe, Sonja. "How to Fix No Child Left Behind." *TIME* 169, no. 23 (June 4, 2007): 34–41. (12)

Willis, Scott. "Mainstreaming the Gifted." *Education Update* 37, no. 2 (February 1995): 1, 3–4, 9. (9)

Wilson, Steven F. *Learning on the Job: When Business Takes on Public Schools.* Cambridge, Mass.: Harvard University Press, 2006. (8)

"The World in the Classroom." *Educational Leadership* 60, no. 2 (October 2002): 6–69. (7)

Worthen, Blaine R. *What Twenty Years of Educational Studies Reveal About Year-Round Education.* ERIC document, 1994. ED373413. (11)

Appendix

Resources for Further Research

Curriculum Journals

Curriculum Inquiry: http://www.blackwellpublishing.com/journal.asp?ref=0362-6784

Curriculum Review: http://www.paper-clip.com/curriculumreview

Educational Leadership: http://www.ascd.org

Journal of Curriculum and Supervision: http://www.ascd.org

Journal of Curriculum Studies: http://www.tandf.co.uk/journals/titles/00220272.asp

Educational Resources Information Center (ERIC)

ERIC provides free access to more than 1.2 million bibliographic records of journal articles and other education-related materials. ERIC is sponsored by the U.S. Department of Education, Institute of Education Sciences. The former sixteen ERIC Clearinghouses ceased operating December 31, 2003.

ERIC websites:

http://www.eric.ed.gov

http://www.eric.ed.gov/ERICWebPortal/Home.portal?_nfpb=true&_pageLabel= JournalPage&logoutLink=false (journals indexed in ERIC)

http://www.eric.ed.gov/ERICWebPortal/Home.portal?_nfpb=true&_pageLabel= Thesaurus&_nfls=false (thesaurus of ERIC descriptors arranged alphabetically and by category)

Institute of Education Sciences

http://www.ed.gov/about/offices/list/ies/index.html?src=mr

The Education Sciences Reform Act of 2002 replaced the U.S. Department of Education's Office of Educational Research and Improvement with the Institute of Education Sciences within which are four national centers.

National Center for Education Evaluation and Regional Assistance: http://ies.ed.gov/ncee

National Center for Education Research: http://ies.ed.gov/ncer

National Center for Education Statistics: http://nces.ed.gov

National Center for Special Education Research: http://nces.ed.gov/ncser

Internet Resources in Education

Internet Resources in Education from the University of California, Santa Barbara, offers hundreds of websites in the following categories:

Associations, Organizations, and Research Centers

Counseling/Clinical/School Psychology

Education (General)

Electronic Journals and News Services

ERIC

Government and Statistics

Graduate Schools of Education

Lesson Plans and Activities for Teachers

Mailing Lists

Publishers

Standards and Frameworks

Students' Pages

Style Guides

Author: Lorna Lueck

http://www.library.ucsb.edu/subjects/education/education.html

Regional Educational Laboratory Program

http://ies.gov/ncee/edlabs/regions

The ten Regional Educational Laboratories are educational research and development organizations supported by contracts with the U.S. Department of Education.

REL Appalachia: http://ies.ed.gov/ncee/edlabs/regions/appalachia/index.asp

REL Central: http://ies.ed.gov/ncee/edlabs/regions/central/index.asp

REL Mid-Atlantic: http://ies.ed.gov/ncee/edlabs/regions/midatlantic/index.asp

REL Midwest: http://ies.ed.gov/ncee/edlabs/regions/midwest/index.asp

REL Northeast and Islands: http://ies.ed.gov/ncee/edlabs/regions/northeast/index.asp

REL Northwest: http://ies.ed.gov/ncee/edlabs/regions/northwest/index.asp

REL Pacific: http://ies/ed/gov/ncee/edlabs/regions/pacific/index.asp

REL Southeast: http://ies.ed.gov/ncee/edlabs/regions/southeast/index.asp

REL Southwest: http://ies.ed.gov/ncee/edlabs/regions/southwest/index.asp

REL West: http://ies.ed.gov/ncee/edlabs/regions/west/index.asp

Research and Development Centers

Center for the Improvement of Early Reading Achievement: http://www.ciera.org

Consortium for Policy Research in Education: http://www.cpre.org/About_CPRE.htm

Learning Research and Development Center: http://www.lrdc.pitt.edu

National Center for Early Development and Learning: http://www.fpg.unc.edu/~ncedl

National Center for Improving Student Learning and Achievement in Mathematics and Science: http://wwwwcer.wisc.edu

National Center for Postsecondary Improvement: http://stanford.edu/group/ncpi/index.html

National Research Center on the Gifted and Talented: http://www.gifted.unconn.edu/nrcgt.html

Name Index

Subject Index

Credits

Excerpts from Ronald C. Doll, *Curriculum Improvement: Decision Making and Process*, 9th ed. (Boston: Allyn and Bacon, 1996). Reprinted by permission of Allyn and Bacon, Inc.

Donald Orlich, from "Educational Reform: Mistakes, Misconceptions, and Miscues," *Phi Delta Kappan* 70, no. 7 (March 1989): 517. Adapted from Donald C. Orlich, *Staff Development: Enhancing Human Potential.* Copyright © 1989 by Allyn and Bacon.

From Louis J. Rubin, ed., *Curriculum Handbook: The Disciplines, Current Movements, and Instructional Methodology* (Boston: Allyn and Bacon, 1977). Reprinted by permission of Louis J. Rubin.

J. Lloyd Trump and Delmar F. Miller, from *Secondary School Curriculum Improvement: Meeting the Challenge of the Times*, 3rd ed. (Boston: Allyn and Bacon, 1979). Reprinted by permission of Allyn and Bacon.

Arthur W. Combs, "A Perceptual View of the Adequate Personality," in *Perceiving, Behaving, Becoming*, 1962 Yearbook (Alexandria, Va.: Association for Supervision and Curriculum Development, 1962). Reprinted by permission of the Association for Supervision and Curriculum Development. Copyright © 1962 by the Association for Supervision and Curriculum Development. All rights reserved.

Rita S. Dunn and Kenneth J. Dunn, "Learning Styles/Teaching Styles: Should They . . . Can They . . . Be Matched?" *Educational Leadership* 36, no. 4 (January 1979). Reprinted with permission of the Association for Supervision and Curriculum Development. Copyright © 1979 by the Association for Supervision and Curriculum Development. All rights reserved.

Susan B. Ellis, "Models of Teaching: A Solution to the Teaching Style/Learning Style Dilemma," *Educational Leadership* 36, no. 4 (January 1979). Reprinted with permission of the Association for Supervision and Curriculum Development. Copyright © 1979 by the Association for Supervision and Curriculum Development. All rights reserved.

Fenwick W. English and Roger A. Kaufman, *Needs Assessment: A Focus for Curriculum Development* (Alexandria, Va.: Association for Supervision and Curriculum Development, 1975). Reprinted with permission of the Association for Supervision and Curriculum Development. Copyright © 1975 by the Association for Supervision and Curriculum Development. All rights reserved.

Barbara Bree Fischer and Louis Fischer, "Styles in Teaching and Learning," *Educational Leadership* 36, no. 4 (January 1979). Reprinted with permission of the Association for Supervision and Curriculum Development. Copyright © 1979 by the Association for Supervision and Curriculum Development. All rights reserved.

Thomas E. Gatewood and Charles A. Dilg, *The Middle School We Need* (Alexandria, Va.: Association for Supervision and Curriculum Development, 1975). Reprinted with permission of the Association for Supervision and Curriculum Development. Copyright © 1975 by the Association for Supervision and Curriculum Development. All rights reserved.

From *The First Amendment in Schools: A Guide from the First Amendment Center* (p. 17), by Charles C. Haynes, Sam Chaltain, John E. Ferguson, Jr., David L. Hudson,